The Norton
Introduction to Poetry

NINTH EDITION

THE NORTON
INTRODUCTION
TO *Poetry*

NINTH EDITION

J. PAUL HUNTER
Emeritus, University of Chicago
University of Virginia

ALISON BOOTH
University of Virginia

KELLY J. MAYS
University of Nevada, Las Vegas

W. W. NORTON & COMPANY
New York, London

W. W. Norton & Company has been independent since its founding in 1923, when William Warder and Mary D. Herter Norton first published lectures delivered at the People's Institute, the adult education division of New York City's Cooper Union. The Nortons soon expanded their program beyond the Institute, publishing books by celebrated academics from America and abroad. By mid-century, the two major pillars of Norton's publishing program—trade books and college texts—were firmly established. In the 1950s, the Norton family transferred control of the company to its employees, and today—with a staff of four hundred and a comparable number of trade, college, and professional titles published each year—W. W. Norton & Company stands as the largest and oldest publishing house owned wholly by its employees.

Editor: Peter Simon
Developmental editor: Michael Fleming
Assistant editor: Birgit Larsson
Electronic media editor: Eileen Connell
Production manager: Diane O'Connor
Photo research: Stephanie Romeo
Permissions clearance: Katrina Washington and Rivka Genesen
Interior design: Charlotte Staub
Managing editor, College: Marian Johnson

Composition: Binghamton Valley Composition
Manufacturing: Courier Companies

Copyright © 2007, 2002, 1999, 1996, 1991, 1986, 1981, 1973
by W. W. Norton & Company, Inc.

Since this page cannot legibly accommodate all the copyright notices, the Permissions Acknowledgments constitute an extension of the copyright page.

Library of Congress Cataloging-in-Publication Data

The Norton introduction to poetry / [collected by] J. Paul Hunter, Alison
   Booth, Kelly J. Mays.—9th ed.
      p. cm.
   Includes bibliographical references and index.

   ISBN 0-393-92857-8 (pbk.)

   1. Poetry—Collections.   I. Hunter, J. Paul, date.   II. Booth, Alison.
   III. Mays, Kelly J.

PN6101.N6 2006
808.1—dc22

                                                            2005055533

W. W. Norton & Company, Inc., 500 Fifth Avenue, New York, N.Y. 10110
www.wwnorton.com

W. W. Norton & Company Ltd., Castle House, 75/76 Wells Street, London
W1T 3QT

   3 4 5 6 7 8 9 0

Brief Contents

Poetry

Contents

[WEB] indicates that a work is featured on *LitWeb*.
[CD] indicates that a work is featured on the Audio Companion.

Understanding the Text 27

Exploring Contexts 303

Critical Approaches   683

Preface

Through nine editions, *The Norton Introduction to Poetry* has been committed to helping students learn to read and enjoy poetry. This edition, like those before it, offers many different ways of building and reinforcing the skills of reading; in addition to studying poems in terms of their elements, this book emphasizes reading works in different contexts—authorial, historical, cultural, and critical. For this edition, I have provided many new selections and have strengthened contextual groups. The Ninth Edition, like its predecessors, offers in a single volume a complete course in reading and writing about poetry. It is both an anthology and a textbook—a teaching anthology—for the indispensable course in which, together with a college teacher, a college student begins to read poetry, and to write about it, seriously. The works are arranged in order to introduce a reader to the study of poetry. The first section, *Poetry: Reading, Responding, Writing*, treats the purpose and nature of poetry, the reading experience, and the first steps one takes to begin writing about poetry. This is followed by the eight-chapter section called *Understanding the Text*, in which poems are analyzed in terms of craft, the so-called elements of poetry; this section ends with "The Whole Text," a chapter that uses the analytical aids offered in the previous chapters, putting them together to view the work as a whole. The third section, *Exploring Contexts*, suggests some ways of seeing a work of poetry interacting with its temporal and cultural contexts and reaching out beyond the page.

The sections on reading, analyzing, and placing the work in context are followed by guidance in taking that final and extremely difficult step—evaluation. *Evaluating Poetry* demonstrates how to assess the merits of several poems; rather than offering definitive judgments, a litmus test, or even a checklist or formula, it discusses ways of bringing to consciousness, defining, modifying, articulating, and negotiating one's judgments about a work of poetry. The section has been further refined in this edition to guide students toward determining and declaring *on what basis* they make their evaluative judgments. *Reading More Poetry* is a reservoir of additional examples, for independent study or a different approach. The book's arrangement facilitates the reader's movement from narrower to broader questions, mirroring the way people read—wanting to learn more as they experience more.

In the section called *Writing about Poetry*, I deal with both the writing process as applied to poetic works—choosing a topic, gathering evidence, developing an argument, and so forth—and with the varieties of a reader's written responses, from summarizing and paraphrasing to analysis and interpretation. I explore not merely the hows but also the whats and whys. In addition, I cover the use and citation of secondary sources. This section, when coupled with the student paper on page 672, provides a brief reference for writers of papers on poetry.

The Ninth Edition includes 497 poems. The 78 new selections are by Virginia Hamilton Adair, Sherman Alexie, John Ashbery, John Bancks, Elizabeth Bishop,

Eavan Boland, Arna Bontemps, Elizabeth Barrett Browning, Lorna Dee Cervantes, Dan Chiasson, Henri Cole, Billy Collins, Henry Constable, Wendy Cope, Countee Cullen, Rita Dove, Carol Ann Duffy, Peter Everwine, George Farwell, Vicki Feaver, Anne Finch (Countess of Winchelsea), Robert Frost, Louise Gluck, Robert Graves, Thomas Gray, Bartholomew Griffin, Angelina Grimke, Rachel Hadas, Joy Harjo, Robert Hass, Langston Hughes, Anthony Hecht, Helene Johnson, John Keats, Galway Kinnell, Yusef Komunyakaa, D. H. Lawrence, Emma Lazarus, Michael Longley, Archibald Macleish, Andrew Marvell, Roger McGough, Heather McHugh, Claude McKay, Edna St. Vincent Millay, Paul Muldoon, Sharon Olds, Robert Pinsky, Sir Philip Sidney, Charles Simic, Dave Smith, Cathy Song, Mark Strand, Jonathan Swift, Derek Walcott, Nancy Willard, C. K. Williams, Charles Wright, and Lady Mary Wroth.

I have retained my editorial procedures, which proved their usefulness in earlier editions. First of all, I have annotated the works, as is customary in Norton anthologies; my notes are informational and not interpretive, for their purpose is to help readers understand and appreciate the work, not to dictate a meaning or a response. Second, to avoid giving the impression that all poetry was written at the same time, I have noted at the right margin after each selection the date of first book or periodical publication; or, when the date appears at the left margin, the year of composition. Finally, in a glossary at the back I define the literary terms used throughout the book.

One exciting feature of *The Norton Introduction to Poetry* isn't bound into the book itself. *LitWeb,* an online provides students and teachers with in-depth reading prompts and exercises designed to inspire creative reading of and writing about literature, as well as links to useful literary resources. To view this unique ancillary, visit *wwnorton.comlitweb.*

Also, because nearly any reading experience can be enhanced by an accompanying *listening* experience, all copies of *The Norton Introduction to Poetry* include a CD audio companion.

In all my work on this edition, I have been guided by teachers in other English departments and in my own, by students who used the textbook and wrote me, and by students in my own classes. I hope that with such capable help I have been able to offer you a solid and stimulating introduction to the experience of poetry.

Acknowledgments   I would like to thank my teachers, for their example in the love of poetry and in the art of sharing that love; my students, for their patience as I learn from them to be a better teacher of poetry; and my family.

I would also like to thank my colleagues, many of whom have taught this book and evaluated my efforts, for their constant encouragement and enlightenment. Of my colleagues, I would like especially to thank Danielle Allen, Martha Bohrer, Matthew Hofer, Janel Mueller, Debbie Nelson, Eirik Steinhoff, Richard Strier, Robert von Hallberg, and Andrew Yaphe (all from the University of Chicago), and Clare Kinney, Jahan Ramazani, Chip Tucker, and Cynthia Wall (all from the University of Virginia).

I would also like to thank the many teachers whose comments on previous editions have helped me plan the Ninth: Professor Lisa Ashby, Concordia University; Dr. Mary Bagley, Missouri Baptist College; Professor Beverly Bailey, Seminole Community College; Professor Charles Bailey, San Jacinto College Central; Professor Carolyn Baker, San Antonio College; Professor Abby Bardi, Prince George's

Community College; Professor Joseph Bathanti, Mitchell Community College; Professor Jim Beggs, Rodesto Junior College; Professor Elaine Bender, El Camino College; Professor Gerri Black, Atlantic-Cape Community College; Professor Tom Caldwell, Lake Land College; Professor Joe Cambridge, Tompkins Cortland Community College; Dr. Peggy Cole, Arapahoe Community College; Professor Daniel Colvin, Western Illinois University; Professor Ruth Corson, Norwalk Community Technical College; Professor Janis Crowe, Furman University; Professor Bonnie Davids, Missouri Valley College; Professor Al Davis, Moorhead State University; Professor Kathleen De Grave, Pittsburg State University; Professor Dixie Durham, Chapman University; Dr. Lamona Evans, University of Central Oklahoma; Professor Susan Fitzgerald, University of Memphis; Professor Julie Fleenes, Harper College; Dr. Deborah Ford, University of Southern Mississippi; Professor Kim Gardner, University of Memphis; Professor John Gery, University of New Orleans; Professor Joseph Green, Lower Columbia College; Dr. Loren Gruber, Missouri Valley College; Professor James Guimond, Rider University; Professor Andrew Gutteridge, Trinity Western University; Professor Janice Hall, St. Petersburg Junior College; Professor Sidney Harrison, Manatee College; Professor Jim Hauser, William Patterson University; Dr. Philip Heldrich, Emporia State University; Professor Nancy Henry, SUNY Binghamton; Professor Jonathan Hershey, Floyd College; Professor Lin Humphrey, Citrus College; Dr. Vernon Ingraham, University of Massachussets, Dartmouth; Professor Claudia Jannone, University of South Florida; Professor Charles Jimenez, Hillsborough Community College; Professor Sally Joranko, John Carroll University; Professor P. Kelly Joyner, George Mason University; Professor Josephine King, Georgia Central and Southern University; Professor Kathy King, University of Montevallo; Professor Elizabeth Kraft, University of Georgia; Professor Dennis Kriewald, Laredo Community College; Dr. Katherine Leffel, University of Alabama, Birmingham; Professor Jerri Lindblad, Frederick Community College; Professor Eileen Maguire, University of North Florida; Professor Paul Marx, University of New Haven; Professor Kelly Mays, University of Nevada, Las Vegas; Professor Susan McClure, Indiana University of Pennsylvania; Dr. Nellie McCrory, Gaston College; Professor Darlene McElfresh, Northern Kentucky University; Professor Jim McKeown, McLennan Community College; Professor Robert McPhillips, Iona College; Professor Karen Miller, St. Petersburg Junior College; Professor Joseph Mills, North Carolina School of the Arts; Dr. Craig Monk, University of Lethbridge; Professor Paul Munn, Saginaw Valley State University; Professor Solveig Nelson, Grand View College; Professor James Obertino, Central Missouri State University; Professor Jeannette Palmer, Motlow State Community College; Professor Leland Person, University of Alabama, Birmingham; Professor Robert Petersen, Middle Tennessee State University; Dr. Rhonda Pettit, University of Cincinnati, Raymond Walters College; Professor Sylvia Rackow, Baruch College; Professor Daniel Robinson, Colorado State University; Professor Marti Robinson, Ulster County Community College; Professor Victoria Rosner, Texas A&M University; Professor Mike Runyan, Saddleback College; Professor Harold Schneider, American River College; Dr. Beverly Schneller, Millersville University; Professor Donald Schweda, Quincy University; Professor Judith Seagle, East Tennessee State University; Professor Karen Sidwell, St. Petersburg Junior College; Professor Judy Sieg, Spartanburg Technical College; Dr. Stephen Sparacio, St. John's University; Professor Linda Stolhancke, University of West Florida; Professor Debra Sutton, Jefferson College; Professor Burt Thorp, University of North

Dakota; Professor James Thorson, University of New Mexico; Professor James Tomck, Delta State University; Professor Susan Trudell, Scott Community College; Professor Richard Turner, Indiana University–Purdue University at Indianapolis; Dr. Von Underwood, Cameron University; Professor John Valone, Sacramento City College; Professor Michael Weiser, Thomas Nelson Community College; Professor Sallie Wolf, Arapahoe Community College; Professor Clarence Wolfshehl, William Woods University; Professor Whitney Womack, Miami University, Ohio; Professor David Zimmerman, Amarillo College; Professor Linda Zionkowski, Ohio University.

The Norton
Introduction to Poetry

NINTH EDITION

Poetry: Reading, Responding, Writing

If you're a reader of poetry, you already know: poetry reading is not just an intellectual and bookish activity; it is about feeling. Reading poetry well means responding to it: if you respond on a feeling level, you are likely to read more accurately, with deeper understanding, and with greater pleasure. And, conversely, if you read poetry accurately, and with attention to detail, you will almost certainly respond to it—or learn how to respond—on an emotional level. Reading poetry involves conscious articulation through language, and reading and responding come to be, for experienced readers of poetry, very nearly one. But those who teach poetry—and there are a lot of us, almost all enthusiasts about both poetry as a subject and reading as a craft—have discovered something else: writing about poetry helps both the reading and the responding pro-cesses. Responding involves remembering and reflect-ing as well. As you recall your own past and make associations between things in the text and things you already know and feel, you will not only respond more fully to a particular poem, but improve your reading skills more generally. Your knowledge and life experi-ence inform your reading of what is before you and allow you to connect elements within the text—events, images, words, sounds—so that meanings and feelings develop and accumulate. Prior learning creates expectations: of pattern, repetition, association, or causality. Reflecting on the text—and on expectations produced by themes and ideas in the text—re-creates old feelings but directs them in new, often unusual ways. Poems, even when they are about things we have no experience of, connect to things we do know and order our memories, thoughts, and feelings in new and newly challenging ways.

> *Poetry is a way of taking life by the throat.*
> —ROBERT FROST

A course in reading poetry can ultimately enrich your life by helping you become more articulate and more sensitive to both ideas and feelings: that's the larger goal. But the more immediate goal—and the route to the larger one—is to make you a better reader of texts and a more precise and careful writer yourself. Close attention to one text makes you appreciate, and understand, textuality and its possibilities more generally. Texts may be complex and even unstable in some ways; they do not affect all readers the same way, and they work through language that has its own volatilities and complexities. But paying attention to how you read—developing specific questions to ask and working on your reading skills systematically—can take a lot of the guesswork out of reading texts and give you a sense of greater satisfaction in your interpretations.

READING

Poems, perhaps even more than other texts, can sharpen your reading skills because they tend to be so compact, so fully dependent on concise expressions of feeling. In poems, ideas and feelings are packed tightly into just a few lines. The experiences of life are very concentrated here, and meanings emerge quickly, word by word. Poems often show us the very process of putting feelings into a language that can be shared with others—to *say* feelings in a communicable way. Poetry can be intellectual too, explaining and exploring ideas, but its focus is more often on how people feel than how they think. Poems work out a shareable language for feeling, and one of poetry's most insistent virtues arises from its attempt to express the inexpressible. How can anyone, for example, put into words what it means to be in love or how it feels to lose someone one cares about? Poetry tries, and it often captures a shade of emotion that feels just right to a reader. No single poem can be said to represent all the things that love or death feels like or means, but one of the joys of experiencing poetry occurs when we read a poem and want to say, "Yes, that is just what it is like; I know exactly what that line means but I've never been able to express it so well." Poetry can be the voice of our feelings even when our minds are speechless with grief or joy. Reading is no substitute for living, but it can make living more abundant and more available.

Here are two poems that talk about the sincerity and depth of love between two people. Each is written as if it were spoken by one person to his or her lover, and each is definite and powerful about the intensity and quality of love; but the poems work in quite different ways—the first one asserting the strength and depth of love, the second implying intense feeling by reminiscing about earlier events in the relationship between the two people.

ELIZABETH BARRETT BROWNING
How Do I Love Thee?

How do I love thee? Let me count the ways.
I love thee to the depth and breadth and height
My soul can reach, when feeling out of sight
For the ends of Being and ideal Grace.
5 I love thee to the level of every day's
Most quiet need, by sun and candlelight.
I love thee freely, as men strive for Right;
I love thee purely, as they turn from Praise;
I love thee with the passion put to use
10 In my old griefs, and with my childhood's faith.
I love thee with a love I seemed to lose
With my lost saints—I love thee with the breath,
Smiles, tears of all my life!—and, if God choose,
I shall but love thee better after death.

1850

JAROLD RAMSEY

The Tally Stick

Here from the start, from our first of days, look:
I have carved our lives in secret on this stick
of mountain mahogany the length of your arms
outstretched, the wood clear red, so hard and rare.
5   It is time to touch and handle what we know we share.

Near the butt, this intricate notch where the grains
converge and join: it is our wedding.
I can read it through with a thumb and tell you now
who danced, who made up the songs, who meant us joy.
10   These little arrowheads along the grain,
they are the births of our children. See,
they make a kind of design with these heavy crosses,
the deaths of our parents, the loss of friends.

Over it all as it goes, of course, I
15   have chiseled Events, History—random
hashmarks cut against the swirling grain.
See, here is the Year the World Went Wrong,
we thought, and here the days the Great Men fell.
The lengthening runes of our lives run through it all.

20   See, our tally stick is whittled nearly end to end;
delicate as scrimshaw, it would not bear you up.
Regrets have polished it, hand over hand.
Yet let us take it up, and as our fingers
like children leading on a trail cry back
25   our unforgotten wonders, sign after sign,
we will talk softly as of ordinary matters,
and in one another's blameless eyes go blind.

                                                        1977

"How Do I Love Thee?" is direct but fairly abstract. It lists several ways in which the poet feels love and connects them to some noble ideas of higher obligations—to justice (line 7), for example, and to spiritual aspiration (lines 2–4). It suggests a wide range of things that love can mean and notices a variety of emotions. It is an ardent statement of feeling and asserts a permanence that will extend even beyond death. It contains admirable thoughts and memorable phrases that many lovers would like to hear said to themselves. What it does not do is say very much about what the relationship between the two lovers is like on an everyday basis, what experiences they have had together, what distinguishes their relationship from that of other devoted or ideal lovers. Its appeal is to our general sense of what love is like and of how intense feelings can be; it does not offer details.

"The Tally Stick" is much more concrete. The whole poem concentrates on a single object that, like "How Do I Love Thee?," "counts" or "tallies" the ways in which this couple love one another. This stick stands for their love and becomes a kind of physical totem for it: its natural features (lines 6, 10, and 12) and the marks carved on it (lines 15–16, 20–21) indicate events in the story of the relationship. We could say that the stick *symbolizes* their love—later on, we will look at terms like this that make it easier to talk about poems—but for now it is enough to notice that the stick serves the lovers as a marker and a reminder of some specific details of their love. It is a special kind of reminder because its language is "secret" (line 2), something they can share privately (except that we as readers of the poem are looking over their shoulders, not intruding but sharing their secret). The poet interprets the particular features of the stick as standing for particular events—their wedding and the births of their children, for example—and carves marks into it as reminders of other events (lines 15 ff.). The stick itself becomes a very personal object, and in the last stanza of the poem it is as if we watch the lovers touching the stick together and reminiscing over it, gradually dissolving into their emotions and each other as they recall the "unforgotten wonders" (line 25) of their lives together.

Both poems are powerful statements of feelings, each in its own way. Various readers will respond differently to each poem; the effect these poems have on their readers will lead some to prefer one and some the other. Personal preference does not mean that objective standards for poetry cannot be found—some poems <u>are</u> <u>better than others</u>, and later we will look in detail at features that help us to evaluate poems—but we need no preconceived standards as to what poetry must be or how it must work. Some good poems are quite abstract, others quite specific. Any poem that helps us to articulate and clarify human feelings and ideas has a legitimate claim on us as readers.

Both "How Do I Love Thee?" and "The Tally Stick" are written as if they were addressed to the partner in the love relationship, and both talk directly about the intensity of the love, as does the following poem:

LINDA PASTAN

love poem

I want to write you
a love poem as headlong
as our creek
after thaw
5 when we stand
on its dangerous
banks and watch it carry
with it every twig
every dry leaf and branch
10 in its path
every scruple
when we see it
so swollen

with runoff
15 that even as we watch
we must grab
each other
and step back
we must grab each
20 other or
get our shoes
soaked we must
grab each other

1988

The directness and simplicity of this poem suggest how the art and craft of poems work. The poem expresses the desire to write a love poem even as the love poem itself begins to proceed; the desire and the resultant poem exist side by side, and in reading the poem we seem to watch and hear the poet's creative process at work in developing appropriate metaphors and means of expression. The poem must be "headlong" (line 2) to match the power of a love that needs to be compared to the irresistible forces of nature. The poem should, like the love it expresses and the swollen creek it describes, sweep everything along, and it should represent (and reproduce) the sense of watching that the lovers have when they observe natural processes at work. The poem, like the action it represents, has to suggest to readers the kind of desire that grabbing each other means to the lovers.

The lovers in this poem seem, at least to themselves, to own the world they observe, but in fact they are controlled by it. The creek on whose banks they stand is "our creek" (line 3), but what they observe as they watch its rising currents requires them ("must," lines 16, 19, 22) to "grab each other" over and over again. It is as if their love is part of nature itself, which subjects them to forces larger than themselves. Everything—twigs, leaves, branches, scruples—is carried along by the powerful currents after the "thaw" (line 4), and the poem replicates the repeated action of the lovers as if to power along observant readers, just as the lovers are powered along by what they see. But the poem (and their love) admits dangers, too; it is the fact of danger that propels the lovers to each other. The poem suggests that love provides a kind of haven, but the haven hardly involves passivity or peace; instead, it requires the kind of grabbing that means activity and boldness and deep passion. Love here is no quiet or simple matter even if the expression of it in poems can be direct and can stem from a simple observation of experience. The "love poem" itself—linked as it is with the headlong currents of the creek from which the lovers are protecting themselves—even represents that which is beyond love and that which, therefore, both threatens love and at the same time makes it happen. The power of poetry is thus affirmed at the center of the poem, but what poetry is about (love and life) is suggested to be more important. Poetry makes things happen but is not itself a substitute for life, just a means to make life more energetic and meaningful.

The next poem talks only indirectly about the quality and intensity of love. It is written as if it were a letter from a woman to her husband, who has gone on a long journey on business. It directly expresses how much she misses him and indirectly suggests how much she cares about him.

EZRA POUND

The River-Merchant's Wife: A Letter

(after Rihaku)[1]

While my hair was still cut straight across my forehead
I played about the front gate, pulling flowers.
You came by on bamboo stilts, playing horse,
You walked about my seat, playing with blue plums.
5 And we went on living in the village of Chokan:
Two small people, without dislike or suspicion.

At fourteen I married My Lord you.
I never laughed, being bashful.
Lowering my head, I looked at the wall.
10 Called to, a thousand times, I never looked back.

At fifteen I stopped scowling,
I desired my dust to be mingled with yours
For ever and for ever and for ever.
Why should I climb the look out?

15 At sixteen you departed,
You went into far Ku-to-yen, by the river of swirling eddies,
And you have been gone five months.
The monkeys make sorrowful noise overhead.

You dragged your feet when you went out.
20 By the gate now, the moss is grown, the different mosses,
Too deep to clear them away!

The leaves fall early this autumn, in wind.
The paired butterflies are already yellow with August
Over the grass in the West garden;
25 They hurt me. I grow older.
If you are coming down through the narrows of the river Kiang,
Please let me know beforehand,
And I will come out to meet you
    As far as Cho-fu-Sa.

1915

The "letter" tells us only a few facts about the nameless merchant's wife: that she is about sixteen and a half years old, that she married at fourteen and fell in love with her husband a year later, that she is now very lonely. About their relationship we know only that they were childhood playmates in a small Chinese village, that their marriage originally was not a matter of personal choice, and that

---

1. The Japanese name for Li Po, an eighth-century Chinese poet. Pound's poem is a loose paraphrase of one by Li Po.

the husband unwillingly went away on a long journey five months ago. But the words tell us a great deal about how the young wife feels, and the simplicity of her language suggests her sincere and deep longing. The daily noises she hears seem "sorrowful" (line 18), and she worries about the dangers of the faraway place where her husband is, thinking of it in terms of its perilous "river of swirling eddies" (line 16). She thinks of how moss has grown up over the unused gate, and more time seems to her to have passed than actually has (lines 22–25). Nostalgically she remembers their innocent childhood, when they played together without deeper love or commitment (lines 1–6), and contrasts that with her later satisfaction in their love (lines 11–14) and with her present anxiety, loneliness, and desire. We do not need to know the geography of the river Kiang or how far Cho-fu-Sa is to sense that her wish to see him is very strong, that her desire is powerful enough to make her venture beyond the ordinary geographical bounds of her existence so that their reunion will happen sooner. The closest she comes to a direct statement about her love is "I desired my dust to be mingled with yours / For ever and for ever and for ever" (lines 12–13). But her single-minded vision of the world, her perception of even the beauty of nature as only a record of her husband's absence and the passage of time, and her plain, apparently uncalculated language about her rejection of other suitors and her shutting out of the rest of the world all show her to be committed, desirous, nearly desperate for his presence. In a different sense, she too has counted the ways that she loves her man.

Poems can be about the meaning of a relationship or about disappointment just as easily as about emotional fulfillment, and poets are often very good at suggesting the contradictions and uncertainties in relationships. Love does not always go smoothly, and the following poem records (in a kind of monologue, part dream and part waking) the complex longings of a married woman whose attitudes toward marriage are quite different from those of Barrett Browning or the river-merchant's wife.

LIZ ROSENBERG

Married Love

The trees are uncurling their first
green messages: Spring, and some man
lets his arm brush my arm in a darkened
theatre. Faint-headed, I fight the throb.
5   Later I dream
the gas attendant puts a cool hand
on my breast, asking a question.
Slowly I rise through the surface of the dream,
brushing his hand and my own heat away.

10   Young, I burned to marry. Married,
the smolder goes on underground;
clutching at weeds, writhing everywhere.
I'm trying to talk to a friend on burning

issues, flaming from the feet up,
15 drinking in his breath, touching his wrist.
I want to grab the pretty woman
on the street, seize the falcon
by its neck, beat my way into whistling steam.

I turn to you in the dark, oh husband,
20 watching your lit breath circle the pillow.
Then you turn to me, throwing first one limb
and then another over me, in the easy brotherly
lust of marriage. I cling to you
as if I were a burning ship and you
25 could save me, as if I won't go sliding down
beneath you soon; as if our lives are made of rise
and fall, and we could ride this out forever,
with longing's thunder rolling heavy in our arms.

1986

The initial expectations of springtime and newness here quickly turn into signs, both conscious and unconscious, of desire ("throb") for anonymous sex attraction ("some man"). Reality and fantasy are nearly one here, as the woman tries to reject arousal she does not wish to feel. All the poem, in fact, is full of fire and burning, which the speaker cannot ignore, subdue, or quench; there is hurt here and bewilderment and fear, and the easy habitual comforts of married love are not exactly reassuring ("brotherly lust") nor do they seem to satisfy desire. The woman feels herself to be a burning (and sinking) ship, and her marital clinging seems an act of desperation; she hopes for salvation (or at least a "rid[ing] out"), but "longing's thunder" remains far more powerful than any sense of satisfaction or solution. Poetry does not always celebrate or make us feel better; sometimes, as here, it challenges easy or familiar notions of how feelings are supposed to work, and even the most appealing subjects may be transformed, challenging our assumptions and understanding.

RESPONDING

The poems we have looked at so far all describe, though in quite different ways, feelings associated with loving or being attached to someone and the expression—either physical or verbal—of those feelings. Watching how poems discover a language for feeling can help us to discover a language for our own feelings, but the process is also reciprocal: being conscious of feelings we already have can lead us into poems more surely and with more satisfaction. Readers with a strong romantic bent—and with strong yearnings or positive memories of desire—will be likely to find "The Tally Stick" and "The River-Merchant's Wife: A Letter" easy to respond to and admire, while those more skeptical of human institutions and male habits may find the wifely despair of "Married Love" more satisfying.

> *If I feel physically as if the top of my head were taken off, I know that is poetry.*
> —EMILY DICKINSON

Poems can be about all kinds of experiences, and not all the things we find in them will replicate (or even relate to) experiences we may have had individually. But sharing through language will often enable us to uncover feelings—of love or anger, fear or confidence—we did not know we had. The next few poems involve another, far less pleasant set of feelings than those usually generated by love, but even here, where our experience may be limited, we are able to respond, to feel the tug of emotions within us that we may not be fully aware of. In the following poem, a father struggles to understand and control his grief over the death of a seven-year-old son. We don't have to be a father or to have lost a loved one to be aware of—and even share—the speaker's pain, because our own experiences will have given us some idea of what such a loss would feel like. And the words and strategies of the poem may arouse expectations created by our previous experiences.

BEN JONSON

On My First Son

Farewell, thou child of my right hand,[1] and joy;
My sin was too much hope of thee, loved boy:
Seven years thou wert lent to me, and I thee pay,
Exacted by thy fate, on the just[2] day.
5   O could I lose all father now! for why
Will man lament the state he should envý,
To have so soon 'scaped world's and flesh's rage,
And, if no other misery, yet age?
Rest in soft peace, and asked, say, "Here doth lie
10 Ben Jonson his[3] best piece of poetry."
For whose sake henceforth all his vows be such
As what he loves may never like too much.

                                                    1616

This poem's attempts to rationalize the boy's death are quite conventional. Although the father tries to be comforted by pious thoughts, his feelings keep showing through. The poem's beginning—with its formal "farewell" and the rather distant-sounding address to the dead boy ("child of my right hand")—cannot be sustained for long: both of the first two lines end with bursts of emotion. It is as if the father is trying to explain the death to himself and to keep his emotions under control, but cannot quite manage it. Even the punctuation suggests the way his feelings compete with conventional attempts to put the death into some sort of perspective that will soften the grief, and the comma near the end of each of the first two lines marks a pause that cannot quite hold back the overflowing

---

1. A literal translation of the son's name, Benjamin.
2. Exact; the son died on his seventh birthday, in 1603.
3. That is, Ben Jonson's (this was a common Renaissance form of the possessive).

emotion. But finally the only "idea" that the poem supports is that the father wishes he did not feel so intensely; in the fifth line he fairly blurts that he wishes he could lose his fatherly emotions, and in the final lines he resolves never again to "like" so much that he can be this deeply hurt. Philosophy and religion offer their useful counsels in this poem, but they prove far less powerful than feeling. Rather than drawing some kind of moral about what death means, the poem presents the actuality of feeling as inevitable and nearly all-consuming.

The poem that follows also tries to suppress the rawness of feelings about the death of a loved one, but here the survivor is haunted by memories of his wife when he sees a physical object—a vacuum cleaner—that he associates with her.

HOWARD NEMEROV

The Vacuum

The house is so quiet now
The vacuum cleaner sulks in the corner closet,
Its bag limp as a stopped lung, its mouth
Grinning into the floor, maybe at my
5   Slovenly life, my dog-dead youth.

I've lived this way long enough,
But when my old woman died her soul
Went into that vacuum cleaner, and I can't bear
To see the bag swell like a belly, eating the dust
10   And the woolen mice, and begin to howl

Because there is old filth everywhere
She used to crawl, in the corner and under the stair.
I know now how life is cheap as dirt,
And still the hungry, angry heart
15   Hangs on and howls, biting at air.

                                    1955

The poem is about a vacuum in the husband's life, but the title refers most obviously to the vacuum cleaner that, like the tally stick we looked at earlier, seems to stand for many of the things that were once important in the life he had together with his wife. The cleaner is a reminder of the dead wife ("my old woman," line 7) because of her devotion to cleanliness. But to the surviving husband buried in the filth of his life it seems as if the machine has become almost human, a kind of ghost of her: it "sulks" (line 2), it has lungs and a mouth (line 3), and it seems to grin, making fun of what has become of him. He "can't bear" (line 8) to see it in action because it then seems too much alive, too much a reminder of her life. The poem records his paralysis, his inability to do more than discover that life is "cheap as dirt" without her ordering and cleansing presence for him. At the end it is *his* angry heart that acts like the haunting machine, howling and biting at air as if he has merged with her spirit and the physical object that memorializes her.

This poem puts a strong emphasis on the stillness of death and the way it makes things seem to stop; it captures in words the hurt, the anger, the inability to understand, the vacuum that remains when a loved one dies and leaves a vacant space. But here we do not see the body or hear a direct good-bye to the dead person; rather we encounter the feeling that lingers and won't go away, recalled through memory by an especially significant object, a mere thing but one that has been personalized to the point of becoming nearly human in itself. (The event described here is, by the way, fictional; the poet's wife did not actually die. Like a dramatist or writer of fiction, the poet may simply *imagine* an event in order to analyze and articulate how such an event might feel in certain circumstances. A work of literature can be *true* without being *actual*.)

Here is another poem about a death:

SEAMUS HEANEY

WEB   *Mid-Term Break*

I sat all morning in the college sick bay
Counting bells knelling classes to a close.
At two o'clock our neighbors drove me home.

In the porch I met my father crying—
5 He had always taken funerals in his stride—
And Big Jim Evans saying it was a hard blow.

The baby cooed and laughed and rocked the pram
When I came in, and I was embarrassed
By old men standing up to shake my hand

10 And tell me they were "sorry for my trouble,"
Whispers informed strangers I was the eldest,
Away at school, as my mother held my hand

In hers and coughed out angry tearless sighs.
At ten o'clock the ambulance arrived
15 With the corpse, stanched and bandaged by the nurses.

Next morning I went up into the room. Snowdrops
And candles soothed the bedside; I saw him
For the first time in six weeks. Paler now,

Wearing a poppy bruise on his left temple,
20 He lay in the four foot box as in his cot.
No gaudy scars, the bumper knocked him clear.

A four foot box, a foot for every year.

1966

If, in "The Vacuum," the grief is displaced onto an object left behind, here grief seems almost wordless. The speaker of the poem, the older brother of the dead four-year-old, cannot really articulate his grief and instead provides a lot of meticulous detail, as if giving us information can substitute for an expression of feeling. He is "embarrassed" (line 8) by the attempts of others to say how they feel and to empathize with him. He records the feelings of other family members in detail, but never fully expresses his own feelings, as if he has taken on a kind of deadness of his own that eludes, and substitutes for, articulation. Only when he confronts the bruised body itself can he begin to come to terms with the loss, and even there he resorts to a kind of mathematical formula to displace the feeling so that he doesn't have to talk about it. Though the feelings in the poem are extremely powerful, the power is expressed (as in the Jonson poem above) by suppression. It is not restraint that holds back the young man's grief, but a silence that cannot be put into any words except those of enumerated facts.

Sometimes poems are a way of confronting feelings. Sometimes they explore feelings in detail and try to intellectualize or rationalize them. At other times, poems generate responses by recalling experiences many years in the past. In the following two poems, for example, memories of childhood provide perspective on two very different events. In the first, written as if the person speaking the poem were in the fifth grade, a child's sense of death is portrayed through her exploration of a photograph that makes her grandfather's presence vivid to her memory—a memory that lingers primarily through smell and touch. In the second poem, another childhood memory—this time of overshoes—takes an adult almost physically back into childhood. As you read the two poems, keep track of (or perhaps even jot down) your responses. How much of your feeling is due to your own past experiences? In which specific places? What family photographs do you remember most vividly? What feelings did they evoke that make them so memorable? How are your memories different from those expressed in "Fifth Grade Autobiography"? in "The Fury of Overshoes"? Which feelings expressed in each poem are similar to your own? Where do your feelings differ most strongly? How would you articulate your responses to such memories differently? In what ways does an awareness of your similar—and different—experiences and feelings make you a better reader of the poem?

RITA DOVE

Fifth Grade Autobiography

I was four in this photograph fishing
with my grandparents at a lake in Michigan.
My brother squats in poison ivy.
His Davy Crockett cap
5 sits squared on his head so the raccoon tail
flounces down the back of his sailor suit.

My grandfather sits to the far right
in a folding chair,
and I know his left hand is on
10 the tobacco in his pants pocket

because I used to wrap it for him
every Christmas. Grandmother's hips
bulge from the brush, she's leaning
into the ice chest, sun through the trees
15 printing her dress with soft
luminous paws.

I am staring jealously at my brother;
the day before he rode his first horse, alone.
I was strapped in a basket
20 behind my grandfather.
He smelled of lemons. He's died—

but I remember his hands.

1989

ANNE SEXTON

The Fury of Overshoes

They sit in a row
outside the kindergarten,
black, red, brown, all
with those brass buckles.
5 Remember when you couldn't
buckle your own
overshoe
or tie your own
shoe
10 or cut your own meat
and the tears
running down like mud
because you fell off your
tricycle?
15 Remember, big fish,
when you couldn't swim
and simply slipped under
like a stone frog?
The world wasn't
20 yours.
It belonged to
the big people.
Under your bed
sat the wolf
25 and he made a shadow
when cars passed by
at night.
They made you give up

your nightlight
30 and your teddy
and your thumb.
Oh overshoes,
don't you
remember me,
35 pushing you up and down
in the winter snow?
Oh thumb,
I want a drink,
it is dark,
40 where are the big people,
when will I get there,
taking giant steps
all day,
each day
45 and thinking
nothing of it?

1974

There is much more going on in the poems we have glanced at than we have taken time to consider, but even the quickest look at these poems suggests the range of feelings that poems offer—the depth of feeling, the clarity, the experience that may be articulately and precisely shared. Not all poems are as accessible as those we've looked at so far, and even the accessible ones yield themselves to us more readily and more fully if we approach them systematically by developing specific reading habits and skills—just as someone learning to play tennis or to make pottery systematically learns the rules, the techniques, the things to watch out for that are distinctive to the pleasures and hazards of that skill or craft. It helps if you develop a sense of what to expect, and the chapters that follow will show you the things that poets can do—and thus what poems can do for you.

But knowing what to expect isn't everything. As a reader of poetry, you should always be open—to new experiences, new feelings, new ideas. Every poem is a potential new experience, and no matter how sophisticated you become, you can still be surprised (and delighted) by new poems—and by rereading old ones. Good poems bear many, many rereadings, and often one discovers something new with every new reading: there is no such thing as "mastering" a poem, and good poems are not exhausted by repeated readings. Let poems surprise you when you come to them, let them come on their own terms, let them be themselves. If you are open to poetry, you are also open to much more that the world can offer you.

No one can give you a method that will offer you total experience of all poems. But because individual poems often share characteristics with other poems, the following guidelines can prompt you to ask the right questions:

1. *Read the syntax literally.* What the words say literally in normal sentences is only a starting point, but it is the place to start. Not all poems use normal prose syntax, but most of them do, and you can save yourself embarrassment by paraphrasing accurately (that is, rephrasing what the poem literally says, in plain prose) and not simply free-associating from an isolated word or phrase.

2. *Articulate for yourself what the title, subject, and situation make you expect.* Poets often use false leads and try to surprise you by doing shocking things, but defining expectation lets you become conscious of where you are when you begin.

3. *Identify the poem's situation.* What is said is often conditioned by where it is said and by whom. Identifying the speaker and his or her place in the situation puts what he or she says in perspective.

4. *Find out what is implied by the traditions behind the poem.* Verse forms, poetic kinds, and metrical patterns all have a frame of reference, traditions of the way they are usually used and for what. For example, the **anapest** (two unstressed syllables followed by a stressed one, as in the word *Tennessee*) is usually used for comic poems, and when poets use it "straight" they are probably making a point with this "departure" from tradition.

5. *Use your dictionary, other reference books, and reliable Web sites.* Look up anything you don't understand: an unfamiliar word (or an ordinary word used in an unfamiliar way), a place, a person, a myth, an idea—anything the poem uses. When you can't find what you need or don't know where to look, ask the reference librarian for help.

6. *Remember that poems exist in time, and times change.* Not only the meanings of words, but whole ways of looking at the universe vary in different ages. Consciousness of time works two ways: your knowledge of history provides a context for reading the poem, and the poem's use of a word or idea may modify your notion of a particular age.

7. *Take a poem on its own terms.* Adjust to the poem; don't make the poem adjust to you. Be prepared to hear things you do not want to hear. Not all poems are about your ideas, nor will they always present emotions you want to feel. But be tolerant and listen to the poem's ideas, not only to your wish to revise them for yourself.

8. *Be willing to be surprised.* Things often happen in poems that turn them around. A poem may seem to suggest one thing at first, then persuade you of its opposite, or at least of a significant qualification or variation.

9. *Assume there is a reason for everything.* Poets do make mistakes, but when a poem shows some degree of verbal control it is usually safest to assume that the poet chose each word carefully; if the choice seems peculiar, you may be missing something. Try to account for everything in a poem, see what kind of sense you can make of it, and figure out a coherent **pattern** that explains the text as it stands.

10. *Argue.* Discussion usually results in clarification and keeps you from being too dependent on personal biases and preoccupations that sometimes mislead even the best readers. Talking a poem over with someone else (especially someone who thinks very differently) can expand your perspective.

WRITING

If you have been keeping notes on your personal responses to the poems you've read, you have already taken an important step toward writing about them. There are many different ways to write about poems, just as there are many different things to say. (The section in the back of the book called "Writing about Poetry" suggests some ways to come up with a good topic.) But all writing begins with a clear sense of the poem itself and your responses to it, so the first steps (long before formally sitting down to write) are to read the poem several times and keep notes on the things that strike you and the questions that remain.

Formulating a clear series of questions will usually suggest an appropriate approach to the poem and a good topic. Learning to ask the right questions can save you a lot of time. Some questions—the kinds of questions implied in the ten guidelines for reading listed above—are basic and apply, more or less, to all poems. But each poem makes demands of its own, too, because of its distinctive way of going about its business, so you will usually want to list what seem to you the crucial questions for that poem. Here, just to give you an example, are some questions that could lead you to a paper topic about the Anne Bradstreet poem on p. 18.

1. How does the **title** affect your reading of and response to the poem?
2. What is the poem about?
3. What makes the poem interesting?
4. Who is the **speaker**? What role does the speaker have?
5. What effect does the poem have on you? Do you think the poet intended such an effect?
6. What is distinctive about the poet's use of language? Which words especially contribute to the poem's effect?

What *is* poetry? Let your definition be cumulative as you read more and more poems. No dictionary definition will cover all that you find, and it is better to discover for yourself poetry's many ingredients, its many effects, its many ways of acting. What can it do for you? Wait and see. Add up its effects after you have read carefully—after you have reread and studied—a hundred or so poems; then continue to read new poems or reread old ones.

PRACTICING READING: SOME POEMS ON LOVE

W. H. AUDEN

[*Stop all the clocks, cut off the telephone*]

Stop all the clocks, cut off the telephone,
Prevent the dog from barking with a juicy bone,
Silence the pianos and with muffled drum
Bring out the coffin, let the mourners come.

5 Let aeroplanes circle moaning overhead
  Scribbling on the sky the message He Is Dead,
  Put crêpe bows round the white necks of the public doves,
  Let the traffic policemen wear black cotton gloves.

  He was my North, my South, my East and West,
10 My working week and my Sunday rest,
  My noon, my midnight, my talk, my song;
  I thought that love would last for ever: I was wrong.

  The stars are not wanted now: put out every one;
  Pack up the moon and dismantle the sun;
15 Pour away the ocean and sweep up the wood;
  For nothing now can ever come to any good.

ca. 1936

- Whom does the speaker of this poem seem to be addressing? Why might the poet have proclaimed his grief with such a public declaration as this poem?

ANDREW MARVELL

The Definition of Love – Perfect, unattainable

1

My love is of a birth as rare
As 'tis for object strange and high:
It was begotten by Despair
Upon Impossibility.

2

5 Magnanimous Despair alone
Could show me so divine a thing,
Where feeble Hope could ne'er have flown
But vainly flapped its tinsel wing.

3

And yet I quickly might arrive
10 Where my extended soul is fixed,
But Fate does iron wedges drive,
And always crowds itself betwixt.

4

For Fate with jealous eye does see
Two perfect loves, nor lets them close:
15 Their union would her ruin be,
And her tyrannic power depose.

5

And therefore her decrees of steel
Us as the distant Poles have placed,
(Though Love's whole world on us doth wheel)
20 Not by themselves to be embraced,

6

Unless the giddy heaven fall,
And earth some new convulsion tear;
And, us to join, the world should all
Be cramped into a planisphere.[1]

7

25 As lines (so loves) oblique may well
Themselves in every angle greet:
But ours so truly parallel,
Though infinite, can never meet.

8

Therefore the love which us doth bind,
30 But Fate so enviously debars,
Is the conjunction of the mind,
And opposition of the stars.

1681

- What, exactly, is Marvell's "definition" of love as implied by the poem? What seems to be the "Impossibility" (line 4) besetting the would-be lovers?

ANNE BRADSTREET

WEB   *To My Dear and Loving Husband*

If ever two were one, then surely we.
If ever man were loved by wife, then thee;
If ever wife was happy in a man,
Compare with me ye women if you can.
5 I prize thy love more than whole mines of gold,
Or all the riches that the East doth hold.
My love is such that rivers cannot quench,
Nor aught but love from thee give recompense.
Thy love is such I can no way repay;
10 The heavens reward thee manifold, I pray.
Then while we live, in love let's so persever,
That when we live no more we may live ever.

1678

---

1. Flat sphere.

- How does Bradstreet's strategy of characterizing her love through a series of comparisons compare with Barrett Browning's strategy in "How Do I Love Thee?"

(CD) **WILLIAM SHAKESPEARE**

[*Let me not to the marriage of true minds*]

Let me not to the marriage of true minds *A*
Admit impediments.[2] Love is not love *B*
Which alters when it alteration finds, *A*
Or bends with the remover to remove: *B*
5 Oh, no! it is an ever-fixéd mark, *C*
That looks on tempests and is never shaken; *D*
It is the star to every wandering bark, *C*
Whose worth's unknown, although his height be taken.[3] *D*
Love's not Time's fool, though rosy lips and cheeks *E*
10 Within his bending sickle's compass come; *F*
Love alters not with his brief hours and weeks, *E*
But bears it out even to the edge of doom. *F*
If this be error and upon me proved, *G*
I never writ, nor no man ever loved. *G*

1609

- What might the speaker mean when he says that love doesn't "ben[d] with the remover to remove"?

ALAN BOLD

A Special Theory of Relativity

According to Einstein
There's no still center of the universe:
Everything is moving
Relative to something else.
5 *My love, I move myself towards you,*
Measure my motion
In relation to yours.

According to Einstein
The mass of a moving body
10 Exceeds its mass

2. The Marriage Service contains this address to the witnesses: "If any of you know cause or just impediments why these persons should not be joined together. . . ."
3. That is, measuring the altitude of stars (for purposes of navigation) is not a way to measure value.

When standing still.
My love, in moving
Through you
I feel my mass increase.

15 According to Einstein
The length of a moving body
Diminishes
As speed increases.
My love, after accelerating
20 *Inside you*
I spectacularly shrink.

According to Einstein
Time slows down
As we approach
25 The speed of light.
My love, as we approach
The speed of light
Time is standing still.

1969

- Why are the final three lines in each stanza italicized? When reading
  the poem aloud, how would you alter the tone of your voice for the
  italicized lines?

SHARON OLDS

Last Night

The next day, I am almost afraid.
Love? It was more like dragonflies
in the sun, 100 degrees at noon,
the ends of their abdomens stuck together, I
5 close my eyes when I remember. I hardly
knew myself, like something twisting and
twisting out of a chrysalis,
enormous, without language, all
head, all shut eyes, and the humming
10 like madness, the way they writhe away,
and do not leave, back, back,
away, back. Did I know you? No kiss,
no tenderness—more like killing, death-grip
holding to life, genitals
15 like violent hands clasped tight
barely moving, more like being closed
in a great jaw and eaten, and the screaming
I groan to remember it, and when we started

to die, then I refuse to remember,
20 the way a drunkard forgets. After,
you held my hands extremely hard as my
body moved in shudders like the ferry when its
axle is loosed past engagement, you kept me
sealed exactly against you, our hairlines
25 wet as the arc of a gateway after
a cloudburst, you secured me in your arms till I slept—
that was love, and we woke in the morning
clasped, fragrant, buoyant, that was
the morning after love.

1996

- What comparison is the speaker of this poem making between "dragonflies / in the sun" and a night of love-making?

STEPHEN DUNN

After Making Love

No one should ask the other
"What were you thinking?"

No one, that is,
who doesn't want to hear about the past

5 and its inhabitants,
or the strange loneliness of the present

filled, even as it may be, with pleasure,
or those snapshots

of the future, different heads
10 on different bodies.

Some people actually desire honesty.
They must never have broken

into their own solitary houses
after having misplaced the key,

15 never seen with an intruder's eyes
what is theirs.

1996

- What does it mean to see something of one's own "with an intruder's eyes" (line 15)? Considering its title, what does the poem imply about the relationship between love and honesty?

DENISE LEVERTOV

Wedding-Ring

My wedding-ring lies in a basket
as if at the bottom of a well.
Nothing will come to fish it back up
and onto my finger again.
5   It lies
among keys to abandoned houses,
nails waiting to be needed and hammered
into some wall,
telephone numbers with no names attached,
10 idle paperclips.
             It can't be given away
for fear of bringing ill-luck.
             It can't be sold
for the marriage was good in its own
15 time, though that time is gone.
             Could some artificer
beat into it bright stones, transform it
into a dazzling circlet no one could take
for solemn betrothal or to make promises
20 living will not let them keep? Change it
into a simple gift I could give in friendship?

1978

- How does the wedding ring's situation—lying "in a basket / as if at
the bottom of a well"—embody the marriage symbolized by the ring?

MARY, LADY CHUDLEIGH

To the Ladies

Wife and servant are the same,
But only differ in the name:
For when that fatal knot is tied,
Which nothing, nothing can divide,
5 When she the word *Obey* has said,
And man by law supreme has made,
Then all that's kind is laid aside,
And nothing left but state[4] and pride.
Fierce as an eastern prince he grows,
10 And all his innate rigor shows:

4. Social position.

Then but to look, to laugh, or speak,
Will the nuptial contract break.
Like mutes, she signs alone must make,
And never any freedom take,
15 But still be governed by a nod,
And fear her husband as her god:
Him still must serve, him still obey,
And nothing act, and nothing say,
But what her haughty lord thinks fit,
20 Who, with the power, has all the wit.
Then shun, oh! shun that wretched state,
And all the fawning flatterers hate.
Value yourselves, and men despise:
You must be proud, if you'll be wise.

                                    1703

- Who do you think is the intended audience for this poem? If the
  speaker overstates her case to some degree, why might she do so?

W. B. YEATS

A Last Confession

What lively lad most pleasured me
Of all that with me lay?
I answer that I gave my soul
And loved in misery,
5 But had great pleasure with a lad
That I loved bodily.

Flinging from his arms I laughed
To think his passion such
He fancied that I gave a soul
10 Did but our bodies touch,
And laughed upon his breast to think
Beast gave beast as much.

I gave what other women gave
That stepped out of their clothes,
15 But when this soul, its body off,
Naked to naked goes,
He it has found shall find therein
What none other knows,

And give his own and take his own
20 And rule in his own right;
And though it loved in misery
Close and cling so tight,

There's not a bird of day that dare
Extinguish that delight.

1933

- What distinction is the speaker making between physical and spiritual love? Why would this poem be someone's "last confession"?

CD WEB LI-YOUNG LEE

Persimmons

In sixth grade Mrs. Walker
slapped the back of my head
and made me stand in the corner
for not knowing the difference
5 between *persimmon* and *precision*.
How to choose
persimmons. This is precision.
Ripe ones are soft and brown-spotted.
Sniff the bottoms. The sweet one
10 will be fragrant. How to eat:
put the knife away, lay down newspaper.
Peel the skin tenderly, not to tear the meat.
Chew the skin, suck it,
and swallow. Now, eat
15 the meat of the fruit,
so sweet,
all of it, to the heart.

Donna undresses, her stomach is white.
In the yard, dewy and shivering
20 with crickets, we lie naked,
face-up, face-down.
I teach her Chinese.
Crickets: *chiu chiu.* Dew: I've forgotten.
Naked: I've forgotten.
25 *Ni, wo:*   you and me.
I part her legs,
remember to tell her
she is beautiful as the moon.

Other words
30 that got me into trouble were
fight and *fright, wren* and *yarn.*
Fight was what I did when I was frightened,
fright was what I felt when I was fighting.
Wrens are small, plain birds,
35 yarn is what one knits with.

Wrens are soft as yarn.
My mother made birds out of yarn.
I loved to watch her tie the stuff;
a bird, a rabbit, a wee man.

40 Mrs. Walker brought a persimmon to class
and cut it up
so everyone could taste
a *Chinese apple.* Knowing
it wasn't ripe or sweet, I didn't eat
45 but watched the other faces.

My mother said every persimmon has a sun
inside, something golden, glowing,
warm as my face.

Once, in the cellar, I found two wrapped in newspaper,
50 forgotten and not yet ripe.
I took them and set both on my bedroom windowsill,
where each morning a cardinal
sang, *The sun, the sun.*
Finally understanding
55 he was going blind,
my father sat up all one night
waiting for a song, a ghost.
I gave him the persimmons,
swelled, heavy as sadness,
60 and sweet as love.

This year, in the muddy lighting
of my parents' cellar, I rummage, looking
for something I lost.
My father sits on the tired, wooden stairs,
65 black cane between his knees,
hand over hand, gripping the handle.

He's so happy that I've come home.
I ask how his eyes are, a stupid question.
All gone, he answers.

70 Under some blankets, I find a box.
Inside the box I find three scrolls.
I sit beside him and untie
three paintings by my father:
Hibiscus leaf and a white flower.
75 Two cats preening.
Two persimmons, so full they want to drop from the cloth.

He raises both hands to touch the cloth,
asks, *Which is this?*

This is persimmons, Father.

80 *Oh, the feel of the wolftail on the silk,*
   the strength, the tense
   precision in the wrist.
   I painted them hundreds of times
   eyes closed. These I painted blind.
85 *Some things never leave a person:*
   scent of the hair of one you love,
   the texture of persimmons,
   in your palm, the ripe weight.

                                                            1986

- How does the tone shift as the focal point of the poem changes? What key words and phrases mark the tone in each stanza?

SUGGESTIONS FOR WRITING

1. Of all the love poems in this chapter, which one seems to reveal the deepest, truest feelings? Which one seems most—or least—likely to stir feelings of love in the recipient of the poem? Write an essay in which you discuss the emotional effect of one or more of the poems in this chapter.

2. Paraphrase, stanza by stanza, Andrew Marvell's "The Definition of Love." How accurately does your paraphrase represent the feelings described by the poem? Write an essay in which you consider what makes a poem "poetry" and why this matters.

3. Consider your responses to all the marriage poems in this chapter. Which one most accurately expresses your ideal of a good marriage? Why do you think so? What does your choice say about you? Write an essay in which you reflect upon how these poems reinforce, refine, or perhaps even challenge your views of marriage.

4. Imagine that one of the love poems in this chapter was written for you. Write a letter in which you respond to the poet, discussing the feelings and the perceptions revealed in the poem.

Understanding the Text

1 TONE

Poetry is full of surprises. Poems express anger or outrage just as effectively as love or sadness, and good poems can be written about going to a rock concert or having lunch or mowing the lawn, as well as about making love or smelling flowers or listening to Beethoven. Even poems on "predictable" subjects can surprise us with unpredicted attitudes, unusual events, or sudden twists. Knowing that a poem is about some particular subject—love, for example, or death—may give us a general idea of what to expect, but it never tells us altogether what we will find in a particular poem. Responding to a poem fully means being open to the poem and its surprises, letting the poem guide us to its own stances, feelings, and ideas—to an illumination of a topic that may be very different from what we expect or what we have thought before. Letting a poem speak to us means listening to *how* the poem says what it says—hearing the tone of voice implied in the way the words are spoken. *What* a poem says involves its **theme**, a statement about its subject. *How* a poem makes that statement involves its **tone**, the poem's attitude or feelings toward the theme.

The following two poems—one about death and one about love—express attitudes and feelings quite different from those in the poems we have read so far.

MARGE PIERCY

Barbie Doll

This girlchild was born as usual
and presented dolls that did pee-pee
and miniature GE stoves and irons
and wee lipsticks the color of cherry candy.
5 Then in the magic of puberty, a classmate said:
You have a great big nose and fat legs.

She was healthy, tested intelligent,
possessed strong arms and back,
abundant sexual drive and manual dexterity.
10 She went to and fro apologizing.
Everyone saw a fat nose on thick legs.

She was advised to play coy,
exhorted to come on hearty,
exercise, diet, smile and wheedle.

[handwritten: Internal Self]

15 Her good nature wore out
    like a fan belt.
    So she cut off her nose and her legs
    and offered them up.

    In the casket displayed on satin she lay
20 with the undertaker's cosmetics painted on,
    a turned-up putty nose,
    dressed in a pink and white nightie.
    Doesn't she look pretty? everyone said.
    Consummation at last.
25 To every woman a happy ending.   *[handwritten: What is a happy ending?]*

                                      1973

W. D. SNODGRASS

Leaving the Motel

    Outside, the last kids holler
    Near the pool: they'll stay the night.
    Pick up the towels; fold your collar
    Out of sight.

5   Check: is the second bed
    Unrumpled, as agreed?
    Landlords have to think ahead
    In case of need,

    Too. Keep things straight: don't take
10 The matches, the wrong keyrings—
    We've nowhere we could keep a keepsake—
    Ashtrays, combs, things

    That sooner or later others
    Would accidentally find.
15 Check: take nothing of one another's
    And leave behind

    Your license number only,
    Which they won't care to trace;
    We've paid. Still, should such things get lonely,
20 Leave in their vase

    An aspirin to preserve
    Our lilacs, the wayside flowers
    We've gathered and must leave to serve
    A few more hours;

25 That's all. We can't tell when
    We'll come back, can't press claims,
    We would no doubt have other rooms then,
    Or other names.

                                        1968

The first poem, "Barbie Doll," has the strong note of sadness that characterizes many death poems, but it emphasizes not the girl's death but the disappointments in her life. The only "scene" in the poem (lines 19–23) portrays the unnamed girl at rest in her casket, but the still body in the casket contrasts not with vitality but with frustration and anxiety: her life since puberty (lines 5–6) had been full of apologies and attempts to change her physical appearance and emotional makeup. The "consummation" she achieves in death is not, however, a triumph, despite what people say (line 23). Although the poem's last two words are "happy ending," this girl without a name has died in embarrassment and without fulfillment, and the final lines are ironic, questioning the whole idea of what "happy" means. The cheerful comments at the end lack force and truth because of what we already know; we understand them as ironic because they underline how unhappy the girl was and how false her cosmeticized corpse is to the sad truth of her life.

The poem suggests the falsity and destructiveness of those standards of female beauty that have led to the tragedy of the girl's life. In an important sense, the poem is not really *about* death at all in spite of the fact that the girl's death and her repaired corpse are central to it. As the title suggests, the poem dramatizes how standardized, commercialized notions of femininity and prettiness can be painful and destructive to those whose bodies do not precisely fit the conformist models, and the poem vigorously attacks those conventional standards and the widespread, unthinking acceptance of them.

"Leaving the Motel" similarly goes in quite a different direction from many poems on the subject of love. Instead of expressing assurance about how love lasts and endures, or about the sincerity and depth of affection, this poem describes a parting of lovers after a brief, surreptitious sexual encounter. But it does not emphasize sexuality or eroticism in the meeting of the nameless lovers (we see them only as they prepare to leave), nor does it suggest why or how they have found each other, or what either of them is like as a person. It focuses on how careful they must be not to get caught, how exact and calculating they must be in their planning, how finite and limited their encounter must be, how sealed off this encounter is from the rest of their lives. The poem relates the tiny details the lovers must think of, the agreements they must observe, and the ritual checklist of their duties ("Check . . . Keep things straight . . . Check . . . ," lines 5, 9, 15). Affection and sentiment have their small place in the poem (notice the care for the flowers, lines 19–24, and the thought of "press[ing] claims," line 26), but the emphasis is on temporariness, uncertainty, and limits. Although it is about an illicit, perhaps adulterous, sexual encounter, there is no sex in the poem, only a kind of archaeological record of lust.

Labeling a poem a "love poem" or a "death poem" is primarily a matter of convenience; such categories indicate the **subject** of a poem, or the event or **topic** it chooses to engage. But as the poems we have been looking at suggest, poems that may be loosely called "love poems" or "death poems" may differ widely from one another, express totally different attitudes or ideas, and concentrate on very different aspects of the subject. The main advantages of grouping poems in this way is that a reader can become conscious of individual differences; a reading of two poems side by side may suggest how each is distinctive in what it has to say and how it says it.

The theme of a poem may be expressed in several different ways, and poems often have more than one theme. We could say, for example, that the theme of "Leaving the Motel" is that illicit love is secretive, careful, transitory, and short on emotion and sentiment, or that secret sexual encounters tend to be brief, calculated, and characterized by restrained or hesitant feelings. "Barbie Doll" suggests that commercialized standards destroy humane values; that rigid and idealized notions of normality cripple those who are different; that people are easily and tragically led to accept evaluations thrust upon them by others; that American consumers tend to be conformists, easily influenced in their outlook by advertising and by commercial products; that children who do not conform to middle-class standards and notions don't have a chance. The poem implies each of these ideas, and all are quite central to it. But none of these assertions individually, nor all of them together, can fully express or explain the poem itself. To state the themes in such a brief and abstract way—though it may help to clarify what the poem does and does not say—cannot do justice to the experience of the poem, the way it works on us as readers, the way we respond. Poems affect us in all sorts of ways—emotional and psychological as well as rational—and often a poem's dramatization of a story, an event, or a moment bypasses our rational responses and affects us far more deeply than a clear and logical argument would.

Here is a poem even more directly about desire and its implications. It too is cautious, even critical, but it represents the appeal of both drugs and sex as powerfully as it depicts the fear of their consequences. The "Plague" is here the AIDS epidemic in America, especially among gay men, in the early 1990s.

THOM GUNN

In Time of Plague

My thoughts are crowded with death
and it draws so oddly on the sexual
that I am confused
confused to be attracted
5 by, in effect, my own annihilation.
Who are these two, these fiercely attractive men
who want me to stick their needle in my arm?
They tell me they are called Brad and John,
one from here, one from Denver, sitting the same
10 on the bench as they talk to me,
their legs spread apart, their eyes attentive.
I love their daring, their looks, their jargon,
and what they have in mind.

Their mind is the mind of death.
15 They know it, and do not know it,
and they are like me in that
(I know it, and do not know it)
and like the flow of people through this bar.
Brad and John thirst heroically together
20 for euphoria—for a state of ardent life
in which we could all stretch ourselves
and lose our differences. I seek
to enter their minds: am I a fool,
and they direct and right, properly
25 testing themselves against risk,
as a human must, and does,
or are they the fools, their alert faces
mere death's heads lighted glamorously?

I weigh possibilities
30 till I am afraid of the strength
of my own health
and of their evident health.

They get restless at last with my indecisiveness
and so, first one, and then the other,
35 move off into the moving concourse of people
who are boisterous and bright
carrying in their faces and throughout their bodies
the news of life and death.

1992

Delicate subject, sensitive poem. The situation and narrative here are quite clear, and the speaker is plainly attracted by the two men and "what they have in mind" (line 13), but the poem is about a mental state rather than physical action. The tone is carefully poised between excitement and fear—so much so that the two emotions don't just coexist but are nearly one, and a lust for life and attraction to death are very close. The speaker realizes that he is "attracted by . . . my own annihilation" (lines 4–5), and his vacillation about action involves an internal debate ("I weigh possibilities," line 29) between desire and self-protection. The tone of voice here is both excited and cautionary—at the same time.

Poems, then, can differ widely from one another even when they share a common subject. And the subjects of poetry can also vary widely. It isn't true that certain subjects are "poetic" and that others aren't appropriate to poetry. Any human activity, thought, or feeling can be the subject of poetry. Poetry often deals with beauty and the softer, more attractive human emotions, but it can deal with ugliness and unattractive human conduct as well, for poetry seeks to represent human beings and human events, showing us ourselves not only as we would like to be but as we are. Good poetry gets written about all kinds of topics, in all kinds of forms, with all kinds of attitudes. Here, for example, is a poem about a prison inmate—and about the conflict between individual and societal values.

ETHERIDGE KNIGHT

Hard Rock Returns to Prison from the Hospital for the Criminal Insane

Hard Rock was "known not to take no shit
From nobody," and he had the scars to prove it:
Split purple lips, lumped ears, welts above
His yellow eyes, and one long scar that cut
5   Across his temple and plowed through a thick
Canopy of kinky hair.

The WORD was that Hard Rock wasn't a mean nigger
Anymore, that the doctors had bored a hole in his head,
Cut out part of his brain, and shot electricity
10 Through the rest. When they brought Hard Rock back,
Handcuffed and chained, he was turned loose,
Like a freshly gelded stallion, to try his new status.
And we all waited and watched, like indians at a corral,
To see if the WORD was true.

15 As we waited we wrapped ourselves in the cloak
Of his exploits: "Man, the last time, it took eight
Screws to put him in the Hole."[1] "Yeah, remember when he
Smacked the captain with his dinner tray?" "He set
The record for time in the Hole—67 straight days!"
20 "Ol Hard Rock! man, that's one crazy nigger."
And then the jewel of a myth that Hard Rock had once bit
A screw on the thumb and poisoned him with syphilitic spit.

The testing came, to see if Hard Rock was really tame.
A hillbilly called him a black son of a bitch
25 And didn't lose his teeth, a screw who knew Hard Rock
From before shook him down and barked in his face.
And Hard Rock did *nothing.* Just grinned and looked silly,
His eyes empty like knot holes in a fence.

And even after we discovered that it took Hard Rock
30 Exactly 3 minutes to tell you his first name,
We told ourselves that he had just wised up,
Was being cool; but we could not fool ourselves for long,
And we turned away, our eyes on the ground. Crushed.
He had been our Destroyer, the doer of things
35 We dreamed of doing but could not bring ourselves to do,
The fears of years, like a biting whip,
Had cut grooves too deeply across our backs.

                                                    1968

---

1. Solitary confinement. *Screws*: guards.

The picture of Hard Rock as a kind of hero to other prison inmates is established early in the poem through a retelling of the legends circulated about him; the straightforward chronology of the poem sets up the mystery of how he will react after his "treatment" in the hospital. The poem identifies with those who wait; they are hopeful that Hard Rock's spirit has not been broken by surgery or shock treatments, and the lines crawl almost to a stop with disappointment in stanza 4. The *"nothing"* (line 27) of Hard Rock's response to taunting and the emptiness of his eyes ("like knot holes in a fence," line 28) reduce the narrator's hopes to despair. The final stanza recounts the observers' attempts to reinterpret, to hang onto hope that their symbol of heroism can stand up against the best efforts to tame him, but the spirit has gone out of the hero-worshipers, too, and the poem records them as beaten, tamed, deprived of their spirit as Hard Rock has been of his. The poem records the despair of the hopeless, and it protests against the cruel exercise of power that can quash even as defiant a figure as Hard Rock.

The following poem is equally full of anger and disappointment, but it expresses its attitudes in a very different way.

 WILLIAM BLAKE

London

    I wander through each chartered street,
    Near where the chartered Thames does flow,
    And mark in every face I meet
    Marks of weakness, marks of woe.

5 In every cry of every man,
    In every Infant's cry of fear,
    In every voice, in every ban,
    The mind-forged manacles I hear.

    How the Chimney-sweeper's cry
10 Every black'ning Church appalls;
    And the hapless Soldier's sigh
    Runs in blood down Palace walls.

    But most through midnight streets I hear
    How the youthful Harlot's curse
15 Blasts the new-born Infant's tear,
    And blights with plagues the Marriage hearse.

1794

The poem gives a strong sense of how London feels to this particular observer; it is cluttered, constricting, oppressive. The wordplay here articulates and connects the strong emotions he associates with London experiences. The repeated words—"every," for example, and "cry"—intensify the sense of total despair in the city and create connections between things not necessarily related, such as the cries of street vendors with the cries for help. The twice-used word "chartered" implies strong feelings, too. The streets, instead of seeming alive with people or bustling with movement, are rigidly, coldly determined, controlled, cramped. Likewise the river seems as if it were planned, programmed, laid out by an oppressor. In actual fact, the course of the Thames through the city had been altered (slightly) by the government before Blake's time, but most important is the word's emotional force, the sense it projects of constriction and artificiality: the speaker experiences London as if human artifice had totally usurped nature. Moreover, according to the poem, people are victimized, "marked" by their confrontations with the city and its faceless institutions: the "Soldier's sigh" that "runs in blood down Palace walls" vividly suggests, through metaphor, both the powerlessness of the individual and the callousness of power. The description of the city has clearly become, by now, a subjective, highly emotional, and vivid expression of how the speaker feels about London and what it represents to him.

> *Poetry makes nothing happen.*
> —W. H. AUDEN

Another thing about "London": at first it looks like an account of a personal experience, as if the speaker is describing and interpreting as he goes along: "I wander through each chartered street." But soon it is clear that he is describing many wanderings, putting together impressions from many walks, re-creating a typical walk—which shows him "every" person in the streets, allows him to generalize about the churches being "appalled" (literally, made white) by the cry of the representative Chimney-sweeper, and leads to his conclusions about soldiers, prostitutes, and infants. We receive not a personal record of an event, but a representation of it in retrospect—not a story, not a narrative or chronological account of events, but a dramatization of self that compresses many experiences and impressions into one.

> *When power leads man toward arrogance, poetry reminds him of his limitations. When power narrows the areas of man's concern, poetry reminds him of the richness and diversity of his existence. When power corrupts, poetry cleanses.*
> —JOHN F. KENNEDY

"London" is somber in spite of the poet's playfulness with words. Wordplay may be witty and funny if it calls attention to its own cleverness, but here it prompts the discovery of unsuspected (but meaningful) connections between things. The tone of the poem is sad, despairing, and angry; reading it aloud, one would try to show in the tone of one's voice the strong feelings that the poem expresses, just as one would try to reproduce tenderness and caring and passion in reading aloud "The Tally Stick" or "How Do I Love Thee?"

The following two poems are "about" animals, although both of them place their final emphasis on human beings: the animal in each case is only the means to the end of exploring human nature. The poems share a common assumption that animal behavior may appear to reflect human habits and conduct and may reveal much about ourselves, and in each case the character central to the poem is revealed to be surprisingly unlike the way she thinks of herself. But the poems are very different. Read each poem aloud, and try to imagine what each main character is like. What tones of voice do you use to help express the character of the "killer" (line 24) in the first poem? What demands on your voice does the second poem make?

MAXINE KUMIN

CD *Woodchucks*

Gassing the woodchucks didn't turn out right.
The knockout bomb from the Feed and Grain Exchange
was featured as merciful, quick at the bone
and the case we had against them was airtight,
5 both exits shoehorned shut with puddingstone,[2]
but they had a sub-sub-basement out of range.

Next morning they turned up again, no worse
for the cyanide than we for our cigarettes
and state-store Scotch, all of us up to scratch.
10 They brought down the marigolds as a matter of course
and then took over the vegetable patch
nipping the broccoli shoots, beheading the carrots.

The food from our mouths, I said, righteously thrilling
to the feel of the .22, the bullets' neat noses.
15 I, a lapsed pacifist fallen from grace
puffed with Darwinian pieties for killing,
now drew a bead on the littlest woodchuck's face.
He died down in the everbearing roses.

Ten minutes later I dropped the mother. She
20 flipflopped in the air and fell, her needle teeth
still hooked in a leaf of early Swiss chard.
Another baby next. O one-two-three
the murderer inside me rose up hard,
the hawkeye killer came on stage forthwith.

25 There's one chuck left. Old wily fellow, he keeps
me cocked and ready day after day after day.
All night I hunt his humped-up form. I dream
I sight along the barrel in my sleep.
If only they'd all consented to die unseen
30 gassed underground the quiet Nazi way.

1972

2. A mixture of cement, pebbles, and gravel.

ADRIENNE RICH

Aunt Jennifer's Tigers

Aunt Jennifer's tigers prance across a screen,
Bright topaz denizens of a world of green.
They do not fear the men beneath the tree;
They pace in sleek chivalric certainty.

5   Aunt Jennifer's fingers fluttering through her wool
Find even the ivory needle hard to pull.
The massive weight of Uncle's wedding band
Sits heavily upon Aunt Jennifer's hand.

When Aunt is dead, her terrified hands will lie
10   Still ringed with ordeals she was mastered by.
The tigers in the panel that she made
Will go on prancing, proud and unafraid.

1951

If you read "Woodchucks" aloud, how would your tone of voice change from beginning to end? What tone would you use to read the ending? How does the hunter feel about her increasing attraction to violence? Why does the poem begin by calling the gassing of the woodchucks "merciful" and end by describing it as "the quiet Nazi way"? What names does the hunter call herself? How does the name-calling affect your feelings about her? Exactly when does the hunter begin to *enjoy* the feel of the gun and the idea of killing? How does the poet make that clear?

In the second poem, why are tigers a particularly appropriate contrast to the quiet and subdued manner of Aunt Jennifer? What words describing the tigers seem particularly significant? How is the tiger an opposite of Aunt Jennifer? In what ways does it externalize her secrets? Why are Aunt Jennifer's hands described as "terrified"? What clues does the poem give about why Aunt Jennifer is so afraid? How does the poem make you feel about Aunt Jennifer? about her tigers? about her life? How would you describe the tone of the poem? How does the poet feel about Aunt Jennifer?

Twenty years after writing "Aunt Jennifer's Tigers," Adrienne Rich said this about the poem:

In writing this poem, composed and apparently cool as it is, I thought I was creating a portrait of an imaginary woman. But this woman suffers from the opposition of her imagination, worked out in tapestry, and her lifestyle, "ringed with ordeals she was mastered by." It was important to me that Aunt Jennifer was a person as distinct from myself as possible—distanced by the formalism of the poem, by its objective, observant tone—even by putting the woman in a different generation. In those years formalism was part of the strategy—like asbestos gloves, it allowed me to handle materials I couldn't pick up bare-handed.[3]

3. From "When We Dead Awaken: Writing as Re-Vision," a talk given in December 1971 at the Women's Forum of the Modern Language Association.

Not often do we have such an explicit comment on a poem by its author, and (although such a statement may clarify why the author chose a particular mode of presentation and how the poem fits into the author's own patterns of thinking and growing) we don't actually need the explanation in order to understand and experience the force of the poem. Most poems contain within them all we need to tap the human and artistic resources they offer us.

Subject, theme, and tone: each of these categories gives us a way to begin considering poems and how one poem differs from another. Comparing poems with the same subject or a similar theme or tone can lead to a clearer understanding of each individual poem and can refine our responses to their subtle differences. The title of a poem ("Leaving the Motel," for example) or the way a poem first introduces its subject can often give us a sense of what to expect, but we must be open to surprise, too. No two poems affect us in exactly the same way; the variety of possible poems multiplies when you think of all the possible themes and tones that can be explored within any single subject. Varieties of feeling often coincide with varieties of thinking, and readers open to the pleasures of the unexpected may find themselves learning, growing, becoming more sensitive to ideas and human issues—as well as more articulate about feelings and thoughts they already have.

MANY TONES: POEMS ABOUT FAMILIES

GALWAY KINNELL

After Making Love We Hear Footsteps

For I can snore like a bullhorn
or play loud music
or sit up talking with any reasonably sober Irishman
and Fergus will only sink deeper
5   into his dreamless sleep, which goes by all in one flash,
but let there be that heavy breathing
or a stifled come-cry anywhere in the house
and he will wrench himself awake
and make for it on the run—as now, we lie together,
10   after making love, quiet, touching along the length of our bodies,
familiar touch of the long-married,
and he appears—in his baseball pajamas, it happens,
the neck opening so small
he has to screw them on, which one day may make him wonder
15   about the mental capacity of baseball players—
and says, "Are you loving and snuggling? May I join?"
He flops down between us and hugs us and snuggles himself to sleep,
his face gleaming with satisfaction at being this very child.

In the half darkness we look at each other
20   and smile
and touch arms across his little, startlingly muscled body—

this one whom habit of memory propels to the ground of his making,
sleeper only the mortal sounds can sing awake,
this blessing love gives again into our arms.

1980

- How does the language in lines 1–5 establish the poem's tone? Do the last lines
  (starting with line 22) alter the tone in any way?

EMILY GROSHOLZ

Eden

In lurid cartoon colors, the big baby
dinosaur steps backwards under the shadow
of an approaching tyrannosaurus rex.
"His mommy going to fix it," you remark,
5   serenely anxious, hoping for the best.

After the big explosion, after the lights
go down inside the house and up the street,
we rush outdoors to find a squirrel stopped
in straws of half-gnawed cable. I explain,
10   trying to fit the facts, "The squirrel is dead."

No, you explain it otherwise to me.
"He's sleeping. And his mommy going to come."
Later, when the squirrel has been removed,
"His mommy fix him," you insist, insisting
15   on the right to know what you believe.

The world is truly full of fabulous
great and curious small inhabitants,
and you're the freshly minted, unashamed
Adam in this garden. You preside,
20   appreciate, and judge our proper names.

Like God, I brought you here.
Like God, I seem to be omnipotent,
mostly helpful, sometimes angry as hell.
I fix whatever minor faults arise
25   with bandaids, batteries, masking tape, and pills.

But I am powerless, as you must know,
to chase the serpent sliding in the grass,
or the tall angel with the flaming sword
who scares you when he rises suddenly
30   behind the gates of sunset.

1992

- How does Grosholz use language to elevate the poem's subject
  matter from the trivial and childish to the biblical and profound?

RACHEL HADAS

The Red Hat

It started before Christmas. Now our son
officially walks to school alone.
Semi-alone, it's accurate to say:
I or his father track him on the way.
5 He walks up on the east side of West End,
we on the west side. Glances can extend
(and do) across the street; not eye contact.
Already ties are feeling and not fact.
Straus Park is where these parallel paths part;
10 he goes alone from there. The watcher's heart
stretches, elastic in its love and fear,
toward him as we see him disappear,
striding briskly. Where two weeks ago,
holding a hand, he'd dawdle, dreamy, slow,
15 he now is hustled forward by the pull
of something far more powerful than school.

The mornings we turn back to are no more
than forty minutes longer than before,
but they feel vastly different—flimsy, strange,
20 wavering in the eddies of this change,
empty, unanchored, perilously light
since the red hat vanished from our sight.

                                        1998

• How does the poem's use of rhyme and meter affect the tone? Does
  this make the poem any less natural or conversational?

DANIEL TOBIN

The Clock

Bored with plastic armies,
he climbs onto the parlor loveseat
and watches the wide expression of the clock.
He doesn't know what time is,
5 doesn't know how in no time
those numbers will fill his days
the way water fills a bath
into which an exhausted man
lowers himself, not wanting to rise.

10 Sun and moon gaze back at him
from the glaze of the silver frame,
each with a human face,
his own face mirrored there.
Look closer, his mother says,
15 and you can see the small hand move.
And he leans closer now, steadied
in her arms, the hand a winded runner
lapped on the track. That's hours,
she says, the big hand's minutes, the quick,
20 seconds. And the boy fingers the pivot
anchoring them, his touch
stirs with the machine.
I'm older now, and now, and now. The gears
start to tick through every room of that house.

1999

- How do the language and tone shift when the boy touches the clock?
  What exactly has changed?

EAVAN BOLAND

The Necessity for Irony

On Sundays,
when the rain held off,
after lunch or later,
I would go with my twelve year old
5 daughter into town,
and put down the time
at junk sales, antique fairs.

There I would
lean over tables,
10 absorbed by
place, wooden frames,
glass. My daughter stood
at the other end of the room,
her flame-coloured hair
15 obvious whenever—
which was not often—

I turned around.
I turned around.
She was gone.
20 Grown. No longer ready
to come with me, whenever

a dry Sunday
held out its promises
25 of small histories. Endings.

When I was young
I studied styles: their use
and origin. Which age
was known for which
ornament: and was always drawn
30 to a lyric speech, a civil tone.
But never thought
I would have the need,
as I do now, for a darker one:

Spirit of irony,
35 my caustic author
of the past, of memory,—
and of its pain, which returns
hurts, stings—reproach me now,
remind me
40 that I was in those rooms,
with my child,
with my back turned to her,
searching—oh irony!—
for beautiful things.

1998

- Why does the speaker say he now needs a "darker" tone (line 33)?
  How does the poem embody this "spirit of irony" (line 34)?

PAT MORA

Elena

My Spanish isn't enough.
I remember how I'd smile
listening to my little ones,
understanding every word they'd say,
5 their jokes, their songs, their plots.
  Vamos a pedirle dulces a mamá. Vamos.[1]
But that was in Mexico.
Now my children go to American high schools.
They speak English. At night they sit around
10 the kitchen table, laugh with one another.
I stand by the stove and feel dumb, alone.

---

1. Let's go ask mama for sweets. Let's go.

I bought a book to learn English.
My husband frowned, drank more beer.
My oldest said, "*Mamá*, he doesn't want you
15 to be smarter than he is." I'm forty,
embarrassed at mispronouncing words,
embarrassed at the laughter of my children,
the grocer, the mailman. Sometimes I take
my English book and lock myself in the bathroom,
20 say the thick words softly,
for if I stop trying, I will be deaf
when my children need my help.

                                        1985

- What does the speaker mean by the first line—"My Spanish isn't enough"? What other words in the poem address the inadequacy of language?

ANDREW HUDGINS

Begotten

I've never, as some children do,
looked at my folks and thought, I *must*
have come from someone else—
rich parents who'd misplaced me, but
5 who would, as in a myth or novel,
return and claim me. Hell, no. I saw
my face in cousins' faces, heard
my voice in their high drawls. And Sundays,
after the dinner plates were cleared,
10 I lingered, elbow propped on red
oilcloth, and studied great-uncles, aunts,
and cousins new to me. They squirmed.
I stared till I discerned the features
they'd gotten from the family larder:
15 eyes, nose, lips, hair? I stared until,
uncomfortable, they'd snap, "Hey, boy—
what are you looking at? At me?"
"No, sir," I'd lie. "No, ma'am." I'd count ten
and then continue staring at them.
20 I never had to ask, What am I?
I stared at my blood-kin, and thought,
So *this*, dear God, is what I am.

                                        1994

- What can you infer from the language in "Begotten" about the speaker's attitude toward his life?

LORNA DEE CERVANTES

Refugee Ship

Like wet cornstarch, I slide
past my grandmother's eyes. Bible
at her side, she removes her glasses.
The pudding thickens.

5 Mama raised me without language.
I'm orphaned from my Spanish name.
The words are foreign, stumbling
on my tongue. I see in the mirror
my reflection: bronzed skin, black hair.

10 I feel I am a captive
aboard the refugee ship.
The ship that will never dock.
El barco que nunca atraca.[2]

1981

- How do the "foreign" Spanish words of the poem's final line affect the tone?

PAUL MULDOON

Milkweed and Monarch

As he knelt by the grave of his mother and father
the taste of dill, or tarragon—
he could barely tell one from the other—

filled his mouth. It seemed as if he might smother.
5 Why should he be stricken
with grief, not for his mother and father,

but a woman slinking from the fur of a sea-otter
in Portland, Maine, or, yes, Portland, Oregon—
he could barely tell one from the other—

10 and why should he now savor
the tang of her, her little pickled gherkin,
as he knelt by the grave of his mother and father?

He looked about. He remembered her palaver
on how both earth and sky would darken—
15 "You could barely tell one from the other"—

2. Spanish version of line 12.

while the Monarch butterflies passed over
in their milkweed-hunger: "A wing-beat, some reckon,
may trigger off the mother and father

of all storms, striking your Irish Cliffs of Mohel[3]
20 with the force of a hurricane."
Then: "Milkweed and Monarch 'invented' each other."

He looked about. Cow's-parsley[4] in a samovar.
He'd mistaken his mother's name, "Regan," for "Anger":
as he knelt by the grave of his mother and father
25 he could barely tell one from the other.

                                        1999

- What is the effect of the repeating words "father" and "other" on
  the tone of the poem? What is the feeling of the poem's final stanza?

MICHAEL LONGLEY

In a Mississauga[5] Garden

The ghosts of the aunt and uncles I never knew
Put in an appearance when I meet my cousin.
Charlie, big in the Union, straightens his plus fours.
Hugh is curing homegrown tobacco in the garage
5 While my grandparents lie upstairs, out of sorts.
Seamstress to the Court, Daisy burns a cigarette hole
In the chesterfield, then makes the tea for everyone.
Maurice keeps fiddling with the wind-up gramophone.
Having come all the way across the Atlantic,
10 From Clapham Common[6] to this Mississauga garden,
They flit out of sight like the different robins
Or the blackbird with flashes of red on its wings.

                                        1991

- How does the poem's old-fashioned vocabulary (e.g., "plus fours,"
  "chesterfield") help to reinforce the tone of the speaker's voice?

---

3. Tall, rocky cliffs on the coast of western Ireland that are constantly buffeted by the Atlantic.
4. Another name for Queen Anne's lace, a flowering plant with small, white blossoms that grows in fields
and on roadsides.   5. A suburb of Toronto.   6. Near London.

SEAMUS HEANEY

Mother of the Groom

What she remembers
Is his glistening back
In the bath, his small boots
In the ring of boots at her feet.

5 Hands in her voided lap,
She hears a daughter welcomed.
It's as if he kicked when lifted
And slipped her soapy hold.

Once soap would ease off
10 The wedding ring
That's bedded forever now
In her clapping hand.

1966

- Which words in the poem appear to have double meanings? How
  does this use of language affect the poem's tone?

KELLY CHERRY

Alzheimer's

He stands at the door, a crazy old man
Back from the hospital, his mind rattling
Like the suitcase, swinging from his hand,
That contains shaving cream, a piggy bank,
5 A book he sometimes pretends to read,
His clothes. On the brick wall beside him
Roses and columbine slug it out for space, claw the mortar.
The sun is shining, as it does late in the afternoon
In England, after rain.
10 Sun hardens the house, reifies it,
Strikes the iron grillwork like a smithy
And sparks fly off, burning in the bushes—
The rosebushes—
While the white wood trim defines solidity in space.
15 This is his house. He remembers it as his,
Remembers the walkway he built between the front room
And the garage, the rhododendron he planted in back,
The car he used to drive. He remembers himself,
A younger man, in a tweed hat, a man who loved
20 Music. There is no time for that now. No time for music,

The peculiar screeching of strings, the luxurious
Fiddling with emotion.
Other things have become more urgent.
Other matters are now of greater import, have more
25 Consequence, must be attended to. The first
Thing he must do, now that he is home, is decide who
This woman is, this old, white-haired woman
Standing here in the doorway,
Welcoming him in.

1997

- How do phrases like "a crazy old man" and "a book he sometimes pretends to read" indicate the speaker's feelings toward her father? Does her attitude shift at some point? Where?

SIMON J. ORTIZ

My Father's Song

Wanting to say things,
I miss my father tonight.
His voice, the slight catch,
the depth from his thin chest,
5 the tremble of emotion
in something he has just said
to his son, his song:

We planted corn one Spring at Aču—
we planted several times
10 but this one particular time
I remember the soft damp sand
in my hand.

My father had stopped at one point
to show me an overturned furrow;
15 the plowshare had unearthed
the burrow nest of a mouse
in the soft moist sand.

Very gently, he scooped tiny pink animals
into the palm of his hand
20 and told me to touch them.
We took them to the edge
of the field and put them in the shade
of a sand moist clod.

I remember the very softness
25 of cool and warm sand and tiny alive mice
and my father saying things.

1976

- What are the "things" that the speaker wants to say in "My Father's Song"? Are they the same things he remembers his father saying? Does the poem itself says these things?

SUSAN MUSGRAVE

You Didn't Fit

for my father

You wouldn't fit in your coffin
but to me it was no surprise.
All your life you had never fit in
anywhere; you saw no reason to
5 begin fitting now.

When I was little I remember
a sheriff coming. You were
taken to court because your
false teeth didn't fit and you
10 wouldn't pay the dentist. It was
your third set, you said none of them
fit properly. I was afraid then
that something would take you from me
as it has done now: death
15 with a bright face and teeth that
fit perfectly.

A human smile that shuts me out.
The Court, I remember, returned
your teeth, now marked an exhibit.
20 You were dismissed with costs—
I never understood. The teeth were
terrible. We liked you better
without them.

We didn't fit, either, into your
25 life or your loneliness, though you
tried, and we did too. Once
I wanted to marry you, and then left;
I'm still the child who won't fit
into the arms of anyone, but is
30 always reaching.
I was awkward for years, my bones
didn't fit in my body but stuck out
like my heart—people used to comment
on it. They said I was very good
35 at office parties where you took me
and let others do the talking—the

crude jokes, the corny men—I saw
how they hurt you and I loved you
harder than ever.

40   Because neither of us fit. Later you
blamed me, said "You must fit in,"
but I didn't and I still think
it made you secretly happy.

Like I am now: you won't fit in your
45   coffin. My mother, after a life
of it, says, "This is the last straw."
And it is. We're all clutching.

                                        1985

- What additional layers of meaning or feeling does the word "fit"
  take on each time it is used?

ALAN DUGAN

Elegy

I know but will not tell
you, Aunt Irene, why there
are soapsuds in the whiskey:
Uncle Robert had to have
5   a drink while shaving. May
there be no bloodshed in your house
this morning of my father's death
and no unkept appearance
in the living, since he has
10   to wear the rouge and lipstick
of your ceremony, mother,
for the first and last time:
father, hello and goodbye.

                                        1963

- How does the use of the word "bloodshed" (line 6) affect the tone
  of the poem?

ROBERT HAYDEN

Those Winter Sundays

Sundays too my father got up early
and put his clothes on in the blueblack cold,
then with cracked hands that ached
from labor in the weekday weather made
5 banked fires blaze. No one ever thanked him.

I'd wake and hear the cold splintering, breaking.
When the rooms were warm, he'd call,
and slowly I would rise and dress,
fearing the chronic angers of that house,

10 Speaking indifferently to him,
who had driven out the cold
and polished my good shoes as well.
What did I know, what did I know
of love's austere and lonely offices?

1966

- Why does the poem begin with the words "Sundays too" (rather
  than, say, "On Sundays")? What are the "austere and lonely offices"
  of love in the poem's final line?

The Whipping

The old woman across the way
  is whipping the boy again
and shouting to the neighborhood
  her goodness and his wrongs.

5 Wildly he crashes through elephant ears,
  pleads in dusty zinnias,
while she in spite of crippling fat
  pursues and corners him.

She strikes and strikes the shrilly circling
10 boy till the stick breaks
in her hand. His tears are rainy weather
  to woundlike memories:

My head gripped in bony vise
  of knees, the writhing struggle
15 to wrench free, the blows, the fear
  worse than blows that hateful

Words could bring, the face that I
  no longer knew or loved. . . .

Well, it is over now, it is over,
20 and the boy sobs in his room,

And the woman leans muttering against
  a tree, exhausted, purged—
avenged in part for lifelong hidings
  she has had to bear.

1962, 1966

- What words in the poem express the violence of the scene? How
  does the tone change in the poem's final stanza?

YVONNE SAPIA

Grandmother, a Caribbean Indian, Described by My Father

Nearly a hundred when she died,
mi viejita[7]
was an open boat,
and I had no map
5 to show her the safe places.
There was much to grieve.
Her shoulders were stooped.
Her hands were never young.
They broke jars
10 at the watering holes,
like bones, like hearts.

When she was a girl,
she was given the island
but no wings.
15 She wanted wings,
though she bruised
like a persimmon.
She was not ruined
before her marriage.
20 But after the first baby died,
she disappeared in the middle
of days to worship
her black saint,
after the second,
25 to sleep with a hand towel
across her eyes.

I had to take care
not to exhume

7. My little old woman or mother [Sapia's note].

from the mound of memory
30 these myths, these lost ones.
Born sleek as swans
on her river, my brother,
the man you have met
who has one arm,
35 and I glided into the sun.
Other children poured forth,
and by the time I was sixteen
I lost my place
in her thatched house.

40 She let me go,
and she did not come to the pier
the day the banana boat
pushed away from her shore
towards Nueva York
45 where I had heard
there would be room for me.

1987

• **What words in this poem set the tone? How does the tone evolve
over the course of the poem?**

ALBERTO ALVARO RÍOS

Mi Abuelo[8]

Where my grandfather is is in the ground
where you can hear the future like an
Indian with his ear at the tracks. A
pipe leads down to him so that sometimes
5 he whispers what will happen to a man
in town or how he will meet the best-
dressed woman tomorrow and how the best
man at her wedding will chew the ground
next to her. Mi abuelo is the man
10 who talks through all the mouths in my house. An
echo of me hitting the pipe sometimes
to stop him from saying "my hair is a
sieve" is the only other sound. It is a
phrase that among all others is the best,
15 he says, and "my hair is a sieve" is sometimes
repeated for hours out of the ground
when I let him, but mostly I don't. "An

---

8. My grandfather.

abuelo should be much more than a man
like you!" He stops then, and speaks: "I am a man
20 who has served ants with the attitude of a
waiter, who has made each smile as only an
ant who is fat can, and they liked me best,
but there is nothing left." Yet, I know he ground
green coffee beans as a child, and sometimes
25 he will talk about his wife, and sometimes
about when he was deaf and a man
cured him by mail and he heard ground
hogs talking, or about how he walked with a
cane he chewed on when he got hungry. At best,
30 mi abuelo is a liar. I see an
old picture of him at nani's with an
off-white yellow center mustache and sometimes
that's all I know for sure. He talks best
about these hills, slowest waves, and where this man
35 is going, and I'm convinced his hair is a
sieve, that his fever is cool now in the ground.
Mi abuelo is an ordinary man.
I look down the pipe, sometimes, and see a
ripple-topped stream in its best suit, in the ground.

                                        1980

- What is the "pipe" in this poem? What might it mean that "my hair
  is a sieve"? What are some of the speaker's attitudes toward his
  grandfather?

JIMMY SANTIAGO BACA

Green Chile

I prefer red chile over my eggs
and potatoes for breakfast.
Red chile *ristras*[9] decorate my door,
dry on my roof, and hang from eaves.
5 They lend open-air vegetable stands
historical grandeur, and gently swing
with an air of festive welcome.
I can hear them talking in the wind,
haggard, yellowing, crisp, rasping
10 tongues of old men, licking the breeze.

---

9. Braided strings of peppers.

But grandmother loves green chile.
When I visit her,
she holds the green chile pepper
in her wrinkled hands.
15 Ah, voluptuous, masculine,
an air of authority and youth simmers
from its swan-neck stem, tapering to a flowery
collar, fermenting resinous spice.
A well-dressed gentleman at the door
20 my grandmother takes sensuously in her hand,
rubbing its firm glossed sides,
caressing the oily rubbery serpent,
with mouth-watering fulfillment,
fondling its curves with gentle fingers.
25 Its bearing magnificent and taut
as flanks of a tiger in mid-leap,
she thrusts her blade into
and cuts it open, with lust
on her hot mouth, sweating over the stove,
30 bandanna round her forehead,
mysterious passion on her face
and she serves me green chile con carne
between soft warm leaves of corn tortillas,
with beans and rice—her sacrifice
35 to her little prince.
I slurp from my plate
with last bit of tortilla, my mouth burns
and I hiss and drink a tall glass of cold water.

All over New Mexico, sunburned men and women
40 drive rickety trucks stuffed with gunny-sacks
of green chile, from Belen, Veguita, Willard, Estancia,
San Antonio y Socorro, from fields
to roadside stands, you see them roasting green chile
in screen-sided homemade barrels, and for a dollar a bag,
45 we relive this old, beautiful ritual again and again.

1989

- What different qualities do the red and green chiles have? Which
  words in the poem help to personify the chiles? How fully do these
  words reflect the differences between the speaker and the grand-
  mother?

POEMS ABOUT ANIMALS AND INSECTS (AND HUMANS)

JOHN HOLLANDER

Adam's Task

And Adam gave names to all cattle, and to the fowl of the air, and to every
beast of the field . . .   —Gen. 2:20

Thou, paw-paw-paw; thou, glurd; thou, spotted
  Glurd; thou, whitestap, lurching through
The high-grown brush; thou, pliant-footed,
  Implex; thou, awagabu.

5 Every burrower, each flier
  Came for the name he had to give:
Gay, first work, ever to be prior,
  Not yet sunk to primitive.

Thou, verdle; thou, McFleery's pomma;
10   Thou; thou; thou—three types of grawl;
Thou, flisket; thou, kabasch; thou, comma-
  Eared mashawk; thou, all; thou, all.

Were, in a fire of becoming,
  Laboring to be burned away,
15 Then work, half-measuring, half-humming,
  Would be as serious as play.

Thou, pambler; thou, rivarn; thou, greater
  Wherret, and thou, lesser one;
Thou, sproal; thou, zant; thou, lily-eater.
20   Naming's over. Day is done.

                       1971

- How does this poem's tone change over the course of its twenty
  lines? What does the repeated use of "thou" contribute to the tone?

SUSAN DONNELLY

Eve Names the Animals

To me, *lion* was sun on a wing
over the garden. *Dove,*
a burrowing, blind creature.

I swear that man
5 never knew animals. Words
he lined up according to size,

while elephants slipped flat-eyed
through water

and trout
10 hurtled from the underbrush, tusked
and ready for battle.

The name he gave me struck
me to him. He did it to comfort me,
for not being first.

15 Mornings, while he slept,
I got away. Pickerel
hopped on the branches above me.
Only spider accompanied me,
nosing everywhere,
20 running up to lick my hand.

Poor finch. I suppose I was
woe to him—
the way he'd come looking for me,
not wanting either of us
25 to be ever alone

But to myself I was
palomino
      raven
           fox . . .

30 I strung words
by their stems and wore them
as garlands on my long walks.

The next day
I'd find them withered.

35 I liked change.

1985

- How would you characterize the tone of this poem—playful? angry?
  ironic? How does Eve's assertion that "The name he gave me stuck /
  me to him" (lines 12–13) help to illuminate the poem?

VIRGINIA HAMILTON ADAIR

God to the Serpent

Beloved Snake, perhaps my finest blueprint,
How can I not take pride in your design?
Your passage without hoof- or paw- or shoe-print
Revels in art's and nature's S-curve line.

5 No ears, no whiskers, fingers, legs or teeth,
No cries, complaints, nor curses from you start;
But silence shares your body in its sheath,
Full-functioning with no superfluous part.

Men try to emulate your forkéd tongue,
10 Their prideful piece dwarfed by your lordly length.
Two arms for blows or hugging loosely hung
Are mocked by Boa Constrictor's single strength.

How dare men claim their image as my own,
With all those limbs and features sticking out?
15 You, Snake, with continuity of bone
Need but a spine to coil and cruise about.

Men fear the force of your hypnotic eyes,
Make myths to damn your being wise and deft.
You, Snake, not men, deserve my cosmic prize.
20 I'm glad you stayed in Eden when they left.

1996

- How do such effects of sound as alliteration, rhythm, and rhyme contribute to the tone of the poem? Which line most fully embodies the tone? Why?

WILLIAM BLAKE

The Tyger

Tyger! Tyger! burning bright
In the forests of the night,
What immortal hand or eye
Could frame thy fearful symmetry?

5 In what distant deeps or skies
Burnt the fire of thine eyes?
On what wings dare he aspire?
What the hand dare seize the fire?

And what shoulder, & what art,
10 Could twist the sinews of thy heart?
And when thy heart began to beat,
What dread hand? & what dread feet?

What the hammer? what the chain?
In what furnace was thy brain?
15 What the anvil? what dread grasp
Dare its deadly terrors clasp?

When the stars threw down their spears
And water'd heaven with their tears,
Did he smile his work to see?
20 Did he who made the Lamb make thee?

Tyger! Tyger! burning bright
In the forests of the night,
What immortal hand or eye
Dare frame thy fearful symmetry?

1790

- How does Blake achieve a tone of "fearful" (line 4) wonderment in this poem? How, in turn, does the tone contribute to the poem's overall meaning and feeling?

RICHARD WILBUR

The Pardon

My dog lay dead five days without a grave
In the thick of summer, hid in a clump of pine
And a jungle of grass and honeysuckle-vine.
I who had loved him while he kept alive

5 Went only close enough to where he was
To sniff the heavy honeysuckle-smell
Twined with another odor heavier still
And hear the flies' intolerable buzz.

Well, I was ten and very much afraid.
10 In my kind world the dead were out of range
And I could not forgive the sad or strange
In beast or man. My father took the spade

And buried him. Last night I saw the grass
Slowly divide (it was the same scene
15 But now it glowed a fierce and mortal green)
And saw the dog emerging. I confess

I felt afraid again, but still he came
In the carnal sun, clothed in a hymn of flies,
And death was breeding in his lively eyes.
20 I started in to cry and call his name,

Asking forgiveness of his tongueless head.
. . . I dreamt the past was never past redeeming:
But whether this was false or honest dreaming
I beg death's pardon now. And mourn the dead.

1950

- Why does the speaker "beg death's pardon now" (line 24)? What words or phrases in this poem create a tone that helps to prepare the reader for the final line?

SEAMUS HEANEY

The Outlaw

Kelly's kept an unlicensed bull, well away
From the road: you risked fine but had to pay

The normal fee if cows were serviced there.
Once I dragged a nervous Friesian on a tether

5 Down a lane of alder, shaggy with catkin,
Down to the shed the bull was kept in.

I gave Old Kelly the clammy silver, though why
I could not guess. He grunted a curt "Go by

Get up on that gate." And from my lofty station
10 I watched the business-like conception.

The door, unbolted, whacked back against the wall.
The illegal sire fumbled from his stall

Unhurried as an old steam engine shunting,
He circled, snored and nosed. No hectic panting,

15 Just the unfussy ease of a good tradesman;
Then an awkward, unexpected jump, and

His knobbed forelegs straddling her flank,
He slammed life home, impassive as a tank,

Dropping off like a tipped-up load of sand.
20 "She'll do," said Kelly and tapped his ash-plant

Across her hindquarters. "If not, bring her back."
I walked ahead of her, the rope now slack

While Kelly whooped and prodded his outlaw
Who, in his own time, resumed the dark, the straw.

1969

- How does the speaker feel about Old Kelly and his business with the
  bull, and how do you know this—that is, what words or phrases
  create the tone of the poem?

C. K. WILLIAMS

The Doe

Near dusk, near a path, near a brook,
we stopped, I in disquiet and dismay
for the suffering of someone I loved,
the doe in her always incipient alarm.

5 All that moved was her pivoting ear
the reddening sun shining through
transformed to a color I'd only seen
in a photo of a new child in a womb.

Nothing else stirred, not a leaf,
10 not the air, but she startled and bolted
away from me into the crackling brush.

The part of my pain which sometimes
releases me from it fled with her, the rest,
in the rake of the late light, stayed.

2003

- How does the speaker's mood of "disquiet and dismay" affect the
  tone with which he relates his encounter with the doe? What feeling
  is conveyed by the words "the rake of the late light" in the poem's
  final line?

ROBERT LOWELL

 ### *Skunk Hour*

for Elizabeth Bishop

Nautilus Island's hermit
heiress still lives through winter in her Spartan cottage;
her sheep still graze above the sea.
Her son's a bishop. Her farmer

5　is first selectman[1] in our village,
　　she's in her dotage.

　　Thirsting for
　　the hierarchic privacy
　　of Queen Victoria's century,
10　she buys up all
　　the eyesores facing her shore,
　　and lets them fall.

　　The season's ill—
　　we've lost our summer millionaire,
15　who seemed to leap from an L. L. Bean[2]
　　catalogue. His nine-knot yawl
　　was auctioned off to lobstermen.
　　A red fox stain covers Blue Hill.

　　And now our fairy
20　decorator brightens his shop for fall,
　　his fishnet's filled with orange cork,
　　orange, his cobbler's bench and awl,
　　there is no money in his work,
　　he'd rather marry.

25　One dark night,
　　my Tudor Ford climbed the hill's skull,
　　I watched for love-cars. Lights turned down,
　　they lay together, hull to hull,
　　where the graveyard shelves on the town. . . .
30　My mind's not right.

　　A car radio bleats,
　　"Love, O careless Love. . . ."[3] I hear
　　my ill-spirit sob in each blood cell,
　　as if my hand were at its throat. . . .
35　I myself am hell;
　　nobody's here—

　　only skunks, that search
　　in the moonlight for a bite to eat.
　　They march on their soles up Main Street:
40　white stripes, moonstruck eyes' red fire
　　under the chalk-dry and spar spire
　　of the Trinitarian Church.

　　I stand on top
　　of our back steps and breathe the rich air—
45　a mother skunk with her column of kittens swills the garbage pail.
　　She jabs her wedge head in a cup

---

1. An elected New England town official.　2. Famous Maine sporting goods firm.
3. A popular folk song recorded many times, as by Frankie Laine (1959).

of sour cream, drops her ostrich tail,
and will not scare.

                                                                1959

- What words or phrases in the poem contribute a sense of what the
  speaker means in saying "My mind's not right" (line 30)? What feel-
  ings does the speaker seem to associate with "skunk hour"?

THOMAS GRAY

Ode on the Death of a Favorite Cat,
Drowned in a Tub of Gold Fishes

'Twas on a lofty vase's side,
Where China's gayest art had dyed
   The azure flowers that blow;
Demurest of the tabby kind,
5 The pensive Selima reclined,
   Gazed on the lake below.

Her conscious tail her joy declared;
The fair round face, the snowy beard,
   The velvet of her paws,
10 Her coat, that with the tortoise vies,
Her ears of jet, and emerald eyes,
   She saw; and purred applause.

Still had she gazed; but 'midst the tide
Two angel forms were seen to glide,
15   The genii of the stream;
Their scaly armor's Tyrian hue[4]
Through richest purple to the view
   Betrayed a golden gleam.

The hapless nymph with wonder saw;
20 A whisker first and then a claw,
   With many an ardent wish,
She stretched in vain to reach the prize.
What female heart can gold despise?
   What cat's averse to fish?

25 Presumptuous maid! with looks intent
Again she stretched, again she bent,
   Nor knew the gulf between.
(Malignant Fate sat by and smiled)
The slipp'ry verge her feet beguiled,
30   She tumbled headlong in.

---

4. Purple.

Eight times emerging from the flood
She mewed to ev'ry watry god,
    Some speedy aid to send.
No dolphin came, no Nereid stirred;
35 Nor cruel Tom, nor Susan heard;
    A favorite has no friend!

From hence, ye beauties, undeceived,
Know, one false step is ne'er retrieved,
    And be with caution bold.
40 Not all that tempts your wandering eyes
And heedless hearts, is lawful prize;
    Nor all that glisters, gold.
                                    1748

• How does the tone of the poem help to convey the allure of "all that
  glisters" (line 42)? What does the tone suggest about the use of
  poetry as an instructional medium in the eighteenth century?

EMILY DICKINSON

CD   *[A narrow Fellow in the Grass]*

A narrow Fellow in the Grass
Occasionally rides—
You may have met Him—did you not
His notice sudden is—

5 The Grass divides as with a Comb—
A spotted shaft is seen—
And then it closes at your feet
And opens further on—

He likes a Boggy Acre
10 A Floor too cool for Corn—
Yet when a Boy, and Barefoot—
I more than once at Noon

Have passed, I thought, a Whip lash
Unbraiding in the Sun
15 When stooping to secure it
It wrinkled, and was gone—

Several of Nature's People
I know, and they know me—
I feel for them a transport
20 Of cordiality—

But never met this Fellow
Attended, or alone

Without a tighter breathing
And Zero at the Bone—

1866

- How does the tone of the poem change in the final stanza? What might account for this change?

JOHN KEATS

On the Grasshopper and the Cricket

The poetry of earth is never dead:
When all the birds are faint with the hot sun,
And hide in cooling trees, a voice will run
From hedge to hedge about the new-mown mead;
5 That is the grasshopper's—he takes the lead
In summer luxury—he has never done
With his delights; for when tired out with fun
He rests at ease beneath some pleasant weed.
The poetry of earth is ceasing never:
10 On a lone winter evening, when the frost
Has wrought a silence, from the stove there shrills
The cricket's song, in warmth increasing ever,
And seems to one in drowsiness half lost,
The grasshopper's among some grassy hills.

December 30, 1816

- What is the tone of the "grasshopper" section of the poem (lines 1–8)? How does the tone change in the "cricket" section (lines 9–14)?

ROBERT BURNS

To a Louse

On Seeing One on a Lady's Bonnet at Church

Ha! whare ya gaun, ye crowlan ferlie![5]
Your impudence protects you sairly:[6]
I canna say but ye strunt[7] rarely,
    Owre gauze and lace;
5 Tho' faith, I fear ye dine but sparely,
    On sic a place.

5. Crawling miracle! 6. Sorely. 7. Strut.

Ye ugly, creepan, blastit wonner,[8]
Detested, shunn'd, by saunt an' sinner,
How daur ye set your fit[9] upon her,
10   Sae fine a Lady!
Gae somewhere else and seek your dinner,
      On some poor body.

Swith, in some beggar's haffet squattle;[1]
There ye may creep, and sprawl, and sprattle,[2]
15 Wi'ither kindred, jumping cattle,
      In shoals and, nations;
Whare horn nor bane[3] ne'er daur unsettle,
      Your thick plantations.

Now haud you there ye're out o'sight,
20 Below the fatt'rels,[4] snug and tight,
Na faith ye yet![5] ye'll no be right,
      Till ye've got on it,
The vera tapmost, towrin height
      O' Miss's bonnet.

25 My sooth! right bauld ye set your nose out,
As plump an' gray as onie grozet:[6]
O for some rank, mercurial rozet,[7]
      Or fell, red smeddum,[8]
I'd gie you sic a hearty dose o't,
30   Wad dress your droddum![9]

I wad na been surpriz'd to spy
You on an auld wife's flainen toy,[1]
Or aiblins some bit duddie boy,[2]
      On 's wylecoat;[3]
35 But Miss's fine Lunardi,[4] fye!
      How daur ye do't?

O Jenny dinna toss your head,
An' set your beauties a' abread![5]
Ye little ken what cursed speed
40   The blastie's[6] makin!
Thae[7] winks and finger-ends, I dread,
      Are notice takin!

O wad some Pow'r the giftie gie us
To see oursels as others see us!
45 It wad frae monie a blunder free us

---

8. Wonder.   9. Foot.   1. Swift, in some beggar's hair sprawl.   2. Struggle.   3. Bone.
4. Ribbon ends.   5. No matter!   6. Gooseberry.   7. Rosin.   8. Or sharp, red powder.
9. Buttocks.   1. Flannel cap.   2. Or perhaps some small ragged boy.   3. Undershirt.   4. Bonnet.
5. Abroad.   6. Creature's.   7. Those.

An foolish notion:
What airs in dress an' gait wad lea'e us,
And ev'n Devotion![8]

1785

- What is the speaker's attitude toward the louse? toward Jenny? What lines best summarize the speaker's main point?

PETER EVERWINE

Lullaby

Last night, in the dark, something
came near and frightened me
and left me turning in my bed, listening
to the hum of a mosquito—almost the timbre
5 of a human voice—as it came and went.
She must have entered from the garden
through the torn screen, looking
to calm a need of her own
and called to—so I've been told—
10 by the sound a heart makes.
No, this isn't another metaphor
meant to adorn a romantic tale.
Like you, I'd kill a mosquito in a moment.
But it does make one stop and think
15 how driven we are, even the least, to hear
the world's incessant undersong—
even if it was never meant for us
or never anything but clamor we wanted to *be* song—
and how much we love it, and with what sadness,
20 knowing we have to turn away
and enter the dark.

2003

- What is "the world's incessant undersong" (line 16)? What words or phrases contribute to the poem's feeling of "sadness" (line 19)?

8. Piety.

WALT WHITMAN

A Noiseless Patient Spider

A noiseless patient spider,
I marked where on a little promontory it stood isolated,
Marked how to explore the vacant vast surrounding,
It launched forth filament, filament, filament, out of itself,
5 Ever unreeling them, ever tirelessly speeding them.

And you O my soul where you stand,
Surrounded, detached, in measureless oceans of space,
Ceaselessly musing, venturing, throwing, seeking the spheres to
       connect them,
Till the bridge you will need be formed, till the ductile anchor hold,
10 Till the gossamer thread you fling catch somewhere, O my soul.

                                                          1881

- How does the description of the spider—"noiseless" and "patient"—
  set the tone for the entire poem? What is the analogy suggested by
  the poem's two stanzas?

ROBERT FROST

Range-Finding

The battle rent a cobweb diamond-strung
And cut a flower beside a groundbird's nest
Before it stained a single human breast.
The stricken flower bent double and so hung.
5 And still the bird revisited her young.
A butterfly its fall had dispossessed,
A moment sought in air his flower of rest,
Then slightly stooped to it and fluttering clung.
On the bare upland pasture there had spread
10 O'ernight 'twixt mullein stalks a wheel of thread
And straining cables wet with silver dew.
A sudden passing bullet shook it dry.
The indwelling spider ran to greet the fly,
But finding nothing, sullenly withdrew.

                                                          1916

- What is the "battle" of line 1? What is the poem's actual subject?

SUGGESTIONS FOR WRITING

1. Both "Eden," by Emily Grosholz, and "The Clock," by Daniel Tobin, use shifts of tone to elevate the poems' subject matter from the narrow concerns of children to the more universal issues that face adults. Where, in each poem, is this shift of tone? How is the shift revealed through language? Write an essay in which you compare and contrast the way each poet accomplishes this broadening of perspective.

2. In what way is precision of language the real subject of Li-Young Lee's "Persimmons"? How does the poem itself embody this subject? Write an essay in which you explore the subtle shifts in tone throughout the poem, and the way these shifts affect a reader's feelings. What, finally, seems to be the poet's attitude toward language as a medium for the precise expression of feeling?

3. What words in Robert Hayden's "Those Winter Sundays" suggest the son's feelings toward his father and his home? What words indicate that the poet's attitudes have changed since the time depicted in the poem? Write an essay in which you compare the speaker's feelings, as a youth and then later as a man, about his father and his home.

4. Kelly Cherry's "Alzheimer's" uses contrasts—especially before and after—to characterize the ravages of Alzheimer's disease. What evidence does the poem provide about what the man used to be like? What specific changes have come about? How does the setting of the poem suggest some of those changes? In what ways do the stabilities of house, landscape, and other people clarify what has happened? Write an essay about the function of the poem's setting.

5. Write an essay in which you consider the use of language to create tone in any grouping of two or more poems in this chapter.

2 SPEAKER: WHOSE VOICE DO WE HEAR?

Poems are personal. The thoughts and feelings they express belong to a specific person, and however general or universal their sentiments seem to be, poems come to us as the expression of an individual human voice. That voice is often the voice of the poet. But not always. Poets sometimes create "characters" just as writers of fiction or drama do—people who speak for them only indirectly. A character may, in fact, be very different from the poet, just as a character in a play or story is not necessarily the author, and that person, the **speaker** of the poem, may express ideas or feelings very different from the poet's own. In the following poem, rather than speaking directly to us himself, the poet has created two speakers, both female, each of whom has a distinctive voice, personality, and character.

THOMAS HARDY

The Ruined Maid

"O 'Melia,[1] my dear, this does everything crown!
Who could have supposed I should meet you in Town?
And whence such fair garments, such prosperi-ty?"—
"O didn't you know I'd been ruined?" said she.

5 —"You left us in tatters, without shoes or socks,
Tired of digging potatoes, and spudding up docks;[2]
And now you've gay bracelets and bright feathers three!"—
"Yes: that's how we dress when we're ruined," said she.

—"At home in the barton[3] you said 'thee' and 'thou,'
10 And 'thik oon,' and 'theäs oon,' and 't'other'; but now
Your talking quite fits 'ee for high compa-ny!"—
"Some polish is gained with one's ruin," said she.

—"Your hands were like paws then, your face blue and bleak
But now I'm bewitched by your delicate cheek,
15 And your little gloves fit as on any la-dy!"—
"We never do work when we're ruined," said she.

---

1. Short for Amelia.   2. Spading up weeds.   3. Farmyard.

—"You used to call home-life a hag-ridden dream,
And you'd sigh, and you'd sock;[4] but at present you seem
To know not of megrims[5] or melancho-ly!"—
20   "True. One's pretty lively when ruined," said she.

—"I wish I had feathers, a fine sweeping gown,
And a delicate face, and could strut about Town!"—
"My dear—a raw country girl, such as you be,
Cannot quite expect that. You ain't ruined," said she.

1866

    The first voice, that of a young woman who has remained back on the farm, is designated typographically (that is, by the way the poem is printed): there are dashes at the beginning and end of all but the first of her speeches. She speaks the first part of each **stanza** (a stanza is a section of a poem designated by spacing), usually the first three lines. The second young woman, a companion and coworker on the farm in years gone by, regularly gets the last line in each stanza (and in the last stanza, two lines), so it is clear who is talking at every point. Also, the two speakers are just as clearly distinguished by what they say, how they say it, and what sort of person each proves to be. The nameless stay-at-home shows little knowledge of the world, and everything surprises her: seeing her former companion at all, but especially seeing her well clothed, cheerful, and polished; and as the poem develops she shows increasing envy of her more worldly friend. She is the "raw country girl" (line 23) that the other speaker says she is, and she still speaks the country dialect ("fits 'ee," line 11, for example) that she notices her friend has lost (lines 9–11). The "ruined" young woman ('Melia), on the other hand, says little except the refrain about having been ruined, but even the slight variations she plays on that theme suggest her sophistication and amusement at her rural friend, although she still uses a country "ain't" at the end. We are not told the full story of their lives (was the "ruined" young woman thrown out? did she run away from home or work?), but we know enough (that they've been separated for some time, that the stay-at-home did not know where the other had gone) to allow the dialogue to articulate the contrast between them: one is still rural, inexperienced, and innocent; the other is sophisticated, citified—and "ruined." Each speaker's style of speech then does the rest.

    It is equally obvious that there is a speaker (or, in this case, a singer) in stanzas 2 through 9 of the following poem:

---

4. Deliver angry blows.   5. Migraine headaches.

X. J. KENNEDY

In a Prominent Bar in Secaucus One Day

*To the tune of "The Old Orange Flute" or the tune of
"Sweet Betsy from Pike"*

In a prominent bar in Secaucus[6] one day
Rose a lady in skunk with a topheavy sway,
Raised a knobby red finger—all turned from their beer—
While with eyes bright as snowcrust she sang high and clear:

5   "Now who of you'd think from an eyeload of me
That I once was a lady as proud as could be?
Oh I'd never sit down by a tumbledown drunk
If it wasn't, my dears, for the high cost of junk.

"All the gents used to swear that the white of my calf
10 Beat the down of a swan by a length and a half.
In the kerchief of linen I caught to my nose
Ah, there never fell snot, but a little gold rose.

"I had seven gold teeth and a toothpick of gold.
My Virginia cheroot was a leaf of it rolled
15 And I'd light it each time with a thousand in cash—
Why the bums used to fight if I flicked them an ash.

"Once the toast of the Biltmore,[7] the belle of the Taft,
I would drink bottle beer at the Drake, never draft,
And dine at the Astor on Salisbury steak
20 With a clean tablecloth for each bite I did take.

"In a car like the Roxy[8] I'd roll to the track,
A steel-guitar trio, a bar in the back,
And the wheels made no noise, they turned over so fast,
Still it took you ten minutes to see me go past.

25 "When the horses bowed down to me that I might choose,
I bet on them all, for I hated to lose.
Now I'm saddled each night for my butter and eggs
And the broken threads race down the backs of my legs.

"Let you hold in mind, girls, that your beauty must pass
30 Like a lovely white clover that rusts with its grass.
Keep your bottoms off barstools and marry you young
Or be left—an old barrel with many a bung.

---

6. A small town on the Hackensack River in New Jersey, a few miles west of Manhattan.
7. Like the Taft, Drake, and Astor, a once-fashionable New York hotel.
8. A luxurious old New York theater and movie house, the site of many "world premieres" in the heyday of Hollywood.

"For when time takes you out for a spin in his car
You'll be hard-pressed to stop him from going too far
35 And be left by the roadside, for all your good deeds,
Two toadstools for tits and a face full of weeds."

All the house raised a cheer, but the man at the bar
Made a phonecall and up pulled a red patrol car
And she blew us a kiss as they copped her away
40 From that prominent bar in Secaucus, N.J.

1961

Again, we learn about the character primarily through her own words, although we may not believe everything she tells us about her past. From her introduction in the first stanza we get some general notion of her appearance and condition, but it is she who tells us that she is a junkie (line 8) and a prostitute (line 27) and that her face and figure have seen better days (lines 32, 36). That information could make her a sad case, and the poem might lament her state or allow us to lament it, but instead she presents herself in a light, friendly, and theatrical way. She is anxious to give advice and sound righteous (line 31, for example), but she's also enormously cheerful about herself, and her spirit repeatedly bursts forth through her song. Her performance gives her a lot of pleasure as she exaggerates outrageously about her former luxury and prominence, and even her departure in a patrol car she chooses to treat as a grand exit, throwing a kiss to her audience. The comedy is bittersweet, perhaps, but she is allowed to present herself, through her own words and attitudes, as a likable character—someone who has survived life's disappointments and retained her dignity. The glorious fiction of her life, narrated with energy and polish in the manner of a practiced and accomplished liar, betrays some rather naive notions of good taste and luxurious living (lines 18–26). But this "lady in skunk" has a picturesque and engaging style, a refreshing sense of humor about herself, and a flair for drama. Like the cheap fur she wears, her experiences in what she considers high life satisfy her sense of style and celebration. The self-portrait accumulates, almost completely through how she talks about herself, and the poet develops our attitude toward her by allowing her to recount her story herself, in her own words—or rather in words chosen for her by the author.

Sometimes poets "borrow" a character from history and ask readers to factor in historical facts and contexts. In the following poem, for example, the Canadian poet Margaret Atwood draws heavily upon facts and traditions about a nineteenth-century émigré from Scotland to Canada:

MARGARET ATWOOD

Death of a Young Son by Drowning

He, who navigated with success
the dangerous river of his own birth
once more set forth

on a voyage of discovery
5   into the land I floated on
but could not touch to claim.

His feet slid on the bank,
the currents took him;
he swirled with ice and trees in the swollen water

10   and plunged into distant regions,
his head a bathysphere;
through his eyes' thin glass bubbles

he looked out, reckless adventurer
on a landscape stranger than Uranus
15   we have all been to and some remember.

There was an accident; the air locked,
he was hung in the river like a heart.
They retrieved the swamped body,

cairn of my plans and future charts,
20   with poles and hooks
from among the nudging logs.

It was spring, the sun kept shining, the new grass
leapt to solidity;
my hands glistened with details.

25   After the long trip I was tired of waves.
My foot hit rock. The dreamed sails
collapsed, ragged.

      I planted him in this country
      like a flag.

                       1970

The poem comes from a volume called *The Journals of Susanna Moodie: Poems by Margaret Atwood* (1970). A frontier pioneer, Moodie herself had written two books about Canada, *Roughing It in the Bush* and *Life in the Clearings,* and Atwood found their observations rather stark and disorganized. She wrote her Susanna Moodie poems to refocus the "character" and to reconstruct Moodie's actual geographical exploration and self-discovery. To truly understand these thoughts and meditations, then, we need to know something of the history behind them. Read in context, they present very powerful psychological and cultural analyses.

Some speakers in poems are not, however, nearly so heroic or attractive, and some poems create a speaker we are made to dislike, as the following poem does. Here the speaker, as the title implies, is a monk, but he shows himself to be most unspiritual: mean, petty, self-righteous, and despicable.

ROBERT BROWNING

WEB   *Soliloquy of the Spanish Cloister*

> Gr-r-r—there go, my heart's abhorrence!
> Water your damned flower-pots, do!
> If hate killed men, Brother Lawrence,
> God's blood, would not mine kill you!
> 5 What? your myrtle-bush wants trimming?
> Oh, that rose has prior claims—
> Needs its leaden vase filled brimming?
> Hell dry you up with its flames!
>
> At the meal we sit together:
> 10   *Salve tibi!*[9] I must hear
> Wish talk of the kind of weather,
> Sort of season, time of year:
> *Not a plenteous cork-crop: scarcely
> Dare we hope oak-galls,*[1] *I doubt:*
> 15 *What's the Latin name for "parsley"?*
> What's the Greek name for Swine's Snout?
>
> Whew! We'll have our platter burnished,
> Laid with care on our own shelf!
> With a fire-new spoon we're furnished,
> 20   And a goblet for ourself,
> Rinsed like something sacrificial
> Ere 'tis fit to touch our chaps[2]—
> Marked with L. for our initial!
> (He-he! There his lily snaps!)
>
> 25 *Saint,* forsooth! While brown Dolores
> —Squats outside the Convent bank
> With Sanchicha, telling stories,
> Steeping tresses in the tank,
> Blue-black, lustrous, thick like horsehairs,
> 30   —Can't I see his dead eye glow,
> Bright as 'twere a Barbary corsair's?[3]
> (That is, if he'd let it show!)
>
> When he finishes refection,
> Knife and fork he never lays
> 35 Cross-wise, to my recollection,
> As do I, in Jesu's praise.
> I the Trinity illustrate,
> Drinking watered orange-pulp—

---

9. Hail to thee (Latin). Italics usually indicate the words of Brother Lawrence.
1. Abnormal growth on oak trees, used for tanning.   2. Jaws.   3. North African pirate's.

In three sips the Arian[4] frustrate;
40 —While he drains his at one gulp.

Oh, those melons? If he's able
    We're to have a feast! so nice!
One goes to the Abbot's table,
    All of us get each a slice.
45 How go on your flowers? None double?
    Not one fruit-sort can you spy?
Strange!—And I, too, at such trouble,
    —Keep them close-nipped on the sly!

There's a great text in Galatians,
50   Once you trip on it, entails
Twenty-nine distinct damnations,[5]
    One sure, if another fails:
If I trip him just a-dying,
    Sure of heaven as sure can be,
55 Spin him round and send him flying
    Off to hell, a Manichee?[6]

Or, my scrofulous French novel
    On gray paper with blunt type!
Simply glance at it, you grovel
60   Hand and foot in Belial's gripe:[7]
If I double down its pages
    At the woeful sixteenth print,
When he gathers his greengages,
    Ope a sieve and slip it in't?

65 Or, there's Satan!—one might venture
    Pledge one's soul to him, yet leave
Such a flaw in the indenture
    —As he'd miss till, past retrieve,
Blasted lay that rose-acacia
70   We're so proud of! Hy, Zy, Hine . . .[8]
'St, there's Vespers! Plena gratiâ
    Ave, Virgo.[9] Gr-r-r—you swine!

                                    1842

Not many poems begin with a growl, and this harsh sound turns out to be fair
warning that we are about to meet a real beast, even though he is in the clothing
of a religious man. In line 1 he shows himself to hold a most uncharitable attitude
toward his fellow monk, Brother Lawrence, and by line 4 he has uttered two pro-

4. A heretical sect that denied the Trinity.
5. Galatians 5.15–23 provides a long list of possible offenses, though they do not add up to twenty-nine.
6. A heretic. According to the Manichean heresy, the world was divided into the forces of good and evil,
equally powerful.   7. In the clutches of Satan.   8. Possibly the beginning of an incantation or curse.
9. The opening words of the Ave Maria, here reversed: "Full of grace, Hail, Virgin" (Latin).

fanities and admitted his intense feelings of hatred and vengefulness. His ranting and roaring is full of exclamation points (four in the first stanza!), and he reveals his own personality and character when he imagines curses and unflattering nicknames for Brother Lawrence or plots malicious jokes on him. By the end, we have accumulated no knowledge of Brother Lawrence that makes him seem a fit target for such rage (except that he is pious, dutiful, and pleasant—perhaps enough to make this sort of speaker despise him), but we have discovered the speaker to be lecherous (stanza 4), full of false piety (stanza 5), malicious in trivial matters (stanza 6), ready to use his theological learning to sponsor damnation rather than salvation (stanza 7), a closet reader and viewer of pornography within the monastery (stanza 8)—even willing to risk his own soul in order to torment Brother Lawrence (last stanza).

The speaker characterizes himself; the details accumulate into a fairly full portrait, and here we do not have even an opening and closing "objective" description (as in Kennedy's "In a Prominent Bar") or another speaker (as in Hardy's "The Ruined Maid") to give us perspective. Except for the moments when the speaker mimics or parodies Brother Lawrence (usually in italic type), we have only the speaker's own words and thoughts. But that is enough; the poet has controlled them so carefully that we know what he thinks of the speaker—that he is a mean-spirited, vengeful hypocrite, a thoroughly disreputable and unlikable character. The whole poem has been about him and his attitudes; the point has been to characterize the speaker and develop in us a dislike of him and what he stands for—hypocrisy.

In reading a poem like this aloud, we would want our voice to suggest all the unlikable features of a hypocrite. We would also need to suggest, through tone of voice, the author's contemptuous mocking of the rage and hypocrisy, and we would want, like an actor, to create strong disapproval in the hearer. The poem's words (the ones the author has given to the speaker) clearly imply those attitudes, and we would want our voice to express them. Usually there is much more to a poem than the characterization of the speaker, but in many cases it is necessary first to identify the speaker and determine his or her character before we can appreciate what else goes on in the poem. And sometimes, as here, in looking for the speaker of the poem, we approach the center of the poem itself.

Sometimes the effect of a poem depends on our recognizing the **temporal setting** as well as the speaker's identity. The following poem, for example, quickly makes plain that a childhood experience is at the center of the action and that the speaker is female:

TESS GALLAGHER

Sudden Journey

Maybe I'm seven in the open field—
the straw-grass so high
only the top of my head makes a curve
of brown in the yellow. Rain then.
5 First a little. A few drops on my

wrist, the right wrist. More rain.
My shoulders, my chin. Until I'm looking up
to let my eyes take the bliss.
I open my face. Let the teeth show. I
10 pull my shirt down past the collar-bones.
I'm still a boy under my breast spots.
I can drink anywhere. The rain. My
skin shattering. Up suddenly, needing
to gulp, turning with my tongue, my arms out
15 running, running in the hard, cold plenitude
of all those who reach earth by falling.

                                        1984

The sense of adventure and wonder here has a lot to do with the childlike syntax and choice of words at the beginning of the poem. Sentences are short, observations direct and simple. The rain becomes exciting and blissful and totally absorbing as the child's actions and reactions take over the poem in lines 2–13. But not all of the poem takes place in a child's mind in spite of the precise and impressive re-creation of childish responses and feelings. The opening line makes clear that we are sliding into a supposition of the past; "maybe I'm seven" makes clear that we, as conspiring adults, are pretending ourselves into earlier time. And at the end the word "plenitude"—crucial to interpreting the poem's full effect and meaning—makes clear that we are now encountering an adult perspective on the incident. Elsewhere, too, the adult world gives the incident meaning. In line 12, for example, the joke about being able to drink anywhere depends on an adult sense of what being a boy might mean. The "journey" of the poem's title is not only the little girl's running in the rain, but also the adult's return to a past re-created and newly understood.

The speaker in the following poem positions herself very differently, but we do not get a full sense of her until we are well into the poem. As you read, try to imagine the tone of voice you think this person would use. Exactly when do you begin to know what she sounds like?

DOROTHY PARKER

A Certain Lady

Oh, I can smile for you, and tilt my head,
    And drink your rushing words with eager lips,
And paint my mouth for you a fragrant red,
    And trace your brows with tutored finger-tips.
5 When you rehearse your list of loves to me,
    Oh, I can laugh and marvel, rapturous-eyed.
And you laugh back, nor can you ever see
    The thousand little deaths my heart has died.
And you believe, so well I know my part,

10 That I am gay as morning, light as snow,
    And all the straining things within my heart
        You'll never know.

    Oh, I can laugh and listen, when we meet,
        And you bring tales of fresh adventurings—
15 Of ladies delicately indiscreet,
        Of lingering hands, and gently whispered things.
    And you are pleased with me, and strive anew
        To sing me sagas of your late delights.
    Thus do you want me—marveling, gay, and true—
20 Nor do you see my staring eyes of nights.
    And when, in search of novelty, you stray,
        Oh, I can kiss you blithely as you go . . .
    And what goes on, my love, while you're away,
        You'll never know.

                                            1937

To whom does the speaker seem to be talking? What sort of person is he? How do you feel about him? Which habits and attitudes of his do you like least? How soon can you tell that the speaker is not altogether happy about his conversation and conduct? In what tone of voice would you read the first twenty-two lines aloud? What attitude would you try to express toward the person spoken to? What tone would you use for the last two lines? How would you describe the speaker's personality? What aspects of her behavior are most crucial to the poem's effect?

It is easy to assume that the speaker in a poem is an extension of the poet, especially when the voice is as distinctively self-assured as in "A Certain Lady." So, is the speaker in this poem Dorothy Parker? Maybe. A lot of Parker's poems present a similar world-weary posture and a wry cynicism about romantic love. But the poem is hardly a case of self-revelation, a giving away of personal secrets. If it were, it would be silly, not to say risky, to address her lover in a way that gives damaging facts about a pose she has been so careful to set up.

In poems such as "The Ruined Maid," "In a Prominent Bar," and "Soliloquy of the Spanish Cloister," we are in no danger of mistaking the speaker for the poet, once we have recognized that poets may create speakers who participate in specific situations, much as in fiction or drama. When there is a pointed discrepancy between the speaker and what we know of the poet—when the speaker is a woman, for example, and the poet is a man—we know we have a created speaker to contend with and that the point (or at least *one* point) in the poem is to observe the characterization carefully. In "A Certain Lady" we may be less sure, and in other poems the discrepancy between speaker and poet may be even more uncertain. What are we to make, for example, of the speaker in "Woodchucks" in the previous chapter? Is that speaker the real Maxine Kumin? At best (without knowing something quite specific about the author) we can only say "maybe" to that question. What we can be sure of is the sort of person the speaker is portrayed to be—someone (a man? a woman?) surprised to discover feelings and attitudes that contradict values apparently held with confidence. And that is exactly what we need to know for the poem to have its effect.

Even when poets present themselves as if they were speaking directly to us in their own voices, their poems present only a partial portrait, something considerably less than the full personality and character of the poet. Even when there is not an obviously created character—someone with distinct characteristics that are different from those of the poet—strategies of characterization are used to present the person speaking in one way and not another. Even in a poem like the following one, which contains identifiable autobiographical details, it is still a good idea to think of the speaker instead of the poet, although here the poet is probably writing about a personal, actual experience, and he is certainly making a character of himself—that is, characterizing himself in a certain way, emphasizing some parts of himself and not others.

WILLIAM WORDSWORTH

She Dwelt among the Untrodden Ways

She dwelt among the untrodden ways
  Beside the springs of Dove,[1]
A Maid whom there were none to praise
  And very few to love:

5 A violet by a mossy stone
  Half hidden from the eye!
—Fair as a star, when only one
  Is shining in the sky.

She lived unknown, and few could know
10 When Lucy ceased to be;
But she is in her grave, and, oh,
  The difference to me!

                    1800

Is this poem more about Lucy or about the speaker's feelings concerning her death? Her simple life, far removed from fame and known only to a few, is said to have been beautiful, but we know little about her beyond her name and where she lived, in a beautiful but then-isolated section of northern England. We don't know if she was young or old, only that the speaker thinks of her as "fair" and compares her to a "violet by a mossy stone." We do know that the speaker is deeply pained by her death, so deeply that he is almost inarticulate with grief, lapsing into simple exclamation ("oh," line 11) and hardly able to articulate the "difference" that her death makes.

Did Lucy actually live? Was she a friend of the poet? We don't know; the poem doesn't tell us, and even biographers of Wordsworth are unsure. What we do know is that Wordsworth was able to represent grief very powerfully. Whether the

---

1. A small stream in the Lake District in northern England, near where Wordsworth lived in Dove Cottage at Grasmere.

speaker is the historical Wordsworth or not, that speaker is a major focus of the poem, and it is his feelings that the poem isolates and expresses. We need to recognize some characteristics of the speaker and be sensitive to his feelings for the poem to work.

The poems we have looked at in this chapter—and the group that follows—all suggest the value of beginning the reading of any poem with simple questions: Who is speaking? What do we know about him or her? What kind of person is she or he? Putting together the evidence that the poem presents in answer to such questions can often take us a long way into the poem. For some poems, such questions won't help a great deal because the speaking voice is too indistinct or the character behind the poem too scantily presented. But starting with such questions will often lead you toward the central experience the poem offers. At the very least, the question of speaker helps clarify the tone of voice, and it often provides guidance to the larger situation the poem explores.

• • •

AUDRE LORDE

WEB   *Hanging Fire*

I am fourteen
and my skin has betrayed me
the boy I cannot live without
still sucks his thumb
5 in secret
how come my knees are
always so ashy
what if I die
before morning
10 and momma's in the bedroom
with the door closed.

I have to learn how to dance
in time for the next party
my room is too small for me
15 suppose I die before graduation
they will sing sad melodies
but finally
tell the truth about me
There is nothing I want to do
20 and too much
that has to be done
and momma's in the bedroom
with the door closed.

Nobody even stops to think
25 about my side of it

[handwritten annotations:] Who is speaker? 14, Girl
Life is unjust, unfair
She doesn't get attention from her mother

I should have been on Math Team
my marks were better than his
why do I have to be
the one
30 wearing braces
I have nothing to wear tomorrow
will I live long enough
to grow up
and momma's in the bedroom
35 with the door closed.

                    1978

- What, precisely, do we know about the speaker? How does she feel
  about herself? How can you tell?

JUDITH ORTIZ COFER

The Changeling

                    As a young girl
vying for my father's attention,
I invented a game that made him look up
from his reading and shake his head
5 as if both baffled and amused.

In my brother's closet, I'd change
into his dungarees—the rough material
molding me into boy shape; hide
my long hair under an army helmet
10 he'd been given by Father, and emerge
transformed into the legendary Ché[2]
of grown-up talk.

Strutting around the room,
I'd tell of life in the mountains,
15 of carnage and rivers of blood,
and of manly feasts with rum and music
to celebrate victories *para la libertad*.[3]
He would listen with a smile
to my tales of battles and brotherhood
20 until Mother called us to dinner.

She was not amused
by my transformations, sternly forbidding me
from sitting down with them as a man.
She'd order me back to the dark cubicle

2. Ernesto "Che" Guevara (1928–1967), Argentinian-born Cuban revolutionary leader.
3. For freedom (Spanish).

25 that smelled of adventure, to shed
    my costume, to braid my hair furiously
    with blind hands, and to return invisible,
    as myself,
    to the real world of her kitchen.

                                                        1993

- Why do you think the speaker's father is amused by her "transformation," and why does her mother forbid it? What does this poem imply about all three of them?

SIR THOMAS WYATT

They Flee from Me

They flee from me, that sometime did me seek,
With naked foot stalking in my chamber.
I have seen them, gentle, tame, and meek,
That now are wild, and do not remember
5 That sometime they put themselves in danger
To take bread at my hand; and now they range,
Busily seeking with a continual change.

Thankéd be Fortune it hath been otherwise,
Twenty times better; but once in special,
10 In thin array, after a pleasant guise,
When her loose gown from her shoulders did fall,
And she me caught in her arms long and small.[4]
And therewith all sweetly did me kiss
And softly said, "Dear heart, how like you this?"

15 It was no dream, I lay broad waking.
But all is turned, thorough[5] my gentleness,
Into a strange fashion of forsaking;
And I have leave to go, of her goodness,
And she also to use newfangleness.[6]
20 But since that I so kindely[7] am servéd,
I fain[8] would know what she hath deservéd.

                                                        1557

- Who are "they" who now "flee" the speaker? What is his explanation for their fleeing?

---

4. Slender.   5. Through.   6. Fondness for novelty.   7. That is, in kind.   8. Eagerly.

FRED CHAPPELL

Recovery of Sexual Desire after a Bad Cold

Toward morning I dreamed of the Ace of Spades reversed
And woke up giggling.
New presence in the bedroom, as if it had snowed;
And an obdurate stranger come to visit my body.

5   This is how it all renews itself, floating down
Mothy on the shallow end of sleep;
How Easter gets here, and the hard-bitten dogwood
Flowers, and waters run clean again.

I am a new old man.
10 As morning sweetens the forsythia and the cats.
Bristle with impudent hungers, I learn to smile.
I am a new baby.

What woman could turn from me now?
Shining like a butter knife, and the fever burned off,
15 My whole skin alert as radar, I can think
Of nothing at all but love and fresh coffee.

                                                                    1985

- What kind of a man is the speaker in this poem? How does he feel
  now that he has "recovered"?

WALT WHITMAN

[WEB]   ## [*I celebrate myself, and sing myself*]

I celebrate myself, and sing myself,
And what I assume you shall assume,
For every atom belonging to me as good belongs to you.
I loafe and invite my soul,
5   I lean and loafe at my ease observing a spear of summer grass.

My tongue, every atom of my blood, form'd from this soil, this air,
Born here of parents born here from parents the same, and their
     parents the same,
I, now thirty-seven years old in perfect health begin,
Hoping to cease not till death.
10 Creeds and schools in abeyance,
Retiring back a while suffced at what they are, but never forgotten,
I harbor for good or bad, I permit to speak at every hazard,
Nature without check with original energy.

                                                                    1855, 1881

- What is characteristically American about the speaker of this poem?

ANDREW HUDGINS

Praying Drunk

Our Father who art in heaven, I am drunk.
Again. Red wine. For which I offer thanks.
I ought to start with praise, but praise
comes hard to me. I stutter. Did I tell you
5 about the woman whom I taught, in bed,
this prayer? It starts with praise; the simple form
keeps things in order. I hear from her sometimes.
Do you? And after love, when I was hungry,
I said, *Make me something to eat.* She yelled,
10 *Poof! You're a casserole!*—and laughed so hard
she fell out of the bed. Take care of her.

Next, confession—the dreary part. At night
deer drift from the dark woods and eat my garden.
They're like enormous rats on stilts except,
15 of course, they're beautiful. But why? What *makes*
them beautiful? I haven't shot one yet.
I might. When I was twelve, I'd ride my bike
out to the dump and shoot the rats. It's hard
to kill your rats, our Father. You have to use
20 a hollow point and hit them solidly.
A leg is not enough. The rat won't pause.
Yeep!Yeep! it screams, and scrabbles, three-legged, back
into the trash, and I would feel a little bad
to kill something that wants to live
25 more savagely than I do, even if
it's just a rat. My garden's vanishing.
Perhaps I'll merely plant more beans, though that
might mean more beautiful and hungry deer.
Who knows?
30   I'm sorry for the times I've driven
home past a black, enormous, twilight ridge.
Crested with mist, it looked like a giant wave
about to break and sweep across the valley,
and in my loneliness and fear I've thought,
35 *O let it come and wash the whole world clean.*
Forgive me. This is my favorite sin: despair—
whose love I celebrate with wine and prayer.

Our Father, thank you for all the birds and trees,
that nature stuff. I'm grateful for good health,
40 food, air, some laughs, and all the other things
I'm grateful that I've never had to do
without. I have confused myself. I'm glad
there's not a rattrap large enough for deer.
While at the zoo last week, I sat and wept

45 when I saw one elephant insert his trunk
into another's ass, pull out a lump,
and whip it back and forth impatiently
to free the goodies hidden in the lump.
I could have let it mean most anything,
50 but I was stunned again at just how little
we ask for in our lives. *Don't look! Don't look!*
Two young nuns tried to herd their giggling
schoolkids away. *Line up,* they called. *Let's go
and watch the monkeys in the monkey house.*
55 I laughed, and got a dirty look. Dear Lord,
we lurch from metaphor to metaphor,
which is—let it be so—a form of praying.

I'm usually asleep by now—the time
for supplication. Requests. As if I'd stayed
60 up late and called the radio and asked
they play a sentimental song. Embarrassed.
I want a lot of money and a woman.
And, also, I want vanishing cream. You know—
a character like Popeye rubs it on
65 and disappears. Although you see right through him,
he's there. He chuckles, stumbles into things,
and smoke that's clearly visible escapes
from his invisible pipe. It makes me think,
sometimes, of you. What makes me think of me
70 is the poor jerk who wanders out on air
and then looks down. Below his feet, he sees
eternity, and suddenly his shoes
no longer work on nothingness, and down
he goes. As I fall past, remember me.

1991

- What words or lines in the poem create an ironic or irreverent tone?
  What words or lines create a tone of sincere devotion? What does
  the poem achieve by mixing the tones in this way?

HENRY REED

Lessons of the War

Judging Distances

Not only how far away, but the way that you say it
Is very important. Perhaps you may never get
The knack of judging a distance, but at least you know
How to report on a landscape: the central sector,

5 The right of arc and that, which we had last Tuesday,
     And at least you know

That maps are of time, not place, so far as the army
Happens to be concerned—the reason being,
Is one which need not delay us. Again, you know
10 There are three kinds of tree, three only, the fir and the poplar,
And those which have bushy tops to; and lastly
     That things only seem to be things.

A barn is not called a barn, to put it more plainly,
Or a field in the distance, where sheep may be safely grazing.
15 You must never be over-sure. You must say, when reporting:
At five o'clock in the central sector is a dozen
Of what appear to be animals; whatever you do,
     Don't call the bleeders *sheep*.

I am sure that's quite clear; and suppose, for the sake of example,
20 The one at the end, asleep, endeavors to tell us
What he sees over there to the west, and how far away,
After first having come to attention. There to the west,
On the fields of summer the sun and the shadows bestow
     Vestments of purple and gold.

25 The still white dwellings are like a mirage in the heat,
And under the swaying elms a man and a woman
Lie gently together. Which is, perhaps, only to say
That there is a row of houses to the left of arc,
And that under some poplars a pair of what appear to be humans
30   Appear to be loving.

Well that, for an answer, is what we might rightly call
Moderately satisfactory only, the reason being,
Is that two things have been omitted, and those are important.
The human beings, now: in what direction are they,
35 And how far away, would you say? And do not forget
     There may be dead ground in between.

There may be dead ground in between; and I may not have got
The knack of judging a distance; I will only venture
A guess that perhaps between me and the apparent lovers,
40 (Who, incidentally, appear by now to have finished,)
At seven o'clock from the houses, is roughly a distance
     Of about one year and a half.

                                                    1946

- What words in the poem are used in unexpected ways? What seems
  to be the speaker's perspective—that of a combatant in the war? an
  observer? a historian?

SYLVIA PLATH

Mirror

I am silver and exact. I have no preconceptions.
Whatever I see I swallow immediately
Just as it is, unmisted by love or dislike.
I am not cruel, only truthful—
5 The eye of a little god, four-cornered.
Most of the time I meditate on the opposite wall.
It is pink, with speckles. I have looked at it so long
I think it is a part of my heart. But it flickers.
Faces and darkness separate us over and over.

10 Now I am a lake. A woman bends over me,
Searching my reaches for what she really is.
Then she turns to those liars, the candles or the moon.
I see her back, and reflect it faithfully.
She rewards me with tears and an agitation of hands.
15 I am important to her. She comes and goes.
Each morning it is her face that replaces the darkness.
In me she has drowned a young girl, and in me an old woman
Rises toward her day after day, like a terrible fish.

                                                        1961

- How does the tone of the poem change in the second stanza? How
  does the word "terrible" in the final line affect the tone of the entire
  poem?

KAREN CHASE

Venison

Paul set the bags down, told how they had split
the deer apart, the ease of peeling it
simpler than skinning a fruit, how the buck
lay on the worktable, how they sawed
5 an anklebone off, the smell not rank.
The sun slipped into night.

Where are you I wondered as I grubbed
through cupboards for noodles at least.
Then came venison new with blood,
10 stray hair from the animal's fur.
Excited, we cooked the meat.

Later, I dreamt against your human chest,
you cloaked me in your large arms, then

went for me the way you squander food sometimes.
15 By then, I was eating limbs in my sleep, somewhere
in the snow alone, survivor of a downed plane,
picking at the freshly dead. Whistles
of a far-off flute—legs, gristle, juice.
I cracked an elbow against a rock, awoke.
20 Throughout the night, we consumed and consumed.

2000

- How does the poet characterize the speaker's relationship with Paul?

PAT MORA

1942 Born in El Paso, TX
TX Western 63

La Migra

I

Let's play *La Migra*[9]
I'll be the Border Patrol.
You be the Mexican maid.
I get the <u>badge</u> and sunglasses.

Authority
Power
Government/
State

5 You can <u>hide</u> and run,
but you can't get away
because I have a jeep
I can take you wherever
I want, but don't ask
10 questions because
I don't speak Spanish.
I can touch you wherever
I want but don't complain
too much because I've got
15 boots and kick—if I have to,
and I have handcuffs.
Oh, and a gun.
Get ready, get set, run.

U.S. Immigration
Poem about Human
emotion/feelings
Traumatic
Anxious

II

Let's play *La Migra*
20 You be the Border Patrol.
I'll be the Mexican woman.
Your jeep has a flat,
and you have been spotted
by the sun.
25 <u>All you have is heavy:</u> hat,
<u>glasses, badge, shoes, gun.</u>

I can run faster

9. Border patrol agents.

I know this desert,
where to rest,
where to drink.
30 Oh, I am not alone.
You hear us singing
and laughing with the wind,
Agua dulce brota aquí,
aquí, aquí,[1] but since you
35 can't speak Spanish,
you do not understand.
Get ready.

1993

- Who seems to be the speaker of this poem? What is the game of "hide and run" the speaker proposes? Who will win?

EDNA ST. VINCENT MILLAY

[*Women have loved before as I love now*]

Women have loved before as I love now;
At least, in lively chronicles of the past—
Of Irish waters by a Cornish prow
Or Trojan waters by a Spartan mast
5 Much to their cost invaded—here and there,
Hunting the amorous line, skimming the rest,
I find some woman bearing as I bear
Love like a burning city in the breast.
I think however that of all alive
10 I only in such utter, ancient way
Do suffer love; in me alone survive
The unregenerate passions of a day
When treacherous queens, with death upon the tread,
Heedless and wilful, took their knights to bed.

1931

WEB   [*I, being born a woman and distressed*]

I, being born a woman and distressed
By all the needs and notions of my kind,
Am urged by your propinquity to find
Your person fair, and feel a certain zest
5 To bear your body's weight upon my breast:

---

1. Sweet water springs here, here, here.

So subtly is the fume of life designed,
To clarify the pulse and cloud the mind,
And leave me once again undone, possessed.
Think not for this, however, the poor treason
10 Of my stout blood against my staggering brain,
I shall remember you with love, or season
My scorn with pity,—let me make it plain:
I find this frenzy insufficient reason
For conversation when we meet again.

1923

- Do both of these poems by Edna St. Vincent Millay seem to have the same speaker? Why or why not?

KATHERINE PHILIPS

L'amitié: To Mrs. M. Awbrey

Soul of my soul, my Joy, my crown, my friend!
A name which all the rest doth comprehend;
How happy are we now, whose souls are grown,
By an incomparable mixture, One:
5 Whose well acquainted minds are now as near
As Love, or vows, or secrets can endear.
I have no thought but what's to thee reveal'd,
Nor thou desire that is from me conceal'd.
Thy heart locks up my secrets richly set,
10 And my breast is thy private cabinet.
Thou shedst no tear but what my moisture lent,
And if I sigh, it is thy breath is spent.
United thus, what horror can appear
Worthy our sorrow, anger, or our fear?
15 Let the dull world alone to talk and fight,
And with their vast ambitions nature fright;
Let them despise so innocent a flame,
While Envy, Pride, and Faction play their game:
But we by Love sublim'd so high shall rise,
20 To pity kings, and conquerors despise,
Since we that sacred union have engrossed,
Which they and all the sullen world have lost.

1667

- Who is the speaker, and whom does the speaker address? Why does the speaker hold her love above "the sullen world"?

CAROL ANN DUFFY

Mrs. Midas²

It was late September. I'd just poured a glass of wine, begun
to unwind, while the vegetables cooked. The kitchen
filled with the smell of itself, relaxed, its steamy breath
gently blanching the windows. So I opened one,
5 then with my fingers wiped the other's glass like a brow.
He was standing under the pear tree snapping a twig.

Now the garden was long and the visibility poor, the way
the dark of the ground seems to drink the light of the sky,
but that twig in his hand was gold. And then he plucked
10 a pear from a branch—we grew Fondante d'Automne—
and it sat in his palm like a light bulb. On.
I thought to myself, Is he putting fairy lights in the tree?

He came into the house. The doorknobs gleamed.
He drew the blinds. You know the mind; I thought of
15 the Field of the Cloth of Gold and of Miss Macready.
He sat in that chair like a king on a burnished throne.
The look on his face was strange, wild, vain. I said,
What in the name of God is going on? He started to laugh.

I served up the meal. For starters, corn on the cob.
20 Within seconds he was spitting out the teeth of the rich.
He toyed with his spoon, then mine, then with the knives, the forks.
He asked where was the wine. I poured with a shaking hand,
a fragrant, bone-dry white from Italy, then watched
as he picked up the glass, goblet, golden chalice, drank.

25 It was then that I started to scream. He sank to his knees.
After we'd both calmed down, I finished the wine
on my own, hearing him out. I made him sit
on the other side of the room and keep his hands to himself.
I locked the cat in the cellar. I moved the phone.
30 The toilet I didn't mind. I couldn't believe my ears:

how he'd had a wish. Look, we all have wishes; granted.
But who has wishes granted? Him. Do you know about gold?
It feeds no one; aurum, soft, untarnishable; slakes
no thirst. He tried to light a cigarette; I gazed, entranced,
35 as the blue flame played on its luteous stem. At least,
I said, you'll be able to give up smoking for good.

Separate beds. In fact, I put a chair against my door,
near petrified. He was below, turning the spare room

2. Legendary King of Phrygia, who asked the gods to give him the power to turn to gold anything that he
touched.

into the tomb of Tutankhamun. You see, we were passionate then,
40 in those halcyon days; unwrapping each other, rapidly,
like presents, fast food. But now I feared his honeyed embrace,
the kiss that would turn my lips to a work of art.

And who, when it comes to the crunch, can live
with a heart of gold? That night, I dreamt I bore
45 his child, its perfect ore limbs, its little tongue
like a precious latch, its amber eyes
holding their pupils like flies. My dream-milk
burned in my breasts. I woke to the streaming sun.

So he had to move out. We'd a caravan
50 in the wilds, in a glade of its own. I drove him up
under cover of dark. He sat in the back.
And then I came home, the woman who married the fool
who wished for gold. At first I visited, odd times,
parking the car a good way off, then walking.

55 You knew you were getting close. Golden trout
on the grass. One day, a hare hung from a larch,
a beautiful lemon mistake. And then his footprints,
glistening next to the river's path. He was thin,
delirious; hearing, he said, the music of Pan
60 from the woods. Listen. That was the last straw.

What gets me now is not the idiocy or greed
but lack of thought for me. Pure selfishness. I sold
the contents of the house and came down here.
I think of him in certain lights, dawn, late afternoon,
65 and once a bowl of apples stopped me dead. I miss most,
even now, his hands, his warm hands on my skin, his touch.

1999

- At what point in the poem does the speaker become clearly identified
  with the "Mrs. Midas" of the title? What strategies does the speaker
  use to veil the connection between the Midas legend and the story
  in the poem?

GWENDOLYN BROOKS

[CD] *We Real Cool*

THE POOL PLAYERS,
SEVEN AT THE GOLDEN SHOVEL.

We real cool. We
Left school. We

Lurk late. We
Strike straight. We

5 Sing sin. We
Thin gin. We

Jazz June. We
Die soon.

1950

- Who are "we" in this poem? Do you think that the speaker and the poet share the same idea of what is "cool"?

SUGGESTIONS FOR WRITING

1. Several of the poems in this chapter create characters and imply situations, as in drama. Write an essay in which you describe and analyze the speaker of either "The Ruined Maid" by Thomas Hardy, "In a Prominent Bar in Secaucus One Day" by X. J. Kennedy, "Soliloquy of the Spanish Cloister" by Robert Browning, "A Certain Lady" by Dorothy Parker, or "Mrs. Midas" by Carol Ann Duffy.

2. Write an essay in which you compare and contrast the speakers in "Sudden Journey" by Tess Gallagher, "Hanging Fire" by Audre Lord, "The Changeling" by Judith Ortiz Cofer, and "We Real Cool" by Gwendolyn Brooks. What kinds of self-image do they have? In each poem, what is the distance between the speaker and the poet?

3. In three of the poems in this chapter—"They Flee from Me" by Sir Thomas Wyatt, "Recovery of Sexual Desire after a Bad Cold" by Fred Chappell, and "Venison" by Karen Chase—the speakers describe dreams. How are these dreams integrated into the poem? How are the dreams similar, or different? Write an essay in which you explore the way these three poems make use of the imagery and emotions of dreams.

4. Choose any of the poems in this or the previous chapter and write an essay about the way a poet can create irony and humor through the use of a speaker who is clearly distinct from the poet him- or herself.

3 SITUATION AND SETTING: WHAT HAPPENS? WHERE? WHEN?

Questions about the speaker ("Who" questions) in a poem almost always lead to questions of "Where?" "When?" and "Why?" Identifying the speaker is, in fact, usually part of a larger process of defining the entire imagined **situation** in a poem: What is happening? Where is it happening? Who is the speaker speaking to? Who else is present? Why is this event occurring? In order to understand the dialogue in Hardy's "The Ruined Maid," for example, we need to recognize that the friends are meeting after an extended period of separation, and that they meet in a town setting rather than the rural area in which they grew up together. We infer (from the opening lines) that the meeting is accidental, and that no other friends are present for the conversation. The poem's whole "story" depends on their situation: after leading separate lives for a while they have some catching up to

> *It is difficult / to get the news from poems / yet men die miserably every day / for lack / of what is found there.*
> —WILLIAM CARLOS WILLIAMS

do. We don't know what specific town, year, season, or time of day is involved because those details are not important to the poem's effect. But crucial to the poem are the where and when questions that define the situation and relationship of the two speakers, and the answer to the why question—that the meeting is by chance—is important, too. In another poem we looked at in the previous chapter, Parker's "A Certain Lady," the specific moment and place are not important, but we do need to notice that the "lady" is talking to (or having an imaginary conversation with) her lover and that they are talking about a relationship of some duration.

Sometimes a *specific* time and place (**setting**) may be important. X. J. Kennedy's "lady in skunk" sings her life story "in a prominent bar in Secaucus," a working-class town in New Jersey, but on no particular occasion ("one day"). In Browning's "Soliloquy of the Spanish Cloister," the setting (a monastery) adds to the irony because of the gross inappropriateness of such sentiments and attitudes in a supposedly holy place, just as the setting of Betjeman's "In Westminster Abbey" (below, page 121) similarly helps us to judge the speaker's ideas, attitudes, and self-conception.

The title of the following poem suggests that place may be important, and it is, although you may be surprised to discover exactly what exists at this address and what uses the speaker makes of it.

JAMES DICKEY

Cherrylog Road

Off Highway 106
At Cherrylog Road I entered
The '34 Ford without wheels,
Smothered in kudzu,
5 With a seat pulled out to run
Corn whiskey down from the hills,

And then from the other side
Crept into an Essex
With a rumble seat of red leather
10 And then out again, aboard
A blue Chevrolet, releasing
The rust from its other color,

Reared up on three building blocks.
None had the same body heat;
15 I changed with them inward, toward
The weedy heart of the junkyard,
For I knew that Doris Holbrook
Would escape from her father at noon

And would come from the farm
20 To seek parts owned by the sun
Among the abandoned chassis,
Sitting in each in turn
As I did, leaning forward
As in a wild stock-car race

25 In the parking lot of the dead.
Time after time, I climbed in
And out the other side, like
An envoy or movie star
Met at the station by crickets.
30 A radiator cap raised its head,

Become a real toad or a kingsnake
As I neared the hub of the yard,
Passing through many states,
Many lives, to reach
35 Some grandmother's long Pierce-Arrow
Sending platters of blindness forth

From its nickel hubcaps
And spilling its tender upholstery
On sleepy roaches,
40 The glass panel in between

Lady and <u>colored driver</u>
<u>Not all the way broken out</u>,

The back-seat phone
Still on its hook.
45 I got in as though to exclaim,
"Let us go to the orphan asylum,
John; I have some old toys
For children who say their prayers."

I popped with sweat as I thought
50 I heard Doris Holbrook scrape
Like a mouse in the southern-state sun
That was eating the paint in blisters
From a hundred car tops and hoods.
She was tapping like code,

55 Loosening the screws,
Carrying off headlights,
Sparkplugs, bumpers,
Cracked mirrors and gear-knobs,
Getting ready, already,
60 To go back with something to show

Other than her lips' new trembling
I would hold to me soon, soon,
Where I sat in the ripped back seat
Talking over the interphone,
65 Praying for Doris Holbrook
To come from her father's farm

And to get back there
With no trace of me on her face
To be seen by her red-haired father
70 Who would change, in the squalling barn,
Her back's pale skin with a strop,
Then lay for me

In a bootlegger's roasting car
With a string-triggered 12-gauge shotgun
75 To blast the breath from the air.
Not cut by the jagged windshields,
Through the acres of wrecks she came
With a wrench in her hand,

Through dust where the blacksnake dies
80 Of boredom, and the beetle knows
The compost has no more life.
Someone outside would have seen
The oldest car's door inexplicably
Close from within:

85 I held her and held her and held her,
   Convoyed at terrific speed
   By the stalled, dreaming traffic around us,
   So the blacksnake, stiff
   With inaction, curved back
90 Into life, and hunted the mouse

   With deadly overexcitement,
   The beetles reclaimed their field
   As we clung, glued together,
   With the hooks of the seat springs
95 Working through to catch us red-handed
   Amidst the gray breathless batting

   That burst from the seat at our backs.
   We left by separate doors
   Into the changed, other bodies
100 Of cars, she down Cherrylog Road
   And I to my motorcycle
   Parked like the soul of the junkyard

   Restored, a bicycle fleshed
   With power, and tore off
105 Up Highway 106, continually
   Drunk on the wind in my mouth,
   Wringing the handlebar for speed,
   Wild to be wreckage forever.

                                   1964

The *exact* location of the junkyard is not important (there is no Highway 106 near the real Cherrylog Road in North Georgia), but we do need to know that the setting is rural, that the time is summer and the summer is hot, and that moonshine whiskey is native to the area. Following the story is no problem once we have sorted out these few facts, and we are prepared to meet the cast of characters: Doris Holbrook, her red-haired father, and the speaker. About each we learn just enough to appreciate the sense of vitality, adventure, power, and disengagement that constitute the major effects of the poem.

The situation of lovemaking in a setting other than the junkyard would not produce the same effects, and the exotic sense of a forbidden meeting in this unlikely place helps to re-create the speaker's sense of the episode. For him, it is memorable (notice all the tiny details he recalls), powerful (notice his reaction when he gets back on his motorcycle), dreamlike (notice the sense of time standing still, especially in lines 85–89), and important (notice how the speaker perceives his environment as changed by their lovemaking, lines 88–91 and 98–100). The wealth of details about setting also helps us to raise other, related questions. Why does the speaker fantasize about being shot by the father (lines 72–75)? Why, in a poem so full of details, do we find out so little about what Doris Holbrook looks like and thinks about? What gives us the sense that this incident is a composite of episodes, an event that was repeated many times? What gives us the impression that the events occurred long ago? What makes the speaker feel so powerful at the end? What does he mean when he talks of himself as being "wild to be wreckage forever"? All of the poem's attention to the speaker's reactions, reflections, and memories is intricately tied up with the particulars of setting. Making love in a junkyard is crucial to the speaker's sense of both power and wreckage, and to him Doris is merely a matter of excitement, adventure, and pale skin, appreciated because she makes the world seem different and because she is willing to take risks and to suffer for meeting him like this. The more we probe the poem with questions about situation, the more likely we are to get a sense of the speaker and to catch the poem's full effect.

The **plot** of "Cherrylog Road" is fairly easy to sort out, but its effect is more complex than the simple story suggests. The next poem we will look at is initially much more difficult to follow. Part of the difficulty is that the poem comes from an earlier age and its language and sentence structure are a bit unfamiliar, and part is that the action in the poem is so closely connected to what is being said. But its opening lines—addressed to someone who is resisting the speaker's suggestions—disclose the situation, and gradually we figure out the scene: a man, trying to convince a woman that they should make love, uses a nearby flea for an unlikely example; it becomes part of his argument. And once we recognize the situation, we can readily follow (and be amused by) the speaker's witty, intricate, and specious argument.

JOHN DONNE

Carpe Diem poem

The Flea

Mark but this flea, and mark in this[1]
How little that which thou deny'st me is;
It sucked me first, and now sucks thee,
And in this flea our two bloods mingled be;
5　Thou know'st that this cannot be said
A sin, nor shame, nor loss of maidenhead.
　　Yet this enjoys before it woo,
　　And pampered[2] swells with one blood made of two,
　　And this, alas, is more than we would do.[3]

10　Oh stay,[4] three lives in one flea spare,
Where we almost, yea more than, married are.
This flea is you and I, and this
Our marriage bed, and marriage temple is;
Though parents grudge, and you, we're met
15　And cloistered in these living walls of jet.
　　Though use[5] make you apt to kill me,

---

1. Medieval preachers and rhetoricians asked their hearers to "mark" (look at) an object that illustrated a moral or philosophical lesson they wished to emphasize.　2. Fed luxuriously.
3. According to the medical theory of Donne's era, conception involved the literal mingling of the lovers' blood.　4. Desist.　5. Habit.

> Let not to that, self-murder added be,
> And sacrilege, three sins in killing three.
>
> Cruel and sudden, hast thou since
> 20 Purpled thy nail in blood of innocence?
> Wherein could this flea guilty be,
> Except in that drop which it sucked from thee?
> Yet thou triumph'st, and say'st that thou
> Find'st not thyself, nor me, the weaker now;
> 25 'Tis true; then learn how false, fears be;
> Just so much honor, when thou yield'st to me,
> Will waste, as this flea's death took life from thee.

1633

The scene in "The Flea" develops, action occurs, even as the poem unfolds. Between stanzas 1 and 2, the woman makes a move to kill the flea (as stanza 2 opens, the speaker is trying to stop her), and between stanzas 2 and 3 she has squashed the flea with her fingernail. Once we make sense of what the speaker says, the action is just as clear from the words as if we had stage directions in the margin. All of the speaker's verbal cleverness and all of his silly arguments follow from the situation, and in this poem (as in Browning's "Soliloquy of the Spanish Cloister") we watch as if we were observing a scene in a play. The speaker is, in effect, giving a dramatic monologue for our benefit.

Neither time nor place is important to "The Flea," except that we assume the speaker and his friend are in the same place and have the leisure for some playfulness. The situation could occur anywhere a man, a woman, and a flea could be together: indoors, outdoors, morning, evening, city, country, in a cottage or a castle, on a boat or in a bedroom. We know, from the date of publication, that Donne was writing about people of almost four centuries ago, but the conduct he describes might occur in any age. Only the habits of language (and perhaps the outmoded medical ideas) date the poem.

The two poems that follow have simpler plots, but in each case the heart of the poem is in the basic situation:

RITA DOVE

Daystar

> She wanted a little room for thinking:
> but she saw diapers steaming on the line,
> a doll slumped behind the door.
>
> So she lugged a chair behind the garage
> 5 to sit out the children's naps.
>
> Sometimes there were things to watch—
> the pinched armor of a vanished cricket,
> a floating maple leaf. Other days

she stared until she was assured
10 when she closed her eyes
she'd see only her own vivid blood.

She had an hour, at best, before Liza appeared
pouting from the top of the stairs.
And just *what* was mother doing
15 out back with the field mice? Why,
building a palace. Later
that night when Thomas rolled over and
lurched into her, she would open her eyes
and think of the place that was hers
20 for an hour—where
she was nothing,
pure nothing, in the middle of the day.

1986

LINDA PASTAN

To a Daughter Leaving Home

When I taught you
at eight to ride
a bicycle, loping along
beside you
5 as you wobbled away
on two round wheels,
my own mouth rounding
in surprise when you pulled
ahead down the curved
10 path of the park,
I kept waiting
for the thud
of your crash as I
sprinted to catch up,
15 while you grew
smaller, more breakable
with distance,
pumping, pumping
for your life, screaming
20 with laughter,
the hair flapping
behind you like a
handkerchief waving
goodbye.

1988

Both poems involve motherhood, but they take entirely different stances about it and have very different tones. The mother in Dove's "Daystar," overwhelmed by the demands of young children, needs a room of her own. All she can manage, however, is a brief hour of respite. The situation is virtually the whole story here. Nothing really happens except that daily events (washing diapers, picking up toys, looking at crickets and leaves, explaining the world to children, having sex) crowd her brief private hour and make it precious. Being "nothing" (lines 21 and 22) takes on great value in these circumstances, and the poem makes much of the setting: an isolated chair behind the garage. Setting in poems often means something much more specific about a particular culture or social history, but here time and place get their value from the circumstances of the situation for one frazzled mother.

The particulars of time and place in Pastan's "To a Daughter Leaving Home" are even less specific; the incident the poem describes happened a long time ago, and its vividness is a function of memory. The speaker here thinks back nostalgically to a moment when her daughter made an earlier (but briefer) departure. Though we learn very little about the speaker, at least directly, we may infer quite a bit about her—her affection for her daughter, the kind of mother she has been, her anxiety at the new departure that seems to reflect the earlier wobbly ride into the distance. The daughter is now, the poem implies, old enough to "leave" home in a full sense, but we do not know the specific reason or what the present circumstances are. Only the title tells us the situation, and (like "Daystar") the poem is all situation.

Some poems, however, depend heavily on historical specifics. In the preceding chapter, for example, we saw how Margaret Atwood based "Death of a Young Son by Drowning" on an actual person's journal entries. While the following poem refers to a particular event, it also draws on the parallels between that event and circumstances surrounding the poet and his immediate readers:

JOHN MILTON

On the Late Massacre in Piedmont

Avenge, O Lord, thy slaughtered saints, whose bones
   Lie scattered on the Alpine mountains cold;
   Even them who kept thy truth so pure of old
   When all our fathers worshiped stocks and stones,[6]
5 Forget not: in thy book record their groans
   Who were thy sheep and in their ancient fold
   Slain by the bloody Piemontese that rolled
   Mother with infant down the rocks. Their moans
The vales redoubled to the hills, and they
10   To heaven. Their martyred blood and ashes sow
   O'er all th' Italian fields, where still doth sway

---

6. Idols of wood and stone.

The triple tyrant:[7] that from these may grow
A hundredfold, who having learnt thy way
Early may fly the Babylonian woe.[8]

1655

The "slaughtered saints" were members of the Waldensians—a heretical sect that had long been settled in southern France and northern Italy (the Piedmont). Though a minority, the Waldensians were allowed freedom of worship until 1655, when their protection under the law was taken away and locals attacked them, killing large numbers. This poem, then, is not a private meditation, but rather a public statement about a well-known "news" event. To fully understand the poem and respond to it meaningfully, the reader must therefore be acquainted with its historical context, including the massacre itself and the significance it had for Milton and his English audience.

Milton wrote the poem shortly after the massacre became known in England, and implicit in its "meaning" is a parallel Milton's readers would have perceived between events in the Piedmont and current English politics. Milton signals the analogy early on by calling the dead Piedmontese "saints," the term then regularly used by English Protestants of the Puritan stamp to describe themselves and to thereby assert their belief that every individual Christian—not just those few "special" religious heroes singled out in the Catholic tradition—lived a heroic life. By identifying the Waldensians with the English Puritans—their beliefs were in some ways quite similar, and both were minorities in a larger political and cultural context—Milton was warning his fellow Puritans that, if the Stuart monarchy were reestablished, what had just happened to the Waldensians could happen to them as well. Indeed, following the Restoration in 1660, tight restrictions were placed on the Puritan "sects" under the new British monarchy. In lines 12 and 14, the poem alludes to dangers of religious rule by dominant groups by invoking standard images of Catholic power and persecution; the heir to the English throne (who succeeded to the throne as Charles II in 1660) was spending his exile in Catholic Europe and was, because of his sympathetic treatment of Catholic associates and friends, suspected of being a Catholic. Chauvinistic Englishmen, who promoted rivalries with Catholic powers like France, considered him a traitor.

Many poems, like this one, make use of historical occurrences and situations to create a widely evocative set of angers, sympathies, and conclusions. Sometimes a poet's intention in recording a particular moment or event is to commemorate it or comment upon it. A poem written about a specific occasion is usually called an **occasional poem,** and such a poem is **referential;** that is, it *refers* to a certain historical time or event. Sometimes, it is hard to place ourselves fully enough in another time or place to imagine sympathetically what a particular historical moment would have been like, and even the best poetic efforts do not necessarily transport us there. For such poems we need, at the least, specific historical information—plus a willingness on our part as readers to be transported by a name, a date, or a dramatic situation.

7. The pope's tiara featured three crowns.
8. In Milton's day, Protestants often likened the Roman Church to Babylonian decadence, called the church "the whore of Babylon," and read Revelation 17 and 18 as an allegory of its coming destruction.

Time or place may, of course, be used much less specifically and still be important to a poem; frequently a poem's setting draws upon common notions of a particular time or place. Setting a poem in a garden, for example, or writing about apples almost inevitably reminds many readers of the Garden of Eden because it is part of the Western heritage of belief or knowledge. Even people who don't read at all or who lack Judeo-Christian religious commitments are likely to know about Eden, and a poet writing in our culture can count on that. An **allusion** is a reference to something outside the poem that carries a history of meaning and strong emotional associations. (For a longer account of allusion, see chapter 11.) For example, gardens may carry suggestions of innocence and order, or temptation and the Fall, or both, depending on how the poem handles the allusion. Well-known places from history or myth may be popularly associated with particular ideas or values or ways of life.

The place involved in a poem is its **spatial setting,** and the time is its **temporal setting.** The temporal setting may be a specific date or an era, a season of the year or a time of day. We tend, for example, to think of spring as a time of discovery and growth, and poems set in spring are likely to make use of that association; morning usually suggests discovery as well—beginnings, vitality, the world fresh and new—even to those of us who in reality take our waking slow. Temporal or spatial setting often influences our expectation of theme and tone, although a poet may surprise us by making something very different of what we had thought was familiar. Setting is often an important factor in creating the mood in poems just as in stories, plays, or films. Often the details of setting have a lot to do with the way we ultimately respond to the poem's subject or theme, as in this poem:

SYLVIA PLATH

Point Shirley

From Water-Tower Hill to the brick prison
The shingle booms, bickering under
The sea's collapse.
Snowcakes break and welter. This year
5 The gritted wave leaps
The seawall and drops onto a bier
Of quahog chips,[9]
Leaving a salty mash of ice to whiten

In my grandmother's sand yard. She is dead,
10 Whose laundry snapped and froze here, who
Kept house against
What the sluttish, rutted sea could do.
Squall waves once danced
Ship timbers in through the cellar window;

9. Chips from quahog clamshells, common on the New England coast.

15 A thresh-tailed, lanced
   Shark littered in the geranium bed—

   Such collusion of mulish elements
   She wore her broom straws to the nub.
   Twenty years out
20 Of her hand; the house still hugs in each drab
   Stucco socket
   The purple egg-stones: from Great Head's knob
   To the filled-in Gut
   The sea in its cold gizzard ground those rounds.

25 Nobody wintering now behind
   The planked-up windows where she set
   Her wheat loaves
   And apple cakes to cool. What is it
   Survives, grieves
30 So, over this battered, obstinate spit
   Of gravel? The waves'
   Spewed relics clicker masses in the wind,

   Gray waves the stub-necked eiders ride.
   A labor of love, and that labor lost.
35 Steadily the sea
   Eats at Point Shirley. She died blessed,
   And I come by
   Bones, bones only, pawed and tossed,
   A dog-faced sea.
40 The sun sinks under Boston, bloody red.

   I would get from these dry-papped stones
   The milk your love instilled in them.
   The black ducks dive.
   And though your graciousness might stream,
45 And I contrive,
   Grandmother, stones are nothing of home
   To that spumiest dove.
   Against both bar and tower the black sea runs.

1960

One does not have to know the New England coast by personal experience to
find it vividly re-created in Plath's poem. A reader who knows that coast or another
like it may have an advantage in being able to respond more quickly to the poem's
precise description, but the poem does not depend on the reader's having such
knowledge. The exact location of Point Shirley, near Boston, is not especially
important, but visualization of the setting is. Crucial to the poem's tone and mood
is the sense of the sea as aggressor, a force powerful enough to change the contours
of the coast and invade the privacy of yards and homes. The energy, relentlessness,
and impersonality of the sea met their match, though only temporarily, in the
speaker's grandmother, who "[k]ept house against / What the sluttish, rutted sea

could do" (lines 11–12). The grandmother *belonged* in this setting, and it seemed hers, but twenty years of her absence (since her death) now begin to show. Still, the marks of her obstinacy and love remain, although ultimately they are doomed by the sea's more enduring power.

Details—and how they are amassed—matter here rather than historic particulars of time and place. The grays and whites and drab colors of the sea and its leavings provide both a visual sense of the scene and the mood for the poem. The stubbornness that the speaker admired in the grandmother seems a part of that tenacious grayness. Nothing happens rapidly here; things wear down. Even the "bloody red" (line 40) of the sun's setting—an ominous sign that adds a vivid fright to the dullness rather than brightening it—makes promises that seem slow and doomed. The toughness of the boarded-up house is a monument to the grandmother's loving care and becomes a way for the speaker to touch her human spirit, but the poem finally emphasizes the relentless black sea, which runs against the landmarks and fortresses that had been identified with the setting in the very first line.

Queries about situation and setting begin as simple questions of identification, but frequently become more complex when we sort out all the implications. Often it takes only a moment to determine a poem's situation, but it may take much longer to discover all the implications of time and place, for their meanings may depend upon visual details, or upon actual historical occurrences, or upon habitual ways of thinking about certain times and places—or all three at once. As you read the following poem, notice how the setting—another shore—prepares us for the speaker's moods and ideas, and then watch how the movement of his mind is affected by what he sees.

MATTHEW ARNOLD

 Dover Beach[1]

> The sea is calm tonight.
> The tide is full, the moon lies fair
> Upon the straits; on the French coast the light
> Gleams and is gone; the cliffs of England stand,
> 5 Glimmering and vast, out in the tranquil bay.
> Come to the window, sweet is the night-air!
> Only, from the long line of spray
> Where the sea meets the moon-blanched land,
> Listen! you hear the grating roar
> 10 Of pebbles which the waves draw back, and fling,
> At their return, up the high strand,
> Begin, and cease, and then again begin,
> With tremulous cadence slow, and bring
> The eternal note of sadness in.

---

1. At the narrowest point on the English Channel. The light on the French coast (lines 3–4) would be about twenty miles away.

15 Sophocles long ago
Heard it on the Aegean, and it brought
Into his mind the turbid ebb and flow
Of human misery;[2] we
Find also in the sound a thought,
20 Hearing it by this distant northern sea.

The Sea of Faith
Was once, too, at the full, and round earth's shore
Lay like the folds of a bright girdle furled.
But now I only hear
25 Its melancholy, long, withdrawing roar,
Retreating, to the breath
Of the night-wind, down the vast edges drear
And naked shingles[3] of the world.

Ah, love, let us be true
30 To one another! for the world, which seems
To lie before us like a land of dreams,
So various, so beautiful, so new,
Hath really neither joy, nor love, nor light,
Nor certitude, nor peace, nor help for pain;
35 And we are here as on a darkling plain
Swept with confused alarms of struggle and flight,
Where ignorant armies clash by night.

ca. 1851

Exactly what is the dramatic situation in "Dover Beach"? How soon are you aware that someone is being spoken to? How much do you learn about the person spoken to? How would you describe the speaker's mood? What does the speaker's mood have to do with time and place? Do any details of present time and place help to account for his tendency to talk repeatedly of the past and the future? How important is it to the poem's total effect that the beach here involves an international border? What particulars of Dover Beach seem especially important to the poem's themes? to its emotional effects?

Not all poems have an identifiable situation or setting, just as not all poems have a speaker who is entirely distinct from the author. Poems that simply present a series of thoughts and feelings directly, in a contemplative, meditative, or reflective way, may not set up any kind of action, plot, or situation at all, preferring to speak directly without the intermediary of a dramatic device. But most poems depend crucially upon a sense of place, a sense of time, and an understanding of human interaction in scenes that resemble the strategies of drama or film. And questions about these matters will often lead you to define not only the "facts" but also the feelings central to the design a poem has upon its readers.

2. In Sophocles' *Antigone*, lines 637–46, the chorus compares the fate of the house of Oedipus to the waves of the sea.   3. Pebble-strewn beaches.

SITUATIONS

MARK STRAND

Black Sea

One clear night while the others slept, I climbed
the stairs to the roof of the house and under a sky
strewn with stars I gazed at the sea, at the spread of it,
the rolling crests of it raked by the wind, becoming
5 like bits of lace tossed in the air. I stood in the long
whispering night, waiting for something, a sign, the approach
of a distant light, and I imagined you coming closer,
the dark waves of your hair mingling with the sea,
and the dark became desire, and desire the arriving light.
10 The nearness, the momentary warmth of you as I stood
on that lonely height watching the slow swells of the sea
break on the shore and turn briefly into glass and disappear . . .
Why did I believe you would come out of nowhere? Why with all
that the world offers would you come only because I was here?

2003

• How does the situation create a tone of loneliness and despair?
  What words and phrases contribute to this tone?

ANDREW MARVELL

To His Coy Mistress

Had we but world enough, and time,
This coyness,[2] lady, were no crime.
We would sit down, and think which way
To walk, and pass our long love's day.
5 Thou by the Indian Ganges' side
Shouldst rubies[3] find: I by the tide
Of Humber would complain.[4] I would
Love you ten years before the Flood,
And you should if you please refuse

---

2. Hesitancy, modesty (not necessarily suggesting calculation).
3. Talismans that are supposed to preserve virginity.
4. Write love complaints, conventional songs lamenting the cruelty of love. *Humber:* a river and estuary in Marvell's hometown of Hull.

10 Till the conversion of the Jews.[5]
     My vegetable love[6] should grow
     Vaster than empires, and more slow;
     An hundred years should go to praise
     Thine eyes, and on thy forehead gaze;
15 Two hundred to adore each breast,
     But thirty thousand to the rest.
     An age at least to every part,
     And the last age should show your heart.
     For, lady, you deserve this state;[7]
20 Nor would I love at lower rate.
        But at my back I always hear
     Time's wingéd chariot hurrying near;
     And yonder all before us lie
     Deserts of vast eternity.
25 Thy beauty shall no more be found,
     Nor, in thy marble vault, shall sound
     My echoing song; then worms shall try
     That long preserved virginity,
     And your quaint honor turn to dust,
30 And into ashes all my lust:
     The grave's a fine and private place,
     But none, I think, do there embrace.
        Now therefore, while the youthful hue
     Sits on thy skin like morning dew,[8]
35 And while thy willing soul transpires[9]
     At every pore with instant fires,
     Now let us sport us while we may,
     And now, like am'rous birds of prey,
     Rather at once our time devour
40 Than languish in his slow-chapped[1] pow'r.
     Let us roll all our strength and all
     Our sweetness up into one ball,
     And tear our pleasures with rough strife
     Thorough[2] the iron gates of life.
45 Thus, though we cannot make our sun
     Stand still,[3] yet we will make him run.[4]

1681

- **Whom is the speaker trying to persuade in this poem? Is his argument persuasive?**

5. Which, according to popular Christian belief, will occur just before the end of the world.
6. Which is capable only of passive growth, not of consciousness. The "vegetable soul" is lower than the other two divisions of the soul, "animal" and "rational."   7. Dignity.
8. The text reads "glew." "Lew" (warmth) has also been suggested as an emendation.   9. Breathes forth.
1. Slow-jawed. Chronos (Time), ruler of the world in early Greek myth, devoured all of his children except Zeus, who was hidden. Later, Zeus seized power (see line 46 and note).   2. Through.
3. To lengthen his night of love with Alcmene, Zeus made the sun stand still.
4. Each sex act was believed to shorten life by one day.

EMILY BRONTË

The Night-Wind

In summer's mellow midnight,
A cloudless moon shone through
Our open parlor window
And rosetrees wet with dew.

5 I sat in silent musing,
The soft wind waved my hair:
It told me Heaven was glorious,
And sleeping Earth was fair.

I needed not its breathing
10 To bring such thoughts to me,
But still it whispered lowly,
"How dark the woods will be!

"The thick leaves in my murmur
Are rustling like a dream,
15 And all their myriad voices
Instinct[5] with spirit seem."

I said, "Go, gentle singer,
Thy wooing voice is kind,
But do not think its music
20 Has power to reach my mind.

"Play with the scented flower,
The young tree's supple bough,
And leave my human feelings
In their own course to flow."

25 The wanderer would not leave me;
Its kiss grew warmer still—
"O come," it sighed so sweetly,
"I'll win thee 'gainst thy will.

"Have we not been from childhood friends?
30 Have I not loved thee long?
As long as thou hast loved the night
Whose silence wakes my song.

"And when thy heart is laid at rest
Beneath the church-yard stone
35 I shall have time enough to mourn
And thou to be alone."

September 11, 1840

---

5. Infused.

- What might it mean that the speaker in "The Night-Wind" feels tempted by the wind to go wandering in the darkness? What might she find there?

MARGARET ATWOOD

Siren Song

This is the one song[6] everyone
would like to learn: the song
that is irresistible:

the song that forces men
5 to leap overboard in squadrons
even though they see the beached skulls

the song nobody knows
because anyone who has heard it
is dead, and the others can't remember.

10 Shall I tell you the secret
and if I do, will you get me
out of this bird suit?

I don't enjoy it here
squatting on this island
15 looking picturesque and mythical

with these two feathery maniacs,
I don't enjoy singing
this trio, fatal and valuable.

I will tell the secret to you,
20 to you, only to you.
Come closer. This song

is a cry for help: Help me!
Only you, only you can,
you are unique

25 at last. Alas
it is a boring song
but it works every time.

                    1974

- Why is the siren song "irresistible," "fatal and valuable," "boring"? Why does it "work every time"?

6. See Homer's *Odyssey* 12.

MARILYN CHIN

Summer Love

The black smoke rising means that I am cooking
dried lotus, bay oysters scrambled with eggs.
If this doesn't please you, too bad, it's all I have.
I don't mind your staying for breakfast—but, please—do not linger;
5 nothing worse in the morning than last night's love.

Your belly is flat and your skin—milk in the moonlight.
I notice your glimmer among a thousand tired eyes.
When we dance closely, fog thickens, all distinctions falter.
I let you touch me where I am most vulnerable,
10 heart of the vulva, vulva of the heart.

Perhaps, I fear, there will not be another like you.
Or you might walk away in the same face of the others—
  —blue with scorn and a troubled life.
But, for now, let the summers be savored and the centuries be forgiven.
15 Two lovers in a field of floss and iris—
where nothing else matters but the dew and the light.

                                                1994

- How does the language of this poem (and its title) echo the situation's sexuality,
  uncertainty, and hope?

RICHARD SNYDER

A Mongoloid Child Handling Shells
on the Beach

She turns them over in her slow hands,
as did the sea sending them to her;
broken bits from the mazarine[7] maze,
they are the calmest things on this sand.
5 The unbroken children splash and shout,
rough as surf, gay as their nesting towels.
But she plays soberly with the sea's
small change and hums back to it its slow vowels.

                                                1971

- How much does this poem's title contribute to setting up its
  situation?

_____

7. Blue.

VIRGINIA HAMILTON ADAIR

Peeling an Orange

Between you and a bowl of oranges I lie nude
Reading *The World's Illusion* through my tears.
You reach across me hungry for global fruit,
Your bare arm hard, furry and warm on my belly.
5 Your fingers pry the skin of a navel orange
Releasing tiny explosions of spicy oil.
You place peeled disks of gold in a bizarre pattern
On my white body. Rearranging, you bend and bite
The disks to release further their eager scent.
10 I say "Stop, you're tickling," my eyes still on the page.
Aromas of groves arise. Through green leaves
Glow the lofty snows. Through red lips
Your white teeth close on a translucent segment.
Your face over my face eclipses *The World's Illusion*.
15 Pulp and juice pass into my mouth from your mouth.
We laugh against each other's lips. I hold my book
Behind your head, still reading, still weeping a little.
You say "Read on, I'm just an illusion," rolling
Over upon me soothingly, gently moving,
20 Smiling greenly through long lashes. And soon
I say "Don't stop. Don't disillusion me."
Snows melt. The mountain silvers into many a stream.
The oranges are golden worlds in a dark dream.

1996

- How does the suggestion of crying alter your perception of the
  situation in this poem?

MARY JO SALTER

Welcome to Hiroshima

is what you first see, stepping off the train:
a billboard brought to you in living English
by Toshiba Electric. While a channel
silent in the TV of the brain

5 projects those flickering re-runs of a cloud
that brims its risen columnful like beer
and, spilling over, hangs its foamy head,
you feel a thirst for history: what year

it started to be safe to breathe the air,
10 and when to drink the blood and scum afloat

on the Ohta River. But no, the water's clear,
they pour it for your morning cup of tea

in one of the countless sunny coffee shops
whose plastic dioramas advertise
15 mutations of cuisine behind the glass:
a pancake sandwich; a pizza someone tops

with a maraschino cherry. Passing by
the Peace Park's floral hypocenter (where
how bravely, or with what mistaken cheer,
20 humanity erased its own erasure),

you enter the memorial museum
and through more glass are served, as on a dish
of blistered grass, three mannequins. Like gloves
a mother clips to coatsleeves, strings of flesh

25 hang from their fingertips; or as if tied
to recall a duty for us, *Reverence*
the dead whose mourners too shall soon be dead,
but all commemoration's swallowed up

in questions of bad taste, how re-created
30 horror mocks the grim original,
and thinking at last *They should have left it all*
you stop. This is the wristwatch of a child.

Jammed on the moment's impact, resolute
to communicate some message, although mute,
35 it gestures with its hands at eight-fifteen
and eight-fifteen and eight-fifteen again

while tables of statistics on the wall
update the news by calling on a roll
of tape, death gummed on death, and in the case
40 adjacent, an exhibit under glass

is glass itself: a shard the bomb slammed in
a woman's arm at eight-fifteen, but some
three decades on—as if to make it plain
hope's only as renewable as pain

45 and as if all the unsung
debasements of the past may one day come
rising to the surface once again—
worked its filthy way out like a tongue

1984

- What arrests the speaker's attention to see beyond the "bad taste"
  (line 29) of the museum's displays? What is it that "works its filthy
  way out like a tongue" (line 48)?

HOWARD NEMEROV

A Way of Life

It's been going on a long time.
For instance, these two guys, not saying much, who slog
Through sun and sand, fleeing the scene of their crime,
Till one turns, without a word, and smacks
5 His buddy flat with the flat of an axe,
Which cuts down on the dialogue
Some, but is viewed rather as normal than sad
By me, as I wait for the next ad.

It seems to me it's been quite a while
10 Since the last vision of blonde loveliness
Vanished, her shampoo and shower and general style
Replaced by this lean young lunk-
head parading along with a gun in his back to confess
How yestereve, being drunk
15 And in a state of existential despair,
He beat up his grandma and pawned her invalid chair.

But here at last is a pale beauty
Smoking a filter beside a mountain stream,
Brief interlude, before the conflict of love and duty
20 Gets moving again, as sheriff and posse expound,
Between jail and saloon, the American Dream
Where Justice, after considerable horsing around,
Turns out to be Mercy; when the villain is knocked off,
A kindly uncle offers syrup for my cough.

25 And now these clean-cut athletic types
In global hats are having a nervous debate
As they stand between their individual rocket ships
Which have landed, appropriately, on some rocks
Somewhere in Space, in an atmosphere of hate
30 Where one tells the other to pull up his socks
And get going, he doesn't say where; they fade,
And an angel food cake flutters in the void.

I used to leave now and again;
No more. A lot of violence in American life
35 These days, mobsters and cops all over the scene.
But there's a lot of love, too, mixed with the strife,
And kitchen-kindness, like a bedtime story
With rich food and a more kissable depilatory.
Still, I keep my weapons handy, sitting here
40 Smoking and shaving and drinking the dry beer.

1967

- What does the succession of images represent to the speaker of "A Way of Life"? Would the situation be different today?

TIMES

WILLIAM SHAKESPEARE

[*Full many a glorious morning have I seen*]

Full many a glorious morning have I seen
Flatter the mountain-tops with sovereign eye,
Kissing with golden face the meadows green,
Gilding pale streams with heavenly alchymy;
5 Anon permit the basest clouds to ride
With ugly rack[1] on his celestial face,
And from the forlorn world his visage hide,
Stealing unseen to west with this disgrace:
Even so my sun one early morn did shine,
10 With all-triumphant splendor on my brow;
But, out! alack! he was but one hour mine,
The region cloud hath mask'd him from me now.
  Yet him for this my love no whit disdaineth;
  Suns of the world may stain when heaven's sun staineth.

1609

- What words and phrases mark the shifts of the clouds back and forth across the face of the sun in "Full many a glorious morning"? What distinction is Shakespeare making between "suns of the world" and "heaven's sun"?

JOHN DONNE

The Good-Morrow

I wonder, by my troth, what thou and I
  Did, till we loved? were we not weaned till then?
But sucked on country pleasures, childishly?
  Or snorted we in the Seven Sleepers' den?[2]   "New religion"
5 'Twas so; but[3] this, all pleasures fancies be.

---

1. Moss.
2. According to legend, seven Christian youths escaped Roman persecution by sleeping in a cave for 187 years. *Snorted:* snored.   3. Except for.

If ever any beauty I did see,
Which I desired, and got,[4] twas but a dream of thee.

Shift

And now good-morrow to our waking souls,
  Which watch not one another out of fear;
10 For love, all love of other sights controls,
  And makes one little room an everywhere.
Let sea-discoverers to new worlds have gone,
Let maps to other,[5] worlds on worlds have shown,
Let us possess one world, each hath one, and is one.

*The world is
in the room*

*Heptet
7 lines*

15 My face in thine eye, thine in mine appears,[6] A
  And true plain hearts do in the faces rest; B
Where can we find two better hemispheres, A
  Without sharp north, without declining west? B
Whatever dies was not mixed equally,[7] C
20 If our two loves be one, or, thou and I C
Love so alike that none do slacken, none can die. C

Quatrain

Triplet

1633

- Like so many of Donne's poems, this one attempts to persuade.
  What is the situation of this poem? What does the speaker wish to
  demonstrate?

SYLVIA PLATH *Alba*
Morning Song

Love set you going like a fat gold watch.
The midwife slapped your footsoles, and your bald cry
Took its place among the elements.

Our voices echo, magnifying your arrival. New statue.
5 In a drafty museum, your nakedness
Shadows our safety. We stand round blankly as walls.

I'm no more your mother
Than the cloud that distils a mirror to reflect its own slow
Effacement at the wind's hand.

10 All night your moth-breath
Flickers among the flat pink roses. I wake to listen:
A far sea moves in my ear.

One cry, and I stumble from bed, cow-heavy and floral
In my Victorian nightgown.
15 Your mouth opens clean as a cat's. The window square

---

4. Sexually possessed.   5. Other people.   6. That is, each is reflected in the other's eyes.
7. Perfectly mixed elements, according to scholastic philosophy, were stable and immortal.

Whitens and swallows its dull stars. And now you try
Your handful of notes;
The clear vowels rise like balloons.

1961

- How does this poem's language emphasize the distinctions between the speaker and her baby? How does the poem's setting in time—morning—affect its meaning?

BILLY COLLINS

Morning

Why do we bother with the rest of the day,
the swale of the afternoon,
the sudden dip into evening,

then night with his notorious perfumes,
5 his many-pointed stars?

This is the best—
throwing off the light covers,
feet on the cold floor,
and buzzing around the house on espresso—

10 maybe a splash of water on the face,
a palmful of vitamins—
but mostly buzzing around the house on espresso,

dictionary and atlas open on the rug,
the typewriter waiting for the key of the head,
15 a cello on the radio,

and, if necessary, the windows—
trees fifty, a hundred years old
out there,
heavy clouds on the way
20 and the lawn steaming like a horse
in the early morning.

1998

- What words and phrases help to color the reader's perceptions of the various times of day mentioned in this poem? Why is morning "the best" (line 6)?

MARK STRAND

A.M.

. . . And here the dark infinitive to feel,
Which would endure and have the earth be still
And the star-strewn night pour down the mountains
Into the hissing fields and silent towns until the last
5 Insomnia turned in, must end, and early risers see
The scarlet clouds break up and golden plumes of smoke
From uniform dark homes turn white, and so on down
To the smallest blade of grass and fallen leaf
Touched by the arriving light. Another day has come,
10 Another fabulous escape from the damages of night,
So even the gulls, in the ragged circle of their flight,
Above the sea's long aisles that flash and fall, scream
Their approval. How well the sun's rays probe
The rotting carcass of a skate, how well
15 They show the worms and swarming flies at work,
How well they shine upon the fatal sprawl
Of everything on earth. How well they love us all.

2001

- What is the setting—the "here" of the opening line? What changes in the poem's tone mark the coming of day?

AUGUST KLEINZAHLER

Aubade on East 12th Street

The skylight silvers
and a faint shudder from the underground
travels up the building's steel.

Dawn breaks across this wilderness
5 of roofs with their old wooden storage tanks
and caps of louvered cowlings

moving in the wind. Your back,
raised hip and thigh
well-tooled as a rounded baluster

10 on a lathe of shadow and light.

1996

- Paraphrase the simile that concludes this poem. How does "a lathe of shadow and light" figure into the comparison?

JONATHAN SWIFT

A Description of the Morning

Now hardly here and there a hackney-coach[8]
Appearing, showed the ruddy morn's approach.
Now Betty[9] from her master's bed had flown,
And softly stole to discompose her own.
5 The slip shod 'prentice from his master's door
Had pared the dirt, and sprinkled round the floor.
Now Moll had whirled her mop with dext'rous airs,
Prepared to scrub the entry and the stairs.
The youth with broomy stumps began to trace
10 The kennel-edge[1] where wheels had worn the place.
The small-coal man[2] was heard with cadence deep,
Till drowned in shriller notes of chimney-sweep:
Duns[3] at his lordship's gate began to meet;
And brick-dust Moll had screamed through half the street.[4]
15 The turnkey now his flock returning sees,
Duly let out a-nights to steal for fees.[5]
The watchful bailiffs take their silent stands,[6]
And schoolboys lag with satchels in their hands.

                                                              1709

- From the poem's brief descriptions of morning routines, what do
  we know about its various characters and the kind of community
  they inhabit? Could a similar poem be written today?

JOY HARJO

Mourning Song

It's early evening here in the small world, where gods gamble for good
weather as the sky turns red. Oh grief rattling around in the bowl of my
skeleton. How I'd like to spit you out, turn you into another human, or
remake the little dog spirit who walked out of our house without its skin

---

8. Hired coach. *Hardly:* scarcely; that is, they are just beginning to appear.
9. A stock name for a servant girl. Moll (lines 7, 14) is a frequent lower-class nickname.
1. Edge of the gutter that ran down the middle of the street. *Trace:* To find old nails [Swift's note].
2. A seller of coal and charcoal.   3. Bill collectors.
4. Selling powdered brick that was used to clean knives.
5. Jailers collected fees from prisoners for their keep and often let them out at night so they could steal to
pay expenses.   6. Looking for those on their "wanted" lists.

5 toward an unseen land. We were left behind to figure it out during a
harvest turned to ashes. I need to mourn with the night, turn to the
gleaming house of bones under your familiar brown skin. The hot stone of
our hearts will make a fire. If we cry more tears we will ruin the land with
salt; instead let's praise that which would distract us with despair. Make a
10 song for death, a song with yellow teeth and bad breath. For loneliness,
the house guest who eats everything and refuses to leave. A song for bad
weather so we can stand together under our leaking roof, and make a
terrible music with our wise and ragged bones.

1994

- **What has caused the speaker to mourn? What will be "praised" by the "terrible
music" of the mourning song?**

LOUISE BOGAN

Evening in the Sanitarium[7]

The free evening fades, outside the windows fastened with decorative
    iron grilles.
The lamps are lighted; the shades drawn; the nurses are watching a
    little.
It is the hour of the complicated knitting on the safe bone needles; of
    the games of anagrams and bridge;
The deadly game of chess; the book held up like a mask.

5 The period of the wildest weeping, the fiercest delusion, is over.
The women rest their tired half-healed hearts; they are almost well.
Some of them will stay almost well always: the blunt-faced woman
    whose thinking dissolved
Under academic discipline; the manic-depressive girl
Now leveling off; one paranoiac afflicted with jealousy.
10 Another with persecution. Some alleviation has been possible.

O fortunate bride, who never again will become elated after childbirth!
O lucky older wife; who has been cured of feeling unwanted!
To the suburban railway station you will return, return,
To meet forever Jim home on the 5:35.
15 You will be again as normal and selfish and heartless as anybody else.

There is life left: the piano says it with its octave smile.
The soft carpets pad the thump and splinter of the suicide to be.
Everything will be splendid: the grandmother will not drink habitually.
The fruit salad will bloom on the plate like a bouquet
20 And the garden produce the blue-ribbon aquilegia.[8]

---

7. Originally published with the subtitle "Imitated from Auden" [Bogan's note]. 8. Columbine.

The cats will be glad; the fathers feel justified; the mothers relieved.
The sons and husbands will no longer need to pay the bills.
Childhoods will be put away, the obscene nightmare abated.

At the ends of the corridors the baths are running.
25 Mrs. C. again feels the shadow of the obsessive idea.
Miss R. looks at the mantel-piece, which must mean something.

                                                                    1941

- Why do you think this poem is set in the evening? How does this setting affect
  the poem?

ARCHIBALD LAMPMAN

Winter Evening

To-night the very horses springing by
Toss gold from whitened nostrils. In a dream
The streets that narrow to the westward gleam
Like rows of golden palaces; and high
5 From all the crowded chimneys tower and die
A thousand aureoles. Down in the west
The brimming plains beneath the sunset rest,
One burning sea of gold. Soon, soon shall fly
The glorious vision, and the hours shall feel
10 A mightier master; soon from height to height,
With silence and the sharp unpitying stars,
Stern creeping frosts, and winds that touch like steel,
Out of the depth beyond the eastern bars,
Glittering and still shall come the awful night.

                                                                    1899

- How does this poem's language create a sense of afternoon's warmth
  and beauty, and then of danger and pain in "the awful night"?

PLACES

JOHN BETJEMAN

In Westminster Abbey[9]

Let me take this other glove off
  As the *vox humana*[1] swells,
And the beauteous fields of Eden
  Bask beneath the Abbey bells.
5 Here, where England's statesmen lie,
  Listen to a lady's cry.

Gracious Lord, oh bomb the Germans.
  Spare their women for Thy Sake,
And if that is not too easy
10   We will pardon Thy Mistake.
But, gracious Lord, whate'er shall be,
Don't let anyone bomb me.

Keep our Empire undismembered
  Guide our Forces by Thy Hand,
15 Gallant blacks from far Jamaica,
    Honduras and Togoland;
Protect them Lord in all their fights,
And, even more, protect the whites.

Think of what our Nation stands for,
20   Books from Boots[2] and country lanes,
Free speech, free passes, class distinction,
    Democracy and proper drains.
Lord, put beneath Thy special care
One-eighty-nine Cadogan Square.[3]

25 Although dear Lord I am a sinner,
  I have done no major crime;
Now I'll come to Evening Service
  Whensoever I have the time.
So, Lord, reserve for me a crown,[4]
30 And do not let my shares go down.

---

9. Gothic church in London in which English monarchs are crowned and many famous Englishmen are buried (see lines 5, 39–40).
1. Organ tones that resemble the human voice.   2. A chain of British pharmacies.
3. Presumably where the speaker lives, in a fashionable section of central London.
4. Coin worth five shillings (but also an afterlife reward).

I will labor for Thy Kingdom,
  Help our lads to win the war,
Send white feathers to the cowards[5]
  Join the Women's Army Corps,[6]
35 Then wash the Steps around Thy Throne
In the Eternal Safety Zone.

Now I feel a little better,
  What a treat to hear Thy Word
Where the bones of leading statesmen,
40   Have so often been interred.
And now, dear Lord, I cannot wait
Because I have a luncheon date.

1940

- How do the poem's setting in place—a historic church in London—
  and time—1940, during the German bombardment of Britain—affect
  the tone?

ELIZABETH ALEXANDER

West Indian Primer

for Clifford L. Alexander, Sr.
1898–1989

"On the road between Spanish Town
and Kingston," my grandfather said,
"I was born." His father a merchant,
Jewish, from Italy or Spain

5 In the great earthquake the ground split
clean, and great-grandfather fell
in the fault with his goat. I don't know
how I got this tale and do not ask.

His black mother taught my grand-
10 father figures, fixed codfish cakes
and fried plantains, drilled cleanliness,
telling the truth, punctuality.

"There is no man more honest,"
my father says. Years later
15 I read that Jews passed through my
grandfather's birthplace frequently.

---

5. White feathers were sometimes given or sent to men not in uniform to suggest that they were cowards and should join the armed forces.
6. The speaker uses the old World War I name (Women's Army Auxiliary Corps) of the Auxiliary Territorial Service, an organization that performed domestic (and some foreign) defense duties.

I know more about Toussaint[7]
and Hispaniola[8] than my own
Jamaica and my family tales.
20 I finger the stories like genie

lamps. I write this West Indian primer.

1990

- Why do you think this poem is presented as a "primer"—that is, a basic introduction—for the speaker's native Jamaica? Does the poem fulfill that function?

AGHA SHAHID ALI

Postcard from Kashmir

(for Pavan Sahgal)

Kashmir shrinks into my mailbox,
my home a neat four by six inches.

I always loved neatness. Now I hold
the half-inch Himalayas in my hand.
5 This is home. And this the closest
I'll ever be to home. When I return,
the colors won't be so brilliant,
the Jhelum's waters[9] so clean,
so ultramarine. My love
10 so overexposed.

And my memory will be a little
out of focus, in it
a giant negative, black
and white, still undeveloped.

1987

- What words characterize the speaker's dreams of home in this poem? What words reveal a more realistic attitude?

7. Self-educated, Haitian black soldier and liberator (1743–1803).
8. The first island claimed by Columbus for Spain in 1492. Now divided into the nations of Haiti and the Dominican Republic.   9. The river Jhelum runs through Kashmir and Pakistan.

DEREK WALCOTT

Midsummer

Certain things here[1] are quietly American—
that chain-link fence dividing the absent roars
of the beach from the empty ball park, its holes
muttering the word umpire instead of empire;
5 the gray, metal light where an early pelican
coasts, with its engine off, over the pink fire
of a sea whose surface is as cold as Maine's.
The light warms up the sides of white, eager Cessnas[2]
parked at the airstrip under the freckling hills
10 of St. Thomas. The sheds, the brown, functional hangar,
are like those of the Occupation in the last war.
The night left a rank smell under the casuarinas,
the villas have fenced-off beaches where the natives walk,
illegal immigrants from unlucky islands
15 who envy the smallest polyp its right to work.
Here the wetback crab and the mollusc are citizens,
and the leaves have green cards. Bulldozers jerk
and gouge out a hill, but we all know that the dust
is industrial and must be suffered. Soon—
20 the sea's corrugations are sheets of zinc
soldered by the sun's steady acetylene. This
drizzle that falls now is American rain,
stitching stars in the sand. My own corpuscles
are changing as fast. I fear what the migrant envies:
25 the starry pattern they make—the flag on the post office—
the quality of the dirt, the fealty changing under my foot.

1984

- What is "American" (line 22) about the images described in this poem? Why does the speaker say he fears "the starry pattern" made by the raindrops in the sand (line 25)?

JOHN ASHBERY

City Afternoon

A veil of haze protects this
Long-ago afternoon forgotten by everybody
In this photograph, most of them now
Sucked screaming through old age and death.

---

1. Trinidad.   2. Small airplanes.

5 If one could seize America
Or at least a fine forgetfulness
That seeps into our outline
Defining our volumes with a stain
That is fleeting too

10 But commemorates
Because it does define, after all:
Gray garlands, that threesome
Waiting for the light to change,
Air lifting the hair of one
15 Upside down in the reflecting pool.

                                                        1975

• What is the "stain" of line 8? How does it help to "define" (line 10)
  the poem's setting?

THOM GUNN

A Map of the City

I stand upon a hill and see
A luminous country under me,
Through which at two the drunk must weave;
The transient's pause, the sailor's leave.

5 I notice, looking down the hill,
Arms braced upon a window sill;
And on the web of fire escapes
Move the potential, the grey shapes.

I hold the city here, complete:
10 And every shape defined by light
Is mine, or corresponds to mine,
Some flickering or some steady shine.

This map is ground of my delight.
Between the limits, night by night,
15 I watch a malady's advance,
I recognize my love of chance.

By the recurrent lights I see
Endless potentiality,
The crowded, broken, and unfinished!
20 I would not have the risk diminished.

                                                        1954

• In what way does the speaker's view of a city at night constitute a
  "map"? How is this map "complete" (line 9)?

MARY OLIVER

Singapore

In Singapore, in the airport,
a darkness was ripped from my eyes.
In the women's restroom, one compartment stood open.
A woman knelt there, washing something
    in the white bowl.

5 Disgust argued in my stomach
and I felt, in my pocket, for my ticket.

A poem should always have birds in it.
Kingfishers, say, with their bold eyes and gaudy wings.
Rivers are pleasant, and of course trees.
10 A waterfall, or if that's not possible, a fountain
    rising and falling.
A person wants to stand in a happy place, in a poem.

When the woman turned I could not answer her face.
Her beauty and her embarrassment struggled together, and
    neither could win.
She smiled and I smiled. What kind of nonsense is this?
15 Everybody needs a job.

Yes, a person wants to stand in a happy place, in a poem.
But first we must watch her as she stares down at her labor,
    which is dull enough.
She is washing the tops of the airport ashtrays, as big as
    hubcaps, with a blue rag.
Her small hands turn the metal, scrubbing and rinsing.
20 She does not work slowly, nor quickly, but like a river.
Her dark hair is like the wing of a bird.

I don't doubt for a moment that she loves her life.
And I want her to rise up from the crust and the slop
    and fly down to the river.
This probably won't happen.
25 But maybe it will.
If the world were only pain and logic, who would want it?

Of course, it isn't.
Neither do I mean anything miraculous, but only
the light that can shine out of a life. I mean
30 the way she unfolded and refolded the blue cloth,
the way her smile was only for my sake; I mean
the way this poem is filled with trees, and birds.

1990

- What "darkness was ripped" from the speaker's eyes (line 2)? Does
  it matter that the poem is set in (and named after) a particular city?

EARLE BIRNEY

Irapuato[3]

For reasons any
                    brigadier
                                      could tell
this is a favorite nook for
5   massacre

Toltex by Mixtex Mixtex by Aztex
Aztex by Spanishtex Spanishtex by
Mexitex by Mexitex by Mexitex by Texaco[4]
So any farmer can see how the strawberries
10 are the biggest and reddest
      in the whole damn continent

but why
          when arranged under
                              the market flies
15 do they look like small clotting hearts?
                                    1962

- What connects "Toltex" and "Texaco" in the speaker's mind
  (lines 6–8)?

DORIANNE LAUX

The Laundromat

My clothes somersault in the dryer. At thirty
I float in and out of a new kind of horniness,
the kind where you get off on words and gestures;
long talks about art are foreplay, the climax
5 is watching a man eat a Napoleon while he drives.
Across from me a fifty year old matron folds clothes,
her eyes focused on the nipples of a young man in
silk jogging shorts. He looks up, catching her.
She giggles and blurts out, "Hot, isn't it?"
10 A man on my right eyes the line of my shorts, waiting
for me to bend over. I do. An act of animal kindness.
A long black jogger swings in off the street to
splash his face in the sink and I watch the room
become a sweet humid jungle. We crowd around

3. A city in central Mexico, northwest of Mexico City.
4. The Toltec, Mixtec, and Aztec peoples lived in pre-Columbian Mexico.

15 the Amazon at the watering hole, twitching our noses
    like wildebeests or buffalo, snorting, rooting out
    mates in the heat. I want to hump every moving thing
    in this place. I want to lie down in the dry dung
    and dust and twist to scratch my back. I want to
20 stretch and prowl and grow lazy in the shade. I want
    to have a slew of cubs. "Do you have change for
    a quarter?" he asks, scratching the inside of his thigh.
    Back in the laundromat my socks are sticking to my
    sheets. Caught in the crackle of static electricity,
25 I fold my underwear. I notice the honey-colored
    stains in each silk crotch. Odd-shaped, like dreams,
    I make my panties into neat squares and drop them,
    smiling, into the wicker basket.

                                                     1990

- What sights and sounds of the laundromat arouse the speaker's
  erotic fantasies? What parallels does the speaker find between the
  laundromat and a "sweet humid jungle" (line 14)?

SUGGESTIONS FOR WRITING

1. Matthew Arnold's "Dover Beach" is a meditation on history and human destiny
   derived from the poet's close observation of the ebb and flow of the sea. Write an
   essay in which you examine the poem's descriptive language and the way this creates
   a suitable setting for Arnold's philosophical musings.
2. Certain seventeenth-century poets, such as John Donne and Andrew Marvell, have
   been called "metaphysical poets" for their ingenuity in using apparently far-fetched
   analogies to create apt and insightful comparisons, usually intended to persuade.
   What is the line of reasoning in Donne's "The Flea" or Marvell's "To His Coy Mis-
   tress"? Who is the intended audience for each poem? Write an essay in which you
   discuss the way that either or both of these poems uses situation as the basis for
   comparison and persuasion.
3. Mary Jo Salter's "Welcome to Hiroshima" and Howard Nemerov's "A Way of Life"
   both use situations—visiting a war museum and watching television, respectively—
   that present a host of ideas about modern society in general and America in partic-
   ular. What is each poem saying about our moral and political values? Write an essay
   in which you examine the way either of these poems uses situation to create an
   implied commentary on American moral and political values.
4. This chapter contains a number of poems about the morning. Some of these, such
   as Shakespeare's "Full many a glorious morning have I seen" and Sylvia Plath's
   "Morning Song," associate morning with love, while others, such as Billy Collins's
   "Morning" and Mark Strand's "A.M.," associate the morning with more general
   feelings of joy. Write an essay in which you compare and contrast the poetic use of
   the morning setting in any two of the poems in this chapter.
5. Choose any of the poems in this or the previous chapters and write an essay about
   the way a poet can use situation and setting to evoke a rich intermingling of lan-
   guage, subject, and feeling.

4 LANGUAGE

Fiction and drama depend upon language just as poetry does, but in a poem almost everything comes down to the particular meanings and implications of individual words. When we read stories and plays, we generally focus our attention on character and plot, and although words determine how we imagine those characters and how we respond to what happens to them, we are not as likely to pause over any one word as we may need to when reading a poem. Because poems are often short, a lot depends on every word in them. Sometimes, as though they were distilled prose, poems contain only the essential words. They say just barely enough to communicate in the most basic way, using elemental signs—with each chosen for exactly the right shade of meaning or feeling or both. But elemental does not necessarily mean simple, and these signs may be very rich in their meanings and complex in their effects. The poet's word choice—the **diction** of a poem— determines not only meaning but just about every effect the poem produces.

PRECISION AND AMBIGUITY

Let's look first at poems that create some of their effects by examining—or playing with—a single word. Often multiple meanings or shiftiness and uncertainty of a word are at issue. The following short poem, for example, depends almost entirely on the way we use the word *play*.

SARAH CLEGHORN
[*The golf links lie so near the mill*]

The golf links lie so near the mill
That almost every day
The laboring children can look out
And see the men at play.
                              1915

While traveling in the American South, Cleghorn had seen, right next to a golf course, a textile mill that employed quite young children. Her poem doesn't *say* that we expect men to work and children to play; it just assumes our expectation and builds an effect of **dramatic irony**—an incongruity between what we expect and what actually occurs—out of the observation. The poem saves almost all of its devastating effect for the final word, after the situation has been carefully described and the irony set up.

In the following two poems, a word used over and over acquires multiple meanings and refuses to be limited to a single one.

ANNE FINCH, COUNTESS OF WINCHELSEA

There's No To-Morrow

A Fable imitated from Sir Roger L'Estrange

    Two long had Lov'd, and now the Nymph desir'd,
    The Cloak of Wedlock, as the Case requir'd;
    Urg'd that, the Day he wrought her to this Sorrow,
    He Vow'd, that he wou'd marry her To-Morrow.
5 Agen he Swears, to shun the present Storm,
    That he, To-Morrow, will that Vow perform.
    The Morrows in their due Successions came;
    Impatient still on Each, the pregnant Dame
    Urg'd him to keep his Word, and still he swore the same.
10 When tir'd at length, and meaning no Redress,
    But yet the Lye not caring to confess,
    He for his Oath this Salvo chose to borrow,
    That he was Free, since there was no To-Morrow;
    For when it comes in Place to be employ'd,
15 'Tis then To-Day; To-Morrow's ne'er enjoy'd.
    The Tale's a Jest, the Moral is a Truth;
    To-Morrow and To-Morrow, cheat our Youth:
    In riper Age, To-Morrow still we cry,
    Not thinking, that the present Day we Dye;
20 Unpractis'd all the Good we had Design'd;
    There's No To-Morrow to a Willing Mind.

                                         1713

CHARLES BERNSTEIN

Of Time and the Line

George Burns[1] likes to insist that he always
takes the straight lines; the cigar in his mouth
is a way of leaving space between the

---

1. American comedian (1896–1996) who played straight man to his wife, Gracie Allen.

lines for a laugh. He weaves lines together
5　by means of a picaresque narrative;
not so Hennie Youngman,[2] whose lines are strict-
ly paratactic. My father pushed a
line of ladies' dresses—not down the street
in a pushcart but upstairs in a fact'ry
10　office. My mother has been more concerned
with her hemline. Chairman Mao[3] put forward
Maoist lines, but that's been abandoned (most-
ly) for the East-West line of malarkey
so popular in these parts. The prestige
15　of the iambic line has recently
suffered decline, since it's no longer so
clear who "I" am, much less who *you* are. When
making a line, better be double sure
what you're lining in & what you're lining
20　out & which side of the line you're on; the
world is made up so (Adam didn't so much
name as delineate). Every poem's got
a prosodic lining, some of which will
unzip for summer wear. The lines of an
25　imaginary are inscribed on the
social flesh by the knifepoint of history.
Nowadays, you can often spot a work
of poetry by whether it's in lines
or no; if it's in prose, there's a good chance
30　it's a poem. While there is no lesson in
the line more useful than that of the pick-
et line, the line that has caused the most ad-
versity is the bloodline. In Russia
everyone is worried about long lines;
35　back in the USA, it's strictly soup-
lines. "Take a chisel to write," but for an
actor a line's got to be cued. Or, as
they say in math, it takes two lines to make
an angle but only one lime to make
40　a Margarita.

1991

The Finch poem repeatedly explores the shifting sands of the word "to-morrow," first noting how different people may think of its meanings differently, then showing how these shifts are anchored in time and the whole process of meaning. The Bernstein poem finds a great variety of completely different meanings of the word "line." How many different meanings can you distinguish in the poem? What does "Time" (in the title) have to do with the poem?

Here is a far more personal and emotional poem, which uses a single word,

---

2. American comedian (1906–1998), stand-up king of the one-liner.
3. Mao Zedong (1893–1976), leader of the revolution that established China as a communist nation.

"terminal," to explore the changing relationship between two people—a father (who speaks the poem) and daughter.

YVOR WINTERS

At the San Francisco Airport

to my daughter, 1954

This is the terminal: the light
Gives perfect vision, false and hard;
The metal glitters, deep and bright.
Great planes are waiting in the yard—
5   They are already in the night.

And you are here beside me, small,
Contained and fragile, and intent
On things that I but half recall—
Yet going whither you are bent.
10   I am the past, and that is all.

But you and I in part are one:
The frightened brain, the nervous will,
The knowledge of what must be done,
The passion to acquire the skill
15   To face that which you dare not shun.

The rain of matter upon sense
Destroys me momently. The score:
There comes what will come. The expense
Is what one thought, and something more—
20   One's being and intelligence.

This is the terminal, the break.
Beyond this point, on lines of air,
You take the way that you must take;
And I remain in light and stare—
25   In light, and nothing else, awake.

1954

In this case, the poem soberly and thoughtfully probes the several possible meanings of its key word. The importance of the word involves its **ambiguity** (its having more than one possible meaning) rather than its **precision** (its exactness).

What does it *mean* to be in a place called a "terminal"? As the parting of father and daughter is explored carefully, the place of parting and the means of transportation take on meanings larger than their simple referential ones. The poem presents contrasts—young and old, light and dark, past and present, security and adventure. The father ("I am the past," line 10) remains in the light, among known objects and experiences familiar to his many years; the daughter is about to depart into the night, the unknown, the uncertain future. But they both share a sense of the necessity of the parting, of the need for the daughter to mature, gain knowledge, acquire experience. Is she going off to school? to college? to her first job? We don't know, but her plane ride clearly means a new departure and a clean break with childhood, dependency, the past.

So much depends upon the word "terminal." It refers to the airport building, of course, but it also implies a boundary, an extremity, a terminus, something that is limited, a junction, a place where a connection may be broken. Important as well is the unambiguous or "dictionary" meaning of certain other words—that is, what these words **denote**. The final stanza is articulated flatly, as if the speaker has recovered from the momentary confusion of stanza 4, when "being and intelligence" are lost in the emotion of the parting itself. The words "break," "point," "way," and "remain" are almost unemotional and colorless; they do not make value judgments or offer personal views, but rather define and describe. The sharp articulation of the last stanza stresses the **denotations** of the words employed, as though the speaker is trying to disengage himself from the emotion of the situation and just give the facts.

Words, however, are more than hard blocks of meaning on whose sense everyone agrees. They also have a more personal side, and they carry emotional force and shades of suggestion. The words we use indicate not only what we mean but how we feel about it, and we choose words that we hope will engage others emotionally and persuasively, in conversation and daily usage as well as in poems. A person who holds office is, quite literally (and unemotionally), an *officeholder*—the word denotes what he or she does. But if we want to convey that a particular officeholder is wise, trustworthy, and deserving of political support we may call that person a *civil servant*, a *political leader*, or an *elected official*, whereas if we want to promote distrust

> *A poet is, before anything else, a person who is passionately in love with language.*
> —W. H. AUDEN

or contempt of that same officeholder we might say *politician* or *bureaucrat* or *political hack*. These latter terms have clear **connotations**—suggestions of emotional coloration that imply our attitude and invite a similar one from our hearers. What words **connote** can be just as important to a poem as what they denote; some poems work primarily through denotation and some more through connotation.

"At the San Francisco Airport," certainly, depends primarily on denotation. The speaker tries to *specify* the meanings and implications of the parting with his daughter, and his tendency to split categories neatly for the two of them at first contributes to the sense of clarity and certainty he wants to project. He is the past (line 10) and what remains (line 24); he has age and experience, his life is the known quantity, he stands in the light. She, on the other hand, is committed to the adventure of going into the night; she seems small, fragile, and her identity blurs into the uncertain future. Yet the connotations of some words carry strong emotional force as well as clear definition: that the daughter seems "small" and "fragile" to the speaker suggests his fear for her, something quite different from her own sense of adventure. The neat, clean categories keep breaking down, and the speaker's feelings keep showing through. In stanza 1, the light in the terminal gives "perfect vision," but the speaker also notices, indirectly, its artificial quality: it is "false" and "hard," suggesting the limits of the rationalism he tries to maintain. That artificial light shines over most of the poem and honors the speaker's effort, but the whole poem represents his struggle, and in stanza 4 the signals of disturbance are very strong as, despite an insistence on a vocabulary of calculation, his rational facade collapses completely. If we have observed his verbal strategies carefully, we should not be surprised to find him at the end just *staring* in the artificial light, merely awake, although the poem has shown him to be unconsciously awake to much more than he will candidly admit.

"At the San Francisco Airport" is an unusually intricate and complicated poem, and it offers us, if we are willing to examine precisely its carefully crafted fabric, rich insight into how complex it is to be human and to have human feelings and foibles when we think we must be rational machines.

But connotations can work more simply. The following epitaph, for example, even though it describes the mixed feelings one person has about another, depends heavily on the connotations of fairly common words.

WALTER DE LA MARE
Slim Cunning Hands

Slim cunning hands at rest, and cozening eyes—
Under this stone one loved too wildly lies;
How false she was, no granite could declare;
  Nor all earth's flowers, how fair.

1950

What the speaker in "Slim Cunning Hands" remembers about the dead woman—her hands, her eyes—tells part of the story; her physical presence was clearly important to him. The poem's other nouns—stone, granite, flowers—all remind us of her death and its finality. All these words denote objects having to do with the rituals that memorialize a departed life. Granite and stone connote finality as well, and flowers connote fragility and suggest the shortness of life (which is why they have become the symbolic language of funerals). The way the speaker talks about the woman expresses, in just a few words, the complexity of his love for her. She was loved, he says, too "wildly"—by him perhaps, and apparently by others. The excitement she offered is suggested by the word, and also the lack of control. The words "cunning" and "cozening" help us interpret both her wildness and her falsity; they suggest her calculation, cleverness, and untrustworthiness as well as her skill, persuasiveness, and ability to please. Moreover, coming at the end of the second line the word "lies" has more than one meaning. The body "lies" under the stone, but the woman's falsity has by now become too prominent to ignore as a second meaning. And the word "fair," a simple yet very inclusive word, suggests how totally attractive the speaker finds her: her beauty can no more be expressed by flowers than her fickleness can be expressed by something as permanent as words in stone. But the word "fair," in the emphatic position as the final word, also implies two other meanings that seem to resonate, ironically, with what we have already learned about her from the speaker: "impartial" and "just." "Impartial" she may be in her preferences (as the word "false" suggests), but to the speaker she is hardly "just," and the final defining word speaks both to her appearance and (ironically) to her character. Simple words here tell us perhaps all we need to know of a long story—or at least the speaker's version of it.

Words like "fair" and "cozening" are loaded. They imply more emotionally than they mean literally. They have strong, clear connotations; they tell us what to think, what evaluation to make; and they suggest the basis for the evaluation. Similarly, both words in the title of the following poem are key to the poem's meaning and effect.

PAT MORA

Gentle Communion

Even the long-dead are willing to move.
Without a word, she came with me from the desert.
Mornings she wanders through my rooms
making beds, folding socks.

5 Since she can't hear me anymore,
Mamande[4] ignores the questions I never knew
to ask, about her younger days, her red
hair, the time she fell and broke her nose
in the snow. I will never know.

10 When I try to make her laugh,
to disprove her sad album face, she leaves
the room, resists me as she resisted
grinning for cameras, make-up, English.

While I write, she sits and prays,
15 feet apart, legs never crossed,
the blue housecoat buttoned high
as her hair dries white, girlish
around her head and shoulders.

She closes her eyes, bows her head,
20 and like a child presses her hands together,
her patient flesh steeple, the skin
worn, like the pages of her prayer book.

Sometimes I sit in her wide-armed
chair as I once sat in her lap.
25 Alone, we played a quiet I Spy.
She peeled grapes I still taste.

She removes the thin skin, places
the luminous coolness on my tongue.
I know not to bite or chew. I wait
30 for the thick melt,
our private green honey.

1991

4. A child's conflation of *mama grande* (Spanish for "grandmother").

Neither of the words in the title appears in the text itself, but both resonate throughout the poem. "Communion" is the more powerful of the words; here, it comes to imply the close ritualized relationship between the speaker and "Mamande." Mamande has long been dead but now returns, recalling to the speaker a host of memories and providing a sense of history and family identity. To the speaker, the reunion has a powerful value, reminding her of rituals, habits, and beliefs that "place" her and affirm her heritage. The past is strong in the speaker's mind and in the poem. Many details are recalled from album photographs—the blue housecoat (line 16), the sad face (line 11), the white hair that was once red (lines 7–8 and 17), the posture at prayer (lines 19–22), the big chair (lines 23–24), the plain old-fashioned style (line 13)—and the speaker's childhood memories fade into them as she recalls a specific intimate moment.

The full effect of the word "communion"—which describes an intimate moment of union and a ritual—comes only in the final lines, when the speaker remembers the secret of the grapes and recalls their sensuous feel and taste. The moment brings together the experience of different generations and cultures and represents a sacred sharing: the Spanish grandmother had resisted English, modernity, and show (line 13), and the speaker is a poet, writing (and publishing) in English, but the two have a common "private" (line 31) moment ritually shared and forever memorable. At the end, too, the full sense of "gentle" becomes evident—a word that sums up the softness, quietness, and understatedness of the experience, the personal qualities of "Mamande," and the unpretentious but dignified social level of the family heritage. Throughout the text, other words—ordinary, simple, and precise—suggest the sense of personal dignity, revealed identity, and verbal power that the speaker comes to accept as her own. Look especially at the words "move" (line 1), "steeple" (line 21), and "luminous" (line 28).

Words are the starting point for all poetry, of course, and almost every word is likely to be significant, either denotatively or connotatively or both. Poets who know their craft pick each word with care to express exactly what needs to be expressed and to suggest every emotional shade that the poem is calculated to evoke in us. Often individual words qualify and amplify one another—suggestions clarify other suggestions, and meanings grow upon meanings—and thus the way the words are put together can be important, too. Notice, for example, that in "Slim Cunning Hands" the final emphasis is on how *fair* in appearance the woman was; the speaker's last word describes the quality he can't forget in spite of her lack of a different kind of fairness and his distrust of her, the quality that, even though it doesn't justify everything else, mitigates all the disappointment and hurt.

That one word does not stand all by itself, however, any more than any other word in a poem can be considered all alone. Every word exists within larger units of meaning—sentences, patterns of comparisons and contrasts, the whole poem—and where the word is and how it is used are often important. The final word or words may be especially emphatic (as in "Slim Cunning Hands"), and words that are repeated take on a special intensity, as "terminal" does in "At the San Francisco Airport," or as "chartered" and "cry" do in "London," or "what did I know?" in "Those Winter Sundays" (both in chapter 1). Certain words often stand out, because they are used in an unusual way (like "chartered" in "London") or because they are given an artificial prominence—through unusual sentence structure, for example, or because the title calls special attention to them.

Sometimes word choice in poems is less dramatic and less obviously "significant" but equally important. Often, in fact, simple appropriateness makes the words in a poem work, and words that do not call special attention to themselves can be the most effective. Precision of denotation may be just as impressive and productive of specific effects as the resonance or ambiguous suggestiveness of connotation. Often poems achieve their power by a combination of verbal effects, setting off elaborate figures of speech (which we will discuss shortly) or other complicated strategies with simple words chosen to mark exact actions, moments, or states of mind. Notice, for example, how carefully the following poem produces its complex description of emotional patterns by delineating and then elaborating precise stages of feeling.

EMILY DICKINSON

CD *[After great pain, a formal feeling comes—]*

After great pain, a formal feeling comes—
The Nerves sit ceremonious, like Tombs—
The stiff Heart questions was it He, that bore,
And Yesterday, or Centuries before?

5 The Feet, mechanical, go round—
Of Ground, or Air, or Ought—
A Wooden way
Regardless grown,
A Quartz contentment, like a stone—

10 This is the Hour of Lead—
Remembered, if outlived,
As Freezing Persons recollect the Snow—
First—Chill—then Stupor—then the letting go—

ca. 1862

As you read the following poem, notice how the title calls upon us to wonder, from the beginning, how playful and how patterned the boy's bedtime romp with his father is. Try to be conscious of the emotional effects created by what seem to be the key words. Which words establish the bond between the two males?

THEODORE ROETHKE

My Papa's Waltz

The whiskey on your breath
Could make a small boy dizzy;
But I hung on like death:
Such waltzing was not easy.

5 We romped until the pans
Slid from the kitchen shelf;
My mother's countenance
Could not unfrown itself.

The hand that held my wrist
10 Was battered on one knuckle;
At every step you missed
My right ear scraped a buckle.

You beat time on my head
With a palm caked hard by dirt,
15 Then waltzed me off to bed
Still clinging to your shirt.

1948

Exactly what is the situation in "My Papa's Waltz"? What are the family's economic circumstances? How can you tell? What indications are there of the family's social class, or of the father's line of work? How would you characterize the speaker? How does the poem indicate his pleasure in the bedtime ritual? Which words suggest the boy's excitement? Which suggest his anxiety? How can you tell the speaker's feelings about his father? What clues are there about what the mother is like? What clues are there in the word choice that an adult is remembering a childhood experience? How scared was the boy at the time? How does the grown adult now evaluate his emotions when he was a boy? In what sense is the poem a tribute to memories of the father? How would you describe the poem's tone?

The subtlety and force of word choice is sometimes very much affected by **word order,** the way the sentences are put together. Some poems employ unusual word order because of the demands of rhyme and meter, but ordinarily poets use word order very much as prose writers do, to create a particular emphasis. When you find an unusual word order, you can be pretty sure that something there merits special attention. Notice the odd constructions in the second and third stanzas of "My Papa's Waltz"—the way the speaker talks about the abrasion of buckle on ear in line 12, for example. He does not say that the buckle scraped his ear, but rather puts it the other way round—a big difference in the kind of effect created, for it avoids placing blame and refuses to specify any unpleasant effect. Had he said that the buckle scraped his ear—the normal way of putting it—we would have to worry about the fragile ear. The **syntax** (sentence structure) of the poem channels our feeling and helps to control what we think of the "waltz."

In the most curious part of the poem, the second stanza, the silent mother appears, and the syntax is peculiar in two places. In lines 5–6, the connection between the romping and the pans falling is stated oddly: "We romped *until* the pans / Slid from the kitchen shelf" (emphasis added). The speaker does not say that they knocked down the pans or imply awkwardness, but he does suggest energetic activity and duration. He implies intensity, almost intention—as though the romping would not be complete until the pans fell. And the sentence about the mother—odd but effective—makes her position clear. A silent bystander in this male ritual, she doesn't seem frightened or angry. She seems to be holding a frown, or to have it molded on her face, as though it were part of her own ritual, and perhaps a facet of her stern character as well. The syntax implies that she *has to* maintain the frown, and the falling of the pans almost seems to be for her benefit. She disapproves, but she remains their audience.

Sometimes poems create, as well, a powerful sense of the way minds and emotions work by varying normal syntactical order in special ways. Listen, for example, in the following poem to the speaker's sudden loss of vocal control in the midst of what seems to be a calm analysis of her feelings about sexual behavior.

SHARON OLDS

Sex without Love

How do they do it, the ones who make love
without love? Beautiful as dancers,
gliding over each other like ice-skaters
over the ice, fingers hooked
5 inside each other's bodies, faces
red as steak, wine, wet as the
children at birth whose mothers are going to
give them away. How do they come to the
come to the   come to the   God   come to the
10 still waters, and not love
the one who came there with them, light
rising slowly as steam off their joined
skin? These are the true religious,
the purists, the pros, the ones who will not
15 accept a false Messiah, love the
priest instead of the God. They do not
mistake the lover for their own pleasure,
they are like great runners: they know they are alone
with the road surface, the cold, the wind,
20 the fit of their shoes, their over-all cardio-
vascular health—just factors, like the partner
in the bed, and not the truth, which is the
single body alone in the universe
against its own best time.

                                            1984

The poem starts calmly enough, with a simple rhetorical question implying that the speaker just cannot understand sex without love. Lines 2–4 compare such sexual activity with some distant aesthetic, with two carefully delineated examples, and the speaker—although plainly disapproving—seems coolly in control of the analysis and evaluation. But by the end of the fourth line, something begins to seem odd: "hooked" seems too ugly and extreme a way to characterize the lovers' fingers, however much the speaker may disapprove, and by line 6 the syntax breaks down. How does "wine" fit the syntax of the line? Is it parallel with "steak," another example of redness? Or is it somehow related to the last part of the sentence, parallel with "faces"? Neither of these possibilities quite works. At best, the punctuation is inadequate; at worst, the speaker's mind is working too fast for the language it generates, scrambling its images. We can't yet be sure what is going on, but by the ninth line the lack of control is manifest with the compulsive repeating (three times) of "come to the" and the interjected "God."

Such verbal behavior—here concretized by the way the poem orders its words—invites us to reevaluate the speaker's moralism relative to her emotional involvement with the issues and with her representation of sexuality itself. The speaker's values, as well as those who have sex without love, become a subject for evaluation.

Words, the basic materials of poetry, come in many kinds and can be used in many ways and in different—sometimes surprising—combinations. They are seldom simple or transparent, even when we know their meanings and recognize their syntactical combinations as conventional. Carefully examining them, individually and collectively, is a crucial part of reading poems, and being able to ask good questions about the words that poems use is one of the most basic—and rewarding—skills a reader of poetry can develop.

• • •

MARTHA COLLINS

Lies

Anyone can get it wrong, laying low
when she ought to lie, but is it a lie
for her to say she laid him when we know
he wouldn't lie still long enough to let
5   her do it? A good lay is not a song,
not anymore; a good lie is something
else: lyrics, lines, what if you say *dear sister*
when you have no sister, what if you say *guns*
when you saw no guns, though you know
10   they're there? *She laid down her arms; she lay
down, her arms by her sides.* If we don't know,
do we lie if we say? If we don't say, do we lie
down on the job? To arms! in any case
dear friends. If we must lie, let's not lie around.

1999

• How many different meanings of "lie" and "lay" does this poem contain? What would you say is the poem's real subject?

PAUL MULDOON

Errata

For "Antrim" read "Armagh."
For "mother" read "other."
For "harm" read "farm."
For "feather" read "father."

5 For "Moncrieff" read "Monteith."
For *"Béal Fierste"* read *"Béal Feirste."*
For "brave" read "grave."
For "revered" read "reversed."

For "married" read "marred."
10 For "pull" read "pall."
For "ban" read "bar."
For "smell" read "small."

For "spike" read "spoke."
For "lost" read "last."
15 For "Steinbeck" read "Steenbeck."
For "ludic" read "lucid."

For "religion" read "region."
For "ode" read "code."
For "Jane" read "Jean."
20 For "rod" read "road."

For "pharoah" read "pharaoh."
For *"Fíor-Gael"* read *"Fíor-Ghael."*
For "Jeffrey" read "Jeffery."
For "vigil" read "Virgil."

25 For "flageolet" read "fava."
For "veto" read "vote."
For "Aiofe" read "Aoife."
For "anecdote" read "antidote."

For "Rosemont" read "Mount Rose."
30 For "plump" read "plumb."
For "hearse" read "hears."
For "loom" read "bloom."

1998

• Does reading the poem aloud seem to alter the tone? Do more suggestions of meaning emerge when the poem is read aloud?

EMILY DICKINSON

[CD]   *[I dwell in Possibility—]*

I dwell in Possibility—
A fairer House than Prose—
More numerous of Windows—
Superior—for Doors—

5 Of Chambers as the Cedars—
Impregnable of Eye—
And for an Everlasting Roof
The Gambrels[5] of the Sky—

Of Visitors—the fairest—
10 For Occupation—This—
The spreading wide my narrow Hands
To gather Paradise—

ca. 1862

- What does Dickinson seem to mean by "Possibility"? How does the poem's ending broaden this meaning?

WILLIAM CARLOS WILLIAMS

The Red Wheelbarrow

so much depends
upon

a red wheel
barrow

5 glazed with rain
water

beside the white
chickens.
          1923

- Why do you think the poet has included the details of the "rain / water" and "the white / chickens"?

5. Roofs with double slopes.

This Is Just to Say

I have eaten
the plums
that were in
the icebox

5 and which
you were probably
saving
for breakfast

Forgive me
10 they were delicious
so sweet
and so cold

                    1934

- What is meant by "This" in the poem's title? What is the apparent occasion for this poem?

OGDEN NASH

Reflections on Ice-Breaking

Candy
Is dandy
But liquor
Is quicker.[6]
        1929

- How does the sound add to the lightheartedness of the sense?

Here Usually Comes the Bride

June means weddings in everyone's lexicon,
Weddings in Swedish, weddings in Mexican.
Breezes play Mendelssohn, treeses play Youmans,
Birds wed birds, and humans wed humans.
5 All year long the gentlemen woo,
But the ladies dream of a June "I do."
Ladies grow loony, and gentlemen loonier;
This year's June is next year's Junior.
                              1949

- Is the poem funnier when read aloud? Is it funnier still when the pronunciations of "Mexican" and "Junior" are altered to preserve the rhyme?

6. Nash later reportedly proposed two more lines: "Pot / Is not."

ROBERT GRAVES

The Cool Web

Children are dumb to say how hot the day is,
How hot the scent is of the summer rose,
How dreadful the black wastes of evening sky,
How dreadful the tall soldiers drumming by.

5 But we have speech, to chill the angry day,
And speech, to dull the rose's cruel scent.
We spell away the overhanging night,
We spell away the soldiers and the fright.

There's a cool web of language winds us in,
10 Retreat from too much joy or too much fear:
We grow sea-green at last and coldly die
In brininess and volubility.

But if we let our tongues lose self-possession,
Throwing off language and its watery clasp
15 Before our death, instead of when death comes,
Facing the wide glare of the children's day,
Facing the rose, the dark sky and the drums,
We shall go mad no doubt and die that way.

                                        1927

- How does speech "chill the angry day" (line 5) or "dull the rose's cruel scent" (line 6)? Why will we die in madness "if we let our tongues lose self-possession" (line 13)?

RITA DOVE

Parsley[7]

1. The Cane Fields

There is a parrot imitating spring
in the palace, its feathers parsley green.
Out of the swamp the cane appears

---

7. On October 2, 1937, Rafael Trujillo (1891–1961), dictator of the Dominican Republic, ordered 20,000 blacks killed because they could not pronounce the letter "r" in *perejil,* the Spanish word for parsley [Dove's note].

to haunt us, and we cut it down. El General
5   searches for a word; he is all the world
there is. Like a parrot imitating spring,

we lie down screaming as rain punches through
and we come up green. We cannot speak an R—
out of the swamp, the cane appears

10 and then the mountain we call in whispers *Katalina.*[8]
The children gnaw their teeth to arrowheads.
There is a parrot imitating spring.

El General has found his word: *perejil.*
Who says it, lives. He laughs, teeth shining
15 out of the swamp. The cane appears

in our dreams, lashed by wind and streaming.
And we lie down. For every drop of blood
there is a parrot imitating spring.
Out of the swamp the cane appears.

2. The Palace

20 The word the general's chosen is parsley.
It is fall, when thoughts turn
to love and death; the general thinks
of his mother, how she died in the fall
and he planted her walking cane at the grave
25 and it flowered, each spring stolidly forming
four-star blossoms. The general

pulls on his boots, he stomps to
her room in the palace, the one without
curtains, the one with a parrot
30 in a brass ring. As he paces he wonders
Who can I kill today. And for a moment
the little knot of screams
is still. The parrot, who has traveled

all the way from Australia in an ivory
35 cage, is, coy as a widow, practising
spring. Ever since the morning
his mother collapsed in the kitchen
while baking skull-shaped candies
for the Day of the Dead,[9] the general
40 has hated sweets. He orders pastries
brought up for the bird; they arrive

dusted with sugar on a bed of lace.
The knot in his throat starts to twitch;

---

8. That is, "Katarina."   9. All Souls' Day, November 1.

he sees his boots the first day in battle
45 splashed with mud and urine
as a soldier falls at his feet amazed—
how stupid he looked—at the sound
of artillery. *I never thought it would sing*
the soldier said, and died. Now

50 the general sees the fields of sugar
cane, lashed by rain and streaming.
He sees his mother's smile, the teeth
gnawed to arrowheads. He hears
the Haitians sing without R's
55 as they swing the great machetes:
Katalina, they sing, *Katalina,*

mi madle, mi amol en muelte.[1] God knows
his mother was no stupid woman; she
could roll an R like a queen. Even
60 a parrot can roll an R! In the bare room
the bright feathers arch in a parody
of greenery, as the last pale crumbs
disappear under the blackened tongue. Someone

calls out his name in a voice
65 so like his mother's, a startled tear
splashes the tip of his right boot.
My mother, my love in death.
The general remembers the tiny green sprigs
men of his village wore in their capes
70 to honor the birth of a son. He will
order many, this time, to be killed

for a single, beautiful word.

1983

- How do the repeated lines in part 1, "The Cane Fields" (a villanelle),
  help to create and sustain a mood that suits the poem's meaning?
- What words and phrases in part 2, "The Palace," are prefigured in
  part 1? How does the sound of the poem create a context for the
  poem's subject—the sound of a word?

---

1. Line 67 translates this phrase.

GERARD MANLEY HOPKINS
Pied Beauty[2]

Glory be to God for dappled things—
    For skies of couple-color as a brinded[3] cow;
       For rose-moles all in stipple[4] upon trout that swim;
Fresh-firecoal chestnut-falls;[5] finches' wings;
5   Landscape plotted and pieced—fold, fallow, and plow;
    And all trades, their gear and tackle and trim.
All things counter, original, spare, strange;
    Whatever is fickle, freckled (who knows how?)
      With swift, slow; sweet, sour; adazzle, dim;
10 He fathers-forth whose beauty is past change;
      Praise him.

                            1887

- How many ways of expressing mixed color can you find in this poem? How does Hopkins expand the meaning of "pied beauty"?

E. E. CUMMINGS
[in Just-][6]

in Just-
spring   when the world is mud-
luscious the little
lame balloonman

5 whistles   far   and wee

and eddieandbill come
running from marbles and
piracies and it's
spring

10 when the world is puddle-wonderful

the queer
old balloonman whistles
far   and   wee
and bettyandisbel come dancing

15 from hop-scotch and jump-rope and

---

2. Parti-colored beauty: having patches or sections of more than one color.
3. Streaked or spotted.   4. Rose-colored dots or flecks.
5. Fallen chestnuts as red as burning coals.   6. The first poem in the series *Chansons innocentes*.

it's
spring
and
    the
20   goat-footed

balloonMan   whistles
far
and
wee[7]

1923

- What are some connotations of "mud-luscious" and "puddle-wonderful"? What are some of the ways in which this poem challenges a reader's expectations of diction and syntax?

MARY OLIVER

Morning

Salt shining behind its glass cylinder.
Milk in a blue bowl. The yellow linoleum.
The cat stretching her black body from the pillow.
The way she makes her curvaceous response to the small, kind gesture.
5 Then laps the bowl clean.
Then wants to go out into the world
where she leaps lightly and for no apparent reason across the lawn,
then sits, perfectly still, in the grass.
I watch her a little while, thinking:
10 what more could I do with wild words?
I stand in the cold kitchen, bowing down to her.
I stand in the cold kitchen, everything wonderful around me.

1992

- How does alliteration contribute to the poem's tone and meaning? What does the speaker aspire to achieve with "wild words"?

---

7. Pan, whose Greek name means "everything," is traditionally represented with a syrinx (or the pipes of Pan). The upper half of his body is human, the lower half goat, and as the father of Silenus he is associated with the spring rites of Dionysus.

BEN JONSON

Still to Be Neat[8]

Still[9] to be neat, still to be dressed,
As you were going to a feast;
Still to be powdered, still perfumed;
Lady, it is to be presumed,
5 Though art's hid causes are not found,
All is not sweet, all is not sound.

Give me a look, give me a face
That makes simplicity a grace;
Robes loosely flowing, hair as free;
10 Such sweet neglect more taketh me
Than all th' adulteries of art.
They strike mine eyes, but not my heart.

1609

- What are some possible meanings of the poem's assertion that "all is not sound"? What are some connotations of "th' adulteries of art"?

ROBERT HERRICK

Delight in Disorder

A sweet disorder in the dress
Kindles in clothes a wantonness.
A lawn[1] about the shoulders thrown
Into a fine distractiön;
5 An erring lace, which here and there
Enthralls the crimson stomacher,[2]
A cuff neglectful, and thereby
Ribbands[3] to flow confusedly;
A winning wave, deserving note,
10 In the tempestuous petticoat;
A careless shoestring, in whose tie
I see a wild civility;
Do more bewitch me than when art
Is too precise[4] in every part.

1648

- What are some of the words that this poem uses to indicate "disorder"? Why do you think the speaker finds disorder "sweet"?

---

8. A song from Jonson's play *The Silent Woman* (1609–10).   9. Continually.   1. Scarf of fine linen.
2. Ornamental covering for the breasts.   3. Ribbons.
4. Puritans were often called Precisians because of their fastidiousness.

JOHN MILTON

From *Paradise Lost*[5]

Of man's first disobedience, and the fruit[6]
Of that forbidden tree whose mortal taste
Brought death into the world, and all our woe,
With loss of Eden, till one greater Man
5 Restore us, and regain the blissful seat,
Sing, Heav'nly Muse,[7] that, on the secret top
Of Oreb, or of Sinai, didst inspire
That shepherd who first taught the chosen seed
In the beginning how the Heav'ns and Earth
10 Rose out of Chaos: or, if Sion hill
Delight thee more, and Siloa's brook that flowed
Fast[8] by the oracle of God, I thence
Invoke thy aid to my adventurous song,
That with no middle flight intends to soar
15 Above th' Aonian mount,[9] while it pursues
Things unattempted yet in prose or rhyme.
And chiefly thou, O Spirit,[1] that dost prefer
Before all temples th' upright heart and pure,
Instruct me, for thou know'st; thou from the first
20 Wast present, and, with mighty wings outspread,
Dovelike sat'st brooding on the vast abyss,
And mad'st it pregnant: what in me is dark
Illumine; what is low, raise and support;

5. The opening lines of Books I and II and a short passage from Book III. The first passage states the poem's subject, and the second describes Satan's beginning address to the council of fallen angels meeting to discuss strategy; in the third, God is looking down from Heaven at his new human creation and watching Satan approaching the Earth.   6. The apple, but also the consequences.

7. Addressing one of the Muses and asking for aid is a convention for the opening lines of an epic; Milton complicates the standard procedure here by describing sources and circumstances of Judeo-Christian revelation rather than specifically invoking one of the nine classical Muses. Sinai is the spur of Mount Oreb, where Moses ("That shepherd," line 8, who was traditionally regarded as author of the first five books of the Bible) received the Law; Sion hill and Siloa (lines 10–11), near Jerusalem, correspond to the traditional mountain (Helicon) and springs of classical tradition.

8. Close.   9. Mount Helicon, home of the classical Muses.

1. The divine voice that inspired the Hebrew prophets. Genesis 1.2 says that "the spirit of God moved upon the face of the waters" as part of the process of Creation; Milton follows tradition in making the inspirational and communicative function of God present in Creation itself. The passage echoes and merges many biblical references to Creation and divine revelation.

That, to the height of this great argument,[2]
25 I may assert Eternal Providence,
And justify the ways of God to men.
    Say first (for Heav'n hides nothing from thy view,
Nor the deep tract of Hell), say first what cause
Moved our grand parents, in that happy state,
30 Favored of Heav'n so highly, to fall off
From their Creator, and transgress his will
For one restraint, lords of the world besides?[3]
Who first seduced them to that foul revolt?
Th' infernal serpent; he it was, whose guile,
35 Stirred up with envy and revenge, deceived
The mother of mankind, what time[4] his pride
Had cast him out from Heav'n, with all his host
Of rebel angels, by whose aid, aspiring
To set himself in glory above his peers,
40 He trusted to have equaled the Most High,
If he opposed; and with ambitious aim
Against the throne and monarchy of God,
Raised impious war in Heav'n and battle proud,
With vain attempt. Him the Almighty Power
45 Hurled headlong flaming from th' ethereal sky,
With hideous ruin and combustion down
To bottomless perdition, there to dwell
In adamantine chains and penal fire,
Who durst defy th' Omnipotent to arms.[5]

*   *   *

   II
High on a throne of royal state, which far
Outshone the wealth of Ormus and of Ind,[6]
Or where the gorgeous East with richest hand
Show'rs on her kings barbaric pearl and gold,
5 Satan exalted sat, by merit raised
To that bad eminence; and, from despair
Thus high uplifted beyond hope, aspires
Beyond thus high, insatiate to pursue
Vain war with Heav'n, and by success[7] untaught,
10 His proud imaginations thus displayed:
    "Powers and Dominions, Deities of Heav'n,
For since no deep within her gulf can hold
Immortal vigor, though oppressed and fall'n,
I give not Heav'n for lost. From this descent

---

2. Subject.   3. In all other respects. *For*: because of.   4. When.
5. After invoking the Muse and giving a brief summary of the poem's subject, an epic regularly begins *in medias res* ("in the midst of things").
6. India. *Ormus:* Hormuz, an island in the Persian Gulf, famous for pearls.
7. Outcome, either good or bad.

15 Celestial virtues rising will appear
   More glorious and more dread than from no fall,
   And trust themselves to fear no second fate.
   Me though just right and the fixed laws of Heav'n
   Did first create your leader, next, free choice,
20 With what besides, in council or in fight,
   Hath been achieved of merit, yet this loss,
   Thus far at least recovered, hath much more
   Established in a safe unenvied throne
   Yielded with full consent. The happier state
25 In Heav'n, which follows dignity, might draw
   Envy from each inferior; but who here
   Will envy whom the highest place exposes
   Foremost to stand against the Thunderer's aim
   Your bulwark, and condemns to greatest share
30 Of endless pain? Where there is then no good
   For which to strive, no strife can grow up there
   From faction; for none sure will claim in hell
   Precédence, none, whose portion is so small
   Of present pain, that with ambitious mind
35 Will covet more. With this advantage then
   To union, and firm faith, and firm accord,
   More than can be in Heav'n, we now return
   To claim our just inheritance of old,
   Surer to prosper than prosperity
40 Could have assured us; and by what best way,
   Whether of open war or covert guile,
   We now debate; who can advise, may speak."

                    *   *   *

          III

                    *   *   *

56   Now had th' Almighty Father from above,
   From the pure empyrean where he sits
   High throned above all height, bent down his eye,
   His own works and their works at once to view:
60 About him all the sanctities of Heav'n[8]
   Stood thick as stars, and from his sight received
   Beatitude past utterance; on his right
   The radiant image of his glory sat,
   His only Son. On earth he first beheld
65 Our two first parents, yet the only two
   Of mankind, in the happy garden placed,
   Reaping immortal fruits of joy and love,
   Uninterrupted joy, unrivaled love,

---

8. The hierarchies of angels.

In blissful solitude. He then surveyed
70 Hell and the gulf between, and Satan there
Coasting the wall of Heav'n on this side Night
In the dun air sublime,[9] and ready now
To stoop[1] with wearied wings and willing feet
On the bare outside of this world, that seemed
75 Firm land embosomed without firmament,
Uncertain which, in ocean or in air.

1667

- Why do you think Milton uses convoluted syntax such as that in, for example, the poem's opening sentence (lines 1–16)? What effects of sound or sense does this make possible?
- In the passage describing Heaven (part III, lines 56–69), what words establish the tone? What words indicate a shift in tone when God looks down upon Satan approaching the Earth (lines 69–76)?

PICTURING: THE LANGUAGES OF DESCRIPTION

The language of poetry is most often visual and pictorial. Rather than depending primarily on abstract ideas and elaborate reasoning, poems depend mainly on concrete and specific words that create images in our minds. Poems thus help us to see things afresh and anew or to feel them suggestively through our other physical senses, such as hearing or touch. But mostly, poetry uses the sense of sight to help us form, in our minds, visual impressions, images that communicate more directly than concepts. We "see" yellow leaves on a branch, a father and son waltzing precariously, or two lovers sitting together on the bank of a stream, so that our response begins from a vivid impression of exactly what is happening. Some people think that those media and arts that challenge the imagination of a hearer or reader—radio drama, for example, or poetry—allow us to respond more fully than those (such as television or theater) that actually show things more fully to our physical senses. Certainly they leave more to our imagination, to our mind's eye.

Visual applications of language stem from the nature and direction of the poetic process itself, and some of them have to do with how poems are conceived and then, gradually, fleshed out in words. Poems are sometimes quite abstract—they can even be *about* abstractions. But usually, they are quite concrete in what they ask us to see. One reason is that they often begin in a poet's mind with a picture or an image: of a person, a place, an event, or an object of observation. That image may be based on something the poet has seen—that is, it may be a picture of something remembered by the poet—but it may also be totally imaginary and only based on the "real world" in the sense that it draws on the poet's physical sense of what the world is like, including the people and things in it. Sometimes a poet represents an imagined scene or object in a highly stylized or feeling-centered way, as do, for example, impressionist or surrealist painters. But that process often begins from a quite specific image in the poet's mind that he or she

---

9. Aloft in the twilight atmosphere.   1. Swoop down, like a bird of prey.

then tries to **represent,** in words, in such a way that readers can "see" it, too, through the poet's vivid verbal representation of what he or she has already "seen" (imagined) in the mind.

Think of it this way: a painter or sculptor uses strategies of form, color, texture, viewpoint, and relationship to create a visual idea, and so the viewer begins with an *actual* image, something that can be seen physically (though the viewer's understanding and interpretation may be many steps away). Even when a poet begins with an idea that draws on visual experience, however, the reader still has to *imagine* (through the poem's words) an image, some person or thing or action that the poem describes. The poet must help the reader to flesh out that mental image on the basis of the words he or she uses. In a sense, then, the reader becomes a visual artist, but the poet directs how the visualization is to be done by evoking specific responses through words. *How* that happens can involve quite complicated verbal strategies—or even *visual* ones that draw on the possibilities of print (see chapter 7).

The languages of description are quite varied. The visual qualities of poetry result partly from the two aspects of poetic language described in the previous section: on the one hand, the precision of individual words, and, on the other hand, precision's opposite—the reach, richness, and ambiguity of suggestion that words sometimes accrue. Visualization can also derive from sophisticated rhetorical and literary devices (figures of speech and symbols, for example, as we will see later in this chapter). But often description begins simply with naming—providing the word (noun, verb, adjective, or adverb) that will trigger images familiar from a reader's own experience. A reader can readily imagine a *dog* or *cat* or *house* or *flower* when each word is named, but not all readers will have the same kind of dog or flower come to mind (because of our individual experiences) until the word is qualified in some way. So the poet may specify that the dog is a greyhound or poodle, or that the flower is a daffodil or a lilac or Queen Anne's lace; or the poet may provide colors, sizes, specific movements, or particular identifying features. Such description can involve either narrowing by category or expansion through detail, and often comparisons are either explicitly or implicitly involved. In Richard Wilbur's "The Beautiful Changes," for example, the similarity between wading through flowers in a meadow and wading among waves in the sea helps to suggest how the first experience feels as well as to etch it visually in our minds. More than just a matter of naming, using precise words, and providing basic information, description involves qualification and comparison; sometimes the poet needs to tell us what a picture is not, dissociating what the poem describes from other possible images we may have in mind. Different features in the language of description add up to something that describes a whole—a picture or scene—as well as a series of individualized objects.

Seeing in the mind's eye—the re-creation of visual experience—requires different skills from poets and readers. Poets use all the language strategies they can think of to re-create for us something they have already "seen." Poets depend on our having had a rich variety of visual experiences and try to draw on those experiences by using common, evocative words and then refining the process through more elaborate verbal devices. We as readers inhabit the process the other way around, trying to draw on our previous knowledge so that we can "see" by following verbal clues. In the poems that follow, notice the ways that description leads to specific images, and pay attention to how shape, color, relationship, and perspective become clear, not only through individual words but also through combinations of words and phrases that suggest appearance and motion.

• • •

JEANNE MARIE BEAUMONT

Rorschach

Snow patches along the creek bank.
Too simple. Wings melting there.

The tops of two maples
beside the window of my childhood bedroom.

5   Stain on a linen napkin left by lip-
stick—why it's called that. *Go on.*

A man's tattered bow tie
put through the wash cycle—by accident.

A dress, haunted by the child who wore it,
10 standing by itself in the center of a room.

A face. *Whose?* A woman's face, lathered up
with soap except around the eyes.

A fluke. *A flute?* A fluke
with two eyes on one side of its head.

15 The cigarette ground into the floor
by Bette Davis in *All About Eve.*

Next. A house that can't be seen
from the road—no, what hides it.

Graffiti of the nearsighted
20 painted by mouth.

And if I say "tree"?
I'd say—death by wood.

Cabinet? Casket.
Tell me again.

25 A map. A map of the island
where I asked to be born.

1997

• What is the meaning of the poem's title, "Rorschach"? What does
that meaning reveal about the nature of the dialogue that follows?

OSCAR WILDE

Symphony in Yellow

An omnibus across the bridge
   Crawls like a yellow butterfly,
   And, here and there, a passer-by
Shows like a little restless midge.[1]

5 Big barges full of yellow hay
   Are moored against the shadowy wharf,
   And, like a yellow silken scarf,
The thick fog hangs along the quay.

The yellow leaves begin to fade
10   And flutter from the Temple[2] elms,
   And at my feet the pale green Thames
Lies like a rod of rippled jade.

                                        1909

- What can you infer about London and its climate and the season
  from each of the yellow images in this poem?

NANCY WILLARD

The Snow Arrives After Long Silence

The snow arrives after long silence
from its high home where nothing leaves
tracks or stains or keeps time.
The sky it fell from, pale as oatmeal,
5 bears up like sheep before shearing.

The cat at my window watches
amazed. So many feathers and no bird!
All day the snow sets its table
with clean linen, putting its house
10 in order. The hungry deer walk

on the risen loaves of snow.
You can follow the broken hearts
their hooves punch in its crust.
Night after night the big plows rumble
15 and bale it like dirty laundry

---

1. Tiny mosquito-like insect.   2. The law-courts area of London.

and haul it to the Hudson.
Now I scan the sky for snow,
and the cool cheek it offers me,
and its body, thinned into petals,
20 and the still caves where it sleeps.

2003

- List all the similes and metaphors in the poem. What is the cumu-
lative effect of so many comparisons applied to the images of snow?

RICHARD WILBUR

The Beautiful Changes

One wading a Fall meadow finds on all sides
The Queen Anne's Lace[3] lying like lilies
On water; it glides
So from the walker, it turns
5 Dry grass to a lake, as the slightest shade of you
Valleys my mind in fabulous blue Lucernes.[4]

The beautiful changes as a forest is changed
By a chameleon's tuning his skin to it;
As a mantis, arranged
10 On a green leaf, grows
Into it, makes the leaf leafier, and proves
Any greenness is deeper than anyone knows.

Your hands hold roses always in a way that says
They are not only yours; the beautiful changes
15 In such kind ways,
Wishing ever to sunder
Things and things' selves for a second finding, to lose
For a moment all that it touches back to wonder.

1947

- What part of speech is "Beautiful" in the poem's title and lines 7
and 14? What part of speech is "Changes"? What is meant by "the
beautiful changes / In such kind ways" (lines 14–15)?

---

3. A plant sometimes called "wild carrot," with delicate, finger-like leaves and flat clusters of small white
flowers.
4. Alfalfa, a plant resembling clover, with small purple flowers. Lake Lucerne is famed for its deep blue color
and picturesque Swiss setting amid limestone mountains.

TED HUGHES

To Paint a Water Lily

A green level of lily leaves
Roofs the pond's chamber and paves

The flies' furious arena: study
These, the two minds of this lady.

5   First observe the air's dragonfly
That eats meat, that bullets by

Or stands in space to take aim;
Others as dangerous comb the hum
Under the trees. There are battle-shouts
10 And death-cries everywhere hereabouts

But inaudible, so the eyes praise
To see the colors of these flies

Rainbow their arcs, spark, or settle
Cooling like beads of molten metal

15 Through the spectrum. Think what worse
Is the pond-bed's matter of course;

Prehistoric bedragonned times
Crawl that darkness with Latin names,

Have evolved no improvements there,
20 Jaws for heads, the set stare,

Ignorant of age as of hour—
Now paint the long-necked lily-flower

Which, deep in both worlds, can be still
As a painting, trembling hardly at all

25 Though the dragonfly alight,
Whatever horror nudge her root.

                                    1960

- What are "the two minds of this lady" (line 4)? Whom do you think
  the speaker is addressing when he commands, "Now paint the long-
  necked lily flower" (line 22)?

JOHN BANCKS

A Description of London

HOUSES, churches, mixed together,
Streets unpleasant in all weather;
Prisons, palaces contiguous,
Gates, a bridge, the Thames irriguous.[4]

5 Gaudy things enough to tempt ye,
Showy outsides, insides empty;
Bubbles, trades, mechanic arts,
Coaches, wheelbarrows and carts.

Warrants, bailiffs, bills unpaid,
10 Lords of laundresses afraid;
Rogues that nightly rob and shoot men,
Hangmen, aldermen and footmen.

Lawyers, poets, priests, physicians,
Noble, simple, all conditions:
15 Worth beneath a threadbare cover,
Villainy bedaubed all over.

Women black, red, fair and grey,
Prudes and such as never pray,
Handsome, ugly, noisy, still,
20 Some that will not, some that will.

Many a beau without a shilling,
Many a widow not unwilling;
Many a bargain, if you strike it:
This is London! How d'ye like it?

1738

- What is the overall effect of the various lists of contrasting things
  and people to be seen in London? How are these lists used to develop
  the poem's tone?

JAMES MERRILL

b o d y

Look closely at the letters. Can you see,
entering (stage right), then floating full,
then heading off—so soon—

---

4. The River Thames threads its way through London, keeping the nearby land moist and fertile ("irri-
guous").

how like a little kohl-rimmed moon
o plots her course from *b* to *d*

—as *y*, unanswered, knocks at the stage door?
Looked at too long, words fail,
phase out. Ask, now that *body* shines
no longer, by what light you learn these lines
10   and what the *b* and *d* stood for.

1995

- Why might *y* be described as "unanswered" in the word "body"?
  What is meant by "Looked at too long, words fail"?

MARY JO SALTER

Home Movies: A Sort of Ode

Because it hadn't seemed enough,
after a while, to memorialize
more Christmases, the three-layer cakes
ablaze with birthday candles, the blizzard
5   Billy took a shovel to,
Phil's lawn mower tour of the yard,
the tree forts, the shoot-'em-ups
between the boys in new string ties
and cowboy hats and holsters,
10   or Mother sticking a bow as big
as Mouseketeer ears in my hair,

my father sometimes turned the gaze
of his camera to subjects more
artistic or universal:
15   rapt close-ups of a rose's face;
a real-time sunset (nearly an hour);
what one assumes were brilliant autumn
leaves before their colors faded
to dry beige on the aging film;
20   a great deal of pacing, at the zoo,
by polar bears and leopards caged,
he seemed to say, like him.

What happened between him and her
is another story. And just as well
25   we have no movie of it, only
some unforgiving scowls she gave
through terrifying, ticking silence
when he must have asked her (no
sound track) for a smile.

30 Yet the scenes I keep reversing to
   are private: not those generic cherry
   blossoms at the full, or the brave
   daffodil after a snowfall;

   instead, it's the re-run surprise
35 of the unshuttered, prefab blanks
   of windows at the back of the house,
   and how the lines of aluminum
   siding are scribbled on with meaning
   only for us who lived there.
40 It's the pair of elephant bookends
   I'd forgotten, with the upraised trunks
   like handles, and the books they sought
   to carry in one block to a future
   that scattered all of us.

45 And look: it's the stoneware mixing bowl
   figured with hand-holding dancers
   handed down so many years
   ago to my own kitchen, still
   valueless, unbroken. Here
50 she's happy, teaching us to dye
   some Easter eggs in it, a Grecian
   urn of sorts near which—a foster
   child of silence and slow time
   myself—I smile because she does,
55 and patiently await my turn.

                               1999

- How does the plainness of the language suit the descriptions in the poem? What story emerges from the accumulated images? What possible meanings arise from the poem's final line?

ANDREW MARVELL

On a Drop of Dew

See how the orient[5] dew
Shed from the bosom of the morn
   Into the blowing roses,
Yet careless of its mansion new
5 For[6] the clear region where 'twas born
   Round in itself incloses,

---

5. Shining.   6. By reason of.

And in its little globe's extent
Frames as it can its native element;
  How it the purple flow'r does slight,
10   Scarce touching where it lies,
But gazing back upon the skies,
  Shines with a mournful light
    Like its own tear,
Because so long divided from the sphere.[7]
15   Restless it rolls and unsecure,
    Trembling lest it grow impure,

  Till the warm sun pity its pain,
And to the skies exhale it back again.
  So the soul, that drop, that ray
20 Of the clear fountain of eternal day,
  Could it within the human flower be seen,
    Rememb'ring still its former height,
    Shuns the sweet leaves and blossoms green;
    And, recollecting its own light,
25 Does, in its pure and circling thoughts, express
The greater Heaven in an Heaven less.
    In how coy[8] a figure wound,
    Every way it turns away;
    So the world excluding round,
30   Yet receiving in the day:
    Dark beneath, but bright above,
    Here disdaining, there in love.

  How loose and easy hence to go,
  How girt and ready to ascend;
35   Moving but on a point below,
    It all about does upwards bend.
Such did the manna's sacred dew distill,
White and entire, though congealed and chill;[9]
Congealed on earth, but does, dissolving, run
Into the glories of th' almighty sun.

1681

- How does the sun "exhale" (line 17) the drop of dew? "Back again"
  to where? Explain the comparison between the dewdrop and the
  human soul.

---

7. Of heaven.   8. Reserved, withdrawn, modest.
9. In the wilderness, the Israelites fed upon manna from heaven (distilled from the dew; see Exodus 16.10–
21); manna became a traditional symbol for divine grace.

BEN JONSON

To Penshurst[1]

Thou art not, Penshurst, built to envious show,
Of touch[2] or marble; nor canst boast a row
Of polished pillars, or a roof of gold;
Thou hast no lantern[3] whereof tales are told,
5 Or stair, or courts; but stand'st an ancient pile,
And, these grudged at, art reverenced the while.[4]
Thou joy'st in better marks, of soil, of air,
Of wood, of water; therein thou art fair.
Thou hast thy walks for health, as well as sport;
10 Thy mount, to which the dryads do resort,
Where Pan and Bacchus[5] their high feasts have made
Beneath the broad beech and the chestnut shade,
That taller tree, which of a nut was set
At his great birth[6] where all the Muses met.
15 There in the writhéd bark are cut the names
Of many a sylvan, taken with his flames;[7]
And thence the ruddy satyrs oft provoke
The lighter fauns to reach thy Lady's Oak.[8]
Thy copse too, named of Gamage,[9] thou hast there,
20 That never fails to serve thee seasoned deer
When thou wouldst feast, or exercise, thy friends.
The lower land, that to the river bends,
Thy sheep, thy bullocks, kine, and calves do feed;
The middle grounds thy mares and horses breed.
25 Each bank doth yield thee conies;[1] and the tops,
Fertile of wood, Ashore and Sidney's copse,
To crown thy open table, doth provide
The purpled pheasant with the speckled side;
The painted partridge lies in every field,
30 And for thy mess is willing to be killed.
And if the high-swollen Medway[2] fail thy dish,
Thou hast thy ponds that pay thee tribute fish,

1. The country seat (in Kent) of the Sidney family, owned by Sir Robert, brother of the poet, Sir Philip. Jonson's celebration of the estate is one of the earliest "house" poems and a prominent example of topographical or didactic-descriptive poetry.
2. Touchstone: basanite, a smooth dark stone similar to black marble.
3. A glassed or open tower or dome atop the roof.
4. I.e., although these (more pretentious structures) are envied anyway.
5. Ancient gods of nature and wine, both associated with spectacular feasting and celebration.
6. Sir Philip Sidney's, on November 30, 1554; the tree stood for nearly 150 years.
7. Inspired by Sidney's love poetry.
8. Where, according to legend, a former lady of the house (Lady Leicester) began labor pains. *Satyrs:* half-men, half-goats who participated in the rites of Bacchus.
9. The maiden name of the owner's wife. *Copse:* thicket.   1. Rabbits.   2. A river bordering the estate.

Fat agéd carps that run into thy net,
And pikes, now weary their own kind to eat,
35 As loath the second draught or cast to stay,[3]
Officiously[4] at first themselves betray;
Bright eels that emulate them, and leap on land
Before the fisher, or into his hand.
Then hath thy orchard fruit, thy garden flowers,
40 Fresh as the air, and new as are the hours.
The early cherry, with the later plum,
Fig, grape, and quince, each in his time doth come:
The blushing apricot and woolly peach
Hang on thy walls, that every child may reach.
45 And though thy walls be of the country stone,
They're reared with no man's ruin, no man's groan;
There's none that dwell about them wish them down,
But all come in, the farmer and the clown,[5]
And no one empty-handed, to salute
50 Thy lord and lady, though they have no suit.[6]
Some bring a capon, some a rural cake,
Some nuts, some apples; some that think they make
The better cheeses bring 'em, or else send
By their ripe daughters, whom they would commend
55 This way to husbands, and whose baskets bear
An emblem of themselves in plum or pear.
But what can this (more than express their love)
Add to thy free[7] provisions, far above
The need of such? whose liberal board doth flow
60 With all that hospitality doth know;
Where comes no guest but is allowed to eat,
Without his fear, and of thy lord's own meat;
Where the same beer and bread, and selfsame wine,
That is his lordship's shall be also mine.
65 And I not fain[8] to sit (as some this day
At great men's tables), and yet dine away.[9]
Here no man tells[1] my cups; nor, standing by,
A waiter doth my gluttony envý,
But gives me what I call, and lets me eat;
70 He knows below he shall find plenty of meat.
Thy tables hoard not up for the next day;
Nor, when I take my lodging, need I pray
For fire, or lights, or livery;[2] all is there,
As if thou then wert mine, or I reigned here:
75 There's nothing I can wish, for which I stay.
That found King James when hunting late this way

3. Await. *Draught:* drawing in of a net.   4. Obligingly.   5. Rustic, peasant.   6. Request for favors.
7. Generous.   8. Obliged.
9. Possibly, "elsewhere," because they do not get enough to eat; or "away" in the sense of far from the party
of honor.   1. Counts.   2. Provisions (or, possibly, servants).

With his brave son, the prince,[3] they saw thy fires
Shine bright on every hearth, as the desires
Of thy Penates[4] had been set on flame
80 To entertain them; or the country came
With all their zeal to warm their welcome here.
What (great I will not say, but) sudden cheer
Didst thou then make 'em! and what praise was heaped
On thy good lady then! who therein reaped
85 The just reward of her high housewifery;[5]
To have her linen, plate, and all things nigh,
When she was far; and not a room but dressed
As if it had expected such a guest!
These, Penshurst, are thy praise, and yet not all.
90 Thy lady's noble, fruitful, chaste withal.
His children thy great lord may call his own,
A fortune in this age but rarely known.
They are, and have been, taught religion; thence
Their gentler spirits have sucked innocence.
95 Each morn and even they are taught to pray,
With the whole household, and may, every day,
Read in their virtuous parents' noble parts
The mysteries of manners, arms, and arts.
Now, Penshurst, they that will proportion[6] thee
100 With other edifices, when they see
Those proud, ambitious heaps, and nothing else,
May say, their lords have built, but thy lord dwells.

1616

- Summarize Jonson's descriptions of the house and grounds of Penshurst. What overall impression of the estate is created by the poem?
- How does Jonson use descriptions of the estate as a means of praising the Sidney family? Why might Jonson have addressed the poem to the estate rather than directly to the family?

METAPHOR AND SIMILE

Being visual does not just mean describing, telling us facts, indicating shapes, colors, and specific details, and giving us precise discriminations through exacting verbs, nouns, adverbs, and adjectives. Often the vividness of the picture in our minds depends upon comparisons through **figures of speech.** What we are trying to imagine is pictured in terms of something else familiar to us, and we are asked to think of one thing as if it were something else. Many such comparisons, in which something is pictured or figured forth in terms of something already familiar to us, are taken for granted in daily life. Things we can't see or that aren't familiar to us are imaged as things we already know; for example, God is said to be like a father; Italy is said to be shaped like a boot; life is compared to a forest,

---

3. Prince Henry, who died in 1612.   4. Roman household gods.   5. Domestic economy.   6. Compare.

a journey, or a sea. When the comparison is explicit—that is, when one thing is directly compared to something else—the figure is called a **simile.** When the comparison is implicit, with something described as if it were something else, it is called a **metaphor.**

Poems use **figurative language** much of the time. A poem may insist that death is like a sunset or sex like an earthquake or that the way to imagine how it feels to be spiritually secure is to think of the way a sheep is taken care of by a shepherd. The pictorialness of our imagination may *clarify* things for us—scenes, states of mind, ideas—but at the same time it stimulates us to think of how those pictures make us *feel.* Pictures, even when they are mental pictures or imagined visions, may be both denotative and connotative, just as individual words are: they may clarify and make precise, and they may evoke a range of feelings. In the poem that follows, the poet helps us visualize the old age and approaching death of the speaker by making comparisons with familiar things—the coming of winter, the approach of sunset, and the dying embers of a fire.

WILLIAM SHAKESPEARE

CD

[*That time of year thou mayst in me behold*]

That time of year thou mayst in me behold
When yellow leaves, or none, or few, do hang
Upon those boughs which shake against the cold,
Bare ruined choirs, where late the sweet birds sang.
5 In me thou see'st the twilight of such day
As after sunset fadeth in the west;
Which by and by[1] black night doth take away,
Death's second self,[2] that seals up all in rest.
In me thou see'st the glowing of such fire,
10 That on the ashes of his youth doth lie,
As the deathbed whereon it must expire,
Consumed with that which it was nourished by.
This thou perceiv'st, which makes thy love more strong,
To love that well which thou must leave ere long.

1609

The first four lines of "That time of year" evoke images of the late autumn; but notice that the poet does not have the speaker say directly that his physical condition and age make him resemble autumn. He draws the comparison without stating it as a comparison: you can see my own state, he says, in the coming of winter, when almost all the leaves have fallen from the trees. The speaker portrays himself *indirectly* by talking about the passing of the year. The poem uses metaphor; that is, one thing is pictured *as if* it were something else. "That time of year" goes on to another metaphor in lines 5–8 and still another in lines 9–12, and each

1. Shortly.   2. Sleep.

Poetry distills words to what is absolutely necessary to ellicit meaning + feeling

metaphor contributes to our understanding of the speaker's sense of his old age and approaching death. More important, however, is the way the metaphors give us feelings, an emotional sense of the speaker's age and of his own attitude toward aging. Through the metaphors we come to understand, appreciate, and to some extent share the increasing sense of urgency that the poem expresses. Our emotional sense of the poem depends largely on the way each metaphor is developed and by the way each metaphor leads, with its own kind of internal logic, to another.

The images of late autumn in the first four lines all suggest loneliness, loss, and nostalgia for earlier times. As in the rest of the poem, the speaker presents our eyes as the main vehicle for noticing his age and condition; in the phrase "thou mayst in me behold" (line 1) he introduces what he is asking us to see, and in both lines 5 and 9 he tells us similarly "In me thou see'st. . . ." The picture of the trees shedding their leaves suggests that autumn is nearly over, and we can imagine trees either with yellow leaves, or without leaves, or with just a trace of foliage remaining—the latter perhaps most feelingly suggesting the bleakness and loneliness that characterize the change of seasons, the ending of the life cycle. But other senses are invoked, too. The boughs shaking against the cold represent an appeal to our tactile sense, and the next line appeals to our sense of hearing, although only by the silence of birds no longer singing. (Notice how exact the visual representation is of the bare, or nearly bare, limbs, even as the speaker notes the cold and the lack of birds; birds lined up like a choir on risers would have made a striking visual image on the barren limbs one above the other, but now there is only the *reminder* of what used to be. The present is quiet, bleak, and lonely; it is the absence of color, song, and life that underscores the visual impression, a reminder of what formerly was.)

The next four lines have a slightly different tone, and the color changes. From a black-and-white landscape with a few yellow leaves, we come upon a rich and almost warm reminder of a faded sunset. But a somber note enters the poem in these lines through another figure of speech, **personification,** which involves treating an abstraction, such as death or justice or beauty, as if it were a person. As the poem talks about the coming of night and of sleep, Sleep is personified as the "second self" of Death (that is, as a kind of "double" for death). The main emphasis is on how night and sleep close in on the twilight, and only secondarily does a reminder of death enter the poem. But it does enter.

The third metaphor—that of the dying embers of a fire—begins in line 9 and continues to color and warm the bleak cold that the poem began with, but it also sharpens the reminder of death. The three main metaphors in the poem work to make our sense of old age and approaching death more familiar but also more immediate: moving from barren trees, to fading twilight, to dying embers suggests a sensuous increase of color and warmth but also an increasing urgency. The first metaphor involves a whole season, or at least a segment of one, a matter of days or possibly weeks; the second involves the passing of a single day, reducing the time scale to a matter of minutes, and the third draws our attention to that split second when a glowing ember dies into a gray ash. The final part of the fire metaphor introduces the most explicit sense of death so far, as the metaphor of embers shifts into a direct reminder of death. Embers, which had been a metaphor of the speaker's aging body, now themselves become, metaphorically, a deathbed; the vitality that nourishes youth is used up just as a log in a fire is. The urgency of the reminder of coming death has now peaked. It is friendlier but now seems immediate and inevitable, a natural part of the life process, and the final two lines then offer an explicit plea to make good and intense use of the remaining moments of human relationship.

"That time of year" represents an unusually intricate use of images to organize a poem and focus its emotional impact. Not all poems are so skillfully made, and not all depend on such a full and varied use of metaphor. But most poems use metaphors for at least part of their effect, and often a poem fully develops a single metaphor as its statement, as in the following poem about the role of a mother and wife.

LINDA PASTAN

Marks

My husband gives me an A
for last night's supper,
an incomplete for my ironing,
a B plus in bed.
5 My son says I am average,
an average mother, but if
I put my mind to it
I could improve.
My daughter believes
10 in Pass/Fail and tells me
I pass. Wait 'til they learn
I'm dropping out.

                              1978

The speaker in "Marks" is obviously less than pleased with the idea of continually being judged, and the metaphor of marks (or grades) as a way of talking about her performance of family duties suggests her irritation. The list of the roles implies the many things expected of her, and the three different systems of marking (letter grades, categories to be checked off on a chart, and pass/fail) detail the difficulties of multiple standards. The poem retains the language of schooldays all the way to the end ("learn," line 11; "dropping out," line 12), and the major effect of the poem depends on the irony of the speaker's surrendering to the metaphor the family has thrust upon her; if she is to be judged as if she were a student, she retains the right to leave the system. Ironically, she joins the system (adopts the metaphor for herself) in order to defeat it.

The following poem depends from the beginning—even from its title—on a single metaphor and the values associated with it.

DAVID WAGONER

My Father's Garden

On his way to the open hearth where white-hot steel
Boiled against furnace walls in wait for his lance
To pierce the fireclay and set loose demons
And dragons in molten tons, blazing
5   Down to the huge satanic caldrons,
Each day he would pass the scrapyard, his kind of garden.

In rusty rockeries of stoves and brake drums,
In grottoes of sewing machines and refrigerators,
He would pick flowers for us: small gears and cogwheels
10   With teeth like petals, with holes for anthers,
Long stalks of lead to be poured into toy soldiers,
Ball bearings as big as grapes to knock them down.

He was called a melter. He tried to keep his brain
From melting in those tyger-mouthed mills
15   Where the same steel reappeared over and over
To be reborn in the fire as something better
Or worse: cannons or cars, needles or girders,
Flagpoles, swords, or plowshares.

But it melted. His classical learning ran
20   Down and away from him, not burning bright.
His fingers culled a few cold scraps of Latin
And Greek, *magna sine laude*,[3] for crosswords
And brought home lumps of tin and sewer grills
As if they were his ripe prize vegetables.

                                                    1987

This poem pays tribute to the speaker's father and the things the father under-
stands and values in his ordinary, workingman's life. The father, a "melter" (line
13) in the steel mills (lines 14–15), values things made from what he helps produce.
His avocation has developed from his vocation: he collects metal objects from the
scrapyard and brings them home just as another man might pick flowers for his
family. The scrapyard is, says the speaker, "his kind of garden" (line 6). The father
has led a hard life, but he shows love for his children in the only way he knows
how—by bringing home things that mean something to him and that can be made
into toys his children will come to value. Describing these scraps as the products
of his garden—"As if they were his ripe prize vegetables" (line 24)—makes them
seem homegrown, carefully tended, nurtured by the father into a useful beauty.
Instead of crude and ugly pieces of scrap, they become—through the metaphor of
the poem—examples of value and beauty corresponding to the warm feelings the

---

3. Without great distinction; a reversal of the usual *magna cum laude*.

speaker has for a father who did what he could with what he knew and what he had.

Sometimes, in poetry as in prose, comparisons are made explicitly, as in the following poem:

ROBERT BURNS

A Red, Red Rose

O, my luve's like a red, red rose
That's newly sprung in June.
O, my luve is like the melodie
That's sweetly played in tune.

5 As fair art thou, my bonnie lass,
So deep in luve am I;
And I will luve thee still, my dear,
Till a' the seas gang[4] dry.

Till a' the seas gang dry, my dear,
10 And the rocks melt wi' the sun;
And I will luve thee still, my dear,
While the sands o' life shall run.

And fare thee weel, my only luve,
And fare thee weel a while!
15 And I will come again, my luve,
Though it were ten thousand mile.

1796

The first four lines make two explicit comparisons: the speaker says that his love is "like a . . . rose" and "like [a] melodie." As we noted earlier, such *explicit* comparisons are called similes, and usually (as here) the comparison involves the word *like* or the word *as*. Similes work much as do metaphors, except that usually they are used more passingly, more incidentally; they make a quick comparison and usually do not elaborate, whereas metaphors often extend over a long section of a poem (in which case they are called **extended metaphors**) or even over the whole poem, as in "Marks" (in which case they are called **controlling metaphors**).

The two similes in "A Red, Red Rose" assume that we already have a favorable opinion of roses and of melodies. Here the poet does not develop the comparison or even remind us of attractive details about roses or tunes. He pays the quick compliment and moves on. Similes sometimes develop more elaborate comparisons than this and occasionally, as in Marvell's "On a Drop of Dew," even govern long sections of a poem (in which case they are called **analogies**). Usually, though, a simile is briefer and relies more fully on something we already know. The speaker

4. Go.

in "My Papa's Waltz" says that he hung on "like death"; he doesn't have to explain or elaborate the comparison: we know the anxiety he refers to.

Like metaphors, similes may imply both meaning and feeling; they may both explain something and invoke feelings about it. All figurative language involves an attempt to clarify something *and* to prompt readers to feel a certain way about it. Saying that one's love is like a rose implies a delicate and fragile beauty and invites our senses into play so that we can share sensuously a response to appealing fragrance and soft touch, just as the shivering boughs and dying embers in "That time of year" suggest separation and loss at the same time that they invite us to share both the cold sense of loneliness and the warmth of old friendship.

Once you start looking for them, you will find figures of speech in poem after poem; they are among the most common devices through which poets share their visions with us.

The following poem uses a variety of metaphors to describe sexual experiences:

ADRIENNE RICH

Two Songs

I

Sex, as they harshly call it,
I fell into this morning
at ten o'clock, a drizzling hour
of traffic and wet newspapers.
5 I thought of him who yesterday
clearly didn't
turn me to a hot field
ready for plowing,
and longing for that young man
10 piercéd me to the roots
bathing every vein, etc.[5]
All day he appears to me
touchingly desirable,
a prize one could wreck one's peace for.
15 I'd call it love if love
didn't take so many years
but lust too is a jewel
a sweet flower and what
pure happiness to know
20 all our high-toned questions
breed in a lively animal.

---

5. See the opening lines of the Prologue to Chaucer's *Canterbury Tales.*

II

That "old last act"!
And yet sometimes
all seems post coitum triste[6]
25   and I a mere bystander.
Somebody else is going off,
getting shot to the moon.
Or, a moon-race!
Split seconds after
30   my opposite number lands
I make it—
we lie fainting together
at a crater-edge
heavy as mercury in our moonsuits
35   till he speaks
in a different language
yet one I've picked up
through cultural exchanges . . .
we murmur the first moonwords:
40   *Spasibo.*[7] *Thanks. O.K.*

1964

The first "song" begins straightforwardly as narration ("Sex . . . I fell into this morning / at ten o'clock"), but the vividness of sex and desire is communicated mostly by figures of speech. The speaker compares her body to "a hot field / ready for plowing" (lines 7–8)—quite unlike her resistant body yesterday—and also describes her longing by metaphor, in this case an elaborate one borrowed from another poem. After so sensual and urgent a beginning, the song turns more thoughtful and philosophical, but even the intellectual sorting between love and lust comes to depend on metaphors: lust is a "jewel" (line 17) and a "flower" (line 18). After the opening pace and excitement, those later figures of speech seem calm and tame, moving the poem from the lust of its beginning to a contemplative reflection on the value and beauty of momentary physical pleasures.

The second song depends on two closely related metaphors, each highly self-conscious and a little comic. The song begins on a plaintive note, considering the classic melancholic feeling after sex; the speaker pictures herself as isolated, left out, "a mere bystander" (line 25), while someone else is having sexual pleasure. She describes the pleasure of others through two colloquial expressions (both metaphors) for sexual climax: "going off" (line 26) and "getting shot to the moon" (line 27). Suddenly the narrator pretends to take sex as space travel seriously and creates a metaphor of her own: sexual partners running a "moon-race" (line 28). In the rest of the poem, she presents the metaphor in the context of the space race between the United States and Russia in the early 1960s, and she describes the race, not exactly even but close enough, in detail. These are international relations—foreign affairs—and the lovers appropriately say their thank-yous separately in Russian and English, then sign off with an international "*O.K.*"

. . .

6. Sadness after sexual union.   7. Russian for "thanks."

WILLIAM SHAKESPEARE

[*Shall I compare thee to a summer's day?*]

Shall I compare thee to a summer's day?
Thou art more lovely and more temperate.
Rough winds do shake the darling buds of May,
And summer's lease hath all too short a date.
5 Sometime too hot the eye of heaven shines,
And often is his gold complexion dimmed;
And every fair from fair sometime declines,
By chance or nature's changing course untrimmed.
But thy eternal summer shall not fade,
10 Nor lose possession of that fair thou ow'st,
Nor shall Death brag thou wand'rest in his shade,
When in eternal lines to time thou grow'st.
    So long as men can breathe or eyes can see,
    So long lives this,[8] and this gives life to thee.
                   1609

- What sort of promise does the speaker make with this poem? Why can he boast that "thy eternal summer shall not fade"?

ANONYMOUS[9]

The Twenty-third Psalm

The Lord is my shepherd; I shall not want.
He maketh me to lie down in green pastures: he leadeth me beside
    the still waters.
He restoreth my soul: he leadeth me in the paths of righteousness
    for his name's sake.
Yea, though I walk through the valley of the shadow of death,
    I will fear no evil: for thou art with me;
    thy rod and thy staff they comfort me.
5 Thou preparest a table before me in the presence of mine enemies:
    thou anointest my head with oil; my cup runneth over.
Surely goodness and mercy shall follow me all the days of my life:
    and I will dwell in the house of the Lord for ever.

- What is the controlling metaphor in this poem? At what point in the psalm does the controlling metaphor shift?

8. This poem.
9. Traditionally attributed to King David. This English translation is from the King James Version of the Bible.

HENRY KING

Sic Vita[1]

Like to the falling of a star,
Or as the flights of eagles are,
Or like the fresh spring's gaudy hue,
Or silver drops of morning dew,
5 Or like a wind that chafes the flood,
Or bubbles which on water stood:
Even such is man, whose borrowed light
Is straight called in, and paid to night.

The wind blows out, the bubble dies,
10 The spring entombed in autumn lies,
The dew dries up, the star is shot,
The flight is past, and man forgot.

                                        1657

- What is a man's "light"? In what way is it "borrowed"? How many similes are there in this poem?

JOHN DONNE

[Batter my heart, three-personed God][2]

Batter my heart, three-personed God; for You
As yet but knock, breathe, shine, and seek to mend;
That I may rise and stand, o'erthrow me, and bend
Your force, to break, blow, burn, and make me new.
5 I, like an usurped town, to another due,
Labor to admit You, but Oh, to no end!
Reason, Your viceroy[3] in me, me should defend,
But is captived, and proves weak or untrue.
Yet dearly I love You, and would be loved fain,[4]
10 But am betrothed unto Your enemy:
Divorce me, untie or break that knot again,
Take me to You, imprison me, for I,
Except You enthrall me, never shall be free,
Nor ever chaste, except You ravish me.

                                        1633

- In the poem's controlling metaphor, who is the speaker? Who, or what, is God? To whom is the speaker "betrothed"?

1. Such is life.   2. *Holy Sonnets*, 14.   3. One who rules as the representative of a higher power.
4. Gladly.

The Computation

For the first twenty years, since yesterday,
I scarce believed thou couldst be gone away;
For forty more, I fed on favors past,
And forty on hopes—that thou wouldst, they might, last.
5 Tears drowned one hundred, and sighs blew out two;
A thousand, I did neither think, nor do,
Or not divide, all being one thought of you;
Or in a thousand more forgot that too.
Yet call not this long life, but think that I
10 Am, by being dead, immortal. Can ghosts die?

1633

- Who, or what, might be "thou" in the second line? What seems to be the cause of the speaker's "death"?

The Canonization

For God's sake hold your tongue and let me love!
    Or⁵ chide my palsy or my gout,
My five gray hairs or ruined fortune flout;
With wealth your state, your mind with arts improve,
5   Take you a course, get you a place,
    Observe his Honor or his Grace,
Or the king's real or his stampéd face⁶
    Contemplate; what you will, approve,
        So you will let me love.

10 Alas, alas, who's injured by my love?
    What merchant's ships have my sighs drowned?
Who says my tears have overflowed his ground?
When did my colds a forward spring remove?
    When did the heats which my veins fill
15   Add one man to the plaguy bill?⁷
Soldiers find wars, and lawyers find out still
    Litigious men which quarrels move,
        Though she and I do love.

Call us what you will, we are made such by love.
20   Call her one, me another fly,
We're tapers too, and at our own cost die;⁸

---

5. Either. 6. On coins. 7. List of plague victims.
8. Tapers—candles—consume themselves. To "die" is Renaissance slang for consummating the sexual act, which was popularly believed to shorten life by one day. *Fly:* a traditional symbol of transitory life.

And we in us find th' eagle and the dove.[9]
   The phoenix riddle hath more wit[1]
   By us; we two, being one, are it.
25 So to one neutral thing both sexes fit,
    We die and rise the same, and prove
     Mysterious by this love.

We can die by it, if not live by love;
   And if unfit for tombs and hearse
30 Our legend be, it will be fit for verse;[2]
   And if no piece of chronicle we prove,
   We'll build in sonnets pretty rooms[3]
  (As well a well-wrought urn becomes[4]
The greatest ashes, as half-acre tombs),
35   And by these hymns all shall approve
    Us canonized for love.

And thus invoke us: "You whom reverent love
   Made one another's hermitage,
You to whom love was peace, that now is rage,
40 Who did the whole world's soul extract, and drove[5]
   Into the glasses of your eyes
   (So made such mirrors and such spies
That they did all to you epitomize)
   Countries, towns, courts; beg from above
45   A pattern of your love!"

1633

- Whom does the speaker address in the first line, "hold your tongue"? Why does the speaker concede that he and his lover may not "prove" a "piece of chronicle" (line 31)?

DAVID FERRY

At the Hospital

She was the sentence the cancer spoke at last,
Its blurred grammar finally clarified.

1983

- What, exactly, has "clarified" the cancer's "blurred grammar"?

---

9. Traditional symbols of strength and purity.
1. Meaning. According to tradition, only one phoenix existed at a time, dying in a funeral pyre of its own making and being reborn from its own ashes. The bird's existence was thus a riddle akin to a religious mystery (line 27), and a symbol sometimes fused with Christian representations of immortality.
2. That is, if we don't turn out to be an authenticated piece of historical narrative.
3. In Italian, *stanza* means room.   4. Befits.   5. Compressed.

DOROTHY LIVESAY

Other

1

Men prefer an island
With its beginning ended:
Undertone of waves
Trees overbended.

5 Men prefer a road
Circling, shell-like
Convex and fossiled
Forever winding inward.

Men prefer a woman
10 Limpid in sunlight
Held as a shell
On a sheltering island . . .

Men prefer an island.

2

But I am mainland
15 O I range
From upper country to the inner core:
From sageland, brushland, marshland
To the sea's floor.

Show me an orchard where I have not slept,
20 A hollow where I have not wrapped
The sage about me, and above, the still
Stars clustering
Over the ponderosa pine, the cactus hill.

Tell me a time
I have not loved,
25 A mountain left unclimbed:
A prairie field
Where I have not furrowed my tongue,
Nourished it out of the mind's dark places;
30 Planted with tears unwept
And harvested as friends, as faces.

O find me a dead-end road
I have not trodden
A logging road that leads the heart away
35 Into the secret evergreen of cedar roots
Beyond sun's farthest ray—
Then, in a clearing's sudden dazzle,
There is no road; no end; no puzzle.
But do not show me! For I know
40 The country I caress:
A place where none shall trespass

None possess:
A mainland mastered
From its inaccess.

––––

45 Men prefer an island.

1955

- What does the speaker mean by "Men prefer an island" (line 1) and "I am mainland" (line 14)? What is important about the distinction between the two?

RANDALL JARRELL

The Death of the Ball Turret Gunner[6]

From my mother's sleep I fell into the State,
And I hunched in its belly till my wet fur froze.
Six miles from earth, loosed from its dream of life,
5 I woke to black flak and the nightmare fighters.
When I died they washed me out of the turret with a hose.

1945

- What is meant by "I fell into the State"? What do the words "sleep," "dream," and "nightmare" suggest about the poem's basic situation?

RICHARD BARNFIELD

A Comparison of the Life of Man

Man's life is well comparèd to a feast,
   Furnished with choice of all variety;
To it comes Time, and as a bidden guest
   He sets him down[7] in pomp and majesty;
5 The threefold age of man the waiters be:
   Then with an earthen voider,[8] made of clay,
Comes Death, and takes the table clean away.

1598

- What is "The threefold age of man"? To what is the speaker comparing "an earthen voider, made of clay"?

6. A ball turret was a plexiglass sphere set into the belly of a B-17 or B-24 and inhabited by two .50 caliber machine-guns and one man, a short, small man. When this gunner tracked with his machine-guns a fighter attacking his bomber from below, he revolved with the turret; hunched upside-down in his little sphere, he looked like the foetus in the womb. The fighters which attacked him were armed with cannon firing explosive shells. The hose was a steam hose. [Jarrell's note]
7. That is, Time seats himself.   8. Tray or basket used for clearing the table.

FRANCIS WILLIAM BOURDILLON

The Night Has a Thousand Eyes

The night has a thousand eyes,
  And the day but one;
Yet the light of the bright world dies
  With the dying sun.

5 The mind has a thousand eyes,
  And the heart but one;
Yet the light of a whole life dies
  When the love is gone.

1889

- What are the "thousand eyes" of the night? the single eye of the day? What, exactly, are the comparisons to the mind and the heart?

EAVAN BOLAND

An Elegy for My Mother in Which She Scarcely Appears

I knew we had to grieve for the animals
a long time ago: weep for them, pity them.
I knew it was our strange human duty
to write their elegies after we arranged their demise.
5 I was young then and able for the paradox.
I am older now and ready with the question:
What happened to them all? I mean to those
old dumb implements which have
no eyes to plead with us like theirs
10 no claim to make on us like theirs? I mean—

there was a singing kettle. I want to know
why no one tagged its neck or ringed the tin
base of its extinct design or crouched to hear
its rising shriek in winter or wrote it down with
15 the birds in their blue sleeves of air
torn away with the trees that sheltered them.

And there were brass fire dogs which lay out
all evening on the grate and in the heat
thrown at them by the last of the peat fire
20 but no one noted down their history or put them
in the old packs under slate-blue moonlight.
There was a wooden clotheshorse, absolutely steady,
without sinews, with no mane and no meadows
to canter in; carrying, instead of
25 landlords or Irish monks, rinsed tea cloths
but still, I would have thought, worth adding to
the catalogue of what we need, what we always need

as is my mother, on this Dublin evening of
fog crystals and frost as she reaches out to test
30 one corner of a cloth for dryness as the prewar
Irish twilight closes in and down on the room
and the curtains are drawn and here am I,
not even born and already a conservationist,
with nothing to assist me but the last
35 and most fabulous of beasts—language, language—
which knows, as I do, that it's too late
to record the loss of these things but does so anyway,
and anxiously, in case it shares their fate.

                                        2005

• How is the speaker's mother represented by the various "dumb
  implements" of the poem—the kettle (line 11), the fire dogs (line 17),
  and the clotheshorse (line 22)? What does the speaker mean by
  "conservationist" (line 33)?

AMY LOWELL

Aubade

As I would free the white almond from the green husk
So would I strip your trappings off,
Beloved.
And fingering the smooth and polished kernel
5 I should see that in my hands glittered a gem beyond counting.

                                        1917

• What are the "trappings" that the speaker would strip from her
  beloved?

MARGARET CAVENDISH, DUCHESS OF NEWCASTLE

Of the Theme of Love

O Love, how thou art tired out with rhyme!
Thou art a tree whereon all poets climb;
And from thy branches every one takes some
Of thy sweet fruit, which fancy feeds upon.
5 But now thy tree is left so bare and poor
That they can hardly gather one plum more.

late 17th century

- Why does the speaker complain that "thy tree is left so bare and poor"?

CHARLES SIMIC

Classic Ballroom Dances

Grandmothers who wring the necks
Of chickens; old nuns
With names like Theresa, Marianne,
Who pull schoolboys by the ear;

5 The intricate steps of pickpockets
Working the crowd of the curious
At the scene of an accident; the slow shuffle
Of the evangelist with a sandwich board;

The hesitation of the early-morning customer
10 Peeking through the window grille
Of a pawnshop; the weave of a little kid
Who is walking to school with eyes closed;

And the ancient lovers, cheek to cheek,
On the dance floor of the Union Hall,
15 Where they also hold charity raffles
On rainy Monday nights of an eternal November.

1980

- What makes each of the "dances" described in the poem "classic"?

EMILY DICKINSON

[*Wild Nights—Wild Nights!*]

Wild Nights—Wild Nights!
Were I with thee
Wild Nights should be
Our luxury!

5 Futile—the Winds—
To a Heart in port—
Done with the Compass—
Done with the Chart!

Rowing in Eden—
10 Ah, the Sea!
Might I but moor—Tonight—
In Thee!

ca. 1861

- To what, exactly, does the speaker compare her love? What are some possible, even opposite, interpretations of the line "Done with the Chart"?

GREG DELANTY

The Blind Stitch

I can't say why rightly, but suddenly it's clear once more
  what holds us together as we sit, recumbent in the old ease
of each other's company, chewing the rag about friends,
  a poem we loved and such-like. Your Portuguese skin,
5 set off by a turquoise dress, doesn't hinder either.
  But there's something more than tan-deep between us.
I sew a button to a waistcoat you made me, ravelled years ago.
  You hemmed it with the stitch you mend a frock with now.
Our hands, without thought for individual movement, sew in
10   and out, entering and leaving at one and the same time.
If truth be told, the thread had frayed between us, unnoticed,
  except for the odd rip. But as we sew, love is
in the mending, and though nothing's said, we feel it
  in a lightness of mood, our ease, our blind stitch.

2001

- In addition to the title, what other words and phrases in this poem contribute to the sewing metaphor?

SYMBOL

The word *symbol* is often used sloppily and sometimes pretentiously, but properly used the term suggests one of the most basic things about poems—their ability to get beyond what words signify and make larger claims about meanings in the verbal world. All words go beyond themselves. They are not simply a collection of sounds: they signify something beyond their sounds, often things or actions or ideas. Words describe not only a verbal universe but also a world in which actions occur, acts have implications, and events have meaning. Sometimes words signify something beyond themselves, say a rock or a tree or a cloud, and symbolize something as well, such as solidity or life or dreams. Words can—when their implications are agreed on by tradition, convention, or habit—stand for things beyond their most immediate meanings or significations and become symbols, and even simple words that have accumulated no special power from previous use may be given special significance in special circumstances—either in poetry or in life itself.

A **symbol** is, put simply, something that stands for something else. The everyday world is full of common examples; a flag, a logo, a trademark, or a skull and crossbones all suggest things beyond themselves, and everyone likely understands what their display indicates, whether or not each viewer shares a commitment to what the object represents. In common usage a prison symbolizes confinement, constriction, and loss of freedom, and in specialized traditional usage a cross may symbolize oppression, cruelty, suffering, death, resurrection, triumph, or the intersection of two separate things, traditions, or ideas (as in crossroads and crosscurrents, for example). The specific symbolic significance depends on the context; a reader, for example, might determine significance by looking at contiguous details in a poem and by examining the poem's attitude toward a particular tradition or body of beliefs. A star means one thing to a Jewish poet and something else to a Christian poet, still something else to a sailor or an actor. In a very literal sense, words themselves are all symbols (they stand for an object, action, or quality, not just for letters or sounds), but symbols in poetry are said to be those words and groups of words that have a range of reference beyond their literal signification or denotation.

Poems sometimes create a symbol out of a thing, action, or event that has no previously agreed on symbolic significance. The following poem, for example, gives a seemingly random gesture symbolic significance:

SHARON OLDS

Leningrad Cemetery, Winter of 1941[1]

That winter, the dead could not be buried.
The ground was frozen, the gravediggers weak from hunger,
the coffin wood used for fuel. So they were covered with something
and taken on a child's sled to the cemetery

---

1. The 900-day siege of Leningrad (now Saint Petersburg) during World War II began in September 1941.

5 in the sub-zero air. They lay on the soil,
some of them wrapped in dark cloth
bound with rope like the tree's ball of roots
when it waits to be planted; others wound in sheets,
their pale, gauze, tapered shapes
10 stiff as cocoons that will split down the center
when the new life inside is prepared;
but most lay like corpses, their coverings
coming undone, naked calves
hard as corded wood spilling
15 from under a cloak, a hand reaching out
with no sign of peace, wanting to come back
even to the bread made of glue and sawdust,
even to the icy winter, and the siege.

1979

All of these corpses—frozen, neglected, uncovered—vividly stamp upon our minds a picture of the horrors of war, one likely to stay in our minds long after we have finished reading the poem. Several details are striking, and the poem's language heightens our sense of them. The corpses wound in sheets, for example, are described in "their pale, gauze, tapered shapes" (line 9), and they are compared to cocoons that one day will split and emit new life; and the limbs that dangle loose when the coverings come undone are "hard as corded wood spilling" (line 14). But clearly the most memorable sight is the hand dangling from one corpse that is coming unwrapped, for the poet invests that hand with special significance, giving its gesture *meaning*. The hand is "reaching out . . . wanting to come back" (lines 15–16); it is as if the dead can still gesture even if they cannot speak, and the gesture seems to signify the desire of the dead to return at any price. They would be glad to live, even under the grim conditions that attend life in Leningrad during the war. Suddenly the grimness that we—the living—have been witnessing pales by comparison with what the dead have lost simply by being dead. The hand has been made to *symbolize* the desire of the dead to return, to live, to be still among us, anywhere. The hand reaches out in the poem as a gesture that means something; the poet has made it a symbol of desire.

The whole array of dead bodies in the poem might be called symbolic as well. As a group, they stand for the war's human waste, and their dramatic presence provides the poem with a dramatic visualization of how war leaves no time for decency, not even the decency of burial. The bodies are a symbol: they stand for what the poem as a whole asserts.

The following poem also arises out of a historical moment. Here, however, the poet gives significance to a personal event by the interpretation he puts upon it.

JAMES DICKEY

The Leap

The only thing I have of Jane MacNaughton
Is one instant of a dancing-class dance.
She was the fastest runner in the seventh grade,
My scrapbook says, even when boys were beginning
5   To be as big as the girls,
But I do not have her running in my mind,
Though Frances Lane is there, Agnes Fraser,
Fat Betty Lou Black in the boys-against-girls
Relays we ran at recess: she must have run

10 Like the other girls, with her skirts tucked up
So they would be like bloomers,
But I cannot tell; that part of her is gone.
What I do have is when she came,
With the hem of her skirt where it should be
15 For a young lady, into the annual dance
Of the dancing class we all hated, and with a light
Grave leap, jumped up and touched the end
Of one of the paper-ring decorations

To see if she could reach it. She could,
20 And reached me now as well, hanging in my mind
From a brown chain of brittle paper, thin
And muscular, wide-mouthed, eager to prove
Whatever it proves when you leap
In a new dress, a new womanhood, among the boys
25 Whom you easily left in the dust
Of the passionless playground. If I said I saw
In the paper where Jane MacNaughton Hill,

Mother of four, leapt to her death from a window
Of a downtown hotel, and that her body crushed-in
30 The top of a parked taxi, and that I held
Without trembling a picture of her lying cradled
In that papery steel as though lying in the grass,
One shoe idly off, arms folded across her breast,
I would not believe myself. I would say
35 The convenient thing, that it was a bad dream
Of maturity, to see that eternal process

Most obsessively wrong with the world
Come out of her light, earth-spurning feet
Grown heavy: would say that in the dusty heels
40 Of the playground some boy who did not depend
On speed of foot, caught and betrayed her.
Jane, stay where you are in my first mind:

It was odd in that school, at that dance.
I and the other slow-footed yokels sat in corners
45 Cutting rings out of drawing paper

Before you leapt in your new dress
And touched the end of something I began,
Above the couples struggling on the floor,
New men and women clutching at each other
50 And prancing foolishly as bears: hold on
To that ring I made for you, Jane—
My feet are nailed to the ground
By dust I swallowed thirty years ago—
While I examine my hands.

                                                    1967

Memory is crucial to "The Leap." The fact that Jane MacNaughton's graceful leap in dancing class has stuck in the speaker's mind all these years means that this leap was important to him, meant something to him, stood for something in his mind. For the speaker, the leap is an "instant" and the "only thing" he has of Jane. He remembers its grace and ease, and he struggles at several points to articulate its meaning (lines 16–26, 44–50), but even without articulation or explanation it remains in his head as a visual memory, a symbol of something beyond himself, something he cannot do, something he wanted to be. What that leap stood for, or symbolized, was boldness, confidence, accomplishment, maturity, Jane's ability to go beyond her fellow students in dancing class—the transcending of childhood by someone entering adulthood. Her feet now seem "earth-spurning" (line 38) in that original leap, and they separate her from everyone else. Jane MacNaughton was beyond the speaker's abilities and any attempt he could make to articulate his hopes, but she was not beyond his dreams. And even before he could say so, she symbolized a dream.

The leap to her death seems cruelly wrong and ironic after the grace of her earlier leap. In memory she is suspended in air, as if there were no gravity, no coming back to earth, as if life could exist as dream. And so the photograph, re-created in precise detail, is a cruel dashing of the speaker's dream—a detailed record of the ending of a leap, a denial of the suspension in which his memory had held her. His dream is grounded; her mortality is insistent. But the speaker still wants to hang on to that symbolic moment (line 42), which he confronts in a more mature context but which he will never altogether replace or surrender.

The leap is ultimately symbolic in the *poem*, too, not just in the speaker's mind. In the poem (and for us as readers) its symbolism is double: the first leap symbolizes aspiration, and the second symbolizes the frustration and grounding of high hopes; the two are complementary, one impossible to imagine without the other. The poem is horrifying in some ways, a dramatic reminder that human beings don't ultimately transcend their mortality, their limits, no matter how heroic or unencumbered by gravity they may have seemed to an observer. But the poem is not altogether sad and despairing, partly because it still affirms the validity of the original leap and partly because it creates and elaborates another symbol: the paper chain.

The chain connects Jane to the speaker both literally and figuratively. It is, in part, *his* paper chain that she had leaped to touch in dancing class (lines 18–19), and he thinks of her first leap as "touch[ing] the end of something I began" (line 47). He and the other earthbound, "slow-footed yokels" (line 44) made the chain, and it connects them to her original leap, just as a photograph glimpsed in the paper connects the speaker to her second leap. The paper in the chain is "brittle" (line 21), and its creators seem dull artisans compared to the artistic performer that Jane was. They are heavy and "left in the dust" (lines 25, 52–53), but she is "light" (line 16) and able to transcend them, even in transcendence touching their lives and what they can do. And so the paper chain becomes the poem's symbol of linkage, connecting lower accomplishment to higher possibility, the artisan to the artist, material substance to the act of imagination. And at the end the speaker examines the hands that made the chain because those hands certify his connection to her and the imaginative leap she had made for him. The chain thus symbolizes not only the lower capabilities of those who cannot leap like the budding Jane could, but (later) the connection with her leap as both transcendence and mortality. Like the leap itself, the chain has been elevated to special meaning, given symbolic significance, by the poet's treatment of it. A leap and a chain have no necessary significance in themselves to most of us—at least no significance that we have all agreed upon—but they may take on significance in specific circumstances or a specific text.

Other objects and acts have a built-in significance because of past usage in literature, or tradition, or the stories a culture develops to explain itself and its beliefs. Over the years some things have acquired an agreed-upon significance, an accepted value in our minds. They already stand for something before the poet cites them; they are **traditional symbols.** Their uses in poetry have to do with the fact that poets can count on a recognition of their traditional suggestions and meanings outside the poem, and the poem does not have to propose or argue a particular symbolic value. Birds, for example, traditionally symbolize flight, freedom from confinement, detachment from earthbound limits, the ability to soar beyond rationality and transcend mortal limits. Traditionally, birds have also been linked with imagination, especially poetic imagination, and poets often identify with them as pure and ideal singers of songs, as in Keats's "Ode to a Nightingale" (see chapter 10). One of the most traditional symbols, the rose, may be a simple and fairly plentiful flower in its season, but it has so long stood for particular qualities that merely to name it raises predictable expectations. Its beauty, delicacy, fragrance, shortness of life, and depth of color have made it a symbol of the transitoriness of beauty, and countless poets have counted on its accepted symbolism— sometimes to compliment a friend (as Burns does in "A Red, Red Rose") or sometimes to make a point about the nature of symbolism. The following poem draws, in quite a traditional way, on the traditional meanings.

EDMUND WALLER

Song

Go, lovely rose!
Tell her that wastes her time and me
　That now she knows,
When I resemble[2] her to thee,
5　How sweet and fair she seems to be.

　Tell her that's young,
And shuns to have her graces spied,
　That hadst thou sprung
In deserts, where no men abide,
10　Thou must have uncommended died.

　Small is the worth
Of beauty from the light retired;
　Bid her come forth,
Suffer herself to be desired,
15　And not blush so to be admired.

　Then die! that she
The common fate of all things rare
　May read in thee;
How small a part of time they share
That are so wondrous sweet and fair!

1645

The speaker in "Song" sends the rose to his love in order to have it speak its traditional meanings of not only beauty but also transitoriness. He counts on accepted symbolism to make his point and hurry her into accepting his advances. Likewise, the poet does not elaborate or argue these things because he does not need to; he counts on the familiarity of the tradition (though, of course, readers unfamiliar with the tradition will not respond in the same way—that is one reason it is difficult to fully appreciate texts from another linguistic or cultural tradition).

Poets may use traditional symbols to invoke predictable responses—in effect using shortcuts to meaning by repeating acts of signification sanctioned by time and cultural habit. But often poets examine the tradition even as they employ it, and sometimes they revise or reverse meanings built into the tradition. Symbols do not necessarily stay the same over time, and poets often turn even the most traditional symbols to their own original uses. Knowing the traditions of poetry—reading a lot of poems and observing how they tend to use certain words, metaphors, and symbols—can be very useful in reading new poems, but traditions evolve and individual poems do highly individual things. Knowing the past never means being able to interpret new texts with confidence. Symbolism makes things

---

2. Compare.

happen, but individual poets and texts determine what will happen and how. The following two poems work important variations on the traditional associations of roses:

D. H. LAWRENCE

I Am Like a Rose

I am myself at last; now I achieve
My very self. I, with the wonder mellow,
Full of fine warmth, I issue forth in clear
And single me, perfected from my fellow.

5 Here I am all myself. No rose-bush heaving
Its limpid sap to culmination has brought
Itself more sheer and naked out of the green
In stark-clear roses, than I to myself am brought.

1917

DOROTHY PARKER

One Perfect Rose

A single flow'r he sent me, since we met.
    All tenderly his messenger he chose;
Deep-hearted, pure, with scented dew still wet—
    One perfect rose.

5 I knew the language of the floweret;
    "My fragile leaves," it said, "his heart enclose."
Love long has taken for his amulet
    One perfect rose.

Why is it no one ever sent me yet
10   One perfect limousine, do you suppose?
Ah no, it's always just my luck to get
    One perfect rose.

1937

Sometimes symbols—traditional or not—become so insistent in the world of a poem that the larger referential world is left almost totally behind. In such cases the symbol is everything, and the poem does not just *use* symbols but becomes a **symbolic poem,** usually a highly individualized one dependent on an internal system introduced by the individual poet.

Here is an example of such a poem:

WILLIAM BLAKE

The Sick Rose[3]

O rose, thou art sick.
The invisible worm
That flies in the night
In the howling storm

5 Has found out thy bed
Of crimson joy,
And his dark secret love
Does thy life destroy.

1794

The poem does not seem to be about a rose, but about what the rose represents—not in this case something altogether understandable through the traditional meanings of *rose*.

We usually associate the rose with beauty and love, often with sex; and here several key terms have sexual connotations: "worm," "bed," and "crimson joy." The violation of the rose by the worm is the poem's main concern; the violation seems to have involved secrecy, deceit, and "dark" motives, and the result is sickness rather than the joy of love. The poem is sad; it involves a sense of hurt and tragedy, nearly of despair. The poem cries out against the misuse of the rose, against its desecration, implying that instead of a healthy joy in sensuality and sexuality, there has been in this case destruction and hurt, perhaps because of misunderstanding and repression and lack of sensitivity.

But to say so much about this poem we have to extrapolate from other poems by Blake, and we have to introduce information from outside the poem. Fully symbolic poems often require that, and thus they ask us to go beyond the formal procedures of reading that we have discussed so far. As presented in this poem, the rose is not part of the normal world that we ordinarily see, and it is symbolic in a special sense. The poet does not simply take an object from our everyday world and give it special significance, making it a symbol in the same sense that the leap or the corpse's hand is a symbol. Here the rose seems to belong to its own world, a world made entirely inside the poem or the poet's head. The rose is not referential, or not primarily so. The whole poem is symbolic; it is not paraphrasable; it lives in its own world. But what is the rose here a symbol of? In general terms, we can say from what the poem tells us; but we may not be as confident as we can be in the more nearly recognizable world of "The Leap" or "Leningrad Cemetery, Winter of 1941." In "The Sick Rose," it seems inappropriate to ask the standard questions: What rose? Where? Which worm? What are the particulars here? In the world of this poem worms can fly and may be invisible. We are altogether in a world of meanings that have been formulated according to a special

3. In Renaissance emblem books, the scarab beetle, worm, and rose are closely associated: the beetle feeds on dung, and the smell of the rose is fatal to it.

system of knowledge and code of belief. We will feel comfortable and confident in that world only if we read many poems written by the poet (in this case William Blake) within the same symbolic system.

Negotiation of meanings in symbolic poems can be very difficult indeed. Reading symbolic poems is an advanced skill that depends on special knowledge of authors and of the special traditions they work from. But usually the symbols you will find in poems *are* referential of meanings we all share and you can readily discover these meanings by carefully studying the poems themselves.

• • •

ROBERT FROST

Fireflies in the Garden

Here come real stars to fill the upper skies,
And here on earth come emulating flies,
That though they never equal stars in size,
(And they were never really stars at heart)
5 Achieve at times a very star-like start.
Only, of course, they can't sustain the part.

1928

- What is the tone of this poem? What does the poem say about the limits of symbolism?

STEPHEN DUNN

Dancing with God

At first the surprise
of being singled out,
the dance floor crowded
and me not looking my best,
5 a too-often-worn dress
and the man with me
a budding casualty
of one repetition too much.
God just touched his shoulder
10 and he left.
Then the confirmation of
an old guess.
God was a wild god,
into the most mindless rock,
15 but graceful,

looking—this excited me—
like no one I could love,
cruel mouth, eyes evocative
of promises unkept.
20 I never danced better, freer,
as if dancing were my way
of saying how easily
I could be with him, or apart.
When the music turned slow
25 God held me close
and I felt for a moment
I'd mistaken him,
that he was Death
and this the famous embrace
30 before the lights go out.
But God kept holding me
and I him
until the band stopped
and I stood looking at a figure
35 I wanted to slap
or forgive for something,
I couldn't decide which.
He left then, no thanks,
no sign
40 that he'd felt anything
more than an earthly moment
with someone who could've been
anyone on earth.
To this day I don't know why
45 I thought he was God,
though it was clear
there was no going back
to the man who brought me,
nice man
50 with whom I'd slept
and grown tired,
who danced wrong,
who never again
could do anything right.

1989

- Does the poem finally state definitively whether or not the dance
  partner really was God, at least in the speaker's mind? How does the
  ambiguity serve the poem?

ADRIENNE RICH

Diving into the Wreck

First having read the book of myths,
and loaded the camera,
and checked the edge of the knife-blade,
I put on
5 the body-armor of black rubber
the absurd flippers
the grave and awkward mask.
I am having to do this
not like Cousteau[4] with his
10 assiduous team
aboard the sun-flooded schooner
but here alone.

There is a ladder.
The ladder is always there
15 hanging innocently
close to the side of the schooner.
We know what it is for,
we who have used it.
Otherwise
20 it's a piece of maritime floss
some sundry equipment.

I go down.
Rung after rung and still
the oxygen immerses me
25 the blue light
the clear atoms
of our human air.
I go down.
My flippers cripple me,
30 I crawl like an insect down the ladder
and there is no one
to tell me when the ocean
will begin.

First the air is blue and then
35 it is bluer and then green and then
black I am blacking out and yet
my mask is powerful
it pumps my blood with power
the sea is another story
40 the sea is not a question of power

---

4. Jacques-Yves Cousteau (1910–1997), French underwater explorer and writer.

I have to learn alone
to turn my body without force
in the deep element.

And now: it is easy to forget
45 what I came for
among so many who have always
lived here
swaying their crenellated fans
between the reefs
50 and besides
you breathe differently down here.

I came to explore the wreck.
The words are purposes.
The words are maps.
55 I came to see the damage that was done
and the treasures that prevail.
I stroke the beam of my lamp
slowly along the flank
of something more permanent
60 than fish or weed

the thing I came for:
the wreck and not the story of the wreck
the thing itself and not the myth
the drowned face always staring
65 toward the sun
the evidence of damage
worn by salt and sway into this threadbare beauty
the ribs of the disaster
curving their assertion
70 among the tentative haunters.

This is the place.
And I am here, the mermaid whose dark hair
streams black, the merman in his armored body
We circle silently
75 about the wreck
we dive into the hold.
I am she: I am he

whose drowned face sleeps with open eyes
whose breasts still bear the stress
80 whose silver, copper, vermeil cargo lies
obscurely inside barrels
half-wedged and left to rot
we are the half-destroyed instruments
that once held to a course
85 the water-eaten log
the fouled compass

We are, I am, you are
by cowardice or courage
the one who find our way
90 back to this scene
carrying a knife, a camera
a book of myths
in which
our names do not appear.

1972   1973

- What word or phrase first signals the reader that "Diving into the
  Wreck" is to be understood symbolically, not literally? What are
  some possible symbolic interpretations of the wreck and the dive?

ROO BORSON

After a Death

Seeing that there's no other way,
I turn his absence into a chair.
I can sit in it,
gaze out through the window.
5 I can do what I do best
and then go out into the world.
And I can return then with my useless love,
to rest,
because the chair is there.

                                             1989

- Why do you think the speaker chooses to symbolize her absent loved
  one with a chair?

HOWARD NEMEROV

The Town Dump

> *"The art of our necessities is strange,*
> *That can make vile things precious."*[5]

A mile out in the marshes, under a sky
Which seems to be always going away
In a hurry, on that Venetian land threaded
With hidden canals, you will find the city
5 Which seconds ours (so cemeteries, too,

_____
5. *King Lear* 3.2.70–71.

Reflect a town from hillsides out of town),
Where Being most Becomingly[6] ends up
Becoming some more. From cardboard tenements,
Windowed with cellophane, or simply tenting
10   In paper bags, the angry mackerel eyes
Glare at you out of stove-in, sunken heads
Far from the sea; the lobster, also, lifts
An empty claw in his most minatory
Of gestures; oyster, crab, and mussel shells
15   Lie here in heaps, savage as money hurled
Away at the gate of hell. If you want results,
These are results.
                   Objects of value or virtue,
However, are also to be picked up here,
20   Though rarely, lying with bones and rotten meat,
Eggshells and mouldy bread, banana peels
No one will skid on, apple cores that caused
Neither the fall of man nor a theory
Of gravitation.[7] People do throw out
25   The family pearls by accident, sometimes,
Not often; I've known dealers in antiques
To prowl this place by night, with flashlights, on
The off-chance of somebody's having left
Derelict chairs which will turn out to be
30   By Hepplewhite,[8] a perfect set of six
Going to show, I guess, that in any sty
Someone's heaven may open and shower down
Riches responsive to the right dream; though
It is a small chance, certainly, that sends
35   The ghostly dealer, heavy with fly-netting
Over his head, across these hills in darkness,
Stumbling in cut-glass goblets, lacquered cups,
And other products of his dreamy midden[9]
Penciled with light and guarded by the flies.

40   For there are flies, of course. A dynamo
Composed, by thousands, of our ancient black
Retainers, hums here day and night, steady
As someone telling[1] beads, the hum becoming
A high whine at any disturbance; then,
45   Settled again, they shine under the sun

---

6. "Being" and "Becoming" have been, since Heraclitus (ca. 540–ca. 480 B.C.), the standard antinomies in Western philosophy, standing for (respectively) the eternal and that which changes.
7. According to legend, Sir Isaac Newton's discovery of the principle of gravitation followed his being hit on the head by a falling apple.
8. A late-eighteenth-century cabinetmaker and furniture designer, famed for his simplification of neoclassic lines. No pieces known to have been made by Hepplewhite survive.
9. Refuse heap. The term usually describes those primitive refuse heaps that have been untouched for centuries and in which archaeologists dig for shards and artifacts of older cultures.   1. Counting.

Like oil-drops, or are invisible as night,
By night.
       All this continually smoulders,
Crackles, and smokes with mostly invisible fires
50 Which, working deep, rarely flash out and flare,
And never finish. Nothing finishes;
The flies, feeling the heat, keep on the move.
Among the flies, the purefying fires,
The hunters by night, acquainted with the art
55 Of our necessities, and the new deposits
That each day wastes with treasure, you may say
There should be ratios. You may sum up
The results if you want results. But I will add
That wild birds, drawn to the carrion and flies,
60 Assemble in some numbers here, their wings
Shining with light, their flight enviably free,
Their music marvelous, though sad, and strange.

                                1958

- As suggested by the poem, in what ways does the town dump "second" (line 5) or "reflect" (line 6) the town itself? What are the "results" (lines 16, 17, and 58)? What might the "wild birds" (line 59) symbolize?

DAN CHIASSON

My Ravine

How will you know what my poem is like
      until you've gone down my ravine and seen

the box springs, mattresses, bookcases, and desks
      the neighboring women's college dumps each year,

5 somebody's hair dryer, someone's Herodotus
      a poem's dream landscape, one half Latin and

one half shit, the neighboring women's college's shit?
      Wheelbarrow upon wheelbarrow, a humpbacked

custodian hauls old dormitory furniture down
10   and launches it, watching it roll into the pile.

You won't know how my poem decides what's in,
      what's out, what decorum means and doesn't mean,

until you follow him home after work and see him
      going wild all night imagining those girls' old beds.

15   You won't know what I'm trying for until you hear
        how every fall in my back yard a swarm of deer

    materializes, scavenging where the raspberries touched
        the radishes, now plowed under, itching the lawn

    for dandelions, stare at each other and wander
20   bewildered down my ravine and turn into skeletons.

                                                              2002

- What might be symbolized by the ravine? The custodian and the old
  dormitory furniture? The scavenging deer?

SUGGESTIONS FOR WRITING

1. List all the neologisms and other unusual words in Hopkins's "Pied Beauty." Find
   the most precise synonym you can for each. How can you tell exactly what these
   words contribute to the poem? Explain the effects of the repeated consonant sounds
   (alliteration) and repeated vowel sounds (assonance) in the poem. What are the
   advantages of making up original words to describe highly individualized effects?
   What are the disadvantages?
2. Compare Dickinson's "I dwell in Possibility—" with two of her other poems, "A
   narrow Fellow in the Grass" (page 36) and "Wild Nights—Wild Nights!" (page 182).
   What patterns of word use do you see in the three poems? What kinds of vocabulary
   do they have in common? what patterns of syntax? what strategies of organization?
3. Read aloud the passages from Milton's *Paradise Lost*. Then ask a friend to read the
   passages aloud as well. As the friend reads, note which words—and which choices
   of word order—provide especially useful guides for reading aloud. Make a list of all
   the lines in which the "normal" word order would be different if the poem were not
   written in a metrical form designed for reading aloud. In each case in which the
   poem uses unusual word order, try to figure out exactly what effect is produced by
   the variation.
4. Consider the poems about roses found in this chapter and write a paragraph about
   each poem showing how it establishes specific symbolism for the rose. What gen-
   eralizations can you draw about the rose's traditional meanings in poetry? If you
   can, find other poems about roses outside of this book to determine if your gener-
   alizations still apply.
5. Research the design of World War II bombers like the B-17 and the B-24. Try to find
   a picture of the gunner in the ball turret of such an airplane, and note carefully his
   body position. Write an essay in which you explain how Randall Jarrell's "The Death
   of the Ball Turret Gunner" uses visual details to create its fetal and birth metaphors.
6. Is there a "correct" interpretation of a richly symbolic poem such as Stephen Dunn's
   "Dancing with God," Adrienne Rich's "Diving into the Wreck," Howard Nemerov's
   "The Town Dump," or Don Chiasson's "My Ravine"? If one interpretation seems to
   fit all the particulars of the poem, does that mean it is better than other possible
   interpretations? Write an essay in which you explore the symbolism in one of these
   poems and then argue for or against the idea that there is a single best way to
   understand the poem. Can ambiguity serve a poet's purpose, or does it ultimately
   undercut a poem's meaning and significance?

5 THE SOUNDS OF POETRY

A lot of what happens in a poem happens in your mind's eye, but some of it happens in your "mind's ear" and in your voice. Poems are full of meaningful sounds and silences as well as words and sentences. Besides choosing words for their meanings, poets sometimes choose words because they have certain sounds, and poems use sound effects to create a mood or establish a tone, just as films do. Sometimes the sounds of words are crucial to what is happening in the text of the poem.

Here is a poem that explores the sounds of a particular word, tries them on, and analyzes them in relation to the word itself.

HELEN CHASIN
The Word Plum

The word *plum* is delicious

pout and push, luxury of
self-love, and savoring murmur

full in the mouth and falling
5 like fruit

taut skin
pierced, bitten, provoked into
juice, and tart flesh

question
10 and reply, lip and tongue
of pleasure.

                    1968

The poem savors the sounds of the word as well as the taste and feel of the fruit itself. It is almost as if the poem is tasting the sounds and rolling them slowly on the tongue. The second and third lines even replicate the *p, l, uh,* and *m* sounds of the word while at the same time imitating the squishy sounds of eating the fruit. Words like "delicious" and "luxury" sound juicy, and other words imitate sounds of satisfaction and pleasure—"murmur," for example. Even the process of eating is in part re-created aurally. The tight, clipped sounds of "taut skin /

pierced" suggest the way teeth sharply break the skin and slice quickly into the soft flesh of a plum, and as they describe the tartness, the words ("provoked," "question") force the lips to pucker and the tongue and palate to meet and hold, as if the mouth were savoring a tart fruit. The poet is having fun here re-creating the sensual appeal of a plum, teasing the sounds and meanings out of available words. The words must mean something appropriate and describe something accurately first of all, of course, but when they can also imitate the sounds and feel of the process, they can do double duty. Not many poems manipulate sound as intensely or as fully as "The Word *Plum,*" but many poems at least contain passages in which the sounds of life are reproduced by the human voice reading the poem. To get the full effect of this poem—and of many others—*you must read aloud*; that way, you can attend to the vocal rhythms and articulate the sounds as the poem calls for them to be reproduced by the human voice.

You will almost always enhance a poem's effect by reading aloud, using your voice to pronounce the words so that the poem becomes a spoken communication. Historically, poetry began as an oral phenomenon, and often poems that seem very difficult when looked at silently come alive when turned into sound. Early bards in many cultures chanted or recited their verses, and the music of poetry—its cadences and rhythms—developed from this kind of performance. The presentation of primitive poetry (and some later work as well) was often accompanied by some kind of musical instrument. The rhythms of any poem become clearer when you say or hear them.

Poetry is almost always a vocal art, dependent on the human voice to become its full self (for some exceptions look at the shaped verse in chapter 7). In a sense, it only begins to exist as a real phenomenon when a reader reads and actualizes it. Poems don't really achieve their full meaning when they exist merely on a page; a poem on a page is more a score or set of stage directions for a poem than a poem itself. Sometimes, in fact, it is hard to experience the poem at all unless you hear it; the actual experience of saying the words aloud or hearing them spoken is very good practice for learning to hear in your mind's ear when you read silently. A good poetry reading might easily convince you of the importance of a good voice sensitive to the poem's requirements, but you can also persuade yourself by reading poems aloud in the privacy of your own room. An audience is even better, however—an occasion to share the pleasure in the sounds themselves and what they imply. At its oral best, much poetry is communal.

MONA VAN DUYN

What the Motorcycle Said

Br-r-r-am-m-m, rackety-am-m, OM, *Am:*
All—r-r-room, r-r-ram, ala-bas-ter—
Am, the world's my oyster.

I hate plastic, wear it black and slick,
5 hate hardhats, wear one on my head,
that's what the motorcycle said.

Passed phonies in Fords, knocked down billboards, landed
on the other side of The Gap, and Whee,
bypassed history.

10 When I was born (The Past), baby knew best.
They shook when I bawled, took Freud's path,
threw away their wrath.

R-r-rackety-am-m. *Am.* War, rhyme,
soap, meat, marriage, the Phantom Jet
15 are shit, and like that.

Hate pompousness, punishment, patience, am into Love,
hate middle-class moneymakers, live on Dad,
that's what the motorcycle said.

Br-r-r-am-m-m. It's Nowsville, man. Passed Oldies, Uglies,
20 Straighties, Honkies. I'll never be
mean, tired or unsexy.

Passed cigarette suckers, souses, mother-fuckers,
losers, went back to Nature and found
how to get VD, stoned.

25 Passed a cow, too fast to hear her moo, "*I* rolled
our leaves of grass into one ball.
I am the grassy All."

Br-r-r-am-m-m, rackety-am-m, OM, *Am:*
All—gr-r-rin, oooohgah, gl-l-utton—
30 *Am,* the world's my smilebutton.

                                        1973

Saying this poem as if you were a motorcycle with the power of speech (sort of) is part of the poem's fun, and the rich, loud sounds of a motorcycle revving up concentrate and intensify the effect and enrich the pleasure. It's a shame not to hear a poem like this aloud; you miss a lot if you don't try to imitate the sounds or to pick up the motor's rhythms. A performance here is clearly worth it: human being as motorcycle, motorcycle as human being.

And it's a good poem, too. It does something interesting, important, and maybe a bit subversive. The speaking motorcycle seems to take on the values of some of its riders, the noisy and obtrusive ones that readers most likely associate with motorcycles. The types of riders made fun of here are themselves somewhat mindless and mechanical; they have cult feelings about their group, they travel in packs, and they seem to have no life beyond their machines. The speaking motorcycle, like such riders, exults in power and speed, lives for the moment, and has little respect for people, the past, institutions, or anything beyond its own small world. It is self-centered, trendy, ignorant, and inarticulate; but it is proud as well, mighty proud, and it glories in the rough thunder of its own sounds. That's what the motorcycle says.

The following poem uses sound effectively, too.

KENNETH FEARING

Dirge

1-2-3 was the number he played but today the number came 3-2-1;
Bought his Carbide at 30, and it went to 29; had the favorite at Bowie[1]
   but the track was slow—

O executive type, would you like to drive a floating-power, knee-
   action, silk-upholstered six? Wed a Hollywood star? Shoot the course
   in 58? Draw to the ace, king, jack?
O fellow with a will who won't take no, watch out for three cigarettes
   on the same, single match; O democratic voter born in August under
   Mars, beware of liquidated rails—

5   Denouement to denouement, he took a personal pride in the certain,
   certain way he lived his own, private life,
But nevertheless, they shut off his gas; nevertheless, the bank foreclosed;
   nevertheless, the landlord called; nevertheless, the radio broke,

And twelve o'clock arrived just once too often,
Just the same he wore one gray tweed suit, bought one straw hat, drank
   one straight Scotch, walked one short step, took one long look, drew
   one deep breath,
Just one too many,

10   And wow he died as wow he lived,
Going whop to the office and blooie home to sleep and biff got married
   and bam had children and oof got fired,
Zowie did he live and zowie did he die,

With who the hell are you at the corner of his casket, and where the
   hell're we going on the right-hand silver knob, and who the hell cares
   walking second from the end with an American Beauty[2] wreath from
   why the hell not,

Very much missed by the circulation staff of the New York Evening Post;
   deeply, deeply mourned by the B.M.T.[3]

15   Wham, Mr. Roosevelt; pow, Sears Roebuck; awk, big dipper; bop, summer
   rain;
Bong, Mr., bong, Mr., bong, Mr., bong.

                                                                1935

---

1. A racetrack in Maryland. *Carbide:* stock in the Union Carbide Corporation.   2. A variety of rose.
3. A New York City subway line.

As the title implies, "Dirge" is a kind of musical lament, in this case for a certain sort of businessman who took many chances and saw his investments and life go down the drain in the depression of the early 1930s. Reading this poem aloud helps a lot, in part because of the expressive cartoon words here that echo the action, words like "oof" and "blooie" (which primarily carry their meaning in their sounds, for they have practically no literal or referential meaning). Reading aloud also helps us notice that the poem employs rhythms much as a song would and that it frequently shifts its pace and mood. Notice how carefully the first two lines are balanced, and then how quickly the rhythm shifts as the "executive type" is addressed directly in line 3. (Line 2 is long and dribbles over in the narrow pages of a book like this; the especially long lines and irregular line lengths here create some of the poem's special sound effects.) In the direct address, the poem first picks up the lingo of advertising, which it recites in rapid-fire order rather like advertising phrases. In stanza 3 here, the rhythm shifts again, but the poem gives us helpful clues about how to read. Line 5 sounds like prose and is long, drawn out, and rather dull (rather like its subject), but line 6 sets up a regular (and monotonous) rhythm with its repeated "nevertheless," which punctuates the rhythm like a drumbeat: "But nevertheless, *tuh-tuh-tuh-tuh-tuh;* nevertheless, *tuh-tuh-tuh-tuh;* nevertheless, *tuh-tuh-tuh-tuh;* nevertheless, *tuh-tuh-tuh-tuh-tuh.*" In the next stanza, the repetitive phrasing comes again, this time guided by the word "one" in cooperation with other words of one syllable: "wore *one* gray tweed suit, bought *one* straw hat, *tuh* one *tuh-tuh, tuh* one *tuh-tuh, tuh* one *tuh-tuh, tuh* one *tuh-tuh.*" And then a new rhythm and a new technique begin in stanza 5, which imitates the language of comic books to describe in violent, exaggerated terms the routine of the businessman's life. You have to say words like "whop" and "zowie" aloud and in the rhythm of the whole sentence to get the full effect of how boring his life is, no matter how he tries to jazz it up with exciting words. And so it goes—repeated words, shifting rhythms, emphasis on routine and averageness—until the final bell ("Bong. . . . bong . . . bong . . . bong") tolls rhythmically for the dead man in the final clanging line.

> *There are only three things . . . that a poem must reach: the eye, the ear, and what we may call the heart or the mind. It is the most important of all to reach the heart of the reader. And the surest way to reach the heart is through the ear.*
> —ROBERT FROST

Sometimes the sounds in poems just provide special effects, rather like a musical score behind a film, setting mood and getting us into an appropriate frame of mind. But often sound and meaning go hand in hand, and the poet finds words that in their sounds echo the action. A word that captures or approximates the sound of what it describes, such as "splash" or "squish" or "murmur," is an **onomatopoeic** word, and the device itself is **onomatopoeia**. And poets can do similar things with pacing and rhythm, sounds and pauses. The punctuation, the length of vowels, and the combination of consonant sounds help to control the way we read so that we use our voice to imitate what is being described. The poems at the end of this chapter suggest several ways that such imitations of pace and pause may occur: by echoing the lapping of waves on a shore, for example ("Like as the waves"), or reproducing the rhythms of a musical style ("Dear John, Dear Coltrane").

Here is a classic passage in which a skillful poet talks about the virtues of making the sound echo the sense—and shows at the same time how to do it:

ALEXANDER POPE

Sound and Sense[4]

337 But most by numbers[5] judge a poet's song,
  And smooth or rough, with them, is right or wrong;
  In the bright muse though thousand charms conspire,[6]
340 Her voice is all these tuneful fools admire,
  Who haunt Parnassus[7] but to please their ear,
  Not mend their minds; as some to church repair,
  Not for the doctrine, but the music there.
  These, equal syllables[8] alone require,
345 Though oft the ear the open vowels tire,
  While expletives[9] their feeble aid do join,
  And ten low words oft creep in one dull line,
  While they ring round the same unvaried chimes,
  With sure returns of still expected rhymes.
350 Where'er you find "the cooling western breeze,"
  In the next line, it "whispers through the trees";
  If crystal streams "with pleasing murmurs creep,"
  The reader's threatened (not in vain) with "sleep."
  Then, at the last and only couplet fraught
355 With some unmeaning thing they call a thought,
  A needless Alexandrine[1] ends the song,
  That, like a wounded snake, drags its slow length along.
  Leave such to tune their own dull rhymes, and know
  What's roundly smooth, or languishingly slow;
360 And praise the easy vigor of a line,
  Where Denham's strength and Waller's[2] sweetness join.
  True ease in writing comes from art, not chance,
  As those move easiest who have learned to dance.
  'Tis not enough no harshness gives offense,
365 The sound must seem an echo to the sense:
  Soft is the strain when Zephyr[3] gently blows,
  And the smooth stream in smoother numbers flows;
  But when loud surges lash the sounding shore,
  The hoarse, rough verse should like the torrent roar.

4. From *An Essay on Criticism,* Pope's poem on the art of poetry and the problems of literary criticism. The passage excerpted here follows a discussion of several common weaknesses of critics—failure to regard an author's intention, for example, or overemphasis on clever metaphors and ornate style.
5. Meter, rhythm, sound. 6. Unite.
7. A mountain in Greece, traditionally associated with the Muses and considered the seat of poetry and music. 8. Regular accents. 9. Filler words, such as "do."
1. A line of six metrical feet, sometimes used in pentameter poems to vary the pace mechanically. Line 357 is an alexandrine.
2. Sir John Denham and Edmund Waller, seventeenth-century poets credited with perfecting the heroic couplet. 3. The west wind.

370 When Ajax[4] strives, some rock's vast weight to throw,
The line too labors, and the words move slow;
Not so, when swift Camilla[5] scours the plain,
Flies o'er th' unbending corn, and skims along the main.
Hear how Timotheus'[6] varied lays surprise,
375 And bid alternate passions fall and rise!
While, at each change, the son of Libyan Jove[7]
Now burns with glory, and then melts with love;
Now his fierce eyes with sparkling fury glow,
Now sighs steal out, and tears begin to flow:
380 Persians and Greeks like turns of nature[8] found,
And the world's victor stood subdued by sound!
The pow'r of music all our hearts allow,
And what Timotheus was, is DRYDEN now.

                                                              1711

A lot of things are going on here simultaneously. The poem uses a number of echoic or onomatopoeic words, and in some lines pleasant and unpleasant consonant sounds underline a particular point or add some mood music. When the poet talks about a particular weakness in poetry, he illustrates it at the same time—by using open vowels (line 345), expletives (line 346), monosyllabic words (line 347), predictable rhymes (lines 350–53), or long, slow lines (line 357). And the good qualities of poetry he talks about and illustrates as well (line 360, for example). But the main effects of the passage come from an interaction of several strategies at once. The effects are fairly simple and easy to spot, but their causes involve a lot of poetic ingenuity. In line 340, for example, Pope achieves a careful cacophonous effect by repeating the $\overline{oo}$ vowel sound and repeating the *l* consonant sound together with (twice) interrupting the rough *f* sound in the middle; no one wants to be caught admiring that music, but the careful harmony of the preceding sounds has set us up beautifully. And the pace of lines 347, 357, and 359 is carefully controlled by clashing consonant sounds as well as by the use of long vowels. Line 347 moves incredibly slowly and seems much longer than it is because almost all the one-syllable words end in a consonant that refuses to blend with the beginning of the next word, making the words hard to say without distinct, awkward pauses between them. In lines 357 and 359, long vowels such as those in "wounded," "snake," "slow," "along," "roundly," and "smooth" help to slow down the pace, and awkward, hard-to-pronounce consonants are again juxtaposed. The commas also provide nearly a full stop in the midst of these lines to slow us down still more. Similarly, the harsh lashing of the shore in lines 368–69 is accomplished partly by onomatopoeia, partly by a shift in the pattern of stress, which creates irregular waves in line 368, and partly by the dominance of rough consonants in

4. A Greek hero of the Trojan War, noted for his strength.   5. A woman warrior in Virgil's *Aeneid*.
6. The court musician of Alexander the Great, celebrated in a famous poem by John Dryden (see line 383) for the power of his music over Alexander's emotions.
7. In Greek tradition, the chief god of any people was often given the name Zeus (Jove), and the chief god of Libya (the Greek name for all of Africa) was called Zeus Ammon. Alexander visited his oracle and was proclaimed son of the god.   8. Similar alternations of emotion.

line 369. (In Pope's time, the English *r* was still trilled gruffly so that it could be made to sound extremely rrrough and harrrsh.) Almost every line in this passage demonstrates how to make sound echo sense.

As "Sound and Sense" and "Dirge" suggest, poets most effectively manipulate sound by carefully controlling the rhythm of the voice so that not only are the proper sounds heard, but they are heard at precisely the right moment. Pace and rhythm are as important to a good poem as they are to a good piece of music. The human voice naturally develops certain rhythms in speech; some syllables and some words receive more stress than others. Just as multisyllabic words put more stress on some syllables than others (dictionaries always indicate which syllables are stressed), words in the context of a sentence receive more or less stress, depending on meaning. One-syllable words are thus sometimes stressed and sometimes not. A careful poet controls the flow of stresses so that, in many poems, a certain basic pattern of rhythm (or **meter**) develops almost like a quiet percussion instrument in the background. Not all poems have meter, and not all metered poems follow a single dominant rhythm, but many poems employ one pervasive pattern, and it is useful to look for patterns of stress.

In the Western world, we can thank the ancient Greeks for systematizing an understanding of meter and giving us a vocabulary (including the words *rhythm* and *meter*) that enables us to discuss the art of poetry. *Meter* comes from a Greek word meaning "measure": what we measure in the English language are the patterns of stressed (or "accented") syllables that occur naturally when we speak, and, just as when we measure length, the unit we use in measuring poetry is the **foot.** Most traditional poetry in English uses the accentual-syllabic form of meter—meaning that its rhythmic pattern is based on both a set number of syllables per line and a regular pattern of accents in each line. The most common metrical pattern is **iambic,** in which each foot contains an unstressed syllable followed by a stressed one. Consider, for example, the first two lines of Alexander Pope's "Sound and Sense," here marked to show the stressed syllables:

> But móst | by núm- | bers júdge | a pó- | et's sóng,
> And smóoth | or róugh, | with thém,| is ríght | or wróng.

These lines, like so many in English literature, provide an example of **iambic pentameter**—that is, the lines are written in a meter consisting of five iambic feet. Notice that there is nothing forced or artificial in the sound of these lines; the words flow easily. In fact, linguists contend that English is naturally iambic, and even the most ordinary, "unpoetic" utterances often fall into this pattern: "Please tell me if you've heard this one before." "They said she had a certain way with words." "The baseball game was televised at nine."

Besides the iamb, other metrical feet include the following:

trochee—an accented syllable followed by an unstressed one ("méter," "Hómer")
anapest—two unaccented syllables followed by a stressed one ("comprehénd," "after yóu")
dactyl—an accented syllable followed by two unstressed ones ("róundabout," "dínnertime")

Line lengths are sometimes described in terms of the number of syllables: a *decasyllabic* line, for example, is ten syllables long; an *octosyllabic* is eight, etc. Much more commonly though, lines are described in terms of the number of feet. It is possible to write regular lines using any of the feet shown above:

iambic pentameter—"In sé- | quent tóil | all fór- | wards dó | con- | ténd . . ." (William Shakespeare)
trochaic octameter—"Ónce u- | pón a | mídnight | dréary, | whíle I | póndered, | wéak and | wéary . . ." (Edgar Allan Poe)
anapestic tetrameter—"There are mán- | y who sáy | that a dóg | has his dáy . . ." (Dylan Thomas)
dactylic hexameter—"Thís is the | fórest pri- | méval. The | múrmuring | pínes and the | hémlocks . . ." (Henry Wadsworth Longfellow)

Notice that this final example is perfectly regular until the final foot, a trochee. Few poems, in fact, are written entirely in regular lines, and substitution of one metrical foot for another—to accommodate idioms and conversational habits or to create a special effect or emphasis—is quite common, especially in the first foot of a line. Shakespeare often begins an iambic line with a trochee:

Líke as | the wáves | make towárds | the péb- | bled shóre . . .

The poet may introduce a **spondee,** for example—a pair of accented syllables. Consider this line from John Milton's *Paradise Lost,* a poem written mainly in iambic pentameter:

Rócks, cáves, | lákes, féns, | bógs, déns, | and Shádes | of Déath . . .

Here Milton substitutes three spondees for the first three iambs in a pentameter line. John Dryden's "To the Memory of Mr. Oldham" begins with two spondees:

Fárewéll, tóo líttle, and tóo látely knówn

A **caesura,** a short pause often (though not always) signaled by a mark of punctuation such as a comma, may interrupt a line, as in the example from Poe's "The Raven," above, or in most lines of more than five or six syllables. (Sometimes, other even more elaborate accentual variations are used—*amphybrachs,* for example, involve an unstressed syllable, a stressed one, and then another unstressed one—but such hybrids are seldom used in English verse.)

In traditional metrical poetry, the poet's art, just like the musician's, consists of establishing metrical patterns and then varying the patterns without breaking them. With just the few rhythmic building blocks shown above, poets can create an almost infinite variety of rhythms.

Here is a poem that names and illustrates many of the meters. If someone read it aloud and you charted the stressed ($-$) and unstressed ($\smile$) syllables, you would have a chart similar to that done by the poet himself in the text.

SAMUEL TAYLOR COLERIDGE

Metrical Feet

Lesson for a Boy

Trōchĕe trīps frŏm lōng tŏ shōrt;⁹
From long to long in solemn sort
Slōw Spōndēe stălks; strōng fŏot! yet ill able
Ēvĕr tŏ cōme ŭp wĭth Dāctȳl trĭsȳllăblĕ.
5 Ĭāmbĭcs mārch frŏm shŏrt tŏ lōng—
Wĭth ă lēap ănd ă bōund thĕ swĭft Ānăpĕsts thrōng;
One syllable long, with one short at each side,
Ămphībrăchȳs hāstes wĭth ă stātelȳ stride—
Fīrst ănd lāst bēing lōng, mĭddlĕ shŏrt, Ămphĭmācer
10 Strīkes hĭs thūndĕrĭng hōofs līke ă prōud hīgh-brĕd Rācer.
If Derwent¹ be innocent, steady, and wise,
And delight in the things of earth, water, and skies;
Tender warmth at his heart, with these meters to show it,
With sound sense in his brains, may make Derwent a poet—
15 May crown him with fame, and must win him the love
Of his father on earth and his Father above.
        My dear, dear child!
Could you stand upon Skiddaw,² you would not from its whole ridge
See a man who so loves you as your fond s. t. COLERIDGE.
1806

The following poem exemplifies dactylic rhythm (– ˘ ˘ or stressed syllable
followed by two unstressed ones).

WENDY COPE

Emily Dickinson

Higgledy-piggledy
Emily Dickinson
Liked to use dashes
Instead of full stops.

5 Nowadays, faced with such
Idiosyncrasy,
Critics and editors
Send for the cops.

        1986

---

9. The long and short marks over syllables are Coleridge's.
1. Written originally for Coleridge's son Hartley, the poem was later adapted for his younger son, Derwent.
2. A mountain in the lake country of northern England (where Coleridge lived in his early years), near the town of Derwent.

Limericks rely on **anapestic** meter (˘ ˘ −, or two unstressed syllables followed by a stressed one), although usually the first two syllables are in iambic meter (see below).

ANONYMOUS

There was a young girl from St. Paul,
Wore a newspaper-dress to a ball.
  The dress caught on fire
  And burned her entire
Front page, sporting section and all.

The following poem is composed in the more common **trochaic** meter (− ˘, a stressed syllable followed by an unstressed one).

SIR JOHN SUCKLING

Song

Why so pale and wan, fond Lover?
  Prithee why so pale?
Will, when looking well can't move her,
  Looking ill prevail?
5 Prithee why so pale?

Why so dull and mute, young Sinner?
  Prithee why so mute?
Will, when speaking well can't win her,
  Saying nothing do 't?
10 Prithee why so mute?

Quit, quit, for shame, this will not move,
  This cannot take her;
If of her self she will not love,
  Nothing can make her,
15 The Devil take her.

                1646

Like Pope's "Sound and Sense," the following poem uses the English language's most common poetic meter, **iambic** (˘ – , an unstressed syllable followed by a stressed one, which some would argue is the most "natural" rhythm for English).

JOHN DRYDEN

To the Memory of Mr. Oldham[3]

[handwritten annotation: Iambic Pentameter]

Farewell, too little, and too lately known, *[handwritten: 1st couplets]*
Whom I began to think and call my own;
For sure our souls were near allied, and thine
Cast in the same poetic mold with mine.
5 One common note on either lyre did strike,
And knaves and fools we both abhorred alike.
To the same goal did both our studies drive;
The last set out the soonest did arrive.
Thus Nisus fell upon the slippery place,
10 While his young friend performed and won the race.[4]
O early ripe! to thy abundant store
What could advancing age have added more?
It might (what nature never gives the young)
Have taught the numbers[5] of thy native tongue.
15 But satire needs not those, and wit will shine
Through the harsh cadence of a rugged line.[6]
A noble error, and but seldom made,
When poets are by too much force betrayed.
Thy generous fruits, though gathered ere their prime,
20 Still showed a quickness; and maturing time
But mellows what we write to the dull sweets of rhyme.
Once more, hail and farewell; farewell, thou young,
But ah too short, Marcellus[7] of our tongue;
Thy brows with ivy, and with laurels bound;
25 But fate and gloomy night encompass thee around.

1684

Scanning a poem line by line—that is, sorting out its metrical pattern—can be hard work, and few people enjoy the process (which is called **scansion**). Doing it right involves listening carefully to your voice as you read aloud, marking the

---

3. John Oldham (1653–1683), who like Dryden (see lines 3–6) wrote satiric poetry.
4. In Virgil's *Aeneid* (Book 5), Nisus (who is leading the race) falls and then trips the second runner so that his friend Euryalus can win.   5. Rhythms.
6. In Dryden's time, the English *r* was pronounced with a harsh, trilling sound.
7. Nephew of the Roman emperor Augustus; Marcellus died at twenty and was celebrated by Virgil in the *Aeneid*, Book 6.

stressed and unstressed syllables, counting the syllables and feet, and checking the rhyme patterns. Though there is no easy substitute for this work, there is often a major payoff in seeing the subtleties of a poet's craft as well as in hearing the poetry itself more fully and resonantly. If, for example, you chart "To the Memory of Mr. Oldham," you will notice some extraordinary variations in the basic iambic pattern, variations that signal special emphasis on certain key terms and that indicate structural changes and directions. Even the first line is highly irreg-ular—even though no pattern has yet been established in our ears. (Often, in fact, you will need to scan several lines before you can be sure of the "controlling" metrical pattern of a poem.) Possibly as many as seven syllables in this first line are stressed, rather than the expected five in a regular iambic pentameter line, and the effect is both to strongly emphasize Oldham's relatively unknown status (*too lit*-tle *and too late*-ly *known*) and to draw out, lengthily, in conjunction with the use of a series of long vowels, the reading of the line.

Hearing a poem properly involves practice—listening to others read poetry and especially to yourself as you read poems aloud, so that you get used to hearing your voice, so that you become confident about where the stresses fall, and so that the rhythms begin to play themselves out "naturally." Your dictionary will show you the stresses for every word of more than one syllable, and the governing stress of individual words will largely control the patterns in a line: if you read a line for its basic sense (almost, for a moment, as if it were prose), you will usually see the line's basic pattern. But single-syllable words can be a challenge because they may or may not get a stress depending on their syntactic function and the full meaning of the sentence. Normally, important functional words, such as nouns and verbs of one syllable, get stressed (as in normal conversation or in prose); but conjunc-tions (such as *and* or *but*), prepositions (such as *on* or *with*), and articles (such as *an* or *the*) do not. But you often need to make decisions as you say words aloud, decisions based on what the words actually convey and what the sentence means. Listen to yourself as you read aloud and be prepared for uncertainties. Sometimes you will even find your "normal" pronunciation being influenced or modified by the pattern your voice develops as you hear basic rhythms. The way you actually read a line, once you have "heard" the basic rhythm, is influenced by two factors: normal pronunciations and prose sense (on the one hand) and the predominant pattern of the poem (on the other). Since these two forces are constantly in tension and are sometimes contradictory, you can almost never fully predict the actual reading of a line, and good reading aloud (like every other art) depends less on formula than on subtlety and flexibility.

Because scanning lines is an imprecise craft, sometimes very good readers plau-sibly disagree about whether or not to stress certain syllables. Then, too, some stresses are stronger than others: the convention of calling syllables "stressed" or "unstressed" fails to measure degrees of stress—and meaning often dictates that some syllables be stressed *much* more heavily than others.

In addition, not every poem relies on a formal pattern of stresses. As we saw in "Sound and Sense" and "To the Memory of Mr. Oldham," a poem dominated by iambic meter might incorporate trochaic, anapestic, spondaic, or dactylic feet in one place or another to create a stylistic effect. Beyond that, a poet tired of or resistant to traditional vocal patterns might follow or create other patterns—or employ patternlessness—to form the sound of a poem. Counting only the number of syllables (and *not* stresses) in a line is one common variation, which early-twentieth-century poets such as Marianne Moore were especially fond of. Even more widespread is **free verse,** which does without any governing pattern of stresses or line lengths.

• • •

EDGAR ALLAN POE

WEB   *The Raven*

Once upon a midnight dreary, while I pondered, weak and weary,
Over many a quaint and curious volume of forgotten lore,
While I nodded, nearly napping, suddenly there came a tapping,
As of some one gently rapping, rapping at my chamber door.
5 " 'Tis some visitor," I muttered, "tapping at my chamber door—
                Only this, and nothing more."

Ah, distinctly I remember it was in the bleak December,
And each separate dying ember wrought its ghost upon the floor.
Eagerly I wished the morrow;—vainly I had sought to borrow
10 From my books surcease of sorrow—sorrow for the lost Lenore—
For the rare and radiant maiden whom the angels name Lenore—
                Nameless here for evermore.

And the silken sad uncertain rustling of each purple curtain
Thrilled me—filled me with fantastic terrors never felt before;
15 So that now, to still the beating of my heart, I stood repeating
" 'Tis some visitor entreating entrance at my chamber door;—
Some late visitor entreating entrance at my chamber door;—
                This it is, and nothing more."

Presently my soul grew stronger; hesitating then no longer,
20 "Sir," said I, "or Madam, truly your forgiveness I implore;
But the fact is I was napping, and so gently you came rapping,
And so faintly you came tapping, tapping at my chamber door,
That I scarce was sure I heard you"—here I opened wide the door;—
                Darkness there, and nothing more.

25 Deep into that darkness peering, long I stood there wondering, fearing,
Doubting, dreaming dreams no mortal ever dared to dream before;
But the silence was unbroken, and the darkness gave no token,
And the only word there spoken was the whispered word, "Lenore!"
This I whispered, and an echo murmured back the word, "Lenore!"—
30   Merely this, and nothing more.

Back into the chamber turning, all my soul within me burning,
Soon I heard again a tapping somewhat louder than before.
"Surely," said I, "surely that is something at my window lattice;
Let me see, then, what thereat is, and this mystery explore—

35 Let my heart be still a moment and this mystery explore;—
                    'Tis the wind and nothing more!"

Open here I flung the shutter, when, with many a flirt and flutter,
In there stepped a stately raven of the saintly days of yore;
Not the least obeisance made he; not an instant stopped or stayed he;
40 But, with mien of lord or lady, perched above my chamber door—
Perched upon a bust of Pallas[8] just above my chamber door—
                    Perched, and sat, and nothing more.

Then this ebony bird beguiling my sad fancy into smiling,
By the grave and stern decorum of the countenance it wore,
45 "Though thy crest be shorn and shaven, thou," I said, "art sure no craven,
Ghastly grim and ancient raven wandering from the Nightly shore—
Tell me what thy lordly name is on the Night's Plutonian[9] shore!"
                    Quoth the raven, "Nevermore."

Much I marvelled this ungainly fowl to hear discourse so plainly,
50 Though its answer little meaning—little relevancy bore,
For we cannot help agreeing that no living human being
Ever yet was blessed with seeing bird above his chamber door—
Bird or beast upon the sculptured bust above his chamber door,
                    With such name as "Nevermore."

55 But the raven, sitting lonely on the placid bust, spoke only
That one word, as if his soul in that one word he did outpour.
Nothing farther then he uttered—not a feather then he fluttered—
Till I scarcely more than muttered "Other friends have flown before—
On the morrow *he* will leave me, as my hopes have flown before."
60   Then the bird said "Nevermore."

Startled at the stillness broken by reply so aptly spoken,
"Doubtless," said I, "what it utters is its only stock and store
Caught from some unhappy master whom unmerciful Disaster
Followed fast and followed faster till his songs one burden bore—
65 Till the dirges of his Hope that melancholy burden bore
                    Of 'Never—nevermore.' "

But the raven still beguiling all my sad soul into smiling,
Straight I wheeled a cushioned seat in front of bird and bust and door;
Then, upon the velvet sinking, I betook myself to linking
70 Fancy unto fancy, thinking what this ominous bird of yore—
What this grim, ungainly, ghastly, gaunt, and ominous bird of yore
                    Meant in croaking "Nevermore."

This I sat engaged in guessing, but no syllable expressing
To the fowl whose fiery eyes now burned into my bosom's core;
75 This and more I sat divining, with my head at ease reclining
On the cushion's velvet lining that the lamplight gloated o'er,

8. Athena, the Greek goddess of wisdom. 9. Dark; Pluto was god of the underworld.

But whose velvet violet lining with the lamplight gloating o'er,
     She shall press, ah, nevermore!

Then, methought, the air grew denser, perfumed from an unseen censer
80 Swung by angels whose faint foot-falls tinkled on the tufted floor.
"Wretch," I cried, "thy God hath lent thee—by these angels he hath sent thee
Respite—respite and nepenthe[1] from thy memories of Lenore!
Quaff, oh quaff this kind nepenthe and forget this lost Lenore!"
     Quoth the raven, "Nevermore."

85 "Prophet!" said I, "thing of evil!—prophet still, if bird or devil!—
Whether Tempter sent, or whether tempest tossed thee here ashore,
Desolate, yet all undaunted, on this desert land enchanted—
On this home by Horror haunted—tell me truly, I implore—
Is there—*is* there balm in Gilead?[2]—tell me—tell me, I implore!"
90   Quoth the raven, "Nevermore."

"Prophet!" said I, "thing of evil—prophet still, if bird or devil!
By that Heaven that bends above us—by that God we both adore—
Tell this soul with sorrow laden if, within the distant Aidenn,[3]
It shall clasp a sainted maiden whom the angels name Lenore—
95 Clasp a rare and radiant maiden whom the angels name Lenore."
     Quoth the raven, "Nevermore."

"Be that word our sign of parting, bird or fiend!" I shrieked upstarting—
"Get thee back into the tempest and the Night's Plutonian shore!
Leave no black plume as a token of that lie thy soul hath spoken!
100 Leave my loneliness unbroken!—quit the bust above my door!
Take thy beak from out my heart, and take thy form from off my door!"
     Quoth the raven, "Nevermore."

And the raven, never flitting, still is sitting, still is sitting
On the pallid bust of Pallas just above my chamber door;
105 And his eyes have all the seeming of a demon's that is dreaming,
And the lamp-light o'er him streaming throws his shadow on the floor;
And my soul from out that shadow that lies floating on the floor
     Shall be lifted—nevermore!

                                             1844

- Describing the composition of "The Raven," Poe wrote of the need to use sounds "in the fullest possible keeping with that melancholy which I had predetermined as the tone of the poem." List at least five of the sound effects (e.g., rhyme, alliteration, etc.) that Poe uses in "The Raven." How does each of these contribute to the poem's tone of "melancholy"?

1. A drug reputed by the Greeks to cause forgetfulness or sorrow (pronounced "ne-PEN-thee").
2. See Jeremiah 8.22.   3. Eden.

WILLIAM SHAKESPEARE

[CD] *[Like as the waves make towards the pebbled shore]*

Like as the waves make towards the pebbled shore,
So do our minutes hasten to their end,
Each changing place with that which goes before,
In sequent toil all forwards do contend.[4]
5 Nativity, once in the main[5] of light,
Crawls to maturity, wherewith being crowned,
Crooked[6] eclipses 'gainst his glory fight,
And Time that gave doth now his gift confound.[7]
Time doth transfix[8] the flourish set on youth
10 And delves the parallels[9] in beauty's brow,
Feeds on the rarities of nature's truth,
And nothing stands but for his scythe to mow.
And yet to times in hope[1] my verse shall stand,
Praising thy worth, despite his cruel hand.

1609

- Which lines in this poem vary the basic iambic metric scheme? What is the effect of these variations?

JAMES MERRILL

Watching the Dance

1. BALANCHINE'S[2]

Poor savage, doubting that a river flows
But for the myriad eddies made
By unseen powers twirling on their toes,

Here in this darkness it would seem
5 You had already died, and were afraid.
Be still. Observe the powers. Infer the stream.

---

4. Struggle. *Sequent:* successive.   5. High seas. *Nativity:* newborn life.   6. Perverse.   7. Bring to nothing.
8. Pierce.   9. Lines, wrinkles.   1. In the future.
2. George Balanchine (1904–1983), Russian-born ballet choreographer and teacher.

2. DISCOTHÈQUE

Having survived entirely your own youth,
Last of your generation, purple gloom
Investing you, sit, Jonah,[3] beyond speech,

10 And let towards the brute volume VOOM whale mouth
VAM pounding viscera VAM VOOM
A teenage plankton luminously twitch.

                                                    1967

• When you read this poem aloud, which lines flow most easily, and
  which contain abrupt pauses? If the first stanza of the poem is an
  imitation of a dance choreographed by Balanchine, what might this
  dance look like?

GERARD MANLEY HOPKINS

[CD] *Spring and Fall:*

to a young child

Márgarét áre you gríeving[4]
Over Goldengrove unleaving?
Leáves, like the things of man, you
With your fresh thoughts care for, can you?
5 Áh! ás the heart grows older
It will come to such sights colder
By and by, nor spare a sigh
Though worlds of wanwood leafmeal[5] lie;
And yet you wíll weep and know why.
10 Now no matter, child, the name:
Sórrow's spríngs áre the same.
Nor mouth had, no nor mind, expressed
What heart heard of, ghost[6] guessed:
It ís the blight man was born for,
15 It is Margaret you mourn for.

                                                    1880

• How does this poem's heavy use of alliteration serve its themes of
  youth and age, life and death?

---

3. According to Jonah 4, Jonah sat in gloom near Nineveh after its residents repented and God decided to
spare the city from destruction.   4. Hopkins's own accent markings.
5. Broken up, leaf by leaf (analogous to "piecemeal"). *Wanwood:* pale, gloomy woods.   6. Soul.

THEODORE ROETHKE

The Waking

I wake to sleep, and take my waking slow.
I feel my fate in what I cannot fear.
I learn by going where I have to go.

We think by feeling. What is there to know?
5 I hear my being dance from ear to ear.
I wake to sleep, and take my waking slow.

Of those so close beside me, which are you?
God bless the Ground! I shall walk softly there,
And learn by going where I have to go.

10 Light takes the Tree; but who can tell us how?
The lowly worm climbs up a winding stair;
I wake to sleep, and take my waking slow.

Great Nature has another thing to do
To you and me; so take the lively air,
15 And, lovely, learn by going where to go.

This shaking keeps me steady. I should know.
What falls away is always. And is near.
I wake to sleep, and take my waking slow.
I learn by going where I have to go.

                                    1953

- What traditional poetic form is employed by this poem? How does
  the pattern of repeated lines and sounds support the assertion in
  line 4 that "We think by feeling"?

LEE ANN BROWN

Foolproof Loofah

Lo! I fill prol pills
Poof! I rail pro lolls
Fool! I ill for lips
O Pale! I foil frail profs
5 Fop! I frill pale roils—
So! I proof oil spills

April Fool's!
                    1999

- Do the lines of this poem have meaning outside of their sound?
  How do the poem's first six lines set up the final one?

CYNTHIA ZARIN

Song

My heart, my dove, my snail, my sail, my
  milktooth, shadow, sparrow, fingernail,
    flower-cat and blossom-hedge, mandrake

root now put to bed, moonshell, sea-swell,
5   manatee, emerald shining back at me,
    nutmeg, quince, tea leaf and bone, zither,

cymbal, xylophone; paper, scissors, then
  there's stone—Who doesn't come through the door
    to get home?

                  1993

- Who might be the speaker—or perhaps the singer—of this poem?
  How else might the poem be arranged into lines in order to empha-
  size the rhyme words and the rhythmic pattern?

CAROL ANN DUFFY

Mrs. Sisyphus

That's him pushing the stone up the hill, the jerk.
I call it a stone—it's nearer the size of a kirk.
When he first started out, it just used to irk,
but now it incenses me, and him, the absolute berk.
5 I could do something vicious to him with a dirk.

Think of the perks, he says.
What use is a perk, I shriek,
when you haven't the time to pop open a cork
or go for so much as a walk in the park?
10 He's a dork.
Folk flock from miles around just to gawk.
They think it's a quirk,
a bit of a lark.
A load of old bollocks is nearer the mark.
15 He might as well bark
at the moon—
that feckin' stone's no sooner up
than it's rolling back
all the way down.

20 And what does he say?
Mustn't shirk—
keen as a hawk,
lean as a shark
Mustn't shirk!

25 But I lie alone in the dark,
feeling like Noah's wife did
when he hammered away at the Ark;
like Frau Johann Sebastian Bach.
My voice reduced to a squawk,
30 my smile to a twisted smirk;
while, up on the deepening murk of the hill,
he is giving one hundred per cent and more to his work.

2001

- How do the repeated sounds drive the poem and establish the tone? What might it indicate that the speaker gives Sisyphus himself the last word?

WORDS AND MUSIC

People often associate poetry with music, and there are good reasons—both historical and theoretical—for doing so. The word **lyric,** for example—the standard term for a short, harmonious, pleasant, and often romantic poem—derives from the ancient Greeks' practice of reciting or singing (and perhaps composing) certain poems to the accompaniment of a stringed, harplike musical instrument, the lyre. Throughout history, poems have been set to music for voices or instruments, and many "lyrics" have been created specifically to fit musical compositions. Many poems, especially during the Renaissance, were simply called "Song" (or "Chanson" or "Lied" or similar terms in other languages), and some were constructed in hybrid musical-poetic forms such as the madrigal, the dirge, the hymn, and so on.

The most fundamental link between poetry and music involves their almost equal dependence on the principles of rhythm. Both art forms have a basis in mathematics—a regular beat or syncopated sound pattern predicts (and to some extent determines) their phrasing and formal movement. Not all composers of either poetry or music have mathematical knowledge, but their crafts depend on an ability to hear (almost instinctively and certainly habitually) pacings, pauses, alternations, and relationships. Just as good musicians learn to listen and count so easily that it seems "natural," poets often develop an ear for rhythm that makes their sound choices effortless and, seemingly, automatic. Readers, too, can develop such an ear, and hearing the rhythms of poems can be crucial to the total effects they create.

There are movements, of course, in both poetry and music to suppress or ignore regular patterns in favor of "freer" sounds and repetitions, but the tendency of both arts to use rhythm predictably makes some comparisons (and some common terminology) desirable and useful for describing strategies and effects. But the parallels are often *not* precise, the relationships metaphoric rather than actual. Both poetry and music use representational or imitative strategies to create the illusion of sounds—bells, waves, motorcycles, for example—but words operate referentially in a way that sounds normally do not, and their syntax is of a different kind from that in musical composition. Readers can better appreciate sound effects in poetry by hearing musical relationships, but the referential fact of language almost always alters the "pure" effects of sound (except in nonsense lyrics or in poems like "Joy Sonnet in a Random Universe" or "What the Motorcycle Said," where simple sounds or tonal expressions are simply recorded and transliterated).

Poems composed to or for music tend to differ from poems that produce or rely on rhythmic, harmonic, or musical effects created solely by words themselves. Reading the lyrics of a song you know well (so that you, in effect, "hear" the music as you read the words) is quite different from reading words that have for you no musical association or history. You probably cannot stop yourself from hearing the music that accompanies lyrics by, say, the Beatles, and the music thus becomes for you, even when you just *read* the words, part of the total effect. But the "music" (or more exactly the percussive rhythms and patterns of sound) created by a poem itself can work in a similar way when there is no musical "source" or co-creation. To say that a poem makes or uses "music" can mean many different things.

The poems that follow were all written for, in conjunction with, or to imitate music. If you "update" this collection with lyrics from your favorite contemporary singers and groups, you may find that some lyrics that are very good when sung do not work well as "separate" poetic texts, whereas some make very good poems indeed. Can you, in the lyrics you know well, separate the actual musical implications from those of the words alone?

THOMAS RANDOLPH

A Song

Music, thou queen of souls, get up and string
Thy powerful lute, and some sad requiem sing,
    Till rocks requite thy echo with a groan,
    And the dull cliffs repeat the duller tone.
5 Then on a sudden with a nimble hand
Run gently o'er the chords, and so command
    The pine to dance, the oak his roots forgo,
    The holm and aged elm to foot it too;
Myrtles shall caper, lofty cedars run,
10 And call the courtly palm to make up one.
    Then, in the midst of all their jolly train,
    Strike a sad note, and fix 'em trees again.

1638

- What natural element does music personify in this poem? How does the poem balance sound and imagery?

THOMAS CAMPION

When to Her Lute Corinna Sings

When to her lute Corinna sings,
Her voice revives the leaden[1] strings,
And doth in highest notes appear
As any challenged[2] echo clear;
5 But when she doth of mourning speak,
Ev'n with her sighs the strings do break.

And as her lute doth live or die,
Led by her passion, so must I:
For when of pleasure she doth sing,
10 My thoughts enjoy a sudden spring;
But if she doth of sorrow speak,
Ev'n from my heart the strings do break.

1601

- How does Campion mimic an "echo" in this poem? What is the effect of this echoing?

WILLIAM SHAKESPEARE

Spring[3]

When daisies pied[4] and violets blue
  And ladysmocks all silver-white
And cuckoobuds of yellow hue
  Do paint the meadows with delight,
5 The cuckoo then, on every tree,
Mocks married men;[5] for thus sings he,
                Cuckoo;
Cuckoo, cuckoo: Oh word of fear,
Unpleasing to a married ear!

10 When shepherds pipe on oaten straws,
  And merry larks are plowmen's clocks,
When turtles tread,[6] and rooks, and daws,
  And maidens bleach their summer smocks,
The cuckoo then, on every tree,
15 Mocks married men; for thus sings he,
                Cuckoo;
Cuckoo, cuckoo: Oh word of fear,
Unpleasing to a married ear!

ca. 1595

- What words or phrases might a singer emphasize in order to enhance this poem's comic effect?

---

1. Heavy.   2. Aroused.   3. A song from *Love's Labour's Lost*.   4. Of varied colors.
5. By the resemblance of its call to the word *cuckold*.   6. Turtledoves copulate.

JOHN NEWTON

Faith's Review and Expectation

[I. Chronicles.] Chap. XVII. 16, 17.

Amazing grace! (how sweet the sound)
   That sav'd a wretch like me!
I once was lost, but now am found,
   Was blind, but now I see.

5 'Twas grace that taught my heart to fear,
   And grace my fears reliev'd;
How precious did that grace appear,
   The hour I first believ'd!

Thro' many dangers, toils and snares,
10   I have already come;
   'Tis grace has brought me safe thus far,
   And grace will lead me home.

The LORD has promis'd good to me,
   His word my hope secures;
15 He will my shield and portion be,
   As long as life endures.

Yes, when this flesh and heart shall fail,
   And mortal life shall cease;
I shall possess, within the vail,
20   A life of joy and peace.

The earth shall soon dissolve like snow,
   The sun forbear to shine;
But GOD, who call'd me here below,
   Will be for ever mine.

                            1779

- How does this poem sound without its well-known musical tune?
  What elements still help it to "sing"?

AUGUSTUS MONTAGUE TOPLADY

A Prayer, Living and Dying

I

ROCK of ages, cleft for me,
Let me hide myself in Thee!
Let the Water and the Blood,
From thy riven Side which flow'd,
5 Be of sin the double cure;
Cleanse me from its guilt and pow'r.

II

Not the labors of my hands
Can fulfill thy Law's demands:
Could my zeal no respite know,
10 Could my tears for ever flow,
All for sin could not atone;
Thou must save, and Thou alone.

III

Nothing in my hand I bring;
Simply to thy Cross I cling;
15 Naked, come to Thee for dress;
Helpless, look to Thee for grace;
Foul, I to the Fountain fly:
Wash me, SAVIOR, or I die!

IV

While I draw this fleeting breath—
20 When my eye-strings break in death—
When I soar to worlds unknown—
See Thee on thy judgment-throne—
ROCK of ages, cleft for me,
Let me hide myself in Thee!

1776

- What aspects of this poem might make it suitable for communal singing by untrained singers?

ROBERT HAYDEN

Homage to the Empress of the Blues[7]

Because there was a man somewhere in a candystripe silk shirt,
gracile and dangerous as a jaguar and because a woman moaned
for him in sixty-watt gloom and mourned him Faithless Love
Twotiming Love Oh Love Oh Careless Aggravating Love,

5   She came out on the stage in yards of pearls, emerging like
      a favorite scenic view, flashed her golden smile and sang.

Because grey laths began somewhere to show from underneath
torn hurdygurdy[8] lithographs of dollfaced heaven;
and because there were those who feared alarming fists of snow
10 on the door and those who feared the riot-squad of statistics,

      She came out on the stage in ostrich feathers, beaded satin,
      and shone that smile on us and sang.

                                                                      1962

- How do the two short stanzas beginning with "She came out" complete the thoughts of the longer stanzas that start with "Because"?

BILLY COLLINS

The Blues

Much of what is said here
must be said twice,
a reminder that no one
takes an immediate interest in the pain of others.

5 Nobody will listen, it would seem,
if you simply admit
your baby left you early this morning
she didn't even stop to say good-bye.

But if you sing it again
10 with the help of the band
which will now lift you to a higher,
more ardent and beseeching key,

people will not only listen;
they will shift to the sympathetic

---

7. Bessie Smith (1894 [or 1898?]–1937); legendary blues singer whose theatrical style grew out of the black American vaudeville tradition.   8. A disreputable kind of dance hall.

15 edges of their chairs,
   moved to such acute anticipation

by that chord and the delay that follows,
they will not be able to sleep
unless you release with one finger
20 a scream from the throat of your guitar

and turn your head back to the microphone
to let them know
you're a hard-hearted man
but that woman's sure going to make you cry.

1995

- What does this poem say about the importance of music in poetry?

MICHAEL HARPER

CD   *Dear John, Dear Coltrane*

  a love supreme, a love supreme
  a love supreme, a love supreme[9]

Sex fingers toes
in the marketplace
near your father's church
in Hamlet, North Carolina—[1]
5 witness to this love
in this calm fallow
of these minds,
there is no substitute for pain:
genitals gone or going,
10 seed burned out,
you tuck the roots in the earth,
turn back, and move
by river through the swamps,
singing: *a love supreme, a love supreme;*
15 what does it all mean?
Loss, so great each black
woman expects your failure
in mute change, the seed gone.
You plod up into the electric city—

9. Coltrane wrote "A Love Supreme" in response to a spiritual experience in 1957 that also led to his quitting heroin and alcohol. Mainly an instrumental improvisation featuring Coltrane's saxophone, the piece begins with the repeated chant of "a love supreme." The record was released in 1965.
1. Coltrane's birthplace. His family shared a house with Coltrane's grandfather, who was the minister of St. Stephen's AME Zion Church.

20 your song now crystal and
  the blues. You pick up the horn
  with some will and blow
  into the freezing night:
  a love supreme, a love supreme—

25 Dawn comes and you cook
  up the thick sin 'tween
  impotence and death, fuel
  the tenor sax cannibal
  heart, genitals and sweat
30 that makes you clean—
  a love supreme, a love supreme—

  Why you so black?
  cause I am
  why you so funky?
35 *cause I am*
  why you so black
  cause I am
  why you so sweet?
  cause I am
40 *why you so black?*
  cause I am
  a love supreme, a love supreme:

  So sick
  you couldn't play *Naima,*[2]
45 so flat we ached
  for song you'd concealed
  with your own blood,
  your diseased liver gave
  out its purity,
50 the inflated heart
  pumps out, the tenor kiss,
  tenor love:
  a love supreme, a love supreme—
  a love supreme, a love supreme—

         1970

- In what ways is this poem, as suggested by the title, both a "Dear John" letter and a poem of praise?

2. A song Coltrane wrote for and named after his wife, recorded in 1959.

CHARLES WRIGHT

Body and Soul

for Coleman Hawkins

The world's body is not our body,
       although we'd have it so.
Our body's not infinite, although
This afternoon, under the underwater slant-shine
5 Of sunlight and cloud shadow,
It almost seems that way in the wind,
        a wind that comes
From a world away with its sweet breath and its tart tongue
And casts us loose, like a cloud,
10 Heaven-ravaged, blue pocket, small change for the hand.

I used to think the power of words was inexhaustible,
That how we said the world
       was how it was, and how it would be.
I used to imagine that word-sway and word-thunder
15 Would silence the Silence and all that,
That words were the Word,
That language could lead us inexplicably to grace,
As though it were geographical.
20 I used to think these things when I was young.
         I still do.

Some poems exist still on the other side of our lives,
And shine out,
    but we'll never see them.
They are unutterable, in a language without an alphabet.
25 Unseen. World-long. Bone music.
Too bad. We'd know them by heart
      if we could summer them out in our wounds.
Too bad. Listening hard.
Clouds, of course, are everywhere, and blue sky in between.
30 Blue sky. Then what comes after the blue.

Our lives, it turns out, are still-lifes, glass bottles and fruit,
Dead animals, flowers,
      the edges of this and that
Which drop off, most often, to indeterminate vacancy.
35 We're beautiful, and hung up to dry.
        Outside the frame,
Mountains are moving, rivers flash, a cloud-scrumbled sky.
Field-patches nudge up to comfort us.
A train crosses a trestle.
40 Across the room, someone gets up and rearranges the things.

Insubstantial as smoke, our words
Drum down like fingertips across the page,

leaving no smudge or mark.
Unlike our purloined selves, they will not rise from the dead.
45 Unlike our whimpers and prayers, they lie low and disappear.
This word, that word, all fall down.
How far from heaven the stars are,
                            how far the heart from the page.

We don't know what counts—
50 It's as simple as that, isn't it,
                            we just don't know what counts.

Mid-winter in Charlottesville,
                            soul-shunt and pat-down, crumbs
Snow-flecked across the back yard, then gone on the sun's tongue.
55 These are the four lessons I have learned,
One from Martha Graham,
                            three others from here and there—
Walk as though you'd been given one brown eye and one blue,
Think as though you thought best with somebody else's brain,
60 Write as though you had in hand the last pencil on earth,
Pray as though you were praying with someone else's soul.

2002

- What musical and linguistic connections are there among the activities in
  Wright's four lessons (58–61): walking, thinking, writing, and praying? How does
  each relate to silence? to body and soul?

JAMES A. EMANUEL

Jazzanatomy

EVERYTHING is jazz:
snails, jails, rails, tails, males, females,
snow-white   cotton bales.

Knee-bone, thigh, hip-bone.
5 Jazz slips you percussion bone
classified "unknown."

Sleek lizard rhythms,
cigar-smoke tunes, straight-gin sky
laced with double moons.

10 Second-chance rhthyms,
don't-give-up riffs: jazz gets HIGH
off can'ts, buts, and ifs.

1999

- How does word choice in this poem create the overall sound and
  rhythm of jazz?

WILLIE PERDOMO

CD   *123rd Street Rap*

A day on
123rd Street

goes a little
something like
5   this:

Automatic bullets bounce
off stoop steps

It's about time to pay
all my debts

10   Church bells bong for
for drunken mourners

Baby men growing on
all the corners

Money that
15   ain't mine

Sun that
don't shine

Trees that
don't grow

20   Wind that
won't blow

Drug posses
ready to rumble

Ceilings starting
25   to crumble

Abuelas[3] close
eyes and pray

While they watch
the children play

30   Not much I
can say

---

3. Grandmothers.

Except day turns
to night

And I can't tell what's
35 wrong from what's right

on 123rd Street
1996

- Read "123rd Street Rap" first silently and then aloud. Does it "work" better one way or the other? Listen to the author reading this poem (on the CD). Has your opinion of it changed?

SUGGESTIONS FOR WRITING

1. Read Pope's "Sound and Sense" carefully twice—once silently and once aloud—and then mark the stressed and unstressed syllables. Draw up a chart indicating, line by line, exactly what the patterns of stress are, and then single out all the lines that have major variations from the basic iambic pentameter pattern. Pick out six lines with variations that seem to you worthy of comment, and write a paragraph on each in which you show how the varied metrical pattern contributes to the specific effects achieved in that line.

2. Try your hand at writing limericks in imitation of "There was a young girl from St. Paul"; study the rhythmic patterns and line lengths carefully, and imitate them exactly in your poem. Begin your limerick with "There once was a _____ from _____" (using a place for which you think you can find a comic rhyme).

3. Read Poe's "The Raven" aloud, paying particular attention to pacing. Do you find yourself speeding up as you continue through the poem? Does a quickening pace suit the speaker's growing exasperation and madness? Write an essay in which you examine the way that Poe underlines the poem's story and emotional flow with a range of poetic devices: line length, punctuation, rhyme, meter, and the sounds of words.

4. Pope's "Sound and Sense" contains this advice for poets: "But when loud surges lash the sounding shore, / The hoarse, rough verse should like the torrent roar" (lines 368–69). In other words, he counsels that the sound of the poet's description should match the sense of what the poem is describing. Write an essay in which you examine the sound and sense in Shakespeare's "[Like as the waves make towards the pebbled shore]"—how does the poem achieve a harmony of meaning and sound?

5. Write an essay in which you discuss any of the poems you have read in this book in which sound seems a more important element than anything else, even the meaning of words. What is the point of writing and reading this kind of poetry? Can it achieve its effects through silent reading, or must it be experienced aloud?

6. Is there a meaningful difference between poetry and song lyrics? between poetry and rap? Is hip-hop a form of literature? Write an essay in which you explore the definitions of "poetry" and "lyrics." Be sure to cite enough examples to illustrate your ideas.

6 INTERNAL STRUCTURE

"Proper words in proper places": that is how one great writer of English prose, Jonathan Swift, described good writing. A good poet finds appropriate words, and already we have looked at some implications for readers of the verbal choices a poet makes. But the poet must also decide where to put those words—how to arrange them for maximum effect—because individual words, metaphors, and symbols exist not only within phrases and sentences and rhythmic patterns but also within the larger whole of the poem. How should the words be arranged and the poem organized? What comes first and what last? Will the poem have a "plot"? What principle or idea of organization will inform it? How can words, sentences, images, ideas, and feelings be combined into a structure that holds together, seems complete, and affects readers?

Considering these questions from the poet's point of view (What is my plan? Where shall I begin?) can help us notice the effects of structural choices. Every poem works in its own unique way, and therefore every poet must make independent decisions about how to organize an individual poem. But poems do fall into patterns of organization, sometimes because of subject matter, sometimes because of effects intended, sometimes for other reasons. A poet may consciously decide on a particular strategy, may reach instinctively for one, or may happen into one that suits the needs of the moment—a framework onto which words and sentences will hang, one by one and group by group.

When a poem tells a story, the organization may be fairly straightforward. The following poem, for example, tells a simple story largely in chronological order:

EDWIN ARLINGTON ROBINSON
Mr. Flood's Party

Old Eben Flood, climbing alone one night
Over the hill between the town below
And the forsaken upland hermitage
That held as much as he should ever know
5 On earth again of home, paused warily.
The road was his and not a native near;
And Eben, having leisure, said aloud,
For no man else in Tilbury Town to hear:

"Well, Mr. Flood, we have the harvest moon
10 Again, and we may not have many more;

The bird is on the wing, the poet says,[1]
And you and I have said it here before.
Drink to the bird." He raised up to the light
The jug that he had gone so far to fill,
15 And answered huskily: "Well, Mr. Flood,
Since you propose it, I believe I will."

Alone, as if enduring to the end
A valiant armor of scarred hopes outworn
He stood there in the middle of the road
20 Like Roland's ghost winding a silent horn.[2]
Below him, in the town among the trees,
Where friends of other days had honored him,
A phantom salutation of the dead
Rang thinly till old Eben's eyes were dim.

25 Then, as a mother lays her sleeping child
Down tenderly, fearing it may awake
He set the jug down slowly at his feet
With trembling care, knowing that most things break;
And only when assured that on firm earth
30 It stood, as the uncertain lives of men
Assuredly did not, he paced away,
And with his hand extended paused again:

"Well, Mr. Flood, we have not met like this
In a long time; and many a change has come
35 To both of us, I fear, since last it was
We had a drop together. Welcome home!"
Convivially returning with himself,
Again he raised the jug up to the light;
And with an acquiescent quaver said:
40 "Well, Mr. Flood, if you insist, I might.

"Only a very little, Mr. Flood—
For auld lang syne. No more, sir; that will do."
So, for the time, apparently it did,
And Eben evidently thought so too;
45 For soon amid the silver loneliness
Of night he lifted up his voice and sang,
Secure, with only two moons listening,
Until the whole harmonious landscape rang—

"For auld lang syne." The weary throat gave out,
50 The last word wavered, and the song was done.
He raised again the jug regretfully
And shook his head, and was again alone.

1. Edward FitzGerald, in "The Rubáiyát of Omar Khayyám" (more or less a translation of a Persian original), so describes the "Bird of Time."
2. According to French legend, the hero Roland used his powerful ivory horn to warn his allies of impending attack.

There was not much that was ahead of him,
And there was nothing in the town below—
55 Where strangers would have shut the many doors
That many friends had opened long ago.

1921

The fairly simple **narrative structure** here is based on the gradual unfolding of the story. After old Eben is introduced and situated in relation to the town and his home, the "plot" unfolds: he sits down in the road, reviews his life, reflects on the present, and has a drink—several drinks, in fact, as he thinks about passing time and growing old; then he sings and considers going "home." Not much happens, really; we get a vignette of Mr. Flood between two places and two times. But there *is* action, and the poem's movement—its organization and structure—depends on it: Mr. Flood in motion, in stasis, and then, again, contemplating motion. This counts as event, and a certain, limited chronological movement. We could say that a spare sort of story takes place, like that in Dickey's "Cherrylog Road" (chapter 15). The poem's organization—its structural principle—involves the passing of time, action moving forward, a larger story being revealed by the few moments depicted here.

"Mr. Flood's Party" presents about as much story as a short poem ever does, but like most poems it doesn't really emphasize the developing action—which all seems fairly predictable once we "get" who Eben is, how old he is, and what place he occupies in the communal memory of Tilbury Town and vice versa. Rather, the movement forward in time dictates the shape of the poem, determines the way it presents its images, ideas, themes. Nearly everything occurs within an easy-to-follow chronology.

But even here, in this most simple narrative structure, we note complications. One complication is in the use of time itself, for "old" time and "present" time seem posed against each other as a structural principle, too, one in tension with the chronological movement: Eben's past, as contrasted with his present and limited future, focuses the poem's attention, and in some ways the contrast between what was and what is seems even more important than the brief movement through present time that gets the most obvious attention in the poem. Then, too, "character"—Eben's character and that of the townspeople of later generations—gets a lot of attention, even as the chronology moves forward. More than one structural principle is at work here. We may identify the main movement of the poem as chronological and its principal structure as narrative, but to be fair and full in our discussion we have to note several other competing organizational forces at work—principles of comparison and contrast, for example, and of descriptive elaboration.

Most poems work with this kind of complexity, and identifying a single structure behind any poem involves a sense of the organizational principle that makes it work, while at the same time recognizing that other principles repeatedly, perhaps continually, compete for our attention. A poem's structure involves its conceptual framework—what principle best explains its organization and movement—and it is often useful to identify one dominating kind of structure, such as narrative structure, that gives the poem its shape. But we need to recognize from the start that most poems follow structural models loosely. Finding an appropriate label to describe the structure of a particular poem can help in analyzing the poem's other aspects, but the label itself has no magic.

Back of the idea of organic form is the concept that there is a form in all things (and in our experience) which the poet can discover and reveal.

—DENISE LEVERTOV

Purely narrative poems are often very long and often include many features that are not, strictly speaking, closely connected to the narrative or linked to a strict chronology. Very often a poem moves from a narrative of an event to some sort of commentary or reflection on it, as in Philip Larkin's "Church Going" (below, in this chapter). Reflection can be included along the way or may be implicit in the way the story is narrated, as in Maxine Kumin's "Woodchucks" (chapter 1), where we focus more on the narrator and her responses than on the events in the story.

Just as poems sometimes take on a structure like that of a story, they sometimes borrow the structures of plays. The following poem has a **dramatic structure;** it consists of a series of scenes, each of which is presented vividly and in detail, as if on stage.

HOWARD NEMEROV

The Goose Fish

On the long shore, lit by the moon
To show them properly alone,
Two lovers suddenly embraced
So that their shadows were as one.
5 The ordinary night was graced
For them by the swift tide of blood
That silently they took at flood.
And for a little time they prized
   Themselves emparadised.

10 Then, as if shaken by stage-fright
Beneath the hard moon's bony light,
They stood together on the sand
Embarrassed in each other's sight
But still conspiring hand in hand,
15 Until they saw, there underfoot,
As though the world had found them out,
The goose fish turning up, though dead,
   His hugely grinning head.

There in the china light he lay,
20 Most ancient and corrupt and gray.
They hesitated at his smile,
Wondering what it seemed to say
To lovers who a little while
Before had thought to understand,
25 By violence upon the sand,

The only way that could be known
To make a world their own.

It was a wide and moony grin
Together peaceful and obscene;
30 They knew not what he would express,
So finished a comedian
He might mean failure or success,
But took it for an emblem of
Their sudden, new and guilty love
35 To be observed by, when they kissed,
    That rigid optimist.

So he became their patriarch,
Dreadfully mild in the half-dark.
His throat that the sand seemed to choke,
40 His picket teeth, these left their mark
But never did explain the joke
That so amused him, lying there
While the moon went down to disappear
Along the still and tilted track
45   That bears the zodiac.
                                        1955

The first stanza sets the scene—a sandy shore in moonlight—and presents, in fact, the major action of the poem. The rest of the poem dramatizes the lovers' reactions: their initial embarrassment and feelings of guilt (stanza 2), their attempt to interpret the goose fish's smile (stanza 3), their decision to make him, whatever his meaning, the "emblem" of their love (stanza 4), and their acceptance of the fish's ambiguity and of their own relationship (stanza 5). The five stanzas do not exactly present five different scenes or angles on the action, but they do present separate dramatic moments, even if little time has elapsed between them. Almost like a play of five very short acts, the poem traces the drama of the lovers' discovery of themselves and their coming to terms with the meaning of their action. As in many plays, the central event (their lovemaking) is not the central focus of the drama, although the drama is based upon that event and could not take place without it. The poem depicts that event swiftly but very vividly through figurative language: "they took at flood" the "swift tide of blood." The lovers then briefly feel "emparadised," but the poem concentrates on their later reactions.

Their sudden discovery of the fish, a rude shock, injects a grotesque, almost macabre, note into the poem. From a vision of paradise, the poem seems for a moment to turn toward gothic horror when the lovers discover that they have, after all, been seen—and by such a ghoulish spectator. The last three stanzas gradually re-create the intruder in their minds, as they admit that their act of love exists not in isolation, but rather as part of a continuum, as part of their relationship to the larger world, even (at the end) within the context of the earth itself, and the moon, and the stars. In retrospect, we can see that even at the moment of passion the lovers were in touch with larger processes controlled by the presiding moon ("the swift *tide* of blood"), but neither they nor we had understood their act as such then, and the poem is about this gradual recognition of their "place" in time and space.

Stages of feeling and knowing rather than specific visual scenes determine the poem's progress, and its dramatic structure depends upon internal perceptions and internal states of mind rather than dialogue and events. Visualization and images help to organize the poem, too. Notice in particular how the two most striking visual features—the fish and the moon—are presented stanza by stanza. In stanza 1, the fish does not appear, and the moon exists plain; it is only mentioned, not described, and its light provides a stage spotlight to assure not center-stage attention, but rather total privacy: the moon serves as a lookout for the lovers. The stage imagery, barely suggested by the light in stanza 1, is articulated in stanza 2, and there the moon is "hard" and its light "bony"; its characteristics seem more appropriate to the fish, which has now become visible. In stanza 3, the moon's light comes to seem fragile ("china") as it exposes the fish directly; the moon's role as lookout and protector seems abandoned, or at least endangered. No moon appears in stanza 4, but the fish's grin is "wide and moony," almost as if the two onlookers, one earthly and dead, the other heavenly and eternal, have merged, as they nearly were by the imagery in stanza 2. And in stanza 5, the fish becomes a friend, a comedian, an optimist, an emblem, and a patriarch of their love—and his new position in collaboration with the lovers is presided over by the moon going about its eternal business. The moon—providing the stage light for the poem and the means by which not only the fish but the meaning of the lovers' act is discovered—has also helped to organize the poem, partly as a dramatic accessory, partly as imagery.

The following dramatic poem represents a composite of several similar experiences (compare Blake's "London" [chapter 1] and Dickey's "Cherrylog Road" [chapter 3]) rather than a single event—a fairly common pattern in dramatic poems:

PHILIP LARKIN

Church Going

Once I am sure there's nothing going on
I step inside, letting the door thud shut.
Another church: matting, seats, and stone,
And little books; sprawlings of flowers, cut
5   For Sunday, brownish now; some brass and stuff
Up at the holy end; the small neat organ;
And a tense, musty, unignorable silence,
Brewed God knows how long. Hatless, I take off
My cycle-clips in awkward reverence,

10   Move forward, run my hand around the font.
From where I stand, the roof looks almost new—
Cleaned, or restored? Someone would know: I don't.
Mounting the lectern, I peruse a few

Hectoring large-scale verses, and pronounce
15 "Here endeth" much more loudly than I'd meant.
The echoes snigger briefly. Back at the door
I sign the book, donate an Irish sixpence,
Reflect the place was not worth stopping for.

Yet stop I did: in fact I often do,
20 And always end much at a loss like this,
Wondering what to look for; wondering, too,
When churches fall completely out of use
What we shall turn them into, if we shall keep
A few cathedrals chronically on show,
25 Their parchment, plate and pyx in locked cases,
And let the rest rent-free to rain and sheep.
Shall we avoid them as unlucky places?

Or, after dark, will dubious women come
To make their children touch a particular stone;
30 Pick simples³ for a cancer; or on some
Advised night see walking a dead one?
Power of some sort or other will go on
In games, in riddles, seemingly at random;
But superstition, like belief, must die,
35 And what remains when disbelief has gone?
Grass, weedy pavement, brambles, buttress, sky,

A shape less recognizable each week,
A purpose more obscure. I wonder who
Will be the last, the very last, to seek
40 This place for what it was; one of the crew
That tap and jot and know what rood-lofts⁴ were?
Some ruin-bibber,⁵ randy for antique,
Or Christmas-addict, counting on a whiff
Of gown-and-bands and organ-pipes and myrrh?
45 Or will he be my representative,

Bored, uninformed, knowing the ghostly silt
Dispersed, yet tending to this cross of ground
Through suburb scrub because it held unspilt
So long and equably what since is found
50 Only in separation—marriage, and birth,
And death, and thoughts of these—for whom was built
This special shell? For, though I've no idea
What this accoutered frowsty barn is worth,
It pleases me to stand in silence here;

3. Medicinal herbs.
4. Galleries atop the screens (on which crosses are mounted) that divide the naves or main bodies of churches from the choirs or chancels.
5. Literally, ruin-drinker: someone extremely attracted to antiquarian objects.

55 A serious house on serious earth it is,
   In whose blent⁶ air all our compulsions meet,
   Are recognized, and robed as destinies.
   And that much never can be obsolete,
   Since someone will forever be surprising
60 A hunger in himself to be more serious,
   And gravitating with it to this ground,
   Which, he once heard, was proper to grow wise in,
   If only that so many dead lie round.

                                                    1955

Ultimately, Larkin's poem focuses on what it means to visit churches, what it might be that church buildings represent, and what we should make of the fact that "church going" (in the usual sense of the word) has declined so much. The poem uses a *different* sort of church going (visitation by tourists) to consider larger questions about the relationship of religion to culture and history. The poem is, finally, a rather philosophical one about the directions of English culture, and through an enumeration of religious objects and rituals it reviews part of the history of that culture. It tells a kind of story first, through one lengthy dramatized scene, in order to comment later on what the place and the experience may mean, and the larger conclusion derives from the particulars of what the speaker does and touches. By the end of stanza 2 the action is over, but that action, we are told, stands for many such visits to similar churches; after that, the next five stanzas present reflection and discussion.

"Church Going" is a curious poem in many ways. It goes to a lot of trouble to characterize its speaker, who seems a rather odd choice as a commentator on the state of religion. His informal attire (he takes off his cycle-clips at the end of stanza 1) and his less than worshipful behavior do not at first make him seem like a serious philosopher. He is not disrespectful or sacrilegious, and before the end of stanza 1 he has tried to describe the "awkward reverence" he feels; but his overly emphatic imitation of part of the service stamps him as playful, a little satirical. He is a tourist here, not someone who regularly drops in for prayer or meditation in the usual sense. And yet those early details give him credentials, in a way; he knows the names of religious objects and has some history of churches in his grasp. Clearly he does this sort of church going habitually ("Yet stop I did: in fact I often do," line 19) because he wonders seriously what it all means—now—in comparison to what it meant to religious worshipers in times past. Ultimately, he takes the church, its cultural meaning, and its function seriously (lines 55 ff.), and he understands the importance of the church in the history of his culture. Thus the relatively brief drama provides a context for the rambling reflections that grow out of the speaker's dramatic experience.

Sometimes poems are organized by contrasts, and they conveniently set one thing up against another that is quite different. Notice, for example, how the following poem carefully contrasts two worlds:

6. Blended.

PAT MORA

Sonrisas

I live in a doorway
between two rooms, I hear
quiet clicks, cups of black
coffee, *click, click* like facts
5   budgets, tenure, curriculum,
from careful women in crisp beige
suits, quick beige smiles
that seldom sneak into their eyes.

I peek
10 in the other room señoras
in faded dresses stir sweet
milk coffee, laughter whirls
with steam from fresh *tamales*
    sh, sh, mucho ruido,[7]
15 they scold one another,
press their lips, trap smiles
in their dark, Mexican eyes.

                         1986

    Here different words, habits, and values characterize the worlds of the two sets of characters, and the poem is organized largely by the contrasts between them. The meaning of the poem (the difference between the two worlds) is very nearly the same as the structure.

    Poems often have **discursive structures,** too; that is, they may be organized like a treatise, an argument, or an essay. "First," they say, "and second . . . and third . . ." This sort of 1–2–3 structure takes a variety of forms depending on what is being enumerated or argued. Discursive structures help organize poems such as Shelley's "Ode to the West Wind" (later in this chapter), where the wind drives a leaf in Part I, a cloud in Part II, and a wave in Part III, and then, after a summary and statement of the speaker's ambitious hope in Part IV, is asked to make the speaker a lyre in Part V.

    Poems may borrow their organizational strategies from many places, imitating chronological, visual, or discursive shapes in reality or in other works of art. Sometimes poems strive to be almost purely descriptive of someone or something (using **descriptive structures**), in which case poets have to make organizational decisions much as painters or photographers would, deciding first how a whole scene should look, then putting the parts into proper place for the whole. Of course, poems must present their details sequentially, not all at once as actual pictures more or less can, so poets must decide where to start a description (at the left? center? top?) and what sort of movement to use (linear across the scene? clockwise?). But if using words instead of paint or film has some drawbacks, it also has particular

7. A lot of noise.

advantages: figurative language can be a part of description, or an adjunct to it. Poets can insert comparisons at any point without necessarily disturbing the unity of their descriptions.

Some poems use **imitative structures,** mirroring as exactly as possible the structure of something that already exists as an object and can be seen—another poem perhaps. Other poems use **reflective (or meditative) structures,** pondering a subject, theme, or event, and letting the mind play with it, skipping (logically or not) from one sound to another, or to related thoughts or objects as the mind encounters them.

Although the following poem employs several organizational principles, it ultimately takes its structure from an important shift in the speaker's attitude as she reviews, ponders, and rethinks events of long ago.

SHARON OLDS

The Victims

When Mother divorced you, we were glad. She took it and
took it, in silence, all those years and then
kicked you out, suddenly, and her
kids loved it. Then you were fired, and we
5   grinned inside, the way people grinned when
Nixon's helicopter lifted off the South
Lawn for the last time.[8] We were tickled
to think of your office taken away,
your secretaries taken away,
10 your lunches with three double bourbons,
your pencils, your reams of paper. Would they take your
suits back, too, those dark
carcasses hung in your closet, and the black
noses of your shoes with their large pores?
15 She had taught us to take it, to hate you and take it
until we pricked with her for your
annihilation, Father. Now I
pass the bums in doorways, the white
slugs of their bodies gleaming through slits in their
20 suits of compressed silt, the stained
flippers of their hands, the underwater
fire of their eyes, ships gone down with the
lanterns lit, and I wonder who took it and
took it from them in silence until they had
25 given it all away and had nothing
left but this.

1984

---

8. When Richard Nixon resigned the U.S. presidency on August 8, 1974, his exit from the White House (by helicopter from the lawn) was televised live.

"The Victims" divides basically into two parts. In the first two-thirds of the poem (from line 1 to the middle of line 17), the speaker evokes her father (the "you" of lines 1, 3, and so forth), who had been guilty of terrible habits and behavior when the speaker was young and was kicked out suddenly and divorced by the speaker's mother (lines 1–3). He was then fired from his job (line 4) and lost his whole way of life (lines 8–12), and the speaker (taught by the mother, lines 15–17) recalls celebrating every defeat and every loss ("we pricked with her for your annihilation," lines 16–17). The mother is regarded as a victim ("She took it and took it, in silence, all those years" [lines 1–2]), and the speaker forms an indivisible unit with her and the other children ("her kids," lines 3–4). They are the "we" of the first part of the poem. They were "glad" (line 1) at the divorce; they "loved it" (line 4) when the mother kicked out the father; they "grinned" (line 5) when the father was fired; they were "tickled" (line 7) when he lost his job, his secretaries, and his daily life. Only at the end of the first section does the speaker (now older but remembering what it was like to be a child) recognize that the mother was responsible for the easy, childish vision of the father's guilt ("She had taught us to take it, to hate you and take it" [line 15]); nevertheless, all sympathy in this part of the poem is with the mother and her children, while all of the imagery is entirely unfavorable to the father. The family reacted to the father's misfortunes the way observers responded to the retreat in disgrace of Richard Nixon from the U.S. presidency. The father seems to have led a luxurious and insensitive life, with lots of support in his office (lines 8–11), fancy clothes (lines 12–14), and decadent lunches (line 10); his artificial identity seemed haunting and frightening (lines 11–14) to the speaker as child.

But in line 17, the poem shifts its focus and tone. The "you" in the poem is now, suddenly, "Father." A bit of sympathy begins to surface for "bums in doorways" (line 18), who begin to seem like victims, too; their bodies are "slugs" (line 19), their suits are made of residual waste (lines 19–20), and their hands are reduced to nearly useless "flippers" (line 21). Their eyes contain fire (line 22), but it is as if they retain only a spark of life in their submerged and dying state. The speaker has not forgotten the cruelty and insensitivity remembered in the first part of the poem, but the blame seems to have shifted somewhat and the father is not the only villain, nor are the mother and children the only victims. Look carefully at how the existence of street people recalls earlier details about the father, how sympathy for his plight is elicited from us, and how the definition of *victim* shifts.

Imagery, words, attitudes, and narrative are different in the two parts of the poem, and the second half carefully qualifies the first, as if to illustrate the more mature and considered attitudes of the speaker in her older years—a qualification of the easy imitation of the earlier years, when the mother's views dominated and set the tone. Change has governed the poem's structure here; differences in age and attitude are supported by an entirely different point of view and frame of reference.

The paradigms (or models) for organizing poems are, finally, not all that different from those of prose. It may be easier to organize something short rather than something long, but the question of intensity becomes comparatively more important in shorter works. Basically, the problem of how to organize one's material is, for the writer, first of all a matter of deciding what kind of thing one wants to create, of having its purposes and effects clearly in mind. That means that every poem will differ somewhat from every other, but it also means that purposeful patterns—narrative, dramatic, descriptive, imitative, or reflective—may help writers organize and develop their ideas. A consciousness of purpose and effect can help the reader see *how* a poem proceeds toward its goal. And seeing how a poem is organized is, in turn, often a good way of seeing where it is going and what its real concerns and purposes may be. Often a poem's organization helps to clarify the particular effects that the poet wishes to generate. In a good poem, means and ends are closely related, and a reader who is a good observer of one will be rewarded with the other.

• • •

ANONYMOUS

Sir Patrick Spens

The king sits in Dumferling toune,[9]
  Drinking the blude-reid[1] wine:
"O whar will I get guid sailor,
  To sail this ship of mine?"

5 Up and spake an eldern knicht,
  Sat at the king's richt knee:
"Sir Patrick Spens is the best sailor
  That sails upon the sea."

The king has written a braid[2] letter
10 And signed it wi' his hand,
And sent it to Sir Patrick Spens,
  Was walking on the sand.

The first line that Sir Patrick read,
  A loud lauch[3] lauched he;
15 The next line that Sir Patrick read,
  The tear blinded his ee.[4]

"O wha is this has done this deed,
  This il deed done to me,
To send me out this time o' the year,
20 To sail upon the sea?

"Make haste, make haste, my merry men all,
  Our guid ship sails the morn."
"O say na sae,[5] my master dear,
  For I fear a deadly storm.

25 "Late, late yestre'en I saw the new moon
  Wi' the auld moon in her arm,
And I fear, I fear, my dear mastér,
  That we will come to harm."

9. Town.   1. Blood-red.   2. Broad: explicit.   3. Laugh.   4. Eye.   5. Not so.

O our Scots nobles were richt laith[6]
30   To weet their cork-heeled shoon,[7]
But lang owre a'[8] the play were played
Their hats they swam aboon.[9]

O lang, lang, may their ladies sit,
Wi' their fans into their hand,
35 Or ere they see Sir Patrick Spens
Come sailing to the land.

O lang, lang, may the ladies stand
Wi' their gold kems[1] in their hair,
Waiting for their ain[2] dear lords,
40   For they'll see them na mair.

Half o'er, half o'er to Aberdour
It's fifty fadom deep,
And there lies guid Sir Patrick Spens
Wi' the Scots lords at his feet.

probably 13th century

- What event is hinted at in line 32 ("Their hats they swam aboon")
  and in the poem's final stanza? What is the effect of depicting the
  poem's principal action indirectly?

JAMES WRIGHT

Arrangements with Earth for Three Dead Friends

Sweet earth, he ran and changed his shoes to go
Outside with other children through the fields.
He panted up the hills and swung from trees
Wild as a beast but for the human laughter
5 That tumbled like a cider down his cheeks.
Sweet earth, the summer has been gone for weeks,
And weary fish already sleeping under water
Below the banks where early acorns freeze.
Receive his flesh and keep it cured of colds.
10 Button his coat and scarf his throat from snow.

And now, bright earth, this other is out of place
In what, awake, we speak about as tombs.
He sang in houses when the birds were still
And friends of his were huddled round till dawn
15 After the many nights to hear him sing.

6. Right loath: very reluctant.
7. To wet their cork-heeled shoes. Cork was expensive, and, therefore, such shoes were a mark of wealth
and status.   8. Before all.   9. Their hats swam above them.   1. Combs.   2. Own.

Bright earth, his friends remember how he sang
Voices of night away when wind was one.
Lonely the neighborhood beneath your hill
Where he is waved away through silent rooms.
20 Listen for music, earth, and human ways.

Dark earth, there is another gone away,
But she was not inclined to beg of you
Relief from water falling or the storm.
She was aware of scavengers in holes
25 Of stone, she knew the loosened stones that fell
Indifferently as pebbles plunging down a well
And broke for the sake of nothing human souls.
Earth, hide your face from her where dark is warm.
She does not beg for anything, who knew
30 The change of tone, the human hope gone gray.

1957

• What is distinct in the tone, language, and imagery of each of the
poem's three sections? What gives the poem an overall unity, making
it one poem, not three?

PERCY BYSSHE SHELLEY

Ode to the West Wind

I

O wild West Wind, thou breath of Autumn's being,
Thou, from whose unseen presence the leaves dead
Are driven, like ghosts from an enchanter fleeing,

Yellow, and black, and pale, and hectic red,
5 Pestilence-stricken multitudes: O thou,
Who chariotest to their dark wintry bed

The wingéd seeds, where they lie cold and low,
Each like a corpse within its grave, until
Thine azure sister of the Spring shall blow

10 Her clarion[3] o'er the dreaming earth, and fill
(Driving sweet buds like flocks to feed in air)
With living hues and odors plain and hill:

Wild Spirit, which art moving everywhere;
Destroyer and preserver; hear, oh, hear!

---

3. Trumpet call.

II

15 Thou on whose stream, mid the steep sky's commotion,
Loose clouds like earth's decaying leaves are shed,
Shook from the tangled boughs of Heaven and Ocean,

Angels[4] of rain and lightning: there are spread
On the blue surface of thine aëry surge,
20 Like the bright hair uplifted from the head

Of some fierce Maenad,[5] even from the dim verge
Of the horizon to the zenith's height,
The locks of the approaching storm. Thou dirge

Of the dying year, to which this closing night
25 Will be the dome of a vast sepulcher,
Vaulted with all thy congregated might

Of vapors, from whose solid atmosphere
Black rain, and fire, and hail will burst: oh, hear!

III

Thou who didst waken from his summer dreams
30 The blue Mediterranean, where he lay,
Lulled by the coil of his crystálline streams,

Beside a pumice isle in Baiae's bay,[6]
And saw in sleep old palaces and towers
Quivering within the wave's intenser day,

35 All overgrown with azure moss and flowers
So sweet, the sense faints picturing them! Thou
For whose path the Atlantic's level powers

Cleave themselves into chasms, while far below
The sea-blooms and the oozy woods which wear
40 The sapless foliage of the ocean, know

Thy voice, and suddenly grow gray with fear,
And tremble and despoil themselves:[7] oh, hear!

IV

If I were a dead leaf thou mightest bear;
If I were a swift cloud to fly with thee;
45 A wave to pant beneath thy power, and share

The impulse of thy strength, only less free
Than thou, O uncontrollable! If even
I were as in my boyhood, and could be

---

4. Messengers.
5. A frenzied female votary of Dionysus, the Greek god of vegetation and fertility who was supposed to die in the fall and rise again each spring.   6. Where Roman emperors had erected villas, west of Naples.
7. The vegetation at the bottom of the sea . . . sympathizes with that of the land in the change of seasons [Shelley's note].

The comrade of thy wanderings over Heaven,
50 As then, when to outstrip thy skyey speed
Scarce seemed a vision; I would ne'er have striven

As thus with thee in prayer in my sore need.
Oh, lift me as a wave, a leaf, a cloud!
I fall upon the thorns of life! I bleed!

55 A heavy weight of hours has chained and bowed
One too like thee: tameless, and swift, and proud.

                    V

Make me thy lyre, even as the forest is:
What if my leaves are falling like its own!
The tumult of thy mighty harmonies

60 Will take from both a deep, autumnal tone,
Sweet though in sadness. Be thou, Spirit fierce,
My spirit! Be thou me, impetuous one!

Drive my dead thoughts over the universe
Like withered leaves to quicken a new birth!
65 And, by the incantation of this verse,

Scatter, as from an unextinguished hearth
Ashes and sparks, my words among mankind!
Be through my lips to unawakened earth

The trumpet of a prophecy! O Wind,
70 If Winter comes, can Spring be far behind?

                                        1820

- What attributes of the West Wind does the speaker want his poetry
  to embody? In what ways is this poem like the wind it describes?

WILLIAM CARLOS WILLIAMS

The Dance

In Brueghel's great picture, The Kermess,[8]
the dancers go round, they go round and
around, the squeal and the blare and the
tweedle of bagpipes, a bugle and fiddles
5 tipping their bellies (round as the thick-
sided glasses whose wash they impound)
their hips and their bellies off balance
to turn them. Kicking and rolling about
the Fair Grounds, swinging their butts, those
10 shanks must be sound to bear up under such

---

8. A painting by Pieter Brueghel the Elder (1525?–1569).

rollicking measures, prance as they dance
in Brueghel's great picture, The Kermess.

1944

- Why is it appropriate to the subject, a painting, to begin and end
  the poem with the same line? In what ways is the poem like the
  dance it depicts?

EMILY DICKINSON

[*The Wind begun to knead the Grass—*]

The Wind begun to knead the Grass—
As Women do a Dough—
He flung a Hand full at the Plain—
A Hand full at the Sky—
5 The Leaves unhooked themselves from Trees—
And started all abroad—
The Dust did scoop itself like Hands—
And throw away the Road—
The Wagons quickened on the Street—
10 The Thunders gossiped low—
The Lightning showed a Yellow Head—
And then a livid Toe—
The Birds put up the Bars to Nests—
The Cattle flung to Barns—
15 Then came one drop of Giant Rain—
And then, as if the Hands
That held the Dams—had parted hold—
The Waters Wrecked the Sky—
20 But overlooked my Father's House—
Just Quartering a Tree—

1864

- What happens in this poem's final line? How is this the work of
  "the Hands"?

GAIL MAZUR

Desire

It was a kind of torture—waiting
to be kissed. A dark car parked away
from the street lamp, away from our house

where my tall father would wait, his face
5 visible at a pane high in the front door.
Was my mother always asleep? A boy
reached for me, I leaned eagerly into him,
soon the windshield was steaming.

Midnight. A neighbor's bedroom light
10 goes on, then off. The street is quiet....

Until I married, I didn't have my own key,
that wasn't how it worked, not at our house.
You had to wake someone with the bell,
or he was there, waiting. Someone let you in.
15 Those pleasures on the front seat of a boy's
father's car were "guilty," yet my body knew
they were the only right thing to do,

my body hated the cage it had become.

One of those boys died in a car crash;
20 one is a mechanic; one's a musician.
They were young and soft and, mostly, dumb.
I loved their lips, their eyebrows, the bones
of their cheeks, cheeks that scraped mine raw,
so I'd turn away from the parent who let me
25 angrily in. And always, the next day,

no one at home could penetrate the fog
around me. I'd relive the precious night
as if it were a bridge to my new state
from the old world I'd been imprisoned by,
30 and I've been allowed to walk on it, to cross
a border—there's an invisible line
in the middle of the bridge, in the fog,
where I'm released, where I think I'm free.

                                        1995

- What gives each of the poem's four longer stanzas its particular
  cohesion? Why do you think lines 9–10 and line 18 are separate from
  the longer stanzas?

ROO BORSON

Save Us From

Save us from night,
from bleak open highways
without end, and the fluorescent
oases of gas stations,

5 from the gunning of immortal
engines past midnight,
when time has no meaning,
from all-night cafés,
their ghoulish slices of pie,
10 and the orange ruffle on the
apron of the waitress,
the matching plastic chairs,
from orange and brown and
all unearthly colors,
15 banish them back to the test tube,
save us from them,
from those bathrooms with a
moonscape of skin in the mirror,
from fatigue, its merciless brightness,
20 when each cell of the body stands on end,
and the sensation of teeth,
and the mind's eternal sentry,
and the unmapped city
with its cold bed.
25 Save us from insomnia,
its treadmill,
its school bells and factory bells,
from living-rooms like the tomb,
their plaid chesterfields
30 and galaxies of dust,
from chairs without arms,
from any matched set of furniture,
from floor-length drapes which
close out the world,
35 from padded bras and rented suits,
from any object in which horror is concealed.
Save us from waking after nightmares,
save us from nightmares,
from other worlds,
40 from the mute, immobile contours
of dressers and shoes,
from another measureless day, save us.

1989

- What is distinct about each section of the poem forming a complete
  sentence—lines 1–24, lines 25–36, and lines 37–42? Is the succession
  of topics and images in each section merely random, or can you
  detect a pattern?

CATHY SONG

Heaven

He thinks when we die we'll go to China.
Think of it—a Chinese heaven
where, except for his blond hair,
the part that belongs to his father,
5   everyone will look like him.
China, that blue flower on the map,
bluer than the sea
his hand must span like a bridge
to reach it.
10   An octave away.

I've never seen it.
It's as if I can't sing that far.
But look—
on the map, this black dot.
15   Here is where we live,
on the pancake plains
just east of the Rockies,
on the other side of the clouds.
A mile above the sea,
20   the air is so thin, you can starve on it.
No bamboo trees
But the alpine equivalent,
reedy aspen with light, fluttering leaves.
Did a boy in Guangzhou[9] dream of this
25   as his last stop?
I've heard the trains at night
whistling past our yards,
what we've come to own,
the broken fences, the whiny dog, the rattletrap cars.
30   It's still the wild west,
mean and grubby,
the shootouts and fistfights in the back alley.
With my son the dreamer
and my daughter, who is too young to walk,
35   I've sat in this spot
and wondered why here?
Why in this short life,
this town, this creek they call a river?

He had never planned to stay,
40   the boy who helped to build

---

9. Usually called Canton, a seaport city in southeastern China.

the railroads for a dollar a day.[1]
He had always meant to go back.
When did he finally know
that each mile of track led him further away,
45   that he would die in his sleep,
dispossessed,
having seen Gold Mountain,[2]
the icy wind tunneling through it,
these landlocked, makeshift ghost towns?

50   It must be in the blood,
this notion of returning.
It skipped two generations, lay fallow,
the garden an unmarked grave.
On a spring sweater day
55   it's as if we remember him.
I call to the children.
We can see the mountains
shimmering blue above the air.
If you look really hard
60   says my son the dreamer,
leaning out from the laundry's rigging,
the work shirts fluttering like sails,
you can see all the way to heaven.

1988

- Who is "He" in this poem's first line? What family history is recounted in the poem?

STEPHEN DUNN

Poetry

It makes no difference where one starts,
doesn't every beginning subvert
the tyrannies of time and place?
New Jersey or Vermont, it's the gray zone
5   where I mostly find myself
with little purpose or design.
An apple orchard, an old hotel—
when I introduce them
I feel I've been taken somewhere
10   I've been before; such comfort,
like the sound of consecutive iambs
to the nostalgic ear.

---

1. The railroads used immigrant day laborers (mostly Chinese) to lay the tracks in the nineteenth century.
2. Chinese term for America, especially common in the nineteenth century.

Yet it helps as well
here in the middle, somewhat amused,
15   to have a fast red car
and a winding, country road.
To forget oneself can be an art.
"Frost was wrong about free verse,"
she said to me. "Tear the net down,
20   turn the court into a dance floor."
She happened to be good looking, too,
which seemed to further enliven her remark.
It always makes a difference
how one ends, aren't endings where you
25   shut but don't lock the door?
Strange music beginning,
the dance floor getting crowded now.

                                        1996

- In what way is this poem an *ars poetica*—that is, a declaration of a
  poet's aims and practices? What is meant by the final two lines?

MARK STRAND

Keeping Things Whole

In a field
I am the absence
of field.
This is
5   always the case.
Wherever I am
I am what is missing.

When I walk
I part the air
10   and always
the air moves in
to fill the spaces
where my body's been.

We all have reasons
15   for moving.
I move
to keep things whole.

                1964

- What is this poem's discursive structure—that is, how does the
  poem's central idea progress through each of the three stanzas?
  What is meant by the concluding lines, "I move / to keep things
  whole"?

CHARLES WRIGHT

Stray Paragraphs in February, Year of the Rat

East of town, the countryside unwrinkles and smooths out
Unctuously toward the tidewater and gruff Atlantic.
A love of landscape's a true affection for regret, I've found,
Forever joined, forever apart,
5   outside us yet ourselves.

Renunciation, it's hard to learn, is now our ecstasy.
However, if God were still around,
                    he'd swallow our sighs in his nothingness.

The dregs of the absolute are slow sift in my blood,
10 Dead branches down after high winds, dead yard grass and undergrowth—
The sure accumulation of all that's not revealed
Rises like snow in my bare places,
                       cross-whipped and openmouthed.

Our lives can't be lived in flames.
15 Our lives can't be lit like saints' hearts,
                    seared between heaven and earth.

February, old head-turner, cut us some slack, grind of bone
On bone, such melancholy music.
Lift up that far corner of landscape,
20   there, toward the west.
Let some of the deep light in, the arterial kind.

                                        2001

- What unifies the five sections of this poem? What ordering principle might account for this?

ROBERT PINSKY

Poem With Lines in Any Order (Poem)

Sonny said, *Then he shouldn't have given Molly the two more babies.*
Dave's sister and her husband adopted the baby, and that was Babe.
You can't live in the past.
Sure he was a tough guy but he was no hero.
5 Sonny and Toots went to live for a while with the Braegers.
It was a time when it seemed like everybody had a nickname.
Nobody can live in the future.
When Rose died having Babe, Dave came after the doctor with a gun.
Toots said, *What would you expect, he was a young man*
10 *and there she was.*

Sonny still a kid himself when Dave moved out on Molly.
The family gave him Rose's cousin Molly to marry so she could
raise the children.
There's no way to just live in the present.
15 In their eighties Toots and Sonny still arguing about their father.
Dave living above the bar with Della and half the family.

2004

- Experiment with different arrangements of the lines of this poem. What re-
ordering would produce the most coherent narrative? How would you reorder
the lines in order to end with line 3, "You can't live in the past"?

SUGGESTIONS FOR WRITING

1. How many different "scenes" can you identify in "Sir Patrick Spens"? Write an essay
in which you first summarize the story recounted by the poem, and then discuss the
methods of storytelling employed by the poem. Consider the transitions from one
scene to another and the almost cinematic "fading" effect between scenes?
2. Write an essay in which you analyze the structure of James Wright's poem "Arrange-
ments with Earth for Three Dead Friends." What pattern do all three stanzas of the
poem follow, or what common elements do all three contain? What ordering prin-
ciples seem to be at work in the succession of "sweet earth," "bright earth," and
"dark earth"?
3. What words and patterns are repeated in the different stanzas of Shelley's "Ode to
the West Wind"? What differences are there from stanza to stanza? What "progress"
does the poem make? Write an essay in which you discuss the ways that meaning
and structure are intertwined in Shelley's poem.
4. What kind of a poem is Roo Borson's "Save Us From"—a prayer? a meditation on
one's fears? Write an essay in which you explore how the structure of the poem
reveals possible meanings. What is the logic in the superficially random progression
of thoughts and images? What might justify the order of the poem's three complete
sentences?
5. Pick out any poem you have read in this book that seems particularly effective in
the way it is put together. Write an essay in which you consider how the poem is
organized—that is, what structural principles it employs. What do the choices of
speaker, situation, and setting have to do with the poem's structure? What other
artistic decisions contribute to its structure?

7 EXTERNAL FORM

Most poems of more than a few lines are divided into **stanzas**—groups of lines divided from other groups by white space on the page. Putting some space between groupings of lines has the effect of sectioning a poem, giving its physical appearance a series of divisions that often mark turns of thought, changes of scene or image, or other shifts in structure or direction. In Donne's "The Flea" (chapter 3), for example, the stanza divisions mark distinct stages in the action: between the first and second stanzas, the speaker stops his companion from killing the flea; between the second and third stanzas, the companion follows through on her intention and kills the flea. In Nemerov's "The Goose Fish" (chapter 6), the stanzas mark stages in the self-perception of the lovers: each stanza is a more or less distinct scene, and the scenes unfold almost like a series of slides. Not all stanzas are quite so neatly patterned as these, but any formal division of a poem into stanzas is important to consider; what appear to be gaps or silences may be structural markers.

Historically, stanzas have most often been organized by patterns of rhyme, and thus stanza divisions have been a visual indicator of patterns in sound. In most traditional stanza forms, the pattern of rhyme is repeated in stanza after stanza throughout the poem, until voice and ear become familiar with the pattern and come to expect and, in a sense, depend on it. The accumulation of pattern allows us to "hear" deviations from the pattern as well, just as we do in music. The rhyme thus becomes an organizational device in the poem—a formal, external determiner of organization, as distinguished from the internal, structural determiners we considered in chapter 6—and ordinarily the metrical patterns stay constant from stanza to stanza. (That is, a formal rhyme scheme is *external* to the unique inner logic of a poem's narrative, descriptive, or discursive design.) In Shelley's "Ode to the West Wind," for example, the first and third lines in each stanza rhyme, and the middle line then rhymes with the first and third lines of the next stanza. (In indicating rhyme, we conventionally use a different letter of the alphabet to represent each rhyme sound; in the following example, if we begin with "being" as *a* and "dead" as *b*, then "fleeing" is also *a*, and "red" and "bed" are *b*.)

O wild West Wind, thou breath of Autumn's being,	*a*
Thou, from whose unseen presence the leaves dead	*b*
Are driven, like ghosts from an enchanter fleeing,	*a*
Yellow, and black, and pale, and hectic red,	*b*
Pestilence-stricken multitudes: O thou,	*c*
Who chariotest to their dark wintry bed	*b*

The wingéd seeds, where they lie cold and low,	*c*
Each like a corpse within its grave, until	*d*
Thine azure sister of the Spring shall blow	*c*

In this stanza form, known as terza rima, the stanzas are linked to each other by a common sound: one rhyme sound from each stanza is picked up in the next stanza, and so on to the end of the poem (though sometimes poems in this form have sections that use varied rhyme schemes). This stanza form was used by Dante in *The Divine Comedy,* written in Italian in the early 1300s. Terza rima is not all that common in English because it is a rhyme-rich stanza form—that is, it requires many rhymes, and thus many different rhyme words—and English is, relatively speaking, a rhyme-poor language (not as rich in rhyme possibilities as Italian or French). One reason for this is that English is derived from so many different language families that it has fewer similar word endings than languages that have remained "pure"—that is, more dependent for vocabulary on the roots and patterns found in a single language family.

Many contemporary poets use rhyme sparingly, finding it neither necessary nor appealing, but until the twentieth century the music of rhyme was central to both the sound and the formal conception of most poems. Because poetry was originally an oral art (and its texts not always written down), various kinds of **memory devices** (sometimes called **mnemonic devices**) were built into poems to help reciters remember them. Rhyme was one such device, and most people still find it easier to memorize poetry that rhymes. The simple pleasure of hearing familiar sounds repeated at regular intervals may also help to account for the traditional popularity of rhyme, and perhaps plain habit (for both poets and hearers) had a lot to do with why rhyme flourished for so many centuries in so many languages as an expected feature of poetry. Rhyme also helps to give poetry a special aural quality that distinguishes it from prose, a significant advantage in ages that worry about decorum and propriety and are anxious to preserve a strong sense of poetic tradition. Some ages have been very concerned that poetry should not in any way be mistaken for prose or made to serve prosaic functions, and the literary critics and theorists in those ages made extraordinary efforts to emphasize the distinctions between poetry, which was thought to be artistically superior, and prose, which was thought to be primarily utilitarian. An elitist pride and a fear that an expanded reading public could ultimately dilute the possibilities of traditional art forms have been powerful cultural forces in Western civilization, and if such forces were not themselves responsible for creating rhyme in poetry, they at least helped to preserve a sense of its necessity. But rhyme and other patterns of repeated sounds are also important, for countless historical and cultural reasons, to non-Western languages and poetic traditions as well.

There are at least two other reasons for rhyme. One is complex and hard to state justly without long explanations. It involves traditional ideas about the symmetrical relationship of different aspects of the world and the function of poetry to reflect the universe as human learning has understood it. Many cultures (especially in earlier centuries) have assumed that rhyme was proper to verse, perhaps even essential. Poets in these ages and cultures would have felt themselves eccentric or even foolish to compose poems any other way. Some English poets (especially in the Renaissance) did experiment—often very successfully—with **blank verse** (that is, verse that did not rhyme but that nevertheless had strict metrical requirements), but the cultural pressure for rhyme was almost constant. Why? As noted above, custom or habit may account in part for the assumption that rhyme was necessary, but there was probably more to it than that. Rather, the poets' sense that poetry was an imitation of larger relationships in the universe made it seem natural to use rhyme to represent or re-create a sense of pattern, harmony, correspondence, symmetry, and order. The sounds of poetry were thus, they reasoned, reminders of the harmonious cosmos, of the music of the spheres that animated the planets, the processes of nature, the interrelationship of all created things and beings. Probably no poet ever thought, "I shall now tunefully emulate the harmony of God's carefully ordered universe," but the tendency to use rhyme and other repetitions or re-echoings of sound (such as **alliteration** or **assonance**) nevertheless stemmed ultimately from basic assumptions about how the universe worked. In a modern world increasingly perceived as fragmented and chaotic, there is less of a tendency to assert a sense of harmony and symmetry. It would be far too easy and too mechanical, of course, to think that rhyme in a poem specifically means that the poet has a firm sense of cosmic order, and that an unrhymed poem testifies to chaos, but cultural assumptions do affect the expectations of both poets and readers, and cultural tendencies create a kind of pressure on the individual creator. If you take a survey course (or a series of related "period" courses) in English or American literature, you will readily notice the diminishing sense that rhyme is an indispensable aspect of poetry. And similarly, other linguistic and national traditions vary usages in different times, depending on their own evolving philosophical and cultural assumptions.

One other reason for using rhyme is that it provides a kind of discipline for the poet, a way of harnessing poetic talents and keeping a rein on the imagination, so that the results are ordered, controlled, put into some kind of meaningful and

Concentration is the very essence of poetry.
—AMY LOWELL

recognizable form. Robert Frost said that writing poems without rhyme or regular meter was pointless, like playing tennis without a net. Writing good poetry does require a lot of discipline, and Frost speaks for many (perhaps most) traditional poets in suggesting that rhyme or rhythm can be a major source of that discipline. But neither one is the only possible source, and more recent poets have usually felt they would rather play by new rules or invent their own as they go along; they have, therefore, sought their sources of discipline elsewhere, preferring the sparer tones that unrhymed poetry provides. It is not that contemporary poets cannot think of rhyme words or that they do not care about the sounds of their poetry; rather, many recent poets have consciously decided not to work with rhyme and to use instead other aural and metrical devices and other strategies for organizing stanzas, just as they have chosen to work with experimental and variable rhythms instead of writing necessarily in the traditional English meters. Nevertheless, many modern poets have continued to write rhymed verse successfully in a more or less traditional way, finding that, in fact, rhyme can be a useful spur to the imagination—the search for a rhyme word can often lead to unexpected discoveries. It might well be, for example, that the need to find a rhyme for "dirt" led Theodore Roethke to the wonderful final line of "My Papa's Waltz" (chapter 4): "Still clinging to your shirt." A free-verse poet might have judged the poem complete after the previous line: "Then waltzed me off to bed."

The amount and density of rhyme vary widely in stanza and verse forms, from elaborate and intricate patterns of rhyme to more casual or spare sound repetitions. The **Spenserian stanza,** for example, is even more rhyme-rich than terza rima, using only three rhyme sounds in nine rhymed lines, as in Keats's *The Eve of St. Agnes:*

Her falt'ring hand upon the balustrade,	*a*
Old Angela was feeling for the stair,	*b*
When Madeline, St. Agnes' charméd maid,	*a*
Rose, like a missioned spirit, unaware:	*b*
With silver taper's light, and pious care,	*b*
She turned, and down the agéd gossip led	*c*
To a safe level matting. Now prepare,	*b*
Young Porphyro, for gazing on that bed;	*c*
She comes, she comes again, like ring dove frayed and fled	*c*

On the other hand, the **ballad stanza** (as in "Sir Patrick Spens") has only one set of rhymes in four lines; lines 1 and 3 in each stanza do not rhyme at all:

The king sits in Dumferling toune,	*a*
Drinking the blude-reid wine:	*b*
"O whar will I get guid sailor,	*c*
To sail this ship of mine?"	*b*

Most stanza forms use a metrical pattern as well as a rhyme scheme. Terza rima, for example, involves **iambic meter** (unstressed and stressed syllables alternating regularly), and each line has five beats (**pentameter**). Most of the Spenserian stanza (the first eight lines) is also in iambic pentameter, but the ninth line in each stanza has one extra foot (thus, the last line is in iambic hexameter). The ballad stanza, also iambic, as are most English stanza and verse forms, alternates three-beat and four-beat lines; lines 1 and 3 are unrhymed iambic tetrameter (four beats), and lines 2 and 4 are rhymed iambic trimeter (three beats).

THE SONNET

The **sonnet,** one of the most persistent verse forms, originated in the Middle Ages as a prominent form in Italian and French poetry. It dominated English poetry in the late sixteenth and early seventeenth centuries and then was revived several times from the early nineteenth century onward. Except for some early experiments with length, the sonnet has always been fourteen lines long, and it usually is written in iambic pentameter. It is most often printed as if it were a *single* stanza, although it actually has several formal divisions that represent its rhyme schemes and formal breaks. As a popular and traditional verse form in English for more than four centuries, the sonnet has been surprisingly resilient even in ages that largely reject rhyme. It continues to attract a variety of poets, including (curiously) radical and even revolutionary poets, who find its formal demands, discipline, and fixed outcome very appealing. Its uses, although quite varied, can be illustrated fairly precisely. As a verse form, the sonnet is contained, compact, demanding; whatever it does, it must do concisely and quickly. To be effective, it must take advantage of the possibilities inherent in its shortness and its relative rigidity. It is best suited to intensity of feeling and concentration of expression. Not too surprisingly, one subject it frequently discusses is confinement itself.

WILLIAM WORDSWORTH

Nuns Fret Not

Nuns fret not at their convent's narrow room;
And hermits are contented with their cells;
And students with their pensive citadels;
Maids at the wheel, the weaver at his loom,
5 Sit blithe and happy; bees that soar for bloom,
High as the highest Peak of Furness-fells,[1]
Will murmur by the hour in foxglove bells:
In truth the prison, unto which we doom
Ourselves, no prison is: and hence for me,
10 In sundry moods,'twas pastime to be bound
Within the sonnet's scanty plot of ground;
Pleased if some souls (for such there needs must be)
Who have felt the weight of too much liberty,
Should find brief solace there, as I have found.

1807

Most sonnets are structured according to one of two principles of division. On one principle, the sonnet divides into three units of four lines each and a final unit of two lines, and sometimes the line spacing reflects this division. On the other, the fundamental break is between the first eight lines (called an octave) and the last six (called a sestet). The 4-4-4-2 sonnet is usually called the **English** or **Shakespearean sonnet,** and ordinarily its rhyme scheme reflects the structure: the scheme of *abab cdcd efef gg* is the classic one, but many variations from that pattern still reflect the basic 4-4-4-2 division. The 8-6 sonnet is usually called the **Italian** or **Petrarchan sonnet** (the Italian poet Petrarch was an early master of this structure), and its "typical" rhyme scheme is *abbaabba cdecde,* although it too produces many variations that still reflect the basic division into two parts, an **octave** and a **sestet.**

The two kinds of sonnet structures are useful for two different sorts of argument. The 4-4-4-2 structure works very well for constructing a poem that wants to make a three-step argument (with a quick summary at the end), or for setting up brief, cumulative images. "That time of year thou mayst in me behold" (chapter 4), for example, uses the 4-4-4-2 structure to mark the progressive steps toward death and the parting of friends by using three distinct images, then summarizing. "Let me not to the marriage of true minds" (page 19) works very similarly, following the kind of organization that in chapter 6 was referred to as the 1-2-3 structure—and doing it compactly and economically.

Here, on the other hand, is a poem that uses the 8-6 pattern:

---

1. Mountains in England's Lake District, where Wordsworth lived.

HENRY CONSTABLE

[*My lady's presence makes the roses red*]

My lady's presence makes the roses red,
Because to see her lips they blush for shame.
The lily's leaves, for envy, pale became,
And her white hands in them this envy bred.
5 The marigold the leaves abroad doth spread,
Because the sun's and her power is the same.
The violet of purple colour came,
Dyed in the blood she made my heart to shed.
In brief: all flowers from her their virtue take;
10 From her sweet breath their sweet smells do proceed;
The living heat which her eyebeams doth make
Warmeth the ground and quickeneth the seed.
The rain, wherewith she watereth the flowers,
Falls from mine eyes, which she dissolves in showers.

1594

The first eight lines argue that the lady's presence is responsible for the color of all of nature's flowers, and the final six lines summarize and extend that argument to smells and heat—and finally to the rain that the lady draws from the speaker's eyes. That kind of two-part structure, in which the octave states a proposition or generalization and the sestet provides a particularization or application of it, has a variety of uses. The final lines may, for example, reverse the first eight and achieve a paradox or irony in the poem, or the poem may nearly balance two comparable arguments. Basically, the 8-6 structure lends itself to poems with two points to make, or to those that wish to make one point and then illustrate it.

Sometimes the neat and precise structure is altered—either slightly, as in Wordsworth's "Nuns Fret Not," above (where the 8-6 structure is more of an 8½-5½ or 7-7 structure), or more radically as particular needs or effects may demand. And the two basic structures certainly do not define all the structural possibilities within a fourteen-line poem, even if they do suggest the most traditional ways of taking advantage of the sonnet's compact and well-kept container.

During the Renaissance, poets regularly employed the sonnet for love poems, and many modern sonnets continue to be about love or private life. And many continue to use a personal, apparently open and sincere tone. But poets often find the sonnet's compact form and rigid demands equally useful for many varieties of subject, theme, and tone. Besides love, sonnets often treat other subjects: politics, philosophy, discovery. And tones vary widely too, from the anger and remorse of "Th' expense of spirit in a waste of shame" (chapter 15) and righteous outrage of "On the Late Massacre in Piedmont" (chapter 3) to the tender awe of "How Do I Love Thee?" (page 2). Many poets seem to take the kind of comfort Wordsworth describes in the careful limits of the form, finding in its two basic variations (the English sonnet, such as "That time of year," and the Italian sonnet, such as "On First Looking into Chapman's Homer" [chapter 11]) a sufficiency of ways to organize their materials into coherent structures.

. . .

DANTE GABRIEL ROSSETTI
A Sonnet Is a Moment's Monument

A Sonnet is a moment's monument—
  Memorial from the Soul's eternity
  To one dead deathless hour. Look that it be,
Whether for lustral[2] rite or dire portent,
5 Of its own arduous fullness reverent.
    Carve it in ivory or in ebony,
    As Day or Night may rule; and let Time see
Its flowering crest impearled and orient.[3]

A Sonnet is a coin: its face reveals
10   The soul—its converse, to what Power 'tis due—
Whether for tribute to the august appeals
    Of Life or dower in Love's high retinue,

It serve; or 'mid the dark wharf's cavernous breath,
In Charon's palm it pay the toll to Death.[4]

1881

- In Rossetti's metaphor comparing the sonnet to a coin (lines 9–14), what are the two "sides" of a sonnet?

JOHN KEATS
On the Sonnet

If by dull rhymes our English must be chained,
And like Andromeda,[5] the sonnet sweet
Fettered, in spite of painèd loveliness,
Let us find, if we must be constrained,
5 Sandals more interwoven and complete

---

2. Purificatory.   3. Sparkling.
4. In classical myth, Charon was the boatman who rowed the souls of the dead across the river Styx. Ancient Greeks put a small coin in the hand of the dead to pay his fee.
5. According to Greek myth, Andromeda was chained to a rock so that she would be devoured by a sea monster. She was rescued by Perseus, who married her. When she died she was placed among the stars.

To fit the naked foot of Poesy:[6]
Let us inspect the lyre, and weigh the stress
Of every chord,[7] and see what may be gained
By ear industrious, and attention meet;
10 Misers of sound and syllable, no less
Than Midas[8] of his coinage, let us be
Jealous of dead leaves in the bay-wreath crown;[9]
So, if we may not let the Muse be free,
She will be bound with garlands of her own.

1819

- What is the rhyme scheme of this poem? How well does this unusual
  structure meet the challenge implied by the poem?

SIR PHILIP SIDNEY

My True Love Hath My Heart[1]

My true love hath my heart, and I have his,
By just exchange, one for the other given.
I hold his dear, and mine he cannot miss,
There never was a better bargain driven.
5 His heart in me keeps me and him in one,
My heart in him, his thoughts and senses guides;
He loves my heart, for once it was his own,
I cherish his, because in me it bides.

His heart[2] his wound received from my sight;
10 My heart was wounded with his wounded heart;
For as from me on him his hurt did light,
So still methought in me his hurt did smart.
   Both equal hurt, in this change sought our bliss,
   My true love hath my heart, and I have his.

1590

- How does this poem illustrate the three-step argument typical of the
  English sonnet? How does the pun on "heart" play out through the
  poem?

---

6. In a letter that contained this sonnet, Keats expressed impatience with the traditional Petrarchan and
Shakespearean sonnet forms: "I have been endeavoring to discover a better sonnet stanza than we have."
7. Lyre string; *Meet*: proper.
8. The legendary king of Phrygia who asked, and got, the power to turn all he touched to gold.
9. The bay tree was sacred to Apollo, god of poetry, and bay wreaths came to symbolize true poetic achievement. The withering of the bay tree is sometimes considered an omen of death. *Jealous*: suspiciously watchful.
1. This poem is embedded in Sidney's prose romance, *Arcadia*, where it is sung by a simple shepherdess named Charita.
2. The pun on hart (deer), pretty much submerged earlier in the poem, begins to operate openly in mid-poem. "Heart" was often spelled 'hart' in the sixteenth century (as it was in early editions of this poem).

HENRY CONSTABLE

[*Wonder it is, and pity*]

Wonder it is, and pity is, that she
in whom all beauty's treasure we may find,
that may enrich the body and the mind,
towards the poor should use no charity.
5 My love is gone a-begging unto thee,
and if that Beauty had not been more kind
than Pity, long ere this he had been pined;
but Beauty is content his food to be.
Oh pity have, when such poor orphans beg
10 Love (naked boy) hath nothing on his back;
and though he wanteth neither arm nor leg,
yet maimed he is, sith³ he his sight doth lack.
And yet (though blind) he beauty can behold,
and yet (though naked) he feels more heat than cold.

1592

- Explain the poem's metaphorical representation of Love.

LADY MARY WROTH

In This Strange Labyrinth

In this strange labyrinth⁴ how shall I turn?
    Ways are on all sides while the way I miss;
    If to the right hand, there in love I burn;
    Let me go forward, therein danger is;
5 If to the left, suspicion hinders bliss;
    Let me turn back: shame cries I ought return
    Nor faint though crosses with my fortunes kiss.
    Stand still is harder, although sure to mourn;
Thus let me take the right, or left hand way;
10   Go forward, or stand still, or back retire;
    I must these doubts endure without allay
    Or help, but travail find for my best hire;
Yet that which most my troubled sense doth move
Is to leave all, and take the thread of love.

1621

- **In what ways is the poem itself a "strange labyrinth"? How does the concluding couplet "solve" the conundrum posed by the three quatrains?**

3. Since.
4. The image of love as a labyrinth is traditional, going back at least to Petrarch. In Greek mythology, Ariadne helps Theseus escape a labyrinth by giving him a skein of thread (line 14) to guide his way.

DIANE ACKERMAN

Sweep Me through Your Many-Chambered Heart

Sweep me through your many-chambered heart
if you like, or leave me here, flushed
amid the sap-ooze and blossom: one more dish
in the banquet called April, or think me hard-
5 won all your days full of women. Weeks
later, till I felt your arms around
me like a shackle, heard all the sundown
wizardries the fired body speaks.
Tell me why, if it was no more than this,
10 the unmuddled tumble, the renegade kiss,
today, rapt in a still life and unaware,
my paintbrush dropped like an amber hawk;
thinking I'd heard your footfall on the stair,
I listened, heartwise, for the knock.

                                            1978

- How does the poet make the poem seem off-balance? How is this
  technique appropriate to the speaker's state of mind?

GWEN HARWOOD

In the Park

She sits in the park. Her clothes are out of date.
Two children whine and bicker, tug her skirt.
A third draws aimless patterns in the dirt.
Someone she loved once passes by—too late

5 to feign indifference to that casual nod.
"How nice," et cetera. "Time holds great surprises."
From his neat head unquestionably rises
a small balloon ... "but for the grace of God ..."

They stand a while in flickering light, rehearsing
10 the children's names and birthdays. "It's so sweet
to hear their chatter, watch them grow and thrive,"
she says to his departing smile. Then, nursing
the youngest child, sits staring at her feet.
To the wind she says, "They have eaten me alive."

                                            1963

- What is the implication of the "small balloon" that rises from the
  head of the man who passes by?

SIR PHILIP SIDNEY

[*Come sleep! Oh sleep*]

Come sleep! Oh sleep, the certain knot of peace,
The bating place⁵ of wit, the balm of woe,
The poor man's wealth, the prisoner's release,
The indifferent judge between the high and low;
5 With shield of proof⁶ shield me from out the press
Of those fierce darts Despair at me doth throw;
Oh make in me those civil wars to cease;
I will good tribute pay, if thou do so.
Take thou of me smooth pillows, sweetest bed,
10 A chamber deaf to noise and blind to light,
A rosy garland and a weary head;
And if these things, as being thine by right,
Move not thy heavy grace, thou shalt in me,
Livelier than elsewhere, Stella's image see.⁷

1591

- What is the speaker's argument? Why is the speaker invoking sleep?

BARTHOLOMEW GRIFFIN

Care-charmer Sleep

Care-charmer sleep, sweet ease in restless misery,
The captive's liberty, and his freedom's song,
Balm of the bruised heart, man's chief felicity,
Brother of quiet death, when life is too, too long!
5 A comedy it is, and now an history—
What is not sleep unto the feeble mind!
It easeth him that toils and him that's sorry,
It makes the deaf to hear, to see the blind.
Ungentle sleep, thou helpest all but me,
10 For when I sleep my soul is vexed most.
It is Fidessa⁸ that doth master thee;
If she approach, alas, they power is lost.
But here she is. See, how he runs amain!⁹
I fear at night he will not come again.

1596

- Why does the speaker call sleep "Ungentle"?

---

5. Resting point in the course of a journey.   6. Armor of proven strength; *Press:* Crowd.
7. This poem is part of a cycle of sonnets addressed to Stella ("star") by the speaker, Astrophel ("star-lover").
8. The poem is part of a cycle of sonnets addressed to Fidessa ("faith").   9. In haste.

JOHN KEATS

Sonnet to Sleep

O soft embalmer of the still midnight,
　　Shutting with careful fingers and benign
Our gloom-pleas'd eyes, embower'd from the light,
　　Enshaded in forgetfulness divine:
5　O soothest[1] Sleep! if so it please thee, close,
　　In midst of this thine hymn, my willing eyes,
Or wait the Amen ere thy poppy[2] throws
　　Around my bed its lulling charities.
Then save me or the passed day will shine
10　　Upon my pillow, breeding many woes:
Save me from curious[3] conscience, that still hoards
　　Its strength for darkness, burrowing like the mole;
Turn the key deftly in the oiled wards,[4]
　　And seal the hushed casket of my soul.

Apr. 1819   1838

- What is the form of this sonnet—English or Italian? How does the organization of the poem's rhyme scheme correspond to the poem's organization of thought?

JOHN MILTON

[When I consider how my light is spent]

When I consider how my light is spent,
　　Ere half my days, in this dark world and wide,
　　And that one talent which is death to hide[5]
Lodged with me useless, though my soul more bent

---

1. Softest.　2. Opium is made from the dried juice of the opium poppy.　3. Scrupulous.
4. The ridges in a lock that correspond to the notches of the key.
5. In the parable of the talents (Matthew 25), the servants who earned interest on their master's money (his talents) while he was away were called "good and faithful"; the one who simply hid the money and then returned it was condemned and sent away.

5 To serve therewith my Maker, and present
   My true account, lest he returning chide;
   "Doth God exact day-labor, light denied?"
   I fondly ask; but Patience to prevent[6]
That murmur, soon replies, "God doth not need
10   Either man's work or his own gifts; who best
   Bear his mild yoke, they serve him best. His state
Is kingly. Thousands at his bidding speed
   And post o'er land and ocean without rest:
   They also serve who only stand and wait."

1652?

- Paraphrase the speaker's question and Patience's reply. Does know-
  ing that Milton was blind alter your interpretation of this poem?

CHRISTINA ROSSETTI

In an Artist's Studio

One face looks out from all his canvases,
   One selfsame figure sits or walks or leans;
   We found her hidden just behind those screens,
That mirror gave back all her loveliness.
5 A queen in opal or in ruby dress,
   A nameless girl in freshest summer-greens,
   A saint, an angel—every canvass means
The same one meaning, neither more nor less.
He feeds upon her face by day and night,
10   And she with true kind eyes looks back on him
Fair as the moon and joyful as the light:
   Not wan with waiting, not with sorrow dim;
Not as she is, but was when hope shone bright;
   Not as she is, but as she fills his dream.

1856

- What do you think is "The same one meaning" the speaker sees in
  every portrait in the studio?

6. Forestall. *Fondly:* foolishly.

Cobwebs

It is a land with neither night nor day,
  Nor heat nor cold, nor any wind, nor rain,
  Nor hills nor valleys; but one even plain
Stretches thro' long unbroken miles away:
5 While thro' the sluggish air a twilight grey
  Broodeth; no moons or seasons wax and wane,
  No ebb and flow are there along the main,
No bud-time no leaf-falling, there for aye[7]:—
No ripple on the sea, no shifting sand,.
10 No beat of wings to stir the stagnant space,
No pulse of life thro' all the loveless land:
And loveless sea; no trace of days before,
  No guarded home, no toil-won resting place,
No future hope no fear for evermore

1855

- What is the "land" that is described throughout this poem? Why do
  you think the poem is entitled "Cobwebs"?

ELIZABETH BARRETT BROWNING

WEB ## [*When our two souls stand up*]

When our two souls stand up erect and strong,
Face to face, silent, drawing nigh and nigher,
Until the lengthening wings break into fire
At either curvéd point,—what bitter wrong
5 Can the earth do to us, that we should not long
Be here contented? Think. In mounting higher,
The angels would press on us and aspire
To drop some golden orb of perfect song
Into our deep, dear silence. Let us stay
10 Rather on earth, Belovéd,—where the unfit
Contrarious moods of men recoil away
And isolate pure spirits, and permit
A place to stand and love in for a day,
With darkness and the death-hour rounding it

1897

- Explain the metaphor of this poem's first four lines. What will cause
  "the lengthening wings" to "break into fire"?

7. Forever.

EDNA ST. VINCENT MILLAY

[*What lips my lips have kissed, and where, and why*]

What lips my lips have kissed, and where, and why,
I have forgotten, and what arms have lain
Under my head till morning; but the rain
Is full of ghosts tonight, that tap and sigh
5 Upon the glass and listen for reply,
And in my heart there stirs a quiet pain
For unremembered lads that not again
Will turn to me at midnight with a cry.
Thus in the winter stands the lonely tree,
10 Nor knows what birds have vanished one by one,
Yet knows its boughs more silent than before:
I cannot say what loves have come and gone;
I only know that summer sang in me
A little while, that in me sings no more.

1923

- What are the poem's principal parts? Why does the Petrarchan model suit this sonnet?

[*I shall forget you presently, my dear*]

I shall forget you presently, my dear,
So make the most of this, your little day,
Your little month, your little half a year,
Ere I forget, or die, or move away,
5 And we are done forever; by and by
I shall forget you, as I said, but now,
If you entreat me with your loveliest lie
I will protest you with my favorite vow.
I would indeed that love were longer-lived,
10 And oaths were not so brittle as they are,
But so it is, and nature has contrived
To struggle on without a break thus far,—
Whether or not we find what we are seeking
Is idle, biologically speaking.

1922

- What is the meaning of this poem's final couplet? What does it indicate about the poem's tone?

GWENDOLYN BROOKS

First Fight. Then Fiddle.

First fight. Then fiddle. Ply the slipping string
With feathery sorcery; muzzle the note
With hurting love; the music that they wrote
Bewitch, bewilder. Qualify to sing
5   Threadwise. Devise no salt, no hempen thing
For the dear instrument to bear. Devote
The bow to silks and honey. Be remote
A while from malice and from murdering.
But first to arms, to armor. Carry hate
10   In front of you and harmony behind.
Be deaf to music and to beauty blind.
Win war. Rise bloody, maybe not too late
For having first to civilize a space
Wherein to play your violin with grace.

                                        1949

- After advising "First Fight. Then fiddle," the speaker discusses first
  music, then conflict. Why do you think the poet has arranged her
  argument this way?

EMMA LAZARUS

The New Colossus

Not like the brazen giant of Greek fame,
With conquering limbs astride from land to land;
Here at our sea-washed, sunset gates shall stand
A mighty woman with a torch,[8] whose flame
5   Is the imprisoned lightning, and her name
Mother of Exiles. From her beacon-hand
Glows world-wide welcome; her mild eyes command
The air-bridged harbor that twin cities frame.
"Keep ancient lands, your storied pomp!" cries she
10   With silent lips. "Give me your tired, your poor,
Your huddled masses yearning to breathe free,
The wretched refuse of your teeming shore.
Send these, the homeless, tempest-tost to me,
I lift my lamp beside the golden door!"

November 1883

- Why is the sonnet form appropriate to this poem's subject and the
  voice it projects?

---

8. The Statue of Liberty, in New York harbor.

SIR CHARLES G. D. ROBERTS

The Potato Harvest

A high bare field, brown from the plough, and borne
   Aslant from sunset; amber wastes of sky
   Washing the ridge; a clamor of crows that fly
In from the wide flats where the spent tides mourn
5 To yon their rocking roosts in pines wind-torn;
   A line of grey snake-fence that zigzags by
   A pond and cattle; from the homestead nigh
The long deep summonings of the supper horn.
Black on the ridge, against that lonely flush,
10   A cart, and stoop-necked oxen; ranged beside
   Some barrels; and the day-worn harvest-folk,
Here emptying their baskets, jar the hush
   With hollow thunders. Down the dusk hillside
   Lumbers the wain; and day fades out like smoke.

1886

- What does the poem gain visually by indenting certain lines to emphasize the Italian sonnet form? What makes this form appropriate to the poem's subject matter and imagery?

DAVE SMITH

Wreck in the Woods

Under that embrace of wild saplings held fast,
surrounded by troops of white mushrooms, by wrens
visiting like news-burdened ministers known
only to some dim life inside, this Model
5 A Ford like my grandfather's entered the earth.
What were fenders, hood, doors, no one washed, polished,
grazed with a tip of finger, or boyhood dream.
I stood where silky blue above went wind-rent,
pines, oaks, dogwood ticking, pushing as if grief
10 called families to see what none understood. What
plot of words, what heart-shudder of men, women
here ended so hard the green world must hide it?
Headlights, large, round. Two pieces of shattered glass.

1996

- In what respects does this poem resemble a traditional sonnet? How does the poem's subject suit its form?

HENRI COLE

White Spine

Liar, I thought, kneeling with the others,
how can He love me and hate what I am?
The dome of St. Peter's[9] shone yellowish
gold, like butter and eggs. *My God*, I prayed
5 anyhow, as if made in the image
and likeness of Him. Nearby, a handsome
priest looked at me like a stone; I looked back,
not desiring to go it alone.
The college of cardinals[1] wore punitive red.
10 The white spine waved to me from his white throne.[2]
Being in a place not my own, much less
myself. I climbed out, a beast in a crib.
Somewhere a terrorist rolled a cigarette.
Reason, not faith, would change him.

1998

- What are the hidden rhymes and near-rhymes that help to knit this poem together? How is the form of this poem itself "a place not my own"?

ROBERT HASS

Sonnet

[handwritten: Failed Sonnet!]

A man talking to his ex-wife on the phone.
He has loved her voice and listens with attention
to every modulation of its tone. Knowing
it intimately. Not knowing what he wants
5 from the sound of it, from the tendered civility.
He studies, out the window, the seed shapes
of the broken pods of ornamental trees.
The kind that grow in everyone's garden, that no one
but horticulturists can name. Four arched chambers
10 of pale green, tiny vegetal proscenium arches,
a pair of black tapering seeds bedded in each chamber.

[handwritten: Fake love]
[handwritten: The speaker's heart]

---

9. St. Peter's Basilica, Rome.   1. The Pope's counselors.
2. The ceremonial chair on which the Pope ("white spine") sits.

A wish geometry, miniature, Indian or Persian,
lovers or gods in their apartments. Outside, white,
patient animals, and tangled vines, and rain.

1996

- Why do you think the poet has chosen, with this title, to identify
  the poem with the traditional sonnet form? What is appropriate in
  the image of the "four arched chambers"?

BILLY COLLINS

Sonnet

All we need is fourteen lines, well, thirteen now,
and after this one just a dozen
to launch a little ship on love's storm-tossed seas,
then only ten more left like rows of beans.
5 How easily it goes unless you get Elizabethan
and insist the iambic bongos must be played
and rhymes positioned at the ends of lines,
one for every station of the cross.
But hang on here while we make the turn
10 into the final six where all will be resolved,
where longing and heartache will find an end,
where Laura will tell Petrarch to put down his pen,
take off those crazy medieval tights,
blow out the lights, and come at last to bed.

1999

- In what respects is Collins's poem a traditional sonnet? In what
  respects is it not?

ANTHONY HECHT

Spring Break

I

The beach is the hot parade ground where brigades
Of suntanned girls disport themselves and thrust
Upon one's notice pelvis, butt, and bust,
And whitened noses bridged with heart-shaped shades.
5 The boys are beery, laying plots to score,
Exhibiting heroic abs and pecs,
The showy animality of sex,
Which the girls make weak pretenses to ignore.

They are viewed by dry, bird-wristed, blue-rinsed crones
10 With diamond rings and teeth of Klondike gold
Mounted on a frail armature of bones;
Their hatted husbands, once, perhaps, adored,
Now paunchy, rheumatoid, and feeling old,
Who joust at chess, assault at shuffleboard.

II

15 As at a signal and like an enormous swarm
Of monarch butterflies, the young ones head
Northward to strict assignments and to bed
Each of them in a rock-star-postered dorm,
And steel themselves for mastering Kant's "Critique"
20 Of impenetrable Reason, Pico's claims
For human dignity, late Henry James,
And insubordinate particles of Greek.

Meanwhile the elders breathe a grateful sigh;
Vanished are rudeness, arrogance, and noise.
25 Yet, a week later, what is their reward?
Views of the changeless ocean leave them bored,
And it would be ungenerous to deny
The girls were pretty and the boys were boys.

2004

- How does the sonnet form underscore the poem's irony and humor?
  How does the rhyme scheme in the second stanza of each section
  play with the conventions of the Italian sonnet?

STANZA FORMS

Many stanza forms are represented in this book. Some have names, because they
have been used over and over by different poets. Others (such as Poe's stanza form
for "The Raven" [chapter 5]) were invented for a particular use in a particular
poem and may never be repeated again. Most traditional stanzas are based on
rhyme schemes, but some use other kinds of predictable sound patterns; early
English poetry, for example, used alliteration to construct a balance between the
first and second half of each line (see Earle Birney's "Anglosaxon Street" [later in
this chapter] for a modern imitation of this principle). Sometimes, especially when
poets interact with each other within a strong community, highly elaborate *verse
forms* have been developed that set up stanzas as part of a scheme for the whole
poem. The poets of medieval Provence were especially inventive, subtle, and elab-
orate in their construction of complex verse forms, some of which have been cop-
ied by poets ever since. The **sestina,** for example, depends on the measured
repetition of words (rather than just sounds) in particular places; see, for example,
Bishop's "Sestina" (later in this chapter) and try to decipher the pattern. (There
are also double and even triple sestinas, tough tests of a poet's ingenuity.) And
the **villanelle,** another Provençal form, depends on the patterned repetition
of whole lines (see Dylan Thomas's "Do Not Go Gentle into That Good Night"

Different cultures and different languages develop their own patterns and measures—not all poetries are parallel to English poetry—and they vary from age to age as well as nation to nation.

You can probably deduce the principles involved in each of the following stanza or verse forms by looking carefully at a poem that uses it; if you have trouble, look at the definitions in the glossary.

heroic couplet	"Sound and Sense"	chapter 5
tetrameter couplet	"To His Coy Mistress"	chapter 3
limerick	"There was a young girl from St. Paul"	chapter 5
free verse	"Dirge"	chapter 5
blank verse	from *Paradise Lost*	chapter 4

What are stanza forms good for? What use is it to recognize them? Why do poets bother? Matters discussed in this chapter so far have suggested two reasons: (1) Breaks between stanzas provide convenient pauses for reader and writer, something roughly equivalent to paragraphs in prose. The eye thus picks up the places where some kind of pause or break or change of focus occurs. (2) Poets sometimes use stanza forms, as they do rhyme itself, as a discipline: writing in a certain kind of stanza form imposes a shape on the act of imagination. But visual spaces and unexpected print divisions also mean that poems sometimes *look* unusual and require special visual attention, attention that does not always follow the logic of sound patterns or syntax. After the following poems illustrating some common stanza forms, you will find a section on poems that employ special configurations and shapes, using spaces and print in other ways, to establish their meanings and effects.

. . .

DYLAN THOMAS

Do Not Go Gentle into That Good Night[1]

Do not go gentle into that good night,
Old age should burn and rave at close of day;
Rage, rage against the dying of the light.

Though wise men at their end know dark is right,
5 Because their words had forked no lightning they
Do not go gentle into that good night.

Good men, the last wave by, crying how bright
Their frail deeds might have danced in a green bay,
Rage, rage against the dying of the light.

10 Wild men who caught and sang the sun in flight,
And learn, too late, they grieved it on its way,
Do not go gentle into that good night.

---

1. Written during the final illness of the poet's father.

Grave men, near death, who see with blinding sight A
Blind eyes could blaze like meteors and be gay, B
15 Rage, rage against the dying of the light. A

And you, my father, there on the sad height, A
Curse, bless, me now with your fierce tears, I pray. B   *Quatrain*
Do not go gentle into that good night. A
Rage, rage against the dying of the light. A

1952

- What do the wise, good, wild, and grave men have in common with
  the speaker's father? Why do you think Thomas chose such a strict
  form, the villanelle, for such an emotionally charged subject?

MARIANNE MOORE

Poetry

I, too, dislike it: there are things that are important beyond all this
    fiddle.
   Reading it, however, with a perfect contempt for it, one discovers in
   it after all, a place for the genuine.
      Hands that can grasp, eyes
5   that can dilate, hair that can rise
         if it must, these things are important not because a

high-sounding interpretation can be put upon them but because they are
   useful. When they become so derivative as to become unintelligible,
   the same thing may be said for all of us, that we
10   do not admire what
   we cannot understand: the bat
      holding on upside down or in quest of something to

eat, elephants pushing, a wild horse taking a roll, a tireless wolf under
   a tree, the immovable critic twitching his skin like a horse that feels a
   flea, the base-
15   ball fan, the statistician—
      nor is it valid
         to discriminate against "business documents and

school-books"[2]; all these phenomena are important. One must make a
   distinction
   however: when dragged into prominence by half poets, the result is not
   poetry,

---

2. *Diary of Tolstoy* (Dutton), p. 84. "Where the boundary between prose and poetry lies, I shall never be able
to understand. The question is raised in manuals of style, yet the answer to it lies beyond me. Poetry is
verse: Prose is not verse. Or else poetry is everything with the exception of business documents and school
books" [Moore's note].

The Year of Magical Thinking

20 nor till the poets among us can be
        "literalists of
        the imagination"[3]—above
            insolence and triviality and can present

    for inspection, "imaginary gardens with real toads in them," shall we
        have
25 it. In the meantime, if you demand on the one hand,
        the raw material of poetry in
            all its rawness and
            that which is on the other hand
                genuine, you are interested in poetry.

                                                          1921

- Is this poem more about the reading or the writing of poetry? What does the poem suggest is the relationship between poetry and "the genuine" (line 3)?

ELIZABETH BISHOP

Sestina

September rain falls on the house.
In the failing light, the old grandmother
sits in the kitchen with the child
beside the Little Marvel Stove,
5 reading the jokes from the almanac,
laughing and talking to hide her tears.

She thinks that her equinoctial tears
and the rain that beats on the roof of the house
were both foretold by the almanac,
10 but only known to a grandmother.
The iron kettle sings on the stove.
She cuts some bread and says to the child,

It's time for tea now; but the child
is watching the teakettle's small hard tears
15 dance like mad on the hot black stove,
the way the rain must dance on the house.
Tidying up, the old grandmother
hangs up the clever almanac

---

3. Yeats, *Ideas of Good and Evil* (A. H. Bullen, 1903), p. 182. "The limitation of [William Blake's] view was from the very intensity of his vision; he was a too literal realist of imagination, as others are of nature; and because he believed that the figures seen by the mind's eye, when exalted by inspiration, were 'eternal existences,' symbols of divine essences, he hated every grace of style that might obscure their lineaments" [Moore's note].

on its string. Birdlike, the almanac
20 hovers half open above the child,
hovers above the old grandmother
and her teacup full of dark brown tears.
She shivers and says she thinks the house
feels chilly, and puts more wood in the stove.

25 *It was to be,* says the Marvel Stove.
I know what I know, says the almanac.
With crayons the child draws a rigid house
and a winding pathway. Then the child
puts in a man with buttons like tears
30 and shows it proudly to the grandmother.

But secretly, while the grandmother
busies herself about the stove,
the little moons fall down like tears
from between the pages of the almanac
35 into the flower bed the child
has carefully placed in the front of the house.

Time to plant tears, says the almanac.
The grandmother sings to the marvellous stove
and the child draws another inscrutable house.

1965

- Try to derive from "Sestina" the "rules" that govern the sestina form.
Why do you think Bishop chose this form for her poem?

ISHMAEL REED

beware : do not read this poem

tonite , *thriller* was
abt an ol woman , so vain she
surrounded herself w /
    many mirrors
5 it got so bad that finally she
locked herself indoors & her
whole life became the
    mirrors

one day the villagers broke
10 into her house , but she was too
swift for them . she disappeared
    into a mirror

each tenant who bought the house
after that   , lost a loved one to
15 the ol woman in the mirror :
first a little girl
then a young woman
then the young woman / s husband

the hunger of this poem is legendary
20 it has taken in many victims
back off from this poem
it has drawn in yr feet
back off from this poem
it has drawn in yr legs

25 back off from this poem
it is a greedy mirror
you are into this poem . from
the waist down
nobody can hear you can they ?
30 this poem has had you up to here
belch
this poem aint got no manners
you cant call out frm this poem
relax now & go w/ this poem
35 move & roll on to this poem
do not resist this poem
this poem has yr eyes
this poem has his head
this poem has his arms
40 this poem has his fingers
this poem has his fingertips
this poem is the reader & the
reader this poem

statistic : the us bureau of missing persons reports
45   that in 1968 over 100,000 people disappeared
leaving no solid clues
nor trace   only
a space   in the lives of their friends

1970

- How does the speaker's repeated use of the word *mirror* help to deter-
mine the form of this poem? How (and why) does the form evolve
in the course of the poem?

ARCHIBALD MacLEISH

Ars Poetica[4]

A poem should be palpable and mute
As a globed fruit,

Dumb
As old medallions to the thumb,

5 Silent as the sleeve-worn stone
Of casement ledges where the moss has grown—

A poem should be wordless
As the flight of birds.

A poem should be motionless in time
10 As the moon climbs.

Leaving, as the moon releases
Twig by twig the night-entangled trees,

Leaving, as the moon behind the winter leaves,
Memory by memory the mind—

15 A poem should be motionless in time
As the moon climbs.

A poem should be equal to:
Not true.

For all the history of grief
20 An empty doorway and a maple leaf.

For love
The leaning grasses and two lights above the sea—

A poem should not mean
But be.

1926

- Can you summarize this poem's ideas about what poetry should be? How does the poem itself illustrate these principles?

THE WAY A POEM LOOKS

Stanza breaks and other kinds of print spaces are important, primarily to guide the voice and the mind to a clearer sense of sound and meaning. But sometimes poems are written to be seen rather than heard, and their appearance on the page

---

4. "The Art of Poetry," title of a poetical treatise by the Roman poet Horace (65–8 B.C.E.).

is crucial to their effect. Cummings's poem "l(a," for example, tries to visualize typographically what the poet asks you to see in your mind's eye.

E. E. CUMMINGS

[*l(a*]

l(a
le
af
fa
5 ll
s)
one
l
iness

1958

Occasionally, too, poems are composed in a specific shape so that they look like physical objects. The poems that follow in this chapter—some very old, some more recent—illustrate ways in which visual effects may be created. Even though poetry has traditionally been thought of as oral—words to be spoken, sung, or performed rather than looked at—the idea that poems can also be related to painting and the visual arts is an old one. Theodoric in ancient Greece is credited with inventing **technopaegnia**—that is, the construction of poems with visual appeal. Once, the shaping of words to resemble an object was thought to have mystical power, but more recent attempts at **concrete poetry** or **shaped verse** are usually playful exercises (such as Hollander's "You Too? Me Too—Why Not? Soda Pop" [chapter 11]) that attempt to supplement (or replace) verbal meanings with devices from painting and sculpture.

Reading a poem like George Herbert's "Easter Wings" aloud wouldn't make much sense. Seeing is everything for a poem like that. A more frequent poetic device involves asking the eyes to become a guide for the voice. The following poem depends on recognition of some standard typographical symbols and knowledge of their names. We have to say those names to read the poem.

FRANKLIN P. ADAMS

Composed in the Composing Room

At stated .ic times
I love to sit and — off rhymes
Till ,tose at last I fall
Exclaiming "I don't ∧ all."

5 Though I'm an * objection
By running this in this here §
This ☞ of the Fleeting Hour,
This lofty -ician Tower—

A ¶er's hope dispels
10 All fear of deadly | |.
You think these [ ] are a pipe?
Well, not on your †eotype.

1914

We create the right terms here when we verbalize, putting the visual signs together with the words or letters printed in the poem, for example making the word "periodic" out of ".ic" or "high Phoenician" out of "-ician" or "daguerreotype" out of "†eotype." Like "Easter Wings," "Composed in the Composing Room" uses typography in an extreme way; here the eyes (and mind) are drawn into a punlike game that offers more puzzle-solving pleasure than emotional effect. More often poets give us—by the visual placement of sounds—a guide to reading, inviting us to regulate the pace of our reading, notice pauses or silences, and pay attention both to the syntax of the poem and to the rhetoric of the voice, thus providing us a kind of musical score for reading.

E. E. CUMMINGS

[Buffalo Bill 's][1]

Buffalo Bill 's
defunct
          who used to
          ride a watersmooth-silver
5   stallion
and break onetwothreefourfive pigeonsjustlikethat
                                                    Jesus
he was a handsome man
                        and what i want to know is
10 how do you like your blueeyed boy
Mister Death

1923

The unusual spacing of words here, with some run together and others widely separated, provides a guide to reading, regulating both speed and sense, so that the poem can capture aloud some of the excitement and wonder that a boy might have felt for a theatrical act as spectacular as that of Buffalo Bill. A good reader-

1. *Portraits* XXI.

aloud, with only this typographical guidance, can capture some of the wide-eyed boy's enthusiasm, remembered now in retrospect from a later perspective (notice how the word "defunct" helps to set the time and point of view).

In prose, syntax and punctuation are the main guides to the voice of a reader, providing indicators of emphasis, pace, and speed; in poetry as well they are more conventional and more common guides than extreme forms of typography, such as in "Buffalo Bill." Reading a poem sensitively is in some ways a lot like reading a piece of prose sensitively: one has to pay close attention to the way the sentences are put together and how they are punctuated. A good reader makes use of appropriate pauses as well as thundering emphasis; silence as well as sound is part of any poem, and reading punctuation is as important as knowing how to say the words.

Beyond punctuation, the placement and spacing of lines on the page may be helpful to a reader even when that placement is not as radical as it is in "Buffalo Bill." The fact that poetry looks different from prose is not an accident; decisions to make lines one length instead of another have as much to do with vocal breaks and phrasing as with functions of syntax or meaning. In a good poem, there are few accidents, not even in the way the poem meets the eye, which provides the most direct route to the voice; the eye is our scanner and director, our prompter and guide.

The eye also may help the ear in another way—guiding us to notice repeated sounds by spotting repeated visual patterns in letters. The most common rhymes in poems occur at the ends of lines, and the arrangement of lines (the typography of the poem) often calls attention to the pattern of sounds because of the similar appearance of line-ending words, as in sonnets and other traditional verse forms. Not all rhymes have similar spellings, of course, but similarities of appearance seem to imply a relationship of sound, too, and many poems hint at their stanza patterns and verse forms by their spatial arrangements and repeated patterns at ends of lines. The following poem takes advantage of such expectations and plays with them by forcing a letter into arbitrary line relationships, forcing words ("stew," line 2) in order to create rhymes, setting up rhyme patterns and then breaking them (lines 9–11), using false or near rhymes (lines 10–11), and creating long lines with multisyllabic rhymes that seem silly (the final two lines).

STEVIE SMITH

The Jungle Husband

Dearest Evelyn, I often think of you
Out with the guns in the jungle stew
Yesterday I hittapotamus
I put the measurements down for you but they got lost in the fuss
5   It's not a good thing to drink out here
You know, I've practically given it up dear.
Tomorrow I am going alone a long way
Into the jungle. It is all grey
But green on top

10   Only sometimes when a tree has fallen
     The sun comes down plop, it is quite appalling.
     You néver want to go in a jungle pool
     In the hot sun, it would be the act of a fool
     Because it's always full of anacondas, Evelyn, not looking ill-fed
15   I'll say. So no more now, from your loving husband, Wilfred.

                                                                    1957

Visual devices can be entertainments to amuse, bewilder, or tease readers of poetry whose chief expectations concern sound, but sometimes poets achieve surprising (and lasting) original effects by manipulations of print space. Stanzas— visual breaks in poems that indicate some kind of unit of meaning or measurement—ultimately are more than visual devices, for they point to structural questions and ultimately frame and formalize the content of poems. But they present— as do the similar visual patterns of words that rhyme—part of the "score" of poems, and suggest one more way that sight becomes a guide to sound in many poems.

                              • • •

GEORGE HERBERT

Easter Wings

Lord, who createdst man in wealth and store,[2]
Though foolishly he lost the same,
Decaying more and more
Till he became
Most poor:
        With thee
        O let me rise
As larks,[3] harmoniously,
And sing this day thy victories:
Then shall the fall further the flight in me.

My tender age in sorrow did begin;
And still with sicknesses and shame
Thou didst so punish sin,
That I became
Most thin.
        With thee
        Let me combine,
And feel this day thy victory;
For, if I imp[4] my wing on thine,
Affliction shall advance the flight in me.

                                                                    1633

2. In plenty.   3. Which herald the morning.
4. Engraft. In falconry, to engraft feathers in a damaged wing, so as to restore the powers of flight *(OED)*.

- How do the decreasing and increasing line lengths correspond to the meaning of the words in "Easter Wings"? Why do you think Herbert has chosen to present the poem "sideways"?

ROBERT HERRICK

The Pillar of Fame

Fame's pillar here, at last, we set,
Out-during *Marble, Brass,* or *Jet,*[5]
Charmed and enchanted so,
As to withstand the blow
Of   overthrow:
5   Nor shall the seas,
Or   OUTRAGES
Of storms o'erbear
What we up-rear;
Tho Kingdoms fall,
10   This pillar never shall
Decline or waste at all;
But stand for ever by his own
Firm and well fixed foundation.

1648

- How does the poem's appearance emphasize the nature of "Fame's pillar"? Would the poem itself have a "well fixed foundation" if it were typeset normally?

---

5. Black lignite or black marble. *Out-during:* outlasting.

MARY ELLEN SOLT

Lilac

1968

- Is "Lilac" a poem, a picture, or both, or neither—and why? How would you read "Lilac" aloud?

ROGER McGOUGH

Here I Am

Here I am
getting on for seventy
and never having gone to work in ladies' underwear

Never run naked at night in the rain
5   Made love to a girl I'd just met on a plane

At that awkward age now between birth and death
I think of all the outrages unperpetrated
                   opportunities missed

10   The dragons unchased
                    The maidens unkissed
                    The wines still untasted
                    The oceans uncrossed
                    The fantasies wasted
                    The mad urges lost

15   Here I am
             as old as Methuselah
           was when he was my age
    and never having stepped outside for a fight

        Crossed on red, pissed[6] on rosé (or white)
20   Pretty dull for a poet, I suppose, eh? Quite.

                                            1992

- What does this poem's shape suggest about its meaning?

EARLE BIRNEY

Anglosaxon Street

Dawn drizzle ended   dampness steams from
blotching brick and   blank plasterwaste
Faded housepatterns   hoary and finicky
unfold stuttering   stick like a phonograph

5 Here is a ghetto   gotten for goyim
O with care denuded   of nigger and kike
No coonsmell rankles   reeks only cellarrot
Ottar[7] of carexhaust   catcorpse and cookinggrease

Imperial hearts   heave in this haven
10 Cracks across windows   are welded with slogans
There'll Always Be An England   enhances geraniums
and V's for Victory   vanquish the housefly

Ho! with climbing sun   march the bleached beldames[8]
festooned with shopping bags   farded[9] flatarched
15 bigthewed Saxonwives   stepping over buttrivers
waddling back wienerladen   to suckle smallfry

Hoy! with sunslope   shrieking over hydrants
flood from learninghall   the lean fingerlings

6. Drunk.   7. Roselike fragrance.   8. Aged women.   9. Rouged.

Nordic nobblecheeked[1]   not all clean of nose
20 leaping Commandowise   into leprous lanes

What! after whistleblow!   spewed from wheelboat
after daylight doughtiness   dire handplay
in sewertrench or sandpit   come Saxonthegns
Junebrown Jutekings[2]   jawslack for meat

25 Sit after supper   on smeared doorsteps
not humbly swearing   hatedeeds on Huns
profiteers politicians   pacifists Jews

Then by twobit magic   to muse in movie
unlock picturehoard   or lope to alehall
30 soaking bleakly   in beer skittleless

Home again to hotbox   and humid husbandhood
in slumbertrough adding   sleepily to Anglekin
Alongside in lanenooks   carling and leman[3]
caterwaul and clip[4]   careless of Saxonry
35 with moonglow and haste   and a higher heartbeat
Slumbers now slumtrack   unstinks cooling
waiting brief for milkmaid   mornstar and worldrise

Toronto 1942, revised 1966

- **Read this poem aloud. How does the poem's appearance help to
  determine the tone and pacing of your reading?**

DAVID FERRY

Evening News

We have been there.
                          and seen nothing
Nothing has been there
                          for us to see
5 In what a beautiful silence
                          the death is inflicted
In a dazzling distance
                          in the fresh dews
And morning lights
10   how radiantly

---

1. Pimpled.
2. The Jutes were the German tribe that invaded England in the fifth century and spearheaded the Anglo-Saxon conquest. *Saxonthegns:* freemen who provided military services for the Saxon lords.
3. Lover. *Carling:* old woman.   4. Embrace.

In the glistening

the village is wasted.

It is by such sights

the eye is instructed.

1983

- How are the eye and the voice guided through this poem? How is the poem's appearance part of its content?

SUGGESTIONS FOR WRITING

1. Chart the rhyme scheme of Keats's "On the Sonnet," and then, after reading the poem aloud, mark the major structural divisions of the poem. At what points do these structural divisions and the breaks in rhyme coincide? At what points do they conflict? Write an essay in which you discuss how these patterns and variations relate to the poem's meaning.
2. Consider carefully the structure of and sequencing in Brooks's "First Fight. Then Fiddle." How do various uses of sound in the poem (rhyme, onomatopoeia, and alliteration, for example) reinforce its themes and tones? Write an essay in which you explore the relationship between "sound and sense" in the poem.
3. Some of the sonnets in this chapter, such as those by Shakespeare, Sidney, and Constable, adhere closely to the classic English model; others, such as those by Keats, Milton, and Roberts, use variations on the Italian model; and some, such as those by Dave Smith and Henri Cole, bear only slight resemblance to either of the traditional sonnet forms. Take any four sonnets found in this chapter as the basis for an essay in which you compare and contrast the various ways poets have used the sonnet form to achieve their unique artistic purposes.
4. Trace the variations on imagery of light and darkness in Thomas's "Do Not Go Gentle into That Good Night." How do we know that light represents life and darkness death (rather than, say, sight and blindness)? How does the poet use the strict formal requirements of the villanelle to emphasize this interplay of light and darkness? Write an essay in which you discuss the interaction of form and content in "Do Not Go Gentle into That Good Night."
5. Every poem has a structure, whether or not it adheres to a traditional form or to conventional ideas about line, rhythm, or spacing. Examine closely the structure of any poem or group of poems in this book. How does the poet use form to shape sound, emotion, and meaning? Write an essay in which you examine the structural choices that determine both the form and the content of these poems.
6. Research Anglo-Saxon poetry and look at classic examples, such as *Beowulf* and "The Seafarer." What are the principles of sound and the function of poetry that inform these Old English poems? Now consider Birney's "Anglosaxon Street." How successful is Birney in applying these principles to a modern poem? Is Birney's poem "serious"? Is it a parody? Write an essay in which you discuss the sound patterns and the form of "Anglosaxon Street" in light of your findings.

8 THE WHOLE TEXT

In the previous seven chapters, we have been thinking about one thing at a time—setting, word choice, symbolism, meter, stanza form, and so on—and we have discussed each poem primarily in terms of a single issue. Learning to deal with one problem at a time is good educational practice and in the long run will make you a more careful and more effective reader of poems. Still, the elements of poems do not work individually but in combination, and in considering even the simplest elements (speaker, for example, or setting) we have noticed how categories overlap—how, for example, the question of setting in Dickey's "Cherrylog Road" quickly merges into questions about the speaker, his state of mind, his personality, his distance from the central events in the poem. Thinking about a single issue never does complete justice to an individual poem; no poem depends for all its effects on just one device or one element of the poet's craft. Poems are complex wholes that demand various kinds of attention, and, ultimately, to read any poem fully and well you need to ask every question about craft, form, and tradition that we've asked so far, and many more questions you may learn to ask after more experience in reading poems. Not all questions are equally relevant to all poems, of course, but moving systematically through your whole repertoire of questions will enable you to get beyond the fragmentation of particular issues in order to approach the whole poem and its multiple effects. In this chapter we will consider how the various elements in poems work together.

Below is a short poem in which several issues we have considered come up almost simultaneously.

ELIZABETH JENNINGS

Delay

The radiance of that star that leans on me
Was shining years ago. The light that now
Glitters up there my eye may never see
And so the time lag teases me with how

5   Love that loves now may not reach me until
Its first desire is spent. The star's impulse
Must wait for eyes to claim it beautiful
And love arrived may find us somewhere else.

1953

In most poems, several issues arise more or less at once, and the analytic practice of separating issues is a convenience rather than an assertion of priorities. In "Delay," a lot of the basic questions (about speaker, situation, and setting, for example) seem to be put on hold in the beginning, but if we proceed systematically the poem opens itself to us. The first line identifies the "I" (or rather, in this case, "me") of the poem as an observer of the bright star that is the main object in the poem and the principal source of its imagery, its "plot," and its analogical argument. But we learn little about the speaker. She surfaces again in lines 4 and 5 and with someone else ("us") in line 8, but she is always "me" in the objective case—acted on rather than acting. All we know for certain about her is that she can speak about the time it takes a star's light to reach her and that she contemplates deeply about the meaning and effect of such time lags. We know even less about the setting and situation; somewhere the speaker watches a bright star and meditates on the fact that she is seeing it long, long after its light was actually sent forth. Her location is not specified, and the time, though probably night, could be any night (in the age of modern astronomy, that is, because the speaker knows about the speed of light and the distance of the stars from Earth); the only other explicit clues we have about the situation involve the "us" of the final line and the fact that the speaker's concern with time seems oddly personal, something that matters to her emotional life—not merely a matter of scientific knowledge.

The poem's language helps us understand much more about the speaker and her situation, as do the poem's structure and stanza form. The most crucial word in the first stanza is probably the verb "leans" (line 1); certainly it is the poem's most unusual and surprising word. Because a star cannot literally *lean* on its observer, the word seems to suggest the speaker's perception of her relationship to the star. Perhaps she feels that the star impinges on her, that she is somehow *subject* to its influence, though not in the popular, astrological sense. Here the star influences the speaker because she understands something about the way the universe works and can apply her knowledge of light and the vastness of space in an analogical way to her own life: it "leans" because it tells her something about how observers are affected by what they observe. And it is worth noticing how fully the speaker thinks of herself as object rather than actor or agent. Here, as throughout the poem, she is acted upon; things happen *to* her—the star leans on her, the time lag teases her (line 4), love may not reach her (line 5), and she (along with someone else) is the object sought in the final line.

Other crucial words also help clarify the speaker and her situation. The words "radiance" (line 1) and "[g]litters" (line 3) are fairly standard ones to describe stars, but here their standard meanings are carefully qualified by their position in time. The actual radiance of the starlight occurred many eons before and seems to be unavailable to the speaker, who now sees only glitter, something far less warm and resonant. And the word "impulse" in line 6 invokes technical knowledge about light. Rather than being impulsive or quickly spent, a star must "wait" for its reception in the eye of the beholder, where it becomes "beautiful"; in physics, an impulse combines force and duration. Hence, the receiver of light—the beholder, the acted-upon—becomes important, and we begin to see why the speaker always appears as the object: she is the receiver and interpreter, and the light is not complete—its duration not established—until she receives and interprets it. The star does, after all, "lean" on (depend on) her in some objective sense as well as the subjective one in which she first seems to report it.

The stanza form suggests that the poem may have stages and that its meaning may emerge in two parts, a suggestion confirmed by the poem's form and structure. The first stanza is entirely about stars and stargazing, but the second stanza establishes the analogy with love that becomes the poem's central metaphor. Now, too, more becomes clear about the speaker and her situation. Her concern is about delay, "time lag" (line 4), and the fact that "[l]ove that loves now may not reach me until / Its first desire is spent" (lines 5–6), a strong indication that her initial observation of the star is driven by feeling and her emotional context. Her attempt to put the remoteness of feeling into a perspective that will enable understanding and patience becomes the "plot" of the poem, and her final calm recognition about "us"—that "love arrived may find us somewhere else"—is, if not comforting, nevertheless a recognition that patience is important and that some things do last. Even the sounds of the poem—in this case the way rhyme is used—help support the meaning of the poem and the tone it achieves. The rhymes in the first part of the poem reflect perfectly the stable sense of ancient stars, while in the second stanza we find near-rhymes: there is harmony here, but in human life and emotion nothing is quite perfect.

Here is another short poem whose several elements deserve detailed attention:

ANONYMOUS

Western Wind

Western wind, when wilt thou blow,
  The small rain down can rain?
Christ, if my love were in my arms
  And I in my bed again!

15th century

Perhaps the most obvious thing here is the poem's structure: its first two lines seem to have little to do with the last two. How can we account for these two distinct and apparently unrelated directions, the calm concern with natural processes in the first part and the emotional outburst about loneliness and lovelessness in the second? The best route to the whole poem is still to begin with the most simple of questions—who? when? where? what is happening?—and proceed to more difficult and complex ones.

As in Jennings's "Delay," the speaker here offers little explicit autobiography. The first two lines provide no personal information but ask a question that could be delivered quite impersonally: they could be part of a philosophical meditation. The abbreviated syntax at the end of line 1 (the question of causality is not fully stated, and we have to supply the "so that" implied at the end of the line) may suggest strong feeling and emotional upset, but it tells us nothing intimate, only that the time is spring (which is when the western wind blows). No place is indicated, no year, no particulars of situation. But lines 3–4, while remaining inexplicit about exact details, make the speaker's situation clear enough: his love is no longer in his arms, and he wishes she were. (We don't know genders here, but we can guess based on what we know of typical practices in fifteenth-century England.)

The poem's language, a study in contrast, guides us to see the two-part structure clearly. The question asked of the wind in lines 1–2 involves straightforward, steady language, but line 3 bursts with agony and personal despair. The power of the first word of line 3—especially in an age of belief—suggests a speaker ready to bewail his loss in the strongest possible terms, and the parallel statements of loss in lines 3 and 4 suggest not only the speaker's physical relationship to his love but also his displacement from home: he is deprived of both place and love, human contact and contact with his past. His longing for a world ordered according to his past experience is structured to parallel his longing for the spring wind that brings the world back to life. The two parts of the poem both express a desire for return—to life, to order, to causal relationships within the world. Setting has in fact become a central theme in the poem, and what the poem expresses tonally involves a powerful desire for stability and belonging—an effect that grows out of our sense of the speaker's situation and character. Speaker, setting, language, and structure here intertwine to create the intense focus of the poem.

In the following short poem, several elements likewise interrelate:

ROBERT HERRICK

Upon Julia's Clothes

Whenas in silks my Julia goes
Then, then, methinks, how sweetly flows
That liquefaction of her clothes.

Next, when I cast mine eyes, and see
5   That brave¹ vibration, each way free,
O, how that glittering taketh me!

1648

The poem is unabashed in its admiration of the way Julia looks, and nearly everything in its six short lines contributes to its celebratory tone. Perhaps the most striking thing about the poem is its unusual, highly suggestive use of words. "[G]oes" at the end of line 1 may be the first word to call special attention to itself, though we will return in a minute to the very first word of the poem. "Walks" or "moves" would seem to be more obvious choices; "goes" is more neutral and less specific and in most circumstances would seem an inferior choice, but here the point seems to be to describe Julia in a kind of seamless and unspecified motion and from a specific angle, because the poem wants to record the effect of Julia's movement on the speaker (already a second element becomes crucial) rather than the specifics of Julia herself. Another word that seems especially important is "liquefaction" (line 3), also an unusual and suggestive word about motion. Again it implies no specific kind of motion, just smoothness and seamlessness, and it applies not to Julia but to her clothes. Other words that might repay a close look

---

1. Handsome, showy.

include "vibration" in line 5 (the speaker is finally a little more direct); "brave" and "free," also in line 5; and "glittering" and "taketh" in line 6.

Had we begun conventionally by thinking about speaker, situation, and setting, we would have quickly noticed the precise way that the speaker clothes Julia: "in silks," which move almost as one with her body. And we would have noticed that the speaker positions himself almost as voyeur (standing for us as observers, of course, but also for himself as the central figure in the poem). Not much detail about situation or setting is given (and the speaker is characterized only as a viewer and appreciator), but one thing about the scene is crucial, and this takes us back to the first word of the poem, "whenas." The slightly quaint quality of the word may at first obscure, to a modern reader, just what it tells us about the situation, that it is a *generic* scene rather than a single event. "Whenas" is very close to "when-ever"; the speaker's claim seems to be that he responds this way *whenever* Julia dons her silks—apparently fairly often, at least in his memory or imagination.

Most of the speaker's language is sensual and rather provocative (he is anxious to share his responses with others so that *everyone* will know just how "taking" Julia is), but one rather elaborate (though somewhat disguised) metaphor suggests his awareness of his own calculation and its consequences. In the beginning of the second stanza he describes how he "cast" his eyes: it is a metaphor from fishing, a frequent one in love poetry about luring, chasing, and catching. Julia, of course, is the object. The metaphor continues two lines later, but the angler has caught himself: he is taken by the "glittering" lure. This turning of the tables, drawing as it does on a traditional, common image that is then modified to help characterize the speaker, gives a little depth to the show: whatever the slither and glitter, there is not just showing off and sensuality but a catch in this angling.

Many other elements deserve comment, especially because they quickly relate to each other. Consider the way the poet uses sounds, first of all in picking words like "liquefaction" that are themselves almost onomatopoeic, but then also using rhyme very cleverly. There are only two rhyme sounds in the poem, one in the first stanza, the other in the second. The long *ee* of the second becomes almost exclamatory, and the three words of the first seem to become linked in a kind of separate grammar of their own, as if "goes," "flows," and "clothes" were all part of a single action—pretty much what the poem claims on a thematic level. A lot happens in this short and simple poem, and although a reader can get at it step by step by thinking about element after element, the interlocking of the elements is finally the most impressive effect of all. Although the plot reenacts familiar stances of woman as object and man as gazer, our analysis and reading need to be flexible enough to consider not only all the analytical categories, but also the ways in which they work together.

Going back to poems read earlier in the book—with the methods and approaches you have learned since then—can help you see how different elements of poems interrelate. Look, for example, at the stanza divisions in Dickey's "Cherry-log Road" (chapter 3) and consider how the neatly spaced, apparently discrete units work against the sometimes frantic pacing of the poem. Or consider the character of the speaker, or the fundamental metaphor of "wreckage" that sponsors the poem, relative to the idea of the speaker. Go back and read Kumin's "Woodchucks" (chapter 1) while thinking about structural questions; or consider how the effaced speaker works in Rich's "Aunt Jennifer's Tigers" (chapter 1); or think about metaphor in Nemerov's "The Vacuum" (page 36).

Here are several more poems to analyze. As you read them, think about the elements discussed in the previous seven chapters—but rather than thinking about a single element at a time, try to consider relationships, how the different elements combine to make you respond not to a single device but to a complex set of strategies and effects.

. . .

CD **W. H. AUDEN**

WEB *Musée des Beaux Arts*[2]

> About suffering they were never wrong,
> The Old Masters: how well they understood
> Its human position; how it takes place
> While someone else is eating or opening a window or just walking
>   dully along;
> 5 How, when the aged are reverently, passionately waiting
> For the miraculous birth, there always must be
> Children who did not specially want it to happen, skating
> On a pond at the edge of the wood:
> They never forgot
> 10 That even the dreadful martyrdom must run its course
> Anyhow in a corner, some untidy spot
> Where the dogs go on with their doggy life and the torturer's horse
> Scratches its innocent behind on a tree.
>
> In Brueghel's *Icarus*,[3] for instance: how everything turns away
> 15 Quite leisurely from the disaster; the plowman may
> Have heard the splash, the forsaken cry,
> But for him it was not an important failure; the sun shone
> As it had to on the white legs disappearing into the green
> Water; and the expensive delicate ship that must have seen
> 20 Something amazing, a boy falling out of the sky,
> Had somewhere to get to and sailed calmly on.

1938

- Find a reproduction of the painting—*Landscape with the Fall of Icarus*, by Pieter Brueghel the Elder—that is the subject of this poem. How is your interpretation affected by examining the painting?

---

2. The Museum of the Fine Arts, in Brussels.

3. *Landscape with the Fall of Icarus,* by Pieter Brueghel the Elder (1525?–1569), located in the Brussels museum. According to Greek myth, Daedalus and his son, Icarus, escaped from imprisonment by using homemade wings of feathers and wax; but Icarus flew too near the sun, the wax melted, and he fell into the sea and drowned. In the Brueghel painting the central figure is a peasant plowing, and several other figures are more immediately noticeable than Icarus, who, disappearing into the sea, is easy to miss in the lower right-hand corner.

GEORGE HERBERT

The Collar

I struck the board[4] and cried, "No more;
       I will abroad!
What? shall I ever sigh and pine?
My lines[5] and life are free, free as the road,
5   Loose as the wind, as large as store.[6]
         Shall I be still in suit?[7]
Have I no harvest but a thorn
To let me blood, and not restore
What I have lost with cordial[8] fruit?
10   Sure there was wine
Before my sighs did dry it; there was corn
  Before my tears did drown it.
Is the year only lost to me?
  Have I no bays[9] to crown it,
15 No flowers, no garlands gay? All blasted?
         All wasted?
Not so, my heart; but there is fruit,
    And thou hast hands.
Recover all thy sigh-blown age
20 On double pleasures: leave thy cold dispute
Of what is fit, and not. Forsake thy cage,[1]
       Thy rope of sands,
Which petty thoughts have made, and made to thee
  Good cable, to enforce and draw,
25   And be thy law,
While thou didst wink[2] and wouldst not see.
      Away! take heed;
      I will abroad.
Call in thy death's-head[3] there; tie up thy fears.
30   He that forbears
  To suit and serve his need,
      Deserves his load."
But as I raved and grew more fierce and wild
    At every word,
35 Methought I heard one calling, *Child!*
  And I replied, *My Lord.*

1633

- How does knowledge of Herbert's profession—clergyman—help you
  to interpret the title and the rest of the poem? What do the many
  metaphors in the poem suggest about the speaker's state of mind?

---

4. Table.   5. Lot.   6. A storehouse; that is, abundance.   7. In service to another.
8. Reviving, restorative.   9. Laurel wreaths of triumph.   1. Moral restrictions.
2. That is, close your eyes to the weaknesses of such restrictions.
3. *Memento mori,* a skull intended to remind people of their mortality.

ROBERT FROST

[WEB] *Design*

I found a dimpled spider, fat and white,
On a white heal-all,[4] holding up a moth
Like a white piece of rigid satin cloth—
Assorted characters of death and blight
5 Mixed ready to begin the morning right,
Like the ingredients of a witches' broth—
A snow-drop spider, a flower like a froth,
And dead wings carried like a paper kite.

What had that flower to do with being white,
10 The wayside blue and innocent heal-all?
What brought the kindred spider to that height,
Then steered the white moth thither in the night?
What but design of darkness to appall?—
If design govern in a thing so small.

1936

- How does this poem confound preconceptions about "light" and "darkness"? How does its elaborate form complement its theme?

D. H. LAWRENCE

Piano

Softly, in the dusk, a woman is singing to me;
Taking me back down the vista of years, till I see
A child sitting under the piano, in the boom of the tingling strings
And pressing the small, poised feet of a mother who smiles as she sings.

5 In spite of myself, the insidious mastery of song
Betrays me back, till the heart of me weeps to belong
To the old Sunday evenings at home, with winter outside
And hymns in the cozy parlor, the tinkling piano our guide.

So now it is vain for the singer to burst into clamor
10 With the great black piano appassionato. The glamour
Of childish days is upon me, my manhood is cast
Down in the flood of remembrance, I weep like a child for the past.

1918

- How does each of the stanzas advance the narrative and the emotional content of the poem? When you read it aloud, what is the combined effect of the regular rhyme scheme and the irregular line lengths?

---

4. A plant, also called the "all-heal" and "self-heal," with tightly clustered violet-blue flowers.

EMILY DICKINSON

[*My Life had stood—a Loaded Gun—*]

My Life had stood—a Loaded Gun—
In Corners—till a Day
The Owner passed—identified—
And carried Me away—

5 And now We roam in Sovereign Woods—
And now We hunt the Doe—
And every time I speak for Him—
The Mountains straight reply—

And do I smile, such cordial light
10 Upon the Valley glow—
It is as a Vesuvian face
Had let its pleasure through—

And when at Night—Our good Day done—
I guard My Master's Head—
15 'Tis better than the Eider-Duck's
Deep Pillow—to have shared—

To foe of His—I'm deadly foe—
None stir the second time—
On whom I lay a Yellow Eye—
20 Or an emphatic Thumb—

Though I than He—may longer live
He longer must—than I—
For I have but the power to kill,
Without—the power to die—

ca. 1863

- How does Dickinson set up and then defy the reader's expectations
  through the poem's central metaphor—the speaker's life as a loaded
  gun? How do the poem's quirks (e.g., the jerky rhythm, the strange
  syntax, the slant rhymes) contribute to its overall effect?

BEN JONSON

Epitaph on Elizabeth, L. H.

Wouldst thou hear what man can say
In a little? Reader, stay.
Underneath this stone doth lie
As much beauty as could die;
5 Which in life did harbor give
To more virtue than doth live.
If at all she had a fault,
Leave it buried in this vault.
One name was Elizabeth;
10 Th' other, let it sleep with death:
Fitter, where it died, to tell,
Than that it lived at all. Farewell.

1616

- How are lines 4 and 6 expressing more than just common court-
liness? In what ways is poetry as much this poem's subject as the
beauty and virtue of Elizabeth?

VIRGINIA HAMILTON ADAIR

Cutting the Cake

Gowned and veiled for tribal ritual
in a maze of tulle and satin
with her eyes rimmed round in cat fur
and the stylish men about her
5 kissing kin and carefree suitors

long she looked unseeing past him
to her picture in the papers
print and photoflash embalming
the demise of the familiar
10 and he trembled as her fingers

took the dagger laid before them
for the ceremonial cutting
of the mounting tiers of sweetness
crowned with manikin and maiden
15 and her chop was so triumphant

that the groomlike little figure
from his lover at the apex
toppled over in the frosting
where a flower girl retrieved him
20 sucked him dry and bit his head off.

1996

- What is the effect on the poem's rhythm of having no punctuation?
  How does that rhythmic effect suit the story of the poem? How does
  the sound of the poem contribute to your understanding of the
  bride's character?

SAMUEL TAYLOR COLERIDGE

Kubla Khan

Or, a Vision in a Dream[5]

In Xanadu did Kubla Khan
A stately pleasure-dome decree:
Where Alph, the sacred river, ran
Through caverns measureless to man
5   Down to a sunless sea.
So twice five miles of fertile ground
With walls and towers were girdled round:
And here were gardens bright with sinuous rills
Where blossomed many an incense-bearing tree;
10 And here were forests ancient as the hills,
Enfolding sunny spots of greenery.

But oh! that deep romantic chasm which slanted
Down the green hill athwart a cedarn cover![6]
A savage place! as holy and enchanted
15 As e'er beneath a waning moon was haunted
By woman wailing for her demon-lover![7]
And from this chasm, with ceaseless turmoil seething,
As if this earth in fast thick pants were breathing,
A mighty fountain momently[8] was forced,
20 Amid whose swift half-intermitted burst
Huge fragments vaulted like rebounding hail,
Or chaffy grain beneath the thresher's flail:
And 'mid these dancing rocks at once and ever

5. Coleridge said he wrote this fragment immediately after waking from an opium dream and that after he
was interrupted by a caller he was unable to finish the poem.
6. From side to side beneath a cover of cedar trees.
7. In a famous and often-imitated German ballad, the lady Lenore is carried off on horseback by the specter
of her lover and married to him at his grave.   8. Suddenly.

It flung up momently the sacred river.
25 Five miles meandering with a mazy motion
Through wood and dale the sacred river ran,
Then reached the caverns measureless to man,
And sank in tumult to a lifeless ocean:
And 'mid this tumult Kubla heard from far
30 Ancestral voices prophesying war!

   The shadow of the dome of pleasure
   Floated midway on the waves;
   Where was heard the mingled measure
   From the fountain and the caves.
35 It was a miracle of rare device,
   A sunny pleasure-dome with caves of ice!

   A damsel with a dulcimer
   In a vision once I saw:
   It was an Abyssinian maid,
40   And on her dulcimer she played,
   Singing of Mount Abora.
   Could I revive within me
   Her symphony and song,
   To such a deep delight 'twould win me,
45 That with music loud and long,
   I would build that dome in air,
   That sunny dome! those caves of ice!
   And all who heard should see them there,
   And all should cry, Beware! Beware!
50 His flashing eyes, his floating hair!
   Weave a circle round him thrice,
   And close your eyes with holy dread,
   For he on honey-dew hath fed,
   And drunk the milk of Paradise.

1798

- In what ways does the poem bear out Coleridge's claim that it is only a "fragment"? In what ways does the poem seem complete? How does the subtitle, "a Vision in a Dream," or the knowledge that Coleridge's "dream" was induced by opium, affect your interpretation of the poem?

SUGGESTIONS FOR WRITING

1. Consider the setting of Auden's "Musée des Beaux Arts" in the sense of both the painting and its location in the museum. In what different ways do the two settings become important? How do they function to frame the story of Icarus, or the theme of suffering? Write an essay in which you discuss the way the poem's setting and structure contribute to the overall effect of the poem.

2. Consider both speaker and situation as you analyze Herbert's "The Collar." How does one of these elements illuminate the other? Write an essay in which you examine the way the poem's whole effect arises from an understanding of the speaker and situation.

3. Discussing Dickinson's "My Life had stood—a Loaded Gun," the poet Adrienne Rich has written, "I think it is a poem about possession by the daemon [of artistic creativity], about the dangers and risks of such possession if you are a woman, about the knowledge that power in a woman can seem destructive, and that you cannot live without the daemon once it has possessed you." Write an essay in which you respond to Rich's interpretation of Dickinson's poem.

4. Consider the interrelationships among speaker, structure, stanza form, and tone in Frost's "Design" or any other sonnet you have read in this book. How do the elements combine to create a unique whole? Write an essay in which you closely analyze a sonnet—its structure and language, as well as its subject, situation, imagery, and theme.

5. Some scholars have disputed Coleridge's claims about "Kubla Khan," contending that, in fact, the poem is not an incomplete fragment of an opium dream and that Coleridge concocted the story about being interrupted by "a person from Porlock." Research the circumstances surrounding the composition of "Kubla Khan," and write an essay in which you argue for or against the assertion that the poem can be considered "complete" on its own terms.

Exploring Contexts

9 READING POETRY IN CONTEXT

The more you know, the better a reader of poetry you will likely be. And that means general knowledge as well as knowledge of other poetry and literary traditions. Poems often draw on a large fund of human knowledge about all sorts of things, asking us to regard a poem in light of facts and values we have taken on from earlier reading or from our experiences in the world. In the previous eight chapters, we have looked at how practice and specific skills make interpretation easier and better; in this "contextual" section we shift our focus to information you need to read richly and fully: information about authors, about events that influenced them or inspired their writing, and about literary traditions that provide a context for their work. Poets always write in a specific time, under unique circumstances, and with some awareness of the world around them, whether or not they explicitly refer to contemporary matters in a particular poem. In this chapter, we will discuss the cultural and historical events, movements, and ideas that directly influence poets or that poets in some way represent in the poems they write.

Very little that you know will ultimately go to waste in your reading of poetry. The best potential reader of poetry has already read widely and thought deeply about all kinds of things, and is supremely wise—wise enough to know exactly how to apply specific knowledge to a given text. We all strive to be that ideal reader, but none of us can fully measure up. Of course, no poet really expects any reader to be perfect, but poems themselves can make special demands: they may require readers to know as much about history, for example, as about the intricacies of language and form. Poems not only *refer* to people, places, and events—things that exist in time—but they also are reflections of given moments, products of both the potentialities and the limitations of the times in which they are created.

Things that happen every day often find their way into poetry in a natural and yet forceful manner. Making love in a junkyard, as in Dickey's "Cherrylog Road" (chapter 3) is a good example; a reader doesn't need to know what particular junkyard was involved—or imaginatively involved—in order to understand the poem, but that reader does need to know what an auto junkyard was like in the mid-twentieth century, with more or less whole car bodies in various states of disintegration roughly arrayed on a large plot of ground. But what if, over the next generation or two, junkyards completely disappear as we find other ways to dispose of old cars? Already, especially in large cities, many old cars are crushed into small metal blocks. But what if the metal is all melted down, or the junk is blasted into space? If that should happen, readers then may have never seen a junkyard, and they will need a footnote to explain what junkyards were like. The history of junkyards will not be lost—people will have pictures, films, and books about the forms and functions of junkyards, probably even the fact that lovers occasionally visited them—but the public memory of junkyards will soon disappear. No social customs, nothing that is made, no institutions or sites can last forever.

Readers may still be able to experience "Cherrylog Road" when junkyards disappear, but they will need some help, and they may think its particulars a little quaint, much as we regard a story that involves a horse and buggy—or even making love in the back-seat of a parked car—as quaint now. Institutions change, habits change, times change, places and settings change—all kinds of particulars change, even when people's wants, needs, and foibles go on in pretty much the same way. Footnotes never provide a precise or adequate substitute for firsthand knowledge, but they can help our understanding and pave the way for feeling. With the aid of footnotes, poems from earlier times can stimulate in readers a kind of imaginative historical sympathy, for poems that refer to specific contemporary details (which have now become to us, in our own time, *historical* details) often describe human nature and human experiences very much as we still know and live them. Today's poem may need tomorrow's footnote, but the poem need not be tomorrow's puzzle—or just a curiosity or fossil.

The following poem, not that many years old, already requires some explanation. Many readers will not know the factual details of the event that occasioned it, and (even more important) most readers will not recall the powerful reaction throughout the United States to the event.

JAMES A. EMANUEL

Emmett Till[1]

I hear a whistling
Through the water.
Little Emmett
Won't be still.
5   He keeps floating
Round the darkness,
Edging through
The silent chill.
Tell me, please,
10   That bedtime story
Of the fairy
River Boy
Who swims forever,
Deep in treasures,
15   Necklaced in
A coral toy.

1968

---

1. In 1955, Till, a black fourteen-year-old from Chicago, was lynched in Mississippi for allegedly making sexual advances toward a white woman.

How do you know what you need to know? The easiest clue is your own puzzlement. When something that you don't recognize happens in a poem—and yet the poem seems not to clarify it—you have a clue that readers at the time the poem was written must have recognized something that is not now common knowledge. Once you know you don't know, it takes only a little work to find out: most college libraries (and, of course, the Internet) contain far more information than you will ever need, and the trick is to search efficiently. Your ability to find the information will depend upon how well you know the printed reference materials and digital resources available to you. Practice helps. Knowledge accumulates. Most poems printed in textbooks like this one will be annotated for you with basic facts, but often you will need additional information before you can interpret a poem's full meaning and feel its resonance. An editor, trying to satisfy the needs of a variety of readers, may not always write the note you particularly need, so you may have to do some digging in the library for the sake of fully appreciating any poem you read—certainly for those you come upon in old magazines and unannotated collections. Few poets like to annotate their own work (they'd rather let you work a little to appreciate it), and besides, many things that now need notes didn't when they were written.

The two poems that follow both require from the reader some specific "referential" information, but they differ considerably in their emphasis on the particularities of time and place. The first poem concerns a moment just before the outbreak of World War I when British naval forces were preparing for combat by taking gunnery practice in the English Channel. The second represents a longer cultural moment in which attitudes and assumptions, rather than a specific event, are at stake.

THOMAS HARDY

Channel Firing

That night your great guns, unawares,
Shook all our coffins as we lay,
And broke the chancel window squares,[2]
We thought it was the Judgment-day

5 And sat upright. While drearisome
Arose the howl of wakened hounds:
The mouse let fall the altar-crumb,[3]
The worms drew back into the mounds,

The glebe cow[4] drooled. Till God called, "No;
10 It's gunnery practice out at sea
Just as before you went below;
The world is as it used to be:

---

2. The windows near the altar in a church.   3. Breadcrumbs from the sacrament of Communion.
4. Parish cow pastured on the meadow next to the churchyard.

"All nations striving strong to make
Red war yet redder. Mad as hatters
15 They do no more for Christés sake
Than you who are helpless in such matters.

"That this is not the judgment-hour
For some of them's a blessed thing,
For if it were they'd have to scour
20 Hell's floor for so much threatening . . .

"Ha, ha. It will be warmer when
I blow the trumpet (if indeed
I ever do; for you are men,
And rest eternal sorely need)."

25 So down we lay again. "I wonder,
Will the world ever saner be,"
Said one, "than when He sent us under
In our indifferent century!"

And many a skeleton shook his head.
30 "Instead of preaching forty year,"
My neighbor Parson Thirdly said,
"I wish I had stuck to pipes and beer."

Again the guns disturbed the hour,
Roaring their readiness to avenge.
35 As far inland as Stourton Tower,
And Camelot, and starlit Stonehenge.[5]

April 1914

SANDRA GILBERT

Sonnet: The Ladies' Home Journal

The brilliant stills of food, the cozy
glossy, bygone life—mashed potatoes
posing as whipped cream, a neat mom
conjuring shapes from chaos, trimming the flame—
5 how we ached for all that,
that dance of love in the living room,
those paneled walls, that kitchen golden
as the inside of a seed: how we leaned

---

5. A circular formation of upright stones dating from about 1600 B.C.E. on Salisbury Plain, Wiltshire; it is thought to have been a ceremonial site for political and religious occasions or perhaps an early astronomical observatory. *Stourton Tower:* a monument in Stourhead Park, Wiltshire, built in the eighteenth century to commemorate King Alfred's ninth-century victory over the Danes. *Camelot:* the legendary site of King Arthur's court, said to have been in Cornwall or Somerset.

on those shiny columns of advice,
10 stroking the *thank yous,* the firm thighs, the wise
closets full of soap.

       But even then
we knew it was the lies we loved, the lies
we wore like Dior coats,[6] the clean-cut airtight
lies that laid out our lives in black and white.

                                    1984

"Channel Firing" is not ultimately *about* World War I, for it presumes that human behavior stays the same from age to age, but it begins from a particular historical vantage point. The composition date was recorded by the author on the manuscript and is considered part of the poem, but even with that clue a reader would not be able to make much sense of the poem without recognizing the specific reference—the dramatic situation here (with a waking corpse as the main speaker) is difficult enough to sort out. The firing of the guns has awakened the dead who are buried near the channel, and in their puzzlement they assume it is Judgment Day, time for them to arise, until God enters and tells them what is happening. Much of the poem's effect depends on character portrayal—a God who laughs and sounds cynical, a parson who regrets his selfless life and wishes he had indulged himself more—as well as the sense that nothing ever changes. But particularity of time and place is crucial to this sense of changelessness; even so important a contemporary moment as the beginning of a world war—a moment viewed by most people at the time as unique and world-changing—fades into a timeless parade of moments that stretches over centuries of history. The geographical particulars cited at the end—as the sound of the guns moves inland to be heard in place after place—make the same point. Great moments in history are all encompassed in the sound of the guns and its message about human behavior. Times, places, and events, however important they seem, all become part of some larger pattern that denies individuality or uniqueness.

The particulars in "Sonnet: The Ladies' Home Journal" work differently—not to remind us of a specific time that readers need to identify but to characterize a way of seeing and thinking. The referentiality here is more cultural than historical; it is based more on ideas and attitudes characteristic of a particular period than on a specific moment or location. The pictures in the *Ladies' Home Journal* stand for a whole way of thinking about women that was characteristic of the time—the mid-twentieth century—when this popular magazine flourished. The poem implicitly contrasts the "lies" (line 13) of the magazine with the truth of the present— that women's lives and values don't reside in some fantasized sense of beautiful food, motherhood, social rituals, and commercial products. Two vastly different cultural attitudes—that of the poem's present, with its skeptical view of women's traditional roles, and that of a past in which carefully posed glossy photographs represented an idealized womanhood—are at the heart of the poem. Readers need to know what the *Ladies' Home Journal* was like generally in order to understand the poem; we do not need to know the date or contents of a specific issue, only

6. Designer coats by Christian Dior.

that this magazine reflected the attitudes and values of a whole age and culture. The referentiality here involves information about ideas and consciousness—about cultural attitudes and their effects on actual human beings—more than the specifics of time and event.

To get at appropriate factual, cultural, and historical information, we need to ask three kinds of questions. One is obvious: it is the "Do I understand the reference to . . . ?" kind. When events, places, or people unfamiliar to you come up, you will need to find out what, where, or who they are. The second kind of question is more difficult: How do you know, in a poem that does *not* refer specifically to events, people, or ideas that you do not recognize, that you *need* to know more? When a poem has no specific references to look up, no people or events to identify, how do you know that it has a specific context? To deal with this sort of question, you have to trust two people: the poet and yourself. Usually, good poets will not puzzle you more than necessary, so you can safely assume that something not self-explanatory will merit close attention and possibly some digging in the library. (Poets do make mistakes and miscalculations about their readers, but at first we should assume they know what they are doing and why they are doing it.) References that are not in themselves clear provide a strong clue that you need more information. And so you need to trust yourself: when something doesn't click, when the information given you does not seem enough, you need to trust your puzzlement and try to find the missing facts that will allow the poem to make sense. But how? Often the date of the poem helps; sometimes the title gives a clue or a point of departure; sometimes you can uncover, by reading about the author, some of the things he or she was interested in or concerned about. There is no single all-purpose way to discover what to look for, but that kind of research—looking for clues, adding up the evidence—can be interesting in itself and very rewarding when it is successful. Meanwhile, the third question, for every factual reference, is *Why?* Why does the poem refer to this particular person instead of some other? What function does the reference serve?

Beyond simply understanding that a particular poem is about an event or place or idea, you often must develop a full sense of historical context, a sense of the larger significance and resonance of the historical background. A poem may expect you already to have some sense of that significance; just as often the poem works to educate you further, both in your understanding and also on the level of feeling.

What we need to bring to our reading varies from poem to poem. For example, Wilfred Owen's "Dulce et Decorum Est" (in this chapter) needs our knowledge that poison gas was used in World War I; the green tint through which the speaker sees the world in lines 13–14 comes from the green glass in the goggles of the gas mask he has just put on. But some broader issues matter as well, such as the climate of opinion that surrounded the war. To idealists, it would become "the war to end all wars," and many soldiers—as well as politicians and propagandists—considered it a sacred mission, regarding the threat of Germany's expansionist policy as dangerous to Western civilization itself. No doubt you will read the poem more intelligently—and with more feeling—the more you know about the context, and the same is true of any poem conscious of its cultural or historical basis. But at the same time, your sense of these subjects will grow as a result of reading sensitively and thoughtfully the poems themselves. Facts are no substitute for skills. Once you have read each of the poems in this section, try taking a breather; and then in one sitting read them all again. Reading poetry can be a form of gaining knowledge as well as an aesthetic experience. Although we don't generally turn to poetry for information as such, poems often give us more than we expect. The ways to wisdom are paved with facts, and although poetry is not primarily a means of transmitting facts, it often requires us to be aware, sometimes in detail, of its context in the real world.

TIMES, PLACES, AND EVENTS

EMMA LAZARUS

1492

Thou two-faced year, Mother of Change and Fate,
Didst weep when Spain cast forth with flaming sword,[1]
The children of the prophets of the Lord,
Prince, priest, and people, spurned by zealot hate.
5 Hounded from sea to sea, from state to state,
The West refused them, and the East abhorred.
No anchorage the known world could afford,
Close-locked was every port, barred every gate.
Then smiling, thou unveil'dst, O two-faced year,
10 A virgin world where doors of sunset part,
Saying, "Ho, all who weary, enter here!"
There falls each ancient barrier that the art
Of race or creed or rank devised, to rear
Grim bulwarked hatred between heart and heart!"

1883

DUDLEY RANDALL

Ballad of Birmingham

(On the bombing of a church in Birmingham, Alabama, 1963)

"Mother dear, may I go downtown
Instead of out to play,
And march the streets of Birmingham
In a Freedom March today?"

---

1. In the same year that Columbus "discovered" America and claimed it for Spain, all Jews were expelled from Spain at the height of the Inquisition.

5   "No, baby, no, you may not go,
     For the dogs are fierce and wild,
     And clubs and hoses, guns and jails
     Aren't good for a little child."

     "But, mother, I won't be alone.
10 Other children will go with me,
     And march the streets of Birmingham
     To make our country free."

     "No, baby, no, you may not go,
     For I fear those guns will fire.
15 But you may go to church instead
     And sing in the children's choir."

     She has combed and brushed her night-dark hair,
     And bathed rose petal sweet,
     And drawn white gloves on her small brown hands,
20 And white shoes on her feet.

     The mother smiled to know her child
     Was in the sacred place,
     But that smile was the last smile
     To come upon her face.

25 For when she heard the explosion,
     Her eyes grew wet and wild.
     She raced through the streets of Birmingham
     Calling for her child.

     She clawed through bits of glass and brick,
30 Then lifted out a shoe.
     "Oh, here's the shoe my baby wore,
     But, baby, where are you?"

                                        1969

WILFRED OWEN

[WEB] *Dulce et Decorum Est*[2]

     Bent double, like old beggars under sacks,
     Knock-kneed, coughing like hags, we cursed through sludge,
     Till on the haunting flares we turned our backs
     And towards our distant rest began to trudge.
5 Men marched asleep. Many had lost their boots

---

2. Part of a phrase from Horace (Roman poet and satirist, 65–8 B.C.E.), quoted in full in the last lines: "It is sweet and proper to die for one's country."

But limped on, blood-shod. All went lame; all blind;
Drunk with fatigue; deaf even to the hoots
Of disappointed shells that dropped behind.

Gas! Gas! Quick, boys!—An ecstasy of fumbling,
10 Fitting the clumsy helmets just in time;
But someone still was yelling out and stumbling
And floundering like a man in fire or lime.—
Dim, through the misty panes and thick green light
As under a green sea, I saw him drowning.

15 In all my dreams, before my helpless sight,
He plunges at me, guttering, choking, drowning.

If in some smothering dreams you too could pace
Behind the wagon that we flung him in,
And watch the white eyes writhing in his face,
20 His hanging face, like a devil's sick of sin;
If you could hear, at every jolt, the blood
Come gargling from the froth-corrupted lungs,
Obscene as cancer, bitter as the cud
Of vile, incurable sores on innocent tongues,—
25 My friend, you would not tell with such high zest
To children ardent for some desperate glory,
The old Lie: Dulce et decorum est
Pro patria mori.

1917

MILLER WILLIAMS

Thinking about Bill, Dead of AIDS

We did not know the first thing about
how blood surrenders to even the smallest threat
when old allergies turn inside out,

the body rescinding all its normal orders
5 to all defenders of flesh, betraying the head,
pulling its guards back from all its borders.

Thinking of friends afraid to shake your hand,
we think of your hand shaking, your mouth set,
your eyes drained of any reprimand.

10 Loving, we kissed you, partly to persuade
both you and us, seeing what eyes had said,
that we were loving and were not afraid.

If we had had more, we would have given more.
As it was we stood next to your bed,
15 stopping, though, to set our smiles at the door.

Not because we were less sure at the last.
Only because, not knowing anything yet,
we didn't know what look would hurt you least.

1989

IRVING LAYTON

From Colony to Nation

A dull people,
but the rivers of this country
are wide and beautiful

A dull people
5 enamoured of childish games,
but food is easily come by
and plentiful

Some with a priest's voice
in their cage of ribs: but
10 on high mountain-tops and in thunderstorms
the chirping is not heard

Deferring to beadle and censor;
not ashamed for this,
but given over to horseplay,
15 the making of money

A dull people, without charm or
ideas,
settling into the clean empty look
of a Mountie or dairy farmer
20 as into a legacy

One can ignore them
(the silences, the vast distances help)
and suppose them at the bottom
of one of the meaner lakes,
25 their bones not even picked for souvenirs.

1956

SEAMUS HEANEY

Punishment[3]

I can feel the tug
of the halter at the nape
of her neck, the wind
on her naked front.

5 It blows her nipples
to amber beads,
it shakes the frail rigging
of her ribs.

I can see her drowned
10 body in the bog,
the weighing stone,
the floating rods and boughs.

Under which at first
she was a barked sapling
15 that is dug up
oak-bone, brain-firkin:

her shaved head
like a stubble of black corn,
her blindfold a soiled bandage,
20 her noose a ring

to store
the memories of love.
Little adulteress,
before they punished you

25 you were flaxen-haired,
undernourished, and your
tar-black face was beautiful.
My poor scapegoat,

I almost love you
30 but would have cast, I know,
the stones of silence.
I am the artful voyeur

---

3. According to the Roman historian Tacitus (ca. A.D. 56–ca. 120), Germanic peoples punished adulterous women by shaving their heads, then either banishing or killing them. In 1951, in Windeby, Germany, the naked body of a young girl from the first century C.E. was pulled from the bog where she had been murdered. In contemporary Ireland, "betraying sisters" (line 38) have sometimes been punished by the IRA for associating with British soldiers.

of your brain's exposed
and darkened combs,
35 your muscles' webbing
and all your numbered bones:

I who have stood dumb
when your betraying sisters,
cauled⁴ in tar,
40 wept by the railings,

who would connive
in civilized outrage
yet understand the exact
and tribal, intimate revenge.

1975

RITA DOVE

The House Slave

The first horn lifts its arm over the dew lit grass
and in the slave quarters there is a rustling—
children are bundled into aprons, cornbread

and water gourds grabbed, a salt pork breakfast taken.
5 I watch them driven into the vague before-dawn
while their mistress sleeps like an ivory toothpick

and Massa dreams of asses, rum and slave-funk.
I cannot fall asleep again. At the second horn,
the whip curls across the backs of the laggards—

10 sometimes my sister's voice, unmistaken, among them.
"Oh! pray," she cries. "Oh! pray!" Those days
I lie on my cot, shivering in the early heat,

and as the fields unfold to whiteness,
and they spill like bees among the fat flowers,
15 I weep. It is not yet daylight.

1980

---

4. Wrapped or enclosed as if in a caul (the inner fetal membrane of higher vertebrates that sometimes covers the head at birth).

Hattie McDaniel[5] Arrives at the Coconut Grove

late, in aqua and ermine, gardenias
scaling her left sleeve in a spasm of scent,
her gloves white, her smile chastened, purse giddy
with stars and rhinestones clipped to her brilliantined hair,
5 on her free arm that fine Negro
Mr. Wonderful Smith.

It's the day that isn't, February 29th,
at the end of the shortest month of the year—
and the shittiest, too, everywhere
10 except Hollywood, California,
where the maid can wear mink and still be a maid,
bobbing her bandaged head and cursing
the white folks under her breath as she smiles
and shoos their silly daughters
15 in from the night dew ... What can she be
thinking of, striding into the ballroom
where no black face has ever showed itself
except above a serving tray?

Hi-Hat Hattie, Mama Mac, Her Haughtiness,
20 the "little lady" from Showboat whose name
Bing forgot, Beulah & Bertha & Malena
& Carrie & Violet & Cynthia & Fidelia,
one half of the Dark Barrymores—
dear Mammy we can't help but hug you crawl into
25 your generous lap tease you
with arch innuendo so we can feel that
much more wicked and youthful
and sleek but oh what

we forgot: the four husbands, the phantom
30 pregnancy, your famous parties, your celebrated
ice box cake. Your giggle above the red petticoat's rustle,
black girl and white girl walking hand in hand
down the railroad tracks
in Kansas City, six years old.
35 The man who advised you, now

---

5. McDaniel (1895-1952) was the first black actor to win an Academy Award—for her portrayal of a maid in *Gone with the Wind* (1939). She was a popular and versatile artist, singer as well as actor, but controversial because she repeatedly played domestic help roles and some felt that she furthered the stereotyping of African Americans, although Dove here recalls her feisty side. The Coconut Grove was an exclusive Hollywood night spot.

that you were famous, to "begin eliminating"
your more "common" acquaintances
and your reply (catching him square
in the eye): "That's a good idea.
40 I'll start right now by eliminating you."

Is she or isn't she? Three million dishes,
a truckload of aprons and headrags later, and here
you are : poised, between husbands
and factions, no corset wide enough
45 to hold you in, your huge face a dark moon split
by that spontaneous smile—your trademark,
your curse. No matter, Hattie: it's a long, beautiful walk
into that flower-smothered standing ovation,
so go on
50 and make them wait.

2004

MBUYISENI OSWALD MTSHALI

Boy on a Swing

Slowly he moves
to and fro, to and fro,
then faster and faster
he swishes up and down.

5 His blue shirt
billows in the breeze
like a tattered kite.

The world whirls by:
east becomes west,
10 north turns to south;
the four cardinal points
meet in his head.

Mother!
Where did I come from?
15 When will I wear long trousers?
Why was my father jailed?

1982

FELICIA DOROTHEA HEMANS

Casabianca[6]

The boy stood on the burning deck
    Whence all but he had fled;
The flame that lit the battle's wreck
    Shone round him o'er the dead.

5 Yet beautiful and bright he stood,
    As born to rule the storm;
A creature of heroic blood,
    A proud, though childlike form.

The flames roll'd on—he would not go
10   Without his father's word;
That father, faint in death below,
    His voice no longer heard.

He call'd aloud:—"Say, Father, say
    If yet my task is done?"
15 He knew not that the chieftain lay
    Unconscious of his son.

"Speak, Father!" once again he cried,
    "If I may yet be gone!"
And but the booming shots replied,
20   And fast the flames roll'd on.

Upon his brow he felt their breath,
    And in his waving hair,
And look'd from that lone post of death
    In still, yet brave despair.

25 And shouted but once more aloud,
    "My Father! must I stay?"
While o'er him fast, through sail and shroud,
    The wreathing fires made way.

They wrapt the ship in splendor wild,
30   They caught the flag on high,
And stream'd above the gallant child,
    Like banners in the sky.

There came a burst of thunder sound—
    The boy—oh! where was he?
35 Ask of the winds that far around
    With fragments strew'd the sea!—

6. Young Casabianca, a boy about thirteen years old, son to the Admiral of the *Orient,* remained at his post (in the Battle of the Nile [1798]) after the ship had taken fire, and all the guns had been abandoned; and perished in the explosion of the vessel, when the flames had reached the powder [Hemans's note].

With mast, and helm, and pennon fair,
  That well had borne their part,
But the noblest thing which perish'd there
40 Was that young faithful heart

1829

ELIZABETH BISHOP

CD *Casabianca*

Love's the boy stood on the burning deck
trying to recite "The boy stood on
the burning deck." Love's the son
  stood stammering elocution
5 while the poor ship in flames went down.

Love's the obstinate boy, the ship,
even the swimming sailors, who
would like a schoolroom platform, too,
  or an excuse to stay
10 on deck. And love's the burning boy.

1946

JONATHAN SWIFT

A Satirical Elegy on the Death of a Late Famous General[7]

His Grace! impossible! what, dead!
Of old age[8] too, and in his bed!
And could that Mighty Warrior fall?
And so inglorious, after all!
5 Well, since he's gone, no matter how,
The last loud trump[9] must wake him now:
And, trust me, as the noise grows stronger,
He'd wish to sleep a little longer.
And could he be indeed so old
10 As by the newspapers we're told?
Threescore, I think, is pretty high;
'Twas time in conscience he should die.
This world he cumbered long enough;
He burnt his candle to the snuff;

---

7. John Churchill, First Duke of Marlborough (1650–1722), British military hero, whose personal reputation became, in the minds of many, tarnished in later life. He died on June 16, 1722. The poem was not published until more than forty years later.   8. Marlborough was seventy-two.   9. See I Corinthians, 15:52.

15 And that's the reason, some folks think,
　　He left behind *so great a stink.*
　　Behold his funeral appears,
　　Nor widow's sighs, nor orphan's tears,
　　Wont at such times each heart to pierce,
20 Attend the progress of his hearse.
　　But what of that, his friends may say,
　　He had those honors in his day.
　　True to his profit and his pride,
　　He made them weep before he died.

25 　　Come hither, all ye empty things,
　　Ye bubbles raised by breath of kings;[1]
　　Who float upon the tide of state,
　　Come hither, and behold your fate.
　　Let pride be taught by this rebuke,
30 How very mean a thing's a Duke;
　　From all his ill-got honors flung,
　　Turned to that dirt from whence he sprung.

1722

ROBERT HAYDEN

Frederick Douglass

When it is finally ours, this freedom,[2] this liberty, this beautiful
and terrible thing, needful to man as air,
usable as earth; when it belongs at last to all,
when it is truly instinct, brain matter, diastole, systole,
5 reflex action; when it is finally won; when it is more
than the gaudy mumbo jumbo of politicians:
this man, this Douglass, this former slave, this Negro
beaten to his knees, exiled, visioning a world
where none is lonely, none hunted, alien,
10 this man, superb in love and logic, this man
shall be remembered. Oh, not with statues' rhetoric,
not with legends and poems and wreaths of bronze alone,
but with the lives grown out of his life, the lives
fleshing his dream of the beautiful, needful thing.

1966

---

1. Monarchs had the power to bestow aristocratic titles.
2. Frederick Douglass (1817–1895), an escaped slave, was involved in the Underground Railroad and became publisher of the famous abolitionist newspaper the *North Star,* in Rochester, New York.

YUSEF KOMUNYAKAA

Facing It

My black face fades,
hiding inside the black granite.
I said I wouldn't,
dammit: No tears.
5 I'm stone. I'm flesh.
My clouded reflection eyes me
like a bird of prey, the profile of night
slanted against morning. I turn
this way—the stone lets me go.
10 I turn that way—I'm inside
the Vietnam Veterans Memorial
again, depending on the light
to make a difference.
I go down the 58,022 names,
15 half-expecting to find
my own in letters like smoke.
I touch the name Andrew Johnson;
I see the booby trap's white flash.
Names shimmer on a woman's blouse
20 but when she walks away
the names stay on the wall.
Brushstrokes flash, a red bird's
wings cutting across my stare.
The sky. A plane in the sky.
25 A white vet's image floats
closer to me, then his pale eyes
look through mine. I'm a window.
He's lost his right arm
inside the stone. In the black mirror
30 a woman's trying to erase names:
No, she's brushing a boy's hair.

1988

ROBERT FROST

The Gift Outright[3]

The land was ours before we were the land's.
She was our land more than a hundred years
Before we were her people. She was ours
In Massachusetts, in Virginia,
5   But we were England's, still colonials,
Possessing what we still were unpossessed by,
Possessed by what we now no more possessed.
Something we were withholding made us weak
Until we found out that it was ourselves
10   We were withholding from our land of living,
And forthwith found salvation in surrender.
Such as we were we gave ourselves outright
(The deed of gift was many deeds of war)
To the land vaguely realizing westward,
15   But still unstoried, artless, unenhanced,
Such as she was, such as she would become.

                                    1942, 1961

CONSTRUCTING IDENTITY, EXPLORING GENDER

ELIZABETH BISHOP

Exchanging Hats

Unfunny uncles who insist
in trying on a lady's hat,
—oh, even if the joke falls flat,
we share your slight transvestite twist

5   in spite of our embarrassment.
Costume and custom are complex.
The headgear of the other sex
inspires us to experiment.

---

3. Frost first "said" this poem publicly on December 5, 1941 (two days before the United States entered World War II) to the Phi Beta Kappa Society at William and Mary College, and published it the following year. Twenty years later, invited to "say" a poem at the presidential inauguration of John F. Kennedy, he read this poem (along with an elaborate poetic preface in which he offered Kennedy "the gift outright of 'The Gift Outright' ") again, substituting (at Kennedy's request) the word "will" for "would" in the final line.

Anandrous[1] aunts, who, at the beach
10 with paper plates upon your laps,
keep putting on the yachtsmen's caps
with exhibitionistic screech,

the visors hanging o'er the ear
so that the golden anchors drag,
15 —the tides of fashion never lag.
Such caps may not be worn next year.

Or you who don the paper plate
itself, and put some grapes upon it,
or sport the Indian's feather bonnet,
20 —perversities may aggravate

the natural madness of the hatter.
And if the opera hats collapse
and crowns grow drafty, then, perhaps,
he thinks what might a miter matter?

25 Unfunny uncle, you who wore a
hat too big, or one too many,
tell us, can't you, are there any
stars inside your black fedora?

Aunt exemplary and slim,
30 with avernal[2] eyes, we wonder
what slow changes they see under
their vast, shady, turned-down brim.

1956

Sonnet

Caught—the bubble
in the spirit-level,
a creature divided;
and the compass needle
5 wobbling and wavering,
undecided.
Freed—the broken
thermometer's mercury
running away;
10 and the rainbow-bird
from the narrow bevel
of the empty mirror,
flying wherever
it feels like, gay!

1999

---

1. Literally, "husbandless."   2. Infernal.

MARIE HOWE

Practicing

I want to write a love poem for the girls I kissed in seventh grade,
a song for what we did on the floor in the basement

of somebody's parents' house, a hymn for what we didn't say but
    thought:
That feels good or *I like that,* when we learned how to open each other's
    mouths

how to move our tongues to make somebody moan. We called it
5   practicing, and
one was the boy, and we paired off—maybe six or eight girls—and
    turned out

the lights and kissed and kissed until we were stoned on kisses, and
    lifted our
nightgowns or let the straps drop, and, Now you be the boy:

concrete floor, sleeping bag or couch, playroom, game room, train room,
    laundry.
10 Linda's basement was like a boat with booths and portholes

instead of windows. Gloria's father had a bar downstairs with stools
    that spun,
plush carpeting. We kissed each other's throats.

We sucked each other's breasts, and we left marks, and never spoke of it
    upstairs
outdoors, in daylight, not once. We did it, and it was

practicing, and slept, sprawled so our legs still locked or crossed, a hand
15   still lost
in someone's hair . . . and we grew up and hardly mentioned who

the first kiss really was—a girl like us, still sticky with the moisturizer
    we'd
shared in the bathroom. I want to write a song

for that thick silence in the dark, and the first pure thrill of unreluctant
    desire,
20 just before we made ourselves stop.

1998

ELIZABETH BARRETT BROWNING

To George Sand

A Desire

Thou large-brained woman and large-hearted man,
Self-called George Sand[3] whose soul, amid the lions
Of thy tumultuous senses, moans defiance
And answers roar for roar, as spirits can:
5   I would some mild miraculous thunder ran
Above the applauded circus,[4] in appliance
Of thine own nobler nature's strength and science,
Drawing two pinions, white as wings of swan,
From thy strong shoulders, to amaze the place
10 With holier light! that thou to woman's claim
And man's, mightst join beside the angel's grace
Of a pure genius sanctified from blame,
Till child and maiden pressed to thine embrace
To kiss upon thy lips a stainless fame.

                                1844

To George Sand

A Recognition

True genius, but true woman! dost deny
The woman's nature with a manly scorn,
And break away the gauds and armlets worn
By weaker women in captivity?
5   Ah, vain denial! that revolted cry
Is sobbed in by a woman's voice forlorn,—
Thy woman's hair, my sister, all unshorn
Floats back dishevelled strength in agony,
Disproving thy man's name: and while before
10 The world thou burnest in a poet-fire,
We see thy woman-heart beat evermore
Through the large flame. Beat purer, heart, and higher,
Till God unsex thee on the heavenly shore
Where unincarnate spirits purely aspire!

                                1844

3. Pseudonym of Amandine-Aurore-Lucie (or-Lucille) Dupin, baronne Dudevant (1804–1876), French
Romantic novelist, famous for her unconventional ideas and behavior.
4. Roman spectacle involving gladiatorial games, brutal athletic contests, and the killing of Christian slaves
by lions.

RICHARD LOVELACE

Song: To Lucasta, Going to the Wars

Tell me not, sweet, I am unkind,
    That from the nunnery
Of thy chaste breast and quiet mind
    To war and arms I fly.

5 True: a new mistress now I chase,
    The first foe in the field;
And with a stronger faith embrace
    A sword, a horse, a shield.

Yet this inconstancy is such
10   As you too shall adore;
I could not love thee, dear, so much,
    Loved I not honor more.

                1649

WILFRED OWEN

Disabled

He sat in a wheeled chair, waiting for dark,
And shivered in his ghastly suit of grey,
Legless, sewn short at elbow. Through the park
Voices of boys rang saddening like a hymn,
5 Voices of play and pleasure after day,
Till gathering sleep had mothered them from him.

About this time Town used to swing so gay
When glow-lamps budded in the light blue trees,
And girls glanced lovelier as the air grew dim,—
10 In the old times, before he threw away his knees.
Now he will never feel again how slim
Girls' waists are, or how warm their subtle hands;
All of them touch him like some queer disease.

There was an artist silly for his face,
15 For it was younger than his youth, last year.
Now, he is old; his back will never brace;
He's lost his color very far from here,
Poured it down shell-holes till the veins ran dry,
And half his lifetime lapsed in the hot race,
20 And leap of purple spurted from his thigh.

One time he liked a blood-smear down his leg,
After the matches,[5] carried shoulder-high
It was after football, when he'd drunk a peg,[6]
He thought he'd better join.—He wonders why.
25 Someone had said he'd look a god in kilts,
That's why; and may be, too, to please his Meg;
Aye, that was it, to please the giddy jilts
He asked to join. He didn't have to beg;
Smiling they wrote his lie; aged nineteen years.

30 Germans he scarcely thought of; all their guilt,
And Austria's, did not move him. And no fears
Of Fear came yet. He thought of jeweled hilts
For daggers in plaid socks; of smart salutes;
And care of arms; and leave; and pay arrears;
35 *Esprit de corps;* and hints for young recruits.
And soon, he was drafted out with drums and cheers.

Some cheered him home, but not as crowds cheer Goal.
Only a solemn man who brought him fruits
Thanked him; and then inquired about his soul.
40 Now, he will spend a few sick years in Institutes,
And do what things the rules consider wise,
And take whatever pity they may dole.
Tonight he noticed how the women's eyes
Passed from him to the strong men that were whole.
45 How cold and late it is! Why don't they come
And put him into bed? Why don't they come?

1917

VICKI FEAVER

Hemingway's Hat

Wearing a copy of the canvas
leather-peaked cap Hemingway wore
at the Finca Vigia—which your mother gave you
to make you look dashing, nerveless,

5 and which makes me feel
like a Shakespearean heroine
dressed as and played by a boy—
I wonder what I'd be like as a man:

not just brave but "needing
10 to be seen to be brave" like Hem;

---

5. Soccer games.   6. A drink, usually brandy and soda.

or like my father, gentle, nervous,
"not a man," as my mother shrieked at him?

She'd wanted a son to replace her brother
lost in the last months of the war in Burma.
15 I tried—when I started to bleed,
getting my hair cut short as a boy's.

Then, while you raced stolen cars
for the thrill, I changed myself
into a girl—stilettos, stiff
20 nylon petticoats, a perm.

You travelled from war to war,
until you came here, where dark butterflies
reconnoitre the lawn, and the cats sleep
in the shade of your chair, and you heard—

25 among oaks and firs and birches—
a silence like the silence at Plei Me
when you saw the dead rising
above the field of battle.

In our games of changing hats,
30 we float free like those ghosts:
last night, me riding you,
our shared penis

a glistening pillar
sliding between us; this morning,
35 you washing me, soaping and rinsing
with a woman's tenderness.

1996

YUSEF KOMUNYAKAA

Tu Do Street

Searching for love, a woman,
someone to help ease down the cocked hammer
of my nerves & senses. The music
divides the evening into black
5 & white—soul, country & western,
acid rock, & Frank Sinatra.
I close my eyes & can see
men drawing lines in the dust,
daring each other to step across.
10 America pushes through the membrane
of mist & smoke, & I'm a small boy

again in Bogalusa[7] skirting tough talk
coming out of bars with *White Only*
signs & Hank Snow. But tonight,
15 here in Saigon, just for the hell of it,
I walk into a place with Hank Williams
calling from the jukebox. The bar girls
fade behind a smokescreen, fluttering
like tropical birds in a cage, not
20 speaking with their eyes & usual
painted smiles. I get the silent
treatment. We have played Judas
for each other out in the boonies
but only enemy machinegun fire
25 can bring us together again.
When I order a beer, the mama-san
behind the counter acts as if she
can't understand, while her
eyes caress a white face;
30 down the street the black GIs
hold to their turf also.
An off-limits sign pulls me
deeper into alleys; I look
for a softness behind these voices
35 wounded by their beauty & war.
Back in the bush at Dak To
& Khe Sahn, we fought
the brothers of these women
we now run to hold in our arms.
40 There's more than a nation divided
inside us, as black & white
soldiers touch the same lovers
minutes apart, tasting
each other's breath,
45 without knowing these rooms
run into each other like tunnels
leading to the underworld.

                                        1988

---

7. Industrial city in southeastern Louisiana.

ROBERT BROWNING

My Last Duchess

Ferrara[8]

That's my last Duchess painted on the wall,
Looking as if she were alive. I call
That piece a wonder, now: Frà Pandolf's hands[9]
Worked busily a day, and there she stands.
5 Will't please you sit and look at her? I said
"Frà Pandolf" by design, for never read
Strangers like you that pictured countenance,
The depth and passion of its earnest glance,
But to myself they turned (since none puts by
10 The curtain I have drawn for you, but I)
And seemed as they would ask me, if they durst,
How such a glance came there; so, not the first
Are you to turn and ask thus. Sir, 'twas not
Her husband's presence only, called that spot
15 Of joy into the Duchess' cheek: perhaps
Frà Pandolf chanced to say "Her mantle laps
Over my lady's wrist too much," or "Paint
Must never hope to reproduce the faint
Half-flush that dies along her throat": such stuff
20 Was courtesy, she thought, and cause enough
For calling up that spot of joy. She had
A heart—how shall I say?—too soon made glad,
Too easily impressed; she liked whate'er
She looked on, and her looks went everywhere.
25 Sir, 'twas all one! My favor at her breast,
The dropping of the daylight in the West,
The bough of cherries some officious fool
Broke in the orchard for her, the white mule
She rode with round the terrace—all and each
30 Would draw from her alike the approving speech,
Or blush, at least. She thanked men,—good! but thanked
Somehow—I know not how—as if she ranked
My gift of a nine-hundred-years-old name
With anybody's gift. Who'd stoop to blame
35 This sort of trifling? Even had you skill
In speech—which I have not—to make your will
Quite clear to such an one, and say, "Just this
Or that in you disgusts me; here you miss,

8. Alfonso II, duke of Ferrara in Italy in the mid-sixteenth century, is the presumed speaker of the poem, which is loosely based on historical events. The duke's first wife—whom he had married when she was fourteen—died under suspicious circumstances at seventeen, and he then negotiated through an agent (to whom the poem is spoken) for the hand of the niece of the count of Tyrol in Austria.
9. Frà Pandolf is, like Claus (line 56), fictitious.

Or there exceed the mark"—and if she let
40 Herself be lessoned so, nor plainly set
Her wits to yours, forsooth, and made excuse,
—E'en then would be some stooping; and I choose
Never to stoop. Oh sir, she smiled, no doubt,
Whene'er I passed her; but who passed without
45 Much the same smile? This grew; I gave commands;
Then all smiles stopped together. There she stands
As if alive. Will't please you rise? We'll meet
The company below, then. I repeat,
The Count your master's known munificence
50 Is ample warrant that no just pretense
Of mine for dowry will be disallowed;
Though his fair daughter's self, as I avowed
At starting, is my object. Nay, we'll go
Together down, sir. Notice Neptune, though,
55 Taming a sea-horse, thought a rarity,
Which Claus of Innsbruck cast in bronze for me!

1842

A Woman's Last Word

1

Let's contend no more, Love,
  Strive nor weep.
All be as before, Love,
  —Only sleep!

2

5 What so wild as words are?
  I and thou
In debate, as birds are,
  Hawk on bough!

3

See the creature stalking
10 While we speak!
Hush and hide the talking
  Cheek on cheek!

4

What so false as truth is,
  False to thee?
15 Where the serpent's tooth is
  Shun the tree—

5

Where the apple reddens
  Never pry—

Lest we lose our Edens,
20   Eye and I

6

Be a god and hold me
    With a charm!
Be a man and fold me
    With thine arm!

7

25 Teach me, only teach, Love!
    As I ought
I will speak thy speech, Love,
    Think thy thought—

8

Meet, if thou require it,
30   Both demands,
Laying flesh and spirit
    In thy hands.

9

That shall be tomorrow
    Not tonight:
35 I must bury sorrow
    Out of sight:

10

—Must a little weep, Love
    (Foolish me!),
And so fall asleep, Love,
40   Loved by thee.

                1855

ESTHER JOHNSON

[*If It Be True*]

If it be true, celestial Powers,
    That you have formed me fair,
And yet in all my vainest hours
    My mind has been my care;
5 Then in return I beg this grace,
    As you were ever kind:
What envious Time takes from my face,
    Bestow upon my mind.

c. 1715

LADY MARY WORTLEY MONTAGU

Written the First Year I Was Marry'd

While thirst of power, and desire of fame,
In every age is every woman's aim;
Of beauty vain, of silly toasters proud,
Fond of a train, and happy in a crowd,
5 On every fop bestowing a kind glance,
Each conquest owing to some loose advance,
Affect to fly, in hopes to be persu'd,
And think they're virtuous, if not grossly lewd:
Let this sure maxim be my virtue's guide,
10 In part to blame she is, who has been try'd;
Too near he has approach'd, who is deny'd.

1712–13

CATHY SONG

Sunworshippers

"Look how they love themselves,"
my mother would lecture as we drove through
the ironwoods, the park on one side,
the beach on the other, where sunworshippers,
5 splayed upon towels, appeared sacrificial,
bodies glazed and glistening like raw fish in the market.
There was folly and irreverence to such exposure,
something only people with dirty feet did.
Who will marry you
10 if your skin is sunbaked and dried up like beef jerky?
We put on our hats and gloves
whenever we went for a drive.
When the sun broke through clouds,
my mother sprouted her umbrella.
15 The body is a temple we worship
secretly in the traveling revivalist tent of our clothes.
The body, hidden, banished to acceptable
rooms of the house, had only a mouth
for eating and a hole for eliminating
20 what the body rejected: the lower forms of life.
Caramel-colored stools, coiled heavily
like a sleeping python, were a sign
we were living right.
But to erect a statue of the body
25 and how the body, insolent and defiant

in a bikini, looked was self-indulgent, sun-
worshipping, fad diets and weight-lifting proof
you loved yourself too much.
We were not allowed to love ourselves too much.
30 So I ate less, and less, and less,
nibbling my way out of meals—
the less I ate, the less
there was of me to love.
I liked it best when standing before the mirror,
35 I seemed to be disappearing into myself,
breasts sunken into the cavity of my bird-cage chest,
air my true element which fed
in those days of college, snow and brick bound,
the coal fire in my eyes.
40 No one knew how I truly felt about myself.
Fueled by my own impending disappearance,
I neither slept nor ate, but devoured radiance,
essential as chlorophyll,
the apple's heated core.
45 Undetected, I slipped in and out of books,
passages of music, brightly painted rooms
where, woven into the signature of voluptuous vines,
was the one who flew one day out the window,
leaving behind an arrangement of cakes and ornamental flowers;
50 to weave one's self, one's breath, ropes of it, whole
and fully formed, was a way of shining
out of this world.

1994

PAULETTE JILES

Paper Matches

My aunts washed dishes while the uncles
squirted each other on the lawn with
garden hoses. Why are we in here,
I said, and they are out there.
5   That's the way it is,
said Aunt Hetty, the shrivelled-up one.
I have the rages that small animals have,
being small, being animal.
Written on me was a message,
10 "At Your Service" like a book of
paper matches. One by one we were
taken out and struck.
We come bearing supper,
our heads on fire.

1973

AMY LOWELL

The Lonely Wife[1]

The mist is thick. On the wide river, the water-plants float smoothly.
No letters come; none go.
There is only the moon, shining through the clouds of a hard, jade-
     green sky,
Looking down at us so far divided, so anxiously apart.
All day, going about my affairs, I suffer and grieve, and press the
5   thought of you closely to my heart.
My eyebrows are locked in sorrow, I cannot separate them.
Nightly, nightly, I keep ready half the quilt,
And wait for the return of that divine dream which is my Lord.

Beneath the quilt of the Fire-Bird, on the bed of the Silver-Crested Love-
     Pheasant,
10 Nightly, nightly, I drowse alone.
The red candles in the silver candlesticks melt, and the wax runs from
     them,
As the tears of your so Unworthy One escape and continue constantly
     to flow.
A flower face endures but a short season,
Yet still he drifts along the river Hsiao and the river Hsiang.
As I toss on my pillow, I hear the cold, nostalgic sound of the water-
15   clock:
Shêng! Shêng! it drips, cutting my heart in two.

I rise at dawn. In the Hall of Pictures
They come and tell me that the snow-flowers are falling.
The reed-blind is rolled high, and I gaze at the beautiful, glittering,
     primeval snow,
20 Whitening the distance, confusing the stone steps and the courtyard.
The air is filled with its shining, it blows far out like the smoke of a
     furnace.
The grass-blades are cold and white, like jade girdle pendants.
Surely the Immortals in Heaven must be crazy with wine to cause such
     disorder,
Seizing the white clouds, crumpling them up, destroying them.

                                                                      1921

---

1. A translation/adaptation of a poem by the Chinese poet Li Po (701–762 C.E.).

LIZ ROSENBERG

The Silence of Women

Old men, as time goes on, grow softer, sweeter,
while their wives get angrier.
You see them hauling the men across the mall
or pushing them down on chairs,
5 "Sit there! and don't you move!"
A lifetime of *yes* has left them
hissing bent as snakes.
It seems even their bones will turn
against them, once the fruitful years are gone.
10 Something snaps off the houselights,
and the cells go dim;
the chicken hatching back into the egg.

Oh lifetime of silence!
words scattered like a sibyl's leaves.
15 Voice thrown into a baritone storm—
whose shrilling is a soulful wind
blown through an instrument
that cannot beat time

but must make music
20 any way it can.

1994

EAVAN BOLAND

Anorexic

Flesh is heretic.
My body is a witch.
I am burning it.

Yes I am torching
5 her curves and paps and wiles.
They scorch in my self-denials.

How she meshed my head
in the half-truths
of her fevers till I renounced
10 milk and honey
and the taste of lunch.

I vomited
her hungers.
Now the bitch is burning.

15 I am starved and curveless.
I am skin and bone.
She has learned her lesson.

Thin as a rib
I turn in sleep.
20 My dreams probe

a claustrophobia
a sensuous enclosure.
How warm it was and wide

once by a warm drum,
25 once by the song of his breath
and in his sleeping side.

Only a little more,
only a few more days
sinless, foodless.

30 I will slip
back into him again
as if I have never been away.

Caged so
I will grow
35 angular and holy

past pain
keeping his heart
such company

as will make me forget
40 in a small space
the fall

into forked dark,
into python needs
heaving to hips and breasts
45 and lips and heat
and sweat and fat and greed.

1980

THOM GUNN

A Blank

The year of griefs being through, they had to merge
In one last grief, with one last property;
To view itself like loosened cloud lose edge,
And pull apart, and leave a voided sky.

5 Watching Victorian porches through the glass,
From the 6 bus, I caught sight of a friend
Stopped on a corner-kerb to let us pass,
A four-year-old blond child tugging his hand,
Which tug he held against with a slight smile.
10 I knew the smile from certain passages
Two years ago, thus did not know him well,
Since they took place in my bedroom and his.

A sturdy-looking admirable young man.
He said "I chose to do this with my life."
15 Casually met he said it of the plan
He undertook without a friend or wife.

Now visibly tugged upon by his decision,
Wayward and eager. So this was his son!
What I admired about his self-permission
20 Was that he turned from nothing he had done,
Or was, or had been, even while he transposed
The expectations he took out at dark
—Of Eros playing, features undisclosed—
Into another pitch, where he might work
25 With the same melody, and opted so
To educate, permit, guide, feed, keep warm,
And love a child to be adopted, though
The child was still a blank then on a form.

The blank was flesh now, running on its nerve,
30 This fair-topped organism dense with charm,
Its braided muscle grabbing what would serve,
His countering pull, his own devoted arm.

                                    1992

SUGGESTIONS FOR WRITING

1. Consider "Hattie McDaniel Arrives at the Coconut Grove" by Rita Dove and "Frederich Douglass" by Robert Hayden. Both treat people of importance within the context of the civil rights movement but who lived before the movement got under way in the 1960s. Dove's poem, written in 2004, speaks about a past cultural event—the 1939 Academy Awards—while Hayden's 1966 poem talks about the death of Frederick Douglass as though it only just occurred. Write an essay in which you explore the way these two poems speak about their own times by pointing to the future.
2. Generations of American schoolchildren were made to memorize and recite Felicia Dorothea Hemans's "Casabianca," a fact reflected by the references to "stammering elocution" and "a schoolroom platform" in Elizabeth Bishop's "Casabianca." Write an essay in which you discuss Bishop's poem in light of Hemans's original. What made Hemans's poem suitable as a recitation piece? How does Bishop's poem "answer" Heman's? How does each poem demonstrate a sense of what poetry is, or what it is for?
3. Research the use of poison gas in World War I and then write an essay in which you analyze Wilfred Owen's "Dulce et Decorum Est." How does the poem dramatize the effects of gas? What statement does it make about this new form of warfare?
4. Write an essay in which you first present a detailed narrative of the 1963 Birmingham bombing, based on research. Then analyze Dudley Randall's "Ballad of Birmingham" in light of this history. To what extent is Randall's poem based on established facts? To what extent is the poem fictitious? How effective is this mingling of fact and fiction?
5. Write an essay in which you analyze either Robert Browning's "My Last Duchess" or his "A Woman's Last Word." Who is the speaker? Who is being addressed? What is the situation? How do details gradually reveal character and "plot"? What is the advantage to the poet in using this form, the dramatic monologue? How does Browning integrate the poetic elements of language and form into the dramatic monologue?

10 THE AUTHOR'S WORK AS CONTEXT: JOHN KEATS AND ADRIENNE RICH

Even though all poets share the medium of language and usually have some common notions about their craft, they put the unique resources of their individual personalities, experiences, and outlooks into every poem they create. A poet may rely on tradition extensively and use devices that others have developed without surrendering his or her individuality, just as any individual shares certain characteristics with others—political affiliations, religious beliefs, tastes in clothes and music—without compromising his or her integrity and uniqueness. Sometimes a person's uniqueness is hard to define. But it is always there, and we recognize and depend on it in our relationships with other people. And so with poets: most don't make a conscious effort to put an individual stamp on their work; they don't have to. The stamp is there in the very subjects, words, images, and forms they choose. Every individual's unique consciousness marks what it records and imagines.

Experienced readers can often identify a poem as the distinctive work of an individual poet even though they may never have seen that poem before, much as experienced listeners can identify a new piece of music as the work of a particular composer, singer, or group after hearing only a few phrases. This ability depends on a lot of reading or a lot of listening to music, and any reasonably sensitive reader can learn, over time, to do it with remarkable accuracy. Yet this ability is not really an end in itself; rather, it is a by-product of learning to appreciate the particular, distinctive qualities of any poet's work. Once you've read several poems by the same poet, you will usually see some features that the poems all share, and gradually you may come to think of those features as characteristic. Many people have favorite poets, just as they have favorite rock groups or rap artists. In both cases, we are attracted to the artist's work precisely because, consciously or not, we recognize and appreciate that artist's distinctive style and outlook.

To perform an experiment, consult the Index of Authors at the back of this book to locate the following poems by Howard Nemerov: "The Vacuum," "The Goose Fish," and "Boom!" (You can also do this experiment with other poets whose work appears in the book several times, such as Emily Dickinson and John Donne.) After reading these poems, list the similarities you find, perhaps by concentrating on each of the literary elements in turn. Then look at Nemerov's "A Way of Life." In what ways is "A Way of Life" like the other Nemerov poems?

The concern with contemporary life, the tendency to concentrate on modern conveniences and luxuries, and the interest in isolating and defining aspects of a distinctively modern sensibility are all characteristic of Nemerov. So, too, is the tendency to create a short drama, with a speaker who is not altogether admirable. Several of Nemerov's poems also share an attitude that seems deeply imbedded in "A Way of Life"—a kind of antiromanticism that emerges when someone tries to sound or feel *too* proud or cheerful and is shown, by events in the poem, to be part of a grimmer reality instead. The concentration upon one or more physical objects is also characteristic, and often (as in "The Vacuum") the main object is a mechanical one that symbolizes modernity and our modern dependency on things. Americanness is emphasized here, too, through a concern with defining not only our time, but also our culture, its habits, and its values. The mood of loneliness is typical of Nemerov, and so is the poem's witty conversational style. The verbal wit here—although not as prominent as the puns and double entendres of "Boom!"—is characteristically informal. Often it seems to derive from the language of commercials and street speech, and Nemerov's undercutting of this language— having a paranoid and simpleminded speaker talk about a gangster in "a state of existential despair"—resembles the strategy of "Boom!" or "The Vacuum." The regular stanzas, rhymed though not in a traditional or regular way and using a number of near-rhymes, are also typical. (Compare, for example, "The Goose Fish.") In short, "A Way of Life" encapsulates Nemerov's thematic interests and ideas, his verbal style, and his cast of mind.

The work of any writer will display a characteristic way of thinking. It will have certain identifiable *tendencies*. But this does not mean that every poem by a particular author will be predictable and contain all of the same features. Poets test their talents and their views—as well as their readers—by experimenting with various subjects and points of view, formal structures and devices. Like all of us, poets also grow and change over time. As readers, then, we want to strive to recognize differences, as well as similarities, among individual poems and to appreciate the ways an author's work does and doesn't change over time.

You will find both continuity and change, similarities and differences, in the work of any good poet, and this chapter introduces you to two great ones. The first, John Keats, enjoyed the briefest of lives and careers, publishing his first poem a mere five years before his death at age 25 (in 1821). As a result, according to one Victorian reviewer, "all Keats's poems are early productions, and there is nothing beyond them but the thought of what he might have become." Thanks to her longevity, the other poet featured in this chapter—Adrienne Rich—gives us the chance to see such "becoming" in action. Indeed, Rich (born in 1929) remains an active, prolific poet, and many readers and critics regard her as the best poet writing today. A careful reader of her work will find similarities of interest and strategy from her earliest poems—published shortly after World War II, in 1951—to her newest ones. A distinctive mind and orientation are at work. And we can speak about characteristic features of Rich's poetry just as surely as we do about characteristic features of Keats's work, even though Rich has written many more poems over a much longer period of time.

But over the years Rich's voice has changed quite a lot, too, and she has modified her views on a number of issues. Such changes were the result both of her personal experiences and of those shared experiences that help to define her era. Many of the changes in Rich's ideas and attitudes, for example, reflect changing concerns among American intellectuals (especially women) in the second half of the twentieth century, and her poems represent both changed social conditions and sharply altered social, political, and philosophical attitudes. But her poems also reflect altered personal circumstances. Rich married in her early twenties and had three children by the time she was thirty; many of her early poems are about heterosexual love, and some of them are quite explicitly about sex. (See, for example, "Two Songs," chapter 4.) More recently, she has been involved in a long-term lesbian relationship and has written, again quite explicitly, about sex between women. (See, for example, "My mouth hovers across your breasts," this chapter.) In Rich's poems, then, we may not only trace the contours of an evolving personal life and outlook, but also—and even more importantly for the study of poetry generally—see how changes *within* the poet and *in her social and cultural context* alter the subjects and themes of her poetry, as well as its formal structure.

Just as information about an author's life and times can help us in this enterprise, so, too, can the essays, letters, and interviews in which an author reflects on the character and aims of his or her poetry and on the subjects the poetry explores. In the case of Rich, we have a bounty of such material from a poet who has also been a remarkably prolific and articulate prose writer. Gathered at the end of the Rich section of this chapter are excerpts from these writings, including both essays that express the author's outlook at a particular moment and retrospective pieces in which the poet gives us her interpretation of the character and development of her work over time. Though Keats wrote no essays of this type, he did leave behind hundreds of letters which both illuminate the ideas about literature and life that animate his poems and vividly display the unique sensibility that produced them.

> *The fear of poetry is an indication that we are cut off from our own reality.*
> —MURIEL RUKEYSER

But before you launch into the poetry and prose of these two great poets, it's worth pausing a moment to ask and answer a key question: of what practical use is it to learn to recognize and understand the distinctive voice and mind of a particular poet? One use is the pleasant surprise that occurs when you recognize something familiar. Reading a new poem by a familiar poet can be like meeting an old friend whose face or conversation reminds you of experiences you have had together. Just as novelty—meeting something or someone altogether new to you—provides one kind of pleasure, so revisiting the familiar provides another, equal and opposite kind. Just *knowing* and *recognizing* often feel good in and of themselves.

In addition, just as you learn from watching other people, seeing how they react and respond to various people, situations, and events, so you can learn from watching poets at work—seeing how they learn and develop, how they change their minds or test alternative points of view, how they discover the reach and limits of their imaginations and talents, how they find their distinctive voices and come to terms with their own identities. Watching a poet at work over a period of years is a little like watching an autobiography unfold, except that the individual poems exist separately and for themselves at the same time that they record the evolution of a distinctive artistic consciousness as it confronts a world that is itself perpetually changing.

Finally, the more you know about a poet and the more of his or her poems you read, the better a reader you will likely be of any individual poem by the poet. External facts of the writer's life may inform whatever he or she writes—be it a poem, an essay, a letter, or an autobiography. But beyond that, when you grow accustomed to a writer's habits and manners and means of expression, you learn what to expect. Coming to a new poem by a poet you already know, you know what to look for and have clear expectations about what the poem will be like. At the same time, you are better prepared to appreciate the surprises each poem holds in store.

JOHN KEATS

Given the brevity of Keats's life and career, readers new to his work may be surprised by the number and variety, as well as the sheer quality, of his poems. In his four short years as a working poet, he completed numerous sonnets (four are included in this book), one of the most haunting of English ballads ("La Belle Dame sans Merci"), and a handful of longer narrative poems. (The most ambitious of these is *Endymion,* the four-book, 4,000-line "poetic romance" that Keats undertook just after abandoning medicine for poetry.) Perhaps even more impressive, Keats wrote the sequence of six great odes—including "Ode to a Nightingale," "Ode on a Grecian Urn," and "To Autumn"—in a mere nine months, between April and September 1819. In addition, Keats left behind the 251 letters that T. S. Eliot described as "the most important ever written by any English poet."

John Keats

To nineteenth-century readers, such achievements were all the more surprising because of Keats's relatively humble upbringing and education. (As one Victorian reviewer marveled, "here is a surgeon's apprentice . . . rivaling in aesthetic perceptions of antique life and thought the most careful scholars of his time and country, and reproducing these impressions in a phraseology as complete and unconventional as if he has mastered the whole history and frequent variations of the English tongue.") Yet it would be a mistake to see Keats as either the "vulgar Cockney" or the untutored genius his contemporaries sometimes took him to be. Well-versed in English poetry past and present, Keats was heavily influenced by poets as diverse as Edmund Spenser, William Shakespeare, John Milton, and William Wordsworth, and was intimately familiar with the literature of ancient Rome (which he read in the original Latin) and ancient Greece (which he read in translation).

Indeed, as you begin to look for patterns in Keats's poems, you may notice that many of them focus on encounters with classical art (a translation of Homer's epics, a group of statues, a funereal urn); take their subjects from classical sources (a fable by Aesop, the myth of Endymion); or allude to classical literature and myth ("Lethe-wards," "Bacchus and his pards"). (Perhaps for this reason, poet Percy Bysshe Shelley declared, "He was a Greek!") As you explore Keats's poetry, then, you may well want to think further about just what the effects of these choices are and what the poems define as most characteristic and attractive about ancient art, life, and thought. Likewise, you will want to think about the implications of Keats's choice to work with traditional poetic forms, especially the sonnet and the ode. (Keats himself somewhat jokingly suggested that he needed such forms in order "to restrain the headlong impetuosity of [his] Muse.")

Ancient artifacts, as well as traditional poetic forms, seem to rank high on Keats's list of "thing[s] of beauty" (*Endymion*). In part this is because their very ancientness shows that they have withstood "the rude / Wasting of old Time," as he says of the Elgin marbles. As a result, they promise not only to remain "a joy forever," but also to grant a kind of immortality both to their subjects and to their creators. Indeed, one of the things that Keats's speakers seem to find so enchanting and so troubling about the various objects they contemplate is that these objects offer at least temporary escape from individual consciousness (or "sole self"), from the constraints of time and space, and from the mutability and mortality to which all living things are subject.

Yet Keats's poetry just as powerfully evokes the beauty of ordinary, living, natural things—of "the sun, the moon, / Trees," and "simple sheep"; of daffodils and musk-rose blooms (*Endymion*, lines 13–14, 15, 19); of nightingales, grasshoppers, and crickets; of "the stubble-plains" and "barred clouds" of a "soft-dying" autumn day ("To Autumn," lines 25–26). And this evocation of natural beauty flows, in part, from a vivid, complex blend of physically rooted "sensations"—of

> *Poetry should surprise by a fine excess and not by singularity—it should strike the reader as wording of his own highest thoughts, and appear almost a remembrance.*
> —JOHN KEATS

sight, sound, smell, touch, and taste—that define our everyday experience and "bind us to the earth" (*Endymion*, line 7). Through rhythm and rhyme, as well as alliteration, assonance, and onomatopoeia ("The murmurous haunt of flies on summer eves"), Keats not only captures physical sensation in language, but also draws our attention to the sensual—visual, tactile, auditory—qualities of words themselves.

One of the reasons the odes are so often singled out for praise and commentary is the fact that they focus so relentlessly on this characteristically Keatsian contrast, even conflict, between the actual, sensual world and the ideal world of art and imagination. Literary critic Miriam Allott suggests that the odes, like "all Keats's major poetry," trace the same singular "movement of thought and feeling," which "at first carries the poet . . . into an ideal world of beauty and permanence, and finally returns him to what is actual and inescapable." Echoing Allott, another critic describes the "recurrent pattern" of the odes as "one of dream and awakening, flight on the wings of imagination into a higher order of reality followed by a disillusioned return to the ordinary, everyday world." Yet as you read these and other of Keats's poems, you will see that each offers a unique perspective on the nature and significance of this contrast and on the desirability of escape. Here, as in any poet's work, then, you will want to look for differences as well as similarities, for evolution and change as well as continuity.

On Seeing the Elgin Marbles[1]

My spirit is too weak—mortality
Weighs heavily on me like unwilling sleep,
And each imagined pinnacle and steep
Of godlike hardship tells me I must die
5 Like a sick eagle looking at the sky.
Yet 'tis a gentle luxury to weep
That I have not the cloudy winds to keep
Fresh for the opening of the morning's eye.
Such dim-conceivéd glories of the brain
10 Bring round the heart an indescribable feud;
So do these wonders a most dizzy pain,
That mingles Grecian grandeur with the rude
Wasting of old Time—with a billowy main—
A sun—a shadow of a magnitude.

1817

From *Endymion* (Book 1)[2]

A thing of beauty is a joy for ever:
Its loveliness increases; it will never
Pass into nothingness; but still will keep
A bower quiet for us, and a sleep
5 Full of sweet dreams, and health, and quiet breathing.
Therefore, on every morrow, are we wreathing
A flowery band to bind us to the earth,
Spite of despondence, of the inhuman dearth
Of noble natures, of the gloomy days,
10 Of all the unhealthy and o'er-darkened ways
Made for our searching: yes, in spite of all,
Some shape of beauty moves away the pall
From our dark spirits. Such the sun, the moon,
Trees old, and young sprouting a shady boon
15 For simple sheep; and such are daffodils
With the green world they live in; and clear rills
That for themselves a cooling covert make
'Gainst the hot season; the mid forest brake,[3]
Rich with a sprinkling of fair musk-rose blooms:

---

1. Figures and friezes from the Athenian Parthenon, they were taken from the site by Lord Elgin, brought to England in 1806, and then sold to the British Museum, where Keats saw them.
2. Keats's long poem about the myth of a mortal (Endymion) loved by the goddess of the moon.
3. Thicket.

20 And such too is the grandeur of the dooms⁴
    We have imagined for the mighty dead;
    All lovely tales that we have heard or read:
    An endless fountain of immortal drink,
    Pouring unto us from the heaven's brink.
25   Nor do we merely feel these essences
    For one short hour; no, even as the trees
    That whisper round a temple become soon
    Dear as the temple's self, so does the moon,
    The passion poesy, glories infinite,
30 Haunt us till they become a cheering light
    Unto our souls, and bound to us so fast,
    That, whether there be shine, or gloom o'ercast,
    They always must be with us, or we die.

1817

Ode to a Nightingale

                    I

My heart aches, and a drowsy numbness pains
    My sense, as though of hemlock I had drunk,
Or emptied some dull opiate to the drains
    One minute past, and Lethe-wards⁵ had sunk:
5 'Tis not through envy of thy happy lot,
    But being too happy in thine happiness,
        That thou, light-wingéd Dryad⁶ of the trees,
            In some melodious plot
    Of beechen green, and shadows numberless,
10   Singest of summer in full-throated ease.

                    II

O, for a draught of vintage! that hath been
    Cooled a long age in the deep-delvéd earth,
Tasting of Flora⁷ and the country green,
    Dance, and Provençal song,⁸ and sunburnt mirth!
15 O for a beaker full of the warm South,
    Full of the true, the blushful Hippocrene,⁹
        With beaded bubbles winking at the brim,
            And purple-stainéd mouth;
    That I might drink, and leave the world unseen,
20   And with thee fade away into the forest dim:

---

4. Judgments.   5. Toward the river of forgetfulness (Lethe) in Hades.   6. Wood nymph.
7. Roman goddess of flowers.   8. The medieval troubadours of Provence were famous for their love songs.
9. The fountain of the Muses on Mt. Helicon, whose waters bring poetic inspiration.

III

Fade far away, dissolve, and quite forget
  What thou among the leaves hast never known,
The weariness, the fever, and the fret
  Here, where men sit and hear each other groan;
25 Where palsy shakes a few, sad, last gray hairs,
    Where youth grows pale, and specter-thin, and dies;
      Where but to think is to be full of sorrow
        And leaden-eyed despairs,
    Where Beauty cannot keep her lustrous eyes,
30   Or new Love pine at them beyond tomorrow.

IV

Away! away! for I will fly to thee,
  Not charioted by Bacchus and his pards,[1]
But on the viewless[2] wings of Poesy,
  Though the dull brain perplexes and retards:
35 Already with thee! tender is the night,
    And haply the Queen-Moon is on her throne,
      Clustered around by all her starry Fays;[3]
        But here there is no light,
    Save what from heaven is with the breezes blown
40   Through verdurous glooms and winding mossy ways.

V

I cannot see what flowers are at my feet,
  Nor what soft incense hangs upon the boughs,
But, in embalméd[4] darkness, guess each sweet
  Wherewith the seasonable month endows
45 The grass, the thicket, and the fruit-tree wild;
    White hawthorn, and the pastoral eglantine;[5]
      Fast fading violets covered up in leaves;
        And mid-May's eldest child,
    The coming musk-rose, full of dewy wine,
50   The murmurous haunt of flies on summer eves.

VI

Darkling[6] I listen; and, for many a time
  I have been half in love with easeful Death,
Called him soft names in many a muséd rhyme,
  To take into the air my quiet breath;
55 Now more than ever seems it rich to die,
    To cease upon the midnight with no pain,
      While thou art pouring forth thy soul abroad
        In such an ecstasy!
    Still wouldst thou sing, and I have ears in vain—
60   To thy high requiem become a sod.

---

1. The Roman god of wine was sometimes portrayed in a chariot drawn by leopards.   2. Invisible.
3. Fairies.   4. Fragrant, aromatic.   5. Sweetbriar or honeysuckle.   6. In the dark.

VII

Thou wast not born for death, immortal Bird!
  No hungry generations tread thee down;
The voice I hear this passing night was heard
  In ancient days by emperor and clown:
65 Perhaps the selfsame song that found a path
    Through the sad heart of Ruth,[7] when, sick for home,
      She stood in tears amid the alien corn;
        The same that ofttimes hath
    Charmed magic casements, opening on the foam
70   Of perilous seas, in faery lands forlorn.

VIII

Forlorn! the very word is like a bell
  To toll me back from thee to my sole self!
Adieu! the fancy cannot cheat so well
  As she is famed to do, deceiving elf.
75 Adieu! adieu! thy plaintive anthem fades
    Past the near meadows, over the still stream,
      Up the hillside; and now 'tis buried deep
        In the next valley-glades:
    Was it a vision, or a waking dream?
80   Fled is that music:—Do I wake or sleep?

May 1819

Ode on a Grecian Urn

I

Thou still unravished bride of quietness,
  Thou foster-child of silence and slow time,
Sylvan historian, who canst thus express
  A flowery tale more sweetly than our rhyme:
5 What leaf-fringed legend haunts about thy shape
    Of deities or mortals, or of both,
      In Tempe or the dales of Arcady?[8]
What men or gods are these? What maidens loath?
    What mad pursuit? What struggle to escape?
10   What pipes and timbrels? What wild ecstasy?

II

Heard melodies are sweet, but those unheard
  Are sweeter; therefore, ye soft pipes, play on;

7. A virtuous Moabite widow who, according to the Old Testament Book of Ruth, left her own country to accompany her mother-in-law, Naomi, back to Naomi's native land. She supported herself as a gleaner.
8. Arcadia. Tempe is a beautiful valley near Mt. Olympus in Greece, and the valleys ("dales") of Arcadia a picturesque section of the Peloponnesus; both came to be associated with the pastoral ideal.

Not to the sensual[9] ear, but, more endeared,
  Pipe to the spirit ditties of no tone:
15 Fair youth, beneath the trees, thou canst not leave
  Thy song, nor ever can those trees be bare;
    Bold Lover, never, never canst thou kiss,
  Though winning near the goal—yet, do not grieve;
    She cannot fade, though thou hast not thy bliss,
20   For ever wilt thou love, and she be fair!

III

Ah, happy, happy boughs! that cannot shed
  Your leaves, nor ever bid the Spring adieu;
And, happy melodist, unweariéd,
  For ever piping songs for ever new;
25 More happy love! more happy, happy love!
  For ever warm and still to be enjoyed,
    For ever panting, and for ever young;
All breathing human passion far above,
  That leaves a heart high-sorrowful and cloyed,
30   A burning forehead, and a parching tongue.

IV

Who are these coming to the sacrifice?
  To what green altar, O mysterious priest,
Lead'st thou that heifer lowing at the skies,
  And all her silken flanks with garlands dressed?
35 What little town by river or sea shore,
  Or mountain-built with peaceful citadel,
    Is emptied of this folk, this pious morn?
And, little town, thy streets for evermore
  Will silent be; and not a soul to tell
40   Why thou art desolate, can e'er return.

V

O Attic shape! Fair attitude! with brede[1]
  Of marble men and maidens overwrought,[2]
With forest branches and the trodden weed;
  Thou, silent form, dost tease us out of thought
45 As doth eternity: Cold Pastoral!
  When old age shall this generation waste,
    Thou shalt remain, in midst of other woe
Than ours, a friend to man, to whom thou say'st,
  Beauty is truth, truth beauty[3]—that is all
50   Ye know on earth, and all ye need to know.

May 1819

---

9. Of the senses, as distinguished from the "ear" of the spirit or imagination.
1. Woven pattern. *Attic:* Attica was the district of ancient Greece surrounding Athens.
2. Ornamented all over.
3. In some texts of the poem "Beauty is truth, truth beauty" is in quotation marks, leading to critical disagreements about whether the last line and a half are also inscribed on the urn or spoken by the poet.

Ode on Melancholy

1

No, no, go not to Lethe,[4] neither twist
    Wolf's-bane, tight-rooted, for its poisonous wine;
Nor suffer thy pale forehead to be kiss'd
    By nightshade, ruby grape of Proserpine,[5]
Make not your rosary of yew-berries,
    Nor let the beetle, nor the death-moth be
        Your mournful Psyche,[6] nor the downy owl
A partner in your sorrow's mysteries,[7]
    For shade to shade will come too drowsily,
10   And drown the wakeful anguish of the soul.

2

But when the melancholy fit shall fall
    Sudden from heaven like a weeping cloud,
That fosters the droop-headed flowers all,
    And hides the green hill in an April shroud,
15 Then glut thy sorrow on a morning rose,
    Or on the rainbow of the salt sand-wave,
        Or on the wealth of globed peonies;
Or if thy mistress some rich anger shows,
    Emprison her soft hand, and let her rave,
20   And feed deep, deep upon her peerless eyes.

3

She dwells with Beauty—Beauty that must die;
    And Joy, whose hand is ever at his lips
Bidding adieu; and aching Pleasure nigh,
    Turning to poison while the bee-mouth sips:
25 Ay, in the very temple of Delight
    Veil'd Melancholy has her sovran shrine,
        Though seen of none save him whose strenuous tongue
Can burst Joy's grape against his palate fine;
His soul shall taste the sadness of her might,
    And be among her cloudy trophies hung.[8]

1819   1820

---

4. In Greek mythology, the river of forgetfulness in Hades.
5. Queen of the infernal regions, wife of Pluto. "Wolf's-bane" and "nightshade" are poisonous plants; yew-berries symbolize death.   6. Psyche (the soul) was sometimes represented as a butterfly or moth.
7. Rites.   8. The Greeks and Romans sometimes hung trophies in the temples of their gods.

To Autumn

I

Season of mists and mellow fruitfulness,
　Close bosom-friend of the maturing sun;
Conspiring with him how to load and bless
　With fruit the vines that round the thatch-eves run;
5　To bend with apples the mossed cottage-trees,
　　And fill all fruit with ripeness to the core;
　　　To swell the gourd, and plump the hazel shells
With a sweet kernel; to set budding more,
　And still more, later flowers for the bees,
10　Until they think warm days will never cease,
　　　For Summer has o'er-brimmed their clammy cells.

II

Who hath not seen thee oft amid thy store?
　Sometimes whoever seeks abroad may find
Thee sitting careless on a granary floor,
15　Thy hair soft-lifted by the winnowing wind;[9]
Or on a half-reaped furrow sound asleep,
　　Drowsed with the fume of poppies, while thy hook[1]
　　　Spares the next swath and all its twinéd flowers:
And sometimes like a gleaner thou dost keep
20　Steady thy laden head across a brook;
　　Or by a cider-press, with patient look,
　　　Thou watchest the last oozings hours by hours.

III

Where are the songs of Spring? Ay, where are they?
　Think not of them, thou hast thy music too—
25 While barréd clouds bloom the soft-dying day,
　And touch the stubble-plains with rosy hue;
Then in a wailful choir the small gnats mourn
　　Among the river sallows, borne aloft
　　　Or sinking as the light wind lives or dies;
30 And full-grown lambs loud bleat from hilly bourn;[2]
　　Hedge-crickets sing; and now with treble soft
　　　The red-breast whistles from a garden-croft;[3]
　　　And gathering swallows twitter in the skies.

September 19, 1819

---

9. Which sifts the grain from the chaff.　1. Scythe or sickle.　2. Domain.
3. An enclosed garden near a house.

PASSAGES FROM LETTERS AND
THE PREFACE TO *ENDYMION*

From *Letter to Benjamin Bailey,*
November 22, 1817[1]

. . . I am certain of nothing but of the holiness of the Heart's affections and the truth of Imagination—What the imagination seizes as Beauty must be truth—whether it existed before or not—for I have the same Idea of all our Passions as of Love they are all in their sublime, creative of essential Beauty. . . . The Imagination may be compared to Adam's dream[2]—he awoke and found it truth. I am the more zealous in this affair, because I have never yet been able to perceive how any thing can be known for truth by consequitive reasoning—and yet it must be—Can it be that even the greatest Philosopher ever ~~when~~ arrived at his goal without putting aside numerous objections—However it may be, O for a Life of Sensations rather than of Thoughts! It is "a Vision in the form of Youth" a Shadow of reality to come—and this consideration has further conv[i]nced me for it has come as auxiliary to another favorite Speculation of mine, that we shall enjoy ourselves here after by having what we called happiness on Earth repeated in a finer tone and so repeated—And yet such a fate can only befall those who delight in sensation rather than hunger as you do after Truth—Adam's dream will do here and seems to be a conviction that Imagination and its empyreal reflection is the same as human Life and its spiritual repetition. But as I was saying—the simple imaginative Mind may have its rewards in the repeti[ti]on of its own silent Working coming continually on the spirit with a fine suddenness—to compare great things with small—have you never by being surprised with an old Melody—in a delicious place—by a delicious voice, fe[l]t over again your very speculations and surmises at the time it first operated on your soul—do you not remember forming to yourself the singer's face more beautiful that [*for* than] it was possible and yet with the elevation of the Moment you did not think so—even then you were mounted on the Wings of Imagination so high—that the Prototype must be here after—that delicious face you will see—What a time! I am continually running away from the subject—sure this cannot be exactly the case with a complex Mind—one that is imaginative and at the same time careful of its fruits—who would exist partly on sensation partly on thought—to whom it is necessary that years should bring the philosophic Mind—such an one I consider your's and therefore it is necessary to your eternal Happiness that you not only ~~have~~ drink this old Wine of Heaven which I shall call the redigestion of our most ethereal Musings on Earth; but also increase in knowledge and know all things. . . .

---

1. Keats's private letters, often carelessly written, are reprinted here uncorrected.
2. In *Paradise Lost* 7.460–90.

From *Letter to George and Thomas Keats,*
December 21, 1817

George Keats

... I spent Friday evening with Wells[3] & went the next morning to see *Death on the Pale horse.*[4] It is a wonderful picture, when West's age is considered; But there is nothing to be intense upon; no women one feels mad to kiss, no face swelling into reality, the excellence of every Art is its intensity, capable of making all disagreeables evaporate, from their being in close relationship with Beauty & Truth—Examine King Lear & you will find this examplified throughout; but in this picture we have unpleasantness without any momentous depth of speculation excited, in which to bury its repulsiveness—The picture is larger than Christ rejected—I dined with Haydon the sunday after you left, & had a very pleasant day, I dined too (for I have been out too much lately) with Horace Smith & met his two Brothers with Hill & Kingston & one Du Bois,[5] they only served to convince me, how superior humour is to wit in respect to enjoyment—These men say things which make one start, without making one feel, they are all alike; their manners are alike; they all know fashionables; they have a mannerism in their very eating & drinking, in their mere handling a

Thomas Keats

Decanter—They talked of Kean[6] & his low company—Would I were with that company instead of yours said I to myself! I know such like acquaintance will never do for me & yet I am going to Reynolds, on wednesday—Brown & Dilke walked with me & back from the Christmas pantomime. I had not a dispute but a disquisition with Dilke, on various subjects; several things dovetailed in my mind, & at once it struck me, what quality went to form a Man of Achievement especially in Literature & which Shakespeare posessed so enormously—I mean *Negative Capability,* that is when man is capable of being in uncertainties, Mysteries, doubts, without any irritable reaching after fact & reason—Coleridge, for instance, would let go

3. Charles Wells (1800–1879), an author.
4. By Benjamin West (1738–1820), American painter and president of the Royal Academy; *Christ Rejected* (mentioned below) is also by West.
5. Thomas Hill (1760–1840), a book collector, and Edward duBois (1774–1850), a journalist.
6. Edmund Kean (1789–1833), a famous Shakespearean actor.

by a fine isolated verisimilitude caught from the Penetralium of mystery, from being incapable of remaining content with half knowledge. This pursued through Volumes would perhaps take us no further than this, that with a great poet the sense of Beauty overcomes every other consideration, or rather obliterates all consideration.

Letter to John Hamilton Reynolds, February 19, 1818

I have an idea that a Man might pass a very pleasant life in this manner—let him on any certain day read a certain Page of full Poesy or distilled Prose and let him wander with it, and muse upon it, and reflect from it, and bring home to it, and prophesy upon it, and dream upon it—untill it becomes stale—but when will it do so? Never—When Man has arrived at a certain ripeness in intellect any one grand and spiritual passage serves him as a starting post towards all "the two-and-thirty Pallaces"[7] How happy is such a "voyage of conception," what delicious diligent Indolence! A doze upon a Sofa does not hinder it, and a nap upon Clover engenders ethereal finger-pointings—the prattle of a child gives it wings, and the converse of middle age a strength to beat them—a strain of musick conducts to "an odd angle of the Isle",[8] and when the leaves whisper it puts a "girdle round the earth",[9] Nor will this sparing touch of noble Books be any irreverance to their Writers—for perhaps the honors paid by Man to Man are trifles in comparison to the Benefit done by great Works to the "Spirit and pulse of good" by their mere passive existence. Memory should not be called knowledge—Many have original minds who do not think it—they are led away by Custom—Now it appears to me that almost any Man may like the Spider spin from

John Hamilton Reynolds

his own inwards his own airy Citadel—the points of leaves and twigs on which the Spider begins her work are few and she fills the Air with a beautiful circuiting: man should be content with as few points to tip with the fine Webb of his Soul and weave a tapestry empyrean—full of Symbols for his spiritual eye, of softness for his spiritual touch, of space for his wandering of distinctness for his Luxury—But the Minds of Mortals are so different and bent on such diverse Journeys that it may at first appear impossible for any common taste and fellowship to exist bettween between two or three under these suppositions—It is however quite the contrary—Minds would leave each other in contrary directions, traverse each other in Numberless points, and all [*for* at] last greet each other at the Journeys

7. "Places of delight" in Buddhism.   8. *The Tempest* 1.2.224.
9. *A Midsummer Night's Dream* 2.1.175–76: "I'll put a girdle round about the earth / In forty minutes."

end—An old Man and a child would talk together and the old Man be led on his Path, and the child left thinking—Man should not dispute or assert but whisper results to his neighbor, and thus by every germ of Spirit sucking the Sap from mould ethereal every human might become great, and Humanity instead of being a wide heath of Furse[1] and Briars with here and there a remote Oak or Pine, would become a grand democracy of Forest Trees. It has been an old Comparison for our urging on—the Bee hive—however it seems to me that we should rather be the flower than the Bee—for it is a false notion that more is gained by receiving than giving—no, the receiver and the giver are equal in their benefits—The f[l]ower I doubt not receives a fair guerdon from the Bee—its leaves blush deeper in the next spring—and who shall say between Man and Woman which is the most delighted? Now it is more noble to sit like Jove that [for than] to fly like Mercury—let us not therefore go hurrying about and collecting honey bee like, buzzing here and there impatiently from a knowledge of what is to be arrived at; but let us open our leaves like a flower and be passive and receptive—budding patiently under the eye of Apollo and taking hints from every noble insect that favors us with a visit—sap will be given us for Meat and dew for drink—I was led into these thoughts, my dear Reynolds, by the beauty of the morning operating on a sense of Idleness—I have not read any Books—the Morning said I was right—I had no Idea but of the Morning, and the Thrush said I was right—seeming to say—

> O thou whose face hath felt the Winter's wind,
> Whose eye has seen the snow-clouds hung in mist,
> And the black elm tops 'mong the freezing stars,
> To thee the spring will be a harvest-time.
> O thou, whose only book has been the light
> Of supreme darkness which thou feddest on
> Night after night when Phœbus was away,
> To thee the spring shall be a triple morn.
> O fret not after knowledge—I have none,
> And yet my song comes native with the warmth.
> O fret not after knowledge—I have none,
> And yet the Evening listens. He who saddens
> At thought of idleness cannot be idle,
> And he's awake who thinks himself asleep.

Now I am sensible all this is a mere sophistication, however it may neighbor to any truths, to excuse my own indolence—so I will not deceive myself that Man should be equal with jove—but think himself very well off as a sort of scullion-Mercury, or even a humble Bee—It is not [for no] matter whether I am right or wrong either one way or another, if there is sufficient to lift a little time from your Shoulders.

---

1. *The Tempest* 1.1.58–59: "Now would I give a thousand furlongs of sea for an acre of barren ground: long heath, broom, furze, anything." (Heather, broom, and furze are all shrubs that grow in poor soil.)

From *Letter to John Taylor, February 27, 1818*

. . . It is a sorry thing for me that any one should have to overcome Prejudices in reading my Verses—that affects me more than any hyper-criticism on any particular Passage. In *Endymion* I have most likely but moved into the Go-cart from the leading strings. In Poetry I have a few Axioms, and you will see how far I am from their Centre. 1ˢᵗ I think Poetry should surprise by a fine excess and not by Singularity—it should strike the Reader as a wording of his own highest thoughts, and appear almost a Remembrance—2ⁿᵈ Its touches of Beauty should never be half way therby making the reader breathless instead of content: the rise, the progress, the setting of imagery should like the Sun come natural natural too him—shine over him and set soberly although in magnificence leaving him in the Luxury of twilight—but it is easier to think what Poetry should be than to write it—and this leads me on to another axiom. That if Poetry comes not as naturally as the Leaves to a tree it had better not come at all. However it may be with me I cannot help looking into new countries with "O for a Muse of fire to ascend!"[2]—If Endymion serves me as a Pioneer perhaps I ought to be content. I have great reason to be content, for thank God I can read and perhaps understand Shakspeare to his depths, and I have I am sure many friends, who, if I fail, will attribute any change in my Life and Temper to Humbleness rather than to Pride—to a cowering under the Wings of great Poets rather than to a Bitterness that I am not appreciated. I am anxious to get Endymion printed that I may forget it and proceed. . . .

From the Preface to *Endymion,* dated April 10, 1818

The imagination of a boy is healthy, and the mature imagination of a man is healthy; but there is a space of life between, in which the soul is in a ferment, the character undecided, the way of life uncertain, the ambition thick-sighted: thence proceeds mawkishness, and all the thousand bitters which those men I speak of must necessarily taste in going over the following pages.

I hope I have not in too late a day touched the beautiful mythology of Greece, and dulled its brightness: for I wish to try once more, before I bid it farewell.

CHRONOLOGY

1795   John Keats born October 31 at Finsbury, just north of London, the eldest child of Thomas and Frances Jennings Keats. Thomas Keats was head ostler at a livery stable.

1797–1803   Birth of three brothers and sisters: George in 1797, Thomas in 1799, Frances Mary (Fanny) in 1803.

---

2. *Henry V* Prologue 1: "O for a muse of fire, that would ascend."

1804   Father killed by a fall from his horse, April 15. On June 27 his mother remarries, and the children go to live with their maternal grandparents at Enfield. The grandfather dies a year later, and the children move with their grandmother to Lower Edmonton.

1809   Begins a literary friendship with Charles Cowden Clarke, the son of the headmaster at the Enfield school, and develops a strong interest in reading.

1810   Mother dies of tuberculosis, after a long illness.

1811   Leaves school to become apprenticed to an apothecary-surgeon in Edmonton; completes a prose translation of the *Aeneid,* begun at school.

1814   Earliest known attempts at writing verse. In December his grandmother dies, and the family home is broken up.

1815   In October moves to next stage of his medical training at Guy's Hospital, south of the Thames in London.

1816   On May 5 his first published poem, "O Solitude," appears in Leigh Hunt's *Examiner.* In October writes "On First Looking into Chapman's Homer," published in December. Meets Hunt, Benjamin Haydon, John Hamilton Reynolds, and Shelley. By the spring of 1817, gives up the idea of medical practice.

1817   In March, moves with brothers to Hampstead, sees the Elgin Marbles with Haydon, and publishes his first collection, *Poems.* Composes *Endymion* between April and November. Reads Milton, Shakespeare, and Coleridge; rereads Wordsworth during the year.

1818   *Endymion* published in April, unfavorably reviewed in September, defended by Reynolds in October. During the summer goes on walking tour of the Lake Country and Scotland, but returns to London in mid-August with a sore throat and severe chills. His brother Tom is also seriously ill by late summer, dying on December 1. In September, Keats first meets Fanny Brawne (eighteen years old), with whom he arrives at an "understanding" by Christmas.

1819   Writes *The Eve of St. Agnes* in January, revises it in September. In April Fanny Brawne and her mother move into the other half of the double house in which Keats lives. During April and May writes "La Belle Dame sans Merci" and all the major odes except "To Autumn," written in September. Rental arrangements force separation from Fanny Brawne during the summer (Keats on Isle of Wight from June to August), and in the fall he tries to break his dependence on her, but they become engaged by Christmas. Earlier in December suffers a recurrence of his sore throat.

1820   In February has a severe hemorrhage and in June an attack of blood-spitting. In July his doctor orders him to Italy for the winter; he sails in September and finally arrives in Rome on November 15. In July a volume of poems published, *Lamia, Isabella, The Eve of St. Agnes and Other Poems.* Fanny Brawne nurses him through the late summer.

1821   Dies at 11 P.M., February 23. Buried in the English Cemetery at Rome.

ADRIENNE RICH

It is fitting that two of Adrienne Rich's books—*A Change of World* (1951) and *The Will to Change* (1971)—bear titles that prominently feature the word *change*. For change has, indeed, been both a continuing concern of her poetry and a hallmark of her poetic career. Published when their author was just twenty-one, poems such as "At a Bach Concert," "Storm Warnings," and "Aunt Jennifer's Tigers" seem, at first glance, preternaturally mature. With their tightly controlled structure, their regular rhythm (and, often, rhyme), and their coolly observant tone, these early poems both embody and celebrate the "discipline" that "masters feelings" and the "proud restraining purity" by which art lends order to life ("At a Bach Concert"). (Versions of the word *master*, in fact, appear in all three poems.) Explaining why he chose *A Change of World* for the Yale Younger Poets Series, poet W. H. Auden singled out just such qualities and attitudes, praising Rich for a "craftsmanship" based in that "capacity for detachment from the self and its emotions without which no art is possible." If "poems are analogous to persons," Auden continued, then these poems are "neatly and modestly dressed, speak quietly but do not mumble, respect their elders but are not cowed by them, and do not tell fibs."

Less than a decade later, however, Rich began to see the very "neatness" and "detachment" of these poems as itself a kind of "fib." As she put it in 1964, the early poems, "even the ones I liked best and in which I felt I'd said most, were queerly limited; . . . in many cases I . . . suppressed, omitted, falsified even, certain disturbing elements to gain the perfection of order." From this point forward, Rich's work is very much an attempt to do the very opposite—to, in Matthew Arnold's words, "see life steadily and see it whole," in all its disturbing, disorderly imperfection. Indeed, one of the major themes of the later poems is both the necessity and the difficulty of breaking through the web of "myth" and illusion in order to get to "the thing itself" ("Diving into the Wreck").

> *By 1956, I had begun dating each of my poems by year. I did this because I was finished with the idea of a poem as a single, encapsulated event, a work of art complete in itself; I knew my life was changing, my work was changing, and I needed to indicate to readers my sense of being engaged in a long, continuous process.*
>
> —ADRIENNE RICH

In its attempt to do just that, Rich's work has itself become less neat and orderly, less quiet, modest, and respectful. Beginning with *Snapshots of a Daughter-in-Law* and its title poem, the poems speak in many radically different voices and tones and are cast in many different forms. Rich's evolution as a poet has not been a matter of pursuing any kind of single-minded mastery over her materials. "I find that I can no longer go to write a poem with a neat handful of materials and express those materials according to a prior plan," Rich explained in 1964; "the poem itself engenders new sensations, new awareness in me as it progresses." What results are "poems that *are* experiences" rather than "poems *about* experiences."

In becoming more informal, exploratory, and emotional, Rich's poems have also become more personal and autobiographical, more willing to enter and lay bare what "Storm Warnings" calls the "troubled regions" of the poet's own life, heart, and mind. In fact, Rich has suggested that her artistic growth has been, in part, a matter of closing the gap between "the woman in the poem and the woman writing the poem." And in "Roofwalker," a 1961 poem that articulates her new

Adrienne Rich circa 1970

poetic ideal, Rich compares herself both to a roofer standing atop a half-built house and to "a naked man fleeing / across" those very roofs. Like both, she now dares to be "exposed, larger than life, / and due to break my neck."

At the same time, Rich's work has also become steadily more social, political, and historical. "History" is, in fact, the title of one poem in this chapter and the subject of many others. Quite a few allude to, or take as their focus, specific women in history—from poet Emily Dickinson to astronomer Caroline Herschel and photographer Tina Modotti. As early as 1956, moreover, Rich began to insist upon the historicity of her own poems by dating each one. "It seems to me now that this was an oblique political statement," Rich insists in the 1984 essay "Blood, Bread, and Poetry": "It was a declaration that placed poetry in a historical continuity, not above or outside history." "For Rich," as one critic argues, "a deepening subjectivity does not mean withdrawal, as it did for [Emily] Dickinson, but, on the contrary, a more searching engagement with people and with social forces."

In Rich's life, as in her work, the movement into the self has fueled the movement outward—into the world and back into the past—and vice versa. On the one hand, it was in part her personal feelings and experiences—the fact that she felt "unfit, disempowered, adrift" as a housewife and mother in the mid-1950s—that sent her to the work of "political" writers like Mary Wollstonecraft, Simone de Beauvoir, and James Baldwin, and, later, into the anti-war, civil rights, and women's movements. On the other hand, it was these writers and movements that eventually encouraged her to see her "private turmoil"—indeed, her consciousness itself—as the product of historically specific social and political forces. As she explains in "Blood, Bread, and Poetry,"

> my personal world view . . . was . . . created by political conditions. I was not a man; I was white in a white-supremacist society; I was . . . educated from the perspective of a particular class; my father was an "assimilated" Jew in an anti-Semitic world, my mother a white southern Protestant; there were particular historical currents on which my consciousness would come together, piece by piece. . . . My personal world view, which like so many young people I carried as a conviction of my own uniqueness, was not original with me, but was, rather, my untutored and half-conscious rendering of the facts of blood and bread, the social and political forces of my time and place.

Rich's mature poetry is, in many ways, an attempt to scrutinize the "social and political forces" that shape our lives and our relationships with each other and with the planet we inhabit. In this way, "the personal is political" for and in Rich—and so, too, is the literary. Yet her poetry works as poetry largely because in it the converse is always equally and palpably true. Her "poems compel us," as critic Albert Gelpi suggests, "precisely because . . . the politics [are] not abstracted and depersonalized but tested on the nerve-ends."

Despite—or even because of—all the changes, Rich's work also demonstrates a real and rare sort of consistency. From the very beginning of her career, Rich has conceived poems with a powerful sense of functional structure and cast them in lyric modes that sensitively reflect their moods and tones. She has engaged readers viscerally and intellectually through vivid images. And in fact certain images and objects—knives and coffee pots, ruins and rubble, maps and monsters, wintry weather—recur in multiple poems, binding the poems together even as they help us to track a process of evolution and change which, Rich reminds us, isn't either simple or complete. "If you think you can grasp me, think again," she warns us in "Delta"; "my story flows in more than one direction."

At a Bach Concert

Coming by evening through the wintry city
We said that art is out of love with life.
Here we approach a love that is not pity.

This antique discipline, tenderly severe,
5   Renews belief in love yet masters feeling,
Asking of us a grace in what we bear.

Form is the ultimate gift that love can offer—
The vital union of necessity
With all that we desire, all that we suffer.

10 A too-compassionate art is half an art.
Only such proud restraining purity
Restores the else-betrayed, too-human heart.

                                        1951

Storm Warnings

The glass has been falling all the afternoon,
And knowing better than the instrument
What winds are walking overhead, what zone
Of gray unrest is moving across the land,
5   I leave the book upon a pillowed chair
And walk from window to closed window, watching
Boughs strain against the sky

And think again, as often when the air
Moves inward toward a silent core of waiting,
10 How with a single purpose time has traveled
By secret currents of the undiscerned
Into this polar realm. Weather abroad
And weather in the heart alike come on
Regardless of prediction.

15 Between foreseeing and averting change
    Lies all the mastery of elements
    Which clocks and weatherglasses cannot alter.
    Time in the hand is not control of time,
    Nor shattered fragments of an instrument
20 A proof against the wind; the wind will rise,
    We can only close the shutters.

    I draw the curtains as the sky goes black
    And set a match to candles sheathed in glass
    Against the keyhole draught, the insistent whine
25 Of weather through the unsealed aperture.
    This is our sole defense against the season;
    These are the things that we have learned to do
    Who live in troubled regions.

                                        1951

Living in Sin

    She had thought the studio would keep itself;
    no dust upon the furniture of love.
    Half heresy, to wish the taps less vocal,
    the panes relieved of grime. A plate of pears,
5   a piano with a Persian shawl, a cat
    stalking the picturesque amusing mouse
    had risen at his urging.
    Not that at five each separate stair would writhe
    under the milkman's tramp; that morning light
10 so coldly would delineate the scraps
    of last night's cheese and three sepulchral bottles;
    that on the kitchen shelf among the saucers
    a pair of beetle-eyes would fix her own—
    envoy from some village in the moldings . . .
15 Meanwhile, he, with a yawn,
    sounded a dozen notes upon the keyboard,
    declared it out of tune, shrugged at the mirror,
    rubbed at his beard, went out for cigarettes;
    while she, jeered by the minor demons,
20 pulled back the sheets and made the bed and found
    a towel to dust the table-top,
    and let the coffee-pot boil over on the stove.
    By evening she was back in love again,
    though not so wholly but throughout the night
25 she woke sometimes to feel the daylight coming
    like a relentless milkman up the stairs.

                                        1955

Snapshots of a Daughter-in-Law

1

You, once a belle in Shreveport,
with henna-colored hair, skin like a peachbud,
still have your dresses copied from that time,
and play a Chopin prelude
5 called by Cortot: *"Delicious recollections*
float like perfume through the memory."

Your mind now, mouldering like wedding-cake,
heavy with useless experience, rich
with suspicion, rumor, fantasy,
10 crumbling to pieces under the knife-edge
of mere fact. In the prime of your life.
Nervy, glowering, your daughter
wipes the teaspoons, grows another way.

2

Banging the coffee-pot into the sink
15 she hears the angels chiding, and looks out
past the raked gardens to the sloppy sky.
Only a week since They said: *Have no patience.*

The next time it was: *Be insatiable.*
Then: *Save yourself; others you cannot save.*[1]
20 Sometimes she's let the tapstream scald her arm,
a match burn to her thumbnail,

or held her hand above the kettle's snout
right in the woolly steam. They are probably angels,
since nothing hurts her any more, except
25 each morning's grit blowing into her eyes.

3

A thinking woman sleeps with monsters.
The beak that grips her, she becomes. And Nature,
that sprung-lidded, still commodious
steamer-trunk of *tempora* and *mores*[2]
30 gets stuffed with it all: the mildewed orange-flowers,
the female pills, the terrible breasts
of Boadicea[3] beneath flat foxes' heads and orchids.

---

1. According to Matthew 27.42, the chief priests, scribes, and elders mocked the crucified Jesus by saying, "He saved others; himself he cannot save."   2. Times and customs.

3. Queen of the ancient Britons. When her husband died, the Romans seized the territory he ruled and scourged Boadicea; she then led a heroic but ultimately unsuccessful revolt. *Female pills:* medicines for menstrual ailments.

Two handsome women, gripped in argument,
each proud, acute, subtle, I hear scream
35 across the cut glass and majolica
like Furies[4] cornered from their prey:
The argument *ad feminam*,[5] all the old knives
that have rusted in my back, I drive in yours,
ma semblable, ma soeur![6]

4

40 Knowing themselves too well in one another:
their gifts no pure fruition, but a thorn,
the prick filed sharp against a hint of scorn . . .
Reading while waiting
for the iron to heat,
45 writing, *My Life had stood—a Loaded Gun—*[7]
in that Amherst pantry while the jellies boil and scum,
or, more often,
iron-eyed and beaked and purposed as a bird,
dusting everything on the whatnot every day of life.

5

50 *Dulce ridens, dulce loquens,*[8]
she shaves her legs until they gleam
like petrified mammoth-tusk.

6

When to her lute Corinna sings[9]
neither words nor music are her own;
55 only the long hair dipping
over her cheek, only the song
of silk against her knees
and these
adjusted in reflections of an eye.

60 Poised, trembling and unsatisfied, before
an unlocked door, that cage of cages,
tell us, you bird, you tragical machine—
is this *fertilisante douleur?*[1] Pinned down
by love, for you the only natural action,

---

4. In Roman mythology, the three sisters were the avenging spirits of retributive justice.
5. To the woman (Latin). The *argumentum ad hominem* (literally, argument to the man) is (in classical rhetoric) an argument aimed at a person's individual prejudices or special interests.
6. My mirror-image (or "double"), my sister. Baudelaire, in the prefatory poem to *Les Fleurs du Mal*, addresses (and attacks) his "hypocrite reader" as "mon semblable, mon frère" (my double, my brother).
7. "My Life had stood—a Loaded Gun—" [Poem No. 754], Emily Dickinson, *Complete Poems*, ed. T. H. Johnson, 1960, p. 369 [Rich's note]. It is reprinted in chapter 8.
8. Sweet laughter, sweet chatter. The phrase (slightly modified here) concludes Horace's *Ode* 1.22, describing the appeal of a mistress.
9. The opening line of a lyric by Thomas Campion (1567–1620). It is reprinted in chapter 5.
1. Enriching pain (French).

65 are you edged more keen
to prise the secrets of the vault? has Nature shown
her household books to you, daughter-in-law,
that her sons never saw?

7

"To have in this uncertain world some stay
70 *which cannot be undermined, is*
of the utmost consequence."[2]
                  Thus wrote
a woman, partly brave and partly good,
who fought with what she partly understood.
75 Few men about her would or could do more,
hence she was labeled harpy, shrew and whore.

8

"You all die at fifteen," said Diderot,[3]
and turn part legend, part convention.
Still, eyes inaccurately dream
80 behind closed windows blankening with steam.
Deliciously, all that we might have been,
all that we were—fire, tears,
wit, taste, martyred ambition—
stirs like the memory of refused adultery
85 the drained and flagging bosom of our middle years.

9

Not that it is done well, but
that it is done at all?[4] Yes, think
of the odds! or shrug them off forever.
This luxury of the precocious child,
90 Time's precious chronic invalid,—
would we, darlings, resign it if we could?
Our blight has been our sinecure:
mere talent was enough for us—
glitter in fragments and rough drafts.

95 Sigh no more, ladies.
                  Time is male
and in his cups drinks to the fair.
Bemused by gallantry, we hear

2. "... is of the utmost consequence," from Mary Wollstonecraft, *Thoughts on the Education of Daughters*, London, 1787 [Rich's note].

3. "Vous mourez toutes a quinze ans," from the *Lettres à Sophie Volland*, quoted by Simone de Beauvoir in *Le Deuxième Sexe*, vol. II, pp. 123–4 [Rich's note]. Editor of the *Encyclopédie* (the central document of the French Enlightenment), Denis Diderot (1713–1784) became disillusioned with the traditional education of women and undertook an experimental education for his own daughter.

4. Samuel Johnson's comment on women preachers: "Sir, a woman's preaching is like a dog's walking on his hinder legs. It is not done well, but you are surprised to find it done at all" (Boswell's *Life of Johnson*, ed. L. F. Powell and G. B. Hill [Oxford: Clarendon, 1934–64], 1.463).

our mediocrities over-praised,
100 indolence read as abnegation,
slattern thought styled intuition,
every lapse forgiven, our crime
only to cast too bold a shadow
or smash the mould straight off.

105 For that, solitary confinement,
tear gas, attrition shelling.
Few applicants for that honor.

10

                  Well,
she's long about her coming, who must be
110 more merciless to herself than history.[5]
Her mind full to the wind, I see her plunge
breasted and glancing through the currents,
taking the light upon her
at least as beautiful as any boy
115 or helicopter,
              poised, still coming,
her fine blades making the air wince

but her cargo
no promise then:
120 delivered
palpable
ours.

1958–60

In her 1972 essay "When We Dead Awaken," Rich describes her consciousness during the time she was writing this poem:

> Over two years I wrote a 10-part poem called "Snapshots of a Daughter-in-Law," in a longer, looser mode than I've ever trusted myself with before. It was an extraordinary relief to write that poem. It strikes me now as too literary, too dependent on allusion; I hadn't found the courage yet to do without authorities, or even to use the pronoun "I"—the woman in the poem is always "she." One section of it, #2, concerns a woman who thinks she is going mad; she is haunted by voices telling her to resist and rebel, voices which she can hear but not obey.

---

5. Cf. *Le Deuxième Sexe,* vol. II, p. 574: ". . . elle arrive du fond des ages, de Thèbes, de Minos, de Chichen Itza; et elle est aussi le totem planté au coeur de la brousse africaine; c'est un helicoptère et c'est un oiseau; et voilà la plus grande merveille: sous ses cheveux peints le bruissement des feuillages devient une pensée et des paroles s'échappent de ses seins" [Rich's note].

Planetarium

(*Thinking of Caroline Herschel, 1750–1848, astronomer, sister of William; and others*)

A woman in the shape of a monster
a monster in the shape of a woman
the skies are full of them

a woman   "in the snow
5   among the Clocks and instruments
or measuring the ground with poles"

in her 98 years to discover
8 comets

she whom the moon ruled
10 like us
levitating into the night sky
riding the polished lenses

Galaxies of women, there
doing penance for impetuousness
15 ribs chilled
in those spaces   of the mind

An eye,
      "virile, precise and absolutely certain"
            from the mad webs of Uranisborg[6]
20   encountering the NOVA

every impulse of light exploding
from the core
as life flies out of us

         Tycho whispering at last
25   "Let me not seem to have lived in vain"

What we see, we see
and seeing is changing

the light that shrivels a mountain
and leaves a man alive

30 Heartbeat of the pulsar
heart sweating through my body

The radio impulse
pouring in from Taurus
         I am bombarded yet   I stand

6. Actually Uraniborg, the elaborate palace-laboratory-observatory of Danish astronomer Tycho Brahe (1546–1601), whose cosmology tried to fuse the Ptolemaic and Copernican systems. Brahe discovered and described (in *De Nova Stella*, 1574) a new star in what had previously been considered a fixed-star system.

35 I have been standing all my life in the
   direct path of a battery of signals
   the most accurately transmitted most
   untranslatable language in the universe
   I am a galactic cloud so deep   so invo-
40 luted that a light wave could take 15
   years to travel through me   And has
   taken   I am an instrument in the shape
   of a woman trying to translate pulsations
   into images   for the relief of the body
45 and the reconstruction of the mind.

1968

Dialogue

   She sits with one hand poised against her head, the
   other turning an old ring to the light
   for hours our talk has beaten
   like rain against the screens
5 a sense of August and heat-lightning
   I get up, go to make tea, come back
   we look at each other
   then she says (and this is what I live through
   over and over)—she says: *I do not know*
10 *if sex is an illusion*

   I do not know
   who I was when I did those things
   or who I said I was
   or whether I willed to feel
15 *what I had read about*
   or who in fact was there with me
   or whether I knew, even then
   that there was doubt about these things

                                        1972

Power

   Living in the earth-deposits of our history

   Today a backhoe divulged out of a crumbling flank of earth
   one bottle amber perfect a hundred-year-old
   cure for fever or melancholy a tonic
5 for living on this earth in the winters of this climate

Today I was reading about Marie Curie:
she must have known she suffered   from radiation sickness
her body bombarded for years   by the element
she had purified
10 It seems she denied to the end
the source of the cataracts on her eyes
the cracked and suppurating skin   of her finger-ends
till she could no longer hold   a test-tube or a pencil

She died   a famous woman   denying
15 her wounds
denying
her wounds   came   from the same source as her power
                                                                                        1978

For the Record

The clouds and the stars didn't wage this war
the brooks gave no information
if the mountain spewed stones of fire into the river
it was not taking sides
5 the raindrop faintly swaying under the leaf
had no political opinions

and if here or there a house
filled with backed-up raw sewage
or poisoned those who lived there
10 with slow fumes, over years
the houses were not at war
nor did the tinned-up buildings

intend to refuse shelter
to homeless old women and roaming children
15 they had no policy to keep them roaming
or dying, no, the cities were not the problem
the bridges were non-partisan
the freeways burned, but not with hatred

Even the miles of barbed-wire
20 stretched around crouching temporary huts
designed to keep the unwanted
at a safe distance, out of sight
even the boards that had to absorb
year upon year, so many human sounds

25 so many depths of vomit, tears
slow-soaking blood
had not offered themselves for this
The trees didn't volunteer to be cut into boards

nor the thorns for tearing flesh
30 Look around at all of it

and ask whose signature
is stamped on the orders, traced
in the corner of the building plans
Ask where the illiterate, big-bellied
35 women were, the drunks and crazies,
the ones you fear most of all: ask where you were.

1983

[My mouth hovers across your breasts][7]

My mouth hovers across your breasts
in the short grey winter afternoon
in this bed   we are delicate
and tough   so hot with joy we amaze ourselves
5 tough   and delicate   we play rings
around each other   our daytime candle burns
with its peculiar light   and if the snow
begins to fall outside   filling the branches
and if the night falls   without announcement
10 these are the pleasures of winter
sudden, wild and delicate   your fingers
exact   my tongue exact at the same moment
stopping to laugh at a joke
my love   hot on your scent   on the cusp of winter

1986

Delta

If you have taken this rubble for my past
raking through it for fragments you could sell
know that I long ago moved on
deeper into the heart of the matter

5 If you think you can grasp me, think again:
my story flows in more than one direction
a delta springing from the riverbed
with its five fingers spread

1989

---

7. This is poem three in Rich's series "Tracking Poems."

History[8]

Should I simplify my life for you?
Don't ask how I began to love men.
Don't ask how I began to love women.
Remember the forties songs, the slowdance numbers
5   the small sex-filled gas-rationed Chevrolet?
Remember walking in the snow and who was gay?
Cigarette smoke of the movies, silver-and-gray
profiles, dreaming the dreams of he-and-she
breathing the dissolution of the wisping silver plume?
10 Dreaming that dream we leaned applying lipstick
by the gravestone's mirror when we found ourselves
playing in the cemetery. In Current Events she said
the war in Europe is over, the Allies
and she wore no lipstick have won the war
15 and we raced screaming out of Sixth Period.

Dreaming that dream
we had to maze our ways through a wood
where lips were knives breasts razors and I hid
in the cage of my mind scribbling
20 *this map stops where it all begins*
into a red-and-black notebook.
Remember after the war when peace came down
as plenty for some and they said we were saved
in an eternal present and we knew the world could end?
25 —remember after the war when peace rained down
on the winds from Hiroshima Nagasaki Utah Nevada?[9]
and the socialist queer Christian teacher jumps from the hotel window?[1]
and L.G. saying *I want to sleep with you but not for sex*
and the red-and-black enamelled coffee-pot dripped slow through the
dark grounds
30 —appetite terror power tenderness
the long kiss in the stairwell the switch thrown
on two Jewish Communists[2] married to each other
the definitive crunch of glass at the end of the wedding?
(When shall we learn, what should be clear as day,
35 *We cannot choose what we are free to love?)*

1995

---

8. This is poem four in Rich's series "Inscriptions."
9. Sites of atomic-bomb explosions, the first two in Japan near the end of World War II, the last two at test sites in the desert.
1. This line alludes to the critic Francis Otto Matthiessen (1902–1950), who taught at Harvard while Rich was an undergraduate there.
2. Julius and Ethel Rosenberg, executed as spies by the United States in 1953.
3. These last two lines are from the opening of W. H. Auden's "Canzone."

Modotti[4]

Your footprints of light on sensitive paper
that typewriter you made famous
my footsteps following you up stair-
wells of scarred oak and shredded newsprint
5 these windowpanes smeared with stifled breaths
corridors of tile and jaundiced plaster
if this is where I must look for you
then this is where I'll find you

From a streetlamp's wet lozenge bent
10 on a curb plastered with newsprint
the headlines aiming straight at your eyes
to a room's dark breath-smeared light
these footsteps I'm following you with
down tiles of a red corridor
15 if this is a way to find you
of course this is how I'll find you

Your negatives pegged to dry in a darkroom
rigged up over a bathtub's lozenge
your footprints of light on sensitive paper
20 stacked curling under blackened panes
the always upstairs of your hideout
the stern exposure of your brows
—these footsteps I'm following you with
aren't to arrest you

25 The bristling hairs of your eyeflash
that typewriter you made famous
your enormous will to arrest and frame
what was, what is, still liquid, flowing
your exposure of manifestos, your
30 lightbulb in a scarred ceiling
well if this is how I find you
Modotti so I find you

In the red wash of your darkroom
from your neighborhood of volcanoes
35 to the geranium nailed in a can

---

4. Tina Modotti (1896–1942): photographer, political activist, revolutionary. Her most significant artistic work was done in Mexico in the 1920s, including a study of the typewriter belonging to her lover, the Cuban revolutionary Julio Antonio Mella. Framed for his murder by the fascists in 1929, she was expelled from Mexico in 1930. After some years of political activity in Berlin, the Soviet Union, and Spain, she returned incognito to Mexico, where she died in 1942.

In my search for Modotti I had to follow clues she left; I did not want to iconize her but to imagine critically the traps and opportunities of her life and choices [Rich's note].

on the wall of your upstairs hideout
in the rush of breath a window
of revolution allowed you
on this jaundiced stair in this huge lashed eye

40   these

footsteps I'm following you with

1996   1999

PERSONAL REFLECTIONS

From *When We Dead Awaken:*
Writing as Re-Vision[1]

Most, if not all, human lives are full of fantasy—passive daydreaming which need not be acted on. But to write poetry or fiction, or even to think well, is not to fantasize, or to put fantasies on paper. For a poem to coalesce, for a character or an action to take shape, there has to be an imaginative transformation of reality which is in no way passive. And a certain freedom of the mind is needed—freedom to press on, to enter the currents of your thought like a glider pilot, knowing that your motion can be sustained, that the buoyancy of your attention will not be suddenly snatched away. Moreover, if the imagination is to transcend and transform experience it has to question, to challenge, to conceive of alter-

Adrienne Rich in 1978

natives, perhaps to the very life you are living at that moment. You have to be free to play around with the notion that day might be night, love might be hate, nothing can be too sacred for the imagination to turn into its opposite or to call experimentally by another name. For writing is re-naming. Now, to be maternally with small children all day in the old way, to be with a man in the old way of marriage, requires a holding-back, a putting-aside of that imaginative activity, and demands instead a kind of conservatism. I want to make it clear that I am *not* saying that in order to write well, or think well, it is necessary to become unavailable to others, or to become a devouring ego. This has been the myth of the masculine artist and thinker; and I do not accept it. But to be a female human being

1. First published in *College English* in 1972; this version, slightly revised, is included in *On Lies, Secrets, and Silence: Selected Prose: 1966–1978* (1979).

trying to fulfill traditional female functions in a traditional way *is* in direct conflict with the subversive function of the imagination. The word traditional is important here. There must be ways, and we will be finding out more and more about them, in which the energy of creation and the energy of relation can be united. But in those earlier years I always felt the conflict as a failure of love in myself. I had thought I was choosing a full life: the life available to most men, in which sexuality, work, and parenthood could coexist. But I felt, at twenty-nine, guilt toward the people closest to me, and guilty toward my own being.

I wanted, then, more than anything, the one thing of which there was never enough: time to think, time to write. The fifties and early sixties were years of rapid revelations: the sit-ins and marches in the South, the Bay of Pigs, the early antiwar movement, raised large questions—questions for which the masculine world of the academy around me seemed to have expert and fluent answers. But I needed to think for myself—about pacifism and dissent and violence, about poetry and society, and about my own relationship to all these things. For about ten years I was reading in fierce snatches, scribbling in notebooks, writing poetry in fragments; I was looking desperately for clues, because if there were no clues then I thought I might be insane. I wrote in a notebook about this time:

> Paralyzed by the sense that there exists a mesh of relationships—e.g., between my anger at the children, my sensual life, pacifism, sex (I mean sex in its broadest significance, not merely sexual desire)—an interconnectedness which, if I could see it, make it valid, would give me back myself, make it possible to function lucidly and passionately. Yet I grope in and out among these dark webs.

I think I began at this point to feel that politics was not something "out there" but something "in here" and of the essence of my condition.

In the late fifties I was able to write, for the first time, directly about experiencing myself as a woman. The poem was jotted in fragments during children's naps, brief hours in a library, or at 3 A.M. after rising with a wakeful child. I despaired of doing any continuous work at this time. Yet I began to feel that my fragments and scraps had a common consciousness and a common theme, one which I would have been very unwilling to put on paper at an earlier time because I had been taught that poetry should be "universal," which meant, of course, nonfemale. Until then I had tried very much *not* to identify myself as a female poet.

How Does a Poet Put Bread on the Table?[2]

But how does a poet put bread on the table? Rarely, if ever, by poetry alone. Of the four lesbian poets at the Nuyorican Poets Café about whose lives I know something, one directs an underfunded community arts project, two are untenured college teachers, one an assistant dean of students at a state university. Of other poets I know, most teach, often part time, without security but year round; two are on disability; one does clerical work; one cleans houses; one is a paid

2. From *What Is Found There: Notebooks on Poetry and Politics* (1993).

organizer; one has a paid editing job. Whatever odd money comes in erratically from readings and workshops, grants, permissions fees, royalties, prizes can be very odd money indeed, never to be counted on and almost always small: checks have to be chased down, grants become fewer and more competitive in a worsening political and economic climate. Most poets who teach at universities are untenured, without pension plans or group health insurance, or are employed at public and community colleges with heavy teaching loads and low salaries. Many give unpaid readings and workshops as part of their political "tithe."

Inherited wealth accounts for the careers of some poets: to inherit wealth is to inherit time. Most of the poets I know, hearing of a sum of money, translate it not into possessions, but into time—that precious immaterial necessity of our lives. It's true that a poem can be attempted in brief interstitial moments, pulled out of the pocket and worked on while waiting for a bus or riding a train or while children nap or while waiting for a new batch of clerical work or blood samples to come in. But only certain kinds of poems are amenable to these conditions. Sometimes the very knowledge of coming interruption dampens the flicker. And there is a difference between the ordinary "free" moments stolen from exhausting family strains, from alienating labor, from thought chained by material anxiety, and those other moments that sometimes arrive in a life being lived at its height though under extreme tension; perhaps we are waiting to initiate some act we believe will catalyze change but whose outcome is uncertain; perhaps we are facing personal or communal crisis in which everything unimportant seems to fall away and we are left with our naked lives, the brevity of life itself, and words. At such times we may experience a speeding-up of our imaginative powers, images and voices rush together in a kind of inevitability, what was externally fragmented is internally recognized, and the hand can barely keep pace.

But such moments presuppose other times: when we could simply stare into the wood grain of a door, or the trace of bubbles in a glass of water as long as we wanted to, *almost* secure in the knowledge that there would be no interruption—times of slowness, or purposelessness.

Often such time feels like a luxury, guiltily seized when it can be had, fearfully taken because it does not seem like work, this abeyance, but like "wasting time" in a society where personal importance—even job security—can hinge on acting busy, where the phrase "keeping busy" is a common idiom, where there is, for activists, so much to be done.

Most, if not all, of the names we know in North American poetry are the names of people who have had some access to freedom in time—that privilege of some which is actually a necessity for all. The struggle to limit the working day is a sacred struggle for the worker's freedom in time. To feel herself or himself, for a few hours or a weekend, as a free being with choices—to plant vegetables and later sit on the porch with a cold beer, to write poetry or build a fence or fish or play cards, to walk without a purpose, to make love in the daytime. To sleep late. Ordinary human pleasures, the self's re-creation. Yet every working generation has to reclaim that freedom in time, and many are brutally thwarted in the effort. Capitalism is based on the abridgment of that freedom.

Poets in the United States have either had some kind of private means, or help from people with private means, have held full-time, consuming jobs, or have chosen to work in low-paying, part-time sectors of the economy, saving their creative energies for poetry, keeping their material wants simple. Interstitial living, where the art itself is not expected to bring in much money, where the artist may move from a clerical job to part-time, temporary teaching to subsistence living on the land to waitressing or doing construction or translating, typesetting, or ghostwriting. In the 1990s this kind of interstitial living is more difficult, risky, and wearing than it has ever been, and this is a loss to all the arts—as much as the shrinkage of arts funding, the censorship-by-clique, the censorship by the Right, the censorship by distribution.

A Communal Poetry[3]

One day in New York in the late 1980s, I had lunch with a poet I'd known for more than twenty years. Many of his poems were—are—embedded in my life. We had read together at the antiwar events of the Vietnam years. Then, for a long time, we hardly met. As a friend, he had seemed to me withheld, defended in a certain way I defined as masculine and with which I was becoming in general impatient; yet often, in their painful beauty, his poems told another story. On this day, he was as I had remembered him: distant, stiff, shy perhaps. The conversation stumbled along as we talked about our experiences with teaching poetry, which seemed a safe ground. I made some remark about how long it was since last we'd talked. Suddenly, his whole manner changed: *You disappeared! You simply disappeared.* I realized he meant not so much from his life as from a landscape of poetry to which he thought we both belonged and were in some sense loyal.

Adrienne Rich in the 2000s

If anything, those intervening years had made me feel more apparent, more visible— to myself and to others—as a poet. The powerful magnet of the women's liberation movement—and the women's poetry movement it released—had drawn me to coffeehouses where women were reading new kinds of poems; to emerging "journals of liberation" that published women's poems, often in a context of political articles and the beginnings of feminist criticism; to bookstores selling chapbooks and pamphlets from the new women's presses; to a woman poet's workshops with women in prison; to meetings with other women poets in Chinese restaurants, coffee shops, apartments, where we talked not only of poetry, but of the conditions that make it possible or impossible. It had never occurred to me that I was disappearing—rather, that I was, along with other women poets, beginning to appear. In fact, we were taking part in an immense shift in human consciousness.

3. From *What Is Found There: Notebooks on Poetry and Politics* (1993).

My old friend had, I believe, not much awareness of any of this. It was, for him, so off-to-the-edge, so out-of-the-way; perhaps so dangerous, it seemed I had sunk, or dived, into a black hole. Only later, in a less constrained and happier meeting, were we able to speak of the different ways we had perceived that time.

He thought there had been a known, defined poetic landscape and that as poetic contemporaries we simply shared it. But whatever poetic "generation" I belonged to, in the 1950s I was a mother, under thirty, raising three small children. Notwithstanding the prize and the fellowship to Europe that my first book of poems had won me, there was little or no "appearance" I then felt able to claim as a poet, against that other profound and as yet unworded reality.

Why I Refused the National Medal for the Arts[4]

July 3, 1997

Jane Alexander, Chair
The National Endowment for the Arts
1100 Pennsylvania Avenue
Washington, D.C. 20506

Dear Jane Alexander,

I just spoke with a young man from your office, who informed me that I had been chosen to be one of twelve recipients of the National Medal for the Arts at a ceremony at the White House in the fall. I told him at once that I could not accept such an award from President Clinton or this White House because the very meaning of art, as I understand it, is incompatible with the cynical politics of this administration. I want to clarify to you what I meant by my refusal.

Anyone familiar with my work from the early sixties on knows that I believe in art's social presence—as breaker of official silences, as voice for those whose voices are disregarded, and as a human birthright. In my lifetime I have seen the space for the arts opened by movements for social justice, the power of art to break despair. Over the past two decades I have witnessed the increasingly brutal impact of racial and economic injustice in our country.

There is no simple formula for the relationship of art to justice. But I do know that art—in my own case the art of poetry—means nothing if it simply decorates the dinner table of power that holds it hostage. The radical disparities of wealth and power in America are widening at a devastating rate. A president cannot meaningfully honor certain token artists while the people at large are so dishonored.

I know you have been engaged in a serious and disheartening struggle to save government funding for the arts, against those whose fear and suspicion of art

---

4. From *Arts of the Possible: Essays and Conversations* (2001).

After the text of my letter to Jane Alexander, then chair of the National Endowment for the Arts, had been fragmentarily quoted in various news stories, Steve Wasserman, editor of the *Los Angeles Times Book Review,* asked me for an article expanding on my reasons. Herewith the letter and the article [Rich's note].

is nakedly repressive. In the end, I don't think we can separate art from overall human dignity and hope. My concern for my country is inextricable from my concerns as an artist. I could not participate in a ritual that would feel so hypocritical to me.

Sincerely,
Adrienne Rich

cc: President Clinton

The invitation from the White House came by telephone on July 3. After several years' erosion of arts funding and hostile propaganda from the religious right and the Republican Congress, the House vote to end the National Endowment for the Arts was looming. That vote would break as news on July 10; my refusal of the National Medal for the Arts would run as a sidebar story alongside in the *New York Times* and the *San Francisco Chronicle*.

In fact, I was unaware of the timing. My refusal came directly out of my work as a poet and essayist and citizen drawn to the interfold of personal and public experience. I had recently been thinking and writing about the shrinking of the social compact, of whatever it was this country had ever meant when it called itself a democracy: the shredding of the vision of *government of the people, by the people, for the people*.

"We the people—still an excellent phrase," said the playwright Lorraine Hansberry in 1962, well aware who had been excluded, yet believing the phrase might someday come to embrace us all. And I had for years been feeling both personal and public grief, fear, hunger, and the need to render this, my time, in the language of my art.

Whatever was "newsworthy" about my refusal was not about a single individual—not myself, not President Clinton. Nor was it about a single political party. Both major parties have displayed a crude affinity for the interests of corporate power, while deserting the majority of the people, especially the most vulnerable. Like so many others, I've watched the dismantling of our public education, the steep rise in our incarceration rates, the demonization of our young black men, the accusations against our teen-age mothers, the selling of health care—public and private—to the highest bidders, the export of subsistence-level jobs in the United States to even lower-wage countries, the use of below-minimum-wage prison labor to break strikes and raise profits, the scapegoating of immigrants, the denial of dignity and minimal security to working and poor people. At the same time, we've witnessed the acquisition of publishing houses, once risk-taking conduits of creativity, by conglomerates driven single-mindedly to fast profits, the acquisition of major communications and media by those same interests, the sacrifice of the arts and public libraries in stripped-down school and civic budgets, and, most recently, the evisceration of the National Endowment for the Arts. Piece by piece the democratic process has been losing ground to the accumulation of private wealth.

There is no political leadership in the White House or the Congress that has spoken to and for the people who, in a very real sense, have felt abandoned by their government.

Lorraine Hansberry spoke her words about government during the Cuban missile crisis, at a public meeting in New York to abolish the House Un-American Activities Committee. She also said in that speech, "My government is wrong." She did not say, I abhor all government. She claimed her government as a citizen, African American, and female, and she challenged it. (I listened to her words again, on an old vinyl recording, this past Fourth of July.)

In a similar spirit many of us today might wish to hold government accountable, to challenge the agendas of private power and wealth that have displaced historical tendencies toward genuinely representative government in the United States. We might still wish to claim our government, to say, *This belongs to us—* we, the people, as we are now.

We would have to start asking questions that have been defined as nonquestions—or as naive, childish questions. In the recent official White House focus on race, it goes consistently unsaid that the all-embracing enterprise of our early history was the slave trade, which left nothing, no single life, untouched, and was, along with the genocide of the native population and the seizure of their lands, the foundation of our national prosperity and power. Promote dialogues on race? apologize for slavery? We would need to perform an autopsy on capitalism itself.

Marxism has been declared dead. Yet the questions Marx raised are still alive and pulsing, however the language and the labels have been co-opted and abused. What is social wealth? How do the conditions of human labor infiltrate other social relationships? What would it require for people to live and work together in conditions of radical equality? How much inequality will we tolerate in the world's richest and most powerful nation? Why and how have these and similar questions become discredited in public discourse?

And what about art? Mistrusted, adored, pietized, condemned, dismissed as entertainment, commodified, auctioned at Sotheby's, purchased by investment-seeking celebrities, it dies into the "art object" of a thousand museum basements. It's also reborn hourly in prisons, women's shelters, small-town garages, community-college workshops, halfway houses, wherever someone picks up a pencil, a wood-burning tool, a copy of *The Tempest,* a tag-sale camera, a whittling knife, a stick of charcoal, a pawnshop horn, a video of *Citizen Kane,* whatever lets you know again that this deeply instinctual yet self-conscious expressive language, this regenerative process, could help you save your life. "If there were no poetry on any day in the world," the poet Muriel Rukeyser wrote, "poetry would be invented that day. For there would be an intolerable hunger." In an essay on the Caribbean poet Aimé Césaire, Clayton Eshleman names this hunger as "the desire, the need, for a more profound and ensouled world." There is a continuing dynamic between art repressed and art reborn, between the relentless marketing of the superficial and the "spectral and vivid reality that employs all means" (Rukeyser again) to reach through armoring, resistances, resignation, to recall us to desire.

Art is both tough and fragile. It speaks of what we long to hear and what we dread to find. Its source and native impulse, the imagination, may be shackled in early life, yet may find release in conditions offering little else to the spirit. For a recent document on this, look at Phyllis Kornfeld's *Cellblock Visions: Prison*

Art in America, notable for the variety and emotional depth of the artworks repro-
duced, the words of the inmate artists, and for Kornfeld's unsentimental and
lucid text. Having taught art to inmates for fourteen years, in eighteen institu-
tions (including maximum-security units), she sees recent incarceration policy as
rapidly devolving from rehabilitation to dehumanization, including the disman-
tling of prison arts programs.

Art can never be totally legislated by any system, even those that reward obe-
dience and send dissident artists to hard labor and death; nor can it, in our
specifically compromised system, be really free. It may push up through cracked
macadam, by the merest means, but it needs breathing space, cultivation, pro-
tection to fulfill itself. Just as people do. New artists, young or old, need edu-
cation in their art, the tools of their craft, chances to study examples from the
past and meet practitioners in the present, get the criticism and encouragement
of mentors, learn that they are not alone. As the social compact withers, fewer
and fewer people will be told *Yes, you can do this; this also belongs to you.* Like
government, art needs the participation of the many in order not to become the
property of a powerful and narrowly self-interested few.

Art is our human birthright, our most powerful means of access to our own
and another's experience and imaginative life. In continually rediscovering and
recovering the humanity of human beings, art is crucial to the democratic vision.
A government tending further and further away from the search for democracy
will see less and less "use" in encouraging artists, will see art as obscenity or hoax.

In 1987, the late Justice William Brennan spoke of "formal reason severed
from the insights of passion" as a major threat to due-process principles. "Due
process asks whether government has treated someone fairly, whether individual
dignity has been honored, whether the worth of an individual has been acknowl-
edged. Officials cannot always silence these questions by pointing to rational
action taken according to standard rules. They must plumb their conduct more
deeply, seeking answers in the more complex equations of human nature and
experience."

It is precisely where fear and hatred of art join the pull toward quantification
and abstraction, where the human face is mechanically deleted, that human dig-
nity disappears from the social equation. Because it is to those "complex equa-
tions of human nature and experience" that art addresses itself.

In a society tyrannized by the accumulation of wealth as Eastern Europe was
tyrannized by its own false gods of concentrated power, recognized artists have,
perhaps, a new opportunity: to work out our connectedness, *as artists,* with other
people who are beleaguered, suffering, disenfranchised—precariously employed
workers, trashed elders, rejected youth, the "unsuccessful," and the art they too
are nonetheless making and seeking.

I wish I didn't feel the necessity to say here that none of this is about imposing
ideology or style or content on artists; it's about the inseparability of art from
acute social crisis in this century and the one now approaching.

We have a short-lived model, in our history, for the place of art in relation to
government. During the Depression of the 1930s, under New Deal legislation,
thousands of creative and performing artists were paid modest stipends to work
in the Federal Writers Project, the Federal Theatre Project, the Federal Art Project.
Their creativity, in the form of novels, murals, plays, performances, public mon-
uments, the providing of music and theater to new audiences, seeded the art and

the consciousness of succeeding decades. By 1939 this funding was discontinued.

Federal funding for the arts, like the philanthropy of private arts patrons, can be given and taken away. In the long run art needs to grow organically out of a social compost nourishing to everyone, a literate citizenry, a free, universal, public education complex with art as an integral element, a society honoring both human individuality and the search for a decent, sustainable common life. In such conditions, art would still be a voice of hunger, desire, discontent, passion, reminding us that the democratic project is never-ending.

For that to happen, what else would have to change?

CHRONOLOGY

1929   Born in Baltimore, Maryland, May 16. Began writing poetry as a child under the encouragement and supervision of her father, Dr. Arnold Rich, from whose "very Victorian, pre-Raphaelite" library, Rich later recalled, she read Tennyson, Keats, Arnold, Blake, Rossetti, Swinburne, Carlyle, and Pater.

1951   A.B., Radcliffe College. *A Change of World* chosen by W. H. Auden for publication in the Yale Younger Poets series.

1952–53   Guggenheim Fellowship; travel in Europe and England. Marriage to Alfred H. Conrad, an economist who taught at Harvard. Residence in Cambridge, Massachusetts, 1953–66.

1955   Birth of David Conrad. Publication of *The Diamond Cutters and Other Poems*.

1957   Birth of Paul Conrad.

1959   Birth of Jacob Conrad.

1960   National Institute of Arts and Letters Award for poetry.

1961–62   Guggenheim Fellowship; residence with family in the Netherlands.

1962   Bollingen Foundation grant for translation of Dutch poetry.

1962–63   Amy Lowell Travelling Fellowship.

1963   *Snapshots of a Daughter-in-Law* published. Bess Hokin Prize of *Poetry* magazine.

1966   *Necessities of Life* published. Move to New York City; residence there from 1966 on. Increasingly active politically in protests against the war in Vietnam.

1966–68   Lecturer at Swarthmore College.

1967–69   Adjunct Professor of Writing in the Graduate School of the Arts, Columbia University.

1968   Began teaching in the SEEK and Open Admissions Programs at City College of New York.

1969   *Leaflets* published.

1970   Death of Alfred Conrad.

1971   *The Will to Change* published. Increasingly active in the women's movement.

1972–73   Fannie Hurst Visiting Professor of Creative Literature at Brandeis University.

1973   *Diving into the Wreck* published.

1974 National Book Award for *Diving into the Wreck*. Rich rejects the award as an individual, but accepts it, in a statement written with Audre Lorde and Alice Walker, two other nominees, in the name of all women. Professor of English, City College of New York.

1975 *Poems: Selected and New* published.

1976 Professor of English at Douglass College. *Of Woman Born: Motherhood as Experience and Institution* published. *Twenty-one Love Poems* published.

1978 *The Dream of a Common Language: Poems 1974–1977* published.

1979 *On Lies, Secrets, and Silence: Selected Prose 1966–1978* published. Leaves Douglass College and New York City; moves to Montague, Massachusetts; edits, with Michelle Cliff, the lesbian-feminist journal *Sinister Wisdom*.

1981 *A Wild Patience Has Taken Me This Far: Poems 1978–1981* published.

1984 *The Fact of a Doorframe: Poems Selected and New 1950–1984* published. Moves to Santa Cruz, California. Professor of English, San Jose State University.

1986 *Blood, Bread, and Poetry: Selected Prose 1979–1985* published. Professor of English, Stanford University.

1989 *Time's Power: Poems 1985–1988* published.

1991 *An Atlas of the Difficult World: Poems 1988–1991* published.

1992 Wins *Los Angeles Times* Book Prize for *An Atlas of the Difficult World: Poems 1988–1991,* the Lenore Marshall/*Nation* Prize for Poetry, and Nicholas Roerich Museum Poet's Prize; is co-winner of the Frost Silver Medal for distinguished lifetime achievement.

1993 *What Is Found There: Notebooks on Poetry and Politics* published.

1994 Awarded MacArthur fellowship.

1995 *Dark Fields of the Republic: Poems 1991–1995* published.

1996 Awarded the Dorothea Tanning Prize, given by the Academy of American Poets.

1999 Elected a chancellor of the Academy. Received Lannan Foundation's Lifetime Achievement Award. *Midnight Salvage: Poems 1995–1998* published.

2001 *Fox: Poems 1998–2000* and *Arts of the Possible: Essays and Conversations* published.

2002 *The Fact of a Doorframe: Poems Selected and New 1950–2000* published.

2005 *The School among the Ruins: Poems 2000–2004* published.

SUGGESTIONS FOR WRITING

1. Write an essay in which you analyze one of Keats's sonnets, either "On First Looking into Chapman's Homer" (chapter 11), "On the Grasshopper and the Cricket" (chapter 1), or "On Seeing the Elgin Marbles" (this chapter). Which sonnet form does the poem employ, and why is this appropriate? What sound effects does Keats use, and why does this enhance the poem? How does Keats use poetic technique to support the poem's theme?

2. John Keats lost both of his parents and his brother while he was still young, and he knew that he was dying of tuberculosis during the final year of his life, when he wrote many of his greatest poems. Write an essay in which you explore the themes of life and death, mortality and immortality, as they reveal themselves in the selections in this chapter. How does Keats's poetry exemplify the Latin dictum *Vita brevis est, ars longa*—"Life is short, art is long"?

3. Write an essay in which you analyze the poetic techniques Keats employs in the passage from *Endymion* in this chapter. What are the relationships between rhymed words? What is the effect of the rhyme scheme? How does Keats create tension with the combination of rhymed couplets and enjambment—the continuation of sentences past the end of a poetic line?

4. Write an essay in which you present a close reading of one of the odes in this chapter. What is the tone, and how is this achieved? What is the relationship between the poem's form (stanzas, rhyme scheme, etc.) and the development of its argument? How does Keats use observed particulars to point to larger themes?

5. What is the relationship between Keats's poems and his theories about poetry? Write an essay in which you discuss how his poems are illuminated by the ideas he expresses in the letters in this chapter.

6. In her 1951 poem "At a Bach Concert," Adrienne Rich wrote that "Form is the ultimate gift that love can offer." What, exactly, is the case for the "discipline" of formalist art argued by this poem? How has Rich's later work both embodied and rejected formalism? Considering as evidence the selections of poetry in this and previous chapters, and prose in this chapter, write an essay in which you discuss how Rich's thoughts about formalism have evolved throughout her career.

7. Carefully considering plot, characterization, and structure, write an essay in which you detail the ways "Diving into the Wreck" (chapter 16) is and is not typical of Rich's work.

8. In poems such as "Snapshots of a Daughter-in-Law," "Planetarium," and "Modotti," Rich considers the creative accomplishments of women throughout history. What role do these women play, separately and together? How is that role both constrained and unconstrained by men? Write an essay in which you examine the way Rich has portrayed creative women. Are they role models in her work, or something else?

9. Rich once said of her college days in the late 1940s, "I had no political ideas of my own, only the era's vague and hallucinatory anti-Communism and the encroaching privatism of the 1950s. Drenched in invisible assumptions of my class and race, unable to fathom the pervasive ideology of gender, I felt 'politics' as distant, vaguely sinister, the province of powerful older men or of people I saw as fanatics. It was in poetry that I sought a grasp on the world and on interior events, 'ideas of order,' even power." Using the poems by Rich included in this book, write an essay that charts the development of the poet's political consciousness.

10. In her prose writings included in this chapter, Rich describes and defends the political passions that, she says, animate her life as an artist. How fully do Rich's poems embody her political beliefs, particularly her commitment to feminism? Write an essay in which you explore Rich's poetry in light of her feminist politics.

11 LITERARY TRADITION AS CONTEXT

The more poetry you read, the better a reader of poetry you will likely become. This is not just because your skills will improve and develop, but also because you will come to know more about poetic traditions and thus understand more fully how poets influence each other. Poets are conscious of other poets, and often they refer to each other's work or use it as a starting point for their own in ways that may not be immediately obvious to an outsider. Poetry can be thought of as a form of argument: poets agree or disagree over basic matters. Sometimes a quiet (or even noisy) competitiveness underlies their concern with what other poets do; at other times, playfulness and a sense of humor take over, and the competitiveness dwindles to poetic fun and games. And often poets simply want to share in the bounty of our artistic heritage. In any case, a poet's consciousness of what others have done leads to a sense of tradition that is often hard to articulate but is nevertheless very important to the effects of poetry—and this sense of tradition may present a problem for a new reader of poetry. How can I possibly read this poem intelligently, we are likely to ask sometimes in exasperation, until I've read all the other poems that inspired it? The problem is real. Poets don't expect their readers to have Ph.D.'s in literature, but sometimes it *seems* as if they do. For some poets—John Milton, T. S. Eliot, and Richard Wilbur, for example—it does help if one has read practically everything.

Why are poets so dependent on each other? What is the point of their relentless consciousness of what has already been done by others? Why do they repeatedly answer, allude to, and echo other poems? Why does tradition matter to them?

A sense of common task, a communality of purpose, accounts for some traditional poetic practice, as does the competitive desire of individual poets to achieve a place in the poetic **tradition**—the ever-growing body of poetic customs and practices. One way of establishing that place is to define the relationship between one's own work and that of others whose place is already secure. Poets may share and wish to pass on a serious and abiding cultural tradition, but they may also share a sense of playfulness, a kind of poetic gamesmanship. Making words dance on the page or in our heads provides in itself a satisfaction and delight for many writers—pride in craft that is like the pride of a painter or potter or tennis player. Often poets set themselves a particular task to see what they can do. One way of doing that is to introduce a standard **motif** (a recurrent device, formula, or situation that deliberately connects a poem with traditional thought), and then to play variations on it much as a musician might do. Another way is to provide an alternative answer to a question that has repeatedly been asked and answered in a traditional way. Poetic playfulness by no means excludes serious intention—the poems in this chapter often make important state-

> *The truest poetry is the most feigning.*
> —WILLIAM SHAKESPEARE

ments about their subjects, however humorous they may be in their method. Some teasing of the tradition and of other poets is pure fun, a kind of kidding among good friends; some is harsher and represents an attempt to see the world very differently—to define and articulate a very different set of attitudes and values.

The Anglophone poetic tradition is a rich and varied heritage, and individual poets draw upon it in countless ways. You have probably noticed, in the poems you have read so far, a number of allusions—glances at the tradition or at individual expressions of it. The more poems you read, the more such allusions you will notice and the more you will become a comfortable member of the audience poets write for. Poets expect a lot from readers—not always, but often enough to make a new reader feel nervous and even, sometimes, inadequate. The discomfort fades when you begin to notice things that other readers don't. The poems in this chapter illustrate some of the ways that the tradition energizes individual poets to make the most of their heritage.

ECHO AND ALLUSION

The poems in this group employ the familiar poetic strategy of echoing or alluding to other texts as a way of importing meaning into a poem, similar to the strategy of "sampling" words or sounds in contemporary music. An **echo** may simply recall a word, phrase, or sound in another text as a way of associating what is going on in *this* poem with something in another, already familiar text. The familiarity itself may sometimes be the point: writers often like to associate what they do with what has already been done, especially if their work sounds like a text that is already much admired. Echoes of Shakespeare, for example, may imply that this new text shares concerns (and, therefore, insight or quality?) with Shakespeare. An **allusion** more insistently connects a particular word, phrase, or section of a poem with some similar formulation in a previous text; it explicitly *invokes* the reader's recognition of the previous text and asks for interpretation based on the implied similarity.

Strategies of echo and allusion can be very complicated, for the question of just how much of one text can carry over—or be forcibly brought over—into another one cannot be answered categorically.

Often poets quote—or echo with variations—a passage from another text in order to suggest some thematic, ideological, tonal, or stylistic link. Sometimes the purpose is simply to invoke an idea or attitude from another text, another place, or another culture. In "Two Songs" (chapter 4), for example, Adrienne Rich employs Chaucer's familiar formulation of the rites of spring (with its description of all things coming to life, their vital juices flowing, as they follow the natural progress of the seasons) to suggest the way the sap rises in ordinary lusty human beings. The quotation thus puts the speaker's attraction to a lover into a larger human perspective, and her sense of herself as a subject and object of lust comes to seem natural, part of the ordinary course of events.

The first poem in "Echo and Allusion" belongs, uncomfortably, in the *carpe diem* ("seize the day") tradition; but unlike ordinary *carpe diem* poems, it is moralistic. It undercuts the speaker by having him allude to familiar biblical passages that imply a condemnation of live-for-today attitudes and ideas. By echoing

Satan's tempting addresses to Eve in Genesis, the speaker in Jonson's "Come, my Celia" condemns himself in the eyes of readers and becomes a seducer-villain instead of a libertine-hero. The other poems here variously recall individual lines, passages, poems, ideas, or traditions in order to establish a particular stance or attitude. The meaning of each poem derives primarily from interpreting the allusion.

Poems certainly do not need earlier texts in order to exist or have meaning, but prior texts may set up what happens in a particular poem or govern how we construe it. Allusion—the strategy of using one text to comment on and influence the interpretation of another—is one of the most popular and familiar poetic strategies.

Carpe Diem

BEN JONSON

Speaker- himself

[*Come, my Celia, let us prove*][1]

slant

Come, my Celia, let us prove,[2]   *Couplets*
While we can, the sports of love;
Time will not be ours forever:
He at length our good will sever.
5   Spend not, then, his gifts in vain;   *Have sex now cause tomorrow we might be dead.*
Suns that set may rise again,
But if once we lose this light,
'Tis with us perpetual night.
Why should we defer our joys?
10 Fame and rumor are but toys.
Cannot we delude the eyes   *Enjambment*
Of a few poor household spies?
Or his easier ears beguile,
Thus removéd by our wile?
15 'Tis no sin love's fruits to steal,   *It's a sin to tell.*
But the sweet thefts to reveal;
To be taken, to be seen,
These have crimes accounted been.

1606

1. A song from *Volpone*, sung by the play's villain and would-be seducer. Part of the poem paraphrases Catullus, poem 5.   2. Experience.

WILLIAM BLAKE

The Lamb

Little Lamb, who made thee?
  Dost thou know who made thee?
Gave thee life, and bid thee feed
By the stream and o'er the mead;
5 Gave thee clothing of delight,
Softest clothing woolly bright;
Gave thee such a tender voice,
Making all the vales rejoice?
  Little Lamb, who made thee?
10   Dost thou know who made thee?

  Little Lamb, I'll tell thee!
  Little Lamb, I'll tell thee:
He is callèd by thy name,
For he calls himself a Lamb,
15 He is meek and he is mild;
He became a little child.
I a child and thou a lamb,
We are callèd by his name.
  Little Lamb, God bless thee!
20 Little Lamb, God bless thee!

1789

HOWARD NEMEROV

Boom!

Sees Boom in Religion, too

*Atlantic City, June 23, 1957 (AP)—President Eisenhower's pastor said
tonight that Americans are living in a period of "unprecedented religious
activity" caused partially by paid vacations, the eight-hour day and mod-
ern conveniences.*

  *"These fruits of material progress," said the Rev. Edward L. R. Elson
of the National Presbyterian Church, Washington, "have provided the lei-
sure, the energy, and the means for a level of human and spiritual val-
ues never before reached."*

Here at the Vespasian-Carlton,[3] it's just one
religious activity after another; the sky

---

3. Vespasian was emperor of Rome 69–79 C.E., shortly after the reign of Nero. In French, *vespasienne* means
"public toilet."

is constantly being crossed by cruciform
airplanes, in which nobody disbelieves
5   for a second and the tide, the tide
of spiritual progress and prosperity
miraculously keeps rising, to a level
never before attained. The churches are full,
the beaches are full, and the filling-stations
10   are full, God's great ocean is full
of paid vacationers praying an eight-hour day
to the human and spiritual values, the fruits,
the leisure, the energy, and the means, Lord,
the means for the level, the unprecedented level,
15   and the modern conveniences, which also are full.
Never before, O Lord, have the prayers and praises
from belfry and phonebooth, from ballpark and barbecue
the sacrifices, so endlessly ascended.

It was not thus when Job in Palestine
20   sat in the dust and cried, cried bitterly;[4]
when Damien kissed the lepers on their wounds
it was not thus;[5] it was not thus
when Francis worked a fourteen-hour day
strictly for the birds;[6] when Dante took
25   a week's vacation without pay and it rained
part of the time,[7] O Lord, it was not thus.

But now the gears mesh and the tires burn
and the ice chatters in the shaker and the priest
in the pulpit and Thy Name, O Lord,
30   is kept before the public, while the fruits
ripen and religion booms and the level rises
and every modern convenience runneth over,
that it may never be with us as it hath been
with Athens and Karnak and Nagasaki,[8]
35   nor Thy sun for one instant refrain from shining
on the rainbow Buick by the breezeway
or the Chris Craft with the uplift life raft;
that we may continue to be the just folks we are,
plain people with ordinary superliners and
40   disposable diaperliners, people of the stop'n'shop

---

4. According to the Book of Job, he was afflicted with the loss of prosperity, children, and health as a test
of his faith. His name means, in Hebrew, "he cries"; see especially Job 2.7–13.
5. "Father Damien" (Joseph Damien de Veuster, 1840–1889), a Roman Catholic missionary from Belgium,
was known for his work among lepers in Hawaii; he ultimately contracted leprosy himself and died there.
6. St. Francis of Assisi, thirteenth-century founder of the Franciscan order, was noted for his love of all
living things, and one of the most famous stories about him tells of his preaching to the birds.
7. Dante's journey through Hell, Purgatory, and Paradise (in *The Divine Comedy*) takes a week, beginning
on Good Friday, 1300. It rains in the third chasm of Hell.
8. A large Japanese port city, virtually destroyed by a U.S. atomic bomb in 1945. *Athens:* the cultural center
of ancient Greek civilization. *Karnak:* a village on the Nile, built on the site of ancient Thebes.

'n'pray as you go, of hotel, motel, boatel,
the humble pilgrims of no deposit no return
and please adjust thy clothing, who will give to Thee,
if Thee will keep us going, our annual
45 Miss Universe, for Thy Name's Sake, Amen.

1960

MARIANNE MOORE

Love in America?

Whatever it is, it's a passion—
a benign dementia that should be   *must forget*
engulfing America, fed in a way
    the opposite of the way
5 in which the Minotaur[9] was fed.
It's a Midas[1] of tenderness;
    from the heart;
nothing else. From one with ability
to bear being misunderstood—
10   take the blame, with "nobility
    that is action,"[2] identifying itself with
    pioneer unperfunctoriness

without brazenness[3] or
bigness of overgrown
15 undergrown shallowness.

Whatever it is, let it be without
affectation.

Yes, yes, yes, *yes.*

1967

9. The Minotaur demanded a virgin to devour once a year [Moore's note; notes 1–3 are also Moore's].
1. Midas, who had the golden touch, was inconvenienced when eating or picking things up.
2. Unamuno said that what we need as a cure for unruly youth is "nobility that is action."
3. *without brazenness or bigness* . . . Winston Churchill: "Modesty becomes a man."

ROBERT HOLLANDER

You Too? Me Too—Why Not? Soda Pop

I am
look
ing at
the Co
caCola
bottle
which is
green wi
th ridges
just–like

   c   c   c
 o   o   o
 l   l   l
 u   u   u
m   m   m
n   n   n
s   s   s

and on itself it says

COCA-COLA
reg.u.s.pat.off.

exactly like an art pop
statue of that kind of
bottle but not so green
that the juice inside
gives other than the co-
lor it has when I pour
it out in a clear glass
glass on this table top
(It's making me thirsty
all this winking and
beading of Hippocrene
please let me pause drink-
ing the fluid in)
ah! it is enticing how each
color is the same
brown in green bottle
brown in uplifted glass
making each utensil on
the table laid a brown
fork in a brown shade
making me long to watch
them harvesting the crop
which makes the deep-aged
rich brown wine of America
that is to say which makes
soda   pop

1968

WILLIAM SHAKESPEARE

[*Not marble, nor the gilded monuments*]

Not marble, nor the gilded monuments
Of princes, shall outlive this powerful rhyme;
But you shall shine more bright in these conténts
Than unswept stone, besmeared with sluttish time.
5   When wasteful war shall statues overturn,
And broils[4] root out the work of masonry,
Nor[5] Mars his sword nor war's quick fire shall burn
The living record of your memory.
'Gainst death and all-oblivious enmity
10 Shall you pace forth; your praise shall still find room
Even in the eyes of all posterity
That wear this world out to the ending doom.[6]
So, till the judgment that yourself arise,
You live in this, and dwell in lovers' eyes.

1609

POETIC "KINDS"

By now you have experienced all sorts of poems, on a variety of subjects and with all kinds of tones—short poems, long poems, poems that rhyme and poems that don't. And there are, of course, many other sorts of poems that we haven't looked at. Some poems, for example, have thousands of lines and differ substantially from the poems that can be included in an anthology like this.

Poems may be classified in a variety of ways—by subject or theme; by their length, appearance, and formal features; by the way they are organized; by the level of language they use; by the poet's intention and the kinds of effects the poem tries to generate.

Classification may be, of course, simply an intellectual exercise. Recognizing that a poem is, for example, an elegy, a parody, or a satire may provide a satisfaction like that of identifying a scarlet tanager, a weeping willow, a French phrase, or a 1967 Ford Thunderbird. Just *knowing* what others don't know may give us a sense of importance, accomplishment, and power. But we can also experience a poem more fully if we understand early on what kind of poem it is, and if we know that the poet has consciously played by certain rules. The **conventions** a poet employs indicate certain standard ways of saying things to achieve certain expected effects, and thus the tradition involved in a particular poetic kind yields certain standard responses—or variations on them, depending on a particular poem's relation to that tradition. For example, the humor and fun of the following poem depend entirely on readers' recognizing the *kind* of poem they are reading.

4. Riots.   5. Neither. *Mars his:* Mars's.   6. Judgment Day.

CHRISTOPHER MARLOWE

[CD] *The Passionate Shepherd to His Love*

Come live with me and be my love,
And we will all the pleasures prove[1]
That valleys, groves, hills, and fields,
Woods, or steepy mountain yields.

5 And we will sit upon the rocks,
Seeing the shepherds feed their flocks,
By shallow rivers to whose falls
Melodious birds sing madrigals.

And I will make thee beds of roses
10 And a thousand fragrant posies,
A cap of flowers, and a kirtle[2]
Embroidered all with leaves of myrtle;

A gown made of the finest wool
Which from our pretty lambs we pull;
15 Fair linéd slippers for the cold,
With buckles of the purest gold;

A belt of straw and ivy buds,
With coral clasps and amber studs:
And if these pleasures may thee move,
20 Come live with me, and be my love.

The shepherd swains[3] shall dance and sing
For thy delight each May morning:
If these delights thy mind may move,
Then live with me and be my love.

1600

A beginning reader of poetry might easily protest that such a plea is unrealistic and fanciful, and thus feel unsure of the poem's tone. What could such a reader think of a speaker who constructs his argument in such a dreamlike way? But the traditions behind the poem and the conventions of the poetic kind make its intention and effects clear. "The Passionate Shepherd to His Love" is a **pastoral poem,** a poetic kind that concerns itself with the simple life of country folk and describes that life in stylized, idealized terms. The people in a pastoral poem are usually (as here) shepherds, although they may be fishermen or other rustics who lead an outdoor life and tend to basic human needs in a simplified society; the world of the poem is one of simplicity, beauty, music, and love. Life always seems timeless in pastoral; people are eternally young, and the season is always spring, usually May. Nature seems endlessly green and the future entirely golden. Difficulty, frus-

---

1. Experience.   2. Gown.   3. Youths.

tration, disappointment, and obligation do not exist in this world, which is blissfully free of problems. Shepherds sing instead of tending sheep, and they make love and play music instead of having to watch out for wolves in the night. If only the shepherd boy and shepherd girl can agree with each other to make love joyously and passionately, they will live happily ever after. Their language, though informal and fairly simple, always seems a bit more sophisticated than that of real shepherds with real problems and real sheep.

Unrealistic? Of course. No real shepherd spends even a single day like that, and certainly the world of simple country folk includes ferocities of nature, human deceit and mischief, disease, bad weather, old age, moments that are not all green and gold. Probably no poet ever thought that shepherds really live that way, but it is an attractive fantasy, and poets who write pastoral simply choose this one formulaic way to isolate a series of idealized moments. Fantasies can be personal and private, of course, but a certain pleasure comes from shared public fantasies, such as the central moment when two people first contemplate the joys of ecstatic love uncomplicated by the realities of duty or limit. To present a certain tone, attitude, and wholeness, poets self-consciously construct this vision of a world that is self-existent, self-contained, and self-referential.

Other poetic kinds included in this book are:

epic	From *Paradise Lost*	p. 150
lyric	"The Lamb"	p. 385
ballad	"Sir Patrick Spens"	p. 242
aubade	"The Sun Rising"	p. 534
meditation	"Love Calls Us to the Things of This World"	p. 498
dramatic monologue	"My Last Duchess"	p. 329
soliloquy	"Soliloquy of the Spanish Cloister"	p. 73
confessional	"Skunk Hour"	p. 59
protest	"Hard Rock Returns . . ."	p. 32

You will find brief definitions of these terms in the glossary. Each kind has its own characteristics and conventions—established by tradition and habit—and each deserves detailed study and discussion. Meanwhile, in the following section we will examine numerous examples of yet another poetic kind.

HAIKU

The **haiku,** an import into the English poetic tradition, has a long history in its original tradition, Japanese. Originally, the haiku (then called *hokku*) was a short section of a longer poem (called a *renga* or *haikai*) composed by several poets who wrote segments in response to one another in a long, cumulative poetic exercise or game. But early on, at least as early as the seventeenth century, the distinctive subject matter and mode of the haiku, together with the creative discipline required by its formal demands, made it an attractive form in itself, and several major poets built their reputations largely on the basis of their skill in the form.

Traditionally, the Japanese haiku was an unrhymed poem consisting of seventeen sounds (or, rather, characters representing seventeen sounds) and distributed over three lines in a five-seven-five pattern—that is, five distinctive sounds in the first line, seven in the second, and five in the third. "Sounds" in the Japanese language are not exactly the same as "syllables" in English, but there is a rough parallel—close enough so that when English writers began to compose haiku about a century ago, they ordinarily translated the sound requirement into syllables. Here, for example, is a haiku (in translation) that conforms in its Japanese original to the standard formal definition:

CHIYOJO

[*Whether astringent*][1]

Whether astringent
I do not know. This is my first
Persimmon picking.

Haiku aim for conciseness and compression. They leave a lot unsaid, suggesting connections and causes but seldom making them explicit. Typically, haiku describe a natural object—a flower, say, or an animal, or a place—and imply a relationship between that perception and some human feeling or state of mind. Haiku thus depend heavily on emotive language, and they try not to be definitive. Instead of conclusions, summaries, closures, and neat answers, haiku seek openings; they alert the mind to possibility.

Three other traditional characteristics of haiku affect readers' expectations. First, haiku have a "seasonal" requirement, so that each poem associates itself with one season of the year and thus "dates" itself in relation to a predictable, revolving pattern of change. This seasonal association may be quite subtle and indirect—through, for example, some flower, event, or condition normally connected with a particular season. Second, haiku more generally involve descriptions of nature: a poem often begins with the observation of a specific natural phenomenon—a plant, an animal, or an aspect of landscape—that becomes connected, implicitly or explicitly, with a human feeling or emotion. This use of nature develops out of the Buddhist sense of nature as orderly and benign but also contingent and transient. Since human beings are a part of that unified order, other parts of nature serve as "natural" reflections of human states. Haiku adapted into other languages and cultures cannot, of course, rely on the same spiritual assumptions or worldview, but most haiku strive to retain a sense of the human and natural as being mutually reflective and interdependent. Third, haiku often connect the "natural" and the human through a combination of observation and imagination. They blur the Western distinction between seeing something literally and having some "vision" of its end or meaning, though they seldom explicitly connect that claim to a larger, visionary perspective.

---

1. Chiyojo (1703–1775) is probably the most famous Japanese woman haiku poet. Tradition has it that she wrote this poem at the time of (and about) her engagement. Translation by Daniel C. Buchanan.

Some of the traditional Japanese "masters" of haiku from the seventeenth to the early twentieth century—Bashō, Issa, and Buson, for example—are represented (in English translations) in the examples that follow. But haiku has become an international form, and during the last half century or so, poets around the world have made conscious, concentrated attempts to create a haiku tradition in at least fifty languages. The habits and traditions of different languages and literatures have influenced and modified the way haiku are written, something that might offend some traditional masters of haiku, just as it would amuse others to see their work so readily but loosely adapted. Later poets and even translators of classic verses have not always observed the seventeen-syllable and three-line requirements, for example. As in any other poetic kind, the conventions prove both demanding and adaptable to the particular needs of different situations, different languages, and different individual poets. (If you would like to try writing haiku, you might consult one of the guides written for this purpose, such as William S. Higginson's *Haiku Handbook: How to Write, Share, and Teach Haiku* [1992].)

BASHŌ

[*A village without bells—*][2]

A village without bells—
   how do they live?
      spring dusk.

[*This road*]

   This road—
no one goes down it,
   autumn evening.

BUSON

[*Coolness—*][3]

Coolness—
   the sound of the bell
     as it leaves the bell.

---

2. Matsuo Bashō (1644–1694) is usually considered the first great master poet of haiku. Translations by Robert Hass.   3. Yosa Buson (1716–1783). Translations by Robert Hass.

[Listening to the moon]

Listening to the moon,
gazing at the croaking of frogs
in a field of ripe rice.

SEIFŪ

[The faces of dolls]⁴

The faces of dolls.
In unavoidable ways
I must have grown old.

ISSA

[The moon and the flowers]⁵

The moon and the flowers,
forty-nine years,
walking around, wasting time.

[Insects on a bough]

Insects on a bough
floating downriver,
still singing.

Perhaps the single most famous haiku poem is by Bashō. Here are four different translations into English of that poem. (The source of these poems, Hiroaki Sato's *One Hundred Frogs: From Matsu [i.e. Matsuo] Basho to Allen Ginsberg*, contains an even greater variety of examples.)

LAFCADIO HEARN

[Old pond—]

Old pond—frogs jumped in—sound of water.

1898

4. Seifū (1650–1721) was a nun. Translation by Daniel C. Buchanan.
5. Kobayashi Issa (1763–1827). Translations by Robert Hass.

CLARA A. WALSH
[*An old-time pond*]

An old-time pond, from off whose shadowed depth
Is heard the splash where some lithe frog leaps in.

1910

EARL MINER
[*The still old pond*]

The still old pond
and as a frog leaps in it
the sound of a splash.

1979

ALLEN GINSBERG
[*The old pond*]

The old pond—a frog jumps in, kerplunk!

1979

The following haiku were all written in English:

BABETTE DEUTSCH
[*The falling flower*][6]

The falling flower
I saw drift back to the branch
Was a butterfly.

1957

---

6. An adaptation of a poem by Arakida Moritake (1473–1549).

ETHERIDGE KNIGHT

[Eastern guard tower]

Eastern guard tower
glints in sunset; convicts rest
like lizards on rocks.

1960

ALLEN GINSBERG

[Looking over my shoulder]

Looking over my shoulder
my behind was covered
with cherry blossoms.

1955

RICHARD WRIGHT

[In the falling snow]

In the falling snow
A laughing boy holds out his palms
Until they are white.

1960

JAMES A. EMANUEL

Ray Charles

His get-aboard smile,
picnic knees, back-up bounce: JAZZ,
all there, ounce by ounce.

1999

POETS ON POETS: IMITATION, HOMAGE, DOUBT

A poem will often respond directly—sometimes point by point or even line by line or word by word—to another poem. The tactic may be teasing or comic, but often, too, a real challenge exists behind such a facetious answer, perhaps a serious criticism of the first poem's point or the tradition it represents, or an attempt to provide a different perspective. While it may follow its model slavishly, the poem may also alter key words or details so that readers will easily notice the differences in tone or attitude.

The result usually seems self-conscious, as if the poet were trying to do something a little different in light of the shared tradition. However "sincere" the poem may be, its sense of play is equally important. The first three poems below, for example, playfully pick on Marlowe's "The Passionate Shepherd to His Love" (earlier in this chapter). In effect, all of them provide "answers" to that poem, as if his "love" were telling the shepherd what is wrong with his argument. Of course, the poets are answering Marlowe, too. These poets know full well what Marlowe was doing in the pastoral fantasy of his original poem, and they clearly enjoy telling him how people in various circumstances might feel about his fantasy. There is in the end a lot of playfulness and not much hostility in their "realistic" deflation of his magic. The poem by Skirrow, for example, pokes gentle fun at another famous work, offering a summary of Keats's "Ode on a Grecian Urn" (in chapter 10). Others make fun of a previous work in less direct ways, but they share the objective of answering an original, even though they use very different styles to alter the poetic intention of that original.

SIR WALTER RALEGH

The Nymph's Reply to the Shepherd

If all the world and love were young,
And truth in every shepherd's tongue,
These pretty pleasures might me move
To live with thee and be thy love.

5 Time drives the flocks from field to fold,
When rivers rage, and rocks grow cold,
And Philomel[1] becometh dumb;
The rest complain of cares to come.

The flowers do fade, and wanton fields
10 To wayward winter reckoning yields:
A honey tongue, a heart of gall,
Is fancy's spring, but sorrow's fall.

---

1. The nightingale.

Thy gowns, thy shoes, thy beds of roses,
Thy cap, thy kirtle, and thy posies
15 Soon break, soon wither, soon forgotten;
In folly ripe, in reason rotten.

Thy belt of straw and ivy buds,
Thy coral clasps and amber studs,
All these in me no means can move
20 To come to thee and be thy love.

But could youth last, and love still breed,
Had joys no date,[2] nor age no need,
Then these delights my mind might move
To live with thee and be thy love.

                                        1600

WILLIAM CARLOS WILLIAMS

Raleigh Was Right

We cannot go to the country
for the country will bring us no peace
What can the small violets tell us
that grow on furry stems in
5 the long grass among lance shaped leaves?

Though you praise us
and call to mind the poets
who sung of our loveliness
it was long ago!
10 long ago! when country people
would plow and sow with
flowering minds and pockets at ease—
if ever this were true.

Not now. Love itself a flower
15 with roots in a parched ground.
Empty pockets make empty heads.
Cure it if you can but
do not believe that we can live
today in the country
20 for the country will bring us no peace.

                                        1941

2. End.

ALLEN GINSBERG

A Further Proposal

Come live with me and be my love,
And we will some old pleasures prove.
Men like me have paid in verse
This costly courtesy, or curse;

5   But I would bargain with my art
(As to the mind, now to the heart),
My symbols, images, and signs
Please me more outside these lines.

For your share and recompense,
10 You will be taught another sense:
The wisdom of the subtle worm
Will turn most perfect in your form.

Not that your soul need tutored be
By intellectual decree,
15 But graces that the mind can share
Will make you, as more wise, more fair,

Till all the world's devoted thought
Find all in you it ever sought,
And even I, of skeptic mind,
20 A Resurrection of a kind.

This compliment, in my own way,
For what I would receive, I pay;
Thus all the wise have writ thereof,
And all the fair have been their love.

1947

E. E. CUMMINGS

[(*ponder,darling,these busted statues*]

(ponder,darling,these busted statues
of yon motheaten forum be aware
notice what hath remained
—the stone cringes
5   clinging to the stone, how obsolete

lips utter their extant smile. . . .
remark

a few deleted of texture
or meaning monuments and dolls

10 resist Them Greediest Paws of careful
time all of which is extremely
unimportant)whereas Life

matters if or

when the your- and my-
15 idle vertical worthless
self unite in a peculiarly
momentary

partnership(to instigate
constructive
20   Horizontal
business. . . . even so, let us make haste
—consider well this ruined aqueduct

lady,
which used to lead something into somewhere)

                                        1926

DESMOND SKIRROW

Ode on a Grecian Urn Summarized

Gods chase
Round vase.
What say?
What play?
5 Don't know.
Nice, though.

        1960

ANTHONY HECHT

The Dover Bitch

A Criticism of Life

for Andrews Wanning

So there stood Matthew Arnold and this girl
With the cliffs of England crumbling away behind them,
And he said to her, "Try to be true to me,
And I'll do the same for you, for things are bad

5 All over, etc., etc."
   Well now, I knew this girl. It's true she had read
   Sophocles in a fairly good translation
   And caught that bitter allusion to the sea,[3]
   But all the time he was talking she had in mind
10 The notion of what his whiskers would feel like
   On the back of her neck. She told me later on
   That after a while she got to looking out
   At the lights across the channel, and really felt sad,
   Thinking of all the wine and enormous beds
15 And blandishments in French and the perfumes.
   And then she got really angry. To have been brought
   All the way down from London, and then be addressed
   As a sort of mournful cosmic last resort
   Is really tough on a girl, and she was pretty.
20 Anyway, she watched him pace the room
   And finger his watch-chain and seem to sweat a bit,
   And then she said one or two unprintable things.
   But you mustn't judge her by that. What I mean to say is,
   She's really all right. I still see her once in a while
25 And she always treats me right. We have a drink
   And I give her a good time, and perhaps it's a year
   Before I see her again, but there she is,
   Running to fat, but dependable as they come.
   And sometimes I bring her a bottle of *Nuit d'Amour*.

                                                    1968

WENDY COPE

[*Not only marble, but the plastic toys*]

Not only marble, but the plastic toys
From cornflake packets will outlive this rhyme:
I can't immortalize you, love—our joys
Will lie unnoticed in the vault of time.
5 When Mrs Thatcher has been cast in bronze
And her administration is a page
In some O-level text-book, when the dons[4]
Have analysed the story of our age,
When travel firms sell tours of outer space
10 And aeroplanes take off without a sound
And Tulse Hill has become a trendy place

---

3. In Sophocles' *Antigone*, lines 583–91. See "Dover Beach," lines 9–18.
4. Academics. *Mrs Thatcher:* Margaret Thatcher (b. 1925), British Conservative politician and prime minister, 1979–90. *O-level text-book:* a book that prepared British secondary-school students for standardized examinations ("ordinary-level").

And Upper Norwood's on the underground[5]
Your beauty and my name will be forgotten—
My love is true, but all my verse is rotten.

1986

JOHN KEATS

On First Looking into Chapman's Homer[6]

Much have I traveled in the realms of gold,
And many goodly states and kingdoms seen;
Round many western islands have I been
Which bards in fealty to Apollo[7] hold.
5 Oft of one wide expanse had I been told
That deep-browed Homer ruled as his demesne;
Yet did I never breathe its pure serene[8]
Till I heard Chapman speak out loud and bold:
Then felt I like some watcher of the skies
10 When a new planet swims into his ken;[9]
Or like stout Cortez[1] when with eagle eyes
He stared at the Pacific—and all his men
Looked at each other with a wild surmise—
Silent, upon a peak in Darien.

1816

D. H. LAWRENCE

When I Read Shakespeare

When I read Shakespeare I am struck with wonder
that such trivial people should muse and thunder
in such lovely language.

Lear, the old buffer, you wonder his daughters
5 didn't treat him rougher,
the old chough, the old chuffer!

---

5. London subway.
6. George Chapman's were among the most famous Renaissance translations; he completed his *Iliad* in 1611, his *Odyssey* in 1616. Keats wrote the sonnet after being led to Chapman by a former teacher and reading the *Iliad* all night long.
7. Greek god of poetry and music. *Fealty:* literally, the loyalty owed by a vassal to his feudal lord.
8. Atmosphere.   9. Range of vision.
1. Actually, Balboa; he first viewed the Pacific from Darien, in Panama.

And Hamlet, how boring, how boring to live with,
so mean and self-conscious, blowing and snoring
his wonderful speeches, full of other folks' whoring!

10 And Macbeth and his Lady, who should have been choring,
such suburban ambition, so messily goring
old Duncan with daggers!

How boring, how small Shakespeare's people are!
Yet the language so lovely! like the dyes from gas-tar.

1929

WILLIAM WORDSWORTH

London, 1802

Milton! thou should'st be living at this hour:
England hath need of thee: she is a fen
Of stagnant waters: altar, sword, and pen,
Fireside, the heroic wealth of hall and bower,
5 Have forfeited their ancient English dower
Of inward happiness. We are selfish men;
Oh! raise us up, return to us again;
And give us manners, virtue, freedom, power.
Thy soul was like a star, and dwelt apart:
10 Thou hadst a voice whose sound was like the sea:
Pure as the naked heavens, majestic, free,
So didst thou travel on life's common way,
In cheerful godliness; and yet thy heart
The lowliest duties on herself did lay.

1802

ARCHIBALD MACLEISH

You, Andrew Marvell[2]

And here face down beneath the sun
And here upon earth's noonward height
To feel the always coming on
The always rising of the night:

5 To feel creep up the curving east
The earthly chill of dusk and slow

---

2. See Marvell's "To His Coy Mistress" (p. 106), especially lines 21–22, which this poem extends and elaborates.

Upon those under lands the vast
And ever climbing shadow grow

And strange at Ecbatan[3] the trees
10 Take leaf by leaf the evening strange
The flooding dark about their knees
The mountains over Persia change

And now at Kermanshah[4] the gate
Dark empty and the withered grass
15 And through the twilight now the late
Few travelers in the westward pass

And Baghdad darken and the bridge
Across the silent river gone
And through Arabia the edge
20 Of evening widen and steal on

And deepen on Palmyra's[5] street
The wheel rut in the ruined stone
And Lebanon fade out and Crete
High through the clouds and overblown

25 And over Sicily the air
Still flashing with the landward gulls
And loom and slowly disappear
The sails above the shadowy hulls

And Spain go under and the shore
30 Of Africa the gilded sand
And evening vanish and no more
The low pale light across the land

Nor now the long light on the sea:

And here face downward in the sun
35 To feel how swift how secretly
The shadow of the night comes on . . .

1930

---

3. Ancient capital of Media (now in Iran).   4. In Iran.   5. Important city in ancient Syria.

GALWAY KINNELL

Shelley[6]

When I was twenty the one true
free spirit I had heard of was Shelley,
Shelley, who wrote tracts advocating
atheism, free love, the emancipation
5 of women, the abolition of wealth and class,
and poems on the bliss of romantic love,
Shelley, who, I learned later, perhaps
almost too late, remarried Harriet,
then pregnant with their second child,
10 and a few months later ran off with Mary,
already pregnant herself, bringing
with them Mary's stepsister Claire,
who very likely also became his lover,

and in this malaise à trois, which Shelley
15 had imagined would be "a paradise of exiles,"
they lived, along with the spectre of Harriet,
who drowned herself in the Serpentine,
and of Mary's half sister Fanny,
who killed herself, maybe for unrequited
20 love of Shelley, and with the spirits
of adored but often neglected
children conceived incidentally
in the pursuit of Eros—Harriet's
Ianthe and Charles, denied to Shelley
25 and consigned to foster parents; Mary's
Clara, dead at one; her Willmouse,
Shelley's favorite, dead at three; Elena,
the baby in Naples, almost surely
Shelley's own, whom he "adopted"
30 and then left behind, dead at one and a half;
Allegra, Claire's daughter by Byron,
whom Byron sent off to the convent
at Bagnacavallo at four, dead at five—

and in those days, before I knew
35 any of this, I thought I followed Shelley,
who thought he was following radiant desire.

2004

---

6. Percy Bysshe Shelley (1792–1822), English poet who lived a turbulent short life (some of which Kinnell details).

HART CRANE

To Emily Dickinson

You who desired so much—in vain to ask—
Yet fed your hunger like an endless task,
Dared dignify the labor, bless the quest—
Achieved that stillness ultimately best,

5 Being, of all, least sought for: Emily, hear!
O sweet, dead Silencer, most suddenly clear
When singing that Eternity possessed
And plundered momently in every breast;

—Truly no flower yet withers in your hand.
10 The harvest you descried and understand
Needs more than wit to gather, love to bind.
Some reconcilement of remotest mind—

Leaves Ormus rubyless, and Ophir[7] chill.
Else tears heap all within one clay-cold hill.

1933

BILLY COLLINS

Taking Off Emily Dickinson's Clothes

First, her tippet made of tulle,
easily lifted off her shoulders and laid
on the back of a wooden chair.

And her bonnet,
5 the bow undone with a light forward pull.

Then the long white dress, a more
complicated matter with mother-of-pearl
buttons down the back,
so tiny and numerous that it takes forever
10 before my hands can part the fabric,
like a swimmer's dividing water,
and slip inside.

---

7. An ancient country from which Solomon secured gold and precious stones. *Ormus:* presumably Ormuz, an ancient city on the Persian Gulf.

You will want to know
that she was standing
15 by an open window in an upstairs bedroom,
motionless, a little wide-eyed,
looking out at the orchard below,
the white dress puddled at her feet
on the wide-board, hardwood floor.

20 The complexity of women's undergarments
in nineteenth-century America
is not to be waved off,
and I proceeded like a polar explorer
through clips, clasps, and moorings,
25 catches, straps, and whalebone stays,
sailing toward the iceberg of her nakedness.

Later, I wrote in a notebook
it was like riding a swan into the night,
but, of course, I cannot tell you everything—
30 the way she closed her eyes to the orchard,
how her hair tumbled free of its pins,
how there were sudden dashes
whenever we spoke.

What I can tell you is
35 it was terribly quiet in Amherst
that Sabbath afternoon,
nothing but a carriage passing the house,
a fly buzzing in a windowpane.

So I could plainly hear her inhale
40 when I undid the very top
hook-and-eye fastener of her corset

and I could hear her sigh when finally it was unloosed,
the way some readers sigh when they realize
that Hope has feathers;
45 that reason is a plank,
that life is a loaded gun
that looks right at you with a yellow eye.

1998

W. H. AUDEN

In Memory of W. B. Yeats

(d. January, 1939)

I

He disappeared in the dead of winter:
The brooks were frozen, the airports almost deserted,
And snow disfigured the public statues;
The mercury sank in the mouth of the dying day.
5 What instruments we have agree
The day of his death was a dark cold day.

Far from his illness
The wolves ran on through the evergreen forests,
The peasant river was untempted by the fashionable quays;
10 By mourning tongues
The death of the poet was kept from his poems.

But for him it was his last afternoon as himself,
An afternoon of nurses and rumors;
The provinces of his body revolted,
15 The squares of his mind were empty,
Silence invaded the suburbs,
The current of his feeling failed; he became his admirers.

Now he is scattered among a hundred cities
And wholly given over to unfamiliar affections,
20 To find his happiness in another kind of wood
And be punished under a foreign code of conscience.
The words of a dead man
Are modified in the guts of the living.

But in the importance and noise of tomorrow
25 When the brokers are roaring like beasts on the floor of the Bourse,[8]
And the poor have the sufferings to which they are fairly accustomed,
And each in the cell of himself is almost convinced of his freedom,
A few thousand will think of this day
As one thinks of a day when one did something slightly unusual.
30 What instruments we have agree
The day of his death was a dark cold day.

II

You were silly like us; your gift survived it all:
The parish of rich women, physical decay,
Yourself. Mad Ireland hurt you into poetry.
35 Now Ireland has her madness and her weather still,
For poetry makes nothing happen: it survives

---

8. The Paris stock exchange.

In the valley of its making where executives
Would never want to tamper, flows on south
From ranches of isolation and the busy griefs,
40 Raw towns that we believe and die in; it survives,
A way of happening, a mouth.

      III

Earth, receive an honored guest:
William Yeats is laid to rest.
Let the Irish vessel lie
45 Emptied of its poetry.

In the nightmare of the dark
All the dogs of Europe bark,
And the living nations wait,
Each sequestered in its hate;

50 Intellectual disgrace
Stares from every human face,
And the seas of pity lie
Locked and frozen in each eye.

Follow, poet, follow right
55 To the bottom of the night,
With your unconstraining voice
Still persuade us to rejoice;

With the farming of a verse
Make a vineyard of the curse,
60 Sing of human unsuccess
In a rapture of distress;

In the deserts of the heart
Let the healing fountain start,
In the prison of his days
65 Teach the free man how to praise.

1939

WENDY COPE

Engineers' Corner

> *Why isn't there an Engineers' Corner in Westminster Abbey?[9] In
> Britain we've always made more fuss of a ballad than a blueprint . . .
> How many schoolchildren dream of becoming great engineers?—
> advertisement placed in* The Times *by the engineering Council*

We make more fuss of ballads than of blueprints—
That's why so many poets end up rich,

---

9. Gothic church in London where British monarchs are crowned. It contains a Poets' Corner in which many of the nation's poets are buried and honored by statuary.

While engineers scrape by in cheerless garrets.
Who needs a bridge or dam? Who needs a ditch?

5 Whereas the person who can write a sonnet
Has got it made. It's always been the way,
For everybody knows that we need poems
And everybody reads them every day.

Yes, life is hard if you choose engineering—
10 You're sure to need another job as well;
You'll have to plan your projects in the evenings
Instead of going out. It must be hell.

While well-heeled poets ride around in Daimlers,
You'll burn the midnight oil to earn a crust,
15 With no hope of a statue in the Abbey,
With no hope, even, of a modest bust.

No wonder small boys dream of writing couplets
And spurn the bike, the lorry and the train.
There's far too much encouragement for poets—
20 That's why this country's going down the drain.

1985

CULTURAL BELIEF AND TRADITION

The poems in this group draw on a tradition that is larger than just "literary." Mythologies involve whole systems of belief, usually cultural in scope, and the familiar literary formulations of these mythologies are just the surface articulations of a larger view of why the world works the way it does.

Every culture develops stories to explain itself. These stories, about who we are and why we are the way we are, constitute what are often called **myths.** Calling something a myth does not mean claiming that it is false. In fact, it means nearly the opposite, for cultures that subscribe or have ever subscribed to particular myths about culture or history become infused with, and even defined by, those views. Myth, in the sense in which it is used here, involves explanations of life that are more or less universally relied on within a particular culture; it is a frame of reference that people within the culture understand and share. This sharing of a frame of reference does not mean that all people within a culture are carbon copies of each other or that popular stereotypes represent reality accurately, nor does it mean that every individual in the culture *knows* the perceived history and can articulate its events, ideas, and values. But it does mean that a shared history and a shared set of symbols lie behind any particular culture and that the culture is to some extent aware of its distinctiveness from other cultures.

A **culture** may be of many sizes and shapes. Often we think of a nation as a culture (and so speak of American culture, American history, the myth of America, the American dream, the American frame of reference), and we may make smaller and larger divisions—as long as the group has some common history and a somewhat cohesive purpose. We speak of southern culture, for example, or of urban culture, or of the drug culture, or of the various popular-music cultures, or of a culture associated with a particular political belief, economic class, or social group. Most of us belong, willingly or not, to a number of such cultures at one time, and to some extent our identities and destinies are linked to the distinctive features of those cultures and the ways each culture perceives its identity, values, and history. Some of these cultures we choose to join; some are thrust upon us by birth and circumstances. It is these larger and more persistent forms of culture—not those chosen by an individual—that we illustrate in this section.

Poets aware of their heritage often like to probe its history and beliefs and plumb its depths, just as they like to articulate and play variations on the poetic tradition they feel a part of. For poetry written in the English language over the last four hundred years or so, both the Judeo-Christian frame of reference and the classical frame of reference (drawing on the civilizations of ancient Greece and Rome) have been important. Western culture, a broad culture that includes many nations and many religious and social groups, is largely defined within these two frames of reference—or it has been until quite recently. As religious belief in the West has changed over the past two or three centuries, and as classical civilization has been less emphasized and less studied, poets have felt less and less comfortable in assuming that their audiences share this cultural knowledge, but many have continued to use it in order to articulate human traits that have cultural continuity and importance. More recently, poets have drawn on other cultural myths—Native American, African, and Asian, for example—to expand our sense of common heritage and give new meaning to the "American" and "Western" experience. The poems that follow draw on different myths in a variety of ways and tones.

ANNE FINCH, COUNTESS OF WINCHILSEA

Adam Posed

Could our first father, at his toilsome plow,
Thorns in his path, and labor on his brow,
Clothed only in a rude, unpolished skin,
Could he a vain fantastic nymph have seen,
5 In all her airs, in all her antic graces,

Her various fashions, and more various faces;
How had it posed that skill, which late assigned
Just appellations to each several kind!
A right idea of the sight to frame;
10 T'have guessed from what new element she came;
T'have hit the wav'ring form, or giv'n this thing a name.

1713

MIRIAM WADDINGTON

Ulysses Embroidered

You've come
at last from
all your journeying
to the old blind woman
5   in the tower,
Ulysses.[1]

After all adventurings
through seas and
mountains through
10 giant battles,
storms and death,
from pinnacles
to valleys;

Past sirens
15 naked on rocks
between Charybdis
and Scylla, from
dragons' teeth,
from sleep in
20 stables choking
on red flowers
walking through weeds
and through shipwreck.

And now you are
25 climbing the stairs,
taking shape,
a figure in shining
thread rising from
a golden shield:
30 a medallion
emblazoned in
tapestry you grew
from the blind hands
of Penelope.

35 Her tapestry
saw everything,
her stitches

---

1. After the Trojan War, Ulysses (or Odysseus), king of Ithaca and one of the Greek heroes of the war, journeyed for ten years to return to his island home and to his wife, Penelope. To ward off suitors, Penelope had craftily been weaving and unraveling a tapestry that had to be finished before she would remarry. *See* Homer's *Odyssey* for accounts of these events and others mentioned in the poem.

embroidered the
painful colors
40 of her breath the
long sighing touch
of her hands.

She made many
journeys.

1992

ALFRED, LORD TENNYSON

The Kraken

Below the thunders of the upper deep,
Far, far beneath in the abysmal sea,
His ancient, dreamless, uninvaded sleep
The Kraken[2] sleepeth: faintest sunlights flee
5 About his shadowy sides; above him swell
Huge sponges of millennial growth and height;
And far away into the sickly light,
From many a wondrous grot and secret cell
Unnumbered and enormous polypi[3]
10 Winnow with giant arms the slumbering green.
There hath he lain for ages, and will lie
Battening upon huge sea worms in his sleep,
Until the latter fire[4] shall heat the deep;
Then once by man and angels to be seen,
15 In roaring he shall rise and on the surface die.

1830

EDNA ST. VINCENT MILLAY

An Ancient Gesture

I thought, as I wiped my eyes on the corner of my apron:
Penelope did this too.
And more than once: you can't keep weaving all day
And undoing it all through the night;
5 Your arms get tired, and the back of your neck gets tight
And along towards morning, when you think it will never be light,
And your husband has been gone, and you don't know where, for years,

2. A gigantic mythical sea beast.   3. Octopuses.
4. According to the biblical Book of Revelation, fire that will consume the world.

Suddenly you burst into tears;
There is simply nothing else to do.
10 And I thought, as I wiped my eyes on the corner of my apron:
This is an ancient gesture, authentic, antique,
In the very best tradition, classic, Greek;
Ulysses did this too.
But only as a gesture,—a gesture which implied
15 To the assembled throng that he was much too moved to speak.
He learned it from Penelope . . .
Penelope, who really cried.

1954

LOUISE BOGAN

Cassandra

To me, one silly task is like another.
I bare the shambling tricks of lust and pride,
This flesh will never give a child its mother,—
Song, like a wing, tears through my breast, my side,
5 And madness chooses out my voice again,
Again, I am the chosen no hand saves:
The shrieking heaven lifted over men,
Not the dumb earth, wherein they set their graves.

1929

LOUISE GLÜCK

Circe's Power[2]

I never turned anyone into a pig.
Some people are pigs; I make them
look like pigs.

I'm sick of your world
5 that lets the outside disguise the inside

Your men weren't bad men;
undisciplined life
did that to them. As pigs,

under the care of
10 me and my ladies, they
sweetened right up.

---

2. In Greek legend, Circe was a sorceress who turned Ulysses' companions into swine.

Then I reversed the spell,
showing you my goodness
as well as my power. I saw

15 we could be happy here,
as men and women are
when their needs are simple. In the same breath,

I foresaw your departure,
your men with my help braving
20 the crying and pounding sea. You think

a few tears upset me? My friend,
every sorceress is
a pragmatist at heart; nobody
sees essence who can't
25 face limitation. If I wanted only to hold you

I could hold you prisoner.

1996

GEORGE FAREWELL

Quaerè[3]

Whether at doomsday (tell, ye reverend wise)
My friend Priapus[4] with myself shall rise?

1733

PHILLIS WHEATLEY

 ## On Being Brought from Africa to America

'Twas mercy brought me from my Pagan land,
Taught my benighted soul to understand
That there's a God, that there's a Saviour too:
Once I redemption neither sought nor knew.
5 Some view our sable race with scornful eye,
"Their colour is a diabolic die."
Remember, Christians, Negroes, black as Cain,[5]
May be refin'd, and join th' angelic train.

1773

---

3. Query, i.e., question.
4. In Greek mythology, the god of fertility; he was later regarded as the chief deity of lasciviousness, and the phallus was his attribute.   5. One of Adam's sons, he killed his brother Abel. See Genesis 4.

JUNE JORDAN

Something Like a Sonnet for Phillis Miracle Wheatley

Girl from the realm of birds florid and fleet
flying full feather in far or near weather
Who fell to a dollar lust coffled like meat
Captured by avarice and hate spit together
5 Trembling asthmatic alone on the slave block
built by a savagery travelling by carriage
viewed like a species of flaw in the livestock
A child without safety of mother or marriage

Chosen by whimsy but born to surprise
10 They taught you to read but you learned how to write
Begging the universe into your eyes:
They dressed you in light but you dreamed with the night.
From Africa singing of justice and grace,
Your early verse sweetens the fame of our Race.

1989

MAYA ANGELOU

CD *Africa*

Thus she had lain
sugar cane sweet
deserts her hair
golden her feet
5 mountains her breasts
two Niles her tears
Thus she has lain
Black through the years.

Over the white seas
10 rime white and cold
brigands ungentled
icicle bold
took her young daughters
sold her strong sons
15 churched her with Jesus
bled her with guns.
Thus she has lain.

Now she is rising
remember her pain

20 remember the losses
    her screams loud and vain
    remember her riches
    her history slain
    now she is striding
25 although she had lain.

1975

DEREK WALCOTT

[CD] *A Far Cry from Africa*

A wind is ruffling the tawny pelt
Of Africa. Kikuyu,[6] quick as flies,
Batten upon the bloodstreams of the veldt.[7]
Corpses are scattered through a paradise.
5   Only the worm, colonel of carrion, cries:
"Waste no compassion on these separate dead!"
Statistics justify and scholars seize
The salients of colonial policy.
What is that to the white child hacked in bed?
10 To savages, expendable as Jews?

Threshed out by beaters,[8] the long rushes break
In a white dust of ibises whose cries
Have wheeled since civilization's dawn
From the parched river or beast-teeming plain.
15 The violence of beast on beast is read
As natural law, but upright man
Seeks his divinity by inflicting pain.
Delirious as these worried beasts, his wars
Dance to the tightened carcass of a drum,
20 While he calls courage still that native dread
Of the white peace contracted by the dead.

Again brutish necessity wipes its hands
Upon the napkin of a dirty cause, again
A waste of our compassion, as with Spain,[9]
25 The gorilla wrestles with the superman.
I who am poisoned with the blood of both,

6. An East African tribe whose members, as Mau Mau fighters, conducted an eight-year insurrection against British colonial settlers in Kenya.   7. Open plains, neither cultivated nor thickly forested (Afrikaans).
8. In big-game hunting, natives are hired to beat the brush, driving birds—such as ibises—and animals into the open.
9. The Spanish Civil War (1936-39), in which the Republican loyalists were supported politically by liberals in the West and militarily by Soviet Communists, and the Nationalist rebels by Nazi Germany and Fascist Italy.

Where shall I turn, divided to the vein?
I who have cursed
The drunken officer of British rule, how choose
30 Between this Africa and the English tongue I love?
Betray them both, or give back what they give?
How can I face such slaughter and be cool?
How can I turn from Africa and live?

1962

OLIVE SENIOR

Ancestral Poem

I

My ancestors are nearer
than albums of pictures
I tread on heels thrust
into broken-down slippers.

II

5 My mother's womb impulsed
harvests perpetually. She
deeply breathed country air
when she labored me.

III

The pattern woven by my
10 father's hands lulled me
to sleep. Certain actions
moved me so: my father
planting.

When my father planted
15 his thoughts took flight.
He did not need to think.
The ritual was ingrained
in the blood, embedded
in the centuries of dirt
20 beneath his fingernails
encased in the memories
of his race.

(Yet the whiplash of my
father's wrath rever-
25 berated days in my
mind with the inten-
sity of tuning forks.
He did not think.

My mother stunned wept
30 and prayed Father
Forgive Them knowing not
what she prayed for.)

One day I did not pray
A gloss of sunlight through
35 the leaves betrayed me so
abstracted me from rituals.
And discarded prayers and
disproven myths
confirmed me freedom.

        IV
40 Now against the rhythms
of subway trains my
heartbeats still drum
worksongs. Some wheels
sing freedom, the others:
45 home.

Still, if I could balance
water on my head I can
juggle worlds
on my shoulders

                    1985

ALBERTO ALVARO RÍOS

Advice to a First Cousin

The way the world works is like this:
for the bite of scorpions, she says,
my grandmother to my first cousin,
because I might die and someone must know,
5 go to the animal jar
the one with the soup of green herbs
mixed with the scorpions I have been putting in
still alive. Take one out
put it on the bite. It has had time to think
10 there with the others—put the lid back tight—
and knows that a biting is not the way to win
a finger or a young girl's foot.
It will take back into itself the hurting
the redness and the itching and its marks.

15 But the world works like this, too:
look out for the next scorpion you see,

she says, and makes a big face to scare me
thereby instructing my cousin, look out!
for one of the scorpion's many
20 illegitimate and unhappy sons.
It will be smarter, more of the devil.
It will have lived longer than these dead ones.
It will know from them something more
about the world, in the way mothers know
25 when something happens to a child, or how
I knew from your sadness you had been bitten.
It will learn something stronger than biting.
Look out most for that scorpion, she says,
making a big face to scare me again and it works
30 I go—crying—she lets me go—they laugh,
the way you must look out for men
who have not yet bruised you.

1985

LOUISE ERDRICH

Jacklight

> *The same Chippewa word is used both for flirting and hunting game,*
> *while another Chippewa word connotes both using force in intercourse*
> *and also killing a bear with one's bare hands.*
>
> —DUNNING 1959

We have come to the edge of the woods,
out of brown grass where we slept, unseen,
out of knotted twigs, out of leaves creaked shut,
out of hiding.

5   At first the light wavered, glancing over us.
Then it clenched to a fist of light that pointed,
searched out, divided us.
Each took the beams like direct blows the heart answers.
Each of us moved forward alone.

10 We have come to the edge of the woods,
drawn out of ourselves by this night sun,
this battery of polarized acids,
that outshines the moon.

We smell them behind it
15 but they are faceless, invisible,
We smell the raw steel of their gun barrels,
mink oil on leather, their tongues of sour barley.
We smell their mother buried chin-deep in wet dirt.

We smell their fathers with scoured knuckles,
20 teeth cracked from hot marrow.
We smell their sisters of crushed dogwood, bruised apples,
of fractured cups and concussions of burnt hooks.

We smell their breath steaming lightly behind the jacklight.
We smell the itch underneath the caked guts on their clothes.
25 We smell their minds like silver hammers
cocked back, held in readiness
for the first of us to step into the open.

We have come to the edge of the woods,
out of brown grass where we slept, unseen,
30 out of leaves creaked shut, out of our hiding.
We have come here too long.

It is their turn now,
their turn to follow us. Listen,
they put down their equipment.
35 It is useless in the tall brush.
And now they take the first steps, not knowing
how deep the woods are and lightless.
How deep the woods are.

1984

SUGGESTIONS FOR WRITING

1. Write an essay in which you examine the way William Blake's "The Lamb" draws its imagery from the Bible. Whom does the speaker refer to in saying "he calls himself a Lamb"? What, exactly, does "Lamb" imply in this context? Is "The Lamb" a Christian poem? Why or why not?

2. What does Howard Nemerov's "Boom!" allude to in its language and its form? What picture of American politics and culture does the poem paint? Write an essay in which you analyze the satire of "Boom!"

3. Consider Christopher Marlowe's "The Passionate Shepherd to His Love" and the "answers" that poem has inspired: Sir Walter Ralegh's "The Nymph's Reply to the Shepherd," William Carlos Williams's "Raleigh Was Right," and Allen Ginsberg's "A Further Proposal." What issues are illuminated by this poetic "debate"? What might account for the vigorous responses to a simple poem written in the well-established tradition of the pastoral? Write an essay examining the phenomenon of Marlowe's original poem and the poems it inspired.

4. What is gained, and what is lost, when an artistic tradition like Japanese haiku is imported, through translation, imitation, and inspiration, into another culture? Using the poems in this chapter and your own research, write an essay in which you analyze the way that haiku has established itself as a part of English-language literary culture.

5. How closely does E. E. Cummings's "(ponder,darling,these busted statues" echo Andrew Marvell's "To His Coy Mistress"? What images are derived from Marvell? In what specific ways does Cummings's poem undercut Marvell's argument, or its own? Write an essay in which you compare and contrast the two poems. What seem to be Marvell's real intentions, and what are Cummings's?

6. Write an essay in which you compare William Shakespeare's sonnet "Not marble, nor the gilded monuments" and Wendy Cope's "Not only marble, but the plastic toys," based on Shakespeare's original. Do the two poems share thematic concerns? Would Cope's poem be amusing to readers unfamiliar with Shakespeare's?

7. Write an essay in which you discuss the adaptation of Greek myth in Miriam Waddington's "Ulysses Embroidered" or in Louise Glück's "Circe's Power." What details of those poems seem consistent with Homer's account in the *Odyssey* or with the myth of Circe? What details seem to challenge the earlier accounts? What might be Waddington and Glück's purpose in adapting a myth in this way?

8. How do cultural beliefs and traditions define our perception of ourselves and the world around us? With reference to Olive Senior's "Ancestral Poem" and Alberto Alvaro Rìos's "Advice to a First Cousin," write an essay discussing the way writers call upon their cultural traditions in order to better see and understand their contemporary experiences.

9. Each of the "Africa" poems in this chapter displays a distinctive mix of anger and sorrow at the way Africa has been ravaged by history, and also pride in the way that Africans have adopted and mastered the Western culture that has been forced upon them. Write an essay in which you compare and contrast the attitudes that inform Phillis Wheatley's "On Being Brought from Africa to America," June Jordan's "Something Like a Sonnet for Phillis Miracle Wheatley," Maya Angelou's "Africa," and Derek Walcott's "A Far Cry from Africa."

10. Using research and your own analysis, write an essay in which you examine the cultural traditions and historical background behind any poem or group of poems in this book.

12 CULTURAL AND HISTORICAL CONTEXTS: THE HARLEM RENAISSANCE

Poetry may be read in private moments or experienced in a great variety of communal settings—in classrooms or theaters, for example, or at poetry slams or public readings. But it is almost always *written* in solitude by a single author. Collaboration is rare in poetry, even rarer than in other arts, though artistic creation in general (with a few exceptions like film) is usually a lonely process. Still, there is a sense in which many poems represent collaborative acts. We have seen, in chapter 11, how themes and poetic traditions and conventions are passed down over centuries so that they reappear in even the most original and experimental of poets and poems, and how the beliefs and ideologies of groups and cultures are identified, recorded, renewed, and reinterpreted by new poets in new poems. And we have seen, in chapter 9, how public events and shared cultural moments are transformed into poetic accounts and reflections. But sometimes traditions, group identities, shared experiences, desires, and communal needs come together in a particular moment and location to produce poetry (and other arts and artifacts) that has a distinctive stamp of time, place, and vision. One such phenomenon was the "Harlem Renaissance," a period of ten or fifteen years early in the twentieth century when an extraordinary (and extraordinarily talented) group of people came together in uptown Manhattan to celebrate (and embody) the awakening of a new American black consciousness. It was an unprecedented moment in American poetry and in American culture more generally, and it produced some of the twentieth century's most dramatic, compelling, and original poems, as well as significant works of art in a variety of other categories.

> *One ever feels his twoness— an American, a Negro; two souls, two thoughts, two unreconciled strivings; two warring ideals in one dark body, whose dogged strength alone keeps it from being torn asunder.*
> —W. E. B. DU BOIS

The Harlem Renaissance was not exactly a movement in the usual sense of structure and leadership; no one originated it or called it to order, and in fact it was not consciously planned or organized by any person or group. There was no founder, no architect, no leader, and it is hard to say why or how—or even exactly when—it began or ended. It happened, as needs and desires of African American intellectuals and artists became manifest and began to coalesce in a particular time and place, and it ended—or rather sputtered and scattered its energy—when conditions and circumstances in the world at large dictated that other priorities, especially economic ones, began to trump the forces that had brought it together. But it was not, of course, independent of history or without cause. It was a product of many circumstances, most of them involving the long-term aftereffects of slavery and the increasingly articulated desire of African Americans to produce a dis-

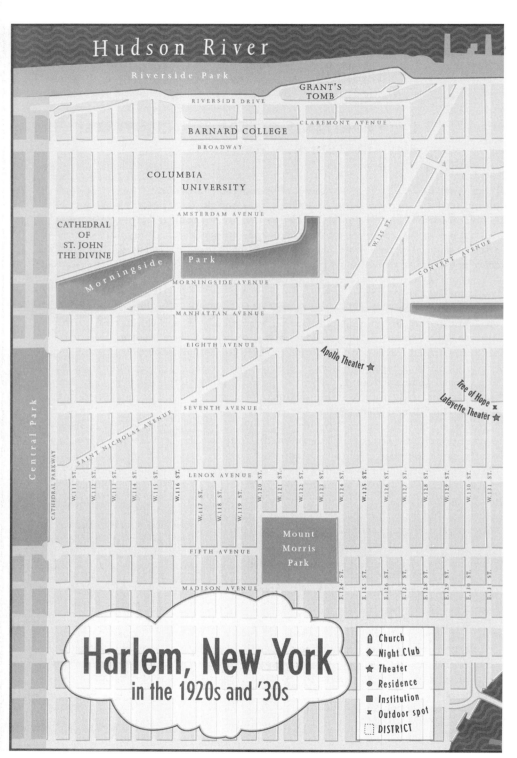

Hudson River

Riverside Park

GRANT'S
TOMB

RIVERSIDE DRIVE

CLAREMONT AVENUE

BARNARD COLLEGE

BROADWAY

COLUMBIA
UNIVERSITY

AMSTERDAM AVENUE

W. 125 ST.

CATHEDRAL
OF
ST. JOHN
THE DIVINE

Morningside   Park

CONVENT AVENUE

MORNINGSIDE AVENUE

MANHATTAN AVENUE

EIGHTH AVENUE

Apollo Theater ★

Tree of Hope ✕
Lafayette Theater ★

SEVENTH AVENUE

Central Park

CATHEDRAL PARKWAY

SAINT NICHOLAS AVENUE

W. 111 ST.
W. 112 ST.
W. 113 ST.
W. 114 ST.
W. 115 ST.
W. 116 ST.
W. 117 ST.
W. 118 ST.
W. 119 ST.

LENOX AVENUE

W. 120 ST.
W. 121 ST.
W. 122 ST.
W. 123 ST.
W. 124 ST.
W. 125 ST.
W. 126 ST.
W. 127 ST.
W. 128 ST.
W. 129 ST.
W. 130 ST.
W. 131 ST.

Mount
Morris
Park

FIFTH AVENUE

E. 124 ST.
E. 125 ST.
E. 126 ST.
E. 127 ST.
E. 128 ST.
E. 129 ST.
E. 130 ST.
E. 131 ST.

MADISON AVENUE

Harlem, New York
in the 1920s and '30s

🏛 Church
◆ Night Club
★ Theater
● Residence
■ Institution
✕ Outdoor spot
⬚ DISTRICT

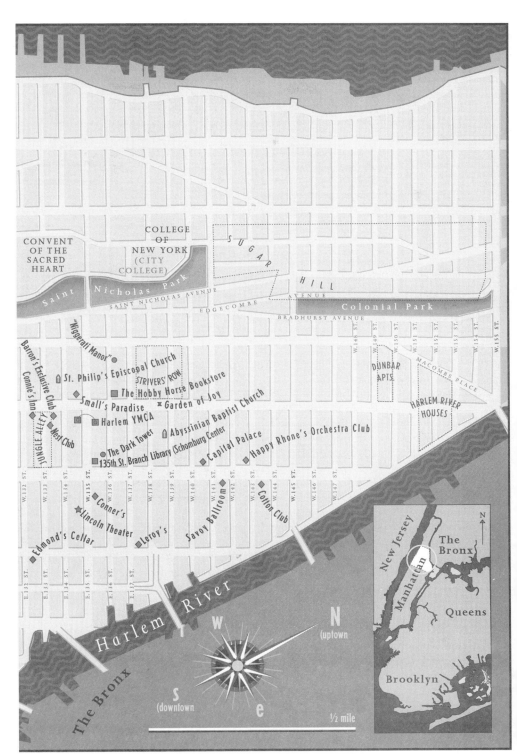

CONVENT OF THE SACRED HEART

COLLEGE OF NEW YORK (CITY COLLEGE)

SUGAR

HILL

Saint Nicholas Park

SAINT NICHOLAS AVENUE

EDGECOMBE

AVENUE

Colonial Park

BRADHURST AVENUE

W.148 ST.
W.149 ST.
W.150 ST.
W.151 ST.
W.152 ST.
W.153 ST.
W.154 ST.
W.155 ST.

MACOMBS PLACE

DUNBAR APTS.

HARLEM RIVER HOUSES

"Niggerati Manor"

Barron's Exclusive Club
Connie's Inn

St. Philip's Episcopal Church

STRIVERS' ROW

The Hobby Horse Bookstore

Small's Paradise
× Garden of Joy

JUNGLE ALLEY
West Club

Harlem YMCA

The Dark Tower

Abyssinian Baptist Church

Capital Palace

Happy Rhone's Orchestra Club

135th St. Branch Library (Schomburg Center)

W.132 ST.
W.133 ST.
W.134 ST.
W.135 ST.
W.136 ST.
W.137 ST.
W.138 ST.
W.139 ST.
W.140 ST.
W.141 ST.
W.142 ST.
W.143 ST.
W.144 ST.
W.145 ST.
W.146 ST.
W.147 ST.

Conner's

Lincoln Theater

Leroy's

Savoy Ballroom

Cotton Club

Edmond's Cellar

E.132 ST.
E.133 ST.
E.134 ST.
E.136 ST.
E.137 ST.

Harlem River

The Bronx

N
W
S (downtown
e
N (uptown)

½ mile

New Jersey

The Bronx

Manhattan

Queens

Brooklyn

N

The Cotton Club, circa 1930

tinctive black American culture within the larger national culture that they had been introduced into forcibly. They drew consciously on features and habits of African culture but imported and naturalized them into a distinctively American, decidedly urban setting. The art they produced—only two generations after slavery—recognized the complications, unhappiness, resistance, awkwardness, and coercive constraints of being black in America, where they were patronized, distrusted, feared, and alternately treated as alien or invisible. But the Harlem Renaissance taught black artists that they were also somehow—though it was not very clear how—central to a melting-pot America that repeatedly tried to define itself without them. The Harlem Renaissance represented powerful assertions: that America had to include the voices of black Americans in order to find its own full definition, and, equally, that artistic creativity—including literary creativity—had to be fully realized and recognized if black Americans were to find their full human identity in their American homeland. To live in Harlem and to be black and creative was not an altogether happy experience, and the poetry that exploded out of that time and place was a poetry of anger, resentment, conflict, and torn loyalties. But it was also a poetry of energy, sensitivity, humanity, and high ideals.

What was the Harlem Renaissance? To call it a movement is to make it seem more coherent, goal-centered, and idealistic than it appeared to be at the time, but out of leaderless and haphazard beginnings it focused needs and desires in a forceful and effective way. It was first of all a migration or, rather, part of a migration: around the end of World War I (the "War to End All Wars"), American blacks relocated in large numbers from the south to the north and from rural agricultural areas to cities. New York was only one of many destinations; Chicago, Philadelphia, Detroit, Washington, Cleveland, Buffalo, and other urban centers all received huge numbers of black migrants. But New York was the largest and most vibrant seat of culture in America, beginning to rival European capitals as a site where active artistic communities produced and consumed culture of all kinds—high, low, and in between. More than 100,000 blacks migrated to Harlem during the 1920s, taking over and transforming a Manhattan neighborhood north of Central Park and turning it into a distinctive, creative, independent, and infectious center of art and performance activities that drew the rest of New York City to it. For most of the 1920s —called "the Roaring 20s" throughout the Western world because of the era's daring, rebellious attitudes and booming economic growth—Harlem was a magnet for avant-garde whites in New York to take their pleasures. They flocked to speakeasies, nightclubs, and theaters (see

A dancer entertains a crowd at Small's Paradise Club, 1929. As at many of Harlem's best-known nightclubs, the entertainers and staff at Small's were primarily African American, and the clientele was mainly white.

Prominent African Americans (including W. E. B. Du Bois, third from the right in the second row) parade down New York's Fifth Avenue on July 28, 1917, to protest a race riot in East St. Louis, Illinois. Thirty-nine African Americans were killed and hundreds were seriously injured in the melee, one of the deadliest outbreaks of racial violence in America.

map, p. 424), and they were fascinated by the kinds of music, dance, and performance art they could find there—productions quite different from those on Broadway or in other parts of the city, though increasingly the white venues tried to capture, in their own productions, something of the life and energy that patrons sought in Harlem. White readers, and many white artists, showed enormous—sometimes mawkish or even ghoulish—curiosity about black life in America.

> I swear to the Lord
> I still can't see
> Why Democracy means
> Everybody but me.
> —LANGSTON HUGHES

Before the Harlem Renaissance had ended, a large number of Broadway productions—Marc Connelly's *Green Pastures*, Eugene O'Neill's *Emperor Jones* and *All God's Chillun Got Wings*, for example—and many novels tried to represent the black experience for white audiences. Black artists and writers (and their readers) were not always happy with the way white writers portrayed black experience and black concerns, but the widespread curiosity—some of it piqued by the flourishing of the Harlem group and some by "intruders" from the white establishment—provided a wider audience for black concerns than had existed in earlier generations.

The height of the Harlem Renaissance was the 1920s, though it is hard to pin down just when the period began and ended. Some historians, pointing to the political ferment caused by U.S. entry into the war in 1917, date the beginnings in the mid to late teens, and some regard it as lasting until the outbreak of World War II in the late 1930s. But the decade of the 1920s saw most of the productivity and creative energy that we associate with the flourishing of Harlem. And it was in the early '20s when most of the leading writers in the group actually moved to New York. Many historians regard the stock-market crash of 1929 and the depression that followed as signs of the end. Certainly the mood of the whole nation changed rapidly then, and by the early 1930s most of the leading figures had moved away from New York, forming smaller communities elsewhere or becoming individually isolated. The Harlem neighborhood itself began a slow economic decline.

Between the wars, though, Harlem's productivity and impact were dramatic. Before 1917, there had been few publishing outlets hospitable to young black writers; only Paul Lawrence Dunbar among African American poets was widely read or known, and he had died in 1906. But rising political and social concerns during and immediately after World War I produced several new periodicals: *The Messenger*, founded in 1917 by A. Philip Randolph and Chandler Owen, claimed to be "The only Radical Negro Magazine in America," and in 1923 the Urban League started its own magazine, *Opportunity*. Both of these new journals saw themselves as activist alternatives to the NAACP's

The cover of Volume I, Number 1 of *Fire!!*, a journal "Devoted to Younger Negro Artists," established by the self-designated "niggerati," the younger generation of African American intellectuals and writers—including Wallace Thurman, Langston Hughes, Zora Neale Hurston, and others—who wanted to (in Hughes's words) "burn up a lot of the old, dead, conventional Negro-white ideas of the past."

Claude McKay, photographed circa 1930 by Carl Van Vechten

Portrait of Alain Locke, by Betsy G. Reyneau

official journal, *Crisis*, edited by W. E. B. Du Bois. Other magazines came and went. *Fire!!* managed only a single issue, but brought verbal and visual art spectacularly together. Meanwhile—and perhaps just as important in a different way—mainstream magazines (*Vanity Fair*, for example) and publishers (Knopf, Macmillan, Harper, and Harcourt Brace) began to feature younger black writers who soon developed a growing readership.

Some historians date the Harlem Renaissance from the composition of Claude McKay's fiery sonnet "If We Must Die," written in the summer of 1919. McKay later denied that the poem referred specifically to blacks and whites, but the many antiblack riots that broke out in several American cities that summer—sometimes called "the Red Summer"—certainly inspired and contextualized the poem. Another milestone was the publication in 1922 of James Weldon Johnson's *Book of American Negro Poetry*, which, in the words of the editors of the *Norton Anthology of African American Literature*, "emphasized the youthful promise of the new writers and established some of the terms of the emerging movement." But it was Alain Locke's landmark anthology, *The New Negro*, that, in 1925, effectively announced the significance of the Harlem Renaissance. Locke, a sociology professor at Howard University and an Oxford graduate as the first African American Rhodes

Langston Hughes, circa 1925, in a pastel portrait by Winold Reiss. The original hangs in the National Portrait Gallery in Washington, D.C.

Countee Cullen, circa 1935

Scholar, gathered all kinds of material—poems, fiction, essays, visual art—by authors old and young, black and white—into a working definition of what the "new Negro" was all about.

The major figures of the Harlem Renaissance were, however, highly individual, and (although they shared many ideals and aspirations) never confined themselves to a creed or hardened into a "school." Langston Hughes, with a wonderful lyric voice and an eye for telling small details, pursued the relationship of poetry to black music and experimented with a variety of forms and rhythms; look, for example, at the award-winning "Weary Blues." Countee Cullen, on the other hand, was deeply committed to conventional poetic forms and felt most at home poetically when he was working in traditional fixed formal structures. Claude McKay, born in Jamaica, lived briefly in New York but mostly in Greenwich Village rather than Harlem, and spent much of his career abroad (Russia, France, North Africa). He always followed his own star in poetry too; his poetry was sometimes violent and incendiary, but equally strong was his sense of nostalgia and natural spiritualism. "The Tropics in New York" shows his sensuous and romantic side, and in spite of setting a militant tone in a founding poem of the Harlem Renaissance, "If We Must Die,"

What is Africa to me?
—COUNTEE CULLEN

he wrote only two poems that were directly about Harlem experiences and themes. Likewise, novelists like Zora Neale Hurston, Jean Toomer, Jesse Fauset, and Nella Larsen pursued individual styles and themes in their fiction. What held the group together conceptually was a dedication to producing first-rate writing, on the one hand and, on the other, a commitment to raising the aspirations of American blacks of all backgrounds and abilities.

The question of who was to benefit from the ambitious art of the Harlem Renaissance was hotly debated. Was it ordinary people, who could stretch the horizons of their reading and their own ambitions? African Americans generally? Or was it primarily intellectuals and artists who might raise expectations for black thought and art? W. E. B. Du Bois, who was a lightning rod for many members of the militant and radical new generation, had famously championed the "talented tenth," a select group whose natural gifts authoritatively raised them above others, and

Vendor selling books and pamphlets from a cart on 125th Street in Harlem, June 1943

The Dark Tower, a forum for African American intellectuals, met frequently in the home of A'Lelia Walker, a prominent Harlem heiress and socialite. Countee Cullen's poem "From the Dark Tower" is painted on the wall.

opinions split over whether the beneficiaries of the Harlem Renaissance were to be ordinary readers and viewers or the creative geniuses themselves, in the service of a higher aesthetic quite distinct from social progress. It's fair to say that the writers themselves remained divided, alternately championing the triumph of art and hoping for a larger cultural impact that would benefit readers (especially black readers) more generally.

The role of whites in the Harlem Renaissance is a matter of some dispute. The most controversial (though undeniably influential) figure was Carl Van Vechten, whose parties legendarily brought young black writers into the company of famous and powerful white celebrities, many of whom could be helpful to their careers. Van Vechten was a gifted photographer whose portraits of many rising figures chronicle the Harlem years brilliantly (see the photo of Arna Bontemps on p. 433), and he undeniably fostered many useful connections that resulted in publication and fame. But some felt his motives were self-serving and meretricious, and his well-meaning novel about everyday Harlem life, *Nigger Heaven,* was widely disparaged, though critics equally suspected "realistic" accounts of everyday life by black writers. (See, for example, the Du Bois review of a Claude McKay novel on p. 455). There is no doubt that figures like Van Vechten fostered considerable interaction between prominent whites and rising figures in the black artistic community, but not everyone regarded the results

Carl Van Vechten, 1926

Known as the "Empress of the Blues," Bessie Smith was one of the most popular entertainers in America during the 1920s. A protégé of the legendary Ma Rainey, Smith spent much of the mid-1920s touring the United States as the star attraction on the vaudeville circuit.

as helpful to the black cause overall. Some historians view white participation in the Harlem Renaissance more generally as exploitative, others as sincere but bumbling; and still others view black-white collaboration then as an early demonstration of racial unity in behalf of art and communal relations.

A second set of issues involves questions about elitism and whether the renaissance had truly salutary effects on the larger black community. Du Bois insisted on the obligation of "the talented tenth" to use their artistic and intellectual gifts to improve the lot of others. Critics of Du Bois find his position divisive and patronizing toward the majority of the black community; defenders see the idea as a strategy for community improvement by emphasizing the responsibility of potential leaders. At the heart of this controversy is disagreement about how leadership works to promote both improved social conditions and audience engagement. (Similar arguments rage today over the stardom of African American athletes and entertainers.) Was the Harlem Renaissance a phenomenon that benefited only a talented few, or did it enhance the lives of ordinary readers, residents of Harlem, and African Americans more generally?

Two related controversies concern the influence of the church on black culture and the relationship of the ambitious new "high art" of poetry, novels, and painting to popular-culture phenomena such as jazz, blues, and dance. Many of the younger writers resisted religion and resented its powerful influence on the black experience, even when they thought highly of the specifically black contributions to religious music. There is little doubt that religion was a powerful force in the black community, but observers continue to debate, as the artists themselves then did, whether it fostered and furthered artistic expression or served as a restraining and discouraging force. Often readers can see in poetry about even the most secular subjects traces of religious ideas and traditions; you will have to decide for yourself whether the effects are positive or not. The relationship of radical art to popular culture was even more vexed. Some central figures in the Harlem Renaissance regarded their own aims as "above" the "attractions" and "spectacles" that drew large numbers of whites to Harlem, and they regarded the performance arts as, at best, distractions from or dilutions of the main thrust of radical artistic expression. And while nearly everyone agrees that the quality of various theatrical arts in the many venues of Harlem was very high, the question of whether, beyond jazz and blues, the influence of popular arts on poetry was good or bad remains open.

. . .

No easy summary of the Harlem Renaissance will do. Its ambitions—often radical, sometimes revolutionary—made enormous waves in both the black urban community and the world of art. The poems of figures like McKay, Hughes, and Cullen, read in the context of their times, provide an invaluable gloss on particular events and issues; the history, in turn, adds resonance to the concerns expressed in the poems. However one measures the Harlem Renaissance in terms of its impact on later writers, black and white, the poems themselves continue to speak to readers across divides of time and culture. You will find that some of the poems can hardly be understood without knowledge of the specific circumstances and conditions that produced them; you will also find that many of the poems reach insistently for connections both to the past and to the enduring concerns of poets and readers in far-flung times and places.

Arna Bontemps, photographed by Carl Van Vechten, 1939

ARNA BONTEMPS

A Black Man Talks of Reaping

I have sown beside all waters in my day.
I planted deep, within my heart the fear
That wind or fowl would take the grain away.
I planted safe against this stark, lean year.

5 I scattered seed enough to plant the land
In rows from Canada to Mexico
But for my reaping only what the hand
Can hold at once is all that I can show.

Yet what I sowed and what the orchard yields
10 My brother's sons are gathering stalk and root,
Small wonder then my children glean in fields
They have not sown, and feed on bitter fruit.

1926

COUNTEE CULLEN

 Yet Do I Marvel

I doubt not God is good, well-meaning, kind,
And did He stoop to quibble could tell why
The little buried mole continues blind,
Why flesh that mirrors Him must some day die,
5 Make plain the reason tortured Tantalus[1]
Is baited by the fickle fruit, declare

---

1. In Greek myth he was condemned, for ambiguous reasons, to stand up to his neck in water he couldn't drink and to be within sight of fruit he couldn't reach to eat.

If merely brute caprice dooms Sisyphus[2]
To struggle up a never-ending stair.
Inscrutable His ways are, and immune
10 To catechism by a mind too strewn
With petty cares to slightly understand
What awful brain compels His awful hand.
Yet do I marvel at this curious thing:
To make a poet black, and bid him sing!

                                    1925

Saturday's Child[3]

Some are teethed on a silver spoon,
  With the stars strung for a rattle;
I cut my teeth as the black raccoon—
  For implements of battle.

5 Some are swaddled in silk and down,
   And heralded by a star;[4]
They swathed my limbs in a sackcloth gown
  On a night that was black as tar.

For some, godfather and goddame
10   The opulent fairies be;
Dame Poverty gave me my name,
  And Pain godfathered me.

For I was born on Saturday—
  "Bad time for planting a seed,"
15 Was all my father had to say,
   And, "One mouth more to feed."

Death cut the strings that gave me life,
  And handed me to Sorrow,
The only kind of middle wife
20   My folks could beg or borrow.

                                    1925

---

2. The king of Corinth who, in Greek myth, was condemned eternally to roll a huge stone uphill.
3. According to a popular nursery rhyme, "Saturday's child works hard for his living."
4. According to Matthew 2.7–10, Jesus' birth was accompanied by the appearance of a new star.

From the Dark Tower

(*To Charles S. Johnson*)[5]

We shall not always plant while others reap
The golden increment of bursting fruit,
Not always countenance, abject and mute,
That lesser men should hold their brothers cheap;
5 Not everlastingly while others sleep
Shall we beguile their limbs with mellow flute,
Not always bend to some more subtle brute;
We were not made eternally to weep.

The night whose sable breast relieves the stark,
10 White stars is no less lovely being dark,
And there are buds that cannot bloom at all
In light, but crumple, piteous, and fall;
So in the dark we hide the heart that bleeds,
And wait, and tend our agonizing seeds.

1927

Angelina Grimke, circa 1905

ANGELINA GRIMKE

The Black Finger

I have just seen a beautiful thing
  Slim and still,
Against a gold, gold sky,
  A straight cypress,
5 Sensitive
  Exquisite,
A black finger
Pointing upwards.
Why, beautiful, still finger are you black?
10 And why are you pointing upwards?

1925

Tenebris[6]

There is a tree, by day,
That, at night,
Has a shadow,
A hand huge and black,

5. Founder and editor of *Opportunity* magazine.   6. In darkness (Latin).

5 With fingers long and black.
   All through the dark,
Against the white man's house,
   In the little wind,
The black hand plucks and plucks
10   At the bricks.
The bricks are the color of blood and very small.
   Is it a black hand,
   Or is it a shadow?

                                        1927

LANGSTON HUGHES

WEB   *The Weary Blues*

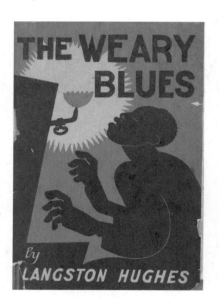

Droning a drowsy syncopated tune,
Rocking back and forth to a mellow croon,
   I heard a Negro play.
Down on Lenox Avenue[7] the other night
5 By the pale dull pallor of an old gas light
   He did a lazy sway. . . .
   He did a lazy sway. . . .
To the tune o' those Weary Blues.
With his ebony hands on each ivory key
10 He made that poor piano moan with melody.
   O Blues!
Swaying to and fro on his rickety stool
He played that sad raggy tune like a musical
      fool.
   Sweet Blues!
15 Coming from a black man's soul.
   O Blues!
In a deep song voice with a melancholy tone
I heard that Negro sing, that old piano moan—
   "Ain't got nobody in all this world,
20   Ain't got nobody but ma self.
   I's gwine to quit ma frownin'
   And put ma troubles on the shelf."
Thump, thump, thump, went his foot on the floor.
He played a few chords then he sang some more—
25   "I got the Weary Blues
   And I can't be satisfied.
   Got the Weary Blues
   And can't be satisfied—
   I ain't happy no mo'
30   And I wish that I had died."

---

7. Major Harlem thoroughfare, now Malcolm X Boulevard.

And far into the night he crooned that tune.
The stars went out and so did the moon.
The singer stopped playing and went to bed
While the Weary Blues echoed through his head.
35 He slept like a rock or a man that's dead.

1923   1925

The Negro Speaks of Rivers

I've known rivers:
I've known rivers ancient as the world and older than the flow of
    human blood in human veins.

My soul has grown deep like the rivers.

I bathed in the Euphrates when dawns were young.
5 I built my hut near the Congo and it lulled me to sleep.
I looked upon the Nile and raised the pyramids above it.
I heard the singing of the Mississippi when Abe Lincoln went down to
    New Orleans, and I've seen its muddy bosom turn all golden in
    the sunset.

I've known rivers:
Ancient, dusky rivers.

10 My soul has grown deep like the rivers.

1926

A pen-and-ink illustration by the artist Aaron Douglas made specifically to accompany
Hughes's "The Negro Speaks of Rivers"

I, Too

I, too, sing America.

I am the darker brother.
They send me to eat in the kitchen
When company comes,
5 But I laugh,
And eat well,
And grow strong.

Tomorrow,
I'll sit at the table.
10 When company comes
Nobody'll dare
Say to me,
"Eat in the kitchen,"
Then.

15 Besides,
They'll see how beautiful I am
And be ashamed—

I, too, am America.

1932

Cross

My old man's a white old man
And my old mother's black.
If ever I cursed my white old man
I take my curses back.

5 If ever I cursed my black old mother
And wished she were in hell,
I'm sorry for that evil wish
And now I wish her well.

My old man died in a fine big house.
10 My ma died in a shack.
I wonder where I'm gonna die,
Being neither white nor black?

1926

HELENE JOHNSON

Sonnet to a Negro in Harlem

You are disdainful and magnificent—
Your perfect body and your pompous gait,
Your dark eyes flashing solemnly with hate,
Small wonder that you are incompetent
5 To imitate those whom you so despise—
Your shoulders towering high above the throng,
Your head thrown back in rich, barbaric song,
Palm trees and mangoes stretched before your eyes.
Let others toil and sweat for labor's sake
10 And wring from grasping hands their meed[8] of gold.
Why urge ahead your supercilious feet?
Scorn will efface each footprint that you make.
I love your laughter arrogant and bold.
You are too splendid for this city street.

1927

CLAUDE McKAY

Harlem Shadows

I hear the halting footsteps of a lass
    In Negro Harlem when the night lets fall
Its veil. I see the shapes of girls who pass
    To bend and barter at desire's call.
5 Ah, little dark girls who in slippered feet
    Go prowling through the night from street to street!

Through the long night until the silver break
    Of day the little gray feet know no rest;
Through the lone night until the last snow-flake
10   Has dropped from heaven upon the earth's white breast,
The dusky, half-clad girls of tired feet
Are trudging, thinly shod, from street to street.

Ah, stern harsh world, that in the wretched way
    Of poverty, dishonor and disgrace,
15 Has pushed the timid little feet of clay,
    The sacred brown feet of my fallen race!
Ah, heart of me, the weary, weary feet
In Harlem wandering from street to street.

1918

8. Reward.

If We Must Die

If we must die, let it not be like hogs
Hunted and penned in an inglorious spot,
While round us bark the mad and hungry dogs,
Making their mock at our accursed lot.
5 If we must die, O let us nobly die,
So that our precious blood may not be shed
In vain; then even the monsters we defy
Shall be constrained to honor us though dead!
O kinsmen! we must meet the common foe!
10 Though far outnumbered let us show us brave,
And for their thousand blows deal one deathblow!
What though before us lies the open grave?
Like men we'll face the murderous, cowardly pack,
Pressed to the wall, dying, but fighting back!

1919

The Tropics in New York

Bananas ripe and green, and ginger-root,
  Cocoa in pods and alligator pears,
And tangerines and mangoes and grape fruit,
  Fit for the highest prize at parish fairs,

5 Set in the window, bringing memories
  Of fruit-trees laden by low-singing rills,
And dewy dawns, and mystical blue skies
  In benediction over nun-like hills.

My eyes grew dim, and I could no more gaze;
10 A wave of longing through my body swept,
And, hungry for the old, familiar ways,
  I turned aside and bowed my head and wept.

1920

The Harlem Dancer

Applauding youths laughed with young prostitutes
And watched her perfect, half-clothed body sway;
Her voice was like the sound of blended flutes
Blown by black players upon a picnic day.

5 She sang and danced on gracefully and calm,
   The light gauze hanging loose about her form;
   To me she seemed a proudly-swaying palm
   Grown lovelier for passing through a storm.
   Upon her swarthy neck black shiny curls
10 Luxuriant fell; and tossing coins in praise,
   The wine-flushed, bold-eyed boys, and even the girls,
   Devoured her shape with eager, passionate gaze;
   But looking at her falsely-smiling face,
   I knew her self was not in that strange place.

                                              1922

The White House

   Your door is shut against my tightened face,
   And I am sharp as steel with discontent;
   But I possess the courage and the grace
   To bear my anger proudly and unbent.
5 The pavement slabs burn loose beneath my feet,
   And passion rends my vitals as I pass,
   A chafing savage, down the decent street,
   Where boldly shines your shuttered door of glass.
   Oh, I must search for wisdom every hour,
10 Deep in my wrathful bosom sore and raw,
   And find in it the superhuman power
   To hold me to the letter of your law!
   Oh, I must keep my heart inviolate
   Against the poison of your deadly hate.

                                              1937

JEAN TOOMER

Song of the Son[9]

   Pour O pour that parting soul in song,
   O pour it in the sawdust glow of night,
   Into the velvet pine-smoke air tonight,
   And let the valley carry it along.
5 And let the valley carry it along.

   O land and soil, red soil and sweet-gum tree,
   So scant of grass, so profligate of pines,
   Now just before an epoch's sun declines

---

9. From the novel *Cane.*

Thy son, in time, I have returned to thee,
10 Thy son, I have in time returned to thee.

In time, for though the sun is setting on
A song-lit race of slaves, it has not set;
Though late, O soil, it is not too late yet
To catch thy plaintive soul, leaving, soon gone,
15 Leaving, to catch thy plaintive soul soon gone.

O Negro slaves, dark purple ripened plums,
Squeezed, and bursting in the pine-wood air,
Passing, before they strip the old tree bare
One plum was saved for me, one seed becomes

20 An everlasting song, a singing tree,
Caroling softly souls of slavery,
What they were, and what they are to me,
Caroling softly souls of slavery.

                                        1923

JAMES WELDON JOHNSON

From the Preface to *The Book of American Negro Poetry*

This power of the Negro to suck up the national spirit from the soil and create something artistic and original, which, at the same time, possesses the note of universal appeal, is due to a remarkable racial gift of adaptability; it is more than adaptability, it is a transfusive[1] quality. And the Negro has exercised this transfusive quality not only here in America, where the race lives in large numbers, but in European countries, where the number has been almost infinitesimal.

Is it not curious to know that the greatest poet of Russia is Alexander Pushkin, a man of African descent; that the greatest romancer of France is Alexandre Dumas,[2] a man of African descent; and that one of the greatest musicians of England is Coleridge-Taylor,[3] a man of African descent?

The fact is fairly well known that the father of Dumas was a Negro of the French West Indies, and that the father of Coleridge-Taylor was a native-born African; but the facts concerning Pushkin's African ancestry are not so familiar.

When Peter the Great[4] was Czar of Russia, some potentate presented him with a full-blooded Negro of gigantic size. Peter, the most eccentric ruler of modern times, dressed this Negro up in soldier clothes, christened him Hannibal,[5] and made him a special body-guard.

---

1. Having the ability to transfer.
2. French novelist and dramatist (1802–1870). Pushkin (1799–1837), Russian man of letters.
3. Samuel Coleridge-Taylor (1875–1912), English composer.
4. Peter I (1672–1725), ruled from 1682 to 1725.
5. After the North African general (247–c. 183 B.C.E.) who made war on Rome.

But Hannibal had more than size, he had brain and ability. He not only looked picturesque and imposing in soldier clothes, he showed that he had in him the making of a real soldier. Peter recognized this, and eventually made him a general. He afterwards ennobled him, and Hannibal, later, married one of the ladies of the Russian court. This same Hannibal was great-grandfather of Pushkin, the national poet of Russia, the man who bears the same relation to Russian literature that Shakespeare bears to English literature.

I know the question naturally arises: If out of the few Negroes who have lived in France there came a Dumas; and out of the few Negroes who have lived in England there came a Coleridge-Taylor; and if from

James Weldon Johnson, circa 1920

the man who was at the time, probably, the only Negro in Russia there sprang that country's national poet, why have not the millions of Negroes in the United States with all the emotional and artistic endowment claimed for them produced a Dumas, or a Coleridge-Taylor, or a Pushkin?

The question seems difficult, but there is an answer. The Negro in the United States is consuming all of his intellectual energy in this grueling race-struggle. And the same statement may be made in a general way about the white South. Why does not the white South produce literature and art? The white South, too, is consuming all of its intellectual energy in this lamentable conflict. Nearly all of the mental efforts of the white South run through one narrow channel. The life of every Southern white man and all of his activities are impassably limited by the ever present Negro problem. And that is why, as Mr. H. L. Mencken[6] puts it, in all that vast region, with its thirty or forty million people and its territory as large as a half dozen Frances or Germanys, there is not a single poet, not a serious historian, not a creditable composer, not a critic good or bad, not a dramatist dead or alive.[7]

*   *   *

This preface has gone far beyond what I had in mind when I started. It was my intention to gather together the best verses I could find by Negro poets and present them with a bare word of introduction. It was not my plan to make this collection inclusive nor to make the book in any sense a book of criticism. I planned to present only verses by contemporary writers; but, perhaps, because this is the first collection of its kind, I realized the absence of a starting-point and was led to provide one and to fill in with historical data what I felt to be a gap.

It may be surprising to many to see how little of the poetry being written by Negro poets today is being written in Negro dialect. The newer Negro poets

6. Henry Louis Mencken (1880–1956), American editor, critic, and essayist.
7. This statement was quoted in 1921. The reader may consider for himself the changes wrought in the decade [Johnson's note, 1931 edition].

show a tendency to discard dialect; much of the subject-matter which went into the making of traditional dialect poetry, 'possums, watermelons, etc., they have discarded altogether, at least, as poetic material. This tendency will, no doubt, be regretted by the majority of white readers; and, indeed, it would be a distinct loss if the American Negro poets threw away this quaint and musical folk speech as a medium of expression. And yet, after all, these poets are working through a problem not realized by the reader, and, perhaps, by many of these poets themselves not realized consciously. They are trying to break away from, not Negro dialect itself, but the limitations on Negro dialect imposed by the fixing effects of long convention.

The Negro in the United States has achieved or been placed in a certain artistic niche. When he is thought of artistically, it is as a happy-go-lucky, singing, shuffling, banjo-picking being or as a more or less pathetic figure. The picture of him is in a log cabin amid fields of cotton or along the levees. Negro dialect is naturally and by long association the exact instrument for voicing this phase of Negro life; and by that very exactness it is an instrument with but two full stops, humor and pathos. So even when he confines himself to purely racial themes, the Aframerican poet realizes that there are phases of Negro life in the United States which cannot be treated in the dialect either adequately or artistically. Take, for example, the phases rising out of life in Harlem, that most wonderful Negro city in the world. I do not deny that a Negro in a log cabin is more picturesque than a Negro in a Harlem flat, but the Negro in the Harlem flat is here, and he is but part of a group growing everywhere in the country, a group whose ideals are becoming increasingly more vital than those of the traditionally artistic group, even if its members are less picturesque.

What the colored poet in the United States needs to do is something like what Synge[8] did for the Irish; he needs to find a form that will express the racial spirit by symbols from within rather than by symbols from without, such as the mere mutilation of English spelling and pronunciation. He needs a form that is freer and larger than dialect, but which will still hold the racial flavor; a form expressing the imagery, the idioms, the peculiar turns of thought, and the distinctive humor and pathos, too, of the Negro, but which will also be capable of voicing the deepest and highest emotions and aspirations, and allow of the widest range of subjects and the widest scope of treatment.

Negro dialect is at present a medium that is not capable of giving expression to the varied conditions of Negro life in America, and much less is it capable of giving the fullest interpretation of Negro character and psychology. This is no indictment against the dialect as dialect, but against the mold of convention in which Negro dialect in the United States has been set. In time these conventions may become lost, and the colored poet in the United States may sit down to write in dialect without feeling that his first line will put the general reader in a frame of mind which demands that the poem be humorous or pathetic. In the meantime, there is no reason why these poets should not continue to do the beautiful things that can be done, and done best, in the dialect.

In stating the need for Aframerican poets in the United States to work out a new and distinctive form of expression I do not wish to be understood to hold any theory that they should limit themselves to Negro poetry, to racial themes;

8. John Middleton Synge (1871–1909), Irish dramatist whose works celebrate Irish traditions.

the sooner they are able to write *American* poetry spontaneously, the better. Nevertheless, I believe that the richest contribution the Negro poet can make to the American literature of the future will be the fusion into it of his own individual artistic gifts.

1921

ALAIN LOCKE

From *The New Negro*

The tide of Negro migration, northward and city-ward, is not to be fully explained as a blind flood started by the demands of war industry coupled with the shutting off of foreign migration, or by the pressure of poor crops coupled with increased social terrorism in certain sections of the South and Southwest. Neither labor demand, the bollweevil[9] nor the Ku Klux Klan is a basic factor, however contributory any or all of them may have been. The wash and rush of this human tide on the beach line of the northern city centers is to be explained primarily in terms of a new vision of opportunity, of social and economic freedom, of a spirit to seize, even in the face of an extortionate and heavy toll, a chance for the improvement of conditions. With each successive wave of it, the movement of the Negro becomes more and more a mass movement toward the larger and the more democratic chance—in the Negro's case a deliberate flight not only from countryside to city, but from medieval America to modern.

Take Harlem as an instance of this. Here in Manhattan is not merely the largest Negro community in the world, but the first concentration in history of so many diverse elements of Negro life. It has attracted the African, the West Indian, the Negro American; has brought together the Negro of the North and the Negro of the South; the man from the city and the man from the town and village; the peasant, the student, the business man, the professional man, artist, poet, musician, adventurer and worker, preacher and criminal, exploiter and social outcast. Each group has come with its own separate motives and for its own special ends, but their greatest experience has been the finding of one another. Proscription and prejudice have thrown these dissimilar elements into a common area of contact and interaction. Within this area, race sympathy and unity have determined a further fusing of sentiment and experience. So what began in terms of segregation becomes more and more, as its elements mix and react, the laboratory of a great race-welding. Hitherto, it must be admitted that American Negroes have been a race more in name than in fact, or to be exact, more in sentiment than in experience. The chief bond between them has been that of a common condition rather than a common consciousness; a problem in common rather than a life in common. In Harlem, Negro life is seizing upon its first chances for group expression and self-determination. It is—or promises at least to be—a race capital. That is why our comparison is taken with those nascent centers of folk-expression and self-determination which are playing a creative part in the world today. Without pretense to their political significance,

---

9. A snout beetle notorious for destroying cotton crops.

Harlem has the same role to play for the New Negro as Dublin has had for the New Ireland or Prague for the New Czechoslovakia.

Harlem, I grant you, isn't typical—but it is significant, it is prophetic. No sane observer, however sympathetic to the new trend, would contend that the great masses are articulate as yet, but they stir, they move, they are more than physically restless. The challenge of the new intellectuals among them is clear enough—the "race radicals" and realists who have broken with the old epoch of philanthropic guidance, sentimental appeal and protest. But are we after all only reading into the stirrings of a sleeping giant the dreams of an agitator? The answer is in the migrating peasant. It is the "man farthest down" who is most active in getting up. One of the most characteristic symptoms of this is the professional man, himself migrating to recapture his constituency after a vain effort to maintain in some Southern corner what for years back seemed an established living and clientele. The clergyman following his errant flock, the physician or lawyer trailing his clients, supply the true clues. In a real sense it is the rank and file who are leading, and the leaders who are following. A transformed and transforming psychology permeates the masses.

When the racial leaders of twenty years ago spoke of developing race-pride and stimulating race-consciousness, and of the desirability of race solidarity, they could not in any accurate degree have anticipated the abrupt feeling that has surged up and now pervades the awakened centers. Some of the recognized Negro leaders and a powerful section of white opinion identified with "race work" of the older order have indeed attempted to discount this feeling as a "passing phase," an attack of "race nerves" so to speak, an "aftermath of the war," and the like. It has not abated, however, if we are to gauge by the present tone and temper of the Negro press, or by the shift in popular support from the officially recognized and orthodox spokesmen to those of the independent, popular, and often radical type who are unmistakable symptoms of a new order. It is a social disservice to blunt the fact that the Negro of the Northern centers has reached a stage where tutelage, even of the most interested and well-intentioned sort, must give place to new relationships, where positive self-direction must be reckoned with in ever increasing measure. The American mind must reckon with a fundamentally changed Negro.

The Negro too, for his part, has idols of the tribe to smash. If on the one hand the white man has erred in making the Negro appear to be that which would excuse or extenuate his treatment of him, the Negro, in turn, has too often unnecessarily excused himself because of the way he has been treated. The intelligent Negro of today is resolved not to make discrimination an extenuation for his shortcomings in performance, individual or collective; he is trying to hold himself at par, neither inflated by sentimental allowances nor depreciated by current social discounts. For this he must know himself and be known for precisely what he is, and for that reason he welcomes the new scientific rather than the old sentimental interest. Sentimental interest in the Negro has ebbed. We used to lament this as the falling off of our friends; now we rejoice and pray to be delivered both from self-pity and condescension. The mind of each racial group has had a bitter weaning, apathy or hatred on one side matching disillusionment or resentment on the other; but they face each other today with the possibility at least of entirely new mutual attitudes.

It does not follow that if the Negro were better known, he would be better liked or better treated. But mutual understanding is basic for any subsequent cooperation and adjustment. The effort toward this will at least have the effect of remedying in large part what has been the most unsatisfactory feature of our present stage of race relationships in America, namely the fact that the more intelligent and representative elements of the two race groups have at so many points got quite out of vital touch with one another.

The fiction is that the life of the races is separate, and increasingly so. The fact is that they have touched too closely at the unfavorable and too lightly at the favorable levels.

While inter-racial councils have sprung up in the South, drawing on forward elements of both races, in the Northern cities manual laborers may brush elbows in their everyday work, but the community and business leaders have experienced no such interplay or far too little of it. These segments must achieve contact or the race situation in America becomes desperate. Fortunately this is happening. There is a growing realization that in social effort the cooperative basis must supplant long-distance philanthropy, and that the only safeguard for mass relations in the future must be provided in the carefully maintained contacts of the enlightened minorities of both race groups. In the intellectual realm a renewed and keen curiosity is replacing the recent apathy; the Negro is being carefully studied, not just talked about and discussed. In art and letters, instead of being wholly caricatured, he is being seriously portrayed and painted.

To all of this the New Negro is keenly responsive as an augury of a new democracy in American culture. He is contributing his share to the new social understanding. But the desire to be understood would never in itself have been sufficient to have opened so completely the protectively closed portals of the thinking Negro's mind. There is still too much possibility of being snubbed or patronized for that. It was rather the necessity for fuller, truer self-expression, the realization of the unwisdom of allowing social discrimination to segregate him mentally, and a counter-attitude to cramp and fetter his own living—and so the "spite-wall" that the intellectuals built over the "color-line" has happily been taken down. Much of this reopening of intellectual contacts has centered in New York and has been richly fruitful not merely in the enlarging of personal experience, but in the definite enrichment of American art and letters and in the clarifying of our common vision of the social tasks ahead.

The particular significance in the re-establishment of contact between the more advanced and representative classes is that it promises to offset some of the unfavorable reactions of the past, or at least to re-surface race contacts somewhat for the future. Subtly the conditions that are molding a New Negro are molding a new American attitude.

However, this new phase of things is delicate; it will call for less charity but more justice; less help, but infinitely closer understanding. This is indeed a critical stage of race relationships because of the likelihood, if the new temper is not understood, of engendering sharp group antagonism and a second crop of more calculated prejudice. In some quarters, it has already done so. Having weaned the Negro, public opinion cannot continue to paternalize. The Negro today is inevitably moving forward under the control largely of his own objectives. What are these objectives? Those of his outer life are happily already well and finally formulated, for they are none other than the ideals of American institutions and democracy. Those of his inner life are yet in process of formation, for the new psychology at present is more of a consensus of feeling than of opinion, of attitude rather than of program. Still some points seem to have crystallized.

Up to the present one may adequately describe the Negro's "inner objectives" as an attempt to repair a damaged group psychology and reshape a warped social perspective. Their realization has required a new mentality for the American Negro. And as it matures we begin to see its effects; at first, negative, iconoclastic, and then positive and constructive. In this new group psychology we note the lapse of sentimental appeal, then the development of a more positive self-respect and self-reliance; the repudiation of social dependence, and then the gradual recovery from hyper-sensitiveness and "touchy" nerves, the repudiation of the double standard of judgment with its special philanthropic allowances and then the sturdier desire for objective and scientific appraisal; and finally the rise from social disillusionment to race pride, from the sense of social debt to the responsibilities of social contribution, and offsetting the necessary working and commonsense acceptance of restricted conditions, the belief in ultimate esteem and recognition. Therefore the Negro today wishes to be known for what he is, even in his faults and shortcomings, and scorns a craven and precarious survival at the price of seeming to be what he is not. He resents being spoken of as a social ward or minor, even by his own, and to being regarded a chronic patient for the sociological clinic, the sick man of American Democracy. For the same reasons, he himself is through with those social nostrums and panaceas, the so-called "solutions" of his "problem," with which he and the country have been so liberally dosed in the past. Religion, freedom, education, money—in turn, he has ardently hoped for and peculiarly trusted these things; he still believes in them, but not in blind trust that they alone will solve his life-problem.

Each generation, however, will have its creed, and that of the present is the belief in the efficacy of collective effort, in race cooperation. This deep feeling of race is at present the mainspring of Negro life. It seems to be the outcome of the reaction to proscription and prejudice; an attempt, fairly successful on the whole, to convert a defensive into an offensive position, a handicap into an incentive. It is radical in tone, but not in purpose and only the most stupid forms of opposition, misunderstanding or persecution could make it otherwise. Of course, the thinking Negro has shifted a little toward the left with the world-trend, and there is an increasing group who affiliate with radical and liberal movements. But fundamentally for the present the Negro is radical on race matters, conservative on others, in other words, a "forced radical," a social protestant rather than a genuine radical. Yet under further pressure and injustice iconoclastic thought and motives will inevitably increase. Harlem's quixotic radicalisms call for their ounce of democracy today lest tomorrow they be beyond cure.

The Negro mind reaches out as yet to nothing but American wants, American ideas. But this forced attempt to build his Americanism on race values is a unique social experiment, and its ultimate success is impossible except through the fullest sharing of American culture and institutions. There should be no delusion about this. American nerves in sections unstrung with race hysteria are often fed the opiate that the trend of Negro advance is wholly separatist, and that the effect of its operation will be to encyst the Negro as a benign foreign body in the body politic. This cannot be—even if it were desirable. The racialism of the Negro is no limitation or reservation with respect to American life; it is only a constructive effort to build the obstructions in the stream of his progress into an efficient dam of social energy and power. Democracy itself is obstructed and stagnated to the extent that any of its channels are closed. Indeed they cannot be selectively closed. So the choice is not between one way for the Negro and another way for the rest, but between American institutions frustrated on the one hand and American ideals progressively fulfilled and realized on the other.

There is, of course, a warrantably comfortable feeling in being on the right side of the country's professed ideals. We realize that we cannot be undone without America's undoing. It is within the gamut of this attitude that the thinking Negro faces America, but with variations of mood that are if anything more significant than the attitude itself. Sometimes we have it taken with the defiant ironic challenge of McKay:[1]

> Mine is the future grinding down to-day
> Like a great landslip moving to the sea,
> Bearing its freight of débris far away
> Where the green hungry waters restlessly
> Heave mammoth pyramids, and break and roar
> Their eerie challenge to the crumbling shore.

Sometimes, perhaps more frequently as yet, it is taken in the fervent and almost filial appeal and counsel of Weldon Johnson's:

> O Southland, dear Southland!
> Then why do you still cling
> To an idle age and a musty page,
> To a dead and useless thing?[2]

But between defiance and appeal, midway almost between cynicism and hope, the prevailing mind stands in the mood of the same author's *To America*,[3] an attitude of sober query and stoical challenge:

> How would you have us, as we are?
>   Or sinking 'neath the load we bear,
> Our eyes fixed forward on a star,
>   Or gazing empty at despair?
>
> Rising or falling? Men or things?
>   With dragging pace or footsteps fleet?
> Strong, willing sinews in your wings,
>   Or tightening chains about your feet?

More and more, however, an intelligent realization of the great discrepancy between the American social creed and the American social practice forces upon the Negro the taking of the moral advantage that is his. Only the steadying and sobering effect of a truly characteristic gentleness of spirit prevents the rapid rise of a definite cynicism and counter-hate and a defiant superiority feeling. Human as this reaction would be, the majority still deprecate its advent, and would gladly see it forestalled by the speedy amelioration of its causes. We wish our race pride to be a healthier, more positive achievement than a feeling based upon a realization of the shortcomings of others. But all paths toward the attainment of a sound social attitude have been difficult; only a relatively few enlightened minds

---

1. Claude McKay.   2. From "O Southland!" (1907).   3. Published in 1917.

have been able as the phrase puts it "to rise above" prejudice. The ordinary man has had until recently only a hard choice between the alternatives of supine and humiliating submission and stimulating but hurtful counter-prejudice. Fortunately from some inner, desperate resourcefulness has recently sprung up the simple expedient of fighting prejudice by mental passive resistance, in other words by trying to ignore it. For the few, this manna may perhaps be effective, but the masses cannot thrive upon it.

Fortunately there are constructive channels opening out into which the balked social feelings of the American Negro can flow freely.

Without them there would be much more pressure and danger than there is. These compensating interests are racial but in a new and enlarged way. One is the consciousness of acting as the advance-guard of the African peoples in their contact with Twentieth Century civilization; the other, the sense of a mission of rehabilitating the race in world esteem from that loss of prestige for which the fate and conditions of slavery have so largely been responsible. Harlem, as we shall see, is the center of both these movements; she is the home of the Negro's "Zionism."[4] The pulse of the Negro world has begun to beat in Harlem. A Negro newspaper carrying news material in English, French and Spanish, gathered from all quarters of America, the West Indies and Africa has maintained itself in Harlem for over five years. Two important magazines,[5] both edited from New York, maintain their news and circulation consistently on a cosmopolitan scale. Under American auspices and backing, three pan-African congresses have been held abroad for the discussion of common interests, colonial questions and the future cooperative development of Africa. In terms of the race question as a world problem, the Negro mind has leapt, so to speak, upon the parapets of prejudice and extended its cramped horizons. In so doing it has linked up with the growing group consciousness of the dark-peoples and is gradually learning their common interests. As one of our writers has recently put it: "It is imperative that we understand the white world in its relations to the non-white world." As with the Jew, persecution is making the Negro international.

As a world phenomenon this wider race consciousness is a different thing from the much asserted rising tide of color. Its inevitable causes are not of our making. The consequences are not necessarily damaging to the best interests of civilization. Whether it actually brings into being new Armadas of conflict or argosies[6] of cultural exchange and enlightenment can only be decided by the attitude of the dominant races in an era of critical change. With the American Negro, his new internationalism is primarily an effort to recapture contact with the scattered peoples of African derivation. Garveyism[7] may be a transient, if spectacular, phenomenon, but the possible role of the American Negro in the future development of Africa is one of the most constructive and universally helpful missions that any modern people can lay claim to.

1925

---

4. An international movement aimed at securing a homeland for the Jewish people.
5. Probably *Opportunity* and the *Crisis*.   6. Merchant ships. *Armadas*: fleets of warships.
7. The Back to Africa movement of Marcus Garvey (1887–1940).

RUDOLPH FISHER

The Caucasian Storms Harlem

I

It might not have been such a jolt had my five years' absence from Harlem been spent otherwise. But the study of medicine includes no courses in cabareting; and, anyway, the Negro cabarets in Washington, where I studied, are all uncompromisingly black. Accordingly I was entirely unprepared for what I found when I returned to Harlem recently.

I remembered one place especially where my own crowd used to hold forth; and, hoping to find some old-timers there still, I sought it out one midnight. The old, familiar plunkety-plunk welcomed me from below as I entered. I descended the same old narrow stairs, came into the same smoke-misty basement, and found myself a chair at one of the ancient white-porcelain, mirror-smooth tables. I drew a deep breath and looked about, seeking familiar faces. "What a lot of 'fays!"[8] I thought, as I noticed the number of white guests. Presently I grew puzzled and began to stare, then I gaped—and gasped. I found myself wondering if this was the right place—if, indeed, this was Harlem at all. I suddenly became aware that, except for the waiters and members of the orchestra, I was the only Negro in the place.

After a while I left it and wandered about in a daze from night-club to night-club. I tried the Nest, Small's, Connie's Inn, the Capitol, Happy's, the Cotton Club. There was no mistake; my discovery was real and was repeatedly confirmed. No wonder my old crowd was not to be found in any of them. The best of Harlem's black cabarets have changed their names and turned white.

Such a discovery renders a moment's recollection irresistible. As irresistible as were the cabarets themselves to me seven or eight years ago. Just out of college in a town where cabarets were something only read about. A year of graduate work ahead. A Summer of rest at hand. Cabarets. Cabarets night after night, and one after another. There was no cover-charge then, and a fifteen-cent bottle of Whistle lasted an hour. It was just after the war[9]—the heroes were home—cabarets were the thing.

How the Lybia prospered in those happy days! It was the gathering place of the swellest Harlem set: if you didn't go to the Lybia, why, my dear, you just didn't belong. The people you saw at church in the morning you met at the Lybia at night. What romance in those war-tinged days and nights! Officers from Camp Upton,[1] with pretty maids from Brooklyn! Gay lieutenants, handsome captains— all whirling the lively onestep. Poor non-coms[2] completely ignored; what sensible girl wanted a corporal or even a sergeant? That white, old-fashioned house, standing alone in 138th street, near the corner of Seventh avenue—doomed to be torn down a few months thence—how it shook with the dancing and laughter of the dark merry crowds!

But the first place really popular with my friends was a Chinese restaurant in 136th street, which had been known as Hayne's Café and then became the Orien-

---

8. Short for "ofays," a derogatory term for whites.   9. I.e., World War I. *Whistle:* a beverage.
1. A military facility near Manhattan.   2. Noncommissioned officers.

tal. It occupied an entire house of three stories, and had carpeted floors and a quiet, superior air. There was excellent food and incredibly good tea and two unusual entertainers: a Cuban girl, who could so vary popular airs that they sounded like real music, and a slender little "brown" with a voice of silver and a way of singing a song that made you forget your food. One could dance in the Oriental if one liked, but one danced to a piano only, and wound one's way between linen-clad tables over velvety, noiseless floors.

Here we gathered: Fritz Pollard, All-American halfback,[3] selling Negro stock to prosperous Negro physicians; Henry Creamer and Turner Layton, who had written "After You've Gone" and a dozen more songs, and were going to write "Strut, Miss Lizzie;" Paul Robeson,[4] All-American end, on the point of tackling law, quite unaware that the stage would intervene; Preacher Harry Bragg, Harvard Jimmie MacLendon and a half a dozen others. Here at a little table, just inside the door, Bert Williams[5] had supper every night, and afterward sometimes joined us upstairs and sang songs with us and lampooned the Actors' Equity Association, which had barred him because of his color. Never did white guests come to the Oriental except as guests of Negroes. But the manager soon was stricken with a psychosis of some sort, became a black Jew, grew himself a bushy, square-cut beard, donned a skull-cap and abandoned the Oriental. And so we were robbed of our favorite resort, and thereafter became mere rounders.

II

Such places, those real Negro cabarets that we met in the course of our rounds! There was Edmonds' in Fifth avenue at 130th street. It was a sure-enough honky-tonk, occupying the cellar of a saloon. It was the social center of what was then, and still is, Negro Harlem's kitchen. Here a tall brown-skin girl, unmistakably the one guaranteed in the song to make a preacher lay his Bible down, used to sing and dance her own peculiar numbers, vesting them with her own originality. She was known simply as Ethel,[6] and was a genuine drawing-card. She knew her importance, too. Other girls wore themselves ragged trying to rise above the inattentive din of conversation, and soon, literally, yelled themselves hoarse; eventually they lost whatever music there was in their voices and acquired that familiar throaty roughness which is so frequent among blues singers, and which, though admired as characteristically African, is as a matter of fact nothing but a form of chronic laryngitis. Other girls did these things, but not Ethel. She took it easy. She would stride with great leisure and self-assurance to the center of the floor, stand there with a half-contemptuous nonchalance, and wait. All would become silent at once. Then she'd begin her song, genuine blues, which, for all their humorous lines, emanated tragedy and heartbreak:

> Woke up this mawnin'
> The day was dawnin'
> And I was sad and blue, so blue, Lord—
> Didn' have nobody
> To tell my troubles to—

---

3. In 1916 at Brown University. He was the first black professional football player (Akron Indians, 1919).
4. A star football player at Rutgers before entering the Columbia University Law School in 1919 (1898–1976).   5. Popular black comedian and actor (c. 1874–1922).   6. Ethel Waters (1896–1977).

It was Ethel who first made popular the song, "Tryin' to Teach My Good Man Right from Wrong," in the slow, meditative measures in which she complained:

> I'm gettin' sick and tired of my railroad man
> I'm gettin' sick and tired of my railroad man—
> Can't get him when I want him—
> I get him when I can.

It wasn't long before this song-bird escaped her dingy cage. Her name is a vaudeville attraction now, and she uses it all—Ethel Waters. Is there anyone who hasn't heard her sing "Shake That Thing!"?

A second place was Connor's in 135th street near Lenox avenue. It was livelier, less languidly sensuous, and easier to breathe in than Edmonds'. Like the latter, it was in a basement, reached by the typical narrow, headlong stairway. One of the girls there specialized in the Jelly-Roll song, and mad habitués[7] used to fling petitions of greenbacks at her feet—pretty nimble feet they were, too—when she sang that she loved 'em but she had to turn 'em down. Over in a corner a group of 'fays would huddle and grin and think they were having a wild time. Slumming. But they were still very few in those days.

And there was the Oriental, which borrowed the name that the former Hayne's Café had abandoned. This was beyond Lenox avenue on the south side of 135th street. An upstairs place, it was nevertheless as dingy as any of the cellars, and the music fairly fought its way through the babble and smoke to one's ears, suffering in transit weird and incredible distortion. The prize pet here was a slim, little lad, unbelievably black beneath his high-brown powder, wearing a Mexican bandit costume with a bright-colored head-dress and sash. I see him now, poor kid, in all his glory, shimmying for enraptured women, who marveled at the perfect control of his voluntary abdominal tremors. He used to let the women reach out and put their hands on his sash to palpate[8] those tremors—for a quarter.

Finally, there was the Garden of Joy, an open-air cabaret between 138th and 139th streets in Seventh avenue, occupying a plateau high above the sidewalk— a large, well-laid, smooth wooden floor with tables and chairs and a tinny orchestra, all covered by a propped-up roof, that resembled an enormous lampshade, directing bright light downward and outward. Not far away the Abysinnian Church used to hold its Summer camp-meetings in a great round circus-tent. Night after night there would arise the mingled strains of blues and spirituals, those peculiarly Negro forms of song, the one secular and the other religious, but both born of wretchedness in travail, both with their soarings of exultation and sinkings of despair. I used to wonder if God, hearing them both, found any real distinction.

There were the Lybia, then, and Hayne's, Connor's, the Oriental, Edmonds' and the Garden of Joy, each distinctive, standing for a type, some living up to their names, others living down to them, but all predominantly black. Regularly I made the rounds among these places and saw only incidental white people. I have seen them occasionally in numbers, but such parties were out on a lark. They weren't in their natural habitat and they often weren't any too comfortable.

But what of Barron's, you say? Certainly they were at home there. Yes, I know

---

7. Regular patrons.   8. Examine by touch.

about Barron's. I have been turned away from Barron's because I was too dark to be welcome. I have been a member of a group that was told, "No more room," when we could see plenty of room. Negroes were never actually wanted in Barron's save to work. Dark skins were always discouraged or barred. In short, the fact about Barron's was this: it simply wasn't a Negro cabaret; it was a cabaret run by Negroes for whites. It wasn't even on the lists of those who lived in Harlem—they'd no more think of going there than of going to the Winter Garden Roof.[9] But these other places were Negro through and through. Negroes supported them, not merely in now-and-then parties, but steadily, night after night.

IV

Some think it's just a fad. White people have always more or less sought Negro entertainment as diversion. The old shows of the early nineteen hundreds, Williams and Walker[1] and Cole and Johnson, are brought to mind as examples. The howling success—literally that—of J. Leubrie Hill[2] around 1913 is another; on the road his "Darktown Follies" played in numerous white theatres. In Harlem it played at the black Lafayette and, behold, the Lafayette temporarily became white. And so now, it is held, we are observing merely one aspect of a meteoric phenomenon, which simply presents itself differently in different circumstances: Roland Hayes and Paul Robeson, Jean Toomer and Walter White, Charles Gilpin[3] and Florence Mills—"Green Thursday," "Porgy," "In Abraham's Bosom"[4]—Negro spirituals—the startling new African groups proposed for the Metropolitan Museum of Art. Negro stock is going up, and everybody's buying.

V

It may be a season's whim, then, this sudden, contagious interest in everything Negro. If so, when I go into a familiar cabaret, or the place where a familiar cabaret used to be, and find it transformed and relatively colorless, I may be observing just one form that the season's whim has taken.

But suppose it is a fad—to say that explains nothing. How came the fad? What occasions the focusing of attention on this particular thing—rounds up and gathers these seasonal whims, and centers them about the Negro? Cabarets are peculiar, mind you. They're not like theatres and concert halls. You don't just go to a cabaret and sit back and wait to be entertained. You get out on the floor and join the pow-wow and help entertain yourself. Granted that white people have long enjoyed the Negro entertainment as a diversion, is it not something different, something more, when they bodily throw themselves into Negro entertainment in cabarets? "Now Negroes go to their own cabarets to see how white people act."

And what do we see? Why, we see them actually playing Negro games. I watch them in that epidemic Negroism, the Charleston. I look on and envy them. They camel and fish-tail and turkey, they geche and black-bottom and scronch, they

9. A prominent Manhattan night club.
1. Bert Williams and George Nash Walker formed an immensely popular vaudeville team in 1895.
2. Songwriter (1869–1916).
3. Actor (1878–1930). Hayes (1887–1976), singer. Toomer (1894–1967), author of *Cane*. White (1893–1955), writer and civil rights leader.
4. A 1926 play by white writer Paul Green. *Porgy* (1925) is a novel by Du Bose Heyward.

skate and buzzard and mess-around[5]—and they do them all better than I! This interest in the Negro is an active and participating interest. It is almost as if a traveler from the North stood watching an African tribe-dance, then suddenly found himself swept wildly into it, caught in its tidal rhythm.

Willingly would I be an outsider in this if I could know that I read it aright— that out of this change in the old familiar ways some finer thing may come. Is this interest akin to that of the Virginians on the veranda of a plantation's big-house—sitting genuinely spellbound as they hear the lugubrious strains floating up from the Negro quarters? Is it akin to that of the African explorer, Stanley,[6] leaving a village far behind, but halting in spite of himself to catch the boom of its distant drum? Is it significant of basic human responses, the effect of which, once admitted, will extend far beyond cabarets? Maybe these Nordics at last have tuned in on our wave-length. Maybe they are at last learning to speak our language.

1927

W. E. B. DU BOIS
Two Novels

Nella Larsen[7] *Quicksand* (Knopf)
Claude McKay *Home to Harlem* (Harper and Brothers)

I have just read the last two novels of Negro America. The one I liked; the other I distinctly did not. I think that Mrs. Imes, writing under the pen name of Nella Larsen, has done a fine, thoughtful and courageous piece of work in her novel. It is, on the whole, the best piece of fiction that Negro America has produced since the heyday of Chesnutt, and stands easily with Jesse Fauset's *There is Confusion*,[8] in its subtle comprehension of the curious cross currents that swirl about the black American.

Claude McKay's *Home to Harlem*, on the other hand, for the most part nauseates me, and after the dirtier parts of its filth I feel distinctly like taking a bath. This does not mean that the book is wholly bad. McKay is too great a poet to make any complete failure in writing. There are bits of *Home to Harlem* beautiful and fascinating: the continued changes upon the theme of the beauty of colored skins; the portrayal of the fascination of their new yearnings for each other which Negroes are developing. The chief character, Jake, has something appealing, and the glimpses of the Haitian, Ray, have all the materials of a great piece of fiction.

But it looks as though, despite this, McKay has set out to cater for that prurient demand on the part of white folk for a portrayal in Negroes of that utter licentiousness which conventional civilization holds white folk back from enjoying—if enjoyment it can be called. That which a certain decadent section of the white American world, centered particularly in New York, longs for with

5. Various popular dances.   6. Sir Henry Morgan Stanley (1841–1904), English explorer.
7. Nella Larsen (1891–1964), novelist.   8. A novel published in 1924.

The cover of the first edition of McKay's *Home to Harlem*

fierce and unrestrained passions, it wants to see written out in black and white, and saddled on black Harlem. This demand, as voiced by a number of New York publishers, McKay has certainly satisfied, and added much for good measure. He has used every art and emphasis to paint drunkenness, fighting, lascivious sexual promiscuity and utter absence of restraint in as bold and as bright colors as he can.

If this had been done in the course of a well-conceived plot or with any artistic unity, it might have been understood if not excused. But *Home to Harlem* is padded. Whole chapters here and there are inserted with no connection to the main plot, except that they are on the same dirty subject. As a picture of Harlem life or of Negro life anywhere, it is, of course, nonsense. Untrue, not so much as on account of its facts, but on account of its emphasis and glaring colors. I am sorry that the author of *Harlem Shadows* stooped to this. I sincerely hope that he will some day rise above it and give us in fiction the strong, well-knit as well as beautiful theme, that it seems to me he might do.

Nella Larsen on the other hand has seized an interesting character and fitted her into a close yet delicately woven plot. There is no "happy ending" and yet the theme is not defeatist like the work of Peterkin and Green.[9] Helga Crane sinks at last still master of her whimsical, unsatisfied soul. In the end she will be beaten down even to death but she never will utterly surrender to hypocrisy and convention. Helga is typical of the new, honest, young fighting Negro woman—the one on whom "race" sits negligibly and Life is always first and its wandering path is but darkened, not obliterated by the shadow of the Veil. White folk will not like this book. It is not near nasty enough for New York columnists. It is too sincere for the South and middle West. Therefore, buy it and make Mrs. Imes write many more novels.

1928

ZORA NEALE HURSTON

How It Feels to Be Colored Me

I am colored but I offer nothing in the way of extenuating circumstances except the fact that I am the only Negro in the United States whose grandfather on the mother's side was *not* an Indian chief.

---

9. Paul Green (1894–1981), white dramatist who often dealt with interracial subjects. Julia Peterkin (1880–1961), white novelist of southern African American life.

I remember the very day that I became colored. Up to my thirteenth year I lived in the little Negro town of Eatonville, Florida. It is exclusively a colored town. The only white people I knew passed through the town going to or coming from Orlando. The native whites rode dusty horses, the Northern tourists chugged down the sandy village road in automobiles. The town knew the Southerners and never stopped cane chewing when they passed. But the Northerners were something else again. They were peered at cautiously from behind curtains by the timid. The more venturesome would come out on the porch to watch them go past and got just as much pleasure out of the tourists as the tourists got out of the village.

The front porch might seem a daring place for the rest of the town, but it was a gallery seat for me. My favorite place was

Zora Neale Hurston

atop the gate-post. Proscenium box[1] for a born first-nighter. Not only did I enjoy the show, but I didn't mind the actors knowing that I liked it. I usually spoke to them in passing. I'd wave at them and when they returned my salute, I would say something like this: "Howdy-do-well-I-thank-you-where-you-goin'?" Usually automobile or the horse paused at this, and after a queer exchange of compliments, I would probably "go a piece of the way" with them, as we say in farthest Florida. If one of my family happened to come to the front in time to see me, of course negotiations would be rudely broken off. But even so, it is clear that I was the first "welcome-to-our-state" Floridian, and I hope the Miami Chamber of Commerce will please take notice.

During this period, white people differed from colored to me only in that they rode through town and never lived there. They liked to hear me "speak pieces" and sing and wanted to see me dance the parse-me-la, and gave me generously of their small silver for doing these things, which seemed strange to me for I wanted to do them so much that I needed bribing to stop. Only they didn't know it. The colored people gave no dimes. They deplored any joyful tendencies in me, but I was their Zora nevertheless. I belonged to them, to the nearby hotels, to the county—everybody's Zora.

But changes came in the family when I was thirteen, and I was sent to school in Jacksonville. I left Eatonville, the town of the oleanders, as Zora. When I disembarked from the river-boat at Jacksonville, she was no more. It seemed that I had suffered a sea change. I was not Zora of Orange County any more, I was now a little colored girl. I found it out in certain ways. In my heart as well as in the mirror, I became a fast[2] brown—warranted not to rub nor run.

---

1. The box seats in a theater on either side of and nearest to the stage.   2. Colorfast.

But I am not tragically colored. There is no great sorrow dammed up in my soul, nor lurking behind my eyes. I do not mind at all. I do not belong to the sobbing school of Negrohood who hold that nature somehow has given them a lowdown dirty deal and whose feelings are all hurt about it. Even in the helter-skelter skirmish that is my life, I have seen that the world is to the strong regardless of a little pigmentation more or less. No, I do not weep at the world—I am too busy sharpening my oyster knife.[3]

Someone is always at my elbow reminding me that I am the grand-daughter of slaves. It fails to register depression with me. Slavery is sixty years in the past. The operation was successful and the patient is doing well, thank you. The terrible struggle that made me an American out of a potential slave said "On the line!" The Reconstruction said "Get set!"; and the generation before said "Go!" I am off to a flying start and I must not halt in the stretch to look behind and weep. Slavery is the price I paid for civilization, and the choice was not with me. It is a bully adventure and worth all that I have paid through my ancestors for it. No one on earth ever had a greater chance for glory. The world to be won and nothing to be lost. It is thrilling to think—to know that for any act of mine, I shall get twice as much praise or twice as much blame. It is quite exciting to hold the center of the national stage, with the spectators not knowing whether to laugh or to weep.

The position of my white neighbor is much more difficult. No brown specter pulls up a chair beside me when I sit down to eat. No dark ghost thrusts its leg against mine in bed. The game of keeping what one has is never so exciting as the game of getting.

I do not always feel colored. Even now I often achieve the unconscious Zora of Eatonville before the Hegira.[4] I feel most colored when I am thrown against a sharp white background.

For instance at Barnard. "Beside the waters of the Hudson" I feel my race. Among the thousand white persons, I am a dark rock surged upon, and overswept, but through it all, I remain myself. When covered by the waters, I am; and the ebb but reveals me again.

Sometimes it is the other way around. A white person is set down in our midst, but the contrast is just as sharp for me. For instance, when I sit in the drafty basement that is The New World Cabaret with a white person, my color comes. We enter chatting about any little nothing that we have in common and are seated by the jazz waiters. In the abrupt way that jazz orchestras have, this one plunges into a number. It loses no time in circumlocutions, but gets right down to business. It constricts the thorax and splits the heart with its tempo and narcotic harmonies. This orchestra grows rambunctious, rears on its hind legs and attacks the tonal veil with primitive fury, rending it, clawing it until it breaks through to the jungle beyond. I follow those heathen—follow them exultingly. I dance wildly inside myself; I yell within, I whoop; I shake my assegai[5] above my head, I hurl it true to the mark *yeeeeooww!* I am in the jungle and living in the jungle way. My face is painted red and yellow and my body is painted blue.

3. An allusion to Shakespeare's *The Merry Wives of Windsor* 2.2.4–5: "Why, then the world's mine oyster, / Which I with sword will open."
4. In Islam, Muhammad's emigration from Mecca to Medina in 622 C.E.; here, the journey to Jacksonville.
5. Spear.

My pulse is throbbing like a war drum. I want to slaughter something—give pain, give death to what, I do not know. But the piece ends. The men of the orchestra wipe their lips and rest their fingers. I creep back slowly to the veneer we call civilization with the last tone and find the white friend sitting motionless in his seat, smoking calmly.

"Good music they have here," he remarks, drumming the table with his fingertips.

Music. The great blobs of purple and red emotion have not touched him. He has only heard what I felt. He is far away and I see him but dimly across the ocean and the continent that have fallen between us. He is so pale with his whiteness then and I am *so* colored.

At certain times I have no race, I am *me*. When I set my hat at a certain angle and saunter down Seventh Avenue, Harlem City, feeling as snooty as the lions in front of the Forty-Second Street Library,[6] for instance. So far as my feelings are concerned, Peggy Hopkins Joyce on the Boule Mich[7] with her gorgeous raiment, stately carriage, knees knocking together in a most aristocratic manner, has nothing on me. The cosmic Zora emerges. I belong to no race nor time. I am the eternal feminine with its string of beads.

I have no separate feeling about being an American citizen and colored. I am merely a fragment of the Great Soul that surges within the boundaries. My country, right or wrong.

Sometimes, I feel discriminated against, but it does not make me angry. It merely astonishes me. How *can* any deny themselves the pleasure of my company? It's beyond me.

But in the main, I feel like a brown bag of miscellany propped against a wall. Against a wall in company with other bags, white, red and yellow. Pour out the contents, and there is discovered a jumble of small things priceless and worthless. A first-water diamond,[8] an empty spool, bits of broken glass, lengths of string, a key to a door long since crumbled away, a rusty knife-blade, old shoes saved for a road that never was and never will be, a nail bent under the weight of things too heavy for any nail, a dried flower or two still a little fragrant. In your hand is the brown bag. On the ground before you is the jumble it held—so much like the jumble in the bags, could they be emptied, that all might be dumped in a single heap and the bags refilled without altering the content of any greatly. A bit of colored glass more or less would not matter. Perhaps that is how the Great Stuffer of Bags filled them in the first place—who knows?

1928

---

6. The headquarters of the New York Public Library.

7. The elegant Boulevard St. Michel in Paris. Peggy Hopkins Joyce was an American showgirl, actress, and celebrity (1893?–1957), famed as "the original gold digger" for her scandalous lifestyle.

8. A diamond of the highest quality.

LANGSTON HUGHES

From *The Big Sea*

Harlem Literati

The summer of 1926, I lived in a rooming house on 137th Street, where Wallace Thurman and Harcourt Tynes[9] also lived. Thurman was then managing editor of the *Messenger*, a Negro magazine that had a curious career. It began by being very radical, racial, and socialistic, just after the war. I believe it received a grant from the Garland Fund[1] in its early days. Then it later became a kind of Negro society magazine and a plugger for Negro business, with photographs of prominent colored ladies and their nice homes in it. A. Phillip Randolph, now President of the Brotherhood of Sleeping Car Porters, Chandler Owen, and George S. Schuyler were connected with it. Schuyler's editorials, à la Mencken,[2] were the most interesting things in the magazine, verbal brickbats that said sometimes one thing, sometimes another, but always vigorously. I asked Thurman what kind of magazine the *Messenger* was, and he said it reflected the policy of whoever paid off best at the time.

Anyway, the *Messenger* bought my first short stories. They paid me ten dollars a story. Wallace Thurman wrote me that they were very bad stories, but better than any others they could find, so he published them.

Thurman had recently come from California to New York. He was a strangely brilliant black boy, who had read everything, and whose critical mind could find something wrong with everything he read. I have no critical mind, so I usually either like a book or don't. But I am not capable of liking a book and then finding a million things wrong with it, too—as Thurman was capable of doing.

Thurman had read so many books because he could read eleven lines at a time. He would get from the library a great pile of volumes that would have taken me a year to read. But he would go through them in less than a week, and be able to discuss each one at great length with anybody. That was why, I suppose, he was later given a job as a reader at Macaulay's—the only Negro reader, so far as I know, to be employed by any of the larger publishing firms.

Later Thurman became a ghost writer for *True Story*, and other publications, writing under all sorts of fantastic names, like Ethel Belle Mandrake or Patrick Casey. He did Irish and Jewish and Catholic "true confessions." He collaborated with William Jordan Rapp[3] on plays and novels. Later he ghosted books. In fact, this quite dark young Negro is said to have written *Men, Women, and Checks*.

Wallace Thurman wanted to be a great writer, but none of his own work ever

---

9. A friend of Thurman's. *House on 137th Street*: the rooming house appears in Thurman's *Infants of the Spring* as "Niggerati Manor."

1. The American Fund for Public Service, established in 1920 by Charles Garland.

2. Henry Louis Mencken (1880-1956), prominent Baltimore essayist, critic, and editor who was a friend of Schuyler's. Randolph (1889-1976) and Owen (1889-1967), editors at the *Messenger*, who hired Schuyler as a writer in 1923. Schuyler (1895-1977), conservative black writer.

3. White playwright (1895-1942), editor of *True Story* magazine. The only work certain to be a collaboration of Thurman and Rapp is the play *Harlem* (1929).

made him happy. *The Blacker the Berry,*[4] his first book, was an important novel on a subject little dwelt upon in Negro fiction—the plight of the very dark Negro woman, who encounters in some communities a double wall of color prejudice within and without the race. His play, *Harlem,* considerably distorted for box office purposes, was, nevertheless, a compelling study—and the only one in the theater—of the impact of Harlem on a Negro family fresh from the South. And his *Infants of the Spring,* a superb and bitter study of the bohemian fringe of Harlem's literary and artistic life, is a compelling book.

But none of these things pleased Wallace Thurman. He wanted to be a *very* great writer, like Gorki or Thomas Mann,[5] and he felt that he was merely a journalistic writer. His critical mind, comparing his pages to the thousands of other pages he had read, by Proust, Melville, Tolstoy, Galsworthy, Dostoyevski, Henry James, Sainte-Beauve, Taine, Anatole France,[6] found his own pages vastly wanting. So he contented himself by writing a great deal for money, laughing bitterly at his fabulously concocted "true stories," creating two bad motion pictures[7] of the "Adults Only" type for Hollywood, drinking more and more gin, and then threatening to jump out of windows at people's parties and kill himself.

During the summer of 1926, Wallace Thurman, Zora Neale Hurston, Aaron Douglas, John P. Davis, Bruce Nugent, Gwendolyn Bennett,[8] and I decided to publish "a Negro quarterly of the arts" to be called *Fire*—the idea being that it would burn up a lot of the old, dead conventional Negro-white ideas of the past, *épater le bourgeois*[9] into a realization of the existence of the younger Negro writers and artists, and provide us with an outlet for publication not available in the limited pages of the small Negro magazines then existing, the *Crisis, Opportunity,* and the *Messenger*—the first two being house organs of inter-racial organizations, and the latter being God knows what.

Sweltering summer evenings we met to plan *Fire.* Each of the seven of us agreed to give fifty dollars to finance the first issue. Thurman was to edit it, John P. Davis to handle the business end, and Bruce Nugent to take charge of distribution. The rest of us were to serve as an editorial board to collect material, contribute our own work, and act in any useful way that we could. For artists and writers, we got along fine and there were no quarrels. But October came before we were ready to go to press. I had to return to Lincoln,[1] John Davis to Law School at Harvard, Zora Hurston to her studies at Barnard, from whence she went about Harlem with an anthropologist's ruler, measuring heads for Franz Boas.[2]

4. Published in 1929.

5. German novelist (1875–1955). Maxim Gorki was the pen name of Russian writer Aleksey Maksimovich Pyeshkov (1868–1936).

6. Pen name of French novelist and essayist Jacques Antole Francois Thibault (1844–1924). Marcel Proust (1871–1922), French novelist. Herman Melville (1819–1891), U.S. writer. Leo Tolstoy (1828–1910), Russian novelist and social critic. John Galsworthy (1867–1933), English novelist. Fyodor Dostoyevski (1821–1881), Russian novelist. James (1843–1916), U.S. novelist and critic. Charles Augustin Sainte-Beuve (1804–1869), French critic and poet. Hippolyte Adolphe Taine (1828–1893), French critic and historian.

7. *Tomorrow's Children* (1934) and *High School Girl* (1935).

8. Poet (1902–1981). Hurston (1891–1960), novelist and folklore collector. Douglas (1898–1979), artist. Davis (1905–1973), lawyer and prominent leftist. Nugent (1906–1987), illustrator and writer.

9. Shock the middle class (French).   1. I.e., Lincoln University in Pennsylvania.

2. German-born American anthropologist (1858–1942).

Only three of the seven had contributed their fifty dollars, but the others faithfully promised to send theirs out of tuition checks, wages, or begging. Thurman went on with the work of preparing the magazine. He got a printer. He planned the layout. It had to be on good paper, he said, worthy of the drawings of Aaron Douglas. It had to have beautiful type, worthy of the first Negro art quarterly. It had to be what we seven young Negroes dreamed our magazine would be—so in the end it cost almost a thousand dollars, and nobody could pay the bills.

I don't know how Thurman persuaded the printer to let us have all the copies to distribute, but he did. I think Alain Locke, among others, signed notes guaranteeing payments. But since Thurman was the only one of the seven of us with a regular job, for the next three or four years his checks were constantly being attached and his income seized to pay for *Fire*. And whenever I sold a poem, mine went there, too—to *Fire*.

None of the older Negro intellectuals would have anything to do with *Fire*. Dr. DuBois[3] in the *Crisis* roasted it. The Negro press called it all sorts of bad names, largely because of a green and purple story by Bruce Nugent, in the Oscar Wilde[4] tradition, which we had included. Rean Graves, the critic for the *Baltimore Afro-American*, began his review by saying: "I have just tossed the first issue of *Fire* into the fire." Commenting upon various of our contributors, he said: "Aaron Douglas who, in spite of himself and the meaningless grotesqueness of his creations, has gained a reputation as an artist, is permitted to spoil three perfectly good pages and a cover with his pen and ink hudge pudge. Countee Cullen has written a beautiful poem in his 'From a Dark Tower,' but tries his best to obscure the thought in superfluous sentences. Langston Hughes displays his usual ability to say nothing in many words."

So *Fire* had plenty of cold water thrown on it by the colored critics. The white critics (except for an excellent editorial in the *Bookman* for November, 1926) scarcely noticed it at all. We had no way of getting it distributed to bookstands or news stands. Bruce Nugent took it around New York on foot and some of the Greenwich Village bookshops put it on display, and sold it for us. But then Bruce, who had no job, would collect the money and, on account of salary, eat it up before he got back to Harlem.

Finally, irony of ironies, several hundred copies of *Fire* were stored in the basement of an apartment where an actual fire occurred and the bulk of the whole issue was burned up. Even after that Thurman had to go on paying the printer.

Now *Fire* is a collector's item, and very difficult to get, being mostly ashes.

That taught me a lesson about little magazines. But since white folks had them, we Negroes thought we could have one, too. But we didn't have the money.

Wallace Thurman laughed a long bitter laugh. He was a strange kind of fellow, who liked to drink gin, but *didn't* like to drink gin; who liked being a Negro, but felt it a great handicap; who adored bohemianism, but thought it wrong to be a bohemian. He liked to waste a lot of time, but he always felt guilty wasting

---

3. W. E. B. Du Bois (1868–1963), African American writer, editor of *Crisis*, and co-founder of the NAACP.
4. Irish playwright (1854–1900), a proponent of the Art for Art's Sake movement. *Green and purple story:* the first installment of a novel called *Smoke, Lilies and Jade*.

time. He loathed crowds, yet he hated to be alone. He almost always felt bad, yet he didn't write poetry.

Once I told him if I could feel as bad as he did *all* the time, I would surely produce wonderful books. But he said you had to know how to *write*, as well as how to feel bad. I said I didn't have to know how to feel bad, because, every so often, the blues just naturally overtook me, like a blind beggar with an old guitar:

> You don't know,
> You don't know my mind—
> When you see me laughin',
> I'm laughin' to keep from cryin'.[5]

About the future of Negro literature Thurman was very pessimistic. He thought the Negro vogue had made us all too conscious of ourselves, had flattered and spoiled us, and had provided too many easy opportunities for some of us to drink gin and more gin, on which he thought we would always be drunk. With his bitter sense of humor, he called the Harlem literati, the "niggerati."

Of this "niggerati," Zora Neale Hurston was certainly the most amusing. Only to reach a wider audience, need she ever write books—because she is a perfect book of entertainment in herself. In her youth she was always getting scholarships and things from wealthy white people, some of whom simply paid her just to sit around and represent the Negro race for them, she did it in such a racy fashion. She was full of side-splitting anecdotes, humorous tales, and tragicomic stories, remembered out of her life in the South as a daughter of a travelling minister of God. She could make you laugh one minute and cry the next. To many of her white friends, no doubt, she was a perfect "darkie," in the nice meaning they give the term—that is a naïve, childlike, sweet, humorous, and highly colored Negro.

But Miss Hurston was clever, too—a student who didn't let college give her a broad *a* and who had great scorn for all pretensions, academic or otherwise. That is why she was such a fine folk-lore collector,[6] able to go among the people and never act as if she had been to school at all. Almost nobody else could stop the average Harlemite on Lenox Avenue and measure his head with a strange-looking, anthropological device and not get bawled out for the attempt, except Zora, who used to stop anyone whose head looked interesting, and measure it.

When Miss Hurston graduated from Barnard she took an apartment in West 66th Street near the park, in that row of Negro houses there. She moved in with no furniture at all and no money, but in a few days friends had given her everything, from decorative silver birds, perched atop the linen cabinet, down to a footstool. And on Saturday night, to christen the place, she had a *hand*-chicken dinner, since she had forgotten to say she needed forks.

She seemed to know almost everybody in New York. She had been a secretary to Fannie Hurst,[7] and had met dozens of celebrities whose friendship she retained. Yet she was always having terrific ups-and-downs about money. She tells this story on herself, about needing a nickel to go downtown one day and

---

5. Hughes later titled a collection of his short stories *Laughing to Keep from Crying* (1952).
6. Hurston published two such collections: *Mules and Men* (1935) and *Tell My Horse* (1938).
7. American fiction writer (1899–1968).

wondering where on earth she would get it. As she approached the subway, she was stopped by a blind beggar holding out his cup.

"Please help the blind! Help the blind! A nickel for the blind!"

"I need money worse than you today," said Miss Hurston, taking five cents out of his cup. "Lend me this! Next time, I'll give it back." And she went on downtown.

Harlem was like a great magnet for the Negro intellectual, pulling him from everywhere. Or perhaps the magnet was New York—but once in New York, he had to live in Harlem, for rooms were hardly to be found elsewhere unless one could pass for white or Mexican or Eurasian and perhaps live in the Village—which always seemed to me a very arty locale, in spite of the many real artists and writers who lived there. Only a few of the New Negroes lived in the Village, Harlem being their real stamping ground.

The wittiest of these New Negroes of Harlem, whose tongue was flavored with the sharpest and saltiest humor, was Rudolph Fisher, whose stories appeared in the *Atlantic Monthly*. His novel, *Walls of Jericho*,[8] captures but slightly the raciness of his own conversation. He was a young medical doctor and X-ray specialist, who always frightened me a little, because he could think of the most incisively clever things to say—and I could never think of anything to answer. He and Alain Locke together were great for intellectual wise-cracking. The two would fling big and witty words about with such swift and punning innuendo that an ordinary mortal just sat and looked wary for fear of being caught in a net of witticisms beyond his cultural ken. I used to wish I could talk like Rudolph Fisher. Besides being a good writer, he was an excellent singer, and had sung with Paul Robeson during their college days. But I guess Fisher was too brilliant and too talented to stay long on this earth. During the same week, in December, 1934, he and Wallace Thurman both died.

Thurman died of tuberculosis in the charity ward at Bellevue Hospital, having just flown back to New York from Hollywood.

1940

SUGGESTIONS FOR WRITING

1. Many poets of the Harlem Renaissance made extensive use of the sonnet form; this chapter contains such examples as Countee Cullen's "From the Dark Tower," Helene Johnson's "Sonnet to a Negro in Harlem," and Claude McKay's "If We Must Die." Write an essay in which you compare and contrast some of the sonnets written during the Harlem Renaissance. How do different approaches to the sonnet form signal different thematic concerns?

2. In 1921, James Weldon Johnson wrote of "the need for Aframerican poets in the United States to work out a new and distinctive form of expression." Judging from the selections in this chapter, do you think that poets such as Langston Hughes and Claude McKay met the need articulated by Johnson? Write an essay in which you examine both traditionalism and innovation in the poetry of the Harlem Renaissance. How distinct are the works of black and white poets during this period?

3. In *The New Negro*, Alain Locke declared, "In Harlem, Negro life is seizing upon its first chances for group expression and self-determination." Do poems such as Arna

8. Published in 1928.

Bontemps's "A Black Man Talks of Reaping," Angelina Grimke's "The Black Finger," and Langston Hughes's "I, Too" achieve a common social consciousness—Locke's "group expression"? What political effect do you think these poets hoped to achieve through their work? Write an essay in which you analyze the political ideas in the poetry of the Harlem Renaissance.

4. Some poems of the Harlem Renaissance—Langston Hughes's "The Weary Blues" and Claude McKay's "The Harlem Dancer," for example—are explicitly about music; others, such as Countee Cullen's "Saturday's Child," with its ballad form, and Angelina Grimke's improvisational "Tenebris," take a distinctly musical approach. Write an essay about the interplay of words and music in the poetry of this period.

5. In his review of Claude McKay's *Home to Harlem*, W. E. B. Du Bois laments that McKay "stooped" to betraying the black cause by portraying "drunkenness, fighting, lascivious sexual promiscuity and utter absence of restraint" in his novel's black characters. Do writers have a particular duty to portray positive role models? Do writers from ethnic groups engaged in social struggle have a particular duty to participate in that struggle? Citing evidence from the selections in this chapter, write an essay in which you weigh the demands of artistic duty against the demands of artistic freedom.

6. What does it mean for a group of artists to be considered a "school"—that is, a group whose work appears to share common themes, styles, and goals? Write an essay in which you discuss whether or not the writers of the Harlem Renaissance spoke with a unified voice. Does a grouping like "the Harlem Renaissance" help our understanding of this period and the art it produced, or does it obscure the individual achievements of the artists themselves?

13 CRITICAL CONTEXTS: A POETRY CASEBOOK

As the previous context chapters have suggested, poems draw on all kinds of earlier texts, experiences, and events. But they also produce new contexts of discussion and interpretation, ongoing conversations about the poems themselves. Different readers of poems see different things in them, so naturally a variety of interpretations and evaluations develop around any poem that is read repeatedly by various readers. Many of those interpretations are published in specialized journals and books (the selections that follow are all reprinted from published sources), and a kind of dialogue develops among readers, producing a body of commentary about the poem. Professional interpreters of texts are called **literary critics,** and the textual analysis they provide is called **criticism**—not because their work is necessarily negative or corrective, but because they ask hard, analytical, "critical" questions and interpret texts through a wide variety of literary, historical, biographical, psychological, aesthetic, moral, political, or social perspectives.

Your own interpretive work may seem to you more private and far removed from such "professional" writing about poems. But once you engage in class discussion with your teacher or even talk informally with a fellow student about a poem, you are in effect practicing your own literary criticism—offering comments, analyzing, judging, putting the poem into some kind of perspective that makes it more knowable and understandable to yourself or to other readers. You are, in effect, joining the ongoing conversation about the poem. The accumulated criticism on any particular poem is, in fact, basically just public conversation and discussion—give and take, competing interpretations, accumulation of relevant facts and information—on the topic of how that poem should be experienced, interpreted, and evaluated. And when you *write* about the poem, you may often engage specifically the opinions of others—your teacher, fellow students, or published "criticism." You may not have the experience or specific expertise of professional critics, but you can modify or answer the work of others and use it in your own work.

There are many different ways to engage literary criticism and put it to work for you. The most common is to draw on published work for specific information about the poem: glossings of particular terms; explanations of references or situations you don't recognize; accounts of how, when, and under what circumstances the poem was written. Another common use of such material is as a springboard for your own interpretation, either building upon what someone else has said or, if you disagree, using it as a point of departure to launch a different view. In either case, your own paper may readily develop out of your reading or out of a class lecture or class discussion, which you may draw on just as you would written accounts. When you use the work of others, you must give full credit, carefully detailing the source of all direct quotations and all borrowed ideas. You must always tell your reader exactly how to find the material you have quoted or summarized. Usually, you do this through careful notes and a list of citations (that is, a bibliography) at the end of your paper. Your instructor will guide you to handbooks—for example, the *MLA Handbook* or *The Chicago Manual of Style*—that demonstrate how to cite each item in the appropriate way.

It can seem intimidating to become involved in critical dialogue, especially with those who are "authorities" or "experts" whose work has been published and widely read. But your own reading experience gives you a legitimate perspective, too, and often you can sharpen your skills by articulating your views against those with extensive interpretive experience. Besides, as you will quickly discover when you read several critical pieces on a particular poem, even the experts disagree. In fact, one measure of a poem's greatness is its ability to stimulate disagreement and a broad range of interpretation.

Procedurally, it is usually best to do your own extensive analysis of a poem *before* consulting what other critics have said. That way, you can confront other views from a firm (if tentative) position. You always want to take in new information and to challenge both your first impressions and your considered analyses—but don't be too quick to adopt somebody else's ideas. The best way to test the views of others is to compare them critically to your own conclusions, which you might then want to supplement, refine, extend, or even scrap altogether. In other words, proceed just as you have been proceeding—asking the questions you have learned to ask, sorting out the evidence you have noticed, and moving toward an integrated interpretation of the poem.

Before you read the criticism on Sylvia Plath's "Daddy" reprinted in this chapter, carefully read the poem itself several times. Ask all the analytical questions you have found useful in other cases: Who is speaking? To whom? When? Under what conditions? What is the full dramatic situation behind the poem? What kind of language does the poem use? To what effect? How does the poem use metaphor? allusion? historical reference? What strategies of rhythm and sound does the poem use? To what effect? What is the poem's tone? In what ways is this poem like other poems or other texts on similar topics? When was the poem written? What do you know about the person who wrote the poem? In what ways is this poem like others you have read by this poet or by this poet's contemporaries? How do the poem's themes and attitudes reflect the culture and times in which it was written?

SYLVIA PLATH

 *Daddy*[1]

You do not do, you do not do
Any more, black shoe
In which I have lived like a foot
For thirty years, poor and white,
5   Barely daring to breathe or Achoo.

---

1. First published in *Ariel*, a volume of poems that appeared two years after Plath's suicide.

Daddy, I have had to kill you.
You died before I had time—
Marble-heavy, a bag full of God,
Ghastly statue with one gray toe[2]
10 Big as a Frisco seal

And a head in the freakish Atlantic
Where it pours bean green over blue
In the waters off beautiful Nauset.[3]
I used to pray to recover you.
15 Ach, du.[4]

In the German tongue, in the Polish town[5]
Scraped flat by the roller
Of wars, wars, wars.
But the name of the town is common.
20 My Polack friend

Says there are a dozen or two.
So I never could tell where you
Put your foot, your root,
I never could talk to you.
25 The tongue stuck in my jaw.

It stuck in a barb wire snare.
Ich,[6] ich, ich, ich,
I could hardly speak.
I thought every German was you.
30 And the language obscene

An engine, an engine
Chuffing me off like a Jew.
A Jew to Dachau, Auschwitz, Belsen.[7]
I began to talk like a Jew.
35 I think I may well be a Jew.

The snows of the Tyrol, the clear beer of Vienna[8]
Are not very pure or true.
With my gypsy-ancestress and my weird luck
And my Taroc[9] pack and my Taroc pack
40 I may be a bit of a Jew.

I have always been scared of *you*,
With your Luftwaffe,[1] your gobbledygoo.
And your neat moustache

---

2. Otto Plath, Sylvia's father, lost a toe to gangrene that resulted from diabetes.   3. An inlet on Cape Cod.
4. Oh, you (German). Plath often portrays herself as Jewish and her oppressors as German.
5. Otto Plath, an ethnic German, was born in Grabow, Poland.   6. German for "I."
7. Sites of World War II Nazi death camps.
8. The snow in the Tyrol (an Alpine region in Austria and northern Italy) is, legendarily, as pure as the beer
is clear in Vienna.   9. Tarot, playing cards used mainly for fortune-telling.
1. The German air force.

And your Aryan[2] eye, bright blue.
45 Panzer[3]-man, panzer-man, O You—

Not God but a swastika
So black no sky could squeak through.
Every woman adores a Fascist,
The boot in the face, the brute
50 Brute heart of a brute like you.

You stand at the blackboard, daddy,
In the picture I have of you,
A cleft in your chin instead of your foot
But no less a devil for that, no not
55 Any less the black man who

Bit my pretty red heart in two.
I was ten when they buried you.
At twenty I tried to die
And get back, back, back to you.
60 I thought even the bones would do

But they pulled me out of the sack,
And they stuck me together with glue.[4]
And then I knew what to do.
I made a model of you,
65 A man in black with a Meinkampf[5] look

And a love of the rack and the screw.
And I said I do, I do.
So daddy, I'm finally through.
The black telephone's off at the root,
70 The voices just can't worm through.

If I've killed one man, I've killed two—
The vampire who said he was you
And drank my blood for a year,
Seven years, if you want to know.
75 Daddy, you can lie back now.

There's a stake in your fat black heart
And the villagers never liked you.
They are dancing and stamping on you.
They always *knew* it was you.
80 Daddy, daddy, you bastard, I'm through.

1966

2. People of Germanic lineage, often blond-haired and blue-eyed.
3. Literally "panther," the Nazi tank corps' term for an armored vehicle.
4. An allusion to Plath's recovery from her first suicide attempt.
5. The title of Adolf Hitler's autobiography and manifesto (1925-27); German for "my struggle."

Once you have a "reading" of your own and have made notes about your conclusions, look at the selections that follow. You can read them in a variety of ways:

- skim them all quickly, and look for things that surprise you or that provide you with specific challenges; or
- read each critical piece carefully, one by one, and keep close track of all the things with which you agree and (even more important) of those things with which you disagree; or
- look specifically for facts or apparently crucial information new to you, examine and question the information carefully, and see how it affects the interpretation you have previously decided on; or
- look for points of disagreement in the different interpretations, make a list of the most important issues raised, and look for the crucial parts of the poem where the basis for these disagreements occurs.

You will also find your own ways to respond to and use the various critical views you come upon here. Working the views of others into your own arguments and your own writing is complicated; while supporting your own conclusions, you must be fair to what others say. But learning to use the facts, opinions, and interpretations of others will clarify your own thoughts, hone or add to your analytical skills, and deepen your views. And participating in the larger conversation about a specific poem—or about poetry in general—will help you read, respond, and write more effectively.

Sylvia Plath

Sylvia Plath's father, Otto Plath

GEORGE STEINER

From *Dying Is an Art**

[N]o group of poems since Dylan Thomas' *Deaths and Entrances* has had as vivid and disturbing an impact on English critics and readers as has *Ariel*. Sylvia Plath's last poems have already passed into legend as both representative of our present tone of emotional life and unique in their implacable, harsh brilliance. Those among the young who read new poetry will know "Daddy," "Lady Lazarus," and "Death & Co." almost by heart, and reference to Sylvia Plath is constant where poetry and the conditions of its present existence are discussed.

The spell does not lie wholly in the poems themselves. The suicide of Sylvia Plath at the age of thirty-one in 1963, and the personality of this young woman who had come from Massachusetts to study and live in England (where she married Ted Hughes, himself a gifted poet), are vital parts of it. To those who knew her and to the greatly enlarged circle who were electrified by her last poems and sudden death, she had come to signify the specific honesties and risks of the poet's condition. Her personal style, and the price in private harrowing she so obviously paid to achieve the intensity and candor of her principal poems, have taken on their own dramatic authority.

All this makes it difficult to judge the poems. I mean that the vehemence and intimacy of the verse is such as to constitute a very powerful rhetoric of sincerity. The poems play on our nerves with their own proud nakedness, making claims so immediate and sharply urged that the reader flinches, embarrassed by the routine discretions and evasions of his own sensibility. Yet if these poems are to take life among us, if they are to be more than exhibits in the history of modern psychological stress, they must be read with all the intelligence and scruple we can muster. They are too honest, they have cost too much, to be yielded to myth.

. . . It requires no biographical impertinence to realize that Sylvia Plath's life was harried by bouts of physical pain, that she sometimes looked on the accumulated exactions of her own nerve and body as "a trash To annihilate each decade." She was haunted by the piecemeal, strung-together mechanics of the flesh, by what could be so easily broken and then mended with such searing ingenuity. The hospital ward was her exemplary ground:

> My patent leather overnight case like a black pillbox,
> My husband and child smiling out of the family photo;
> Their smiles catch onto my skin, little smiling hooks.

This brokenness, so sharply feminine and contemporary, is, I think, her principal realization. It is by the graphic expression she gave to it that she will be judged and remembered. Sylvia Plath carries forward, in an intensely womanly and aggravated note, from Robert Lowell's *Life Studies*, a book that obviously had a great impact on her. This new frankness of women about the specific hurts and tangles of their nervous-physiological makeup is as vital to the poetry of

---

* From George Steiner, *Language and Silence: Essays on Language, Literature, and the Inhuman* (1967; New York: Atheneum, 1974), pp. 295–302.

Sylvia Plath as it is to the tracts of Simone de Beauvoir or to the novels of Edna
O'Brien and Brigid Brophy. Women speak out as never before:

> The womb
> Rattles its pod, the moon
> Discharges itself from the tree with nowhere to go.
> ("Childless Woman")

> They have swabbed me clear of my loving associations.
> Scared and bare on the green plastic-pillowed trolley. . . .
> ("Tulips")

It is difficult to think of a precedent to the fearful close of "Medusa" (the whole
poem is extraordinary):

> I shall take no bite of your body,
> Bottle in which I live,
>
> Ghastly Vatican.
> I am sick to death of hot salt.
> Green as eunuchs, your wishes
> Hiss at my sin.
> Off, off, eely tentacle!
>
> There is nothing between us.

The ambiguity and dual flash of insight in this final line are of a richness and
obviousness that only a very great poem can carry off.

The progress registered between the early and the mature poems is one of
concretion. The general Gothic means with which Sylvia Plath was so fluently
equipped become singular to herself and therefore fiercely honest. What had been
style passes into need. It is the need of a superbly intelligent, highly literate young
woman to cry out about her especial being, about the tyrannies of blood and
gland, of nervous spasm and sweating skin, the rankness of sex and childbirth
in which a woman is still compelled to be wholly of her organic condition. Where
Emily Dickinson could—indeed was obliged to—shut the door on the riot and
humiliations of the flesh, thus achieving her particular dry lightness, Sylvia Plath
"fully assumed her own condition." This alone would assure her of a place in
modern literature. But she took one step further, assuming a burden that was
not naturally or necessarily hers.

Born in Boston in 1932 of German and Austrian parents, Sylvia Plath had no
personal, immediate contact with the world of the concentration camps. I may
be mistaken, but so far as I know there was nothing Jewish in her background.
But her last, greatest poems culminate in an act of identification, of total com-
munion with those tortured and massacred. The poet sees herself on

> An engine, an engine
> Chuffing me off like a Jew.
> A Jew to Dachau, Auschwitz, Belsen.
> I began to talk like a Jew.
> I think I may well be a Jew.
>
> The snows of the Tyrol, the clear beer of Vienna
> Are not very pure or true.
> With my gypsy ancestress and my weird luck

> And my Taroc pack and my Taroc pack
> I may be a bit of a Jew.

Distance is no help; nor the fact that one is "guilty of nothing." The dead men cry out of the yew hedges. The poet becomes the loud cry of their choked silence:

> Herr God, Herr Lucifer
> Beware
> Beware.
> Out of the ash
> I rise with my red hair
> And I eat men like air.

Here the almost surrealistic wildness of the gesture is kept in place by the insistent obviousness of the language and beat; a kind of Hieronymus Bosch[1] nursery rhyme.

Sylvia Plath is only one of a number of young contemporary poets, novelists, and playwrights, themselves in no way implicated in the actual holocaust, who have done most to counter the general inclination to forget the death camps. Perhaps it is only those who had no part in the events who *can* focus on them rationally and imaginatively; to those who experienced the thing, it has lost the hard edges of possibility, it has stepped outside the real.

Committing the whole of her poetic and formal authority to the metaphor, to the mask of language, Sylvia Plath *became* a woman being transported to Auschwitz on the death trains. The notorious shards of massacre seemed to enter into her own being:

> A cake of soap,
> A wedding ring,
> A gold filling.

In "Daddy" she wrote one of the very few poems I know of in any language to come near the last horror. It achieves the classic act of generalization, translating a private, obviously intolerable hurt into a code of plain statement, of instantaneously public images which concern us all. It is the "Guernica"[2] of modern poetry. And it is both histrionic and, in some ways, "arty," as is Picasso's outcry.

Are these final poems entirely legitimate? In what sense does anyone, himself uninvolved and long after the event, commit a subtle larceny when he invokes the echoes and trappings of Auschwitz and appropriates an enormity of ready emotion to his own private design? Was there latent in Sylvia Plath's sensibility, as in that of many of us who remember only by fiat of imagination, a fearful envy, a dim resentment at not having been there, of having missed the rendezvous with hell? In "Lady Lazarus" and "Daddy" the realization seems to me so complete, the sheer rawness and control so great, that only irresistible need could have brought it off. These poems take tremendous risks, extending Sylvia Plath's essentially austere manner to the very limit. They are a bitter triumph, proof of the capacity of poetry to give to reality the greater permanence of the imagined. She could not return from them.

---

1. Dutch artist (c. 1450–c. 1516) whose nightmarish paintings are filled with obscure symbolism.
2. Picasso's famous painting (1937) depicting the brutalities of war.

IRVING HOWE

From *The Plath Celebration: A Partial Dissent**

Sylvia Plath's most famous poem, adored by many sons and daughters, is "Daddy." It is a poem with an affecting theme, the feelings of the speaker as she regathers the pain of her father's premature death and her persuasion that he has betrayed her by dying:

> I was ten when they buried you.
> At twenty I tried to die
> And get back, back, back to you.

In the poem Sylvia Plath identifies the father (we recall his German birth) with the Nazis ("Panzer-man, panzer-man, O You") and flares out with assaults for which nothing in the poem (nor, so far as we know, in Sylvia Plath's own life) offers any warrant: "A cleft in your chin instead of your foot / But no less a devil for that. . . ." Nor does anything in the poem offer warrant, other than the free-flowing hysteria of the speaker, for the assault of such lines as, "There's a stake in your fat black heart / And the villagers never liked you." Or for the snappy violence of

> Every woman adores a Fascist,
> The boot in the face, the brute
> Brute heart of a brute like you.

What we have here is a revenge fantasy, feeding upon filial love-hatred, and thereby mostly of clinical interest. But seemingly aware that the merely clinical can't provide the materials for a satisfying poem, Sylvia Plath tries to enlarge upon the personal plight, give meaning to the personal outcry, by fancying the girl as victim of a Nazi father:

> An engine, an engine
> Chuffing me off like a Jew.
> A Jew to Dachau, Auschwitz, Belsen.
> I began to talk like a Jew.
> I think I may well be a Jew.

The more sophisticated admirers of this poem may say that I fail to see it as a dramatic presentation, a monologue spoken by a disturbed girl not necessarily to be identified with Sylvia Plath, despite the similarities of detail between the events of the poem and the events of her life. I cannot accept this view. The personal-confessional element, strident and undisciplined, is simply too obtrusive to suppose the poem no more than a dramatic picture of a certain style of disturbance. If, however, we did accept such a reading of "Daddy," we would fatally narrow its claims to emotional or moral significance, for we would be confining it to a mere vivid imagining of pathological state. That, surely, is not how its admirers really take the poem.

---

* From Irving Howe, *The Critical Point of Literature and Culture* (1973; New York: Horizon Press, 1977), pp. 231–33.

It is clearly not how the critic George Steiner takes the poem when he calls it "the 'Guernica' of modern poetry." But then, in an astonishing turn, he asks: "In what sense does anyone, himself uninvolved and long after the event, commit a subtle larceny when he invokes the echoes and trappings of Auschwitz and appropriates an enormity of ready emotion to his own private design?" The question is devastating to his early comparison with "Guernica." Picasso's painting objectifies the horrors of Guernica, through the distancing of art; no one can suppose that he shares or participates in them. Plath's poem aggrandizes on the "enormity of ready emotion" invoked by references to the concentration camps, in behalf of an ill-controlled if occasionally brilliant outburst. There is something monstrous, utterly disproportionate, when tangled emotions about one's father are deliberately compared with the historical fate of the European Jews; something sad, if the comparison is made spontaneously. "Daddy" persuades once again, through the force of negative example, of how accurate T. S. Eliot was in saying, "The more perfect the artist, the more completely separate in him will be the man who suffers and the mind which creates."

A. ALVAREZ

From *Sylvia Plath**

The reasons for Sylvia Plath's images are always there, though sometimes you have to work hard to find them. She is, in short, always in intelligent control of her feelings. Her work bears out her theories:

> I think my poems come immediately out of the sensuous and emotional experiences I have, but I must say I cannot sympathise with these cries from the heart that are informed by nothing except a needle or a knife or whatever it is. I believe that one should be able to control and manipulate experiences, even the most terrifying—like madness, being tortured, this kind of experience—and one should be able to manipulate these experiences with an informed and intelligent mind. I think that personal experience shouldn't be a kind of shut box and mirror-looking narcissistic experience. I believe it should be generally relevant, to such things as Hiroshima and Dachau, and so on.

It seems to me that it was only by her determination both to face her most inward and terrifying experiences and to use her intelligence in doing so—so as not to be overwhelmed by them—that she managed to write these extraordinary last poems, which are at once deeply autobiographical and yet detached, generally relevant.

"Lady Lazarus" is a stage further on from "Fever 103°"; its subject is the total purification of achieved death. It is also far more intimately concerned with the drift of Sylvia Plath's life. The deaths of Lady Lazarus correspond to her own crises: the first just after her father died, the second when she had her nervous breakdown, the third perhaps a presentiment of the death that was shortly to come. Maybe this closeness of the subject helped make the poem so direct. The

* From A. Alvarez, *Beyond All This Fiddle* (London: Penguin, 1968), pp. 56–57.

details don't clog each other: they are swept forward by the current of immediate feeling, marshalled by it and ordered. But what is remarkable about the poem is the objectivity with which she handles such personal material. She is not just talking about her own private suffering. Instead, it is the very closeness of her pain which gives it a general meaning; through it she assumes the suffering of all the modern victims. Above all, she becomes an imaginary Jew. I think this is a vitally important element in her work. For two reasons. First, because anyone whose subject is suffering has a ready-made modern example of hell on earth in the concentration camps. And what matters in them is not so much the physical torture—since sadism is general and perennial—but the way modern, as it were industrial, techniques can be used to destroy utterly the human identity. Individual suffering can be heroic provided it leaves the person who suffers a sense of his own individuality—provided, that is, there is an illusion of choice remaining to him. But when suffering is mass-produced, men and women become as equal and identity-less as objects on an assembly line, and nothing remains—certainly no values, no humanity. This anonymity of pain, which makes all dignity impossible, was Sylvia Plath's subject. Second, she seemed convinced, in these last poems, that the root of her suffering was the death of her father, whom she loved, who abandoned her, and who dragged her after him into death. And in her fantasies her father was pure German, pure Aryan, pure anti-semite.

It all comes together in the most powerful of her last poems, "Daddy" . . . , about which she wrote the following bleak note:

> The poem is spoken by a girl with an Electra complex. Her father died while she thought he was God. Her case is complicated by the fact that her father was also a Nazi and her mother very possibly part Jewish. In the daughter the two strains marry and paralyse each other—she has to act out the awful little allegory once over before she is free of it.[1]

. . . What comes through most powerfully, I think, is the terrible *unforgivingness* of her verse, the continual sense not so much of violence—although there is a good deal of that—as of violent resentment that this should have been done to *her*. What she does in the poem is, with a weird detachment, to turn the violence against herself so as to show that she can equal her oppressors with her self-inflicted oppression. And this is the strategy of the concentration camps. When suffering is there whatever you do, by inflicting it upon yourself you achieve your identity, you set yourself free.

Yet the tone of the poem, like its psychological mechanisms, is not single or simple, and she uses a great deal of skill to keep it complex. Basically, her trick is to tell this horror story in a verse form as insistently jaunty and ritualistic as a nursery rhyme. And this helps her to maintain towards all the protagonists— her father, her husband and herself—a note of hard and sardonic anger, as though she were almost amused that her own suffering should be so extreme, so grotesque. The technical psychoanalytic term for this kind of insistent gaiety to protect you from what, if faced nakedly, would be insufferable, is "manic defence." But what, in a neurotic, is a means of avoiding reality can become, for an artist, a source of creative strength, a way of handling the unhandleable, and

---

1. From the introductory notes to "New Poems," a reading prepared for the BBC Third Programme but never broadcast [Alvarez's note].

presenting the situation in all its fullness. When she first read me the poem a few days after she wrote it, she called it a piece of "light verse." It obviously isn't, yet equally obviously it also isn't the racking personal confession that a mere description or précis of it might make it sound.

Yet neither is it unchangingly vindictive or angry. The whole poem works on one single, returning note and rhyme, echoing from start to finish:

> You do not do, you do not do . . .
> . . . I used to pray to recover you.
> Ach, du . . .

There is a kind of cooing tenderness in this which complicates the other, more savage note of resentment. It brings in an element of pity, less for herself and her own suffering than for the person who made her suffer. Despite everything, "Daddy" is a love poem.

JUDITH KROLL

From *Rituals of Exorcism: "Daddy"**

Poems explicitly about the protagonist's father, read in order of composition, show that the attitude toward him evolves from nostalgic mournfulness, regret, and guilt, to resentment and a bitter resolve to break his hold on her. . . .

The recital of the myth in "Daddy" ends in a ritual intended to cancel the earlier "sacred marriage" which has suffocated her:

> You do not do, you do not do
> Any more, black shoe
> In which I have lived like a foot
> For thirty years, poor and white,
> Barely daring to breathe or Achoo.[1]

In this image of passive and victimized domesticity, the speaker implicitly compares her past self to the "old woman who lived in a shoe" who "didn't know what to do"; now, however, she makes it clear that she does know what to do.

As a preamble to the exorcism, she recounts the development of her father's image, beginning with his earlier status as a "bag full of God, / Ghastly statue" (that is, a godlike colossus—mentioning the ghastliness, the ghostly, deathlike, pallid nature of the statue, anticipates the inversions to come) and then introduces the revised images: "panzer-man," "swastika," "Fascist," "brute," "devil," "bastard." Daddy must be cast in this new light, transformed from god to devil, if he is to be successfully expelled, but there must also be some real basis for it. To be effectively exposed, he must first appear as godly. But the speaker soon

* From Judith Kroll, *Chapters in a Mythology: The Poetry of Sylvia Plath* (New York: Harper & Row, 1976), pp. 122–26. Unless otherwise specified, all notes are Kroll's.
1. When Plath introduced "Daddy" as being about "a girl with an Electra complex" (with, in effect, the female version of an Oedipus complex), she gave a clue to what may be a play on words in the poem. "Oedipus" means "swell-foot," and therefore the speaker's identification of herself as a "foot" may be a private way of saying "I am Oedipus" and incorporating into the poem an allusion to the Electra complex.

shows that she now attributes his godliness in part to his authoritarianism and personal inaccessibility—qualities which became intensified through his death, and which later became transferred to "a model of you"—her husband. Both men are really variations on a familiar type, even a stereotype: the "god" who, like Marco the "woman-hater" in *The Bell Jar,* is "chock-full of power" . . . over women precisely because of his deadness, or ultimate inaccessibility, to them. Loving a man literally or metaphorically dead ("The face that lived in this mirror is the face of a dead man" ["The Courage of Shutting-Up"]) becomes a kind of perse-cution or punishment; and so, by the end of the incantation, Daddy deserves to be cast out. The "black telephone . . . off at the root," conveys the finality of the intended exorcism.

The "venomousness," ambiguous from the beginning, is not the whole story. "Daddy" is not primarily a poem of "father-hatred" or abuse as Robert Lowell, Elizabeth Hardwick, and others have contended. The need for exorcising her father's ghost lies, after all, in the extremity of her attachment to him. Alvarez very justly remarks that

> The whole poem works on one single, returning note and rhyme, echoing from start to finish:
>
> > You do not do, you do not do . . .
> > . . . I used to pray to recover you.
> > Ach, du . . .
>
> There is a kind of cooing tenderness in this which complicates the other, more savage note of resentment. It brings in an element of pity, less for herself and her own suffering than for the person who made her suffer. Despite everything, "Daddy" is a love poem.[2]

The love is not merely conveyed by the rhythm and sound of the poem, it is a necessary part of the poem's meaning, a part of the logic of its act.

The exorcism serves another purpose because through it she attempts to reject the pattern of being abandoned and made to suffer by a god, a man who is "chock-full of power": she creates "a model of you"—an image of her father—and marries this proxy. Then she kills both father and husband at once, magically using each as the other's representative.[3] Each death entails that of the other: the stake in her father's heart also kills the "vampire who said he was you"; and the killing of her marriage (for which she now claims to take responsibility, as she does for having allowed her marriage to perpetuate, by proxy, her relationship to her father) finally permits Daddy to "lie back." Formerly an acquiescent victim, she now vengefully cancels that role. The marriage to and killing of her father by proxy are acts of what Frazer[4] calls "sympathetic magic," in which "things act on each other at a distance through a secret sympathy". . . . Such magic, which assumes that human beings can either directly influence the course of nature or can induce gods to influence nature in the desired way, nearly always constitutes the logic of the rituals Frazer discusses. The ritual marriage of a Whitsun bride and bridegroom, for example, aims at assuring abundant crops by sympatheti-

---

2. Alvarez, "Sylvia Plath," p. 66.
3. The biographical basis for this identification is evident in *Letters Home.* . . .
4. Sir James George Frazer (1854–1941), Scottish anthropologist whose book *The Golden Bough* analyzes early religious and magical practices [Editor's note].

cally encouraging a marriage between the powers of fertility. Likewise, diseases may be either inflicted or drawn off by sympathetic magic on the principle that "as the image suffers, so does the man". . . .

Plath was familiar with and used such ideas; for example, she transcribed, from *The Golden Bough,* Frazer's remark about the fertility or barrenness of a man's wife affecting his garden; and she echoes Frazer again in a line, excised from her poem "The Other," in which opening doors and windows is connected with the facilitation of childbirth. (Also, being "lame in the memory" and self, associated with the lameness and death of her father, is at once a homeopathic wound and a sympathetic attachment to him.) The notion that "as the image suffers, so does the man"—affecting the real subject through a proxy—nicely describes marriage to a model of Daddy, and explains why "If I've killed one man, I've killed two." The earlier attempt of the speaker in "Daddy" to recover her father also involved sympathetic magic; she had tried to rejoin him by dying and becoming like him:

> At twenty I tried to die
> And get back, back, back to you.

She finally exorcises her father as if he were a scapegoat invested with the evils of her spoiled history. Frazer's discussion of rituals in which the dying god is also a scapegoat is germane here. He conjectures that two originally separate rituals merged to form this combination, and the father in "Daddy" may well be described as such a divine scapegoat figure.[5]

Sometimes it is a place from which a devil must be cast out, but usually it is a person who is possessed. In Plath's mythology the speaker is not possessed by her father in this sense, but by the false self who is in his thrall. That is why the true self is released (as in "Purdah" and "Lady Lazarus") when the oppressor is made hateful, and thereby overthrown. Rituals of exorcism in Plath's poetry therefore inherently involve the idea of rebirth. When exorcism, or attempted exorcism, of father or proxy occurs, it is preliminary to a rebirth which will entail expulsion of the false self and spoiled history. And even when a ritual of rebirth does not involve an explicit exorcism, one is usually implied.

The logic of sympathetic magic, which appears widely in Plath's late poetry, might well be called one of the physical laws of her poems. . . . Such a logic seems poetically appropriate for a mythology: that the Moon-muse (or one of her agents, such as "The Rival") governs and affects her by a "secret sympathy" seems natural to a mythic drama.

The motifs "released"—or triggered—in her late poems contain the potential for a sympathetic association of those details which express the same motif. Because the details are not incidental, called forth as they are by her mythology, the sympathy is in a sense guaranteed. The images of blood, violent death, and red poppies, all of which release the death and rebirth motif, have the potential

---

5. Frazer says:"If we ask why a dying god should be chosen to take upon himself and carry away the sins and sorrows of the people, it may be suggested that in the practice of using the divinity as a scapegoat we have a combination of two customs. . . . [T]he result would be the employment of the dying god as a scapegoat. He was killed, not originally to take away sin, but to save the divine life from the degeneracy of old age; but, since he had to be killed at any rate, people may have thought that they might as well seize the opportunity to lay upon him the burden of their sufferings and sins, in order that he might bear it away with him to the unknown world beyond the grave" [pp. 667–68]. . . .

for sympathetically affecting one another through their family resemblance. "Tulips" contains an example of the secret sympathy which operates through such resemblance (that is, through expressing the same motif):

> The tulips are too red in the first place, they hurt me.
> . . .
> Their redness talks to my wound, it corresponds.[6]

The word "corresponds" refers both to the communication between tulips and wound and to their underlying likeness. The tulips stand in the same relation to the incipient health or normalcy of the speaker that the poppies in later poems do to her suppressed true self, to (or with) which the poppies correspond. In a sense, this correspondence, and the contrast between it and the speaker's death-in-life existence, *is* the underlying motif in these poems.

It has already been suggested that the Moon-muse has a "sympathetic"—even though not entirely welcome—relation with the speaker[7] (as mother, totem, familiar, emblem) which can be activated without her consent, just as in "Tulips" she cannot prevent her wound from corresponding with the red flowers. Similarly, the coldness and sterility of the Moon-muse may infect the speaker, causing and not merely representing her state of being. The Moon therefore functions as both "emblem" and "real agent."

MARY LYNN BROE

From *Protean Poetic**

Among the other poems that display the performing self, "Daddy" and "Lady Lazarus" are two of the most often quoted, but most frequently misunderstood, poems in the Plath canon. The speaker in "Daddy" performs a mock poetic exorcism of an event that has already happened—the death of her father, who she feels withdrew his love from her by dying prematurely: "Daddy, I have had to kill you. / You died before I had time—."

The speaker attempts to exorcise not just the memory of her father but her own *Mein Kampf* model of him as well as her inherited behavioral traits that lead her graveward under the Freudian banner of death instinct or Thanatos's libido. But her ritual reenactment simply does not take. The event comically backfires

---

6. By the time "Tulips" was written, she had clearly developed much of the technique, imagery, and themes (such as the logic of sympathetic magic) of the late poems.

7. The belief Frazer mentions, that "a barren wife infects her husband's garden with her own sterility," is the sort of contagion that occurs in *Three Women,* in which the Secretary has been infected by the Moon's sterility and by that of the men with whom she works. Men, who cannot bear children, have the disease of "flatness," for they create only negations of and abstractions about life rather than life itself. This disease can (through the mediumship of the Moon) be caught from men, and it is therefore also an inversion or parody of conception. Referring to her miscarriage, the Secretary says: "I watched the men walk about me in the office. They were so flat! / There was something about them like cardboard, and now I had caught it. . . ."

* From Mary Lynn Broe, *Protean Poetic: The Poetry of Sylvia Plath* (Columbia and London: University of Missouri Press, 1980), pp. 172–75.

as pure self-parody: the metaphorical murder of the father dwindles into Hollywood spectacle, while the poet is lost in the clutter of the collective unconscious.

Early in the poem, the ritual gets off on the wrong foot both literally and figuratively. A sudden rhythmic break midway through the first stanza interrupts the insistent and mesmeric chant of the poet's own freedom:

> You do not do, you do not do
> Any more, black shoe
> In which I have lived like a foot
> For thirty years, poor and white,
> Barely daring to breathe or Achoo.

The break suggests, on the one hand, that the nursery-rhyme world of contained terror is here abandoned; on the other, that the poet-exorcist's mesmeric control is superficial, founded in a shaky faith and an unsure heart—the worst possible state for the strong, disciplined exorcist.

At first she kills her father succinctly with her own words, demythologizing him to a ludicrous piece of statuary that is hardly a Poseidon or the Colossus of Rhodes:[1]

> Marble-heavy, a bag full of God,
> Ghastly statue with one grey toe
> Big as a Frisco seal
>
> And a head in the freakish Atlantic
> Where it pours bean green over blue
> In the waters off beautiful Nauset.
> I used to pray to recover you.
> Ach, du.

Then as she tries to patch together the narrative of him, his tribal myth (the "common" town, the "German tongue," the war-scraped culture), she begins to lose her own powers of description to a senseless Germanic prattle ("The tongue stuck in my jaw. / It stuck in a barb wire snare. / Ich, ich, ich, ich"). The individual man is absorbed by his inhuman archetype, the "panzer man," "an engine / Chuffing me off like a Jew." Losing the exorcist's power that binds the spirit and then casts out the demon, she is the classic helpless victim of the swastika man. As she calls up her own picture of him as a devil, he refuses to adopt this stereotype. Instead he jumbles his trademark:

> A cleft in your chin instead of your foot
> But no less a devil for that, no not
> Any less the black man who
>
> Bit my pretty red heart in two.

The overt Nazi-Jew allegory throughout the poem suggests that, by a simple inversion of power, father and daughter grow more alike. But when she tries to imitate his action of dying, making all the appropriate grand gestures, she once again fails: "but they pulled me out of the sack, / And they stuck me together

---

1. One of the seven wonders of the ancient world, a gigantic statue of the Greek sun god, Helios; *Poseidon:* the chief sea god in the Greek pantheon [Editor's note].

with glue." She retreats to a safe world of icons and replicas, but even the doll image she constructs turns out to be "the vampire who said he was you." At last, she abandons her father to the collective unconscious where it is *he* who is finally recognized ("they always *knew* it was you"). *She* is lost, impersonally absorbed by his irate persecutors, bereft of both her power and her conjuror's discipline, and possessed by the incensed villagers. The exorcist's ritual, one of purifying, cleansing, commanding silence and then ordering the evil spirit's departure, has dwindled to a comic picture from the heart of darkness. Mad villagers stamp on the devil-vampire creation.

In the course of performing the imaginative "killing," the speaker moves through a variety of emotions, from viciousness ("a stake in your fat black heart"), to vengefulness ("You bastard, I'm through"), finally to silence ("the black telephone's off at the root"). It would seem that the real victim is the poet-performer who, despite her straining toward identification with the public events of holocaust and destruction of World War II, becomes more murderously persecuting than the "panzer-man" who smothered her, and who abandoned her with a paradoxical love, guilt, and fear. Unlike him, she kills three times: the original subject, the model to whom she said "I do, I do," and herself, the imitating victim. But each of these killings is comically inverted. Each backfires. Instead of successfully binding the spirits, commanding them to remain silent and cease doing harm, and then ordering them to an appointed place, the speaker herself is stricken dumb.

The failure of the exorcism and the emotional ambivalence are echoed in the curious rhythm. The incantatory safety of the nursery-rhyme thump (seemingly one of controlled, familiar terrors) also suggests some sinister brooding by its repetition. The poem opens with a suspiciously emphatic protest, a kind of psychological whistling-in-the-dark. As it proceeds, "Daddy" 's continuous life-rhythms—the assonance, consonance, and especially the sustained *oo* sounds—triumph over either the personal or the cultural-historical imagery. The sheer sense of organic life in the interwoven sounds carries the verse forward in boisterous spirit and communicates an underlying feeling of comedy that is also echoed in the repeated failure of the speaker to perform her exorcism.

Ultimately, "Daddy" is like an emotional, psychological, and historical autopsy, a final report. There is no real progress. The poet is in the same place in the beginning as in the end. She begins the poem as a hesitant but familiar fairy-tale daughter who parodies her attempt to reconstruct the myth of her father. Suffocating in her shoe house, she is unable to do much with that "bag full of God." She ends as a murderous member of a mythical community enacting the ritual or vampire killing, but only for a surrogate vampire, not the real thing ("the vampire who said he was you"). Although it seems that the speaker has moved from identification with the persecuted to identity as persecutor, Jew to vampire-killer, powerless to powerful, she has simply enacted a performance that allows her to live with what is unchangeable. She has used her art to stave off suffocation, and performs her self-contempt with a degree of bravado.[2]

---

2. What remains the most thorough and enlightening account of the poem is A. R. Jones, "On 'Daddy,' " *The Art of Sylvia Plath,* [ed. Newman], pp. 230–36 [Broe's note].

MARGARET HOMANS

From *A Feminine Tradition**

To place an exclusive valuation on the literal, expecially to identify the self as literal, is simply to ratify women's age-old and disadvantageous position as the other and the object. Contemporary poetry by women that takes up this self-defeating strategy risks encounters with death that are destructive both poetically and actually. The current belief in a literal "I" present in poetry is responsible for the popular superstition that Sylvia Plath's death was the purposeful completion of her poetry's project, the assumption being that if the speaker is precisely the same as the biographical Plath, the poetry's self-destructive violence is directed toward Plath herself, not toward an imagined speaker. This reading of Plath is unfair to the woman and, by calling it merely unmediated self-expression, obscures her poetry's real power. In poem after poem depicting or wishing for physical violence, the imagery of violence is part of a symmetrical figurative system, and death is figured as a way of achieving rebirth or some other transcendence.[1] Plath's project may not thus be very different from that of Dickinson, who speaks quite often from beyond the grave, reimagining and repossessing death as her own in order to dispel the terrors of literal death. However, within that figurative system the poet embraces a self-destructive program that must soon have been poetically terminal, even if it did not bring about the actual death.

Several of Plath's late poems come to terms with a father figure (who may include the poetic fathers she acknowledges in *The Colossus*), whose crime, no different from that identified by nineteenth-century women, is of attempting to transform the feminine self into objects. "Lady Lazarus" borrows the most appalling of Nazi imagery to accuse a generalized figure of male power of the ultimate reification. Not only is the dead victim of "Herr Doktor" and "Herr Enemy" an object in being dead, but she is also reduced to the actual physical objects from which the Nazis profited by destroying human bodies: "a Nazi lampshade,"

> A cake of soap,
> A wedding ring,
> A gold filling.

The poem combines the tradition of woman as medium of exchange with that of woman as object to produce a desperately concise picture of literalization.

> I am your opus,
> I am your valuable,
> The pure gold baby
>
> That melts to a shriek.

* From Margaret Homans, *Women Writers and Poetic Identity: Dorothy Wordsworth, Emily Brontë, and Emily Dickinson* (Princeton: Princeton University Press, 1982), pp. 218–21.
1. I am indebted here, for their persuasively positive readings of Plath, to Judith Kroll, *Chapters in a Mythology: The Poetry of Sylvia Plath* (New York: Harper & Row, 1976), and to Stacy Pies, "Coming Clear of the Shadow: The Poetry of Sylvia Plath," unpublished essay (Yale University, 1979) [Homans's note].

Though the poet is here objecting to literalization, not embracing it, the poetic myth of suicide through which the oppression may be lifted amounts to the same thing: the speaker must submit to this literalization in order to transcend it.

> Out of the ash
> I rise with my red hair
> And I eat men like air.

Their death costs her death, and powerful though the poem is, this is an extraordinarily high price for retribution. And as always, it is the process of objectification that makes up the poem, not the final, scarcely articulable transcendence.

"Daddy" uses Nazi imagery to make the same accusation about objectification brought against men as oppressors in "Lady Lazarus" and makes the corollary accusation against the father (and the husband modelled after him) that objectification has silenced her:

> I never could talk to you.
> The tongue stuck in my jaw.
>
> It stuck in a barb wire snare.
> Ich, ich, ich, ich,
> I could hardly speak.

In this context defiance and retribution take the form of her speaking, but again this counterattack is counterproductive. Punning on the expression "being through" to mean both establishing a telephone connection and being finished, she at once makes and conclusively severs communication:

> So daddy, I'm finally through.
> The black telephone's off at the root,
> The voices just can't worm through.

The poem concludes, "Daddy, daddy, you bastard, I'm through." Suppressing the power of the one who silenced her, she simultaneously returns herself to the silence that the poem came into being to protest.

PAMELA J. ANNAS

From *A Disturbance in Mirrors**

... [T]he particular sexual metaphor in "Daddy" is sado-masochism, which stands for the authority structure of a partriarchal and war-making society.... "Daddy" is an analysis of the structure of the society in which the individual is enmeshed. Intertwined with the image of sadist and masochist in "Daddy" is a parallel image of vampire and victim. In "Daddy," father, husband, and a larger patriarchal and competitive authority structure, which the speaker of the poem sees as having been responsible for the various imperialisms of the twentieth

* From Pamela J. Annas, *A Disturbance in Mirrors: The Poetry of Sylvia Plath,* Contributions in Women's Studies no. 89 (New York, Westport, and London: Greenwood Press, 1988), pp. 139–43. All notes are Annas's.

century, all melt together and become demonic, finally a gigantic vampire figure. In the modulation from one image to another to form an accumulated image that is characteristic of many of Plath's late poems, the male figure at the center of "Daddy" takes four major forms: the statue, the Gestapo officer, the professor, and the vampire. The poem begins, however, with an image of a black shoe, an image which, like the black shoe in "The Munich Mannequins" and like the black suit in "The Applicant," can be seen to stand for corporate man. The second stanza of the poem refers back to the title poem of *The Colossus,* where the speaker's father, representative of a gigantic male other, so dominated her world that her horizon was bounded by his scattered pieces. In "Daddy," she describes him as:

> Marble-heavy, a bag full of God,
> Ghastly statue with one grey toe
> Big as a Frisco seal
>
> And a head in the freakish Atlantic
> Where it pours bean green over blue
> In the waters off beautiful Nauset.

Between "The Colossus" and "Daddy" there has been a movement from a mythic and natural landscape to one with social and political boundaries. Here the image of her father, grown larger than the earlier Colossus of Rhodes, stretches across and subsumes the whole of the United States, from the Pacific to the Atlantic ocean.

The next seven stanzas of "Daddy" construct the image of the Gestapo officer, using her family background—her parents were both of German origin—to mediate between her personal sense of suffocation and the social history of the Nazi invasions. The black shoe of the first stanza in which she says she has been wedged like a foot "barely daring to breathe" becomes in stanza ten, at the end of the Nazi section, a larger social image of suffocation: "Not God but a swastika / So black no sky could squeak through." The Gestapo figure recurs briefly three stanzas later as the speaker of the poem transfers the image from father to husband and incidentally suggests that the victim has some control in a brutalized association—at least to the extent she chooses to be there.[1]

---

1. See Wilhelm Reich's *The Mass Psychology of Fascism* (New York: Simon and Schuster, 1969), particularly his chapter on "The Authoritarian Personality," for an analysis of how an oppressed class can contribute to its own oppression. Judith Lewis Herman, in *Father-Daughter Incest* (Cambridge, Mass.: Harvard University Press, 1981), discusses the history of the suppression of incest beginning with Freud and continuing into contemporary psychological literature, the attribution of reports of incest to hysterical female oedipal fantasizing or, when the fact of incest is impossible to deny, assigning blame to the victim: what Herman calls the Seductive Daughter and/or the Collusive Mother (Chapter 1, "A Common Occurence"). Writing in the early 1960s and familiar with some of these attitudes, . . . Plath [not surprisingly] assigns some culpability to the victim. Herman goes on to say, "Even when the girl does give up her erotic attachment to her father, she is encouraged to persist in the fantasy that some other man, like her father, will some day take possession of her, raising her above the common lot of womankind" (p. 57).

I am not of course suggesting that Plath literally had an incestuous relationship with her father—there is no evidence one way or the other—but she does make recurrent use of father/daughter incest as a symbol for male/female relations in a patriarchal society. . . .

> I made a model of you,
> A man in black with a Meinkampf look
>
> And a love of the rack and the screw.
> And I said I do, I do.

The Gestapo figure becomes "Herr Professor" in stanza eleven, an actual image of Plath's father, and also an image of what has for centuries been seen as the prototypical and even ideal relationship between a man and a woman.[2] The professor, who is a man, talks and is active; the woman, who is a student, listens and is passive. A patriarchal social structure is at its purest and, superficially, at its most benign in the stereotyped relationship of male teacher and female student and is a stock romantic fantasy even in women's literature—Emma and Mr. Knightley, Lucy Snowe and the professor in *Villette*.[3] But Plath places this image between the images of Nazi/Jew and vampire/victim so that it becomes the center of a series. Indeed, the image of daddy as teacher turns almost immediately into a devil/demon/vampire:

> A cleft in your chin instead of your foot
> But no less a devil for that, no not
> Any less the black man who
>
> Bit my pretty red heart in two.

The last two stanzas of "Daddy" are like the conclusion of "Lady Lazarus" in their assertion that the speaker of the poem is breaking out of the cycle and that, in order to do so, she must turn on and kill Herr God, Herr Lucifer in the one poem, and Daddy in his final metamorphosis as vampire in the other poem. Plath explained this in Freudian terms in an introductory note to the poem for a BBC Third Programme reading:

> The poem is spoken by a girl with an Electra complex. The father died while she thought he was God. Her case is complicated by the fact that her father was also a Nazi and her mother very possibly part Jewish. In the daughter the two strains marry and paralyze each other—she has to act out the awful little allegory once over before she is free of it.[4]

This reenacting of the allegory becomes at the end of "Daddy" a frenzied communal ritual of exorcism.

> Daddy, you can lie back now.
>
> There's a stake in your fat black heart
> And the villagers never liked you.
> They are dancing and stamping on you.
> They always *knew* it was you.
> Daddy, daddy, you bastard, I'm through.

This cycle of victim/vampire is, left alone, a closed and repetitious cycle, like the repeated suicides of "Lady Lazarus." According to the legends and the Holly-

---

2. This photograph of Otto Plath is reproduced on page 17 of *Letters Home*.
3. [Mary] Ellmann, *Thinking About Women* [New York: Harcourt Brace Jovanovich, 1968], pp. 119–23.
4. Quoted in [M. L.] Rosenthal, *The New Poets* [New York: Oxford University Press, 1967], p. 82.

wood film versions of these legends we all grew up on, once consumed by a vampire, one dies and is reborn a vampire and preys upon others, who in their turn die and become vampires. The vampire imagery in Sylvia Plath's poetry intersects on one level with her World War II imagery and its exploitation and victimization and on another level intersects with her images of a bureaucratic, fragmented, and dead—in the sense of numbed and unaware—society. The connections are sometimes confused, but certainly World War II is often imaged in her poetry as a kind of grisly, vampiric feast. . . .

The whole of "Daddy" is an exorcism to banish the demon, put a stake through the vampire's heart, and thus break the cycle of vampire→victim. It is crucial to the poem that the exorcism is accomplished through communal action by the "villagers." The rhythm of the poem is powerfully and deliberately primitive: a child's chant, a formal curse. The hard sounds, short lines, and repeated rhymes of "do," "you," "Jew," and "through" give a hard pounding quality to the poem that is close to the sound of a heart beat. "Daddy," as well as "Lady Lazarus" and, to a lesser extent, "Fever 103°," is structured as a magical formula or incantation. In the *Colossus* poems, Plath also used poetry as a ritual incantation, but in those early poems it was most often directed toward transformation of self. By 1961, she is less often attempting to transform self into some other, but rather attempting to rid herself and her world of demons. That is, rebirth cannot occur until after the demons have been exorcised. In all three of these poems, the possibilities of the individual are very much tied to those of her society.

Purity, which is what exorcism aims at, is for Plath an ambiguous concept. On the one hand it means integrity of self, wholeness rather than fragmentation, as unspoiled state of being, rest, perfection, aesthetic beauty, and loss of self through transformation into some reborn other. On the other hand, it also means absence, isolation, blindness, a kind of autism which shuts out the world, stasis and death, and a loss of self through dispersal into some other. In "Lady Lazarus" and "Fever 103°" the emphasis is on exorcising the poet's previous selves, though within a social context that makes that unlikely. "Daddy," however, is a purification of the world; in "Daddy" it is the various avatars of the other—the male figure who represents the patriarchal society she lives in—that are being exorcised. In all three cases, the exorcism is violent and, perhaps, provisional. Does she believe, in any of these cases, that a rebirth under such conditions is really possible, that an exorcism is truly taking place, that once the allegory is reenacted, she will be rid of it? The more the speaker of the poems defines her situation as desperate, the more violent and vengeful becomes the agent of purification and transformation. All three of these poems are retaliatory fantasies: in "Lady Lazarus" she swallows men, in "Fever 103°" she leaves them behind, in "Daddy" she kills them. . . .

STEVEN GOULD AXELROD

From *Jealous Gods**

[Although "Daddy"] has traditionally been read as "personal" (Aird 78)[1] or "confessional" (M. L. Rosenthal 82),[2] Margaret Homans has more recently suggested that it concerns a woman's dislocated relations to speech (*Women Writers* 220–21).[3] Plath herself introduced it on the BBC as the opposite of confession, as a constructed fiction: "Here is a poem spoken by a girl with an Electra complex. Her father died while she thought he was God. Her case is complicated by the fact that her father was also a Nazi and her mother very possibly part Jewish. In the daughter the two strains marry and paralyze each other—she has to act out the awful little allegory once over before she is free of it" (*CP* 293).[4] We might interpret this preface as an accurate retelling of the poem; or we might regard it as a case of an author's estrangement from her text, on the order of Coleridge's preface to "Kubla Khan" in which he claims to be unable to finish the poem, having forgotten what it was about. However we interpret Plath's preface, we must agree that "Daddy" is dramatic and allegorical, since its details depart freely from the facts of her biography. In this poem she again figures her unresolved conflicts with paternal authority as a textual issue. Significantly, her father was a published writer, and his successor, her husband, was also a writer. Her preface asserts that the poem concerns a young woman's paralyzing self-division, which she can defeat only through allegorical representation. Recalling that paralysis was one of Plath's main tropes for literary incapacity, we begin to see that the poem evokes the female poet's anxiety of authorship and specifically Plath's strategy of delivering herself from that anxiety by making it the topic of her discourse. Viewed from this perspective, "Daddy" enacts the woman poet's struggle with "daddy-poetry." It represents her effort to eject the "buried male muse" from her invention process and the "jealous gods" from her audience (*J* 223;[5] *CP* 179).

Plath wrote "Daddy" several months after Hughes left her, on the day she learned that he had agreed to a divorce (October 12, 1962). George Brown and Tirril Harris have shown that early loss makes one especially vulnerable to subsequent loss (Bowlby 250–59),[6] and Plath seems to have defended against depression by almost literally throwing herself into her poetry. She followed "Daddy" with a host of poems that she considered her greatest achievement to date: "Medusa," "The Jailer," "Lady Lazarus," "Ariel," the bee sequence, and others. The letters she wrote to her mother and brother on the day of "Daddy," and then again four days later, brim with a sense of artistic self-discovery: "Writing like mad.... Terrific stuff, as if domesticity had choked me" (*LH* 466).[7] Composing

---

* From Steven Gould Axelrod, *Sylvia Plath: The Wound and the Cure of Words* (Baltimore: Johns Hopkins University Press, 1990), pp. 51–70, 237. Unless otherwise indicated, all notes are Axelrod's.
1. Eileen Aird, *Sylvia Plath: Her Life and Work* (New York: Harper & Row, 1973).
2. M. L. Rosenthal, *The New Poets: American and British Poetry since World War II* (London: Oxford University Press, 1967).
3. Margaret Homans, *Women Writers and Poetic Identity: Dorothy Wordsworth, Emily Brontë, and Emily Dickinson* (Princeton: Princeton University Press, 1980).   4. *CP = The Collected Poems.*   5. *J = The Journals.*
6. John Bowlby, *Attachment and Loss,* III: *Loss: Sadness and Depression* (London: Hogarth, 1980).
7. *LH = Letters Home.*

at the "still blue, almost eternal hour before the baby's cry, before the glassy music of the milkman, settling his bottles" (quoted in Alvarez, *Savage God* 21),[8] she experienced an "enormous" surge in creative energy (*LH* 467). Yet she also expressed feelings of misery: "The half year ahead seems like a lifetime, and the half behind an endless hell" (*LH* 468). She was again contemplating things German: a trip to the Austrian Alps, a renewed effort to learn the language. If "German" was Randall Jarrell's "favorite country," it was not hers, yet it returned to her discourse like clock work at times of psychic distress. Clearly Plath was attempting to find and to evoke in her art what she could not find or communicate in her life. She wished to compensate for her fragmenting social existence by investing herself in her texts: "Hope, when free, to write myself out of this hole" (*LH* 466). Desperately eager to sacrifice her "flesh," which was "wasted," to her "mind and spirit," which were "fine" (*LH* 470), she wrote "Daddy" to demonstrate the existence of her voice, which had been silent or subservient for so long. She wrote it to prove her "genius" (*LH* 468).

Plath projected her struggle for textual identity onto the figure of a partly Jewish young woman who learns to express her anger at the patriarch and at his language of male mastery, which is as foreign to her as German, as "obscene" as murder (st. 6), and as meaningless as "gobbledygoo" (st. 9). The patriarch's death "off beautiful Nauset" (st. 3) recalls Plath's journal entry in which she associated the "green seaweeded water" at "Nauset Light" with "the deadness of a being . . . who no longer creates" (*J* 164). Daddy's deadness—suggesting Plath's unwillingness to let her father, her education, her library, or her husband inhibit her any longer—inspires the poem's speaker to her moment of illumination. At a basic level, "Daddy" concerns its own violent, transgressive birth as a text, its origin in a culture that regards it as illegitimate—a judgment the speaker hurls back on the patriarch himself when she labels *him* a bastard (st. 16). Plath's unaccommodating worldview, which was validated by much in her childhood and adult experience, led her to understand literary tradition not as an expanding universe of beneficial influence (as depicted in Eliot's "Tradition and the Individual Talent") but as a closed universe in which every addition required a corresponding subtraction—a Spencerian agon in which only the fittest survived. If Plath's speaker was to be born as a poet, a patriarch must die.

As in "The Colossus," the father here appears as a force or an object rather than as a person. Initially he takes the form of an immense "black shoe," capable of stamping on his victim (st. 1). Immediately thereafter he becomes a marble "statue" (st. 2), cousin to the monolith of the earlier poem. He then transforms into Nazi Germany (st. 6–7, 9–10), the archetypal totalitarian state. When the protagonist mentions Daddy's "boot in the face" (st. 10), she may be alluding to Orwell's comment in *1984*, "If you want a picture of the future, imagine a boot stomping on a human face—forever" (3.3). Eventually the father declines in stature from God (st. 2) to a devil (st. 11) to a dying vampire (st. 15). Perhaps he shrinks under the force of his victim's denunciation, which de-creates him as a power as it creates him as figure. But whatever his size, he never assumes human dimensions, aspirations, and relations—except when posing as a teacher in a photograph (st. 11). Like the colossus, he remains figurative and symbolic, not individual.

8. A. Alvarez, *The Savage God: A Study of Suicide* (1971; New York, Bantam, 1973).

Nevertheless, the male figure of "Daddy" does differ significantly from that of "The Colossus." In the earlier poem, which emphasizes his lips, mouth, throat, tongue, and voice, the colossus allegorically represents the power of speech, however fragmented and resistant to the protagonist's ministrations. In the later poem Daddy remains silent, apart from the gobbledygoo attributed to him once (st. 9). He uses his mouth primarily for biting and for drinking blood. The poem emphasizes his feet and, implicitly, his phallus. He is a "black shoe" (st. 1), a statue with "one gray toe" (st. 2), a "boot" (st. 10). The speaker, estranged from him by fear, could never tell where he put his "foot," his "root" (st. 5). Furthermore, she is herself silenced by his shoe: "I never could talk to you" (st. 5). Daddy is no "male muse" (*J* 223), not even one in ruins, but frankly a male censor. His boot in the face of "every woman" is presumably lodged in her mouth (st. 10). He stands for all the elements in the literary situation and in the female ephebe's internalization of it, that prevent her from producing any words at all, even copied or subservient ones. Appropriately, Daddy can be killed only by being stamped on: he lives and dies by force, not language. If "The Colossus" tells a tale of the patriarch's speech, his grunts and brays, "Daddy" tells a tale of the daughter's effort to speak.

Thus we are led to another important difference between the two poems. The "I" of "The Colossus" acquires her identity only through serving her "father," whereas the "I" of "Daddy" actuates her gift only through opposition to him. The latter poem precisely inscribes the plot of Plath's dream novel of 1958: "a girl's search for her dead father—for an outside authority which must be developed, instead, from the inside" (*J* 258). As the child of a Nazi, the girl could "hardly speak" (st. 6), but as a Jew she begins "to talk" and to acquire an identity (st. 7). In Plath's allegory, the outsider Jew corresponds to "the rebel, the artist, the odd" (*JP* 55),[9] and particularly to the woman artist. Otto Rank's *Beyond Psychology*,[1] which had a lasting influence on her, explicitly compares women to Jews, since "woman . . . has suffered from the very beginning a fate similar to that of the Jew, namely, suppression, slavery, confinement, and subsequent persecution" (287–88). Rank, whose discourse I would consider tainted by anti-Semitism, argues that Jews speak a language of pessimistic "self-hatred" that differs essentially from the language of the majority cultures in which they find themselves (191, 281–84). He analogously, though more sympathetically, argues that woman speaks in a language different from man's, and that as a result of man's denial of woman's world, "woman's 'native tongue' has hitherto been unknown or at least unheard" (248). Although Rank's essentializing of woman's "nature" lapses into the sexist clichés of his time ("intuitive," "irrational" [249]), his idea of linguistic difference based on gender and his analogy between Jewish and female speech seem to have embedded themselves in the substructure of "Daddy" (and in many of Plath's other texts as well). For Plath, as later for Adrienne Rich, the Holocaust and the patriarchy's silencing of women were linked outcomes of the masculinist interpretation of the world. Political insurrection and female self-assertion also interlaced symbolically. In "Daddy," Plath's speaker finds her voice and motive by identifying herself as antithetical to her Fascist father. Rather than getting the colossus "glued" and properly jointed, she wishes to stick herself

9. *JP = Johnny Panic and the Bible of Dreams.*
1. Otto Rank, *Beyond Psychology* (Baltimore: Johns Hopkins University Press, 1990).

"together with glue" (st. 13), an act that seems to require her father's dismemberment. Previously devoted to the patriarch—both in "The Colossus" and in memories evoked in "Daddy" of trying to "get back" to him (st. 12)—she now seeks only to escape from him and to see him destroyed.

Plath has unleashed the anger, normal in mourning as well as in revolt, that she suppressed in the earlier poem. But she has done so at a cost. Let us consider her childlike speaking voice. The language of "Daddy," beginning with its title, is often regressive. The "I" articulates herself by moving backward in time, using the language of nursery rhymes and fairy tales (the little old woman who lived in a shoe, the black man of the forest). Such language accords with a child's conception of the world, not an adult's. Plath's assault on the language of "daddy-poetry" has turned inward, on the language of her own poem, which teeters precariously on the edge of a preverbal abyss—represented by the eerie, keening "oo" sound with which a majority of the verses end. And then let us consider the play on "through" at the poem's conclusion. Although that last line allows for multiple readings, one interpretation is that the "I" has unconsciously carried out her father's wish: her discourse, by transforming itself into cathartic oversimplifications, has undone itself.

Yet the poem does contain its verbal violence by means more productive than silence. In a letter to her brother, Plath referred to "Daddy" as "gruesome" (*LH* 472), while on almost the same day she described it to A. Alvarez as a piece of "light verse" (Alvarez, *Beyond* 56).[2] She later read it on the BBC in a highly ironic tone of voice. The poem's unique spell derives from its rhetorical complexity: its variegated and perhaps bizarre fusion of the horrendous and the comic. As Uroff has remarked, it both shares and remains detached from the fixation of its protagonist (159).[3] The protagonist herself seems detached from her own fixation. She is "split in the most complex fashion," as Plath wrote of Ivan Karamazov[4] in her Smith College honors thesis. Plath's speaker uses potentially self-mocking melodramatic terms to describe both her opponent ("so black no sky could squeak through" [st. 10]) and herself ("poor and white" [st. 1]). While this aboriginal speaker quite literally expresses black-and-white thinking, her civilized double possesses a sensibility sophisticated enough to subject such thinking to irony. Thus the poem expresses feelings that it simultaneously parodies—it may be parodying the very idea of feeling. The tension between erudition and simplicity in the speaker's voice appears in her pairings that juxtapose adult with childlike diction: "breathe or Achoo," "your Luftewaffe, your gobbledygoo" (st. 1, 9). She can expound such adult topics as Taroc packs, Viennese beer, and Tyrolean snowfall; can specify death camps by name; and can employ an adult vocabulary of "recover," "ancestress," "Aryan," *"Meinkampf,"* "obscene," and "bastard." Yet she also has recourse to a more primitive lexicon that includes "chuffing," "your fat black heart," and "my pretty red heart." She proves herself capable of careful intellectual discriminations ("so I never could tell" [st. 5]), conventionalized description ("beautiful Nauset" [st. 3]), and moral analogy ("if I've killed one man, I've killed two" [st. 15], while also exhibiting regressive fantasies (vam-

---

2. A. Alvarez, *Beyond All This Fiddle* (London: Allen Lane-Penguin, 1968).

3. Margaret Dickie Uroff, *Sylvia Plath and Ted Hughes* (Urbana: University of Illinois Press, 1979).

4. A character in Fyodor Dostoyevsky's novel *The Brothers Karamazov* who suffers debilitating guilt for having wished for his father's death [Editor's note].

pires), repetitions ("wars, wars, wars" [st. 4]), and inarticulateness ("panzer-man, panzer-man, O You—" [st. 9]). She oscillates between calm reflection ("You stand at the blackboard, daddy, / In the picture I have of you" [st. 11]) and mad incoherence ("Ich, ich, ich, ich" [st. 6]). Her sophisticated language puts her wild language in an ironic perspective, removing the discourse from the control of the archaic self who understands experience only in extreme terms.

The ironies in "Daddy" proliferate in unexpected ways, however. When the speaker proclaims categorically that "every woman adores a Fascist" (st. 10), she is subjecting her victimization to irony by suggesting that sufferers choose, or at least accommodate themselves to, their suffering. But she is also subjecting her authority to irony, since her claim about "every woman" is transparently false. It simply parodies patriarchal commonplaces, such as those advanced by Helene Deutsch concerning "feminine masochism" (192–99, 245–85).[5] The adult, sophisticated self seems to be speaking here: Who else would have the confidence to make a sociological generalization? Yet the content of the assertion, if taken straightforwardly, returns us to the regressive self who is dominated by extravagant emotions she cannot begin to understand. Plath's mother wished that Plath would write about "decent, courageous people" (LH 477), and she herself heard an inner voice demanding that she be a perfect "paragon" in her language and feeling (J 176). But in the speaker of "Daddy," she inscribed the opposite of such a paragon: a divided self whose veneer of civilization is breached and infected by unhealthy instincts.

Plath's irony cuts both ways. At the same time that the speaker's sophisticated voice undercuts her childish voice, reducing its melodrama to comedy, the childish or maddened voice undercuts the pretensions of the sophisticated voice, revealing the extremity of suffering masked by its ironies. While demonstrating the inadequacy of thinking and feeling in opposites, the poem implies that such a mode can locate truths denied more complex cognitive and affective systems. The very moderation of the normal adult intelligence, its tolerance of ambiguity, its defenses against the primal energies of the id, results in falsification. Reflecting Schiller's idea that the creative artist experiences a "momentary and passing madness" (quoted by Freud in a passage of The Interpretation of Dreams [193][6] that Plath underscored), "Daddy" gives voice to that madness. Yet the poem's sophisticated awareness, its comic vision, probably wins out in the end, since the poem concludes by curtailing the power of its extreme discourse. . . . Furthermore, Plath distanced herself from the poem's aboriginal voice by introducing her text as "a poem spoken by a girl with an Electra complex"—that is, as a study of the girl's pathology rather than her father's—and as an allegory that will "free" her from that pathology. She also distanced herself by reading the poem in a tone that emphasized its irony. And finally, she distanced herself by laying the poem's wild voice permanently to rest after October. The aboriginal vision was indeed purged. "Daddy" represents not Dickinson's madness that is divinest sense, but rather an entry into a style of discourse and a mastery of it. The poem realizes the trope of suffering by means of an inherent irony that both questions and validates the trope in the same gestures, and that finally allows the speaker

5. Helen Deutsch, The Psychology of Women, I: Girlhood (1944; repr. New York: Bantam, 1973).
6. Sigmund Freud, The Interpretation of Dreams, ed. James Strachey, Standard Edition, IV (1900; New York: Norton, 1976).

to conclude the discourse and to remove herself from the trope with a sense of completion rather than wrenching, since the irony was present from the very beginning.

Plath's poetic revolt in "Daddy" liberated her pent-up creativity, but the momentary success sustained her little more than self-sacrifice had done. "Daddy" became another stage in her development, an unrepeatable experiment, a vocal opening that closed itself at once. The poem is not only an elegy for the power of "daddy-poetry" but for the powers of speech Plath discovered in composing it.

When we consider "Daddy" generically, a further range of implications presents itself. Although we could profitably consider the poem as the dramatic monologue Plath called it in her BBC broadcast, let us regard it instead as the kind of poem most readers have taken it to be: a domestic poem. I have chosen this term, rather than M. L. Rosenthal's better-known "confessional poem" or the more neutral "autobiographical poem," because "confessional poem" implies a confession rather than a making (though Steven Hoffman[7] and Lawrence Kramer[8] have recently indicated the mode's conventions) and because "autobiographical poem" is too general for our purpose. I shall define the domestic poem as one that represents and comments on a protagonist's relationship to one or more family members, usually a parent, child, or spouse. To focus our discussion even further, I shall emphasize poetry that specifically concerns a father.

. . . In the 1950s the "domestic poem" proper appeared on the scene, with its own conventions and expectations, and with its own complex cultural and literary reasons for being. Perhaps the precursive poems made the genre's eventual flowering inevitable, while its precise timing depended on a reaction against modernism's aesthetic of impersonality. Theodore Roethke wrote several early poems that initiated the genre: "My Papa's Waltz" (1948), "The Lost Son" (1948), and "Where Knock Is Open Wide" (1951). Lowell's "Life Studies" sequence (1959) was, and is, the genre's most prominent landmark. Other poems in the genre include John Berryman's *The Dream Songs* (1969); Frank Bidart's "Golden State" (1973) and "Confessional" (1983); Robert Duncan's "My Mother Would Be a Falconress" (1968); Allen Ginsberg's *Kaddish* (1960); Randall Jarrell's "The Lost World" (1965); Maxine Kumin's "The Thirties Revisited" (1975), "My Father's Neckties" (1978), and "Marianne, My Mother, and Me" (1989); Stanley Kunitz's "Father and Son" (1958) and "The Testing Tree" (1971); Lowell's "To Mother" (1977), "Robert T. S. Lowell" (1977), and "Unwanted" (1977); James Merrill's "Scenes of Childhood" (1962); Adrienne Rich's "After Dark" (1966); Anne Sexton's "Division of the Parts" (1960) and "The Death of the Fathers" (1972); W. D. Snodgrass' "Heart's Needle" (1959); Diane Wakoski's "The Father of My Country" (1968); and of course Sylvia Plath's "Daddy" (1962). In all these poems, the parent-child relationship serves as a locus for psychological investigation. In many of them it also serves as a means of representing the acquisition of poetic identity and of exploring the bounds of textuality itself. Because later writers

7. Steven Hoffman, "Impersonal Personalism: The Making of a Confessional Poetic," *English Literary History* 45 (Winter 1978): 687–709.

8. Lawrence Kramer, "Freud and the Skunks: Genre and Language in *Life Studies*," in *Robert Lowell: Essays on the Poetry*, ed. Steven Gould Axelrod and Helen Deese (New York: Cambridge University Press, 1986).

were conscious of the Roethke-Lowell domestic poem as at least a genre in embryo, they chose to use its features, or perhaps the power of the genre was such that the features chose them. The "domestic poem" became a system of signs in which each individual text's adherence to the system and deviations within the system produced its particular literary meaning.

In 1959 Plath did not consciously attempt to write in the domestic poem genre, perhaps because she was not yet ready to assume her majority. Her journal entries of that period bristle with an impatience at herself that may derive from this reluctance. She may have feared asserting her "I am I am I am," which seemed to carry with it a countervailing impulse of self-retribution. But by fall 1962, when she had already lost so much, she was ready to chance tackling poetic tradition, and specifically her chief male instructors, Roethke and Lowell. In "Daddy" she achieved her victory in two ways. First, as we have seen, she symbolically assaults a father figure who is identified with male control of language. All her anxiety of influence comes to the fore in the poem: her sense of belatedness, her awareness of constraint, her fears of inadequacy, her furious need to overcome her dependency, her guilt at her own aggressivity. Since the precursors "do not do / Any more" (st. 1), she wishes to escape their paralyzing influence and to empty the "bag full of God" that has kept her tongue stuck in her jaw for so long (st. 2, 5). The father whose power she attacks is not simply Roethke or Lowell, or even Hughes or Otto Plath, but a literary character who includes reference to all of them as categories of masculine authority. Although the Daddy of poetry has already "died" (st. 2)—the fate of all published texts in Plath's postromantic perspective—the speaker must symbolically "kill" him from her own discourse. The poem ironically depicts poetry as both an aggression and a suicide. The female ephebe herself becomes a "brute" in the act of voicing (st. 10), just as have her teachers before her. But the aggression of her speech yields to the self-annihilation of language. By the end of the poem she too, like her male precursors, is "through." The speaker's textual life will be misread on innumerable occasions in innumerable ways, whereas her own misreading and miswriting of the precursors is finished. In its conclusion, the poem acknowledges its alienation from itself, confessing the transitoriness of its unbounded power.

In addition to killing the father in its fictional plot, the poem seeks to discredit the forefathers through its status as poetic act. Taking a genre established by Roethke and Lowell, "Daddy" fundamentally alters it through antithesis and parody. Like all strong poems, it transforms its genre and therefore the way we perceive the precursive examples, making them seem not fulfillments but anticipations. Thus the later work projects its anxiety retrospectively back through its predecessors. Haunted by fears of inadequacy and redundancy, it seeks to make the earlier poems seem incompetent by comparison—a kind of juvenilia in the career of the genre, to represent the final possible stroke, or at the very least to inaugurate some new and important genre, of which the whole domestic genre was but a foreshadowing.

This point comes clearer if we compare "Daddy" with two analogues, Roethke's "The Lost Son" (1948) and Lowell's "Commander Lowell" (1959). In the Freudian drama of "The Lost Son," the protagonist subjectively relives his childhood fears and fantasies. Like the speaker of the companion piece, "My Papa's Waltz," he is still enmeshed in the family romance, remembering the father ambivalently as powerful, protective, and threatening. After locating himself at his father's grave, where he feels both grief and estrangement (in a scene that adumbrates "Electra on Azalea Path"), he descends into his unconscious, seeking, as Roethke later explained, "some clue to existence" (*Poet* 38).[9] He encounters his death wish, his memory of his father as "Father Fear," his sexual anxieties, and finally the "dark swirl" of a blackout, after which a childhood memory of his "Papa" shouting "order" in German returns him to consciousness. Although the figure of "Papa" blends earthly and heavenly father (*Poet* 39), he also symbolizes the superego, restoring order to a psyche and a poem that had fallen into chaos. At the poem's conclusion, as the "lost son" waits for his "understandable spirit" to revive, he appears to be purged, though not cured, of the conflicts that incapacitated him.

The speaker of "Commander Lowell," in contrast, is objective, precise, and witty. His discourse reflects a detached perspective on the past rather than a psychic reimmersion in it. He portrays his father as one who threatened him only through weakness. This father "was nothing to shout / about to the summer colony at 'Matt' "; took "four shots with his putter to sink his putt"; sang "Anchors Aweigh" in the bathtub; was fired from his job; and squandered his inheritance. Whereas Roethke's poem represents a cathartic experience, Lowell's converts chaotic feelings into intellectual irony. Whereas Roethke's poem can be read as an allegory of man's relationship to God or as a model of the Freudian psyche, Lowell's remains a realistic narrative, though it does suggest the cultural and financial decline of a social class.

Plath's poem combines features of both of these precursors: Roethke's evocation of a German-speaking authoritarian with Lowell's sarcastic deflation of a man without qualities; Roethke's subjective anguish with Lowell's social comedy. Like Roethke's Papa, Plath's title character is an intimidating patriarch; like Lowell's Father, he is a buffoon ("big as a Frisco seal"). Finally, Plath's poem, like those of her predecessors, has little to do with psychological cure: the speaker's defenses remain in place. But in a deeper sense, "Daddy" swerves sharply from its precursors, curtailing their power. It turns the psychological depth of Roethke's poem and the ironically detached surface of Lowell's poem into a fury of denunciation, an extravagance of emotion, an exaggeration of acts and effects, perhaps revealing the subtexts of both precursors. If in a sense the texts by Roethke and Lowell constitute what Ned Lukacher[1] might term the primal scene of "Daddy," the latter poem's raw intensity succeeds in reversing the relationship, making itself resemble *their* primal scene. It unmasks Roethke's implicitly oppressive father figure as a monster and Lowell's sophisticated comedy as slapstick. It transforms the domestic genre alternately into a horror show, encapsulating every political, cultural, and familial atrocity of the age, and a theater of cruelty, evoking nervous laughter. "Daddy" takes the genre as far as it can go—and then further.

9. *On the Poet and His Craft: Selected Prose of Theodore Roethke*, ed. Ralph J. Mills, Jr. (Seattle and London: University of Washington Press, 1965).

1. Ned Lukacher, *Primal Scenes: Literature, Philosophy, Psychoanalysis* (Ithaca and London: Cornell University Press, 1986).

SUGGESTIONS FOR WRITING

1. In his essay "Dying Is an Art," George Steiner argues that Plath's poems "are too honest, they have cost too much, to be yielded to myth." Do you think that "Daddy" is an "honest" poem? Write an essay exploring what "honesty" means in modern poetry and whether or not "Daddy" is an "honest" poem. Draw on the critical essays found in this chapter, and be sure to cite them as appropriate.

2. Several of the critics in this chapter make competing claims about the meaning and significance of the form of "Daddy," particularly its nursery-rhyme-like qualities. Using those claims as a springboard, write an essay in which you make your own argument about the relationship between form and content in "Daddy."

3. In "The Plath Celebration: A Partial Dissent," Irving Howe argues, "There is something monstrous, utterly disproportionate, when tangled emotions about one's father are deliberately compared with the historical fate of the European Jews." Is Plath's personal, artistic use of a great historical tragedy truly "monstrous," as Howe says, or is it simply a case of what George Steiner calls "subtle larceny"? Write an essay in which you discuss whether or not it is appropriate for an artist to use the sufferings of others as material for personal artistic expression.

4. Broe, Kroll, Homans, Annas, and Axelrod all claim that "Daddy" portrays the speaker's attempt to successfully "exorcise" one demon or another, though they disagree rather dramatically both about what that demon is and about whether and how that exorcism (not the poem) succeeds. Using their arguments as a starting point, write an essay in which you offer your own interpretation of the process of exorcism enacted in the poem.

5. In "Sylvia Plath," A. Alvarez quotes Plath's own interpretation of "Daddy" as a poem "spoken by a girl with an Electra complex." Research the term "Electra complex," which originated with Sigmund Freud. Is it useful to interpret "Daddy" through the lens of the "Electra complex"? Citing critics included in this chapter, write an essay in which you discuss Plath's Freudian explanation of "Daddy" and, more generally, the reliability of artists' interpretations of their own works.

6. Write an essay comparing Plath's "Daddy" to at least two of the "domestic poems" mentioned by Axelrod in "Jealous Gods." To what extent do you agree and disagree with Axelrod's interpretation of the similarities and differences between "Daddy" and these other poems by Plath's contemporaries?

7. Is "Daddy" a "feminist" poem? Does examination of the poem from a feminist viewpoint, like that of Margaret Homans, help to illuminate the poem, or does it obscure understanding? Citing the essays by Homans and other critics in this chapter, write an essay in which you discuss a feminist reading of "Daddy" and then argue for or against its validity.

14 THE PROCESS OF CREATION

Poems do not write themselves. Even if the idea for a poem comes in a flash (as it sometimes does), poets often struggle to get the final effect just right. For some poems that means draft after draft, and sometimes poets write more than one version of a poem and allow the different versions to compete as rival authorized texts, or poets develop a text that seems to be complete and set but then later alter it in some crucial way. Often a study of the manuscript or of the several drafts suggests the various kinds of decisions a poet may make as a poem moves toward its final form. In this chapter you will find examples of several poems as they take shape—or take different forms—in the poet's mind.

The first example involves early drafts of the first stanza of Richard Wilbur's "Love Calls Us to the Things of This World," which in its finished form is printed right after the drafts. Wilbur is one of the most careful craftsmen writing today, and in the early drafts of the first stanza we can see him moving toward the brilliant and surprising effects he achieves in the "final" version, that is, the version he decided to publish. Someone is just awaking, and through a window sees laundry on a clothesline blowing in the breeze. But he is not quite awake and not quite sure what he sees: his body and soul, the poet says playfully in lines 26 and 27, are not yet quite reunited, and he seems for a moment still sus-

I find laundry a great help to the conception of angels, and I suppose one thing I'm saying in ["Love Calls Us to the Things of This World"*] is that I don't really want to have much truck with angels who aren't in the laundry, who aren't involved in the everyday world. It's a poem against dissociated and abstracted spirituality.*

—RICHARD WILBUR

pended in a world of spirit and dream; the blowing clothes look like disembodied angels. Ultimately, the poem captures that sense of suspension between worlds, the uncertainty of where one is and what is happening in that first half-conscious moment when normal physical laws don't seem to apply. It is a delicate moment to catch, and in the six successive drafts printed below we can see the poet moving toward the more precise effect of the completed poem.

In the first three drafts the speaker seems to speak about himself—not quite right because that device makes him too conscious, and part of the basic effect of the finished poem involves a lack of consciousness and control. By the fourth draft "My eyes came open" has become "The eyes open," and the effect of being a little lost and unsure of identity is becoming clearer. Another major change in the early drafts is that the sound of the laundry pulley changes from "squeak" to "shriek" to "cry": the first two words capture the shrill sound of a moving pulley faithfully, but "cry" makes it seem personal and human, and now it is as if the pulleys were in fact calling the speaker from sleep. The image changes, too: in the first draft the world of sleep is a brothel, but that connotation is eliminated in later drafts, and instead by the sixth draft the "spirit" has become "soul" and is bodiless. Every new draft changes the conception just a little, and in the drafts printed here we can see effects gradually getting clearer in the poet's mind and falling into place. Notice how rhyme appears in draft and then disappears again, notice how the poet tries out and rejects words that don't have quite the right connotation: "wallow" (draft c), "frothing" (draft d), "rout" (draft f). In a detailed set of drafts like this one, we can see the poet weighing different visual and verbal possibilities, choosing every single word with care.

The other poems and passages similarly give us a chance to compare the effects of more than one version of a poem or passage. In several cases, a poem is "finished" in more than one version, and the poets invite us to choose among the competing versions instead of choosing one themselves. In each selection a few crucial words create significant differences in the text.

1. Early drafts of the first stanza of "Love Calls Us to the Things of This World," reprinted by permission of the author:

(a) My eyes came open to the squeak of pulleys
     My spirit, shocked from the brothel of itself

(b) My eyes came open to the shriek of pulleys,
     And the soul, spirited from its proper wallow,
     Hung in the air as bodiless and hollow

(c) My eyes came open to the pulleys' cry.
     The soul, spirited from its proper wallow,
     Hung in the air as bodiless and hollow
     As light that frothed upon the wall opposing;
     But what most caught my eyes at their unclosing
     Was two gray ropes that yanked across the sky.
     One after one into the window frame
     . . . the hosts of laundry came

(d)   The eyes open to a cry of pulleys,
     And the soul, so suddenly spirited from sleep,
     As morning sunlight frothing on the floor,
        While just outside the window
     The air is solid with a dance of angels.

(e)   The eyes open to a cry of pulleys,
     And spirited from sleep, the astounded soul
     Hangs for a moment bodiless and simple
     As dawn light in the moment of its breaking:
        Outside the open window
     The air is crowded with a

(f)   The eyes open to a cry of pulleys,
     And spirited from sleep, the astounded soul
     Hangs for a moment bodiless and simple
     As false dawn
        Outside the open window,

Their air is leaping with a rout of angels.
  Some are in bedsheets, some are in dresses,
  it does not seem to matter

Final version, 1956:

`CD`

The eyes open to a cry of pulleys,
And spirited from sleep, the astounded soul
Hangs for a moment bodiless and simple
As false dawn.
5   Outside the open window
  The morning air is all awash with angels.

  Some are in bed-sheets, some are in blouses,
Some are in smocks: but truly there they are.
Now they are rising together in calm swells
10 Of halcyon[1] feeling, filling whatever they wear
     With the deep joy of their impersonal breathing;
     Now they are flying in place,[2] conveying
The terrible speed of their omnipresence, moving
And staying like white water; and now of a sudden
15 They swoon down into so rapt a quiet
     That nobody seems to be there.
                                  The soul shrinks

     From all that it is about to remember,
From the punctual rape of every blessèd day,
20 And cries,
            "Oh, let there be nothing on earth but laundry,
Nothing but rosy hands in the rising steam
And clear dances done in the sight of heaven."

  Yet, as the sun acknowledges
25 With a warm look the world's hunks and colors,
     The soul descends once more in bitter love
To accept the waking body, saying now
In a changed voice as the man yawns and rises,

     "Bring them down from their ruddy gallows;
30 Let there be clean linen for the backs of thieves;
     Let lovers go fresh and sweet to be undone,
And the heaviest nuns walk in a pure floating
Of dark habits,
              keeping their difficult balance."

---

1. Serene.   2. Like planes in a formation.

2. Two versions of Keats's "Bright star! would I were stedfast as thou art!"

Original version, 1819:

> Bright star! would I were stedfast as thou art!
> Not in lone splendor hung amid the night;
> Not watching, with eternal lids apart,
> Like Nature's devout sleepless Eremite,
> 5 The morning waters at their priestlike task
> Of pure ablution round earth's human shores;
> Or, gazing on the new soft fallen mask
> Of snow upon the mountains and moors:—
> No;—yet still stedfast, still unchangeable.
> 10 Cheek-pillow'd on my Love's white ripening breast,
> To touch, for ever, its warm sink and swell,
> Awake, for ever, in a sweet unrest;
> To hear, to feel her tender taken breath,
> Half-passionless, and so swoon on to death.

Revised version, 1820:

> Bright star! would I were steadfast as thou art—
>   Not in lone splendor hung aloft the night
> And watching, with eternal lids apart,
>   Like nature's patient, sleepless Eremite,
> 5 The moving waters at their priestlike task
>   Of pure ablution round earth's human shores,
> Or gazing on the new soft fallen mask
>   Of snow upon the mountains and the moors—
>
> No—yet still steadfast, still unchangeable,
> 10   Pillowed upon my fair love's ripening breast,
> To feel for ever its soft fall and swell,
>   Awake for ever in a sweet unrest,
> Still, still to hear her tender-taken breath,
> And so live ever—or else swoon to death.

3. The following stanza was originally the first stanza of "Ode on Melancholy" (p. 349). Keats cancelled the stanza before publishing the ode.

> Though you should build a bark of dead men's bones,
>   And rear a phantom gibbet for a mast,
> Stitch creeds together for a sail, with groans
>   To fill it out, bloodstained and aghast;
> 5 Although your rudder be a Dragon's tail,
>   Long sever'd, yet still hard with agony,
>   Your cordage large uprootings from the skull
> Of bald Medusa: certes you would fail
>   To find the Melancholy, whether she
> 10   Dreameth in any isle of Lethe dull.

4. Manuscript and transcription of Keats's "To Autumn."

Manuscript:

Season of Mist and mellow fruitfulness,
Close bosom friend of the maturing sun;
Conspiring with him how to load and bless
The Vines with fruit that round the thatch eves run
   To bend with apples the mossd Cottage trees,
      And fill all fruits with sweetness to the core
         To swell the gourd, and plump the hazle shells
With a white kernel; to set budding more
   And still more, later flowers for the bees,
      Until they think warm days will never cease
         For Summer has o'er brimm'd their clammy cells—

Who hath not seen thee oft amid thy stores?
Sometimes whoever seeks for thee may find
Thee sitting careless on a granary floor
Thy hair soft lifted by the winnowing wind
   Or on a half reap'd furrow sound asleep
      Dos'd with red poppies, while thy reaping hook
         Spares the next swath and all its twined flowers

Or on a half reap'd furrow sound asleep
Dos'd with the fume of poppies, while thy hook
Spares the next swath, and all its twined flowers;

And sometimes like a gleaner thou dost keep
   Steady thy laden head across the brook;
      Or by a Cyder-press with patient look
         Thou watchest the last oozing hours by hours

Season of Mists and mellow fruitfulness
  Close bosom friend of the naturring sun;
Conspiring with him how to load and bless
  The Vines with fruit that round the thatch eves run
5   To bend with apples the moss'd Cottage trees
    And fill all furuits with sweeness to the core
      To swell the gourd, and plump the hazle shells
  With a white kernel; to set budding more
  And still more later flowers for the bees
10   Until they think wam days with never cease
    For Summer has o'erbrimm'd their clammy cells—

              oft amid thy stores?
Who hath not seen thee? ~~for thy haunts are many~~
         abroad
Sometimes whoever seeks ~~for thee~~ may find
Thee sitting careless on a granary floorr
15   Thy hair soft lifted by the winnowing wind

                     ~~husky~~
~~While bright the Sun slants through the barn;~~
  ~~orr on a half reap d furrow sound asleep~~
~~Or sound asleep in a half reaped eld~~
  ~~Dose'd with read poppies; while thy reeping hook~~
~~Spares form Some slumbrous~~
20   ~~minutes while wam slumpers creep~~
Or on a half reap d furrow sound asleep
  Dos d with the fume of poppies, while thy hook
  Spares the next swath and all its twined ouers
~~Spares for some slumbrous minutes the next swath;~~
  And sometimes like a gleans thost dost keep
25   Steady thy laden head across the brook;
  Or by a Cyder-press with patent look
Thou watchest the last oozing hours by hours

5. Three versions of Alexander Pope's "Ode on Solitude."

1709 manuscript version:

Happy the man, who free from care,
The business and the noise of towns,
Contented breathes his native air,
    In his own grounds.

5 Whose herds with milk, whose fields with bread,
Whose flocks supply him with attire,
Whose trees in summer yield him shade,
    In winter fire.

Blest! who can unconcern'dly find
10 His years slide silently away,

In health of body, peace of mind,
    Quiet by day,

Repose at night; study and ease
Together mix'd; sweet recreation,
15 And innocence, which most does please,
    With meditation.

Thus let me live, unseen, unknown;
Thus unlamented let me die;
Steal from the world, and not a stone
20   Tell where I lie.

First printed version, 1717:

How happy he, who free from care,
The rage of courts, and noise of towns;
Contented breathes his native air,
    In his own grounds.
5 Whose herds with milk, whose fields with bread,
Whose flocks supply him with attire.
Whose trees in summer yield him shade,
    In winter fire.
Blest! who can unconcern'dly find
10 Hours, days, and years slide swift away,
In health of body, peace of mind,
    Quiet by day,
Sound sleep by night; study and ease
Together mix'd; sweet recreation,
15 And innocence, which most does please,
    With meditation.
Thus let me live, unheard, unknown;
Thus unlamented let me die;
Steal from the world, and not a stone
20   Tell where I lie.

Final version, 1736:

Happy the man, whose wish and care
A few paternal acres bound,
Content to breathe his native air,
    In his own ground.
5 Whose herds with milk, whose fields with bread,
Whose flocks supply him with attire,
Whose trees in summer yield him shade,
    In winter fire.
Blest! who can unconcern'dly find
10 Hours, days, and years slide soft away,
In health of body, peace of mind,
    Quiet by day,
Sound sleep by night; study and ease
Together mix'd; sweet recreation,
15 And innocence, which most does please,

With meditation.
Thus let me live, unseen, unknown;
Thus unlamented let me die;
Steal from the world, and not a stone
20   Tell where I lie.

6. This famous folk ballad was sung and recited in many variations; here are two written versions. Neither version can be dated precisely.

"O where ha' you been, Lord Randal, my son?
And where ha' you been, my handsome young man?"
"I ha' been at the greenwood; mother, mak my bed soon,
For I'm wearied wi' huntin', and fain wad[3] lie down."

5   "And wha met ye there, Lord Randal, my son?
And wha met you there, my handsome young man?"
"O I met wi' my true-love; mother, mak my bed soon,
For I'm wearied wi' huntin', and fain wad lie down."

"And what did she give you, Lord Randal, my son?
10 And what did she give you, my handsome young man?"
"Eels fried in a pan; mother, mak my bed soon,
For I'm wearied wi' huntin', and fain wad lie down."

"And wha gat your leavin's, Lord Randal, my son?
And wha gat your leavin's, my handsome young man?"
15 "My hawks and my hounds; mother, mak my bed soon,
For I'm wearied wi' huntin', and fain wad lie down."

"And what becam of them, Lord Randal, my son?
And what becam of them, my handsome young man?"
"They stretched their legs out and died; mother, mak my bed soon,
20 For I'm wearied wi' huntin', and fain wad lie down."

"O I fear you are poisoned, Lord Randal, my son!
I fear you are poisoned, my handsome young man!"
"O yes, I am poisoned; mother, mak my bed soon,
For I'm sick at the heart, and I fain wad lie down."

25 "What d'ye leave to your mother, Lord Randal, my son?
What d'ye leave to your mother, my handsome young man?"
"Four and twenty milk kye;[4] mother, mak my bed soon,
For I'm sick at the heart, and I fain wad lie down."

"What d'ye leave to your sister, Lord Randal, my son?
30 What d'ye leave to your sister, my handsome young man?"
"My gold and my silver; mother, mak my bed soon,
For I'm sick at the heart, and I fain wad lie down."

"What d'ye leave to your brother, Lord Randal, my son?
What d'ye leave to your brother, my handsome young man?"
35 "My houses and my lands; mother, mak my bed soon,
For I'm sick at the heart, and I fain wad lie down."

---

3. Would like to.   4. Cows.

"What d'ye leave to your true-love, Lord Randal, my son?
What d'ye leave to your true-love, my handsome young man?"
"I leave her hell and fire; mother, mak my bed soon,
40 For I'm sick at the heart, and I fain wad lie down."

Shorter version:

"O where hae ye been, Lord Randal, my son?
O where hae ye been, my handsome young man?"
"I hae been to the wild wood; mother, make my bed soon,
For I'm weary wi' hunting, and fain wald lie down."

5 "Where gat ye your dinner, Lord Randal, my son?
Where gat ye your dinner, my handsome young man?"
"I dined wi' my true-love; mother, make my bed soon,
For I'm weary wi' hunting, and fain wald lie down."

"What gat ye to your dinner, Lord Randal, my son?
10 What gat ye to your dinner, my handsome young man?"
"I gat eels boiled in broo; mother, make my bed soon,
For I'm weary wi' hunting, and fain wald lie down."

"What became of your bloodhounds, Lord Randal, my son?
What became of your bloodhounds, my handsome young man?"
15 "O they swelled and they died; mother, make my bed soon,
For I'm weary wi' hunting, and fain wald lie down."

"O I fear ye are poisoned, Lord Randal, my son!
O I fear ye are poisoned, my handsome young man!"
"O yes! I am poisoned; mother, make my bed soon,
20 For I'm sick at the heart, and I fain wald lie down."

7. "Poetry," by Marianne Moore, appears on page 276 in a version that was originally published in 1921. Here are two later versions.

The 1925 version:

I too, dislike it:
there are things that are important beyond all this fiddle.
The bat, upside down; the elephant pushing,
the tireless wolf under a tree,
5 the base-ball fan, the statistician—
"business documents and schoolbooks"—
these phenomena are pleasing,
but when they have been fashioned
into that which is unknowable,
10 we are not entertained.
It may be said of all of us
that we do not admire what we cannot understand;
enigmas are not poetry.

The version Moore chose to print in her *Complete Poems* in 1967:

I, too, dislike it.
    Reading it, however, with a perfect contempt for it, one discovers
in it after all, a place for the genuine.

8. Two versions of Emily Dickinson's "Safe in their Alabaster Chambers—":

1859 version:

> Safe in their Alabaster Chambers—
> Untouched by Morning
> And untouched by Noon—
> Sleep the meek members of the Resurrection—
> 5 Rafter of satin,
> And Roof of stone.
>
> Light laughs the breeze
> In her Castle above them—
> Babbles the Bee in a stolid Ear,
> 10 Pipe the Sweet Birds in ignorant cadence—
> Ah, what sagacity perished here!

1861 version:

> Safe in their Alabaster Chambers—
> Untouched by Morning—
> And untouched by Noon—
> Lie the meek members of the Resurrection—
> 5 Rafter of Satin—and Roof of Stone!
>
> Grand go the Years—in the Crescent—above them—
> Worlds scoop their Arcs—
> And Firmaments—row—
> Diadems—drop—and Doges—surrender—
> 10 Soundless as dots—on a Disc of Snow—

9. Drafts of "The Tyger" by William Blake. The final version, published in 1790, can be found on page 56.

First draft:[5]

> The Tyger

1

> Tyger Tyger burning bright
> In the forests of the night
> What immortal hand or eye
> Dare ~~Could~~ frame thy fearful symmetry

2

> Burnt in
> ~~In what~~ distant deeps or skies
> ~~The cruel~~ ~~Burnt the~~ fire of thine eyes
> On what wings dare he aspire
> What the hand dare sieze the fire

3

> And what shoulder & what art
> Could twist the sinews of thy heart

---

5. These drafts have been taken from a notebook used by William Blake called the Rossetti MS because it was once owned by Dante Gabriel Rossetti, the Victorian poet and painter; David V. Erdman's edition of *The Notebook of William Blake* (1973) contains a photographic facsimile. The stanza numbers were written by Blake in the manuscript.

And when they heart began to beat
What dread hand & what dread feet

~~Could fetch it from the furnace deep~~
~~And in thy horrid ribs dare steep~~
~~In the well of sanguine woe~~
~~In what clay & what mould~~
Were thy eyes of fury rolld

~~Where~~   ~~where~~
4   ~~What~~ the hammer ~~what~~ the chain
In what furnace was thy brain

                                        dread grasp
What the anvil what ~~the arm~~ ~~arm~~ ~~grasp~~ ~~clasp~~
Dare ~~Could~~ its deadly terrors ~~clasp~~ ~~grasp~~ clasp

6   Tyger Tyger burning bright
In the forests of the night
What immortal hand & eye
          frame
Dare ~~form~~ thy fearful symmetry

Trial stanzas:
Burnt in distant deeps or skies
The cruel fire of thine eye,
Could heart descend or wings aspire
What the hand dare sieze the fire

          dare he ~~smile~~ ~~laugh~~
5 3̶ And ~~did he laugh~~ his work to see
          ankle
What the ~~shoulder~~ ~~what the knee~~
          Dare
4 ~~Did~~ he who made the lamb make thee
1 When the stars threw down their spears
2 And waterd heaven with their tears

Second full draft:
Tyger Tyger burning bright
In the forests of the night
What Immortal hand & eye
Dare frame thy fearful symmetry

And what shoulder & what art
Could twist the sinews of thy heart
And when thy heart began to beat
What dread hand & what dread feet

When the stars threw down their spears
And waterd heaven with their tears
Did he smile his work to see
Did he who made the lamb make thee

Tyger Tyger burning bright
In the forests of the night
What immortal hand & eye
Dare frame thy fearful symmetry

15 EVALUATING POETRY

How do you know a good poem when you see one? This is not an easy question to answer—partly because deciding about the *value* of poems is a complex, difficult, and often lengthy process, and partly because no single and absolute criterion will measure texts and neatly divide the good from the not so good. People who long for a nice, infallible sorter—some test that will automatically pick out the best poems and distinguish variations of quality much as a litmus test separates acids from bases—often bemoan the "relativity" in evaluating poems. But even if no simple and absolute standard exists, we nevertheless can make distinctions. Some poems are better—that is, more consistently effective with talented and experienced readers—than others. Even if we cannot sensibly rate poems on a 1-to-10 scale or universally agree on the excellence of a single poem, we still can set out criteria to help readers who have not yet developed confidence in their own judgments. As a reader, of course, you don't need to spend all your time asking about quality and being judgmental about poetry. But because life isn't long enough to read everything, you often must separate those poems likely to be worth your time from those that aren't. Besides, the process of sorting—in which you begin to articulate your own judgments and poetic values—can help make you a better reader and a more informed, sophisticated, and wiser person. Evaluating poems can be, among other things, a way to learn about yourself, for what you like in poetry says a lot about where your values lie.

> *Poetry is a language that tells us, through a more or less emotional reaction, something that cannot be said.*
>
> —EDWIN ARLINGTON ROBINSON

"I like it." That simple, unreflective statement about a poem can begin your articulation of standards—as long as you next ask yourself why. Answers to *why* may be, at first, quite basic, even from experienced and sophisticated readers. "I like the way it sounds" or "I like its rhythm and pace" might be good, if partial, reasons for liking a poem. The popularity of nursery rhymes, simple childish ditties, or even Poe's "The Raven" owes a lot (if not necessarily everything) to the use of sound. Another frequent answer might be "Because it is true" or "Because I agree with what it says." We all tend to like sentiments or ideas that resemble our own more than those that challenge or disturb us, though bad formulations of some idea we treasure, like bad behavior in someone we love, can prove more embarrassing than comforting. But the longer we struggle with our reasons for liking a poem, the more complex and revealing our answers will likely be: "I like the *way* it expresses something I had thought but never quite articulated." "I like the way its sounds and rhythms imitate the sounds of what is being described." "I like the way it presents conflicting emotions, balancing negative and positive feelings that seem to exist at the same time in about equal intensity." "I like its precision in describing just how something like that affects a person." Such statements as "I like . . ." quietly cross the border into the area of "I admire," and when you include a second clause, beginning with "because" and offering complex reasons for that admiration, you move into the process of critical evaluation.

What reasons might different readers agree on? *Groups* of readers might agree on certain ideas—questions of politics or economics or religion, for example—but not readers across the board. More likely to generate consensus are technical criteria, questions of craft. How precise are the word choices at crucial moments in the poem? How rich, suggestive, and resonant are the words that open up the poem to larger statements and claims? How appropriate, original, and imaginative are the metaphors and other figures of speech? How carefully and clearly is the poem's situation set up? How fully and appropriately is the speaker characterized? How well matched are the speaker, situation, and setting with the poem's sentiments and ideas? How consistent and appropriate to its themes is the poem's tone? How carefully worked out is the poem's structure? How appropriate to the desired effects are the line breaks, the stanza breaks, and the pattern of rhythms and sounds?

Sometimes you can see how good a poem is in its various aspects by looking at what it is not—considering the choices *not* made by the poet. Often you can consider what a poem would be like if a different artistic choice had been made, as a way of seeing the importance of the choice actually made. What if, for example, Sylvia Plath had described a black *crow* in rainy weather instead of a rook? What if William Carlos Williams had described a *white* wheelbarrow? Sometimes you have the benefit, by referring to a working manuscript or an autobiographical account of composition, of actually watching the process of selection. Look again, for example, at the several drafts of the first stanza of Richard Wilbur's "Love Calls Us to the Things of This World" (from chapter 14):

(a) My eyes came open to the squeak of pulleys
    My spirit, shocked from the brothel of itself

(b) My eyes came open to the shriek of pulleys,
    And the soul, spirited from its proper wallow,
    Hung in the air as bodiless and hollow

(c) My eyes came open to the pulleys' cry.
    The soul, spirited from its proper wallow,
    Hung in the air as bodiless and hollow
    As light that frothed upon the wall opposing;
    But what most caught my eyes at their unclosing
    Was two gray ropes that yanked across the sky.
    One after one into the window frame
    . . . the hosts of laundry came

(d)   The eyes open to a cry of pulleys,
    And the soul, so suddenly spirited from sleep,
    As morning sunlight frothing on the floor,
       while just outside the window
    The air is solid with a dance of angels.

(e)   The eyes open to a cry of pulleys,
       And spirited from sleep, the astounded soul
       Hangs for a moment bodiless and simple
       As dawn light in the moment of its breaking:
         Outside the open window
       The air is crowded with a

(f)   The eyes open to a cry of pulleys,
       And spirited from sleep, the astounded soul
       Hangs for a moment bodiless and simple
       As false dawn
         Outside the open window,
       Their air is leaping with a rout of angels.
         Some are in bedsheets, some are in dresses,
         it does not seem to matter

Notice how much more appropriate to the total poem is the choice of "cry" over "shriek" or "squeak" to describe the sound of pulleys or how much more effective than the metaphor of a spirit's "brothel" is the image of the soul hanging "bodiless." Notice the things Wilbur excised from the early drafts as well as the things he added when the poem became clearer and more of a piece in his mind.

Let's look again at one of the first poems we discussed, Adrienne Rich's "Aunt Jennifer's Tigers" (page 36). This poem gets some of its power from the poet's clear and sympathetic engagement with Aunt Jennifer's situation, but its effects derive from a series of specific technical choices. Rich may or may not have made all these choices consciously; her later comments on the poem suggest that her creative instincts, as well as her then-repressed sense of gender, may have governed some decisions. But however conscious, the choices of speaker, situation, metaphor, and connotative words work brilliantly together to create a strong feminist statement, almost a manifesto on the subject of mastery and compliance, even while (at the same time) making powerful assertions about the power of art to overcome human circumstances.

In a sense this poem has no speaker, no specified personality—only a faceless niece who observes the central character—but the effacing of this speaker in the light of the vivid Jennifer amounts to a brilliant artistic decision. Jennifer, powerless to articulate and possibly even to understand her own plight, nevertheless almost speaks for herself, primarily through her hands. The narrator's seeming refusal to do more than simply describe Jennifer's hands and their product gives Jennifer the crucial central role; she is the center of attention throughout, and the poem emphasizes only what can be seen, with little apparent "editorial" comment (though the speaker does make three evaluative statements, saying that Jennifer was "mastered" by her ordeals [line 10], and noting that her hands are "terrified" [line 9] and that the wedding band "sits heavily" [line 8] on one of them). The tigers are ultimately more eloquent than the speaker: they "prance" (lines 1 and 12) and "pace" (line 4), and they are "proud" (line 12) and unafraid of men (lines 3 and 12), embodying the guarded message Jennifer sends to the world even though she herself is "mastered" and "ringed" (line 10). The brightly conceived colors in the tapestry, the expressive description of Jennifer's fingers and hands (note especially the excitement implied in "fluttering" [line 5]), and the action of the panel itself combine with the characterization of Jennifer to present a strong statement of generational repression—and boldness. The image of knitting as art, suggesting the way the classical Fates determine the future and the nature of things, also hints at what is involved in Rich's art. The quality of the poem lies in the precision and imaginativeness of Rich's craft. In later years, Rich has become clearer and more vocal about her values, but the direction and intensity of her vision are already apparent in this excellent poem taken from her first book, published half a century ago.

The following celebrated poem similarly accomplishes a great deal in a short space:

WILLIAM SHAKESPEARE

[Th' expense of spirit in a waste of shame]

Th' expense of spirit in a waste[1] of shame
Is lust in action; and, till action, lust
Is perjured, murderous, bloody, full of blame,
Savage, extreme, rude, cruel, not to trust;
5 Enjoyed no sooner but despiséd straight;
Past reason hunted; and no sooner had,
Past reason hated, as a swallowed bait,
On purpose laid to make the taker mad:
Mad in pursuit, and in possession so;
10 Had, having, and in quest to have, extreme;
A bliss in proof;[2] and proved, a very woe;
Before, a joy proposed; behind, a dream.
All this the world well knows; yet none knows well
To shun the heaven that leads men to this hell.

1609

This poem fully characterizes its speaker, and it does so with economical skill. It sets up the situation slowly and, at first, somewhat unclearly, but the delay in clarity serves a purpose: we know that whatever disturbs the speaker concerns "lust in action" (line 2); we don't know what the disturbance is, but we gather that it stems from personal experience. Because the two explosive *p*'s in the first half of the first line start the poem swiftly and powerfully, we know that the speaker has strong feelings, and by the fourth line he has listed nine separate unpleasant human characteristics driven by lust. He virtually spits them out.

But the speaker expresses more than just anger and negativity. He admits that lust has definite, and powerful, pleasures: it is anticipated with pleasure ("a joy proposed," line 12) and "enjoyed" (line 5) at the time ("a bliss in proof," line 11). Such inconsistencies (or at least complexities) in the speaker's opinion give the

1. Using up; also, desert. *Expense:* expending. 2. In the act.

poem its unique flavor. His views—like lust itself, according to him—are "extreme" (line 10). The first twelve lines present no easy conclusions, only a confusing vacillation between positives and negatives. The strong condemnation of lust in the beginning—detailed in terms of how it makes people feel about themselves and how it affects their actions—quickly shifts into admissions of pleasure and joy, then shifts back again. No opinion sticks for long, except for the speaker's certainty about the power of lust to drive people to behavior they may love or hate. The "moral" he offers at the end will comfort no one. Everyone agrees with what I've been saying, he concludes, but no one knows how to avoid lust and its consequences because its pleasures are so sensational, both in prospect and in actuality ("the heaven that leads men to this hell").

The speaker's vacillating opinions and moods are not the only confusing thing about the poem's organization. His account of lust repeatedly shifts in time. Does he mean lust as it is being satisfied ("lust in action")? Or does he mean desire and anticipation? Or does he mean what happens afterward? He discusses all three, and hardly systematically. The first line and a half describe the present, and the meter of the first line even imitates the rhythms and force of male ejaculation: note how the basic iambic-pentameter strategy of the poem does not regularize until near the end of the second line. But by line 2 he is talking about what happens before lust in action ("till action"), and by line 5, after. Lines 6 and 7 contrast before and after, and line 9 compares before and during. Line 10 describes all three positions in time ("Had, having, and in quest to have"). Line 11 compares during and after; line 12, before and after. The speaker seems unable to decide exactly what he wants to talk about and what he thinks of his subject.

> *Poems may or may not follow classical patterns— they explode out of everyday experience.*
>
> —DOROTHY LIVESAY

All this shifting around in focus and in feelings could be regarded as a serious flaw. Don't we expect a short poem, especially a sonnet, to be carefully organized and focused toward a single end? Shouldn't the poet make up his mind about what he thinks and what the poem is about? We could easily construct an argument, on the basis of consistency or clarity of purpose, that this is not a very good poem, that perhaps the greatest poet in the English language was not, here, at the top of his form. But doing so would ignore the power of the poem's effects and underrate another principle of consistency—that of character. If we regard the poem as representative of a mind wrestling with the complex feelings brought about by lust—someone out of control because of lust, conscious enough to see his plight but unable to do anything about it—we can see a higher consistency that explains the poem's grip on many readers. This is an account of a human mind grappling with an often-repeated human truism, the subject of many much longer works of literature: lust is beautiful but terrifying, certainly to be avoided but impossible to avoid. Shakespeare has managed, in the unlikely space of fourteen lines and in a form in which we expect tight organization and intense focus, to portray succinctly the human recognition of confusion and powerlessness in the face of a passion larger than our ability to control it.

Here is another poem that is something of a challenge to evaluate:

JOHN DONNE

Song

Go, and catch a falling star,
   Get with child a mandrake root,[3]
Tell me, where all past years are,
   Or who cleft the devil's foot,
5 Teach me to hear mermaids singing
Or to keep off envy's stinging,
     And find
     What wind
Serves to advance an honest mind.

10 If thou beest born to strange sights,[4]
   Things invisible to see,
Ride ten thousand days and nights,
   Till age snow white hairs on thee;
Thou, when thou return'st, wilt tell me
15 All strange wonders that befell thee,
     And swear
     No where
Lives a woman true, and fair.

If thou find'st one, let me know:
20   Such a pilgrimage were sweet.
Yet do not, I would not go,
   Though at next door we might meet:
Though she were true when you met her,
And last till you write your letter,
25   Yet she
     Will be
False, ere I come, to two, or three.

               1633

First we need to consider the irregular, jerky rhythm. Since the poem is called "Song," we expect music, harmony, something pleasant and (within limits) predictable in its rhythm and movement. But this "song" presents nothing like that. At first its message sounds lyrical and romantic: to go and catch a falling star is, if impossible, a romantic thing to propose, a motif that often comes up (and has for centuries) in love poems and popular songs; and lines 3 and 5 propose similar traditional romantic activities that evoke wonder and pleasure in contemplation. But the activities suggested in the alternate lines (2, 4, and 6) contrast sharply; they are just as bold in their unromantic or antiromantic sentiments. Making a mandrake root pregnant does not sound like an especially pleasant activity, however much such a root may look like a female body, and knowledge of the devil's

---

3. The forked mandrake root looks vaguely human.   4. That is, if you have supernatural powers.

cleft foot or envy's stinging are not usually the stuff of romantic poems or songs. Besides, the strange interruptions of easy rhythm (indicated by commas) in otherwise pleasant lines like 1 and 3 suggest that something less than lyrical goes on there, too.

By the time we reach the last stanza, what is going on has become clearer. We have here a portrait of an angry and disillusioned man who is obsessed with the infidelity of women. He is talking to another man, apparently someone who has far more positive, perhaps even romantic, notions of women, and the poem is a kind of argument, except that the disillusioned speaker does all the talking. He pretends to take into account some traditional romantic rhetoric, but turns it all on its head, intermixing the traditional impossible quests of lovers with a quest of his own—to find a "woman true, and fair" (line 18). But he knows cynically— he would probably say from experience, though he offers no evidence of his experience and no account of why he feels the way he does—that all these quests are impossible. A bitter man, he wants nothing to do with love or romance.

If we were to evaluate this "song" on the basis of harmonic and romantic expectations, looking for evenness of rhythms, pleasant sounds, and an attractive series of images consonant with romantic attitudes, we would certainly find it wanting. But again (as with the Shakespeare poem above) a larger question of appropriateness begs to be applied. Do the sounds, tone, images, and organization of the poem "work" in terms of the speaker portrayed here and the kind of artistic project this poem represents? The displeasure we feel in the speaker's words, images, feelings, and attitudes ultimately needs to be directed toward the speaker; the poet has done a good job of portraying a character whose bitterness, however generated, is unpleasant and off-putting. The poem "works" on its own terms. We may or may not like to hear attitudes like this expressed in a poem; we may or may not approve of using a pretended "song" to mouth such sentiments. But whether or not we "like" the poem in terms of what it says, we can evaluate, through close analysis of its several different elements (much as we have been doing analytically in earlier chapters), how *well* it does what it does. Remaining, of course, are still larger questions of whether what it tries to do is worth doing, and readers of different philosophical or political persuasions may differ widely in their opinions and evaluations of that matter.

Different people admire different things, and when we talk about criteria for evaluating poetry, we talk about, at best, elements that a fairly large number of people have, over a long period of time, agreed on as important. A substantial agreement about political or social values may exist within a particular group— misogynists or feminists, say, may reach a consensus among themselves about the value of Donne's "Song." But more general agreements that bridge social and ideological divisions will more likely involve the kinds of matters that have come up for analysis in earlier chapters, matters involving how well a poem *works,* how well it uses the resources within its conceptual limits. For some readers, ideology is everything, and quality has no meaning beyond political views or moral conclusions. But for others, different, more pluralistic evaluations can be made about accomplishment and quality. You need to decide on your own criteria.

Consistency. Appropriateness. Coherence. Effectiveness. Such terms play key roles in most readers' evaluations—as they have done in this discussion. But individual critics or readers will have their own emphases, their own highly personal preferences, their own axes to grind. For some critics in past generations, *organic unity*—whether a poem achieved, like something grown in nature, a wholeness of conception and effect—was the key to all evaluation. With experience, you will develop your own set of criteria, which may or may not involve a single ruling concept or term—*tension* or *ambiguity* or *complexity* or *simplicity* or *authenticity* or *cultural truth* or *representation* or *psychological accuracy*. But wherever (and whenever) you come out, you will learn something about yourself and your values in the process of articulating exactly what you like and admire—and why.

• • •

IRVING LAYTON

Street Funeral

Tired of chewing
the flesh
of other animals;
Tired of subreption and conceit;
5 of the child's
bewildered conscience
fretting the sly man;
Tired of holding down
a job; of giving insults,
10 taking insults;
Of excited fornication,
failing heart valves,
septic kidneys . . .

This frosty morning,
15 the coffin wood bursting
into brilliant flowers,
Is he glad
that after all the lecheries,
betrayals, subserviency,
20 After all the lusts,
false starts, evasions
he can begin
the unobstructed change
into clean grass
25 Done forever
with the insult
of birth,
the long adultery
with illusion?

1956

GEOFFREY HILL

In Memory of Jane Fraser

When snow like sheep lay in the fold
And winds went begging at each door
And the far hills were blue with cold
And a cold shroud lay on the moor

5   She kept the siege. And every day
We watched her brooding over death
Like a strong bird above its prey.
The room filled with the kettle's breath.

Damp curtains glued against the pane
10 Sealed time away. Her body froze
As if to freeze us all and chain
Creation to a stunned repose.

She died before the world could stir.
In March the ice unloosed the brook
15 And water ruffled the sun's hair.
Dead cones upon the alder shook.

                                        1959

GALWAY KINNELL

Blackberry Eating

I love to go out in late September
among the fat, overripe, icy, black blackberries
to eat blackberries for breakfast,
the stalks very prickly, a penalty
5   they earn for knowing the black art
of blackberry-making; and as I stand among them
lifting the stalks to my mouth, the ripest berries
fall almost unbidden to my tongue,
as words sometimes do, certain peculiar words
10 like *strengths* or *squinched,*
many-lettered, one-syllabled lumps,
which I squeeze, squinch open, and splurge well
in the silent, startled, icy, black language
of blackberry-eating in late September.

                                        1980

DEREK WALCOTT

Dry Season

In the country of the ochre afternoon
it is always still and hot, the dry leaves stirring
infrequently sometimes with the rattling pods
of what they call "women's tongues," in
5 the afternoon country the far hills are very quiet
and heat-hazed, but mostly in the middle
of the country of the afternoon I see the brown heat
of the skin of my first love, so still, so perfect,
so unaltered, and I see how she walked
10 with her sunburnt hands against the still sea almonds,
to a remembered cove, where she stood on the small dock—
that was when I thought we were immortal
and that love would be folded doves and folded oars
and water lapping against eroding stone
15 in the ochre country of the afternoon.

2004

WALLACE STEVENS

Anecdote of the Jar

I placed a jar in Tennessee,
And round it was, upon a hill.
It made the slovenly wilderness
Surround that hill.

5 The wilderness rose up to it,
And sprawled around, no longer wild.
The jar was round upon the ground
And tall and of a port in air.

It took dominion everywhere.
10 The jar was gray and bare.
It did not give of bird or bush,
Like nothing else in Tennessee.

1923

JOHN CROWE RANSOM

Bells for John Whiteside's Daughter

There was such speed in her little body,
And such lightness in her footfall,
It is no wonder her brown study[5]
Astonishes us all.

5   Her wars were bruited in our high window.
We looked among orchard trees and beyond
Where she took arms against her shadow,
Or harried unto the pond

The lazy geese, like a snow cloud
10 Dripping their snow on the green grass,
Tricking and stopping, sleepy and proud,
Who cried in goose, Alas,

For the tireless heart within the little
Lady with rod that made them rise
15 From their noon apple-dreams and scuttle
Goose-fashion under the skies!

But now go the bells, and we are ready,
In one house we are sternly stopped
To say we are vexed at her brown study,
20 Lying so primly propped.

                                    1924

MARK STRAND

The Idea

        for Nolan Miller[6]

For us, too, there was a wish to possess
Something beyond the world we knew, beyond ourselves,
Beyond our power to imagine, something nevertheless
In which we might see ourselves; and this desire
5   Came always in passing, in waning light, and in such cold
That ice on the valley's lakes cracked and rolled,
And blowing snow covered what earth we saw,
And scenes from the past, when they surfaced again,
Looked not as they had, but ghostly and white
10 Among false curves and hidden erasures;

---

5. Stillness, as if in meditation or deep thought.
6. College teacher and editor who, according to Strand, inspired him to begin writing poetry.

And never once did we feel we were close
Until the night wind said, 'Why do this,
Especially now? Go back to the place you belong';
And there appeared, with its windows glowing, small,

15 In the distance, in the frozen reaches, a cabin;
And we stood before it, amazed at its being there,
And would have gone forward and opened the door,
And stepped into the glow and warmed ourselves there,
But that it was ours by not being ours,
20 And should remain empty. That was the idea.

1990

EMILY DICKINSON

[*The Brain—is wider than the Sky—*]

The Brain—is wider than the Sky—
For—put them side by side—
The one the other will contain
With ease—and You—beside—

5 The Brain is deeper than the sea—
For—hold them—Blue to Blue—
The one the other will absorb—
As Sponges—Buckets—do—

The Brain is just the weight of God—
10 For—Heft them—Pound for Pound—
And they will differ—if they do—
As Syllable from Sound—

ca. 1862

KATHERINE PHILIPS

Song

'Tis true our life is but a long dis-ease,
Made up of real pain and seeming ease.
You stars, who these entangled fortunes give,
  O tell me why
5   It is so hard to die,
    Yet such a task to live?

If with some pleasure we our griefs betray,
It costs us dearer than it can repay.

> For time or fortune all things so devours,
> 10   Our hopes are crossed,
>   Or else the object lost,
>   Ere we can call it ours.

1667

RICHARD WILBUR

Museum Piece

The good gray guardians of art
Patrol the halls on spongy shoes,
Impartially protective, though
Perhaps suspicious of Toulouse.[7]

5 Here dozes one against the wall,
Disposed upon a funeral chair.
A Degas[8] dancer pirouettes
Upon the parting of his hair.

See how she spins! The grace is there,
10 But strain as well is plain to see.
Degas loved the two together:
Beauty joined to energy.

Edgar Degas purchased once
A fine El Greco,[9] which he kept
15 Against the wall beside his bed
To hang his pants on while he slept.

1950

MURIEL RUKEYSER

Reading Time : 1 Minute 26 Seconds

The fear of poetry is the
fear : mystery and fury of a midnight street
of windows whose low voluptuous voice
issues, and after that there is no peace.

---

7. Henri-Marie-Raymond de Toulouse-Lautrec (1864–1901), French painter famous for his posters, drawings, and paintings of singers, dancers, and actresses.
8. Edgar Degas (1834–1917), French impressionist, usually considered the master of the human figure in movement.
9. El Greco (1541–1614), Cretan-born Spanish painter, known for the mannered disproportion of his figures.

5   That round waiting moment in the
   theatre : curtain rises, dies into the ceiling
   and here is played the scene with the mother
   bandaging a revealed son's head. The bandage is torn off.
   Curtain goes down. And here is the moment of proof.

10 That climax when the brain acknowledges the world,
   all values extended into the blood awake.
   Moment of proof. And as they say Brancusi did,
   building his bird to extend through soaring air,[1]
   as Kafka planned stories that draw to eternity
15 through time extended. And the climax strikes.

   Love touches so, that months after the look of
   blue stare of love, the footbeat on the heart
   is translated into the pure cry of birds
   following air-cries, or poems, the new scene.
20 Moment of proof. That strikes long after act.

   They fear it. They turn away, hand up palm out
   fending off moment of proof, the straight look, poem.
   The prolonged wound-consciousness after the bullet's shot.
   The prolonged love after the look is dead,
25 the yellow joy after the song of the sun.

                                      1939

HEATHER McHUGH

Earthmoving Malediction

   Bulldoze the bed where we made love,
   bulldoze the goddamn room.
   Let rubble be our evidence
   and wreck our home.

5   I can't give touching up by inches,
   can't give beating up
   by heart. So set
   the comforter on fire and turn the dirt

   to some advantage—palaces of
10 pigweed, treasuries of turd. This fist
   will vindicate the hand; the tooth
   and nail refuse to burn, and I

---

1. Constantin Brancusi (1876–1957), Romanian-born French sculptor, was famous for his increasingly abstract sculptures of birds in flight.

must not look back, as
Mrs. Lot[2] was named for such
15   a little—something
in a cemetery,

or a man. Bulldoze the coupled
ploys away, the cute exclusives
in the social mall. We dwell

20   on earth, where beds are brown,
where swoops are fell. Bulldoze
it all, up to the pearly gates:

if paradise comes down
there is no other hell.

1988

_____

QUESTIONS

1. What is the single most important factor in whether you like or dislike a poem? Read back over the poems that you have liked most; what do they have in common?
2. How adaptable are you in adjusting to a poem's emphases? Which poems have you liked though you didn't especially like the conclusions they came to?
3. How important to you is the *precision* of words in a poem? Do you tend to like poems better if they are definite and explicit in what they say? or if they are ambiguous, uncertain, or complex?
4. Which issues and concepts in chapters 1 through 14 have you found most useful? most surprising? Which chapters did you enjoy most? From which did you learn the most about yourself and your tastes and values?
5. What do you value most in poetry generally? Do you read poems that are not assigned? How do you choose them? Do you read poems outside this textbook or outside the course? If so, what kinds of poems do you seek out? Do specific titles draw you in?
6. Are certain subjects or themes always appealing to you? always unappealing?
7. How important to you is the *tone* of a poem? Do you tend to like funny poems more than serious ones? tragic situations more than comic ones? unusual treatments of standard or predictable subjects and themes?
8. Which poem in this chapter did you most enjoy? Which one did you like best after reading the commentary about it? Have you particularly disliked any poems you have read this term? What about them irritated you? Have you changed your mind about some poems after you have reread or discussed them? How did your criteria change?

_____

2. According to Genesis 13 and 19, Lot's wife was turned into a pillar of salt, because she looked back after leaving a condemned city.

WRITING SUGGESTIONS

1. Choose one poem that you admire and one that you do not. Write a two-page essay about each in which you show what led you to your evaluative conclusions. Treat each poem in detail, and fully discuss not only how but *why* things "work"—or don't work. Try to construct your argument as objectively as possible so that you are not simply pitting your personal judgment against someone else's. (Alternative: find two poems that are very much alike in subject matter, theme, or situation, but that seem unequally successful. Write one *comparative* essay in which you account for the difference in quality by showing in detail the difference between what works and what does not.)

2. Discuss with classmates a variety of poems you have read this term, and choose one poem about which a number of you disagree. Discuss among yourselves the different perspectives you have on the poem, and try to sort out in the discussion exactly what issues are at stake. Take notes on the discussion, trying to be clear about how your position differs from that of other students. Once you believe that you have the issues sorted out and can be clear about your own position, write a two- or three-page personal letter to your instructor in which you outline a position contrary to your own and then answer it point by point. Be sure to make clear in your letter the *grounds* for your evaluative position, positive or negative—that is, the principles or values on which you base your evaluation. (Hint: in the conversation with classmates, try to steer the discussion to a clear disagreement on no more than two or three points, and in your letter focus carefully on these points. State the arguments of your classmates as effectively and forcefully as you can so that your own argument will be as probing and sophisticated as you can make it.)

3. Choose a poem you have read this term that you admire but really don't like very much. In thinking over the poem again, try to account for the conflict between your feelings and your intellectual judgment: what questions of content or form, social or political assumption, personal style, or manner of argument in the poem make it less attractive to you? In a personal letter to a friend who is not in the class and who thus has not heard the class discussions of the issues, describe your dilemma, being careful to first outline why you think the poem is admirable. Say frankly what your personal reservations about the poem are, and at the end use the discussion of the poem to talk about your own values, as they pertain to poetry in general.

Reading More Poetry

SHERMAN ALEXIE

On the Amtrak from Boston to New York City

The white woman across the aisle from me says, "Look,
look at all the history, that house
on the hill there is over two hundred years old,"
as she points out the window past me

5 into what she has been taught. I have learned
little more about American history during my few days
back East than what I expected and far less
of what we should all know of the tribal stories

whose architecture is 15,000 years older
10 than the corners of the house that sits
museumed on the hill. "Walden Pond,"[1]
the woman on the train asks, "Did you see Walden Pond?"

and I don't have a cruel enough heart to break
her own by telling her there are five Walden Ponds
15 on my little reservation out West
and at least a hundred more surrounding Spokane,

the city I pretend to call my home. Listen,
I could have told her. "I don't give a shit
about Walden. I know the Indians were living stories
20 around that pond before Walden's grandparents were born

and before his grandparents' grandparents were born.
I'm tired of hearing about Don-fucking-Henley[2] saving it, too,
because that's redundant. If Don Henley's brothers and sisters
and mothers and fathers hadn't come here in the first place

25 then nothing would need to be saved."
But I didn't say a word to the woman about Walden
Pond because she smiled so much and seemed delighted
that I thought to bring her an orange juice

back from the food car. I respect elders
30 of every color. All I really did was eat

1. Where Henry David Thoreau (1817–62) lived and wrote his classic *Walden* (1854).
2. Rock star Don Henley (b. 1947) helped start a preservation project for the woodlands around Walden Pond.

my tasteless sandwich, drink my Diet Pepsi
and nod my head whenever the woman pointed out

another little piece of her country's history
while I, as all Indians have done
35 since this war began, made plans
for what I would do and say the next time

somebody from the enemy thought I was one of their own.

1993

JOHN ASHBERY

Of the Light

That watery light, so undervalued
except when evaluated, which never happens
much, perhaps even not at all—I intend to conserve it
somehow, in a book, in a dish, even at night,
5 like an insect in a light bulb.

Yes, day may just be breaking. The importance isn't there
but in the beautiful flights of the trees
accepting their own flaccid destiny,
or the tightrope of seasons.
10 We get scared when we look at them up close
but the king doesn't mind. He has the tides to worry about,

and how fitting is the new mood of contentment
and how long it will wear thin.

I looked forward to seeing you so much
15 I have dragged the king from his lair: There,
take that, you old wizard. Wizard enough, he replies,
but this isn't going to save us from the light
of breakfast, or mend the hole in your stocking.
"Now wait"—and yet another day has consumed itself,
20 brisk with passion and grief, crisp as an illustration in a magazine
from the thirties, when we and this light were all that mattered.

2000

Paradoxes and Oxymorons

This poem is concerned with language on a very plain level.
Look at it talking to you. You look out a window
Or pretend to fidget. You have it but you don't have it.
You miss it, it misses you. You miss each other.

5 The poem is sad because it wants to be yours, and cannot.
What's a plain level? It is that and other things,
Bringing a system of them into play. Play?
Well, actually, yes, but I consider play to be

A deeper outside thing, a dreamed role-pattern,
10 As in the division of grace these long August days
Without proof. Open-ended. And before you know
It gets lost in the steam and chatter of typewriters.

It has been played once more. I think you exist only
To tease me into doing it, on your level, and then you aren't there
15 Or have adopted a different attitude. And the poem
Has set me softly down beside you. The poem is you.

1981

W. H. AUDEN

As I Walked Out One Evening

As I walked out one evening,
  Walking down Bristol Street,
The crowds upon the pavement
  Were fields of harvest wheat.

5 And down by the brimming river
  I heard a lover sing
Under an arch of the railway:
  "Love has no ending.

"I'll love you, dear, I'll love you
10   Till China and Africa meet,
And the river jumps over the mountain
  And the salmon sing in the street,

"I'll love you till the ocean
  Is folded and hung up to dry
15 And the seven stars go squawking
  Like geese about the sky.

"The years shall run like rabbits,
  For in my arms I hold

The Flower of the Ages,
20 And the first love of the world."

But all the clocks in the city
    Began to whirr and chime:
"O let not Time deceive you,
    You cannot conquer Time.

25 "In the burrows of the Nightmare
    Where Justice naked is,
Time watches from the shadow
    And coughs when you would kiss.

"In headaches and in worry
30 Vaguely life leaks away,
And Time will have his fancy
    To-morrow or to-day.

"Into many a green valley
    Drifts the appalling snow;
35 Time breaks the threaded dances
    And the diver's brilliant bow.

"O plunge your hands in water,
    Plunge them in up to the wrist;
Stare, stare in the basin
40 And wonder what you've missed.

"The glacier knocks in the cupboard,
    The desert sighs in the bed,
And the crack in the tea-cup opens
    A lane to the land of the dead.

45 "Where the beggars raffle the banknotes
    And the Giant is enchanting to Jack,
And the Lily-white Boy is a Roarer,
    And Jill goes down on her back.

"O look, look in the mirror,
50 O look in your distress;
Life remains a blessing
    Although you cannot bless.

"O stand, stand at the window
    As the tears scald and start;
55 You shall love your crooked neighbour
    With your crooked heart."

It was late, late in the evening,
    The lovers they were gone;
The clocks had ceased their chiming,
60 And the deep river ran on.

November 1937

WILLIAM BLAKE
Holy Thursday[3]

'Twas on a Holy Thursday, their innocent faces clean,
The children walking two & two, in red & blue & green;
Grey headed beadles walkd before with wands as white as snow,
Till into the high dome of Paul's they like Thames' waters flow.

5 O what a multitude they seemd, these flowers of London town!
Seated in companies they sit with radiance all their own.
The hum of multitudes was there, but multitudes of lambs,
Thousands of little boys & girls raising their innocent hands.

Now like a mighty wind they raise to heaven the voice of song,
10 Or like harmonious thunderings the seats of heaven among.
Beneath them sit the agèd men, wise guardians of the poor;
Then cherish pity, lest you drive an angel from your door.[4]

1789

Holy Thursday

Is this a holy thing to see,
In a rich and fruitful land,
Babes reduced to misery,
Fed with cold and usurous hand?

5 Is that trembling cry a song?
Can it be a song of joy?
And so many children poor?
It is a land of poverty!

And their sun does never shine,
10 And their fields are bleak & bare,
And their ways are fill'd with thorns;
It is eternal winter there.

For where-e'er the sun does shine,
And where-e'er the rain does fall,
15 Babe can never hunger there,
Nor poverty the mind appall.

1794

3. In the English Church, the Thursday celebrating Christ's ascension, thirty-nine days after Easter. It was customary on this day to march the poor, frequently orphaned children from the charity schools of London to a service at St. Paul's Cathedral.
    This poem is from Blake's *Songs of Innocence*. The one that follows—with the same title—is from his *Songs of Experience*.
4. See Hebrews 13.2: "Be not forgetful to entertain strangers: for thereby some have entertained angels unawares."

GWENDOLYN BROOKS

WEB *To the Diaspora*

you did not know you were Afrika

When you set out for Afrika
you did not know you were going.
Because
you did not know you were Afrika.
5 You did not know the Black continent
that had to be reached
was you.

I could not have told you then that some sun
would come,
10 somewhere over the road,
would come evoking the diamonds
of you, the Black continent—
somewhere over the road.
You would not have believed my mouth.

15 When I told you, meeting you somewhere close
to the heat and youth of the road,
liking my loyalty, liking belief,
you smiled and you thanked me but very little believed me.

Here is some sun. Some.
20 Now off into the places rough to reach.
Though dry, though drowsy, all unwillingly a-wobble,
into the dissonant and dangerous crescendo.
Your work, that was done, to be done to be done to be done.

1981

ROBERT BROWNING

Porphyria's Lover[5]

The rain set early in tonight,
    The sullen wind was soon awake,
It tore the elm-tops down for spite,
    And did its worst to vex the lake:
5   I listened with heart fit to break.
When glided in Porphyria; straight
    She shut the cold out and the storm,

5. A monologue originally published under the title "Madhouse Cells."

And kneeled and made the cheerless grate
    Blaze up, and all the cottage warm;
10   Which done, she rose, and from her form
Withdrew the dripping cloak and shawl,
    And laid her soiled gloves by, untied
Her hat and let the damp hair fall,
    And, last, she sat down by my side
15   And called me. When no voice replied,
She put my arm about her waist,
    And made her smooth white shoulder bare,
And all her yellow hair displaced,
    And, stooping, made my cheek lie there,
20   And spread, o'er all, her yellow hair,
Murmuring how she loved me—she
    Too weak, for all her heart's endeavor,
To set its struggling passion free
    From pride, and vainer ties dissever,
25   And give herself to me forever.
But passion sometimes would prevail,
    Nor could tonight's gay feast restrain
A sudden thought of one so pale
    For love of her, and all in vain:
30   So, she was come through wind and rain.
Be sure I looked up at her eyes
    Happy and proud; at last I knew
Porphyria worshiped me: surprise
    Made my heart swell, and still it grew
35   While I debated what to do.
That moment she was mine, mine, fair,
    Perfectly pure and good: I found
A thing to do, and all her hair
    In one long yellow string I wound
40   Three times her little throat around,
And strangled her. No pain felt she;
    I am quite sure she felt no pain.
As a shut bud that holds a bee,
    I warily oped her lids: again
45   Laughed the blue eyes without a stain.
And I untightened next the tress
    About her neck; her cheek once more
Blushed bright beneath my burning kiss:
    I propped her head up as before,
50   Only, this time my shoulder bore
Her head, which droops upon it still:
    The smiling rosy little head,
So glad it has its utmost will,
    That all it scorned at once is fled,
55   And I, its love, am gained instead!
Porphyria's love: she guessed not how

Her darling one wish would be heard.
And thus we sit together now,
  And all night long we have not stirred
60 And yet God has not said a word!

1836, 1842

CD **EMILY DICKINSON**

WEB **[*Because I could not stop for Death—*]**

Because I could not stop for Death—
He kindly stopped for me—
The Carriage held but just Ourselves—
And Immortality.

5 We slowly drove—He knew no haste
And I had put away
My labor and my leisure too,
For His Civility—

We passed the School, where Children strove
10 At Recess—in the Ring—
We passed the Fields of Gazing Grain—
We passed the Setting Sun—

Or rather—He passed Us—
The Dews drew quivering and chill—
15 For only Gossamer,[6] my Gown—
My Tippet—only Tulle[7]—

We paused before a House that seemed
A Swelling of the Ground—
The Roof was scarcely visible—
20 The Cornice—in the Ground—

Since then—'tis Centuries—and yet
Feels shorter than the Day
I first surmised the Horses' Heads
Were toward Eternity—

ca. 1863

[Handwritten annotations: Allusion, Enjambment, Anaphora, Alliteration]

6. A soft, sheer fabric.   7. A fine net fabric. *Tippet:* scarf.

[I reckon—when I count at all—]

I reckon—when I count at all—
First—Poets—Then the Sun—
Then Summer—Then the Heaven of God—
And then—the List is done—

5   But, looking back—the First so seems
To Comprehend the Whole—
The Others look a needless Show—
So I write—Poets—All—

Their Summer—lasts a Solid Year—
10 They can afford a Sun
The East—would deem extravagant—
And if the Further Heaven—

Be Beautiful as they prepare
For Those who worship Them—
15 It is too difficult a Grace—
To justify the Dream—

ca. 1862

[I stepped from Plank to Plank]

I stepped from Plank to Plank
A slow and cautious way
The Stars about my Head I felt
About my Feet the Sea.

5   I knew not but the next
Would be my final inch—
This gave me that precarious Gait
Some call Experience.

ca. 1864

[We do not play on Graves—]

We do not play on Graves—
Because there isn't Room—
Besides—it isn't even—it slants
And People come—

5 And put a Flower on it—
And hang their faces so—
We're fearing that their Hearts will drop—
And crush our pretty play—

And so we move as far
10 As Enemies—away—
Just looking round to see how far
It is—Occasionally—

ca. 1862

[*She dealt her pretty words like Blades—*]

She dealt her pretty words like Blades—
How glittering they shone—
And every One unbared a Nerve
Or wantoned with a Bone—

5 She never deemed—she hurt—
That—is not Steel's Affair—
A vulgar grimace in the Flesh—
How ill the Creatures bear—

To Ache is human—not polite—
10 The Film upon the eye
Mortality's old Custom—
Just locking up—to Die.

1862

JOHN DONNE

[*Death, be not proud*]

Death be not proud, though some have callèd thee
Mighty and dreadful, for thou art not so;
For those whom thou think'st thou dost overthrow
Die not, poor Death, nor yet canst thou kill me.
5 From rest and sleep, which but thy pictures[8] be,
Much pleasure; then from thee much more must flow,
And soonest[9] our best men with thee do go,
Rest of their bones, and soul's delivery.[1]
Thou art slave to Fate, Chance, kings, and desperate men,
10 And dost with Poison, War, and Sickness dwell;

---

8. Likenesses.   9. Most willingly.   1. Deliverance.

And poppy or charms can make us sleep as well,
And better than thy stroke; why swell'st² thou then?
One short sleep past, we wake eternally
And death shall be no more; Death, thou shalt die.

1633

The Sun Rising

Busy old fool, unruly sun,
    Why dost thou thus,
Through windows, and through curtains, call on us?
Must to thy motions lovers' seasons run?
5   Saucy pedantic wretch, go chide
        Late schoolboys, and sour prentices,³
    Go tell court-huntsmen that the king will ride,
    Call country ants⁴ to harvest offices;
Love, all alike, no season knows, nor clime,
10 Nor hours, days, months, which are the rags of time.
        Thy beams, so reverend and strong
        why shouldst thou think?
I could eclipse and cloud them with a wink,
But that I would not lose her sight so long:
15   If her eyes have not blinded thine,
        Look, and tomorrow late, tell me
    Whether both the Indias⁵ of spice and mine
    Be where thou left'st them, or lie here with me.
Ask for those kings whom thou saw'st yesterday,
20 And thou shalt hear, all here in one bed lay.

        She is all states, and all princes I,
        Nothing else is.
Princes do but play us; compared to this,
All honor's mimic,⁶ all wealth alchemy.
25   Thou, sun, art half as happy as we,
        In that the world's contracted thus;
    Thine age asks⁷ ease, and since thy duties be
    To warm the world, that's done in warming us.
Shine here to us, and thou art every where;
30 This bed thy center⁸ is, these walls thy sphere.

1633

2. Puff with pride.   3. Apprentices.   4. Farmworkers.
5. The East and West Indies, commercial sources of spices and gold.   6. Hypocritical.
7. Requires.   8. Of orbit.

WEB *A Valediction: Forbidding Mourning*

As virtuous men pass mildly away,
    And whisper to their souls to go,
Whilst some of their sad friends do say,
    "The breath goes now," and some say, "No,"

5 So let us melt, and make no noise,
    No tear-floods, nor sigh-tempests move;
'Twere profanation of our joys
    To tell the laity our love.

Moving of the earth[9] brings harms and fears,
10   Men reckon what it did and meant;
But trepidation of the spheres,[1]
    Though greater far, is innocent.

Dull sublunary[2] lovers' love
    (Whose soul is sense) cannot admit
15 Absence, because it doth remove
    Those things which elemented[3] it.

But we, by a love so much refined
    That our selves know not what it is,
Inter-assured of the mind,
20   Care less, eyes, lips, and hands to miss.

Our two souls therefore, which are one,
    Though I must go, endure not yet
A breach, but an expansion,
    Like gold to airy thinness beat.

25 If they be two, they are two so
    As stiff twin compasses are two:
Thy soul, the fixed foot, makes no show
    To move, but doth, if the other do;

And though it in the center sit,
30   Yet when the other far doth roam,
It leans, and hearkens after it,
    And grows erect, as that comes home.

Such wilt thou be to me, who must,
    Like the other foot, obliquely run;

---

9. Earthquakes.
1. The Renaissance hypothesis that the celestial spheres trembled and thus caused unexpected variations in their orbits. Such movements are "innocent" because earthlings do not observe or fret about them.
2. Below the moon—that is, changeable. According to the traditional cosmology that Donne invokes here, the moon was considered the dividing line between the immutable celestial world and the earthly mortal one.   3. Comprised.

35   Thy firmness makes my circle[4] just,
     And makes me end where I begun.

1611?

PAUL LAURENCE DUNBAR

Sympathy

I know what the caged bird feels, alas!
  When the sun is bright on the upland slopes;
When the wind stirs soft through the springing grass,
  And the river flows like a stream of glass;
5   When the first bird sings and the first bud opens,
And the faint perfume from its chalice steals—
I know what the caged bird feels!

I know why the caged bird beats his wing
  Till its blood is red on the cruel bars;
10 For he must fly back to his perch and cling
When he fain[5] would be on the bough a-swing;
  And a pain still throbs in the old, old scars
And they pulse again with a keener sting—
I know why he beats his wing!

15 I know why the caged bird sings, ah me,
  When his wing is bruised and his bosom sore,—
When he beats his bars and he would be free;
It is not a carol of joy or glee,
  But a prayer that he sends from his heart's deep core,
20 But a plea, that upward to Heaven he flings—
I know why the caged bird sings!

1893

We Wear the Mask

We wear the mask that grins and lies,
It hides our cheeks and shades our eyes,—
This debt we pay to human guile;
With torn and bleeding hearts we smile,
5 And mouth with myriad subtleties.

Why should the world be over-wise,
In counting all our tears and sighs?

---

4. A traditional symbol of perfection.   5. Gladly.

Nay, let them only see us, while
    We wear the mask.

10 We smile, but, O great Christ, our cries
To thee from tortured souls arise.
We sing, but oh the clay is vile
Beneath our feet, and long the mile;
But let the world dream otherwise,
15   We wear the mask!

                                        1895

T. S. ELIOT

Journey of the Magi[6]

"A cold coming we had of it,
Just the worst time of the year
For a journey, and such a long journey:
The ways deep and the weather sharp,
5 The very dead of winter."[7]
And the camels galled, sore-footed, refractory,
Lying down in the melting snow.
There were times we regretted
The summer palaces on slopes, the terraces,
10 And the silken girls bringing sherbet.
Then the camel men cursing and grumbling
And running away, and wanting their liquor and women,
And the night-fires going out, and the lack of shelters,
And the cities hostile and the towns unfriendly
15 And the villages dirty and charging high prices:
A hard time we had of it.
At the end we preferred to travel all night,
Sleeping in snatches,
With the voices singing in our ears, saying
20 That this was all folly.

    Then at dawn we came down to a temperate valley,
Wet, below the snow line, smelling of vegetation;
With a running stream and a water-mill beating the darkness,
And three trees on the low sky,[8]
25 And an old white horse galloped away in the meadow.

6. The wise men who followed the star of Bethlehem. See Matthew 2.1–12.
7. An adaptation of a passage from a 1622 sermon by Lancelot Andrewes.
8. Suggesting the three crosses of the Crucifixion (Luke 23.32–33). The Magi see several objects that suggest later events in Christ's life: pieces of silver (see Matthew 26.14–16), the dicing (see Matthew 27.35), the white horse (see Revelation 6.2 and 19.11–16), and the empty wine skins (see Matthew 9.17, possibly relevant also to lines 41–42).

Then we came to a tavern with vine-leaves over the lintel,
Six hands at an open door dicing for pieces of silver,
And feet kicking the empty wine-skins.
But there was no information, and so we continued
30 And arrived at evening, not a moment too soon
Finding the place; it was (you may say) satisfactory.

All this was a long time ago, I remember,
And I would do it again, but set down
This set down
35 This: were we led all that way for
Birth or Death? There was a Birth, certainly,
We had evidence and no doubt. I had seen birth and death,
But had thought they were different; this Birth was
Hard and bitter agony for us, like Death, our death.
40 We returned to our places, these Kingdoms,[9]
But no longer at ease here, in the old dispensation,
With an alien people clutching their gods.
I should be glad of another death.

1927

The Love Song of J. Alfred Prufrock

S'io credesse che mia risposta fosse
A persona che mai tornasse al mondo,
Questa fiamma staria senza piu scosse.
Ma perciocche giammai di questo fondo
Non torno vivo alcun, s'i'odo il vero,
Senza tema d'infamia ti rispondo.[1]

Let us go then, you and I,
When the evening is spread out against the sky
Like a patient etherized upon a table;
Let us go, through certain half-deserted streets,
5 The muttering retreats
Of restless nights in one-night cheap hotels
And sawdust restaurants with oyster-shells:
Streets that follow like a tedious argument
Of insidious intent

9. The Bible identifies the wise men only as "from the east," and subsequent tradition has made them kings. In Persia, magi were members of an ancient priestly caste.
1. Dante's *Inferno* 27.61–66. In the Eighth Chasm, Dante and Virgil meet Count Guido de Montefeltrano, one of the False Counselors. The spirits there are in the form of flames, and Guido speaks from the trembling tip of the flame, responding to Dante's request that he tell his life story: "If I thought that my answer were to someone who would ever go back to Earth, this flame would be still, without any more movement. But because no one has ever gone back alive from this chasm (if what I hear is true) I answer you without fear of infamy."

10 To lead you to an overwhelming question . . .
  Oh, do not ask, "What is it?"
  Let us go and make our visit.

  In the room the women come and go
  Talking of Michelangelo.

15　The yellow fog that rubs its back upon the window-panes,
  The yellow smoke that rubs its muzzle on the window-panes
  Licked its tongue into the corners of the evening,
  Lingered upon the pools that stand in drains,
  Let fall upon its back the soot that falls from chimneys,
20 Slipped by the terrace, made a sudden leap,
  And seeing that it was a soft October night,
  Curled once about the house, and fell asleep.

  And indeed there will be time[2]
  For the yellow smoke that slides along the street,
25 Rubbing its back upon the window-panes;
  There will be time, there will be time
  To prepare a face to meet the faces that you meet;
  There will be time to murder and create,
  And time for all the works and days[3] of hands
30 That lift and drop a question on your plate;
  Time for you and time for me,
  And time yet for a hundred indecisions,
  And for a hundred visions and revisions,
  Before the taking of a toast and tea.

35　In the room the women come and go
  Talking of Michelangelo.

  And indeed there will be time
  To wonder, "Do I dare?" and, "Do I dare?"
  Time to turn back and descend the stair,
40 With a bald spot in the middle of my hair—
  (They will say: "How his hair is growing thin!")
  My morning coat, my collar mounting firmly to the chin,
  My necktie rich and modest, but asserted by a simple pin—
  (They will say: "But how his arms and legs are thin!")
45 Do I dare
  Disturb the universe?

  In a minute there is time
  For decisions and revisions which a minute will reverse.

---

2. See Ecclesiastes 3.1 ff.: "To everything there is a season, and a time to every purpose under the heaven: A time to be born, and a time to die; a time to plant, and a time to pluck up that which is planted; A time to kill, and a time to heal. . . ." Also see Marvell's "To His Coy Mistress": "Had we but world enough, and time. . . ."

3. Hesiod's ancient Greek didactic poem *Works and Days* prescribed in practical detail how to conduct one's life.

For I have known them all already, known them all:—
50 Have known the evenings, mornings, afternoons,
I have measured out my life with coffee spoons;
I know the voices dying with a dying fall
Beneath the music from a farther room.
        So how should I presume?

55   And I have known the eyes already, known them all—
The eyes that fix you in a formulated phrase,
And when I am formulated, sprawling on a pin,
When I am pinned and wriggling on the wall,
Then how should I begin
60 To spit out all the butt-ends of my days and ways?
        And how should I presume?

And I have known the arms already, known them all—
Arms that are braceleted and white and bare
(But in the lamplight, downed with light brown hair!)
65 Is it perfume from a dress
That makes me so digress?
Arms that lie along a table, or wrap about a shawl.
        And should I then presume?
        And how should I begin?

                    • • •

70 Shall I say, I have gone at dusk through narrow streets
And watched the smoke that rises from the pipes
Of lonely men in shirt-sleeves, leaning out of windows? . . .

    I should have been a pair of ragged claws
Scuttling across the floors of silent seas

                    • • •

75 And the afternoon, the evening, sleeps so peacefully!
Smoothed by long fingers,
Asleep . . . tired . . . or it malingers,
Stretched on the floor, here beside you and me.
Should I, after tea and cakes and ices,
80 Have the strength to force the moment to its crisis?
But though I have wept and fasted, wept and prayed,
Though I have seen my head (grown slightly bald) brought
        in upon a platter,[4]
I am no prophet—and here's no great matter;
I have seen the moment of my greatness flicker,
85 And I have seen the eternal Footman hold my coat, and
        snicker,
And in short, I was afraid.

---

4. See Matthew 14.1–12 and Mark 6.17–29: John the Baptist was decapitated, upon Salome's request and at Herod's command, and his head delivered on a platter.

And would it have been worth it, after all,
After the cups, the marmalade, the tea,
Among the porcelain, among some talk of you and me,
90 Would it have been worth while,
To have bitten off the matter with a smile,
To have squeezed the universe into a ball[5]
To roll it toward some overwhelming question,
To say: "I am Lazarus,[6] come from the dead,
95 Come back to tell you all, I shall tell you all"—
If one, settling a pillow by her head,
    Should say: "That is not what I meant at all.
    That is not it, at all."

And would it have been worth it, after all,
100 Would it have been worth while,
    After the sunsets and the dooryards and the sprinkled
      streets,
After the novels, after the teacups, after the skirts that trail
      along the floor—
And this, and so much more?—
It is impossible to say just what I mean!
105 But as if a magic lantern[7] threw the nerves in patterns on a
      screen:
Would it have been worth while
If one, settling a pillow or throwing off a shawl,
And turning toward the window, should say:
    "That is not it at all,
110   That is not what I meant, at all."

                              • • •

No! I am not Prince Hamlet, nor was meant to be;
Am an attendant lord,[8] one that will do
To swell a progress,[9] start a scene or two,
Advise the prince; no doubt, an easy tool,
115 Deferential, glad to be of use,
Politic, cautious, and meticulous;
Full of high sentence, but a bit obtuse;
At times, indeed, almost ridiculous—
Almost, at times, the Fool.

120   I grow old . . . I grow old . . .
I shall wear the bottoms of my trousers rolled.

---

5. See Marvell's "To His Coy Mistress," lines 41–42: "Let us roll all our strength and all / our sweetness up into one ball."
6. One Lazarus was raised from the dead by Jesus (see John 11.1–44), and another (in the parable of the rich man Dives) returned from the dead to warn the living (Luke 16.19–31).
7. A nonelectric projector used as early as the seventeenth century.
8. Like Polonius in *Hamlet*, who is full of maxims ("high sentence," line 117).   9. Procession of state.

Shall I part my hair behind? Do I dare to eat a peach?
I shall wear white flannel trousers, and walk upon the
  beach.
I have heard the mermaids singing, each to each.

125   I do not think that they will sing to me.

I have seen them riding seaward on the waves
Combing the white hair of the waves blown back.
When the wind blows the water white and black.

We have lingered in the chambers of the sea
130 By sea-girls wreathed with seaweed red and brown
Till human voices wake us, and we drown.

1917

ROBERT FROST

CD   *The Road Not Taken*

Two roads diverged in a yellow wood,
And sorry I could not travel both
And be one traveler, long I stood
And looked down one as far as I could
5 To where it bent in the undergrowth;

Then took the other, as just as fair,
And having perhaps the better claim,
Because it was grassy and wanted wear;
Though as for that the passing there
10 Had worn them really about the same,

And both that morning equally lay
In leaves no step had trodden black.
Oh, I kept the first for another day!
Yet knowing how way leads on to way,
15 I doubted if I should ever come back.

I shall be telling this with a sigh
Somewhere ages and ages hence:
Two roads diverged in a wood, and I—
I took the one less traveled by,
20 And that has made all the difference.

1916

Stopping by Woods on a Snowy Evening

Whose woods these are I think I know.
His house is in the village, though;
He will not see me stopping here
To watch his woods fill up with snow.

5 My little horse must think it queer
To stop without a farmhouse near
Between the woods and frozen lake
The darkest evening of the year.

He gives his harness bells a shake
10 To ask if there is some mistake.
The only other sound's the sweep
Of easy wind and downy flake.

The woods are lovely, dark, and deep,
But I have promises to keep,
15 And miles to go before I sleep,
And miles to go before I sleep.

1923

ALLEN GINSBERG

[CD] ## A Supermarket in California

What thoughts I have of you tonight, Walt Whitman,[1] for I walked down the sidestreets under the trees with a headache self-conscious looking at the full moon.

In my hungry fatigue, and shopping for images, I went into the neon fruit supermarket, dreaming of your enumerations![2]

What peaches and what penumbras! Whole families shopping at night! Aisles full of husbands! Wives in the avocados, babies in the tomatoes!—and you, Garcia Lorca,[3] what were you doing down by the watermelons?

I saw you, Walt Whitman, childless, lonely old grubber, poking among the meats in the refrigerator and eyeing the grocery boys.

5   I heard you asking questions of each: Who killed the pork chops? What price bananas? Are you my Angel?

1. Whitman's free verse, strong individualism, and passionate concern with America as an idea have led many modern poets to consider him the father of a new poetry.
2. Whitman's highly rhetorical poetry often contains long lists or parallel constructions piled up for cumulative effect.
3. Federico García Lorca (1898–1936), Spanish poet and playwright, author of *Blood Wedding*, murdered at the beginning of the Spanish Civil War; his works were banned by the Franco government.

I wandered in and out of the brilliant stacks of cans following you,
and followed in my imagination by the store detective.

We strode down the open corridors together in our solitary fancy
tasting artichokes, possessing every frozen delicacy, and never passing
the cashier.

Where are we going, Walt Whitman? The doors close in an hour.
Which way does your beard point tonight?

(I touch your book and dream of our odyssey in the supermarket and
feel absurd.)

Will we walk all night through solitary streets? The trees add shade
to shade, lights out in the houses, we'll both be lonely.

10   Will we stroll dreaming of the lost America of love past blue auto-
mobiles in driveways, home to our silent cottage?

Ah, dear father, graybeard, lonely old courage-teacher, what America
did you have when Charon quit poling his ferry and you got out on a
smoking bank and stood watching the boat disappear on the black
waters of Lethe?[4]

Berkeley 1955

Velocity of Money

For Lee Berton

I'm delighted by the velocity of money as it whistles through
            windows of Lower East Side
Delighted skyscrapers rise grungy apartments fall on 84th Street's
            pavement
Delighted this year inflation drives me out on the street
with double digit interest rates in Capitalist worlds
5   I always was a communist, now we'll win
as usury makes walls thinner, books thicker & dumber
Usury makes my poetry more valuable
Manuscripts worth their weight in useless gold—
The velocity's what counts as the National Debt gets trillions higher
10 Everybody running after the rising dollar
Crowds of joggers down Broadway past City Hall on the way to the
            Fed
Nobody reads Dostoyevsky books anymore so they'll have to give
            passing ear
to my fragmented ravings in between President's speeches
Nothing's happening but the collapse of the Economy
15 so I can go back to sleep till the landlord wins his eviction suit in
            court

February 18, 1986, 10:00 A.M.

---

4. The River of Forgetfulness in Hades. Charon is the boatman who, according to classical myth, ferries
souls to Hades.

THOMAS GRAY

Elegy Written in a Country Churchyard

The curfew tolls the knell of parting day,
   The lowing herd wind slowly o'er the lea,
The plowman homeward plods his weary way,
   And leaves the world to darkness and to me.

5 Now fades the glimmering landscape on the sight,
   And all the air a solemn stillness holds,
Save where the beetle wheels his droning flight,
   And drowsy tinklings lull the distant folds;

Save that from yonder ivy-mantled tower
10   The moping owl does to the moon complain
Of such, as wandering near her secret bower,
   Molest her ancient solitary reign.

Beneath those rugged elms, that yew tree's shade,
   Where heaves the turf in many a moldering heap,
15 Each in his narrow cell forever laid,
   The rude⁵ forefathers of the hamlet sleep.

The breezy call of incense-breathing Morn,
   The swallow twittering from the straw-built shed,
The cock's shrill clarion, or the echoing horn.⁶
20   No more shall rouse them from their lowly bed.

For them no more the blazing hearth shall burn,
   Or busy housewife ply her evening care;
No children run to lisp their sire's return,
   Or climb his knees the envied kiss to share.

25 Oft did the harvest to their sickle yield,
   Their furrow oft the stubborn glebe⁷ has broke;
How jocund did they drive their team afield!
   How bowed the woods beneath their sturdy stroke!

Let not Ambition mock their useful toil,
30   Their homely joys, and destiny obscure;
Nor Grandeur hear with a disdainful smile
   The short and simple annals of the poor.

The boast of heraldry,⁸ the pomp of power,
   And all that beauty, all that wealth e'er gave,
35 Awaits alike the inevitable hour.
   The paths of glory lead but to the grave.

5. Unlearned.   6. The hunter's horn.   7. Soil.   8. Noble birth.

Nor you, ye proud, impute to these the fault,
　　If Memory o'er their tomb no trophies[9] raise,
Where through the long-drawn aisle and fretted[1] vault
40　　The pealing anthem swells the note of praise

Can storied urn or animated[2] bust
　　Back to its mansion call the fleeting breath?
Can Honor's voice provoke the silent dust,
　　Or Flattery soothe the dull cold ear of Death?

45　Perhaps in this neglected spot is laid
　　Some heart once pregnant with celestial fire;
Hands that the rod of empire might have swayed,
　　Or waked to ecstasy the living lyre.

But Knowledge to their eyes her ample page
50　　Rich with the spoils of time did ne'er unroll;
Chill Penury repressed their noble rage,
　　And froze the genial current of the soul.

Full many a gem of purest ray serene,
　　The dark unfathomed caves of ocean bear:
55　Full many a flower is born to blush unseen,
　　And waste its sweetness on the desert air.

Some village Hampden,[3] that with dauntless breast
　　The little tyrant of his fields withstood;
Some mute inglorious Milton[4] here may rest,
60　　Some Cromwell[5] guiltless of his country's blood.

The applause of listening senates to command,
　　The threats of pain and ruin to despise,
To scatter plenty o'er a smiling land,
　　And read their history in a nation's eyes,

65　Their lot forbade: nor circumscribed alone
　　Their growing virtues, but their crimes confined;
Forbade to wade through slaughter to a throne,
　　And shut the gates of mercy on mankind,

The struggling pangs of conscious truth to hide,
70　　To quench the blushes of ingenuous shame,
Or heap the shrine of Luxury and Pride
　　With incense kindled at the Muse's flame.

---

9. An ornamental or symbolic group of figures depicting the achievements of the deceased.

1. Decorated with intersecting lines in relief.

2. Lifelike. *Storied urn*: a funeral urn with an epitaph or pictured story inscribed on it.

3. John Hampden (1594–1643), who, both as a private citizen and as a member of Parliament, zealously defended the rights of the people against the autocratic policies of Charles I.

4. John Milton (1608–1674), great English poet.

5. Oliver Cromwell (1599–1658), lord protector of England during the Interregnum, noted for military genius but also cruelty and intolerance.

Far from the madding crowd's ignoble strife,
  Their sober wishes never learned to stray;
75 Along the cool sequestered vale of life
  They kept the noiseless tenor of their way.

Yet even these bones from insult to protect
  Some frail memorial still erected nigh,
With uncouth rhymes and shapeless sculpture decked,[6]
80 Implores the passing tribute of a sigh.

Their name, their years, spelt by the unlettered Muse,
  The place of fame and elegy supply:
And many a holy text around she strews,
  That teach the rustic moralist to die.

85 For who to dumb Forgetfulness a prey,
  This pleasing anxious being e'er resigned,
Left the warm precincts of the cheerful day,
  Nor cast one longing lingering look behind?

On some fond breast the parting soul relies,
90 Some pious drops the closing eye requires;
Even from the tomb the voice of Nature cries,
  Even in our ashes live their wonted fires.

For thee, who mindful of the unhonored dead
  Dost in these lines their artless tale relate;
95 If chance, by lonely contemplation led,
  Some kindred spirit shall inquire thy fate,

Haply some hoary-headed swain may say,
  "Oft have we seen him at the peep of dawn
Brushing with hasty steps the dews away
100 To meet the sun upon the upland lawn.

"There at the foot of yonder nodding beech
  That wreathes its old fantastic roots so high,
His listless length at noontide would he stretch,
  And pore upon the brook that babbles by.

105 "Hard by yon wood, now smiling as in scorn,
  Muttering his wayward fancies he would rove,
Now drooping, woeful wan, like one forlorn,
  Or crazed with care, or crossed in hopeless love.

"One morn I missed him on the customed hill,
110 Along the heath and near his favorite tree;
Another came; nor yet beside the rill,
  Nor up the lawn, nor at the wood was he;

"The next with dirges due in sad array
  Slow through the churchway path we saw him borne.

6. Cf. the "storied urn or animated bust" (line 41) dedicated inside the church to the "proud" (line 37).

115 Approach and read (for thou canst read) the lay,
　　　Graved on the stone beneath yon aged thorn."

The Epitaph

　　Here rests his head upon the lap of Earth
　　　A youth to Fortune and to Fame unknown.
　　Fair Science⁷ frowned not on his humble birth,
120　*And Melancholy marked him for her own.*

　　Large was his bounty, and his soul sincere,
　　　Heaven did a recompense as largely send:
　　He gave to Misery all he had, a tear,
　　　He gained from Heaven ('twas all he wished) a friend.

125 *No farther seek his merits to disclose,*
　　　Or draw his frailties from their dread abode
　　(There they alike in trembling hope repose),
　　　The bosom of his Father and his God.

　　　　　　　　　　　　　　　　　　　　　1751

THOMAS HARDY

The Darkling Thrush

　　I leant upon a coppice gate
　　　When Frost was specter gray,
　　And Winter's dregs made desolate
　　　The weakening eye of day.
5 The tangled bine-stems scored the sky
　　　Like strings of broken lyres,
　　And all mankind that haunted nigh
　　　Had sought their household fires.

　　The land's sharp features seemed to be
10　The Century's corpse outleant,
　　His crypt the cloudy canopy,
　　　The wind his death-lament.
　　The ancient pulse of germ and birth
　　　Was shrunken hard and dry,
15 And every spirit upon earth
　　　Seemed fervorless as I.

　　At once a voice arose among
　　　The bleak twigs overhead
　　In a full-hearted evensong
20　Of joy illimited;
　　An aged thrush, frail, gaunt, and small,

___
7. Learning.

In blast-beruffled plume,
Had chosen thus to fling his soul
   Upon the growing gloom.

25 So little cause for carolings
   Of such ecstatic sound
Was written on terrestrial things
   Afar or nigh around,
That I could think there trembled through
30   His happy good-night air
Some blessed Hope, whereof he knew
   And I was unaware.

December 31, 1900

Neutral Tones

We stood by a pond that winter day,
And the sun was white, as though chidden of God,
And a few leaves lay on the starving sod;
   —They had fallen from an ash, and were gray.

5 Your eyes on me were as eyes that rove
Over tedious riddles of years ago;
And some words played between us to and fro
   On which lost the more by our love.

The smile on your mouth was the deadest thing
10 Alive enough to have strength to die;
And a grin of bitterness swept thereby
   Like an ominous bird a-wing . . .

Since then, keen lessons that love deceives,
And wrings with wrong, have shaped to me
15 Your face, and the God-curst sun, and a tree,
   And a pond edged with grayish leaves.

                      1898

ROBERT HASS

Then Time

In winter, in a small room, a man and a woman
Have been making love for hours. Exhausted,
Very busy wringing one another's bodies out,
They look at each other suddenly and laugh.
5 "What is this?" he says. "I can't get enough of you,"

She says, a woman who thinks of herself as not given
To cliché. She runs her fingers across his chest,
Tentative touches, as if she were testing her wonder.
He says, "Me too." And she, beginning to be herself

10 Again: "You mean you can't get enough of you, either?"
"I mean," he takes her arms in his hands and shakes them,
"Where does this come from?" She cocks her head
And looks into his face. "Do you really want to know?"
"Yes," he says. "Self-hatred," she says. "Longing for God."

15 Kisses him again. "It's not what it is"—a wry shrug—
"It's where it comes from." Kisses his bruised mouth
A second time, a third. Years later, in another city,
They're having dinner in a quiet restaurant near a park.
Fall. Earlier that day, hard rain: leaves, brass-colored

20 And smoky crimson, flying everywhere. Twenty years older,
She is very beautiful. An astringent person. She'd become,
She said, an obsessive gardener, her daughters grown.
He's trying not to be overwhelmed by love or pity
Because he sees she has no hands. He thinks

25 She must have given them away. He imagines,
Very clearly, how she wakes some mornings
(He has a vivid memory of her younger self, stirred
From sleep, flushed, just opening her eyes)
To momentary horror because she can't remember

30 What she did with them, why they are gone,
And then remembers, and calms herself, so that the day
Takes on its customary sequence once again.
She asks him if he thinks about her. "Occasionally,"
He says, smiling. "And you?" "Not much," she says.

35 "I think it's because we never existed inside time."
He studies her long fingers, a pianist's hands,
Or a gardener's, strong; much-used, as she fiddles
With her wineglass and he understands, vaguely,
That it must be his hands that are gone. Then

40 He's describing a meeting he sat in all day,
Chaired by someone they'd felt, many years before,
Mutually superior to . . . "You know the expression,
'A perfect fool,'" she'd said. And he had liked her tone
Of voice. Now she begins a story of the company

45 In Maine she orders bulbs from, begun by a Polish refugee
Married to a French-Canadian separatist from Quebec.
It's a story with many surprising turns and a rare
Chocolate-black lily at the end. He's listening,
Studying her face, still turning over her remark.

50 He decides that she thinks more symbolically
Than he does and that it seemed to have saved her,
For all her fatalism, from certain kinds of pain.
She finds herself thinking what a literal man he is,
Notices, as if she were recalling it, his pleasure.

55 In the menu, and the cooking, and the architecture of the room.

It moves her—in the way that earnest limitation
Can be moving, and she is moved by her attraction to him.
Also by what he was to her. She sees her own avidity
To live then, or not to not have lived might be more accurate,
60 From a distance, the way a driver might see from the road
A startled deer running across an open field in the rain.
Wild thing. Here and gone. Death made it poignant, or,
If not death exactly, which she'd come to think of
As creatures seething in a compost heap, then time.

2004

SEAMUS HEANEY

Digging

Between my finger and my thumb
The squat pen rests; snug as a gun.

Under my window, a clean rasping sound
When the spade sinks into gravelly ground:
5 My father, digging. I look down

Till his straining rump among the flowerbeds
Bends low, comes up twenty years away
Stooping in rhythm through potato drills[8]
Where he was digging.

10 The coarse boot nestled on the lug, the shaft
Against the inside knee was levered firmly.
He rooted out tall tops, buried the bright edge deep
To scatter new potatoes that we picked
Loving their cool hardness in our hands.

15 By God, the old man could handle a spade.
Just like his old man.

My grandfather cut more turf[9] in a day
Than any other man on Toner's bog.
Once I carried him milk in a bottle
20 Corked sloppily with paper. He straightened up
To drink it, then fell to right away
Nicking and slicing neatly, heaving sods
Over his shoulder, going down and down
For the good turf. Digging.

25 The cold smell of potato mould, the squelch and slap
Of soggy peat, the curt cuts of an edge

---

8. Small furrows in which seeds are sown.
9. Peat cut into slabs and dried to be used as fuel in stoves and furnaces.

Through living roots awaken in my head.
But I've no spade to follow men like them.

Between my finger and my thumb
30   The squat pen rests.
I'll dig with it.

1966

GERARD MANLEY HOPKINS

God's Grandeur

The world is charged with the grandeur of God.
    It will flame out, like shining from shook foil;[1]
    It gathers to a greatness, like the ooze of oil
Crushed. Why do men then now not reck his rod?[2]
5   Generations have trod, have trod, have trod;
    And all is seared with trade; bleared, smeared with toil;
    And wears man's smudge and shares man's smell: the soil
Is bare now, nor can foot feel, being shod.

And for all this, nature is never spent;
10   There lives the dearest freshness deep down things;
And though the last lights off the black West went
    Oh, morning, at the brown brink eastward, springs—
Because the Holy Ghost over the bent
    World broods with warm breast and with ah! bright wings.

1918

The Windhover[3]

To Christ our Lord

I caught this morning morning's minion,[4] king-
    dom of daylight's dauphin,[5] dapple-dawn-drawn Falcon, in his riding
Of the rolling level underneath him steady air, and striding
High there, how he rung upon the rein of a wimpling[6] wing
5 In his ecstasy! then off, off forth on swing,
    As a skate's heel sweeps smooth on a bow-bend: the hurl and gliding

1. "I mean foil in its sense of leaf or tinsel.... Shaken goldfoil gives off broad glares like sheet lightning and also, and this is true of nothing else, owing to its zig-zag dints and creasings and network of small many cornered facets, a sort of fork lightning too" (*Letters of Gerard Manley Hopkins to Robert Bridges,* ed. C. C. Abbott [1955], p. 169).   2. Heed his authority.
3. A small hawk, the kestrel, which habitually hovers in the air, headed into the wind.
4. Favorite, beloved.   5. Heir to regal splendor.   6. Rippling.

Rebuffed the big wind. My heart in hiding
Stirred for a bird,—the achieve of, the mastery of the thing!

Brute beauty and valor and act, oh, air, pride, plume, here
10   Buckle![7] AND the fire that breaks from thee then, a billion
Times told lovelier, more dangerous, O my chevalier![8]

No wonder of it: shéer plód makes plow down sillion[9]
Shine, and blue-bleak embers, ah my dear,
Fall, gall themselves, and gash gold-vermilion.

1877

A. M. KLEIN

Heirloom

My father bequeathed me no wide estates;
No keys and ledgers were my heritage;
Only some holy books with *yahrzeit*[1] dates
Writ mournfully upon a blank front page—

5   Books of the Baal Shem Tov,[2] and of his wonders;
Pamphlets upon the devil and his crew;
Prayers against road demons, witches, thunders;
And sundry other tomes for a good Jew.

Beautiful: though no pictures on them, save
10   The scorpion crawling on a printed track;
The Virgin floating on a scriptural wave,
Square letters twinkling in the Zodiac.

The snuff left on this page, now brown and old,
The tallow stains of midnight liturgy—
15   These are my coat of arms, and these unfold
My noble lineage, my proud ancestry!

And my tears, too, have stained this heirloomed ground,
When reading in these treatises some weird
Miracle, I turned a leaf and found
20   A white hair fallen from my father's beard.

1940

7. Several meanings may apply: to join closely, to prepare for battle, to grapple with, to collapse.
8. Horseman, knight.
9. The narrow strip of land between furrows in an open field divided for separate cultivation.
1. Anniversary of the death of a parent or near relative.
2. A title given to someone who possesses the secret knowledge of Jewish holy men and who, therefore, could work miracles.

ANDREW MARVELL

The Garden

How vainly men themselves amaze[3]
To win the palm, the oak, or bays,[4]
And their incessant labors see
Crowned from some single herb, or tree,
5   Whose short and narrow-vergèd[5] shade
Does prudently their toils upbraid;
While all flowers and all trees do close[6]
To weave the garlands of repose!

Fair Quiet, have I found thee here,
10   And Innocence, thy sister dear?
Mistaken long, I sought you then
In busy companies of men.
Your sacred plants,[7] if here below,
Only among the plants will grow;
15   Society is all but rude[8]
To[9] this delicious solitude.

No white nor red was ever seen
So am'rous as this lovely green.
Fond lovers, cruel as their flame,
20   Cut in these trees their mistress' name:
Little, alas, they know, or heed
How far these beauties hers exceed!
Fair trees, wheresoe'er your barks I wound,
No name shall but your own be found.

25   When we have run our passion's heat,
Love hither makes his best retreat.
The gods, that mortal beauty chase,
Still in a tree did end their race:
Apollo hunted Daphne so,
30   Only that she might laurel grow;
And Pan did after Syrinx speed,
Not as a nymph, but for a reed.[1]

What wondrous life is this I lead!
Ripe apples drop about my head;
35   The luscious clusters of the vine
Upon my mouth do crush their wine;

3. Become frenzied.   4. Awards for athletic, civic, and literary achievements.   5. Narrowly cropped.
6. Unite.   7. Cuttings.   8. Barbarous.   9. Compared to.
1. In Ovid's *Metamorphoses*, Daphne, pursued by Apollo, is turned into a laurel, and Syrinx, pursued by Pan,
into a reed that Pan makes into a flute.

The nectarine and curious[2] peach
Into my hands themselves do reach;
Stumbling on melons, as I pass,
40 Insnared with flowers, I fall on grass.

Meanwhile the mind, from pleasure less,
Withdraws into its happiness;[3]
The mind, that ocean where each kind
Does straight its own resemblance find;[4]
45 Yet it creates, transcending these,
Far other worlds and other seas,
Annihilating[5] all that's made
To a green thought in a green shade.

Here at the fountain's sliding foot,
50 Or at some fruit tree's mossy root,
Casting the body's vest[6] aside,
My soul into the boughs does glide:
There, like a bird, it sits and sings,
Then whets[7] and combs its silver wings,
55 And, till prepared for longer flight,
Waves in its plumes the various[8] light.

Such was that happy garden-state,
While man there walked without a mate:
After a place so pure, and sweet,
60 What other help could yet be meet![9]
But 'twas beyond a mortal's share
To wander solitary there:
Two paradises 'twere in one
To live in paradise alone.

65 How well the skillful gardener drew
Of flowers and herbs this dial[1] new,
Where, from above, the milder sun
Does through a fragrant zodiac run;
And as it works, th' industrious bee
70 Computes its time as well as we!
How could such sweet and wholesome hours
Be reckoned but with herbs and flowers?

1681

---

2. Exquisite.   3. That is, the mind withdraws from lesser-sense pleasure into contemplation.
4. All land creatures supposedly had corresponding sea creatures.
5. Reducing to nothing by comparison.
6. Vestment, clothing; the flesh is being considered as simply clothing for the soul.   7. Preens.
8. Many-colored.   9. Appropriate.   1. A garden planted in the shape of a sundial, complete with zodiac.

JOHN MILTON

Lycidas[2]

In this monody the author bewails a learned friend, unfortunately drowned in his passage from Chester on the Irish Seas, 1637.[3] And by occasion foretells the ruin of our corrupted clergy then in their height.

Yet once more, O ye laurels, and once more
Ye myrtles brown, with ivy never sere,[4]
I come to pluck your berries harsh and crude,[5]
And with forced fingers rude,
5　Shatter your leaves before the mellowing year.
Bitter constraint, and sad occasion dear,[6]
Compels me to disturb your season due:
For Lycidas is dead, dead ere his prime,
Young Lycidas, and hath not left his peer.
10　Who would not sing for Lycidas? He knew
Himself to sing, and build the lofty rhyme.
He must not float upon his wat'ry bier
Unwept, and welter[7] to the parching wind,
Without the meed[8] of some melodious tear.
15　　Begin then, sisters of the sacred well,[9]
That from beneath the seat of Jove doth spring,
Begin, and somewhat loudly sweep the string.
Hence with denial vain and coy excuse;
So may some gentle muse[1]
20　With lucky words favor my destined urn,
And as he passes turn,
And bid fair peace be to my sable shroud.
For we were nursed upon the self-same hill,
Fed the same flock, by fountain, shade, and rill.
25　　Together both, ere the high lawns[2] appeared
Under the opening eyelids of the morn,
We drove afield, and both together heard
What time the gray-fly winds[3] her sultry horn,
Batt'ning[4] our flocks with the fresh dews of night,
30　Oft till the star that rose, at ev'ning, bright,
Towards Heav'n's descent had sloped his westering wheel.

---

2. The name of a shepherd in Virgil's *Eclogues*. Milton's elegy works from the convention of treating the dead man as if he were a shepherd and also transforms other details to a pastoral setting and situation.
3. Edward King, a student with Milton at Cambridge, and at the time of his death a young clergyman. *Monody*: a song sung by a single voice.
4. Withered. The laurel, myrtle, and ivy were all materials used to construct traditional evergreen garlands signifying poetic accomplishment. *Brown*: dusky, dark.　5. Unripe.　6. Dire.
7. Tumble about.　8. Tribute.
9. The Muses, who lived on Mt. Helicon. At the foot of the mountain were two fountains, or wells, where the Muses danced around Jove's altar.　1. Poet.　2. Grasslands, pastures.
3. Blows; that is, the insect hum of midday.　4. Feeding.

Meanwhile the rural ditties were not mute,
Tempered to the oaten flute;[5]
Rough satyrs danced, and fauns with clov'n heel,
35 From the glad sound would not be absent long,
And old Damaetas[6] loved to hear our song.
   But O the heavy change, now thou art gone,
Now thou art gone, and never must return!
Thee, shepherd, thee the woods and desert caves,
40 With wild thyme and the gadding[7] vine o'ergrown,
And all their echoes mourn.
The willows and the hazel copses[8] green
Shall now no more be seen,
Fanning their joyous leaves to thy soft lays.
45 As killing as the canker[9] to the rose,
Or taint-worm to the weanling herds that graze,
Or frost to flowers, that their gay wardrobe wear,
When first the white-thorn blows:[1]
Such, Lycidas, thy loss to shepherd's ear.
50   Where were ye, nymphs,[2] when the remorseless deep
Closed o'er the head of your loved Lycidas?
For neither were ye playing on the steep,
Where your old Bards, the famous Druids, lie,
Nor on the shaggy top of Mona high,
55 Nor yet where Deva spreads her wizard stream:[3]
Ay me, I fondly[4] dream!
Had ye been there—for what could that have done?
What could the Muse[5] herself that Orpheus bore,
The Muse herself, for her enchanting[6] son
60 Whom universal nature did lament,
When by the rout that made the hideous roar,
His gory visage down the stream was sent,
Down the swift Hebrus to the Lesbian shore?
   Alas! What boots[7] it with uncessant care
65 To tend the homely slighted shepherd's trade,
And strictly meditate the thankless Muse?
Were it not better done, as others use[8]
To sport with Amaryllis in the shade,
Or with the tangles of Neaera's hair?
70 Fame is the spur that the clear spirit doth raise

5. Shepherds' pipes.   6. A traditional pastoral name, possibly referring here to a Cambridge tutor.
7. Wandering.   8. Thickets.   9. Cankerworm.   1. Blossoms.   2. Nature deities.
3. The River Dee, reputed to have prophetic powers. *Mona:* the Isle of Anglesey. The steep (line 52) may be a burial ground, in northern Wales, for Druids, ancient priests and magicians; all three locations are near the place where King drowned.   4. Foolishly.
5. Calliope, the Muse of epic poetry, whose son Orpheus was torn limb from limb by frenzied orgiasts. His head, thrown into the Hebrus (lines 62–63), floated into the sea and finally to Lesbos, where it was buried.
6. Orpheus reputedly charmed even inanimate things with his music; he once persuaded Pluto to release his dead wife, Eurydice, from the infernal regions.   7. Profits.
8. Customarily do. Amaryllis (line 68) and Neaera (line 69) are stock names of women celebrated in pastoral love poetry.

(That last infirmity of noble mind)
To scorn delights, and live laborious days;
But the fair guerdon⁹ when we hope to find,
And think to burst out into sudden blaze,
75 Comes the blind Fury¹ with th' abhorréd shears,
And slits the thin-spun life. "But not the praise,"
Phoebus replied, and touched my trembling ears:²
"Fame is no plant that grows on mortal soil,
Nor in the glistering foil³
80 Set off to th' world, nor in broad rumor lies,
But lives and spreads aloft by those pure eyes
And perfect witness of all-judging Jove;
As he pronounces lastly on each deed,
Of so much fame in Heav'n expect thy meed."
85   O fountain Arethuse,⁴ and thou honored flood,
Smooth-sliding Mincius, crowned with vocal reeds,
That strain I heard was of a higher mood.
But now my oat⁵ proceeds,
And listens to the herald of the sea,⁶
90 That came in Neptune's plea.
He asked the waves and asked the felon-winds,
What hard mishap hath doomed this gentle swain,⁷
And questioned every gust of rugged wings
That blows from off each beakéd promontory.
95 They knew not of his story,
And sage Hippotades⁸ their answer brings:
That not a blast was from his dungeon strayed;
The air was calm, and on the level brine,
Sleek Panopë⁹ with all her sisters played.
100 It was that fatal and perfidious bark
Built in th' eclipse, and rigged with curses dark,
That sunk so low that sacred head of thine,
    Next Camus,¹ reverend sire, went footing slow,
His mantle hairy, and his bonnet sedge,
105 Inwrought with figures dim, and on the edge
Like to that sanguine flower inscribed with woe.²
"Ah! who hath reft," quoth he, "my dearest pledge?"
Last came, and last did go,

9. Reward.
1. Atropos, the Fate who cuts the threads of human life after they are spun and measured by her two sisters.
2. In Roman tradition, touching the ears of one's hearers meant asking them to remember what they heard.
Phoebus: Apollo, god of poetic inspiration.   3. Flashy setting, used to make inferior gems glitter.
4. A Sicilian fountain, associated with the pastoral poetry of Theocritus. The River Mincius (line 86) is
associated with Virgil's pastorals.   5. Oaten pipe: pastoral song.
6. Triton, who maintains the innocence of Neptune, the Roman god of the sea, in the death of Lycidas.
7. Youth, shepherd, poet.   8. Aeolus, god of the winds and son of Hippotas.
9. According to Virgil, the greatest of the Nereids (sea nymphs).
1. God of the river Cam, which flows through Cambridge.
2. The hyacinth, which supposedly bore marks that meant "alas" because the flower was created by Phoebus
from the blood of a youth he had killed accidentally.

The pilot of the Galilean Lake;[3]
110 Two massy keys he bore of metals twain
(The golden opes, the iron shuts amain).
He shook his mitered locks, and stern bespake:
"How well could I have spared for thee, young swain,
Enow[4] of such as for their bellies' sake
115 Creep and intrude, and climb into the fold![5]
Of other care they little reck'ning make,
Than how to scramble at the shearers' feast,
And shove away the worthy bidden guest.
Blind mouths! that scarce themselves know how to hold
120 A sheep-hook,[6] or have learned aught else the least
That to the faithful herdman's art belongs!
What recks it[7] them? What need they? They are sped,[8]
And when they list,[9] their lean and flashy songs
Grate on their scrannel[1] pipes of wretched straw.
125 The hungry sheep look up and are not fed,
But swoln with wind, and the rank mist they draw,
Rot inwardly, and foul contagion spread,
Besides what the grim wolf with privy paw[2]
Daily devours apace, and nothing said;
130 But that two-handed engine[3] the door
Stands ready to smite once, and smite no more."
    Return, Alpheus, the dread voice is past,
That shrunk thy streams; return, Sicilian Muse,[4]
And call the vales, and bid them hither cast
135 Their bells and flowrets of a thousand hues.
Ye valleys low, where the mild whispers use,[5]
Of shades and wanton winds and gushing brooks,
On whose fresh lap the swart star[6] sparely looks,
Throw hither all your quaint enameled eyes,
140 That on the green turf suck the honeyed showers,
And purple all the ground with vernal flowers.
Bring the rathe[7] primrose that forsaken dies,
The tufted crow-toe, and pale jessamine,
The white pink, and the pansy freaked[8] with jet,

---

3. St. Peter, a fisherman before he became a disciple. According to Matthew 16.19, Christ promised him "the keys of the kingdom of heaven"; he was traditionally regarded as the first head of the Church, hence the bishop's miter in line 112.   4. The old plural of "enough."

5. According to John 10.1, "He that entereth not by the door into the sheepfold, but climbeth up some other way . . . is a thief and a robber."

6. A bishop's staff was shaped like a sheephook to suggest his role as "pastor" (shepherd) of the flock of saints.   7. Does it matter to.   8. Have attained their purpose—but also, destroyed.

9. Desire.   1. Feeble.   2. The Roman Catholic Church.

3. Not identified. Guesses include the two-handed sword of the archangel Michael, the two houses of Parliament, and St. Peter's keys.

4. The muse of Theocritus. *Alpheus:* a river god who, according to Ovid, fell in love with Arethusa. She fled in the form of an underground stream and became a fountain in Sicily, but Alpheus dived under the sea, and at last his waters mingled with hers. See above, line 85.   5. Frequent.

6. Sirius, the Dog Star, which supposedly withers plants in late summer.   7. Early.   8. Flecked.

145 The glowing violet,
     The musk-rose, and the well-attired woodbine,
     With cowslips wan that hang the pensive head,
     And every flower that sad embroidery wears.
     Bid amaranthus[9] all his beauty shed,
150 And daffodillies fill their cups with tears,
     To strew the laureate hearse[1] where Lycid lies.
     For so to interpose a little ease,
     Let our frail thoughts dally with false surmise.
     Ay me! Whilst thee the shores and sounding seas
155 Wash far away, where'er thy bones are hurled,
     Whether beyond the stormy Hebrides,[2]
     Where thou perhaps under the whelming tide
     Visit'st the bottom of the monstrous world;[3]
     Or whether thou to our moist vows denied,
160 Sleep'st by the fable of Bellerus old,[4]
     Where the great vision of the guarded mount
     Look toward Namancos and Bayona's hold;
     Look homeward, Angel, now, and melt with ruth.[5]
     And, O ye dolphins,[6] waft the hapless youth.
165   Weep no more, woeful shepherds, weep no more,
     For Lycidas your sorrow is not dead,
     Sunk though he be beneath the wat'ry floor,
     So sinks the day-star[7] in the ocean bed,
     And yet anon repairs his drooping head,
170 And tricks[8] his beams, and with new-spangled ore
     Flames in the forehead of the morning sky:
     So Lycidas sunk low, but mounted high,
     Through the dear might of him that walked the waves,[9]
     Where, other groves and other streams along,
175 With nectar pure his oozy locks he laves,
     And hears the unexpressive nuptial song,[1]
     In the blest kingdoms meek of joy and love.
     There entertain him all the saints above,
     In solemn troops and sweet societies
180 That sing, and singing in their glory move,
     And wipe the tears forever from his eyes.
     Now, Lycidas, the shepherds weep no more;

---

9. A legendary flower that cannot fade.   1. Bier.
2. Islands off Scotland, the northern edge of the sea where King drowned.
3. World where monsters live.
4. A legendary giant, supposedly buried at Land's End in Cornwall. At the tip of Land's End is St. Michael's Mount (line 161), from which the archangel is pictured looking south across the Atlantic toward Spanish (Catholic) strongholds (Namancos and Bayona, line 162).   5. Pity.
6. According to Roman legend, dolphins brought the body of a drowned youth, Melicertes, to land, where a temple was erected to him as the protector of sailors.   7. The sun.   8. Dresses.
9. Christ. See Matthew 14.25-26.
1. Sung at the "marriage of the Lamb," according to Revelation 19; *unexpressive:* inexpressible.

Henceforth thou art the genius[2] of the shore,
In thy large recompense, and shalt be good
185 To all that wander in that perilous flood.
　　　Thus sang the uncouth swain[3] to th' oaks and rills,
While the still morn went out with sandals gray;
He touched the tender stops of various quills,[4]
With eager thought warbling his Doric[5] lay.
190 And now the sun had stretched out all the hills,
And now was dropped into the western bay.
At last he rose, and twitched his mantle blue:
Tomorrow to fresh woods, and pastures new.

1637

SHARON OLDS

I Go Back to May 1937

I see them standing at the formal gates of their colleges,
I see my father strolling out
under the ochre sandstone arch, the
red tiles glinting like bent
5 plates of blood behind his head, I
see my mother with a few light books at her hip
standing at the pillar made of tiny bricks with the
wrought-iron gate still open behind her, its
sword-tips black in the May air,
10 they are about to graduate, they are about to get married,
they are kids, they are dumb, all they know is they are
innocent, they would never hurt anybody.
I want to go up to them and say Stop,
don't do it—she's the wrong woman,
15 he's the wrong man, you are going to do things
you cannot imagine you would ever do,
you are going to do bad things to children,
you are going to suffer in ways you never heard of,
you are going to want to die. I want to go
20 up to them there in the late May sunlight and say it,
her hungry pretty blank face turning to me,
her pitiful beautiful untouched body,
his arrogant handsome blind face turning to me,
his pitiful beautiful untouched body,
25 but I don't do it. I want to live. I
take them up like the male and female
paper dolls and bang them together

---

2. Protecting deity.　3. Unlettered shepherd: that is, Milton.　4. Reeds in the shepherd's pipes.
5. The Greek dialect of Theocritus, Bion, and Moschus, the first writers of pastoral.

at the hips like chips of flint as if to
strike sparks from them, I say
30 Do what you are going to do, and I will tell about it.

1987

The Glass

I think of it with wonder now,
the glass of mucus that stood on the table
next to my father all weekend. The cancer
is growing fast in his throat now,
5 and as it grows it sends out pus like the
sun sending out flares, those pouring
tongues. So my father has to gargle, hack,
spit a mouth full of thick stuff
into the glass every ten minutes or so,
10 scraping the rim up his lower lip to
get the last bit off his skin, then he
sets the glass down on the table and it
sits there, like a glass of beer foam,
shiny and faintly golden, he gurgles and
15 coughs and reaches for it again and
gets the heavy sputum out,
full of bubbles and moving around like yeast—
he is like some god producing food from his own mouth.
He himself can eat nothing anymore,
20 just a swallow of milk sometimes,
cut with water, and even then it
can't always get past the tumor,
and the next time the saliva comes up it's
chalkish and ropey, he has to roll it in his
25 throat to form it and get it up and dis-
gorge the elliptical globule into the cup—
and the wonder to me is that it did not disgust me,
that glass of phlegm that stood there all day and
filled slowly with compound globes and I'd
30 empty it and it would fill again and
shimmer there on the table until the
room seemed to turn around it
in an orderly way, a model of the solar system
turning around the gold sun,
35 my father the dark earth that used to
lie at the center of the universe
now turning with the rest of us
around the bright glass of spit
on the table, these last mouthfuls.

1990

My Son the Man

Suddenly his shoulders get a lot wider,
the way Houdini would expand his body
while people were putting him in chains. It seems
no time since I would help him to put on his sleeper,
5 guide his calves into the gold interior,
zip him up and toss him up and
catch his weight. I cannot imagine him
no longer a child, and I know I must get ready,
get over my fear of men now my son
10 is going to be one. This was not
what I had in mind when he pressed up through me like a
sealed trunk through the ice of the Hudson,
snapped the padlock, unsnaked the chains,
and appeared in my arms, what I had always wanted,
15 my son the baby. Now he looks at me
the way Houdini studied a box
to learn the way out, then smiled and let himself be manacled.

1995

SYLVIA PLATH

Barren Woman

Empty, I echo to the least footfall,
Museum without statues, grand with pillars, porticoes, rotundas.
In my courtyard a fountain leaps and sinks back into itself,
Nun-hearted and blind to the world. Marble lilies
5 Exhale their pallor like scent.

I imagine myself with a great public,
Mother of a white Nike and several bald-eyed Apollos.[6]
Instead, the dead injure me with attentions, and nothing can happen.
The moon lays a hand on my forehead,
10 Blank-faced and mum as a nurse.

February 21, 1963

---

6. That is, gods of poetic inspiration. *Nike:* goddess of victory.

Black Rook in Rainy Weather

On the stiff twig up there
Hunches a wet black rook
Arranging and rearranging its feathers in the rain.
I do not expect a miracle
5 Or an accident

To set the sight on fire
In my eye, nor seek
Any more in the desultory weather some design,
But let spotted leaves fall as they fall,
10 Without ceremony, or portent

Although, I admit, I desire,
Occasionally, some backtalk
From the mute sky, I can't honestly complain:
A certain minor light may still
15 Leap incandescent

Out of kitchen table or chair
As if a celestial burning took
Possession of the most obtuse objects now and then—
Thus hallowing an interval
20 Otherwise inconsequent

By bestowing largesse, honor,
One might say love. At any rate, I now walk
Wary (for it could happen
Even in this dull, ruinous landscape); skeptical,
25 Yet politic; ignorant

Of whatever angel may choose to flare
Suddenly at my elbow. I only know that a rook
Ordering its black feathers can so shine
As to seize my senses, haul
30 My eyelids up, and grant

A brief respite from fear
Of total neutrality. With luck,
Trekking stubborn through this season
Of fatigue, I shall
35 Patch together a content

Of sorts. Miracles occur,
If you care to call those spasmodic

Tricks of radiance miracles. The wait's begun again,
The long wait for the angel,
40 For that rare, random descent.[7]

1960

Lady Lazarus

I have done it again.
One year in every ten
I manage it—

A sort of walking miracle, my skin
5 Bright as a Nazi lampshade,
My right foot

A paperweight,
My face a featureless, fine
Jew linen.[8]

10 Peel off the napkin
O my enemy.
Do I terrify?—

The nose, the eye pits, the full set of teeth?
The sour breath
15 Will vanish in a day.

Soon, soon the flesh
The grave cave ate will be
At home on me

And I a smiling woman.
20 I am only thirty.
And like the cat I have nine times to die.

This is Number Three.
What a trash
To annihilate each decade.

25 What a million filaments.
The peanut-crunching crowd
Shoves in to see

Them unwrap me hand and foot—
The big strip tease.
30 Gentlemen, ladies

7. According to Acts 2, the Holy Ghost at Pentecost descended like a tongue of fire upon Jesus' disciples.
8. During World War II, in some Nazi camps, prisoners were gassed to death and their body parts then turned into objects such as lampshades and paperweights.

These are my hands
My knees.
I may be skin and bone,

Nevertheless, I am the same, identical woman.
35 The first time it happened I was ten.
It was an accident.

The second time I meant
To last it out and not come back at all.
I rocked shut

40 As a seashell.
They had to call and call
And pick the worms off me like sticky pearls.

Dying
Is an art, like everything else.
45 I do it exceptionally well.

I do it so it feels like hell.
I do it so it feels real.
I guess you could say I've a call.

It's easy enough to do it in a cell.
50 It's easy enough to do it and stay put.
It's the theatrical

Comeback in broad day
To the same place, the same face, the same brute
Amused shout:

55 "A miracle!"
That knocks me out.
There is a charge

For the eyeing of my scars, there is a charge
For the hearing of my heart—
60 It really goes.

And there is a charge, a very large charge
For a word or a touch
Or a bit of blood

Or a piece of my hair or my clothes.
65 So, so Herr Doktor.
So, Herr Enemy.

I am your opus,
I am your valuable,
The pure gold baby

70 That melts to a shriek.
I turn and burn.
Do not think I underestimate your great concern

Ash, ash—
You poke and stir.
75 Flesh, bone, there is nothing there—

A cake of soap,
A wedding ring,
A gold filling.

Herr God, Herr Lucifer
80 Beware
Beware.

Out of the ash
I rise with my red hair
And I eat men like air.

1965

EZRA POUND

In a Station of the Metro[9]

The apparition of these faces in the crowd;
Petals on a wet, black bough.

1913

A Virginal

No, no! Go from me. I have left her lately.
I will not spoil my sheath with lesser brightness,
For my surrounding air hath a new lightness;
Slight are her arms, yet they have bound me straitly
5 And left me cloaked as with a gauze of aether;
As with sweet leaves; as with a subtle clearness.
Oh, I have picked up magic in her nearness
To sheathe me half in half the things that sheathe her.
No, no! Go from me, I have still the flavor,
10 Soft as spring wind that's come from birchen bowers.
Green come the shoots, aye April in the branches,
As winter's wound with her sleight hand she staunches,
Hath of the trees a likeness of the savor:
As white their bark, so white this lady's hours.

1912

9. The Paris subway.

FRANCIS QUARLES

On Change of Weathers

And were it for thy profit, to obtain
All sunshine? No vicissitude of rain?
Think'st thou that thy laborious plough requires
Not winter frosts as well as summer fires?
5 There must be both: sometimes these hearts of ours
Must have the sweet, the seasonable showers
Of tears; sometimes the frost of chill despair
Makes our desired sunshine seem more fair;
Weathers that most oppose the flesh and blood
10 Are such as help to make our harvest good.
We may not choose, great God: it is thy task;
We know not what to have, nor how to ask.

1632

WALLACE STEVENS

CD   *The Idea of Order at Key West*

She sang beyond the genius of the sea.
The water never formed to mind or voice,
Like a body wholly body, fluttering
Its empty sleeves; and yet its mimic motion
5 Made constant cry, caused constantly a cry,
That was not ours although we understood,
Inhuman, of the veritable ocean.

The sea was not a mask. No more was she.
The song and water were not medleyed sound
10 Even if what she sang was what she heard,
Since what she sang was uttered word by word.
It may be that in all her phrases stirred
The grinding water and the gasping wind;
But it was she and not the sea we heard.

15 For she was the maker of the song she sang.
The ever-hooded, tragic-gestured sea
Was merely a place by which she walked to sing.
Whose spirit is this? we said, because we knew
It was the spirit that we sought and knew
20 That we should ask this often as she sang.

If it was only the dark voice of the sea
That rose, or even colored by many waves;

If it was only the outer voice of sky
And cloud, of the sunken coral water-walled,
25 However clear, it would have been deep air,
The heaving speech of air, a summer sound
Repeated in a summer without end
And sound alone. But it was more than that,
More even than her voice, and ours, among
30 The meaningless plungings of water and the wind,
Theatrical distances, bronze shadows heaped
On high horizons, mountainous atmospheres
Of sky and sea.
              It was her voice that made
The sky acutest at its vanishing.
35 She measured to the hour its solitude.
She was the single artificer of the world
In which she sang. And when she sang, the sea,
Whatever self it had, became the self
That was her song, for she was the maker. Then we,
40 As we beheld her striding there alone,
Knew that there never was a world for her
Except the one she sang and, singing, made.

Ramon Fernandez,[1] tell me, if you know,
Why, when the singing ended and we turned
45 Toward the town, tell why the glassy lights,
The lights in the fishing boats at anchor there,
As the night descended, tilting in the air,
Mastered the night and portioned out the sea,
Fixing emblazoned zones and fiery poles,
50 Arranging, deepening, enchanting night.

Oh! Blessed rage for order, pale Ramon,
The maker's rage to order words of the sea,
Words of the fragrant portals, dimly-starred,
And of ourselves and of our origins,
55 In ghostlier demarcations, keener sounds.

                              1935

1. French classicist and critic (1894–1944), who emphasized the ordering role of a writer's consciousness upon the materials he or she used. Stevens denied that he had Fernandez in mind, saying that he combined a Spanish first name and surname at random: "I knew of Ramon Fernandez, the critic, and had read some of his criticisms, but I did not have him in mind" (*Letters of Wallace Stevens*, ed. Holly Stevens [1966], p. 798). Later, Stevens wrote to another correspondent that he did not have the critic "consciously" in mind (*Letters*, p. 823).

The Emperor of Ice-Cream

Call the roller of big cigars,
The muscular one, and bid him whip
In kitchen cups concupiscent curds.[2]
Let the wenches dawdle in such dress
5   As they are used to wear, and let the boys
Bring flowers in last month's newspapers.
Let be be finale of seem.[3]
The only emperor is the emperor of ice-cream.

Take from the dresser of deal,
10   Lacking the three glass knobs, that sheet
On which she embroidered fantails[4] once
And spread it so as to cover her face.
If her horny feet protrude, they come
To show how cold she is, and dumb.
15   Let the lamp affix its beam.
The only emperor is the emperor of ice-cream.

1923

Sunday Morning

[handwritten: Alba]

I

Complacencies of the peignoir, and late
[handwritten: woman's light dressing gown]
Coffee and oranges in a sunny chair,
And the green freedom of a cockatoo
Upon a rug mingle to dissipate
5   The holy hush of ancient sacrifice.
She dreams a little, and she feels the dark
Encroachment of that old catastrophe,[5]
As a calm darkens among water-lights.
The pungent oranges and bright, green wings
10   Seem things in some procession of the dead,
Winding across wide water, without sound,
The day is like wide water, without sound,

2. "The words 'concupiscent curds' have no genealogy; they are merely expressive: at least, I hope they are expressive. They express the concupiscence of life, but, by contrast with the things in relation in the poem, they express or accentuate life's destitution, and it is this that gives them something more than a cheap lustre" (*Letters*, p. 500).
3. "[T]he true sense of Let be be the finale of seem is let being become the conclusion of denouement of appearing to be: in short, ice cream is an absolute good. The poem is obviously not about ice cream, but about being as distinguished from seeming to be" (*Letters*, p. 341).   4. Fantall pigeons.
5. The Crucifixion.

Stilled for the passing of her dreaming feet
Over the seas, to silent Palestine,
15 Dominion of the blood and sepulchre.

   II

Why should she give her bounty to the dead?
What is divinity if it can come
Only in silent shadows and in dreams?
Shall she not find in comforts of the sun,
20 In pungent fruit and bright, green wings, or else
In any balm or beauty of the earth,
Things to be cherished like the thought of heaven?
Divinity must live within herself
Passions of rain, or moods in falling snow;
25 Grievings in loneliness, or unsubdued
Elations when the forest blooms; gusty
Emotions on wet roads on autumn nights;
All pleasures and all pains, remembering
The bough of summer and the winter branch.
30 These are the measures destined for her soul.

   III

Jove in the clouds has his inhuman birth.
No mother suckled him, no sweet land gave
Large-mannered motions to his mythy mind
He moved among us, as a muttering king,
35 Magnificent, would move among his hinds,[6]
Until our blood, commingling, virginal,
With heaven, brought such requital to desire
The very hinds discerned it, in a star.[7]
Shall our blood fail? Or shall it come to be
40 The blood of paradise? And shall the earth
Seem all of paradise that we shall know?
The sky will be much friendlier then than now,
A part of labor and a part of pain,
And next in glory to enduring love,
45 Not this dividing and indifferent blue.

   IV

She says, "I am content when wakened birds,
Before they fly, test the reality
Of misty fields, by their sweet questionings;
But when the birds are gone, and their warm fields
50 Return no more, where, then, is paradise?"
There is not any haunt of prophecy,
Nor any old chimera of the grave,
Neither the golden underground, nor isle

6. Lowliest rural subjects.   7. The star of Bethlehem.

Melodious, where spirits gat[8] them home,
55 Nor visionary south, nor cloudy palm
Remote on heaven's hill, that has endured
As April's green endures, or will endure
Like her remembrance of awakened birds,
Or her desire for June and evening, tipped
60 By the consummation of the swallow's wings.

V

She says, "But in contentment I still feel
The need of some imperishable bliss."
Death is the mother of beauty; hence from her,
Alone, shall come fulfillment to our dreams
65 And our desires. Although she strews the leaves
Of sure obliteration on our paths,
The path sick sorrow took, the many paths
Where triumph rang its brassy phrase, or love
Whispered a little out of tenderness,
70 She makes the willow shiver in the sun
For maidens who were wont to sit and gaze
Upon the grass, relinquished to their feet.
She causes boys to pile new plums and pears
On disregarded plate.[9] The maidens taste
75 And stray impassioned in the littering leaves.

VI

Is there no change of death in paradise?
Does ripe fruit never fall? Or do the boughs
Hang always heavy in that perfect sky,
Unchanging, yet so like our perishing earth,
80 With rivers like our own that seek for seas
They never find, the same receding shores
That never touch with inarticulate pang?
Why set the pear upon those river-banks
Or spice the shores with odors of the plum?
85 Alas, that they should wear our colors there,
The silken weavings of our afternoons,
And pick the strings of our insipid lutes!
Death is the mother of beauty, mystical,
Within whose burning bosom we devise
90 Our earthly mothers awaiting, sleeplessly.

---

8. Got.
9. "Plate is used in the sense of so-called family plate. Disregarded refers to the disuse into which things fall that have been possessed for a long time. I mean, therefore, that death releases and renews. What the old have come to disregard, the young inherit and make use of" (*Letters*, pp. 183–84).

VII

Supple and turbulent, a ring of men
Shall chant in orgy[1] on a summer morn
Their boisterous devotion to the sun,
Not as a god, but as a god might be,
95 Naked among them, like a savage source.
Their chant shall be a chant of paradise,
Out of their blood, returning to the sky;
And in their chant shall enter, voice by voice,
The windy lake wherein their lord delights,
100 The trees, like serafin,[2] and echoing hills,
That choir among themselves long afterward.
They shall know well the heavenly fellowship
Of men that perish and of summer morn.
And whence they came and whither they shall go
105 The dew upon their feet shall manifest.

VIII

She hears, upon that water without sound,
A voice that cries, "The tomb in Palestine
Is not the porch of spirits lingering.
It is the grave of Jesus, where he lay."
110 We live in an old chaos of the sun,
Or old dependency of day and night,
Or island solitude, unsponsored, free,
Of that wide water, inescapable.
Deer walk upon our mountains, and the quail
115 Whistle about us their spontaneous cries;
Sweet berries ripen in the wilderness;
And, in the isolation of the sky,
At evening, casual flocks of pigeons make
Ambiguous undulations as they sink,
120 Downward to darkness, on extended wings.

1915

ALFRED, LORD TENNYSON

Now Sleeps the Crimson Petal[3]

Now sleeps the crimson petal, now the white;
Nor waves the cypress in the palace walk;
Nor winks the gold fin in the porphyry font;[4]
The firefly wakens; waken thou with me.

---

1. Ceremonial revelry.   2. Seraphim, the highest of the nine orders of angels.
3. A song from *The Princess*, a long narrative poem about what the mid-nineteenth century called the "new woman."   4. Stone fishbowl. *Porphyry:* a red stone containing fine white crystals.

5   Now droops the milk-white peacock like a ghost,
And like a ghost she glimmers on to me.

Now lies the Earth all Danaë[5] to the stars,
And all thy heart lies open unto me.

Now slides the silent meteor on, and leaves
10 A shining furrow, as thy thoughts in me.

Now folds the lily all her sweetness up,
And slips into the bosom of the lake;
So fold thyself, my dearest, thou, and slip
Into my bosom and be lost in me.

1847

Tears, Idle Tears[6]

Tears, idle tears, I know not what they mean,
Tears from the depth of some divine despair
Rise in the heart, and gather to the eyes,
In looking on the happy autumn-fields,
5 And thinking of the days that are no more.

Fresh as the first beam glittering on a sail,
That brings our friends up from the underworld,
Sad as the last which reddens over one
That sinks with all we love below the verge;
10 So sad, so fresh, the days that are no more.

Ah, sad and strange as in dark summer dawns
The earliest pipe of half-awakened birds
To dying ears, when unto dying eyes
The casement slowly grows a glimmering square;
15 So sad, so strange, the days that are no more.

Dear as remembered kisses after death,
And sweet as those by hopeless fancy feigned
On lips that are for others; deep as love,
Deep as first love, and wild with all regret;
20 O Death in Life, the days that are no more!

1847

---

5. A princess in Greek mythology, seduced by Zeus after he became a shower of gold to enter the tower in which she was confined.   6. A song from *The Princess*.

Tithonus[7]

The woods decay, the woods decay and fall,
The vapors weep their burthen[8] to the ground,
Man comes and tills the field and lies beneath,
And after many a summer dies the swan.
5 Me only cruel immortality
Consumes; I wither slowly in thine arms,
Here at the quiet limit of the world,
A white-haired shadow roaming like a dream
The ever-silent spaces of the East,
10 Far-folded mists, and gleaming halls of morn.
　　Alas! for this gray shadow, once a man—
So glorious in his beauty and thy choice,
Who madest him thy chosen, that he seemed
To his great heart none other than a God!
15 I asked thee, "Give me immortality."
Then didst thou grant mine asking with a smile,
Like wealthy men who care not how they give.
But thy strong Hours indignant worked their wills,
And beat me down and marred and wasted me,
20 And though they could not end me, left me maimed
To dwell in presence of immortal youth,
Immortal age beside immortal youth,
And all I was in ashes. Can thy love,
Thy beauty, make amends, though even now,
25 Close over us, the silver star, thy guide,
Shines in those tremulous eyes that fill with tears
To hear me? Let me go; take back thy gift.
Why should a man desire in any way
To vary from the kindly race of men,
30 Or pass beyond the goal of ordinance
Where all should pause, as is most meet[9] for all?
　　A soft air fans the cloud apart; there comes
A glimpse of that dark world where I was born.
Once more the old mysterious glimmer steals
35 From thy pure brows, and from thy shoulders pure
And bosom beating with a heart renewed.
Thy cheek begins to redden through the gloom,
Thy sweet eyes brighten slowly close to mine,
Ere yet they blind the stars, and the wild team
40 Which love thee, yearning for thy yoke, arise,
And shake the darkness from their loosened manes,
And beat the twilight into flakes of fire.

---

7. Prince of Troy, loved by Aurora, goddess of the dawn, to whom he speaks the poem. Aurora obtained for him the gift of eternal life but forgot to ask for eternal youth.　　8. Burden.　　9. Proper.

Lo! ever thus thou growest beautiful
In silence, then before thine answer given
45 Departest, and thy tears are on my cheek.
   Why wilt thou ever scare me with thy tears,
And make me tremble lest a saying learnt,
In days far-off, on that dark earth, be true?
"The Gods themselves cannot recall their gifts."
50   Ay me! ay me! with what another heart
In days far-off, and with what other eyes
I used to watch—if I be he that watched—
The lucid outline forming round thee; saw
The dim curls kindle into sunny rings;
55 Changed with thy mystic change, and felt my blood
Glow with the glow that slowly crimsoned all
Thy presence and thy portals, while I lay,
Mouth, forehead, eyelids, growing dewy-warm
With kisses balmier than half-opening buds
60 Of April, and could hear the lips that kissed
Whispering I knew not what of wild and sweet,
Like that strange song I heard Apollo sing,
While Ilion like a mist rose into towers.[1]
   Yet hold me not forever in thine East;
65 How can my nature longer mix with thine?
Coldly thy rosy shadows bathe me, cold
Are all thy lights, and cold my wrinkled feet
Upon thy glimmering thresholds, when the steam
Floats up from those dim fields about the homes
70 Of happy men that have the power to die,
And grassy barrows of the happier dead.
Release me, and restore me to the ground.
Thou seest all things, thou wilt see my grave;
Thou wilt renew thy beauty morn by morn,
75 I earth in earth forget these empty courts,
And thee returning on thy silver wheels.

                                        1860

Ulysses[2]

It little profits that an idle king,
By this still hearth, among these barren crags,
Matched with an agéd wife,[3] I mete and dole

---

1. According to Ovid's *Heroides*, music by the god of poetic inspiration accompanied the creation of walls and towers around Troy (Ilion).
2. After the end of the Trojan War, Ulysses (or Odysseus), king of Ithaca and one of the Greek heroes of the war, returned to his island home (line 34). Homer's account of the situation is in the *Odyssey* 11, but Dante's account of Ulysses in the *Inferno* 26 is the more immediate background of the poem.
3. Penelope.

Unequal laws unto a savage race,
5 That hoard, and sleep, and feed, and know not me.

   I cannot rest from travel; I will drink
Life to the lees.[4] All times I have enjoyed
Greatly, have suffered greatly, both with those
That loved me, and alone; on shore, and when
10 Through scudding drifts the rainy Hyades[5]
Vexed the dim sea. I am become a name;
For always roaming with a hungry heart
Much have I seen and known—cities of men
And manners, climates, councils, governments,
15 Myself not least, but honored of them all—
And drunk delight of battle with my peers,
Far on the ringing plains of windy Troy.
I am a part of all that I have met;
Yet all experience is an arch wherethrough
20 Gleams that untraveled world, whose margin fades
For ever and for ever when I move.
How dull it is to pause, to make an end,
To rust unburnished, not to shine in use!
As though to breathe were life. Life piled on life
25 Were all too little, and of one to me
Little remains; but every hour is saved
From that eternal silence, something more,
A bringer of new things; and vile it were
For some three suns to store and hoard myself,
30 And this gray spirit yearning in desire
To follow knowledge like a sinking star,
Beyond the utmost bound of human thought.

   This is my son, mine own Telemachus,
To whom I leave the scepter and the isle—
35 Well-loved of me, discerning to fulfill
This labor by slow prudence to make mild
A rugged people, and through soft degrees
Subdue them to the useful and the good.
Most blameless is he, centered in the sphere
40 Of common duties, decent not to fail
In offices of tenderness, and pay
Meet adoration to my household gods,
When I am gone. He works his work, I mine.

   There lies the port; the vessel puffs her sail:
45 There gloom the dark, broad seas. My mariners,
Souls that have toiled, and wrought, and thought with me—
That ever with a frolic welcome took
The thunder and the sunshine, and opposed

---

4. All the way down to the bottom of the cup.
5. A group of stars that were supposed to predict the rain when they rose at the same time as the sun.

Free hearts, free foreheads—you and I are old;
50   Old age hath yet his honor and his toil.
Death closes all; but something ere the end,
Some work of noble note, may yet be done,
Not unbecoming men that strove with Gods.
The lights begin to twinkle from the rocks;
55   The long day wanes; the slow moon climbs; the deep
Moans round with many voices. Come, my friends.
'Tis not too late to seek a newer world.
Push off, and sitting well in order smite
The sounding furrows; for my purpose holds
60   To sail beyond the sunset, and the baths
Of all the western stars, until I die.
It may be that the gulfs will wash us down;[6]
It may be we shall touch the Happy Isles,[7]
And see the great Achilles, whom we knew.
65   Though much is taken, much abides; and though
We are not now that strength which in old days
Moved earth and heaven, that which we are, we are:
One equal temper of heroic hearts,
Made weak by time and fate, but strong in will
70   To strive, to seek, to find, and not to yield.

1833

DYLAN THOMAS

Fern Hill

Now as I was young and easy under the apple boughs
About the lilting house and happy as the grass was green,
    The night above the dingle starry,
        Time let me hail and climb
5   Golden in the heydays of his eyes,
And honored among wagons I was prince of the apple towns
And once below a time I lordly had the trees and leaves
        Trail with daisies and barley
    Down the rivers of the windfall light.

10   And as I was green and carefree, famous among the barns
About the happy yard and singing as the farm was home,
    In the sun that is young once only,
        Time let me play and be
    Golden in the mercy of his means,
15   And green and golden I was huntsman and herdsman, the calves

6. Beyond the Gulf of Gibraltar was supposed to be a chasm that led to Hades.
7. Elysium, the Islands of the Blessed, where heroes like Achilles (line 64) go after death.

Sang to my horn, the foxes on the hills barked clear and cold,
   And the sabbath rang slowly
  In the pebbles of the holy streams.

All the sun long it was running, it was lovely, the hay
20 Fields high as the house, the tunes from the chimneys, it was air
   And playing, lovely and watery
    And fire green as grass.
   And nightly under the simple stars
  As I rode to sleep the owls were bearing the farm away,
25 All the moon long I heard, blessed among stables, the nightjars⁸
   Flying with the ricks,⁹ and the horses
    Flashing into the dark.

And then to awake, and the farm, like a wanderer white
With the dew, come back, the cock on his shoulder: it was all
30   Shining, it was Adam and maiden,
    The sky gathered again
   And the sun grew round that very day.
So it must have been after the birth of the simple light
In the first, spinning place, the spellbound horses walking warm
35   Out of the whinnying green stable
    On to the fields of praise.

And honored among foxes and pheasants by the gay house
Under the new made clouds and happy as the heart was long,
  In the sun born over and over,
40   I ran my heedless ways,
   My wishes raced through the house-high hay
And nothing I cared, at my sky-blue trades, that time allows
In all his tuneful turning so few and such morning songs
   Before the children green and golden
45   Follow him out of grace,

Nothing I cared, in the lamb white days, that time would take me
Up to the swallow-thronged loft by the shadow of my hand,
  In the moon that is always rising,
   Nor that riding to sleep
50   I should hear him fly with the high fields
And wake to the farm forever fled from the childless land.
Oh as I was young and easy in the mercy of his means,
   Time held me green and dying
   Though I sang in my chains like the sea.

               1946

8. Birds also known as goatsuckers.   9. Haystacks.

WALT WHITMAN

Facing West from California's Shores

Facing west, from California's shores,
Inquiring, tireless, seeking what is yet unfound,
I, a child, very old, over waves, towards the house of maternity,[1] the
     land of migrations, look afar,
Look off the shores of my Western sea, the circle almost circled:
5   For starting westward from Hindustan, from the vales of Kashmere,
From Asia, from the north, from the God, the sage, and the hero,
From the south, from the flowery peninsulas and the spice islands,
Long having wandered since, round the earth having wandered,
Now I face home again, very pleased and joyous;
10 (But where is what I started for, so long ago?
And why is it yet unfound?)

                                                        1860

I Hear America Singing

I hear America singing, the varied carols I hear,
Those of mechanics, each one singing his as it should be blithe and
     strong,
The carpenter singing his as he measures his plank or beam,
The mason singing his as he makes ready for work, or leaves off work,
5   The boatman singing what belongs to him in his boat, the deckhand
     singing on the steamboat deck,
The shoemaker singing as he sits on his bench, the hatter singing as he
     stands,
The wood-cutter's song, the ploughboy's on his way in the morning,
     or at noon intermission or at sundown,
The delicious singing of the mother, or of the young wife at work, or
     of the girl sewing or washing,
Each singing what belongs to him or her and to none else,
10 The day what belongs to the day—at night the party of young fellows,
     robust, friendly,
Singing with open mouths their strong melodious songs.

                                                        1860

---

1. Asia, as the supposed birthplace of the human race.

When Lilacs Last in the Dooryard Bloomed[2]

1

When lilacs last in the dooryard bloomed,
And the great star early drooped in the western sky in the night,
I mourned, and yet shall mourn with ever-returning spring.
Ever-returning spring, trinity sure to me you bring,
5 Lilac blooming perennial and drooping star in the west,
And thought of him I love.

2

O powerful western fallen star!
O shades of night—O moody, tearful night!
O great star disappeared—O the black murk that hides the star!
10 O cruel hands that hold me powerless—O helpless soul of me!
O harsh surrounding cloud that will not free my soul.

3

In the dooryard fronting an old farm-house near the white-washed
        palings,
Stands the lilac-bush tall-growing with heart-shaped leaves of rich
        green,
With many a pointed blossom rising delicate, with the perfume
        strong I love,
15 With every leaf a miracle—and from this bush in the dooryard,
With delicate-colored blossoms and heart-shaped leaves of rich green,
A sprig with its flower I break.

4

In the swamp in secluded recesses,
A shy and hidden bird is warbling a song.

20 Solitary the thrush,
The hermit withdrawn to himself, avoiding the settlements,
Sings by himself a song.

Song of the bleeding throat,
Death's outlet song of life (for well dear brother I know,
25 If thou wast not granted to sing thou would'st surely die).

5

Over the breast of the spring, the land, amid cities,
Amid lanes and through old woods, where lately the violets peeped
        from the ground, spotting the gray debris,
Amid the grass in the fields each side of the lanes, passing the endless
        grass,

2. The "occasion" of the poem is the assassination of Abraham Lincoln.

Passing the yellow-speared wheat, every grain from its shroud in the
  dark-brown fields uprisen,
30 Passing the apple-tree blows of white and pink in the orchards,
Carrying a corpse to where it shall rest in the grave,
Night and day journeys a coffin.

6

Coffin that passes through lanes and streets,[3]
Through day and night with the great cloud darkening the land,
35 With the pomp of the inlooped flags with the cities draped in black,
With the show of the States themselves as of crepe-veiled women
  standing,
With processions long and winding and the flambeaus of the night,
With the countless torches lit, with the silent sea of faces and the
  unbared heads,
With the waiting depot, the arriving coffin, and the somber faces,
10 With dirges through the night, with the thousand voices rising
  strong and solemn,
With all the mournful voices of the dirges poured around the coffin,
The dim-lit churches and the shuddering organs—where amid these
  you journey,
With the tolling tolling bells' perpetual clang,
Here, coffin that slowly passes,
45 I give you my sprig of lilac.

7

(Nor for you, for one alone,
Blossoms and branches green to coffins all I bring,
For fresh as the morning, thus would I chant a song for you O sane
  and sacred death.

All over bouquets of roses,
50 O death, I cover you over with roses and early lilies,
But mostly and now the lilac that blooms the first,
Copious I break, I break the sprigs from the bushes,
With loaded arms I come, pouring for you,
For you and the coffins all of you O death.)

8

55 O western orb sailing the heaven,
Now I know what you must have meant as a month since I walked,
As I walked in silence the transparent shadowy night,
As I saw you had something to tell as you bent to me night after
  night,
As you drooped from the sky low down as if to my side (while the
  other stars all looked on),

3. The funeral cortege stopped at many towns between Washington and Springfield, Illinois, where Lincoln
was buried.

60 As we wandered together the solemn night (for something I know
      not what kept me from sleep),
   As the night advanced, and I saw on the rim of the west how full you
      were of woe,
   As I stood on the rising ground in the breeze in the cool transparent
      night,
   As I watched where you passed and was lost in the netherward black
      of the night,
   As my soul in its trouble dissatisfied sank, as where you sad orb,
65 Concluded, dropped in the night, and was gone.

        9

   Sing on there in the swamp,
   O singer bashful and tender, I hear your notes, I hear your call,
   I hear, I come presently, I understand you,
   But a moment I linger, for the lustrous star has detained me,
70 The star my departing comrade holds and detains me.

        10

   O how shall I warble myself for the dead one there I loved?
   And how shall I deck my song for the large sweet soul that has gone?
   And what shall my perfume be for the grave of him I love?

   Sea-winds blown from east and west,
75 Blown from the Eastern sea and blown from the Western sea, till
      there the prairies meeting,
   These and with these and the breath of my chant,
   I'll perfume the grave of him I love.

        11

   O what shall I hang on the chamber walls?
   And what shall the pictures be that I hang on the walls,
80 To adorn the burial-house of him I love?

   Pictures of growing spring and farms and homes,
   With the Fourth-month eve at sundown, and the gray smoke lucid
      and bright,
   With floods of the yellow gold of the gorgeous, indolent, sinking sun,
      burning, expanding the air,
   With the fresh sweet herbage under foot, and the pale green leaves of
      the trees prolific,
85 In the distance the flowing glaze, the breast of the river, with a wind-
      dapple here and there,
   With ranging hills on the banks, with many a line against the sky,
      and shadows,
   And the city at hand with dwellings so dense, and stacks of chim-
      neys,
   And all the scenes of life and the workshops, and the workmen
      homeward returning.

12

Lo, body and soul—this land,
90 My own Manhattan with spires, and the sparkling and hurrying
    tides, and the ships,
The varied and ample land, the South and the North in the light,
    Ohio's shores and flashing Missouri,
And ever the far-spreading prairies covered with grass and corn.

Lo, the most excellent sun so calm and haughty,
The violet and purple morn with just-felt breezes,
95 The gentle soft-born measureless light,
The miracle spreading bathing all, the fulfilled noon,
The coming eve delicious, the welcome night and the stars,
Over my cities shining all, enveloping man and land.

13

Sing on, sing on you gray-brown bird,
100 Sing from the swamps, the recesses, pour your chant from the
    bushes,
Limitless out of the dusk, out of the cedars and pines.

Sing on dearest brother, warble your reedy song,
Loud human song, with voice of uttermost woe.

O liquid and free and tender!
105 O wild and loose to my soul—O wondrous singer!
You only I hear—yet the star holds me (but will soon depart),
Yet the lilac with mastering odor holds me.

14

Now while I sat in the day and looked forth,
In the close of the day with its light and the fields of spring, and the
    farmers preparing their crops,
110 In the large unconscious scenery of my land with its lakes and for-
    ests,
In the heavenly aerial beauty (after the perturbed winds and the
    storms),
Under the arching heavens of the afternoon swift passing, and the
    voices of children and women,
The many-moving sea-tides, and I saw the ships how they sailed,
And the summer approaching with richness, and the fields all busy
    with labor,
115 And the infinite separate houses, how they all went on, each with its
    meals and minutia of daily usages,
And the streets how their throbbings throbbed, and the cities pent—
    lo, then and there,
Falling upon them all and among them all, enveloping me with the
    rest,
Appeared the cloud, appeared the long black trail,
And I knew death, its thought, and the sacred knowledge of death.

120 Then with the knowledge of death as walking one side of me,
And the thought of death close-walking the other side of me,
And I in the middle as with companions, and as holding the hands
of companions,
I fled forth to the hiding receiving night that talks not,
Down to the shores of the water, the path by the swamp in the dim-
ness,
125 To the solemn shadowy cedars and ghostly pines so still.
And the singer so shy to the rest received me,
The gray-brown bird I know received us comrades three,
And he sang the carol of death, and a verse for him I love.

From deep secluded recesses,
130 From the fragrant cedars and the ghostly pines so still,
Came the carol of the bird.

And the charm of the carol rapt me,
As I held as if by their hands my comrades in the night,
And the voice of my spirit tallied the song of the bird.

135 *Come lovely and soothing death,*
Undulate round the world, serenely arriving, arriving,
In the day, in the night, to all, to each,
Sooner or later delicate death.

Praised be the fathomless universe,
140 *For life and joy, and for objects and knowledge curious,*
And for love, sweet love—but praise! praise! praise!
For the sure-enwinding arms of cool-enfolding death.

Dark mother always gliding near with soft feet,
Have none chanted for thee a chant of fullest welcome?
145 *Then I chant it for thee, I glorify thee above all,*
I bring thee a song that when thou must indeed come, come unfalteringly.

Approach strong deliveress,
When it is so, when thou hast taken them I joyously sing the dead,
Lost in the loving floating ocean of thee,
150 *Laved in the flood of thy bliss O death.*

From me to thee glad serenades,
Dances for thee I propose saluting thee, adornments and feastings for thee,
And the sights of the open landscape and the high-spread sky are fitting,
And life and the fields, and the huge and thoughtful night.

155 *The night in silence under many a star,*
The ocean shore and the husky whispering wave whose voice I know,
And the soul turning to thee O vast and well-veiled death,
And the body gratefully nestling close to thee.

Over the tree-tops I float thee a song,
160 *Over the rising and sinking waves, over the myriad fields and the prairies*
wide,

Over the dense-packed cities all and the teeming wharves and ways,
I float this carol with joy, with joy to thee O death.

15

To the tally of my soul,
Loud and strong kept up the gray-brown bird,
165 With pure deliberate notes spreading filling the night.
Loud in the pines and cedars dim,
Clear in the freshness moist and the swamp-perfume,
And I with my comrades there in the night.

While my sight that was bound in my eyes unclosed,
170 As to long panoramas of visions.

    And I saw askant[4] the armies,
I saw as in noiseless dreams hundreds of battle-flags,
Borne through the smoke of the battles and pierced with missiles I
        saw them,
And carried hither and yon through the smoke, and torn and bloody,
175 And at last but a few shreds left on the staffs (and all in silence),
And the staffs all splintered and broken.

I saw battle-corpses, myriads of them,
And the white skeletons of young men, I saw them,
I saw the debris and debris of all the slain soldiers of the war,
180 But I saw they were not as was thought,
They themselves were fully at rest, they suffered not,
The living remained and suffered, the mother suffered,
And the wife and the child and the musing comrade suffered,
And the armies that remained suffered.

16

185 Passing the visions, passing the night,
Passing, unloosing the hold of my comrades' hands,
Passing the song of the hermit bird and the tallying song of my soul,
Victorious song, death's outlet song, yet varying ever-altering song,
As low and wailing, yet clear the notes, rising and falling, flooding
        the night,
190 Sadly sinking and fainting, as warning and warning, and yet again
        bursting with joy,
Covering the earth and filling the spread of the heaven,
As that powerful psalm in the night I heard from recesses,
Passing, I leave thee lilac with heart-shaped leaves,
I leave thee there in the door-yard, blooming, returning with spring.

195 I cease from my song for thee,
From my gaze on thee in the west, fronting the west, communing
        with thee,
O comrade lustrous with silver face in the night.

4. Askance: sideways.

Yet each to keep and all, retrievements out of the night,
The song, the wondrous chant of the gray-brown bird,
200 And the tallying chant, the echo aroused in my soul,
With the lustrous and drooping star with the countenance full of
    woe,
With the holders holding my hand nearing the call of the bird,
Comrades mine and I in the midst, and their memory ever to keep,
    for the dead I loved so well,
For the sweetest, wisest soul of all my days and lands—and this for
    his dear sake,
205 Lilac and star and bird twined with the chant of my soul,
There in the fragrant pines and the cedars dusk and dim.

1865–66, 1881

WILLIAM WORDSWORTH

Lines Written a Few Miles above Tintern Abbey, On Revisiting the Banks of the Wye during a Tour, July 13, 1798[5]

Five years have passed; five summers, with the length
Of five long winters! and again I hear
These waters, rolling from their mountain-springs
With a soft inland murmur. Once again
5 Do I behold these steep and lofty cliffs,
That on a wild secluded scene impress
Thoughts of more deep seclusion; and connect
The landscape with the quiet of the sky.
The day is come when I again repose
10 Here, under this dark sycamore, and view
These plots of cottage-ground, these orchard tufts,
Which at this season, with their unripe fruits,
Are clad in one green hue, and lose themselves
'Mid groves and copses.[6] Once again I see
15 These hedge-rows, hardly hedge-rows, little lines
Of sportive wood run wild: these pastoral farms,
Green to the very door; and wreaths of smoke
Sent up, in silence, from among the trees!
With some uncertain notice, as might seem
20 Of vagrant dwellers in the houseless woods,

---

5. Wordsworth had first visited the Wye valley and the ruins of the medieval abbey there in 1793, while on
a solitary walking tour. He was twenty-three then, twenty-eight when he wrote this poem.
6. Thickets.

Or of some hermit's cave, where by his fire
The hermit sits alone.

                    These beauteous forms,
Through a long absence, have not been to me
As is a landscape to a blind man's eye;
25 But oft, in lonely rooms, and 'mid the din
Of towns and cities, I have owed to them,
In hours of weariness, sensations sweet,
Felt in the blood, and felt along the heart;
And passing even into my purer mind,
30 With tranquil restoration—feelings too
Of unremembered pleasure: such, perhaps,
As have no slight or trivial influence
On that best portion of a good man's life,
His little, nameless, unremembered acts
35 Of kindness and of love. Nor less, I trust,
To them I may have owed another gift,
Of aspect more sublime; that blesséd mood,
In which the burthen[7] of the mystery,
In which the heavy and the weary weight
40 Of all this unintelligible world,
Is lightened—that serene and blesséd mood,
In which the affections gently lead us on—
Until, the breath of this corporeal frame
And even the motion of our human blood
45 Almost suspended, we are laid asleep
In body, and become a living soul;
While with an eye made quiet by the power
Of harmony, and the deep power of joy,
We see into the life of things.

                         If this
50 Be but a vain belief, yet, oh! how oft—
In darkness and amid the many shapes
Of joyless daylight; when the fretful stir
Unprofitable, and the fever of the world,
Have hung upon the beatings of my heart—
55 How oft, in spirit, have I turned to thee,
O sylvan Wye! thou wanderer through the woods,
How often has my spirit turned to thee!

    And now, with gleams of half-extinguished thought,
With many recognitions dim and faint,
60 And somewhat of a sad perplexity,
The picture of the mind revives again;
While here I stand, not only with the sense
Of present pleasure, but with pleasing thoughts

---

7. Burden.

That in this moment there is life and food
65 For future years. And so I dare to hope,
Though changed, no doubt, from what I was when first
I came among these hills; when like a roe
I bounded o'er the mountains, by the sides
Of the deep rivers, and the lonely streams,
70 Wherever nature led: more like a man
Flying from something that he dreads than one
Who sought the thing he loved. For nature then
(The coarser[8] pleasures of my boyish days,
And their glad animal movements all gone by)
75 To me was all in all—I cannot paint
What then I was. The sounding cataract
Haunted me like a passion; the tall rock,
The mountain, and the deep and gloomy wood,
Their colors and their forms, were then to me
80 An appetite; a feeling and a love,
That had no need of a remoter charm,
By thought supplied, nor any interest
Unborrowed from the eye. That time is past,
And all its aching joys are now no more,
85 And all its dizzy raptures. Not for this
Faint I,[9] nor mourn nor murmur; other gifts
Have followed; for such loss, I would believe,
Abundant recompense. For I have learned
To look on nature, not as in the hour
90 Of thoughtless youth; but hearing oftentimes
The still, sad music of humanity,
Nor[1] harsh nor grating, though of ample power
To chasten and subdue. And I have felt
A presence that disturbs me with the joy
95 Of elevated thoughts, a sense sublime
Of something far more deeply interfused,
Whose dwelling is the light of setting suns,
And the round ocean and the living air,
And the blue sky, and in the mind of man:
100 A motion and a spirit, that impels
All thinking things, all objects of all thought,
And rolls through all things. Therefore am I still
A lover of the meadows and the woods
And mountains; and of all that we behold
105 From this green earth; of all the mighty world
Of eye, and ear—both what they half create,
And what perceive; well pleased to recognize
In nature and the language of the sense
The anchor of my purest thoughts, the nurse,

---

8. Physical.   9. Am I discouraged.   1. Neither.

110 The guide, the guardian of my heart, and soul
Of all my moral being.

                              Nor perchance,
    If I were not thus taught, should I the more
    Suffer my genial spirits[2] to decay:
    For thou art with me here upon the banks
115 Of this fair river; thou my dearest Friend,[3]
    My dear, dear Friend; and in thy voice I catch
    The language of my former heart, and read
    My former pleasures in the shooting lights
    Of thy wild eyes. Oh! yet a little while
120 May I behold in thee what I was once,
    My dear, dear Sister! and this prayer I make,
    Knowing that Nature never did betray
    The heart that loved her; 'tis her privilege,
    Through all the years of this our life, to lead
125 From joy to joy: for she can so inform
    The mind that is within us, so impress
    With quietness and beauty, and so feed
    With lofty thoughts, that neither evil tongues,
    Rash judgments, nor the sneers of selfish men,
130 Nor greetings where no kindness is, nor all
    The dreary intercourse of daily life,
    Shall e'er prevail against us, or disturb
    Our cheerful faith that all which we behold
    Is full of blessings. Therefore let the moon
135 Shine on thee in thy solitary walk;
    And let the misty mountain-winds be free
    To blow against thee: and, in after years,
    When these wild ecstasies shall be matured
    Into a sober pleasure; when thy mind
140 Shall be a mansion for all lovely forms,
    Thy memory be as a dwelling-place
    For all sweet sounds and harmonies; oh! then,
    If solitude, or fear, or pain, or grief,
    Should be thy portion, with what healing thoughts
145 Of tender joy wilt thou remember me,
    And these my exhortations! No, perchance—
    If I should be where I no more can hear
    Thy voice, nor catch from thy wild eyes these gleams
    Of past existence—wilt thou then forget
150 That on the banks of this delightful stream
    We stood together; and that I, so long
    A worshiper of Nature, hither came
    Unwearied in that service; rather say
    With warmer love—oh! with far deeper zeal

2. Natural disposition; that is, the spirits are part of his individual genius.   3. His sister Dorothy.

155 Of holier love. Nor wilt thou then forget,
That after many wanderings, many years
Of absence, these steep woods and lofty cliffs,
And this green pastoral landscape, were to me
More dear, both for themselves and for thy sake!

                                                    1798

W. B. YEATS

[CD] *The Lake Isle of Innisfree*[4]

I will arise and go now, and go to Innisfree,
And a small cabin build there, of clay and wattles made,
Nine bean-rows will I have there, a hive for the honey-bee,
And live alone in the bee-loud glade.

5 And I shall have some peace there, for peace comes dropping slow,
Dropping from the veils of the morning to where the cricket sings;
There midnight's all a glimmer, and noon a purple glow,
And evening full of the linnet's wings.

I will arise and go now, for always night and day
10 I hear lake water lapping with low sounds by the shore;
While I stand on the roadway, or on the pavements grey,
I hear it in the deep heart's core.

1890

All Things Can Tempt Me

All things can tempt me from this craft of verse:
One time it was a woman's face, or worse—
The seeming needs of my fool-driven land;
Now nothing but comes readier to the hand
5 Than this accustomed toil. When I was young,
I had not given a penny for a song
Did not the poet sing it with such airs
That one believed he had a sword upstairs;
Yet would be now, could I but have my wish,
10 Colder and dumber and deafer than a fish.

                                                    1910

4. Island in Lough Gill, County Sligo, Ireland.

Easter 1916[5]

I have met them at close of day
Coming with vivid faces
From counter or desk among gray
Eighteenth-century houses.
5 I have passed with a nod of the head
Or polite meaningless words,
Or have lingered awhile and said
Polite meaningless words,
And thought before I had done
10 Of a mocking tale or a gibe
To please a companion
Around the fire at the club,
Being certain that they and I
But lived where motley is worn:
15 All changed, changed utterly:
A terrible beauty is born.

That woman's[6] days were spent
In ignorant good-will,
Her nights in argument
20 Until her voice grew shrill.
What voice more sweet than hers
When, young and beautiful,
She rode to harriers?
This man[7] had kept a school
25 And rode our wingèd horse;[8]
This other[9] his helper and friend
Was coming into his force;
He might have won fame in the end,
So sensitive his nature seemed,
30 So daring and sweet his thought.
This other man[1] I had dreamed
A drunken, vainglorious lout.

5. On Easter Monday, 1916, nationalist leaders proclaimed an Irish Republic. After a week of street fighting, the British government put down the Easter Rebellion and executed a number of prominent nationalists, including the four mentioned in lines 75–76, all of whom Yeats knew personally.
6. Countess Constance Georgina Markiewicz, a beautiful and well-born young woman from County Sligo who became a vigorous and bitter nationalist. At first she was condemned to death, but her sentence was later commuted to life imprisonment, and she was granted amnesty in 1917.
7. Patrick Pearse, who led the assault on the Dublin Post Office, from which the proclamation of a republic was issued. A schoolmaster by profession, he had vigorously supported the restoration of the Gaelic language in Ireland and was an active political writer and poet.
8. Pegasus, a traditional symbol of poetic inspiration.   9. Thomas MacDonagh, also a writer and teacher.
1. Major John MacBride, who had married Yeats's beloved Maud Gonne in 1903 but separated from her two years later.

He had done most bitter wrong
To some who are near my heart,
35 Yet I number him in the song;
He, too, has resigned his part
In the casual comedy;
He, too, has been changed in his turn,
Transformed utterly:
40 A terrible beauty is born.

Hearts with one purpose alone
Through summer and winter seem
Enchanted to a stone
To trouble the living stream.
45 The horse that comes from the road,
The rider, the birds that range
From cloud to tumbling cloud,
Minute by minute they change;
A shadow of cloud on the stream
50 Changes minute by minute;
A horse-hoof slides on the brim,
And a horse plashes within it;
The long-legged moor-hens dive,
And hens to moor-cocks call;
55 Minute by minute they live:
The stone's in the midst of all.

Too long a sacrifice
Can make a stone of the heart.
O when may it suffice?
60 That is Heaven's part, our part
To murmur name upon name,
As a mother names her child
When sleep at last has come
On limbs that had run wild.
65 What is it but nightfall?
No, no, not night but death;
Was it needless death after all?
For England may keep faith[2]
For all that is done and said.
70 We know their dream; enough
To know they dreamed and are dead;
And what if excess of love
Bewildered them till they died?
I write it out in a verse—
75 MacDonagh and MacBride
And Connolly[3] and Pearse
Now and in time to be,

2. Before the uprising the English had promised eventual home rule to Ireland.
3. James Connolly, the leader of the Easter uprising.

Wherever green is worn,
Are changed, changed utterly;
80 A terrible beauty is born.

1916

The Second Coming[4]

Turning and turning in the widening gyre[5]
The falcon cannot hear the falconer;
Things fall apart; the center cannot hold;
Mere anarchy is loosed upon the world,
5 The blood-dimmed tide is loosed, and everywhere
The ceremony of innocence is drowned;
The best lack all conviction, while the worst
Are full of passionate intensity.
Surely some revelation is at hand;
10 Surely the Second Coming is at hand.
The Second Coming! Hardly are those words out
When a vast image out of *Spiritus Mundi*[6]
Troubles my sight: somewhere in sands of the desert
A shape with lion body and the head of a man,
15 A gaze blank and pitiless as the sun,
Is moving its slow thighs, while all about it
Reel shadows of the indignant desert birds.[7]
The darkness drops again; but now I know
That twenty centuries of stony sleep
20 Were vexed to nightmare by a rocking cradle,
And what rough beast, its hour come round at last,
Slouches towards Bethlehem to be born?

January 1919

---

4. The Second Coming of Christ, according to Matthew 24.29–44, will be after a time of "tribulation." Disillusioned by Ireland's continued civil strife, Yeats saw his time as the end of another historical cycle. In *A Vision* (1937), Yeats describes his view of history as dependent on cycles of about two thousand years: the birth of Christ had ended the cycle of Greco-Roman civilization, and now the Christian cycle seemed near an end, to be followed by an antithetical cycle, ominous in its portents.
5. Literally, the widening spiral of a falcon's flight. "Gyre" is Yeats's term for a cycle of history, which he diagrammed as a series of interpenetrating cones.
6. Or *Anima Mundi*, the spirit or soul of the world. Yeats considered this universal consciousness or memory a fund from which poets drew their images and symbols.
7. Yeats later wrote of the "brazen winged beast . . . described in my poem *The Second Coming*" as "associated with laughing, ecstatic destruction."

Leda and the Swan[8]

A sudden blow: the great wings beating still
Above the staggering girl, her thighs caressed
By the dark webs, her nape caught in his bill,
He holds her helpless breast upon his breast.

5   How can those terrified vague fingers push
The feathered glory from her loosening thighs?
And how can body, laid in that white rush,
But feel the strange heart beating where it lies?

A shudder in the loins engenders there
10 The broken wall, the burning roof and tower
And Agamemnon dead.
                   Being so caught up,
So mastered by the brute blood of the air,
Did she put on his knowledge with his power
Before the indifferent beak could let her drop?

1923

Sailing to Byzantium[9]

I

That[1] is no country for old men. The young
In one another's arms, birds in the trees
—Those dying generations—at their song,
The salmon-falls, the mackerel-crowded seas,
5   Fish, flesh, or fowl, commend all summer long
Whatever is begotten, born, and dies.
Caught in that sensual music all neglect
Monuments of unaging intellect.

II

An aged man is but a paltry thing,
10 A tattered coat upon a stick, unless

8. According to Greek myth, Zeus took the form of a swan to rape Leda, who became the mother of Helen of Troy; of Castor; and also of Clytemnestra, Agamemnon's wife and murderer. Helen's abduction from her husband, Menelaus, brother of Agamemnon, began the Trojan War (line 10). Yeats described the visit of Zeus to Leda as an annunciation like that to Mary (see Luke 1.26–38); "I imagine the annunciation that founded Greece as made to Leda" (*A Vision*).
9. The ancient name of Istanbul, the capital and holy city of Eastern Christendom from the late fourth century until 1453. It was famous for its stylized and formal mosaics; its symbolic, nonnaturalistic art; and its highly developed intellectual life. Yeats repeatedly uses it to symbolize a world of artifice and timelessness, free from the decay and death of the natural and sensual world.
1. Ireland, as an instance of the natural, temporal world.

Soul clap its hands and sing, and louder sing
For every tatter in its mortal dress,
Nor is there singing school but studying
Monuments of its own magnificence;
15 And therefore I have sailed the seas and come
To the holy city of Byzantium.

III

O sages standing in God's holy fire
As in the gold mosaic of a wall,
Come from the holy fire, perne in a gyre,[2]
20 And be the singing-masters of my soul.
Consume my heart away; sick with desire
And fastened to a dying animal
It knows not what it is; and gather me
Into the artifice of eternity.

IV

25 Once out of nature I shall never take
My bodily form from any natural thing,
But such a form as Grecian goldsmiths make
Of hammered gold and gold enameling
To keep a drowsy Emperor awake;[3]
30 Or set upon a golden bough[4] to sing
To lords and ladies of Byzantium
Of what is past, or passing, or to come.

1927

Among School Children

I

I walk through the long schoolroom questioning;
A kind old nun in a white hood replies;
The children learn to cipher and to sing,
To study reading-books and history,
5 To cut and sew, be neat in everything
In the best modern way—the children's eyes
In momentary wonder stare upon
A sixty-year-old smiling public man.[5]

---

2. That is, whirl in a coiling motion, so that his soul may merge with its motion as the timeless world invades the cycles of history and nature. "Perne" is Yeats's coinage (from the noun *pim*): to spin around in the kind of spiral pattern that thread makes as it comes off a bobbin or spool.
3. "I have read somewhere that in the Emperor's palace at Byzantium was a tree made of gold and silver, and artificial birds that sang" [Yeats's note].
4. In Book 6 of the *Aeneid*, the sibyl tells Aeneas that he must pluck a golden bough from a nearby tree in order to descend to Hades. Each time Aeneas plucks the one such branch there, an identical one takes its place.   5. At sixty (in 1925), Yeats had been a senator of the Irish Free State.

II

I dream of a Ledaean body,[6] bent
10 Above a sinking fire, a tale that she
Told of a harsh reproof, or trivial event
That changed some childish day to tragedy—
Told, and it seemed that our two natures blent
Into a sphere from youthful sympathy,
15 Or else, to alter Plato's parable,
Into the yolk and white of the one shell.[7]

III

And thinking of that fit of grief or rage
I look upon one child or t'other there
And wonder if she stood so at that age—
20 For even daughters of the swan can share
Something of every paddler's heritage—
And had that color upon cheek or hair,
And thereupon my heart is driven wild:
She stands before me as a living child.

IV

25 Her present image floats into the mind—
Did Quattrocento finger[8] fashion it
Hollow of cheek as though it drank the wind
And took a mess of shadows for its meat?
And I though never of Ledaean kind
30 Had pretty plumage once—enough of that,
Better to smile on all that smile, and show
There is a comfortable kind of old scarecrow.

V

What youthful mother, a shape upon her lap
Honey of generation[9] had betrayed,
35 And that must sleep, shriek, struggle to escape
As recollection or the drug decide,
Would think her son, did she but see that shape
With sixty or more winters on its head,
A compensation for the pang of his birth,
40 Or the uncertainty of his setting forth?

6. Like that of Helen of Troy, daughter of Leda. The memory dream is of Maud Gonne (see also lines 29–30), with whom Yeats had long been hopelessly in love.
7. In Plato's *Symposium,* the origin of human love is explained by parable: Human beings were once spheres, but Zeus feared their power and cut them in half; now each half longs to be reunited with its missing half. Helen and Pollux were hatched from one of two eggs born to Leda after her union with Zeus in the form of a swan; the other contained Castor and Clytemnestra. According to Yeats in *A Vision,* "from one of [Leda's] eggs came Love and from the other War."
8. The hand of a fifteenth-century artist. Yeats especially admired Botticelli, and in *A Vision* praises his "deliberate strangeness everywhere [that] gives one an emotion of mystery which is new to painting."
9. Porphyry, a third-century Greek scholar and Neoplatonic philosopher, says "honey of generation" means the "pleasure arising from copulation" that draws souls "downward" to generation.

VI

Plato thought nature but a spume that plays
Upon a ghostly paradigm of things;[1]
Solider Aristotle played the taws
Upon the bottom of a king of kings;[2]
45 World-famous golden-thighed Pythagoras[3]
Fingered upon a fiddle-stick or strings
What a star sang and careless Muses heard:
Old clothes upon old sticks to scare a bird.

VII

Both nuns and mothers worship images,
50 But those the candles light are not as those
That animate a mother's reveries
But keep a marble or a bronze repose.
And yet they too break hearts—O Presences
That passion, piety or affection knows,
55 And that all heavenly glory symbolize—
O self-born mockers of man's enterprise;

VIII

Labor is blossoming or dancing where
The body is not bruised to pleasure soul,
Nor beauty born out of its own despair,
60 Nor blear-eyed wisdom out of midnight oil.
O chestnut-tree, great-rooted blossomer,
Are you the leaf, the blossom or the bole?
O body swayed to music, O brightening glance,
How can we know the dancer from the dance?

1927

Byzantium

The unpurged images of day recede;
The Emperor's drunken soldiery are abed;
Night resonance recedes, night-walkers' song
After great cathedral gong;
5 A starlit or a moonlit dome[4] disdains

1. Plato considered the real world an imperfect and illusory copy of the ideal world.
2. Aristotle, the teacher of Alexander the Great, disciplined him with a strap ("taws," line 43). His philosophy, insisting on the interdependence of form and matter, took the real world far more seriously than did Plato's.
3. Greek mathematician and philosopher (580?–500? B.C.E.); one legend describes his godlike golden thighs.
4. According to Yeats's philosophy, the full moon ("moonlit") represents the mind "completely absorbed in being."

All that man is,
All mere complexities,
The fury and the mire of human veins.

Before me floats an image, man or shade,
10 Shade more than man, more image than a shade;
For Hades' bobbin bound in mummy-cloth
May unwind the winding path;
A mouth that has no moisture and no breath
Breathless mouths may summon;
15 I hail the superhuman;
I call it death-in-life and life-in-death.

Miracle, bird or golden handiwork,
More miracle than bird or handiwork,
Planted on the star-lit golden bough
20 Can like the cocks of Hades crow,[5]
Or, by the moon embittered, scorn aloud
In glory of changeless metal
Common bird or petal
And all complexities of mire or blood.

25 At midnight on the Emperor's pavement flit
Flames that no faggot[6] feeds, nor steel has lit,
Nor storm disturbs, flames begotten of flame,
Where blood-begotten spirits come
And all complexities of fury leave,
30 Dying into a dance,
An agony of trance,
An agony of flame that cannot singe a sleeve.

Astraddle on the dolphin's mire and blood,[7]
Spirit after spirit! The smithies break the flood,
35 The golden smithies of the Emperor!
Marbles of the dancing floor
Break bitter furies of complexity,
Those images that yet
Fresh images beget,
40 That dolphin-torn, that gong-tormented sea.

1932

---

5. As the bird of dawn, the cock has from antiquity symbolized rebirth and resurrection.

6. Bundle of sticks used as fuel.

7. In ancient art, dolphins symbolize the soul moving from one state to another, and sometimes they provide a vehicle for the dead.

Biographical Sketches

Sketches are included for all poets represented by two or more poems.

VIRGINIA HAMILTON ADAIR (1913–2004)

In 1996, eighty-three years old and blind from glaucoma, Virginia Hamilton Adair published her first collection of poetry, *Ants on the Melon*. Adair, a professor of English at California State Polytechnic University for many years, had occasionally contributed poems to periodicals such as *The New Yorker*, but had concentrated on marriage, motherhood, and teaching. Yet her first collection received significant acclaim, despite (or perhaps because of) her relative seclusion from the poetic profession. Her poems are modest and understated, nonallusive and unambiguous; their subjects range from everyday domestic life to the atomic bomb to the suicide of her husband. Adair continued to publish new work in various periodicals until the time of her death.

JOHN ASHBERY (b. 1927)

John Ashbery was born in Rochester, New York, and raised on a farm near Lake Ontario. He was educated at Harvard University, where he wrote his thesis on Auden, who selected his first book, *Some Trees* (1956), for the Yale Series of Younger Poets. He received his M.A. from Columbia University and attended New York University before working as a copywriter in New York City. Beginning in 1955, he worked for a decade as an art reviewer in Paris. He has since served as poetry editor of the *Partisan Review* and art critic for *New York* and *Newsweek* magazines. He joined the faculty of Brooklyn College in 1974. In addition to poetry, Ashbery has written three plays and (with James Schuyler) a collaborative novel. Loosely connected to what has been called the New York school—along with Schuyler and fellow poets Frank O'Hara and Kenneth Koch—he frequently adopts and adapts the techniques of musicians as well as Abstract Expressionist and Surrealist painters. Ashbery is one of the most prolific and influential poets of the last half-century.

MARGARET ATWOOD (b. 1939)

Margaret Atwood spent her first eleven years in sparsely populated areas of northern Ontario and Quebec, where her father worked as an entomologist. Educated at the University of Toronto and Harvard, Atwood published her first poem at nineteen and has won numerous prizes for her poetry as well as her fiction. Her many novels include *The Edible Woman* (1969), *Surfacing* (1972), *The Handmaid's Tale* (1985), *Cat's Eye* (1988), *Alias Grace* (1996), *The Blind Assassin* (2000), and *Oryx and Crake* (2003); her story collections include *Murder in the Dark* (1983), *Bluebeard's Egg* (1983), *Wilderness Tips* (1991), and *Good Bones* (1992). *Morning in the Burned House* (1995) is her most recent collection of poems.

W. H. AUDEN (1907–1973)

Wystan Hugh Auden was born in York, England, to a medical officer and a nurse. Intending at first to become a scientist, Auden studied at Oxford, where he became the center of the "Oxford Group" of poets and leftist intellectuals. His travels during the 1930s led him to Germany, Iceland, China, Spain (where he was an ambulance driver in the civil war), and the United States (where he taught at various universities and, in 1946, became a naturalized citizen). A prolific writer of poems, plays, essays, and criticism, Auden won the Pulitzer Prize in 1948 for his collection of poems *The Age of Anxiety*, set in a New York City bar. Late in life he returned to Christ Church College, Oxford, where he was writer in residence. He is regarded as a masterly poet of political and intellectual conscience as well as one of the twentieth century's greatest lyric craftsmen.

BASHŌ (1644–1694)

Born Matsuo Munefusa, the second son of a low-ranking provincial samurai, the haiku poet who came to be known as Bashō at first put aside his literary interests and entered into service with the local ruling military house. In 1666, following the feudal lord's death, Bashō left for Edo (now Tokyo), the military capital of the shogun's new government, to pursue a career as a professional poet. He supported himself as a teacher and editor of other people's poetry but ultimately developed a following and a sizable group of students. A seasoned traveler, Bashō maintained an austere existence on the road as well as at home, casting himself in travel narratives such as *Oku no hosomichi* (*The Narrow Road to the Interior,* 1694) as a pilgrim devoted to nature and Zen.

EARLE BIRNEY
(1904–1995)

Born in Calgary, Alberta, Earle Birney was educated in Canada and eventually earned a Ph.D. from the University of Toronto before teaching at the University of Utah. After serving as a major in the Canadian army during World War II, Birney returned to the University of British Columbia, where he had received his B.A. twenty years earlier, and developed the first course there in creative writing. Birney's many books include novels and criticism, but he is best known as a poet. His first collection, *David and Other Poems,* won the Governor General's Medal for Poetry in 1942; many volumes and many awards later, his final collection, *Last Makings,* appeared in 1991.

ELIZABETH BISHOP
(1911–1979)

Born in Worcester, Massachusetts, Elizabeth Bishop endured the death of her father before she was a year old and the institutionalization of her mother when she was five. Bishop was raised by her maternal grandmother in Nova Scotia, then by her paternal grandparents back in Worcester. At Vassar College she met the poet Marianne Moore, who encouraged her to give up plans for medical school and pursue a career in poetry. Bishop traveled through Canada, Europe, and South America, finally settling in Rio de Janeiro, where she lived for nearly twenty years. Her four volumes of poetry are *North and South* (1946); *A Cold Spring* (1955), which won the Pulitzer Prize; *Questions of Travel* (1965); and *Geography III* (1976), which won the National Book Critics' Circle Award. *Complete Poems 1929–1979* and *Collected Prose* gather most of her published work.

WILLIAM BLAKE
(1757–1828)

The son of a London haberdasher and his wife, William Blake studied drawing at ten and at fourteen was apprenticed to an engraver for seven years. After a first book of poems, *Poetical Sketches* (1783), he began experimenting with what he called "illuminated printing"—the words and pictures of each page were engraved in relief on copper, which was used to print sheets that were then partly colored by hand—a laborious and time-consuming process that resulted in books of singular beauty, no two of which were exactly alike. His great *Songs of Innocence* (1789) and *Songs of Experience* (1794) were produced in this manner, as were his increasingly mythic and prophetic books, including *The Marriage of Heaven and Hell* (1793), *The Four Zoas* (1803), *Milton* (1804), and *Jerusalem* (1809). Blake devoted his later life to pictorial art, illustrating *The Canterbury Tales,* the Book of Job, and *The Divine Comedy,* on which he was hard at work when he died.

LOUISE BOGAN
(1897–1970)

Louise Bogan was the close contemporary of modernists such as T. S. Eliot and William Carlos Williams, yet she modeled her own work on sixteenth-and seventeenth-century Metaphysical poetry. Her preference for poetic order may have arisen from a decidedly disordered childhood; Bogan's parents had a tumultuous marriage. Though born in Maine, Bogan attended schools in Boston, leaving Boston University in 1916 to move to New York. Bogan was a distinguished critic and commentator, serving as poetry editor for *The New Yorker* from 1931 to 1969. She followed her verse collections *Body of This Death* (1923), *Dark Summer* (1929), and *The Sleeping Fury* (1937) with translations, commentaries, works of criticism, and the comprehensive collection *The Blue Estuaries: Poems 1923–1968* (1968).

EAVAN BOLAND
(b. 1944)

Eavan Boland, the daughter of the Irish diplomat F. H. Boland and the painter Frances Kelley, was born in Dublin, but educated in London, where her father was Irish ambassador, and New York, where he was a representative to the United Nations. After graduating from Trinity College, Dublin, she lectured in English there but found herself "completely unsuited to being an academic," and subsequently taught on a short-term basis at institutions in Ireland and the United States in order to devote her energies to writing. She has written essays on contemporary Irish literature, translated Irish poetry and work by Horace, Mayakovsky, and Nelly Sachs, and is a well-regarded reviewer and broadcaster. Her *Collected Poems* (1995) brought together seven collections published over twenty years. She is professor of English at Stanford University.

ROO BORSON (b. 1952)

Though considered a Canadian poet, Ruth Elizabeth Borson was born in Berkeley, California. She attended the University of California at Santa Barbara and earned her B.A. from Goddard College. In 1977, she published her first book, *Landfall*, in addition to receiving her M.F.A. from the University of British Columbia, where she was awarded the Macmillan Prize for Poetry. Her work suggests what she calls the "intricacy of the physical world" and recognizes the powers of sensuality and memory. Collections include *The Whole Night Coming Home* (1984), *Intent, or the Weight of the World* (1989), and *Water Memory* (1996).

GWENDOLYN BROOKS
(1917–2000)

Gwendolyn Brooks was born in Topeka, Kansas, and raised in Chicago, where she began writing poetry at the age of seven, and where she graduated from Wilson Junior College in 1936. Shortly after beginning her formal study of modern poetry at Chicago's Southside Community Art Center, Brooks produced her first book of poems, *A Street in Bronzeville* (1945). With her second volume, *Annie Allen* (1949), she became the first African American to win the Pulitzer Prize. Though her early work focused on what Langston Hughes called the "ordinary aspects of black life," during the mid-1960s she devoted her poetry to raising African American consciousness and to social activism. In 1968, she was named the Poet Laureate of Illinois; from 1985 to 1986, she served as poetry consultant to the Library of Congress. Her *Selected Poems* appeared in 1999.

ELIZABETH BARRETT BROWNING
(1806–1861)

Elizabeth Barrett was born into a wealthy family in Durham, England, and raised in Herefordshire. She received no formal schooling, but was very well educated at home in the classics and in English literature, and published her first volume of poetry at the age of thirteen. Despite her status as a prominent woman of letters, deteriorating health forced Barrett to live in semi-seclusion. Her collection *Poems* (1844) inspired the poet Robert Browning to write to her in May 1845, and thus began a courtship that resulted in their eloping to Italy in 1846. Following the publication of *Sonnets from the Portuguese* (1850), Barrett Browning received serious consideration to succeed Wordsworth as Poet Laureate (although the laureateship went instead to Tennyson); one critic hailed her as "the greatest female poet that England has produced." Her most admired work is *Aurora Leigh* (1857), a nine-book verse novel.

ROBERT BROWNING
(1812–1889)

Born in London, Robert Browning attended London University but was largely self-educated, learning Latin, Greek, French, and Italian by the time he was fourteen. He was an accomplished but little-known poet and playwright when he began courting the already famous poet Elizabeth Barrett. After they eloped to Italy in 1846, the Brownings enjoyed a period of happiness during which they produced most of their best-known work. Following Elizabeth's death in 1861, Robert returned to England with their son and for the rest of his life enjoyed great literary and social success. His major collections are *Men and Women* (1855), dedicated to his wife, and *Dramatis Personae* (1864), which contains some of his finest dramatic monologues. Lionized as one of England's greatest poets by the time of his death, Browning is buried in the Poets' Corner at Westminster Abbey.

ROBERT BURNS
(1759–1796)

Robert Burns was born and raised in Ayrshire, Scotland. The son of impoverished tenant farmers, he attended school sporadically but was largely self-taught. He collected subscriptions to publish his first collection, *Poems, Chiefly in the Scottish Dialect* (1786), which made his reputation in both Edinburgh and London. These poems were new in their rebellious individualism and in their pre-Romantic sensitivity to nature, yet they seemed to speak in an authentic "auld Scots" voice. A perennial failure as a farmer, Burns became a tax inspector and settled in the country town of Dumfries. Despite financial difficulties and failing health, he continued to write poems and songs (including "Auld Lang Syne") and devoted his last years to collecting Scottish folk songs for a cultural-preservation project. His work, frequently bawdy, politically zealous, and critical of organized religion, remains deeply loved throughout the world.

BUSON (1716–1784)

Born into a wealthy family in Kemu, Settsu province, Japan, Taniguchi Buson renounced a life of privilege to pursue a career in the arts. In 1751, after several years of traveling and studying under haiku masters in northeastern Japan, he settled in Kyoto and established himself as a professional painter. Known in later life as Yosa Buson, or simply Buson, he was responsible for a revival of the work of his prominent predecessor, Bashō. His own poems, regarded in Japan as second only to those of Bashō, display a subtle complexity and painterly attention to visual detail.

SAMUEL TAYLOR COLE-RIDGE (1772–1834)

Born in the small town of Ottery St. Mary in rural Devonshire, England, Samuel Taylor Coleridge is among the greatest and most original of the nineteenth-century Romantic poets. He wrote three of the most haunting and powerful poems in English—*The Rime of the Ancient Mariner* (1798), *Christabel* (1816), and "Kubla Khan" (1816)—as well as immensely influential literary criticism and a treatise on biology. In 1795, in the midst of a failed experiment to establish a "Pantisocracy" (his form of ideal community), he met William Wordsworth, and in 1798 they jointly published their enormously influential *Lyrical Ballads*. Coleridge's physical ailments, addiction to opium, and profound sense of despair made his life difficult and tumultuous and certainly affected his work. Still, he remains a central figure in English literature.

BILLY COLLINS (b. 1941)

Born in New York, Billy Collins received a B.A. from the College of the Holy Cross in Massachusetts and a Ph.D. from the University of California at Riverside before becoming a professor of English at Lehman College, City University of New York. His publications, several of which have broken sales records for poetry, include *Pokerface* (1977), *Video Poems* (1980), *The Apple That Astonished Paris* (1988), *Questions about Angels* (1991), *The Art of Drowning* (1995), *Picnic, Lightning* (1998), *Sailing around the Room: New and Selected Poems* (2000), *Taking off Emily Dickinson's Clothes* (2000), and *Nine Horses: Poems* (2002). He reads regularly on National Public Radio, performs live, and has recorded a spoken-word CD, *The Best Cigarette* (1997). He was named Poet Laureate of the United States in 2001.

HENRY CONSTABLE (1562–1613)

Henry Constable, the son of Sir Robert Constable, was educated at Cambridge University. A Roman Catholic during a period of fierce religious conflict in England, Constable spent most of his life in exile in Paris, where he served as agent for the Pope in pressing the Scottish king James VI's claims to the English throne (though he may have secretly worked in the service of the English government). As was the fashion for courtiers, Constable composed sonnets; in fact, his collection *Diana* (1592) was one of the first sonnet sequences, in which the poems create a fictional love narrative. His small body of poetry also includes his "Spiritual Sonnets" and a pastoral, "Venus and Adonis," said to have influenced Shakespeare. In 1604, Constable returned to England only to be imprisoned in the Tower of London on suspicion of treason; upon his release two years later he returned to the Continent and died, in 1613, in Liège.

WENDY COPE (b. 1945)

Born in Kent, England, Wendy Cope studied modern history at Oxford University, where she went on to receive a postgraduate degree in education. While working as a primary-school teacher in the 1970s, she began writing poetry. Her trademark optimistic and witty verses have been collected in the volumes *Making Cocoa for Kingsley Amis* (1986); *Serious Concerns* (1992); a children's book, *Twiddling Your Thumbs: Hand Rhymes* (1988); and *If I Don't Know,* which was short-listed for the Whitbread Poetry Award in 2002. Discussing her work, Cope has stated, "I dislike the term 'light verse' because it is used as a way of dismissing poets who allow humor into their work. I believe that a humorous poem can also be 'serious,' deeply felt and saying something that matters."

COUNTEE CULLEN
(1903–1946)

During his lifetime, Countee Cullen was the most celebrated and honored poet of the Harlem Renaissance, and he claimed New York City as his birthplace. In fact, he may have been born in Louisville, Kentucky, and the circumstances of his childhood adoption by the Reverend Frederick Cullen remain obscure. It is certain, though, that the poet received a good education at New York's DeWitt Clinton High School and then New York University. After receiving his M.A. at Harvard, Cullen returned to New York in 1926 and soon established himself as the leading figure in the active Harlem literary world, winning numerous awards for his poetry and editing the influential monthly column "The Dark Tower" for

Opportunity: Journal of Negro Life. A playwright, novelist, translator, and anthologist, Cullen is best remembered as a poet; his work has been collected in the volume *My Soul's High Song: The Collected Writings of Countee Cullen, Voice of the Harlem Renaissance* (1991).

E. E. CUMMINGS
(1894–1962)

Born in Cambridge, Massachusetts, the son of a Congregationalist minister, Edward Estlin Cummings attended Harvard University, where he wrote poetry in the Pre-Raphaelite and Metaphysical traditions. He joined the ambulance corps in France the day after the United States entered World War I but was imprisoned by the French due to his outspokenness against the war; he transmuted the experience into his first literary success, the novel *The Enormous Room* (1922). After the war, Cummings established himself as a poet and artist in New York City's Greenwich Village, made frequent trips to France and New Hampshire, and showed little interest in wealth or his growing celebrity. His variety of modernism was distinguished by its playfulness, its formal experimentation, its lyrical directness, and above all its celebration of the individual. His poetry is collected in *Complete Poems 1904–62* (1991).

JAMES DICKEY
(1923–1997)

James Dickey did not become seriously interested in poetry until he joined the Air Force in 1942. When he returned from World War II, he earned a B.A. and an M.A. at Vanderbilt University, publishing his first poem in *Sewanee Review* in his senior year. Following the publication of his first volume of poems, *Into the Stone* (1960), Dickey, while primarily a poet, worked in advertising, wrote novels, and taught at various universities. His 1965 collection, *Buckdancer's Choice,* received the National Book Award, and from 1967 to 1969 Dickey was consultant in poetry to the Library of Congress. He is widely known for his bestselling novel, *Deliverance* (1970), which he later adapted for Hollywood. Other publications include *The Whole Motion: Collected Poems 1949–1992* (1992) and another novel, *To the White Sea* (1993).

EMILY DICKINSON
(1830–1886)

From childhood on, Emily Dickinson led a sequestered and obscure life. Yet her verse has traveled far beyond the cultured yet relatively circumscribed environment in which she lived: her room, her father's house, her family, a few close friends, and the small town of Amherst, Massachusetts. Indeed, along with Walt Whitman, her far more public contemporary, she all but invented American poetry. Born in Amherst, the daughter of a respected lawyer whom she revered ("His heart was pure and terrible," she once wrote), Dickinson studied for less than a year at the Mount Holyoke Female Seminary, returning permanently to her family home. She became more and more reclusive, dressing only in white, seeing no visitors, yet working ceaselessly at her poems—nearly eighteen hundred in all, only a few of which were published during her lifetime. After her death, her sister Lavinia discovered the rest in a trunk, neatly bound into packets with blue ribbons—among the most important bodies of work in all of American literature.

JOHN DONNE
(1572–1631)

The first and greatest of the English writers who came to be known as the Metaphysical poets, John Donne wrote in a revolutionary style that combined highly intellectual conceits with complex, compressed phrasing. Born into an old Roman Catholic family at a time when Catholics were subject to constant harassment, Donne quietly abandoned his religion and had a promising legal career until a politically disastrous marriage ruined his worldly hopes. He struggled for years to support a large family; impoverished and despairing, he even wrote a treatise (*Biathanatos*) on the lawfulness of suicide. King James (who had ambitions for him as a preacher) eventually pressured Donne to take Anglican orders in 1615, and Donne became one of the great sermonizers of his day, rising to the position of dean of St. Paul's Cathedral in 1621. Donne's private devotions ("Meditations") were published in 1624, and he continued to write poetry until a few years before his death.

RITA DOVE (b. 1952)

A native of Akron, Ohio, Rita Dove attended Miami University in Ohio, studied for a year in West Germany as a Fulbright scholar, and received an MFA in creative writing from the University of Iowa. She is now a professor of English at the University of Virginia as well as associate editor of *Callaloo,* a journal of African American arts and letters. In 1987, Dove became the second African American poet (after Gwendolyn Brooks, in 1950) to win the Pulitzer Prize (for *Thomas and Beulah*). In 1993, she was appointed Poet Laureate of the United States. Her books include *The Yellow House on the Corner* (1980), *Museum* (1983), *Grace Notes* (1989), *Mother Love* (1995), *On the Bus with Rosa Parks* (1999), and, most recently, *American Smooth* (2004). A tireless advocate for poetry, Dove edited *The Best American Poetry 2000* and, from 2000 to 2002, authored the weekly column "Poet's Choice" in the *Washington Post Book World.*

CAROL ANN DUFFY
(b. 1955)

Carol Ann Duffy was born in Glasgow, Scotland, brought up in Staffordshire, England, and studied philosophy at the University of Liverpool. She has been a visiting professor and a writer-in-residence at a number of institutions. A regular reviewer and broadcaster, she now lectures in poetry at Manchester Metropolitan University. Her book *Mean Time* (1993) won both the Whitbread Prize for Poetry and the Forward Prize. The hallmarks of her poetry—her ability to invent plausible characters, to explore a range of points of view, and to pace her poetry so as to surprise readers—derive in large part from her experience of writing for the stage.

PAUL LAURENCE
DUNBAR (1872–1906)

The son of former slaves, Paul Laurence Dunbar was born in Dayton, Ohio. He attended a white high school, where he showed an early talent for writing and was elected class president. Unable to afford further education, he then worked as an elevator operator, writing poems and newspaper articles in his spare time. Dunbar took out a loan to subsidize the printing of his first book, *Oak and Ivy* (1893), but with the publication of *Majors and Minors* (1895) and *Lyrics of Lowly Life* (1896), his growing reputation enabled him to support himself by writing and lecturing. Though acclaimed during his lifetime for his lyrical use of rural black dialect in volumes such as *Candle-Lightin' Time* (1902), Dunbar was later criticized for adopting "white" literary conventions and accused of pandering to racist images of slaves and ex-slaves. He wrote novels and short stories in addition to poetry, and dealt frankly with racial injustice in works such as *The Sport of the Gods* (1903) and *The Fourth of July and Race Outrages* (1903).

STEPHEN DUNN
(b. 1939)

Born in New York, Stephen Dunn received a B.A. in history from Hofstra University, served in the armed forces, played professional basketball in Pennsylvania for a year, and afterward worked in advertising. In 1966, Dunn went to Spain "to try to change my life and see if I could write poetry"; in 1970, he earned an M.A. in creative writing from Syracuse University. Known for his clear, quietly powerful poems, Dunn has taught poetry at several universities, including Columbia, and has published many collections. Some of these are *Five Impersonations* (1971), *Full of Lust and Good Usage* (1976), *Work and Love* (1981), *Local Time* (1986), *Between Angels* (1989), *New and Selected Poems: 1974–1994* (1994), *Loosestrife* (1996), and *Different Hours* (2000), which won the Pulitzer Prize.

T. S. ELIOT (1888–1965)

Thomas Stearns Eliot—from his formally experimental and oblique writings to his brilliant arguments in defense of "orthodoxy" and "tradition"—dominated the world of English poetry between the world wars. Born in St. Louis, Missouri, into a family that hailed from New England, Eliot studied literature and philosophy at Harvard and later in France and Germany. He went to England in 1914, read Greek philosophy at Oxford, and published his first major poem, "The Love Song of J. Alfred Prufrock," the next year. In 1922, with the help

of Ezra Pound, Eliot published *The Waste Land*, which profoundly influenced a generation of poets and became a cornerstone of literary modernism. In his later work, particularly the *Four Quartets* (completed in 1945), Eliot explored religious questions in a quieter, more controlled idiom. By the middle of the twentieth century, Eliot was regarded as a towering figure in modern literature, renowned as a poet, critic, essayist, editor, and dramatist. He was awarded the Nobel Prize for Literature in 1948.

JAMES A. EMANUEL
(b. 1921)

Raised in Nebraska, James A. Emanuel earned a B.A. from Howard University, an M.A. from Northwestern, and a Ph.D. from Columbia; he then became an assistant professor of English at the City College of New York. As the 1960s passed, Emanuel became increasingly committed to reading and writing practices grounded in consciousness of his own racial identity, and he began to write poetry as well as literary criticism. His collections include *The Treehouse and Other Poems* (1968), *Panther Man* (1970), *Black Man Abroad: The Toulouse Poems* (1978), *A Chisel in the Dark: Poems Selected and New* (1980), *The Broken Bowl: New and Uncollected Poems* (1983), *Deadly James and Other Poems* (1987), *Whole Grain: Collected Poems 1958–1989* (1991), and *Jazz: From the Haiku King* (1999). Emanuel has lived in Paris for many years.

DAVID FERRY (b. 1924)

Born in Orange, New Jersey, David Ferry received a B.A. from Amherst College and an M.A. and a Ph.D. from Harvard. A professor of English at Wellesley College, he has published several widely acclaimed translations: *Gilgamesh* (1992), *The Odes of Horace* (1997), *The Eclogues of Virgil* (1999), and *The Epistles of Horace* (2001). His own poetry, informed by his multilingual scholarship, has been collected in such volumes as *On the Way to the Island* (1960), *A Letter and Some Photographs: A Group of Poems* (1981), *Strangers: A Book of Poems* (1983), *Dwelling Places: Poems and Translations* (1993), and *Of No Country I Know: New and Selected Poems and Translations* (1999), which won the Lenore Marshall Prize and the New Yorker Prize for Poetry in 2000.

ANNE FINCH, COUNT-
ESS OF WINCHILSEA
(1661–1720)

Anne Finch was born in Sydmonton, Berkshire, England. After the deaths of her parents, she was raised and educated by an uncle. In 1683, with the poet Anne Killigrew, Finch became a maid of honor to Mary Modena, the duchess of York and future wife of King James II, and at court met Colonel Heneage Finch, future earl of Winchilsea, who became her husband. Colonel Finch was arrested while attempting to follow James to France after the king was deposed in 1688; following his release, he and his wife retired to their estate in Eastwell, Kent. Encouraged by her husband, Anne Finch began to write in the 1680s, and her long poem "The Spleen' was anthologized in 1701. In 1709, Jonathan Swift addressed a poem, "Apollo Outwitted,' to her, and she exchanged poems with Alexander Pope about the representation of "female wits' in his *The Rape of the Lock* (1714). In 1713, she published her *Miscellany Poems on Several Occasions*, which included a tragedy, *Aristomenes*, but many of her poems remained in manuscript at her death. William Wordsworth praised her nature poems, especially "A Nocturnal Reverie." Only recently, however, have Finch's satiric poems and meditations on the problems of women writers achieved their due recognition.

ROBERT FROST
(1874–1963)

Though his poetry identifies Frost with rural New England, he was born and lived to the age of eleven in San Francisco. Moving to New England after his father's death, Frost studied classics in high school, entered and dropped out of both Dartmouth and Harvard, and spent difficult years as an unrecognized poet before his first book, *A Boy's Will* (1913), was accepted and published in England. Frost's character was full of contradiction—he held "that we get forward as much by hating as by loving"—yet by the end of his long life he was one of the most honored poets of his time, and the most widely read. In 1961, two years before his death, he was invited to read a poem at John F. Kennedy's presidential inauguration ceremony. Frost's poems—masterfully crafted, sometimes deceptively simple—are collected in *The Poetry of Robert Frost* (1969).

ALLEN GINSBERG
(1926–1997)

After a childhood in Paterson, New Jersey, overshadowed by his mother's mental illness, Allen Ginsberg enrolled at Columbia University, intent upon following his father's advice and becoming a labor lawyer. At the center of a circle that included Lucien Carr, Jack Kerouac, William S. Burroughs, and Neal Cassady, Ginsberg became interested in experimental poetry and alternative lifestyles. He graduated in 1948 and then joined the literary scene in San Francisco. In 1956, he published *Howl and Other Poems*, with an introduction by his mentor William Carlos Williams. The title poem, which condemned bourgeois culture and celebrated the emerging counterculture, became a manifesto for the Beat movement and catapulted Ginsberg to fame. Deeply involved in radical politics and Eastern spiritualism, Ginsberg went on to write such prose works as *Declaration of Independence for Dr. Timothy Leary* (1971) in addition to many volumes of poetry. His *Collected Poems, 1947–1980* appeared in 1984 and *Selected Poems 1947–1995* in 1996.

THOMAS GRAY
(1716–1771)

Thomas Gray was born in Cornhill, London, the son of a scrivener and his wife, and the only child of twelve to survive infancy. Educated at Eton and Peterhouse College, Cambridge, he divided his time between London and Stoke Poges before settling into a fellowship at Cambridge, where he pursued his studies in Classics, early English poetry, and ancient Welsh and Norse literatures. Other than brief stays in London and tours of the Lake District and Scotland in search of the picturesque, Gray rarely left the university. He embarked on a tour of France and Italy with the writer Horace Walpole in 1739, but after a quarrel returned alone. He began to write English poetry in about 1741. Little of his work was published in his lifetime, but his poems circulated in manuscript among friends. In Gray's "Elegy Written in a Country Churchyard," Samuel Johnson found "sentiments to which every bosom returns an echo" and "images which find a mirror in every mind."

ANGELINA GRIMKE
(1880–1958)

Born in Boston, Angelina Grimke was the descendent of black slaves, white slaveholders, free blacks, and prominent white abolitionists, including her namesake, Angelina Weld Grimke. As a child, Angelina was abandoned by her white mother, whose middle-class family disapproved of her marriage to Archibald Grimke, a biracial lawyer and author who eventually became vice president of the NAACP. Grimke graduated from the Boston Normal School of Gymnastics in 1902 and then moved with her father to Washington, D.C., where she worked as a teacher and began to write poetry, essays, short stories, and plays. By the 1920s, she was publishing her work in the leading journals and anthologies of the Harlem Renaissance—*The Crisis, Opportunity*, Alain Locke's *The New Negro* (1925), Countee Cullen's *Caroling Dusk* (1927), and Robert Kerlin's *Negro Poets and Their Poems* (1928). Much of her finest writing can be found in *Selected Works of Angelina Weld Grimke* (1991).

THOM GUNN
(1929–2004)

With the irony that characterizes much of his poetry, Thom Gunn once claimed, "I am a completely anonymous person—my life contains no events, and I lack any visible personality." Nevertheless, Gunn impressed himself on American poetry, producing more than thirty volumes and winning the Lenore Marshall Prize for *The Man with Night Sweats* (1992). Although he was born and educated in England, earning by 1958 both a B.A. and an M.A. from Trinity College, Cambridge, he lived and worked in California for many years. His poetry combines an appreciation of formal tradition with frank treatments of such subjects as homosexuality and hallucinogens. Much of his best work can be found in his *Selected Poems 1950–1975* (1979) and *Collected Poems* (1994). His last collection is *Boss Cupid* (2000). In 2003, Gunn received the David Cohen British Literature Award for lifetime achievement.

THOMAS HARDY
(1840–1928)

In a preface dated 1901, Thomas Hardy called his poems "unadjusted impressions," which nevertheless might, by "humbly recording diverse readings of phenomena as they are forced upon us by chance and change," lead to a philosophy. Indeed, though he was essentially retrospective in his outlook and traditional in his technique, Hardy anticipated the concerns of modern poetry by treating the craft as an awkward, often skeptical means of penetrating the facade of language. Born at Upper Bockhampton in Dorset, England, the son of a master mason and his wife, Hardy began to write fiction while pursuing an architectural career. His eight novels, now considered classics, brought him moderate commercial and critical success, but when *Jude the Obscure* (1896) was attacked as indecent, Hardy, disgusted, turned exclusively to poetry, producing a body of work that is as distinguished as his fiction. His major novels include *Far from the Madding Crowd* (1887) and *Tess of the D'Urbervilles* (1891); his poems have been selected and collected in various editions.

ROBERT HASS (b. 1941)

Robert Hass was born in San Francisco, California. He was educated at St. Mary's College and at Stanford University, where he studied under the poet Yvor Winters. He has taught at the State University of New York at Buffalo, St. Mary's College, and the University of California at Berkeley. In addition to poetry, he has written essays and criticism and translated much European poetry, most notably that of Czeslaw Milosz. He was poet laureate of the United States in 1995–96.

ROBERT HAYDEN (1913–1980)

Robert Hayden was born Asa Bundy Sheffey, in Detroit, Michigan, and raised by foster parents. He studied at Detroit City College (later Wayne State University), but left in 1936 to work for the Federal Writers' Project, where he researched black history and folk culture. He received an M.A. from the University of Michigan, taught at Fisk University from 1949 until 1969, and then taught at Michigan until his retirement. Although he published ten volumes of poetry, he did not receive acclaim until late in life. His collections include *Heart-Shape in the Dust* (1940), *The Lion and the Archer, Figures of Time* (1955), *A Ballad of Remembrance* (1962), *Selected Poems* (1966), *Words in the Mourning Time* (1970), *Night-Blooming Cereus* (1972), *Angle of Ascent* (1975), *American Journal* (1978 and 1982), and *Collected Poems* (1985).

SEAMUS HEANEY
(b. 1939)

Seamus Heaney, whose poems explore themes of rural life, memory, and history, was born on a farm in Mossbawn, County Derry (Castledawson, Londonderry), Northern Ireland. Educated at Queen's University in Belfast, he has taught at the University of California at Berkeley, Carysfort College in Dublin, and Oxford University; he currently teaches at Harvard. Once called by Robert Lowell "the most important Irish poet since Yeats," Heaney received the 1995 Nobel Prize for Literature. His poetry collections include *Eleven Poems* (1965), *Death of a Naturalist* (1966), *Wintering Out* (1972), *The Haw Lantern* (1987), *Seeing Things* (1991), *The Spirit Level* (1996), and *Electric Light* (2001). Heaney's translation of *Beowulf* (2000) from Anglo-Saxon into modern English gave new life to the oldest of English poems; it not only won Britain's prestigious Whitbread Award but also became a best-seller.

ANTHONY HECHT
(1923–2004)

Anthony Hecht was born in New York City. After graduation from Bard College, he joined the army and was stationed in Europe and Japan. He later taught at Kenyon College, then returned to New York and did graduate work at Columbia University. In the years following, he taught at, among other schools, Smith College, the University of Rochester, and Georgetown University. He published books of criticism—including a study of Auden (a key influence)—and undertook translation, most notably of Aeschylus and Joseph Brodsky. He also collaborated with artist Leonard Baskin on several sequences of poems. A gifted writer of light verse, he co-invented (with John Hollander) the comic "double dactyl,' and even his graver poems often register a dark humor.

He lived in Washington, D.C., where in 1982–84 he served as consultant in poetry to the Library of Congress.

GEORGE HERBERT
(1593–1633)

After the early death of his Welsh father, George Herbert was raised by his mother, a literary patron of John Donne. Herbert graduated with honors from Cambridge and was subsequently elected public orator at the university. He twice represented Montgomery, Wales, as a member of Parliament in the 1620s, but in 1626 he set aside his secular ambitions in favor of service to the Anglican Church. He married, took holy orders in 1630, and spent the rest of his brief life as a country parson in Bemerton, near Salisbury, where he was beloved as "Holy Mr. Herbert." Dying of consumption in 1633, he handed over to a friend the manuscript of *The Temple,* asking him to publish it only if he thought these quietly meditative poems might do good to "any dejected poor soul." The book proved a popular success and placed Herbert, along with Donne, at the forefront of the Metaphysical poets.

ROBERT HERRICK
(1591–1674)

The son of a London goldsmith and his wife, Robert Herrick would have liked nothing better than a life of leisured study, spent discussing literature and drinking sack with his hero, Ben Jonson. Instead, he answered the call of religion, taking holy orders and reluctantly accepting a remote parish in Devonshire. Herrick eventually made himself at home there, inventing dozens of imaginary mistresses with exotic names and practicing, half-seriously, his own peculiar form of paganism. When the Puritans came to power, Herrick was driven from his post to London, where in 1648 he published a volume of over fourteen hundred poems with two titles: *Hesperides* for the secular poems and *Noble Numbers* for those with sacred subjects. The poems did not fit the harsh atmosphere of Puritanism, but after the restoration of the Stuart monarchy in 1660, Herrick was eventually returned to his Devonshire parish, where he lived out his last years quietly.

GERARD MANLEY HOPKINS (1844–1889)

Born the eldest of eight children of a marine-insurance adjuster and his wife, Gerard Manley Hopkins attended Oxford, where his ambition was to become a painter—until, at the age of 22, he converted to Roman Catholicism and burned all his early poetry as too worldly. Not until after his seminary training and ordination as a Jesuit priest, in 1877, did he resume writing poetry, though he made few attempts to publish his verse, which many of his contemporaries found nearly incomprehensible. Near the end of his life, Hopkins was appointed professor of Greek at University College, Dublin, where—out of place, deeply depressed, and all but unknown—he died of typhoid. His poetry, collected and published by his friends, has been championed by modern poets, who admire its controlled tension, strong rhythm, and sheer exuberance.

ANDREW HUDGINS (b. 1951)

Texas-born Andrew Hudgins, son of a career Air Force officer and his wife, lived all over the American South as a boy. He earned an M.A. from the University of Alabama in 1976, then taught English and composition for several years before turning to poetry. After receiving his MFA from the University of Iowa in 1983, Hudgins produced *Saints and Strangers* (1985); astonishingly, this first collection was short-listed for the 1986 Pulitzer Prize. Many reviewers called Hudgins's work "Southern Gothic" for its eerie, graphic imagery, though he came to dislike this label. His second book, *After the Lost War* (1988), is a narrative poem based on the life of Sidney Lanier, an all-but-forgotten Civil War poet and Confederate soldier. Hudgins's subsequent works include *The Never-Ending: New Poems* (1991), *The Glass Hammer: A Southern Childhood* (1994), *Babylon in a Jar* (1998), and *Ecstatic in the Poison: New Poems* (2003).

LANGSTON HUGHES (1902–1967)

Born in Joplin, Missouri, Langston Hughes was raised mainly by his maternal grandmother, though he lived intermittently with each of his par-ents. He studied at Columbia University, but left to travel and work at a variety of jobs. Having already published poems in periodicals, anthologies, and his own first collection, *The Weary Blues* (1926), he graduated from Lincoln University; published a successful novel, *Not without Laughter* (1930); and became a major writer in the intellectual and literary movement called the Harlem Renaissance. During the 1930s, he became involved in radical politics and traveled the world as a correspondent and columnist; during the 1950s, though, the FBI classified him as a security risk and limited his ability to travel. In addition to poems and novels, he wrote essays, plays, screenplays, and an autobiography; he also edited anthologies of literature and folklore. His *Collected Poems* appeared in 1994.

ISSA (1763–1827)

Issa was the pen name of a Japanese poet of the Edo period (1600–1868). At thirteen, Issa left his home in Kashiwabara for Edo (now Tokyo). At about twenty-five, he began to study at the Katsushika haiku school, where he was elected a teacher in 1791. Preferring a nomadic life, he left the school to roam through Japan for many years. In 1814, having inherited his father's property, he returned to his childhood home and started a family; his wife and he had four children, all of whom died in infancy, and she herself died in childbirth. Issa chronicled this tragedy in *The Year of My Life* (1820). His other published works were *The Diary of My Father's Death* (1801) and *My Springtime* (1819)—personal but masterly uses of the haiku form.

BEN JONSON (1572?–1637)

Poet, playwright, actor, scholar, critic, and translator, Ben Jonson was the posthumous son of a clergyman and the stepson of a master bricklayer of Westminster. Jonson had an eventful early life, going to war against the Spanish, working as an actor, killing an associate in a duel, and converting to Roman Catholicism. Meanwhile, Jonson wrote a number of plays that have remained popular to this day, including *Every Man in His Humour* (in which Shakespeare acted a leading role; 1598), *Volpone* (1606), and *The Alchemist* (1610). He was named Poet Laureate in 1616 and spent the latter part of his life at the center of a large circle of friends and admirers known as the "Tribe of Ben." Often considered the first English author to deem writing his primary career, he published *The Works of Benjamin Jonson* in 1616.

JOHN KEATS (1795–1821)

John Keats was the son of a London livery stable owner and his wife; reviewers would later disparage him as a working-class "Cockney poet." At fifteen he was apprenticed to a surgeon, and at twenty-one he became a licensed pharmacist—in the same year that his first two published poems, including the sonnet "On First Looking into Chapman's Homer," appeared in *The Examiner*, a journal edited by the critic and poet Leigh Hunt. Hunt introduced Keats to such literary figures as the poet Percy Bysshe Shelley and helped him publish his *Poems by John Keats* (1817). When his second book, the long poem *Endymion* (1818), was fiercely attacked by critics, Keats, suffering from a steadily worsening case of tuberculosis, knew that he would not live to realize his poetic promise. In July 1820, he published *Lamia, Isabella, The Eve of St. Agnes, and Other Poems,* which contained the poignant "To Autumn" and three great odes: "Ode on a Grecian Urn," "Ode on Melancholy," and "Ode to a Nightingale"; early the next year, he died in Rome. In the years after Keats's death, his letters became almost as famous as his poetry.

GALWAY KINNELL
(b. 1927)

Born in Providence, Rhode Island, Galway Kinnell earned a B.A. from Princeton and an M.A. from the University of Rochester. He served in the navy and has been a journalist, a civil-rights field-worker, and a teacher at numerous colleges and universities. His early poetry, collected in *What a Kingdom It Was* (1960) and *First Poems 1946–1954* (1970), is highly formal; his subsequent work employs a more colloquial style. "Poetry," he has said, "is the attempt to find a language that can speak the unspeakable." He received both a Pulitzer Prize and the American Book Award for *Selected Poems* (1982), and in 2000 he culled *A New Selected Poems* from eight collections spanning twenty-four years. He lives in New York and Vermont.

ETHERIDGE KNIGHT
(1931–1991)

A native of Corinth, Mississippi, Etheridge Knight spent much of his adolescence carousing in pool halls, bars, and juke joints, developing a skillful oratorical style in an environment that prized verbal agility. During this time he also became addicted to narcotics. He served in the U.S. Army from 1947 to 1951; in 1960 he was sentenced to eight years in prison for robbery. At the Indiana State Prison in Michigan City, he began to write poetry and in 1968 published his first collection, *Poems from Prison.* After his release, Knight joined the Black Arts movement, taught at a number of universities, and published works including *Black Voices from Prison* (1970), *Belly Song and Other Poems* (1973), and *Born of a Woman* (1980).

YUSEF KOMUNYAKAA
(b. 1947)

Yusef Komunyakaa was born in Bogalusa, Louisiana. He served in Vietnam as a war correspondent and for a time edited the *Southern Cross.* Decorated with a Bronze Star, he later wrote poems deriving from his Vietnam experience, first collected in *Dien Cai Dau* (1988). Following his years in the military, Komunyakaa studied at the University of Colorado, Colorado State, and the University of California at Irvine. He has also lived in Australia, Saint Thomas, Puerto Rico, and Japan. He teaches at Princeton University. Many of his poems harken back to his childhood in a poor, rural, and largely black Southern community. They grapple with hard realities, including race and social class, and take some of their rhythms and melodic effects from jazz and the blues.

D. H. LAWRENCE
(1885–1930)

The son of a coal miner and a schoolteacher, David Herbert Lawrence was able to attend high school only briefly. He worked for a surgical-appliance manufacturer, attended Nottingham University College, and taught school in Croydon, near London. After publishing his first novel, *The White Peacock* (1911), he devoted his time exclusively to writing; *Sons and Lovers*

(1913) established him as a major literary figure. In 1912, he eloped with Frieda von Richthofen, and in 1914, after her divorce, they were married. During World War I, both his novels and his wife's German nationality gave him trouble: *The Rainbow* was published in September 1915 and suppressed in November. In 1919, the Lawrences left England and began years of wandering: first Italy, then Ceylon, Australia, Mexico, and New Mexico, then back to England and Italy. Lawrence published *Women in Love* in 1920 and *Lady Chatterley's Lover,* his most sexually explicit novel, in 1928. Through it all he suffered from tuberculosis and eventually died from the disease.

IRVING LAYTON
(1912–2006)

Irving Layton was born in Romania, to a Jewish family that emigrated to Canada one year later. After a series of unrelated jobs, Layton earned a degree in agriculture before embarking on a writing career. Considered Canada's most prolific poet, he was critical of both literary tradition and the poetry of modernists such as T. S. Eliot. He served on the editorial boards of several literary magazines, most prominently the *Black Mountain Review,* and his poems are collected in numerous volumes, including *Fornalutx: Selected Poems, 1928–1990* (1992).

EMMA LAZARUS
(1849–1887)

Emma Lazarus was born in New York City, to a prominent Sephardic (Spanish Jewish) family. She was educated at home. In 1868, she met the writer Ralph Waldo Emerson, who became her literary mentor. Lazarus translated medieval Hebrew poets from the German and wrote impassioned essays on behalf of the wave of Jewish immigrants seeking refuge from persecution in Europe after the assassination of Russian Czar Alexander II in 1881. Lazarus was appalled by the squalid conditions in which many of these refugees were forced to live and sympathetic to their difficulty in finding employment. The last five lines of "The New Colossus," the poem for which she is best-remembered, are engraved on the pedestal of the Statue of Liberty, which was dedicated in 1886.

AMY LOWELL
(1874–1925)

Born into a prominent family in Brookline, Massachusetts, and mainly self-educated, Amy Lowell produced her first book, *Dream Drops, or Stories from Fairy Land, by a Dreamer,* in 1887. She did not seriously define herself as a poet until 1902, however, and published her first, rather conventional collection ten years later. In 1913, after reading several poems by H. D., Lowell traveled to England to meet with the Imagist circle. When Ezra Pound abandoned Imagism for Vorticism, Lowell succeeded him as the leading figure of what Pound later derisively called "Amy-gism." Under her eccentric influence, the Imagists experimented with free verse and mystical expression. Credited with popularizing "polyphonic prose," which employed poetic methods of rhyme and alliteration, Lowell published collections of her own poetry, including *Sword Blades and Poppy Seed* (1914), *Men, Women, and Ghosts* (1916), *Can Grande's Castle* (1918), and *What's O'Clock* (1925), as well as several critical and biographical works.

ANDREW MARVELL
(1621–1678)

The son of a clergyman and his wife, Andrew Marvell was born in Yorkshire, England, and educated at Trinity College, Cambridge. There is no evidence that he fought in the English Civil War, which broke out in 1642, but his poem "An Horatian Ode upon Cromwell's Return from Ireland" appeared in 1650, shortly after the beheading of King Charles I in 1649, and may represent straightforward praise of England's new Puritan leader. Some regard it as strong satire, however—Marvell was known in his day for his satirical prose and verse. Today he is better known for lyric poems, such as the carpe diem manifesto "To His Coy Mistress," which he probably wrote while serving as tutor to a Yorkshire noble's daughter. In 1657, on the recommendation of John Milton, Marvell accepted a position in Cromwell's government that he held until his election to Parliament in 1659. After helping restore the monarchy in 1660, he continued to write and to serve as a member of Parliament until the end of his life.

CLAUDE McKAY
(1889–1948)

Festus Claudis McKay was born and raised in Sunny Ville, Clarendon Parish, Jamaica, the youngest of eleven children. He worked as a wheelwright and cabinetmaker, then briefly as a police constable, before writing and publishing two books of poetry in Jamaican dialect. In 1912, he emigrated to the United States, where he attended Booker T. Washington's Tuskegee Institute in Alabama, studied agricultural science at Kansas State College, and then moved to New York City. McKay supported himself through various jobs while becoming a prominent literary and political figure. The oldest Harlem Renaissance writer, McKay was also the first to publish, with the poetry collection *Harlem Shadows* (1922); his other works include the novels *Home to Harlem* (1928) and *Banana Bottom* (1933) and his autobiography, *A Long Way from Home* (1937).

ARCHIBALD MACLEISH
(1892–1982)

Archibald MacLeish was born and raised in Illinois. He was educated at Yale University and Harvard Law School. During World War I, he volunteered to serve at the front. In the early 1920s, he lived in Paris, and throughout the 1930s he served on the editorial board of *Fortune* magazine. MacLeish was influential in the upper echelons of American government under Franklin Delano Roosevelt and held the posts of librarian of Congress and assistant secretary of state, among others. After leaving government, he taught at Harvard University. In addition to poetry, he wrote prose; verse plays, most famously *J.B.* (1957); radio plays; and the Oscar-winning screenplay for *The Eleanor Roosevelt Story* (1965). In his later work, MacLeish attempted to reconcile the conflict between his famous dictum "A poem should not mean / but be" and his political commitment.

JAMES MERRILL
(1926–1995)

Born to wealth in New York City (his father co-founded the Merrill Lynch brokerage house), James Merrill was a precocious poet whose first collec-

tion, *Jim's Book*, was printed privately when he was only sixteen. After college at Amherst, which was interrupted by a year of military service, Merrill began teaching at Bard College and soon started publishing poetry, plays, and fiction. *First Poems* (1951) was followed by many other verse collections, including two National Book Award winners, *Nights and Days* (1966) and *Mirabell* (1979); the Pulitzer Prize–winning *Divine Comedies* (1976); *From the First Nine: Poems 1946–1976* (1982); and *The Inner Room* (1988). His masterpiece, *The Changing Light at Sandover* (1982), grew out of spiritualist sessions with a Ouija board that Merrill conducted with his partner, David Jackson. Merrill served as Chancellor of the Academy of American Poets from 1979 until his death.

EDNA ST. VINCENT MILLAY (1892–1950)

Born in Rockland, Maine, Edna St. Vincent Millay published her first poem at twenty, her first poetry collection at twenty-five. After graduating from Vassar College, she moved to New York City's Greenwich Village, where, as she gained a reputation as a brilliant poet, she also became notorious for her bohemian life and her association with prominent artists, writers, and radicals. In 1923, she won the Pulitzer Prize for her collection *The Ballad of the Harp-Weaver;* in 1925, growing weary of fame, she and her husband moved to Austerlitz, New York, where she lived for the rest of her life. Although her work fell out of favor with mid-twentieth century modernists, who rejected her formalism as old-fashioned, her poetry—witty, acerbic, and superbly crafted—has found many new admirers today.

JOHN MILTON
(1608–1674)

Born in London, the elder son of a self-made businessman and his wife, John Milton exhibited unusual literary and scholarly gifts at an early age; even before entering Cambridge University, he was adept at Latin and Greek and was well on his way to mastering Hebrew and a number of European languages. After graduation, he spent six more years of intense study and composed, among other works, his great pastoral elegy, "Lycidas" (1637). After a year of travel in Europe, Milton return to England

and found his country embroiled in religious strife and civil war. Milton took up the Puritan cause and, in 1641, began writing pamphlets defending everything from free speech to Cromwell's execution of Charles I; Milton also served as Cromwell's Latin secretary until, in 1651, he lost his sight. After the monarchy was restored in 1660, Milton was briefly imprisoned and his property was confiscated. Blind, impoverished, and isolated, he devoted himself to the great spiritual epics of his later years: *Paradise Lost* (1667), *Paradise Regained* (1671), and *Samson Agonistes* (1671).

MARIANNE MOORE
(1887–1972)

Born in Kirkwood, Missouri, Marianne Moore was raised in Carlisle, Pennsylvania. After receiving a degree in biology from Bryn Mawr College, she studied business at Carlisle Commercial College, taught stenography at the U.S. Industrial Indian School in Carlisle, and traveled to Europe. She and her mother moved to New Jersey and New York's Greenwich Village before settling, in 1918, in Brooklyn, New York. From 1921 to 1925, Moore was a librarian at the New York Public Library. She had written and published poetry while still in college, but did not publish her first collection until 1921. A prolific critic, she also edited the influential modernist magazine *Dial* from 1926 to 1929. Her *Collected Poems* (1951) won the Bollingen Prize, the Pulitzer Prize, and a National Book Award and made her a public figure. Her *Complete Poems* appeared in 1967.

PAT MORA (b. 1942)

Born to Mexican American parents in El Paso, Texas, Pat Mora earned a B.A. and an M.A. from the University of Texas at El Paso. She has been a consultant on U.S.–Mexico youth exchanges; a museum director and administrator at her alma mater; and a teacher of English at all levels. Her poetry—collected in *Chants* (1985), *Borders* (1986), *Communion* (1991), *Agua Santa* (1995), and *Aunt Carmen's Book of Practical Saints* (1997)—reflects and addresses her Chicana and southwestern background. Mora's other publications include *Nepantla: Essays from the Land in the Middle* (1993); a family memoir, *House of Houses* (1997); and many works for children.

PAUL MULDOON
(b. 1951)

Paul Muldoon was born in Portadown, County Armagh, Northern Ireland, and was raised in The Moy, a small village featured prominently in many of his poems. He was educated at Queen's University, Belfast, where he met Seamus Heaney, Michael Longley, and other poets of the Belfast "Group." Muldoon worked for the BBC in Belfast until the mid-1980s, when he became a freelance writer and moved to the United States, where he has taught at a number of institutions. He was professor of poetry at Oxford from 1999 to 2004, and is now professor of humanities and creative writing at Princeton. He has written a children's book, translated Gaelic verse, and collaborated on the opera *Shining Brow*.

OGDEN NASH
(1902–1971)

A native of Rye, New York, Ogden Nash attended Harvard University for one year, taught French, sold bonds, and wrote copy for streetcar advertisements before embarking on a literary career peppered with wordplays and sly limericks. After working for Doubleday and Rinehart Press, he joined the staff at the fledgling *New Yorker* magazine. In addition to producing volumes of humorous and unorthodox poetry such as *Hard Lines* (1931), *The Primrose Path* (1935), *Good Intentions* (1942), *Musical Zoo* (1947), and *You Can't Get There from Here* (1957), Nash wrote children's books, collaborated on several musicals, and lectured across the country.

HOWARD NEMEROV
(1920–1991)

Born and raised in New York City, Howard Nemerov graduated from Harvard University, served in the U.S. Army Air Corps during World War II, and returned to New York to complete his first book, *The Image and the Law* (1948). He taught at a number of colleges and universities and published books of poetry, plays, short stories, novels, and essays. His *Collected Poems* won the Pulitzer Prize and the National Book Award in 1978. He served as Consultant in

Poetry to the Library of Congress from 1963 to 1964, and Poet Laureate of the United States from 1988 to 1990. *Trying Conclusions: New and Selected Poems 1961–1991* was published in 1991.

SHARON OLDS (b. 1942)

Born in San Francisco, Sharon Olds earned a B.A. from Stanford University and a Ph.D. from Columbia University. She was founding chair of the Writing Program at Goldwater Hospital (a public facility for the severely physically disabled), and she currently chairs New York University's Creative Writing Program. She has received a National Endowment for the Arts Grant and a Guggenheim Fellowship and was named New York State Poet in 1998. Her books include *Satan Says* (1980); the National Book Critics Circle Award–winning *The Dead and the Living* (1983); *The Gold Cell* (1987); *The Father* (1992); *The Wellspring* (1997); *Blood, Tin, Straw* (1999); and *The Unswept Room,* a National Book Award nominee in 2002.

MARY OLIVER (b. 1935)

Born in Cleveland, Ohio, Mary Oliver attended Ohio State University and Vassar College. A longtime resident of Provincetown, Massachusetts, she has taught at several universities and has received National Endowment of the Arts and Guggenheim fellowships. She published her first volume of poetry, *No Voyage,* in 1963, and has followed it with such collections as the Pulitzer Prize–winning *American Primitive* (1983), *House of Light* (1990), the National Book Award–winning *New and Selected Poems* (1992), and *The Leaf and the Cloud* (2000). Her prose works include two well-received books on poetic technique, *A Poetry Handbook* (1994) and *Rules for the Dance: A Handbook for Reading and Writing Metrical Verse* (1998), and a collection of nature writing, *Blue Pastures* (1995).

WILFRED OWEN
(1893–1918)

Born in Oswestry, Shropshire, England, Wilfred Owen left school in 1911, having failed to win a scholarship to London University. He served as assistant to a vicar in Oxfordshire until 1913, when he left to teach English at a Berlitz school in Bordeaux. In 1915, Owen returned to England to enlist in the army and was sent to the front lines in France. Suffering from shell shock two years later, he was evacuated to Craiglockhart War Hospital, where he met the poets Siegfried Sassoon and Robert Graves. Five of Owen's poems were published in 1918, the year he returned to combat; he was killed one week before the signing of the armistice. His poems, which portray the horror of trench warfare and satirize the unthinking patriotism of those who cheered the war from their armchairs, are collected in the two-volume *Complete Poems and Fragments* (1983).

DOROTHY PARKER
(1893–1967)

Born in West End, New Jersey, Dorothy Rothschild worked for both *Vogue* and *Vanity Fair* magazines before becoming a freelance writer. In 1917, she married Edwin Pond Parker II, whom she divorced in 1928. Her first book of verse, *Enough Rope* (1926), was a best-seller and was followed by *Sunset Gun* (1928), *Death and Taxes* (1931), and *Collected Poems: Not So Deep as a Well* (1936). In 1927, Parker became a book reviewer for *The New Yorker,* to which she contributed for most of her career. In 1933, Parker and her second husband, Alan Campbell, moved to Hollywood, where they collaborated as film writers. In addition, Parker wrote criticism, two plays, short stories, and news reports from the Spanish Civil War. She is probably best remembered, though, as the reigning wit at the "Round Table" at Manhattan's Algonquin Hotel, where, in the 1920s and '30s, she traded barbs with other prominent writers and humorists.

LINDA PASTAN (b. 1932)

Linda Pastan was born in New York City and raised in nearby Westchester County. After graduating from Radcliffe College, she received an M.A. in literature from Brandeis University. Although her first published poems appeared in *Mademoiselle* in 1955, Pastan spent many years concentrating on her husband and children—indeed, much of her poetry deals with her own family life. Her many collections include *A Perfect Circle of Sun* (1971), *The Five Stages of Grief* (1978), American Book Award–nominee *PM/AM: New and Selected Poems* (1982), *A Fraction of Darkness* (1985), *The Imperfect Paradise* (1988), *An Early Afterlife* (1995), *Carnival Evening: New and Selected Poems 1968–1998* (1998), and *The Last Uncle: Poems* (2002). She lives in Potomac, Maryland, and was named Poet Laureate of Maryland in 1991.

KATHERINE PHILIPS
(1632–1664)

Daughter of a London merchant and his wife, Katherine Philips first went to school in Hackney, then moved to Pembrokeshire in 1646, when her widowed mother remarried. At sixteen, she married a much older man, James Philips, who served for twelve years in Wales as a member of Oliver Cromwell's Parliament. Despite being born, and having married, a Puritan, Katherine had Royalist sympathies and wrote tributes to the returning monarchy, although her husband's fortunes declined after the Restoration. She privately circulated her poetry, but gained fame for her translations of Pierre Corneille's plays and eventually became the best-known female poet of her age. An unauthorized edition of her poems (*By the Incomparable Mrs. K. P.*) appeared in 1664; an authorized edition, in 1667.

SYLVIA PLATH
(1932–1963)

Sylvia Plath was born in Boston; her father, a Polish immigrant, died when she was eight. After graduating from Smith College, Plath attended Cambridge University on a Fulbright scholarship, and there she met and married the poet Ted Hughes, with whom she had two children. As she documented in her novel *The Bell Jar* (1963), in 1953—between her junior and senior years of college—Plath became seriously depressed, attempted suicide, and was hospitalized. In 1963, the break-up of her marriage led to another suicide attempt, this time successful. Plath has attained cult status as much for her poems as for her "martyrdom" to art and life. In addition to her first volume of poetry, *The Colossus* (1960), Plath's work has been collected in *Ariel* (1966), *Crossing the Water* (1971), and *Winter Trees* (1972). Her selected

letters were published in 1975; her expurgated journals, in 1983; and her unabridged journals, in 2000.

ALEXANDER POPE
(1688–1744)

Alexander Pope was born in London, to a Catholic linen-draper and his wife. Debarred from university by his religion, he learned Greek, Latin, Italian, and French with the help of a local priest. At age twelve, he contracted a form of tuberculosis, probably Pott's Disease, which left his spine weakened, his growth stunted, and his health permanently damaged. His family moved to Binfield, in Windsor Forest, where at age sixteen Pope composed his "Pastorals' (published 1709). His friend the playwright William Wycherley introduced him to London literary society, and his *Essay on Criticism* (1711) attracted the attention of Joseph Addison, though Pope was to leave Addison's circle for the "Scriblerus Club,' which included John Gay, Jonathan Swift, and other writers. *The Rape of the Lock* appeared in 1712, and the first volume of his translation of the *Iliad* into heroic couplets followed in 1715. This, together with his translation of the *Odyssey* (1725–26), brought him financial security, and he moved to Twickenham, the Jacobite rebellion having made Catholics no longer welcome in the city center. There he wrote *The Dunciad* (1728–42, revised 1743), a satire on the alleged dullness of contemporary culture; the wittily and wickedly satirical "Epistle to Dr. Arbuthnot" (1735); and the *Essay on Man,* the first volume of a projected work in four books, reflecting Pope's interest in philosophical and intellectual speculation.

EZRA POUND
(1885–1972)

Born in Hailey, Idaho, Ezra Pound studied at the University of Pennsylvania and Hamilton College before traveling to Europe in 1908. He remained there, living in Ireland, England, France, and Italy, for much of his life. Pound's tremendous ambition—to succeed in his own work and to influence the development of poetry and Western culture in general—led him to found the Imagist school of poetry, to advise and assist many great writers (Eliot, Joyce, Williams, Frost, and Hemingway, to name a few), and to write a number of highly influential critical works. His increasingly fiery and erratic behavior led to a charge of treason (he served as a propagandist for Mussolini during World War II), a diagnosis of insanity, and twelve years at St. Elizabeth's, an institution for the criminally insane. His verse is collected in *Personae: The Collected Poems* (1949) and *The Cantos* (1976).

HENRY REED
(1914–1986)

Henry Reed was born in Birmingham, England, and educated at Birmingham University. From 1937 to 1941, he worked as a teacher and as a journalist. During World War II, he served in the Royal Army Ordnance Corps and as a cryptographer in the department of Naval Intelligence. In 1945, he went to work as a broadcaster, journalist, and playwright for the BBC, where his coworkers included the poets W. H. Auden, Louis MacNeice, and Dylan Thomas. He later taught at the University of Washington in Seattle. His reputation as a poet rests almost exclusively on the five-part "Lessons of the War," which may be the most anthologized poem of World War II. He also wrote some famously funny radio plays.

ADRIENNE RICH
(b. 1929)

Adrienne Rich was born in Baltimore. Since the selection of her first volume by W. H. Auden for the Yale Series of Younger Poets (1951), her work has continually evolved, from the tightly controlled early poems to the politically and personally charged verse for which she is known today. Rich's books of poetry include *Collected Early Poems 1950–1970* (1993), *The Dream of a Common Language* (1978), *Your Native Land, Your Life* (1986), *Time's Power* (1988), *An Atlas of the Difficult World* (1991), *Dark Fields of the Republic* (1995), *Midnight Salvage* (1999), *Fox* (2001), and *The School among the Ruins* (2004). Her prose works include *Of Woman Born: Motherhood as Experience and Institution* (1976), *On Lies, Secrets, and Silence* (1979), and *Blood, Bread, and Poetry* (1986), all influential feminist texts; *What Is Found There: Notebooks on Poetry and Politics* (1993); and *Arts of the Possible: Essays and Conversations* (2001). Her many awards include a MacArthur Fellowship and a Lanning Foundation Lifetime Achievement Award.

ALBERTO RÍOS
(b. 1952)

Alberto Álvaro Ríos was born in Nogales, Arizona, to a Mexican father and an English mother. After attending the University of Arizona, where he received B.A. and MFA degrees, Ríos published his first collection of poems, *Elk Heads on the Wall* (1979). He has since been a prolific poet and short-story writer. His collection *The Smallest Muscle in the Human Body* was a nominee for the 2002 National Book Award in poetry; his most recent volume of poems is *The Theater of Night* (2006). Ríos's prose includes *The Iguana Killer: Twelve Stories of the Heart* (1984) and *Capriatada: A Nogales Memoir* (1999). Since 1982 Ríos has taught English at Arizona State University.

THEODORE ROETHKE
(1908–1963)

Born in Saginaw, Michigan, Theodore Roethke grew up around his father's twenty-five-acre greenhouse complex—plants and their associations with nurture and growth were an important subject in his later poetry. He worked for a time at Lafayette College, where he was professor of English and tennis coach, and later at the University of Washington, which appointed him poet-in-residence one year before he died. Roethke suffered from periodic mental breakdowns, yet the best of his poetry, with its reverence for and fear of the physical world, seems destined to last. His books include *Open House* (1942), *Praise to the End!* (1951), *The Far Field* (1964), which received a posthumous National Book Award, and *Collected Poems* (1966).

LIZ ROSENBERG
(b. 1956)

A native of Long Island, New York, Liz Rosenberg received a B.A. from Bennington College, an M.A. from Johns Hopkins University, and a Ph.D. from the State University of New York at Binghamton, where she teaches English and currently directs the creative writing program. She has published several books of poetry, including *The Angel Poems* (1984), *The Fire Music* (1985), *Children of Paradise* (1994), and *These Happy Days* (2000); a novel, *Heart and Soul* (1996); and numerous children's books, such as *Eli's Night-Light,* illustrated by Joanna Yardley (2001), and *We Wanted You,* illustrated by Peter Catalanotto (2002). In addition, she is a book columnist for *The Boston Globe.*

CHRISTINA ROSSETTI
(1830–1894)

The daughter of Italian political refugees, Christina Rossetti was born in London and educated at home. Though associated with the Pre-Raphaelite group of artists and writers through her brother, Dante Gabriel Rossetti, Christina withdrew into the more personal world of her quiet but intense devotion to poetry and Anglican spirituality. Published under the pseudonym "Ellen Alleyn," her first poems appeared when she was only eighteen; her first adult collection, *Goblin Market and Other Poems* (1862), was a popular and critical success. Never marrying, Rossetti instead devoted herself to her writing and to a variety of moral and educational causes. Her collected *Poetical Works* (1904) was published a decade after her death.

MARY JO SALTER
(b. 1954)

Born in Grand Rapids, Michigan, and raised in Detroit and Baltimore, Mary Jo Salter received her B.A. from Harvard and her M.A. from Cambridge. Her first poetry collection, *Henry Purcell in Japan* (1985), draws on her years of teaching English in Japan. Salter has published three more collections—*Unfinished Painting* (1989), *Sunday Skaters* (1994), *A Kiss in Space* (1999), and *Open Shutters* (2003)—as well as a children's book, *The Moon Comes Home* (1994). She lives in South Hadley, Massachusetts, teaches poetry at Mount Holyoke College, is a co-editor of *The Norton Anthology of Poetry,* and frequently writes for periodicals such as the *Yale Review* and the *New York Times Book Review.*

WILLIAM SHAKESPEARE
(1554–1616)

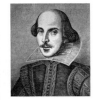

Considering the great fame of his work, surprisingly little is known of William Shakespeare's life. Between 1585 and 1592, he left his birthplace of Stratford-upon-Avon for London to begin a career as playwright and actor. No dates of his professional career are recorded, however, nor can the order in which he composed his plays and poetry be determined with any certainty. By 1594, he had established himself as a poet with two long works—*Venus and Adonis* and *The Rape of Lucrece*—and his more than 150 sonnets are supreme expressions of the form. His reputation, though, rests on the works he wrote for the theater. Shakespeare produced perhaps thirty-five plays in twenty-five years, proving himself a master of every dramatic genre: tragedy (in works such as *Macbeth, Hamlet, King Lear,* and *Othello*); historical drama (for example, *Richard III* and *Henry IV*); comedy (*Twelfth Night, As You Like It,* and many more); and romance (in plays such as *The Tempest* and *Cymbaline*). Without question, Shakespeare is the most quoted, discussed, and beloved writer in English literature.

SIR PHILIP SIDNEY
(1554–1586)

Philip Sidney was born at Penshurst, in Kent, England, to an aristocratic family that included among its poets Sidney's brother Robert, his sister Mary, and his niece, Mary Wroth. His mother, also Mary, was the sister of Queen Elizabeth I's sometime favorite, Robert Dudley, earl of Leicester, and his father, Sir Henry, had served the queen as lord deputy of Ireland. After attending Shrewsbury School, Sidney spent time at Oxford and Cambridge. From 1572 until 1575, he traveled in Europe, during which time he established a firm friendship with Hubert Languet, who encouraged his zealous Protestantism. When in 1580 Queen Elizabeth considered marrying a French Catholic, Sidney criticized the idea in a letter and was consequently banished from court. He spent his enforced "idleness" composing poetry; his famous work of literary criticism, the *Defense of Poesy;* and two versions of his pastoral romance, the *Arcadia,* which was dedicated to his sister Mary and which she published after his death in a widely read version that conflates his first text, the *Old Arcadia,* with his unfinished revision, the *New Arcadia.* Legendary in life and death as the quintessential Elizabethan gentleman, Sidney was in reality more marked by the "great expectation" he mentions in one of his sonnets than by political or romantic success. His *Astrophil*

and Stella, the first great sonnet sequence in English—like his other poetic works, circulated in manuscript but not published until after his death—uses (and revises) Petrarchan conventions to record various experiences of unfulfilled desire. These include, but are not exhausted by, the erotic frustration caused by his failure to win Penelope Devereux, the historical model for Stella, as his wife. Sidney was married to Frances, daughter of the powerful courtier Sir Francis Walsingham, in 1583, the same year he was knighted. Sidney was granted a chance to fight for Protestantism in the Low Countries after being made governor of Flushing (an English possession in the Low Countries) in 1586. He died of gangrene from a wound in the leg.

CATHY SONG
(b. 1955)

Born in Honolulu to a Chinese American mother and a Korean American father, Cathy Song earned her B.A. at Wellesley College and her M.A. at Boston University. Her first collection of poems, *Picture Bride* (1983), won the Yale Younger Poets Award; the poems told the story of a Korean woman embarking on a marriage to an American she knows only through letters and photos. Song has since published three more volumes: *Frameless Windows, Squares of Light* (1991), *School Figures* (1994), and *The Land of Bliss* (2001). Song teaches at the University of Hawaii at Manoa and has received the Hawaii Award for Literature.

WALLACE STEVENS
(1879–1955)

Born and raised in Reading, Pennsylvania, Wallace Stevens attended Harvard University and New York Law School. In New York City, he worked for a number of law firms, published poems in magazines, and befriended such literary figures as William Carlos Williams and Marianne Moore. In 1916, Stevens moved to Connecticut and began working for the Hartford Accident and Indemnity Company, where he became a vice-president in 1934 and where he worked for the rest of his life, writing poetry at night and during vacations. He published his first collection, *Harmonium,* in 1923, and followed it with a series of volumes

from 1935 until 1950, establishing himself as one of the twentieth century's most important poets. His lectures were collected in *The Necessary Angel: Essays on Reality and Imagination* (1951); his *Collected Poems* appeared in 1954.

MARK STRAND (b. 1934)

Born in Summerside, Prince Edward Island, Canada, Mark Strand was raised in both North and South America before earning his B.A. from Antioch College in 1957, a B.F.A. in painting from Yale in 1959, and an M.A. from the University of Iowa's Writers' Workshop. Strand has been, as he says, "eating poetry" ever since. He is the author of many collections of verse, including *Sleeping with One Eye Open* (1964), *Selected Poems* (1980), the Pulitzer Prize-winning *Blizzard of One* (1998), and *The Weather of Words* (2000). His numerous awards include a Fulbright Fellowship and a MacArthur Fellowship; in 1990 he was named United States Poet Laureate. Strand presently teaches poetry at the University of Chicago's Committee on Social Thought.

ALFRED, LORD TENNYSON (1809–1892)

Perhaps the most important and certainly the most popular of the Victorian poets, Alfred, Lord Tennyson demonstrated his talents at an early age; he published his first volume in 1827. Encouraged to devote his life to poetry by a group of undergraduates at Cambridge University known as the "Apostles," Tennyson was particularly close to Arthur Hallam, whose sudden death in 1833 inspired the long elegy *In Memoriam* (1850). With that poem he achieved lasting fame and recognition; he was appointed Poet Laureate the year of its publication, succeeding Wordsworth. Despite the great popularity of his "journalistic" poems—"The Charge of the Light Brigade" (1854) is perhaps the best known—Tennyson's great theme was the past, both personal (*In the Valley of Cauteretz,* 1864) and national (*Idylls of the King,* 1869). Tennyson was made a baron in 1884; when he died, eight years later, he was buried in Poets' Corner in Westminster Abbey.

DYLAN THOMAS
(1914–1953)

Born in Swansea, Wales, into what he called "the smug darkness of a provincial town," Dylan Thomas published his first book, *Eighteen Poems* (1934), at twenty, in the same year that he moved to London. Thereafter he had a successful, though turbulent, career publishing poetry, short stories, and plays, including the highly successful *Under Milk Wood* (1954). In his last years he supported himself with lecture tours and poetry readings in the United States, but his excessive drinking caught up with him and he died in New York City of chronic alcoholism. His *Collected Poems, 1934–1952* (1952) was the last book he published during his short lifetime; his comic novel, *Adventures in the Skin Trade,* was never completed.

DEREK WALCOTT
(b. 1930)

Born of mixed heritage on the West Indian island of St. Lucia, Derek Walcott grew up speaking French and patois but was educated in English. In 1953, he earned his B.A. in English, French, and Latin from the University College of the West Indies in Jamaica. In 1950, with his twin brother, Roderick, he founded the St. Lucia Arts Guild, a dramatic society; nine years later, he founded the Little Carib Theatre Workshop in Trinidad, which he ran until 1976, writing many plays for production there. Walcott has published many volumes of poetry, including *In a Green Night* (1962), *The Castaway* (1965), *Another Life* (1973), *Sea Grapes* (1976), *The Fortunate Traveller* (1981), *Omeros* (1990), *The Bounty* (1997), *Tiepolo's Hound* (2000), and *The Prodigal* (2004). His work draws on diverse influences, from West Indian folk tales to Homer to Yeats. The first Caribbean poet to win the Nobel Prize (in 1992), Walcott now lives and teaches in the United States.

WALT WHITMAN
(1819–1892)

Walt Whitman was born on a farm in West Hills, Long Island, to a British father and a Dutch mother. After working as a journalist throughout New York for many years, he taught for a while and founded his own newspaper, *The Long Islander,* in 1838; he then left journalism to work on *Leaves of Grass,* originally intended as a poetic treatise on American democratic idealism. Published privately in multiple editions from 1855 to 1874, the book at first failed to reach a mass audience. In 1881, Boston's Osgood and Company published another edition of *Leaves of Grass,* which sold well until the district attorney called it "obscene literature" and stipulated that Whitman remove certain poems and phrases. He refused, and it was many years before his works were again published, this time in Philadelphia. By the time Whitman died, his work was revered, as it still is today, for its greatness of spirit and its exuberant American voice.

RICHARD WILBUR
(b. 1921)

Born in New York City and raised in New Jersey, Richard Wilbur received his B.A. from Amherst College and his M.A. from Harvard. He started to write while serving as an army cryptographer during World War II, and his collections *The Beautiful Changes* (1947) and *Ceremony* (1950) established his reputation as a serious poet. In addition to subsequent volumes such as the Pulitzer Prize–winning *Things of This World* (1956), *Walking to Sleep* (1969), *The Mind Reader* (1976), the Pulitzer Prize–winning *New and Collected Poems* (1988), and *Mayflies: New Poems and Translations* (2000), he has published children's books, critical essays, and numerous translations of classic French works by Racine and Molière. He has taught at various colleges and universities, including Harvard, Wellesley, Wesleyan, and Smith. In 1987, he was named Poet Laureate of the United States.

WILLIAM CARLOS WILLIAMS (1883–1963)

Born in Rutherford, New Jersey, William Carlos Williams attended school in Switzerland and New York and studied medicine at the University of Pennsylvania and the University of Leipzig in Germany. He spent most of his life in Rutherford, practicing medicine and gradually establishing himself as one of the great figures in American poetry. Early in his writing career he left the European-inspired Imagist movement in favor of a more uniquely American poetic style comprised of vital, local language and "no ideas but in things." His shorter poems have been published in numerous collected editions and other volumes, including the Pulitzer Prize–winning *Brueghel, and Other Poems* (1963); his five-volume philosophical poem, *Paterson,* was published in 1963. Among his other works are plays such as *A Dream of Love* (1948) and *Many Loves* (1950); a trilogy of novels: *White Mules* (1937), *In the Money* (1940), and *The Build-Up* (1952); his *Autobiography* (1951); his *Selected Essays* (1954); and his *Selected Letters* (1957).

WILLIAM WORDS-
WORTH (1770–1850)

Regarded by many as the greatest of the Romantic poets, William Wordsworth was born in Cockermouth in the English Lake District, a beautiful, mountainous region that figured as a deep inspiration for his poetry. He studied at Cambridge and then spent a year in France, hoping to witness the French Revolution firsthand; as the Revolution's "glorious renovation" dissolved into anarchy and then tyranny, Wordsworth was forced to return to England. Remarkably, he managed to establish "a saving intercourse with my true self" and to write some of his finest poetry, including the early version of his masterpiece, *The Prelude,* which first appeared in 1805 and then again, much altered, in 1850. In 1798, Wordsworth and his friend Samuel Taylor Coleridge published *Lyrical Ballads,* which contained many of their greatest poems and can be considered the founding document of English Romanticism. Wordsworth was revered by the reading public and in 1843 was named Poet Laureate.

CHARLES WRIGHT
(b. 1935)

Charles Wright was born in Pickwick Dam, Tennessee. After his graduation from Davidson College, he served in the Intelligence Corps of the U.S. Army, in Italy. Having further studied at the University of Iowa (under Donald Justice) and in Rome, he published his first book, *Six Poems,* in 1965. He has taught widely, at several institutions in Italy and at the University of California at Irvine. He now lives in Charlottesville, Virginia, where he has been on the faculty of the University of Virginia since 1983. He is known both for his erudition (Italian and East Asian literature are among the influences in his poems) and for his attachment to rural life and landscape, especially that of Appalachia.

WILLIAM BUTLER YEATS
(1865–1939)

William Butler Yeats was born in Dublin and, though he spent most of his youth in London, became the pre-eminent Irish poet of the twentieth century. Immersed in Irish history, folklore, and politics, as well as spiritualism and the occult, he attended art school for a time, but left to devote himself to poetry that was, early in his career, self-consciously dreamy and ethereal. Yeats's poems became tighter and more passionate with his reading of philosophers such as Nietzsche, his involvement (mainly through theater) with the Irish nationalist cause, and his desperate love for the actress and nationalist Maud Gonne. He was briefly a senator in the newly independent Irish government before withdrawing from active public life to Thoor Ballylee, a crumbling Norman tower that Yeats and his wife fashioned into a home. There he developed an elaborate mythology (published as *A Vision* in 1925) and wrote poems that explored fundamental questions of history and identity. He was awarded the Nobel Prize for Literature in 1923. His works, in many genres, have been selected and collected in various editions.

Writing about Poetry

When it comes to the study of poetry, reading and writing are closely interrelated—even mutually dependent—activities. On the one hand, the quality of whatever we write about a poem depends entirely upon the quality of our work as readers. On the other hand, our reading isn't truly complete until we've tried to capture our sense of a text in writing. Indeed, we often read a poem much more actively and attentively when we integrate informal writing into the reading process—pausing periodically to mark especially important or confusing passages, to jot down significant facts, to describe the impressions and responses the text provokes—or when we imagine our reading (and our informal writing) as preparation for writing about the work in a more sustained and formal way.

Writing about poetry can take any number of forms, ranging from the very informal and personal to the very formal and public. In fact, your instructor may well ask you to try your hand at more than one form. However, the essay is by far the most common and complex form that writing about literature takes. As a result, the following chapters will focus on the essay. A first, short chapter covers three basic ways of writing about literature. The second chapter, "The Elements of the Essay," seeks to answer a very basic set of questions: *When an instructor says, "Write an essay," what precisely does that mean? What is the purpose of an essay, and what form does it need to take in order to achieve that purpose?* The third chapter, "The Writing Process," addresses questions about how an essay is produced, while the fourth chapter explores the special steps and strategies involved in writing a research essay—a type of essay about literature that draws on secondary sources. "Quotation, Citation, and Documentation" explains the rules and strategies involved in quoting and citing both literary texts and secondary sources using the documentation system recommended by the Modern Language Association (MLA). And, finally, we present a sample research essay, annotated to point out some of its most important features.

16 PARAPHRASE, SUMMARY, DESCRIPTION

Before turning to the essay, let's briefly consider three other basic ways of writing about poetry: *paraphrase*, *summary*, and *description*. Each of these can be useful both as an exercise to prepare for writing an essay and as part of a completed essay. That is, an essay about a literary text must do more than paraphrase, summarize, or describe the text; yet a good essay about a literary text almost always incorporates some paraphrase, summary, and description of the literature and, in the case of a research essay, of secondary sources as well.

16.1 PARAPHRASE

To paraphrase a statement is to restate it in your own words. Since the goal of paraphrase is to represent a statement fully and faithfully, paraphrases tend to be at least as long as the original, and one usually wouldn't try to paraphrase an entire work of any length. The following example offers a paraphrase of a poem (W. B. Yeats's "All Things Can Tempt Me").

ORIGINAL SENTENCE	PARAPHRASE
All things can tempt me from this craft of verse: One time it was a woman's face, or worse— The seeming needs of my fool-driven land; Now nothing but comes readier to the hand Than this accustomed toil. . . .	Anything can distract me from writing poetry: One time I was distracted by a woman's face, but I was even more distracted by (or I found an even less worthy distraction in) the attempt to fulfill what I imagined to be the needs of a country governed by idiots. At this point in my life I find any task easier than the work I'm used to doing (writing poetry).

Paraphrase resembles translation. Indeed, the paraphrase of Yeats is essentially a "translation" of poetry into prose. But what good is that? First, paraphrasing tests that you truly understand what you've read; it can be especially helpful when an author's diction and syntax seem difficult, complex, or "foreign" to you. Second, paraphrasing can direct your attention to nuances of tone or potentially significant details. For example, paraphrasing Yeats might help you to think about all that he gains by making himself the object rather than the subject of his sentence. Paraphrase can also help you begin generating the kind of interpretive questions that can drive an essay.

16.2 SUMMARY

A summary is a fairly succinct restatement or overview of the content of an entire text or source (or a significant portion thereof). Like paraphrases, summaries should always be stated in your own words.

A summary of a literary text is generally called a *plot summary* because it focuses on the action or plot. Here, for example, is a summary of Edgar Allan Poe's "The Raven":

> The speaker of Poe's "The Raven" is sitting in his room late at night reading in order to forget the death of his beloved Lenore. There's a tap at the door; after some hesitation he opens it and calls Lenore's name, but there is only an echo. When he goes back into his room he hears the rapping again, this time at his window, and when he opens it a raven enters. He asks the raven its name, and it answers very clearly, "Nevermore." As the speaker's thoughts run back to Lenore, he realizes the aptness of the raven's word: she shall sit there nevermore. But, he says, sooner or later he will forget her, and the grief will lessen. "Nevermore," the raven says again, too aptly. Now the speaker wants the bird to leave, but "Nevermore," the raven says once again. At the end, the speaker knows he'll never escape the raven or its dark message.

Though a summary should be significantly shorter than the original, it can be any length you need it to be. Above, the 108 lines of Poe's poem have been reduced to about 160 words. But one could summarize this or any other work in as little as one sentence.

Different readers—or even the same reader on different occasions—will almost certainly summarize the same text in dramatically different ways. Summarizing entails selection and emphasis. As a result, any summary reflects a particular point of view and may even imply a particular interpretation or argument. When writing a summary, you should try to be as objective as possible; nevertheless, your summary will reflect your own understanding and attitudes. For this reason, summarizing a literary text may help you to begin figuring out just what your particular understanding of a text is, especially if you then compare your summary to those of other readers.

16.3 DESCRIPTION

Whereas both summary and paraphrase focus on content, a description of a literary text focuses on its overall form or structure or some particular aspect thereof. Here, for example, is a description (rather than a summary) of the rhyme scheme of "The Raven":

> Poe's "The Raven" is a poem of 108 lines divided into eighteen six-line stanzas. If you were to look just at the ends of the lines, you would notice only one or two unusual features: not only is there only one rhyme sound per stanza—lines 2, 4, 5, and 6 rhyming—but one rhyme sound is the same in all eighteen stanzas, so that seventy-two lines end with the sound "ore." In addition, the fourth and fifth lines of each stanza end with an identical word; in six of the stanzas that word is "door" and in four others "Lenore." There is even more repetition: the last line of six of the first seven stanzas ends with the words "nothing more," and the last eleven stanzas end with the word "Nevermore." The rhyming lines—other than the last, which is very short—in each stanza are fifteen syllables long, the rhymed line sixteen. The longer lines give the effect of shorter ones, however, and add still further to the frequency of repeated sounds, for the first half of each opening line rhymes with the second half of the line, and so do the halves of line 3. There is still more: the first half of line 4 rhymes with the halves of line 3 (in the first stanza the rhymes are "dreary" / "weary" and "napping" / "tapping" / "rapping"). So at least nine words in each six-line stanza are involved in the regular rhyme scheme, and many stanzas have added instances of rhyme or repetition. As if this were not enough, all the half-line rhymes are rich feminine rhymes, where both the accented and the following unaccented syllables rhyme—"dreary" / "wary."

You could similarly describe many other formal elements of the poem—images and symbols, for example. You can describe a play in comparable terms—acts, scenes, settings, time lapses, perhaps—and you might describe a novel in terms of chapters, books, summary narration, dramatized scenes. In addition to describing the narrative structure or focus and voice of a short story, you might describe the diction (word choice), the sentence structure, the amount and kind of description of characters or landscape, and so on.

17 THE ELEMENTS OF THE ESSAY

As you move from reading literary works to writing essays about them, remember that the essay—like the short story, poem, or play—is a distinctive subgenre with unique elements and conventions. Just as you come to a poem with a certain set of expectations, so will readers approach your essay. They will be looking for particular elements, anticipating that the work will unfold in a specific way. This chapter explains and explores those elements so that you can develop a clear sense of what makes a piece of writing an essay and why some essays are more effective than others.

An essay has particular elements and a particular form because it serves a specific purpose. Keeping this in mind, consider what an essay is and what it does. An essay is a relatively short written composition that articulates, supports, and develops an idea or claim. Like any work of expository prose, it aims to explain something complex. Explaining in this case entails both *analysis* (breaking the complex "thing" down into its constituent parts and showing how they work together to form a meaningful whole) and *argument* (working to convince someone that the analysis is valid). In an essay about literature, the literary work is the complex thing that you are helping a reader to better understand. The essay needs to show the reader a particular way to understand the work, to interpret or read it. That interpretation or reading starts with the essayist's own personal response. But an essay also needs to persuade the reader that this interpretation is reasonable and enlightening—that it is, though it is distinctive and new, it is more than merely idiosyncratic or subjective.

To achieve these ends, an essay must incorporate four elements: an appropriate *tone*, a clear *thesis*, a coherent *structure*, and ample, appropriate *evidence*.

17.1 TONE (AND AUDIENCE)

Although your reader or audience isn't an element *in* your essay, tone is. And tone and audience are closely interrelated. In everyday life, the tone we adopt has everything to do with whom we are talking to and what situation we're in. For example, we talk very differently to our parents than to our best friends. And in different situations we talk to the same person in different ways. What tone do you adopt with your best friends when you want to borrow money? when you need advice? when you're giving advice? when you're deciding whether to eat pizza or sushi? In each case you act on your knowledge of who your friends are, what information they already have, and what their response is likely to be. But you also try to adopt a tone that will encourage them to respond in a certain way.

In writing, as in everyday life, your audience, situation, and purpose should shape your tone. Conversely, your tone will shape your audience's response. You need to figure out both who your readers are and what response you want to elicit. Who is your audience? When you write an essay for class, the obvious answer is your instructor. But in an important sense, that is the wrong answer. Although your instructor could literally be the only person besides you who will ever read your essay, you write about literature to learn how to write for an audience of peers—people a lot like you who are sensible and educated and who will appreciate having a literary work explained so that they can understand it more fully. Picture your reader as someone about your own age with roughly the same educational background. Assume the person has some experience in reading literature, but that he or she has read this particular work only once and has not yet closely analyzed it. You should neither be insulting and explain the obvious nor assume that your reader has noticed, considered, and remembered every detail.

Should you, then, altogether ignore the obvious fact that an instructor—who probably has a master's degree or doctorate in literature—is your actual reader? Not altogether: you don't want to get so carried away with speaking to people of your own age and interests that you slip into slang, or feel the need to explain what a stanza is, or leave unexplained an allusion to your favorite movie. Even though you do want to learn from the advice and guidelines your instructor has given, try not to be preoccupied with the idea that you are writing for someone "in authority" or someone utterly different from yourself.

Above all, don't think of yourself as writing for a captive audience, for readers who have to read what you write or who already see the text as you do. (If that were the case, there wouldn't be much point in writing at all.) It is not always easy to know how interested your readers will be or how their views might differ from yours, so you must make the most of every word. Remember that the purpose of your essay is to persuade readers to see the text your way. That process begins with persuading them that you deserve their attention and respect. The tone of your paper should be serious and straightforward, respectful toward your readers and the literary work. But its approach and vocabulary, while formal enough for academic writing, should be lively enough to interest someone like you. Try to imagine, as your ideal reader, the person in class whom you most respect but who often seems to see things differently from you. Write to capture and hold that person's attention and respect. Encourage your reader to adopt a desirable stance *toward* your essay by adopting that same stance *in* your essay. Engage and convince your reader by demonstrating your engagement and conviction. Encourage your reader to keep an open mind by showing that you have done the same.

17.2 THESIS

A thesis is to an essay what a theme is to a poem: it's the governing idea, proposition, claim, or point. Good theses come in many shapes and sizes. A thesis cannot always be conveyed in one sentence, nor will it always appear in the same place in every essay. But you will risk both appearing confused and confusing the reader if you can't state the thesis in one to three sentences or if the thesis doesn't appear somewhere in your introduction, usually near its end.

Regardless of its length or location, a thesis must be debatable—a claim that all readers won't automatically accept. It's a proposition that *can* be proven with evidence from the text. Yet it's one that *has* to be proven, that isn't obviously true or factual, that must be supported with evidence in order to be fully understood or accepted by the reader. The following examples juxtapose a series of inarguable topics or fact statements—ones that are merely factual or descriptive—with thesis statements, each of which makes a debatable claim about the topic or fact:

TOPIC OR FACT STATEMENTS	THESIS STATEMENTS
The experience of the speaker in "How I Discovered Poetry" is very ambiguous.	In "How I Discovered Poetry," what the speaker discovers is the ambiguous power of words—their capacity both to inspire and unite and to denigrate and divide.
"London" consists of three discrete stanzas that each end with a period; two-thirds of the lines are end-stopped.	In "London," William Blake uses a variety of formal techniques to suggest the unnatural rigidity and constraints of urban life.

The thesis statements above are arguable, but they share other traits as well. All are clear and emphatic. Each implicitly answers a compelling interpretive question. Yet each statement entices us to read further by generating more questions in our minds. An effective thesis enables the reader to enter the essay with a clear sense of what its writer will try to prove, and it inspires the reader with the desire to see the writer do it. We want to understand how the writer arrived at this view, to test whether it's valid, and to see how the writer will answer the other questions the thesis has generated in our minds. A good thesis captures the reader's interest and shapes his or her expectations. It also makes promises that the rest of the essay should fulfill.

At the same time, an arguable claim is not one-sided or narrow-minded. A thesis needs to stake out a position, but a position can and should admit complexity. Literary texts tend to focus more on exploring problems, conflicts, and questions than on offering solutions, resolutions, and answers. Their goal is to complicate, not simplify, our way of looking at the world. The best essays about literature and the theses that drive them often share a similar quality.

17.2.1 Interpretive versus Evaluative Claims

The theses in the previous examples involve *interpretive* claims—claims about how a literary text works, what it says, how one should understand it. And interpretive claims generally work best as theses.

Yet it's useful to remember that in reading and writing about poetry we often make (and debate) a different type of claim—the *evaluative*. Evaluation entails judging or assessing. Evaluative claims about literature tend to be of two kinds. The first involves aesthetic judgment, the question being whether a text (or a part or element thereof) succeeds in artistic terms. (This kind of claim features prominently in book reviews, for example.) The second involves philosophical, ethical, or even socially or politically based judgment, the question being whether an idea or action is wise or good, valid or admirable. All interpretive and evaluative claims involve informed opinion (which is why they are debatable). But whereas interpretive claims aim to elucidate the opinions expressed *in* and *by* the text, the second kind of evaluative claim assesses the value or validity of those opinions, often by comparing them with the writer's own.

The following example juxtaposes an interpretive claim with evaluative claims of both types:

INTERPRETIVE CLAIM	EVALUATIVE CLAIMS
The speaker of John Donne's "Song" is an angry and disillusioned man obsessed with the infidelity of women.	In "Song," John Donne does a very effective job of characterizing the speaker, an angry and disillusioned man obsessed with the infidelity of women.
	John Donne's "Song" is a horribly misogynistic poem because it ends up endorsing the idea that women are incapable of fidelity.

In practice, the line between these different types of claims can become very thin. An essay defending an interpretive claim about a text implies that it is at least aesthetically or philosophically worthy enough to merit interpretation. Conversely, defending and developing an evaluative claim about a text always requires a certain amount of interpretation. (You have to figure out what the text says in order to figure out whether the text says it well or says something worthwhile.)

To some extent, then, the distinctions are ones of emphasis. But they are important nonetheless. And unless instructed otherwise, you should generally make your thesis an interpretive claim, reserving evaluative claims for conclusions. (On conclusions, see 17.3.3.)

17.3 STRUCTURE

Like any literary text, an essay needs to have a beginning (or introduction), a middle (or body), and an ending (or conclusion). Each of these parts has a distinct function.

17.3.1 Beginning: The Introduction

Your essay's beginning, or introduction, should draw readers in and prepare them for what's to come by:

- articulating the thesis;
- providing whatever basic information—about the text, the author, and/or the topic—readers will need to follow the argument; and
- creating interest in the thesis by demonstrating that there is a problem or question that it resolves or answers.

This final task involves showing readers why your thesis isn't dull or obvious, establishing a specific *motive* for the essay and its readers. There are numerous possible motives, but writing expert Gordon Harvey has identified three especially common ones:

1. The truth isn't what one would expect or what it might appear to be on a first reading.
2. There's an interesting wrinkle in the text—a paradox, a contradiction, a tension.
3. A seemingly tangential or insignificant matter is actually important or interesting.

(On motives specific to research essays, see 19.1.1.)

17.3.2 Middle: The Body

The middle, or body, of your essay is its beating heart, the place where you do the essential work of supporting and developing the thesis by presenting and analyzing evidence. Each of the body paragraphs needs to articulate, support, and develop one specific claim—a debatable idea directly related to, but smaller and more specific than, the thesis. This claim should be stated fairly early in the paragraph in a *topic sentence*. And every sentence in the paragraph should help prove, or elaborate on, that claim. Indeed, each paragraph ideally should build from an initial, general statement of the claim to the more complex form of it that you develop by presenting and analyzing evidence. In this way, each paragraph functions like a miniature essay with its own thesis, body, and conclusion.

Your essay as a whole should develop logically just as each paragraph does. To ensure that that happens, you need to:

- order your paragraphs so that each builds on the last, with one idea following another in a logical sequence. The goal is to lay out a clear path for the reader. Like any path, it should go somewhere. Don't just prove your point; develop it.
- present each idea/paragraph so that the logic behind the sequential order is clear. Try to start each paragraph with a sentence that functions as a bridge, carrying the reader from one point to the next. Don't make the reader have to leap.

17.3.3 Ending: The Conclusion

In terms of their purpose (not their content), conclusions are introductions in reverse. Whereas introductions draw readers away from their world and into your essay, conclusions send them back. Introductions work to convince readers that they should read the essay. Conclusions work to show them why and how the experience was worthwhile. You should approach conclusions, then, by thinking about what sort of lasting impression you want to create. What precisely do you want readers to take with them as they journey back into the "real world"?

Effective conclusions often consider three things:

1. *Implications*—What picture of your author's work or worldview does your argument imply or suggest? Alternatively, what might your argument imply about some real-world issue or situation?
2. *Evaluation*—What might your argument about the text reveal about the literary quality or effectiveness of the text as a whole or of some specific element? Alternatively, to what extent and how do you agree and/or disagree with the author's conclusions about a particular issue?
3. *Areas of ambiguity or unresolved questions*—Are there any remaining puzzles or questions that your argument and/or the text itself doesn't resolve or answer? Alternatively, might your argument suggest a new question or puzzle worth investigating?

Above all, don't repeat what you've already said. If the essay has done its job to this point, and especially if the essay is relatively short, your readers may feel bored and insulted if they get a mere summary. You should clarify anything that needs clarifying, but go a little beyond that. The best essays are rounded wholes in which conclusions do, in a sense, circle back to the place where they started. However, the best essays remind readers of where they began only in order to give them a more palpable sense of how far they've come.

17.4 EVIDENCE

In terms of convincing readers that your claims are valid, both the amount and the quality of your evidence count. And the quality of your evidence will depend, in great part, on how you prepare and present it. Each of the ideas that makes up the body of your essay must be supported and developed with ample, appropriate evidence. Colloquially speaking, the term *evidence* simply refers to facts. But it's helpful to remember that a fact by itself isn't really evidence for anything, or rather that—as lawyers well know—any one fact can be evidence for many things. Like lawyers, essayists turn a fact into evidence by interpreting it; drawing an inference from it; giving the reader a vivid sense of why and how the fact supports a specific claim. You need, then, both to present specific facts and to actively interpret them. *Show* readers why and how each fact matters.

Quotations are an especially important form of evidence in essays about literature; indeed, an essay about literature that contains no quotations will likely be relatively weak. The reader of such an essay may doubt whether its argument emerges out of a thorough knowledge of the work. However, quotations are by no means the only facts on which you should draw. Indeed, a quotation will lead your reader to expect commentary on, and interpretation of, its language. As a general rule, you should quote directly from the text only when its wording is significant. Otherwise, simply paraphrase, describe, or summarize. The following example, from an essay about Thomas Hardy's novel *Far from the Madding Crowd*, demonstrates the use of both summary and quotation. (On effective quotation, see 20.1; on paraphrase, summary, and description, see ch. 16.)

> At many points in the novel, religion is represented as having degenerated into a system of social control by farmers over workers. Only respectable young men can come courting at Upper Weatherbury farm, and no swearing is allowed (ch. 8). Similarly, the atmosphere in Boldwood's farm kitchen is "like a Puritan Sunday lasting all the week." Bathsheba tries to restrict her workers to drinking mild liquor, and church attendance is taken as the mark of respectability.
> —Fred Reid, "Art and Ideology in *Far from the Madding Crowd*," *Thomas Hardy Annual 4* (London: Macmillan, 1986)

> NOTE: Pay special attention to the way this writer uses paraphrase, summary, and quotation. At the beginning of the paragraph, he simply paraphrases certain rules; at its end, he summarizes or describes one character's action. Here, he can use his own words because it's the rules and actions that illustrate his point, not the words that the novelist uses to describe them. However, Reid does quote the text when its (religious) language is the crucial, evidentiary element.

17.5 CONVENTIONS THAT CAN CAUSE PROBLEMS

A mastery of basic mechanics and writing conventions is essential to convincing your readers that you are a knowledgeable and careful writer whose ideas they should respect. This section explores three conventions that are crucial to essays about literature.

17.5.1 Tenses

Essays about literature tend to function almost wholly in the present tense, a practice that can take some getting used to. The rationale is that the action within any literary work never stops: a text simply, always *is*. Thus yesterday, today, and tomorrow, Ophelia *goes* mad; Wordsworth *sees* nature as an avenue to God; and so on. When in doubt, stick to the present tense when writing about literature.

An important exception to this general rule is demonstrated in the following example. As you read the excerpt, pay attention to the way the writer shifts between tenses, using various past tenses to refer to completed actions that took place in the actual past, and using the present tense to refer to actions that occur within, or are performed by, the text.

> In 1959 Plath **did not** consciously **attempt** to write in the domestic poem genre, perhaps because she **was not** yet ready to assume her majority. Her journal entries of that period **bristle** with an impatience at herself that **may derive** from this reluctance.... But by fall 1962, when she **had** already **lost** so much, she **was** ready.... In "Daddy" she **achieved** her victory in two ways. First, ... she symbolically **assaults** a father figure who **is identified** with male control of language.
> —Steven Gould Axelrod, "Jealous Gods" (ch. 13)

17.5.2 Titles

Underline or italicize the titles of books and works published independently, including:

- long poems (*Endymion; Paradise Lost*)
- periodicals: newspapers, magazines, scholarly journals, and the like (*New York Times; College English*)

Use quotation marks for the titles of works that have been published as part of longer works, including:

- essays and periodical articles ("A Rose for 'A Rose for Emily' "; "Art and Ideology in *Far from the Madding Crowd*")
- poems ("Daddy"; "Ode to a Nightingale")

Generally speaking, you should capitalize the first word of every title, as well as all the other words that aren't either articles (e.g., *the, a*); prepositions (e.g., *among, in, through*); or conjunctions (e.g., *and, but*). One exception to this rule is the poem in which the first line substitutes for a missing title (a category that includes everything by Emily Dickinson, as well as the sonnets of Shakespeare and Edna St. Vincent Millay). In such cases, only the first word is capitalized. Often, the entire phrase is placed in brackets—as in "[Let me not to the marriage of true minds]"—but you will just as often see such titles without brackets.

17.5.3 Names

When first referring to an author, use his or her full name; thereafter, use the last name. (For example, although you may feel a real kinship with Robert Frost, you will appear disrespectful if you refer to him as Robert.)

18 THE WRITING PROCESS

It's fairly easy to describe the purpose and formal elements of an essay. Actually writing one is more difficult. So, too, is prescribing a precise formula for how to do so. In practice, the writing process will vary from writer to writer and from assignment to assignment. No one can give you a recipe. However, this chapter presents a menu of possible approaches and exercises, which you should test out and refine for yourself.

As you do so, keep in mind that writing needn't be a solitary enterprise. Most writers—working in every genre, at every level—get inspiration, guidance, help, and feedback from other people throughout the writing process, and so can you. Your instructor may well create opportunities for collaboration, having you and your colleagues work together to plan essays, critique drafts, and so on. Even if that isn't the case, you can always reach out to others on your own. Since every essay will ultimately have to engage readers, why not bring some actual readers and fellow writers into the writing process? Use class discussions to generate and test out essay topics and theses. Ask the instructor to clarify assignments or to talk with you about your plans. Have classmates, friends, or roommates read your drafts.

Of course, your essay ultimately needs to be your own work. You, the individual writer, must be the ultimate arbiter, critically scrutinizing the advice you receive, differentiating valid reader responses from idiosyncratic ones. But in writing about literature, as in reading it, we all can get a much better sense of what we think by considering others' views.

18.1 GETTING STARTED

18.1.1 Scrutinizing the Assignment

For student essayists, as for most professional ones, the writing process usually begins with an assignment. Though assignments vary greatly, all impose certain restrictions. These are designed not to hinder your creativity but to direct it into productive channels, ensuring that you hone certain skills, try out various approaches, and avoid common pitfalls. Your first task as a writer is thus to scrutinize the assignment. Make sure that you fully understand what you are being asked to do (and not do), and ask questions about anything unclear or puzzling.

Almost all assignments restrict the length of the essay by giving word or page limits. Keep those limits in mind as you generate and evaluate potential essay topics, making sure that you choose a topic you can handle in the space allowed. Many assignments impose further restrictions, often indicating the texts and/or topics to be explored. As a result, any given assignment will significantly shape the rest of the writing process—determining, for example, whether and how you should tackle a step such as "Choosing a Text" or "Identifying Topics."

Here is a representative essay assignment:

> Write an essay analyzing one of the following sonnets: "The New Colossus," "Range-Finding," or "London, 1802." Be sure to consider how the poem's form contributes to its meaning.

This assignment limits your choice of texts to three. Though it also requires that your essay address the effects of the poet's choice to use the sonnet form, it doesn't require this to be the main topic of the essay. Rather, it leaves you free to pursue any topic that focuses on the poem's meaning.

18.1.2 Choosing a Text

If the assignment allows you to choose which text to write about, try letting your initial impressions or "gut reactions" guide you. If you do so, your first impulse may be to choose a text that you like or "get" right away. Perhaps its language resembles your own; it depicts speakers, characters, or situations that you easily relate to; or it explores issues that you care deeply about. Following that first impulse can be a great idea. Writing an engaging essay requires being engaged with whatever we're writing about, and we all find it easier to engage with texts, authors, and/or characters that we like immediately.

You may discover, however, that you have little interesting or new to say about such a text. Perhaps you're too emotionally invested to analyze it closely, or maybe its meaning seems so obvious that there's no puzzle or problem to drive an argument. You might, then, find it more productive to choose a work that provokes the opposite reaction—one that initially puzzles or angers you, one whose characters or situations seem alien, one that investigates an issue you haven't previously thought much about or that articulates a theme you don't agree with. Sometimes such negative responses can have surprisingly positive results when it comes to writing. One student writer, for example, summed up her basic response to William Blake's *The Marriage of Heaven and Hell* with the words "He's crazy." Initially, the poem made no sense to her. And that's precisely why she decided to write about it: she needed to do so, to make sense of it for other readers, in order to make sense of it for herself. In the end, she wrote a powerful essay exploring how the poem defined, and why it celebrated, seeming insanity.

When writing about a text that you've discussed in class, you might make similar use of your "gut responses" to that conversation. Did you strongly agree or disagree with one of your classmate's interpretations of a particular text? If so, why not write about it?

18.1.3 Identifying Topics

When an assignment allows you to create your own topic, you will much more likely build a lively and engaging essay from a particular insight or question that captures your attention and makes you want to say something, solve a problem, or stake out a position. The best papers originate in an individual response to a text and focus on a genuine question about it. Even when an instructor assigns a topic, the effectiveness of your essay will largely depend on whether or not you have made the topic your own, turning it into a question to which you discover your own answer.

Often we refer to "finding" a topic, as if there are a bevy of topics "out there" just waiting to be plucked like ripe fruit off the topic-tree. In at least two ways, that's true. For one thing, as we read a literary work, certain topics often do jump out and say, "Hey, look at me! I'm a topic!" A title alone may have that effect: Why is Keats so keen on that darn nightingale; what does it symbolize for him? Why did Plath write a poem called "Daddy"—how would the poem be different if she'd titled it "Father"?

For another thing, certain general topics can be adapted to fit almost any literary work. In fact, that's just another way of saying that there are certain common types (or subgenres) of literary essays, just as there are of short stories, plays, and poems. For example, one very common kind of literary essay explores the significance of a seemingly insignificant aspect or element of a work—a word or group of related words, an image or image-cluster, an incident or action, and so on. Especially when you're utterly befuddled about where to begin, it can be very useful to keep in mind such a general topic and use it as a starting point. But remember that it's just a starting point. One always has to adapt and narrow a generic topic such as "imagery" in order to produce an effective essay. In practice, then, no writer simply "finds" a topic; he or she *makes* one.

Similarly, though the topic that leaps out at you immediately might end up being the one you find most interesting, you can only discover that by giving yourself some options. It's always a good idea to initially come up with as many topics as you can. Test out various topics to see which one will work best. Making yourself identify multiple topics will lead you to think harder, look more closely, and reach deeper into yourself and the work.

Here are some additional techniques to identify potential topics. In each case, write your thoughts down. Don't worry at this point about what form your writing takes or how good it is.

- *Analyze your initial response.*
  If you've chosen a poem that you feel strongly about, start with those responses. Try to describe your feelings and trace them to their source. Be as specific as possible. What moments, aspects, or elements of the poem most affected you? Exactly how and why did they affect you? What was most puzzling? amusing? annoying? intriguing? Try to articulate the question behind your feelings. Often, strong responses result when a work either challenges or affirms an expectation, assumption, or conviction that you, the reader, bring to the work. Think about whether and how that's true here. Define the specific expectation, assumption, or conviction. How, where, and why does the text challenge it? fulfill and affirm it? Which of your responses and expectations are objectively valid, likely to be shared by other readers?

- *Think through the elements.*
  Start with a list of elements and work your way through them, thinking about what's unique or interesting or puzzling about the text in terms of each. When it comes to tone, what stands out? What about the speaker? the situation? other elements? Come up with a statement about each. Look

for patterns among your statements. Also, think about the questions implied or overlooked by your statements.

- *Pose motive questions.*
  In articulating a motive in your essay's introduction, your concern is primarily with the readers, your goal being to give them a solid reason to keep on reading. But you can often work your way toward a topic (or topics) by considering motive. As suggested earlier (17.3.1), there are three common motives. Turn each one into a question in order to identify potential topics:

  1. What element(s) or aspect(s) of this work might a casual reader misinterpret?
  2. What interesting paradox(es), contradiction(s), or tension(s) do you see in this text?
  3. What seemingly minor, insignificant, easily ignored element(s) or aspect(s) of this text might in fact have major significance?

18.1.4 Formulating a Question and a Thesis

Almost any element, aspect, or point of interest in a text can become a topic for a short essay. Before you can begin writing an essay on that topic, however, you need to come up with a thesis or hypothesis—an arguable statement about the topic. Quite often, one comes up with topic and thesis simultaneously: you might well decide to write about a topic precisely because you've got a specific claim to make about it. At other times, that's not the case: the topic comes much more easily than the thesis. In those cases, it helps to formulate a specific question about the topic and to develop a specific answer. That answer will be your thesis.

Again, remember that your question and thesis should focus on something specific, yet they need to be generally valid, involving more than your personal feelings. Who, after all, can really argue with you about how you feel?

Regardless of how you arrive at your thesis or how strongly you believe in it, it's still helpful at this early stage to think of it as a working hypothesis—a claim that's provisional, still open to rethinking and revision.

18.2 PLANNING

Once you've formulated a tentative thesis, you need to (1) identify the relevant evidence, and (2) figure out how to structure your argument, articulating and ordering your claims or sub-ideas. Generally speaking, it works best to tackle structure first—that is, to first figure out your claims and create an outline—because doing so will help you get a sense of what kind of evidence you need. However, you may sometimes get stuck and need to reverse this process, gathering evidence first in order to then formulate and order your claims.

18.2.1 Moving from Claims to Evidence

If you want to focus first on structure, start by looking closely at your thesis. As in many other aspects of writing, it helps to temporarily fill your readers' shoes, trying to see your thesis and the promises it makes from the readers' point of view. What will they need to be shown, and in what order?

If a good thesis shapes readers' expectations, it can also guide you, as a writer. A good thesis often implies what the essay's claims should be and how they should be ordered. For instance, a thesis that focuses on the development of a character implies both that the first body paragraphs will explain what the character is initially like and that later paragraphs will explore how and why that character changes over the course of the work.

At this stage, it's very helpful to create an outline. Write down or type out your thesis, and then list each claim (to create a *sentence outline*) or each of the topics to be covered (to create a *topic outline*). Now you can return to the text, rereading it in order to gather evidence for each claim. In the process, you might discover facts that seem relevant to the thesis but that don't relate directly to any of the claims you've articulated. In that case, you may need to insert a new claim into the outline. Additionally, you may find (and should actively look for) facts that challenge your argument. Test and reassess your claims against those facts.

18.2.2 Moving From Evidence to Claims

If you are focusing first on evidence, start by rereading the poem in a more strategic way, searching for everything relevant to your topic—words, phrases, structural devices, changes of tone, and so forth. As you read (slowly and single-mindedly, with your thesis in mind), keep your pen constantly poised to mark or note down useful facts. Be ready to say something about the facts as you come upon them; immediately write down any ideas that occur to you. Some of these will appear in your essay; some won't. Just like most of the footage shot in making a film, many of your notes will end up on the cutting-room floor. As in film-making, however, having too much raw material is preferable to not having enough.

No one can tell you exactly how to take notes. But here is one process that you might try. Be forewarned: this process involves using notecards or uniform sheets of paper. Having your notes on individual cards makes it easier to separate and sort them, a concrete, physical process that can aid the mental process of organizing thoughts and facts. If you are working on a computer, create notecards by putting page breaks between each note or by leaving enough space so that you can cut each page down to a uniform size.

1. Keep your thesis constantly in mind as you reread and take notes. Mark all the passages in the text that bear on your thesis. For each, create a notecard that contains a single sentence describing how the line or image relates to your thesis. Also, make cards for other relevant, evidentiary facts—like aspects of a poem's rhyme scheme.

2. Keep reading and taking notes until you experience any of the following:
   - get too tired and lose your concentration. (Stop, take a break, come back later.)
   - stop finding relevant evidence or perceive a noticeable drying up of your ideas. (Again, it's time to pause. Later, when your mind is fresh, read the text one more time to ensure that you didn't miss anything.)
   - find yourself annotating every line, with the evidence all running together into a single blob. (If this happens, your thesis is probably too broad. Simplify and narrow it. Then continue notetaking.)

- become impatient with your notetaking and can't wait to get started writing. (Start drafting immediately. But be prepared to go back to systematic notetaking if your ideas stop coming or your energy fades.)
- find that the evidence is insufficient for your thesis, that it points in another direction, or that it contradicts your thesis. (Revise your thesis to accommodate the evidence, and begin rereading once more.)

3. When you think you have finished notetaking, read all your notecards over slowly, one by one, and jot down any further ideas as they occur to you, each one on a separate notecard.

Use your notecards to work toward an outline. Again, there are many ways to go about doing this. Here's one process:

1. Sort your cards into logical groups or clusters. Come up with a keyword for that group, and write that word at the top of each card in the group.

2. Set your notecards aside. On a fresh sheet of paper or in a new document on your computer, write all the major points you want to make. Write them randomly, as they occur to you. Then read quickly through your notecards, and add to your list any important points you have left out.

3. Now it's time to order your points. Putting your points in order is something of a guess at this point, and you may well want to re-order later. For now, take your best guess. Taking your random list, put a "1" in front of the point you will probably begin with, a "2" before the probable second point, and so on.

4. Copy the list in numerical order, revising (if necessary) as you go.

5. Match up your notes (and examples) with the points on your outline. Prepare a title card for each point in the outline, writing on it the point and its probable place in the essay. Then line them up in order before you begin writing. If you're working on a computer, use the search function to find each instance of a keyword, phrase, or name. Then cut and paste in order to arrange your electronic "cards" under the headings you've identified.

6. At this point, you may discover cards that resist classification, cards that belong in two or more places, and/or cards that don't belong anywhere at all. If a card relates to more than one point, put it in the pile with the lowest number, but write on it the number or numbers of other possible locations. Try to find a place for the cards that don't seem to fit, and then put any that remain unsorted into a special file marked "?" or "use in revision."

Before you begin drafting, you may want to develop a more elaborate outline, incorporating examples and including topic sentences for each paragraph; or you may wish to work directly from your sketchy outline and cards.

18.3 DRAFTING

If you've taken enough time with the planning process, you may already be quite close to a first draft. If you've instead jumped straight into writing, you may have to move back and forth between composing and taking some of the steps described in the last section. Either way, remember that first drafts are often called *rough drafts* for a reason. Think of yourself as a painter "roughing out" a sketch in preparation for the more detailed painting to come. The most important thing is to start writing and keep at it.

Try to start with your thesis and work your way step by step through the entire body of the essay at one sitting. (However, you don't actually have to sit the whole time; if you get stuck, jump up and down, walk around the room, water your plants. Then get back to work.) You will almost certainly feel frustrated at times—as you search for the right word, struggle to decide how the next sentence should begin, or discover that you need to tackle ideas in a different order from what you originally had planned.

Stick to it. If you become truly stuck, try to explain your point to another person, or get out a piece of paper or open a new computer file and try working out your ideas or freewriting for a few minutes before returning to your draft. Or, if you get to a section you simply can't write at the moment, make a note about what needs to go in that spot. Then move on and come back to that point later.

Whatever it takes, stay with your draft until you've at least got a middle, or body, that you're relatively satisfied with. Then take a break. Later or even tomorrow come back and take another shot, attaching an introduction and conclusion to the body, filling in any gaps, doing your utmost to create a relatively satisfying whole. Now pat yourself on the back and take another break.

18.4 REVISING

Revision is one of the most important and difficult tasks for any writer. It's a crucial stage in the writing process, yet one that is all too easy to ignore or mismanage. The difference between a so-so essay and a good one, between a good essay and a great one, often depends entirely on effective revision. Give yourself time to revise and develop revision strategies that work for you; the investment in time and effort will pay rich dividends.

Ideally, the process of revision should involve three distinct tasks: assessing the elements, improving the argument, and editing and proofreading. Each of these may require a separate draft. Before considering those three tasks, however, you should be aware of the following three general tips.

First, effective revision requires you to temporarily play the role of reader, as well as writer, of your essay. Take a step back from your draft, doing your utmost to look at it from a more objective point of view. Revision demands re-vision—looking again, seeing anew. As a result, this is an especially good time to involve other people. Have a classmate or friend read and critique your draft.

Second, at this stage it helps to think less in absolute terms (right and wrong, good and bad) than in terms of strengths and weaknesses (elements and aspects of the draft that work well and those that can be improved through revision). If you can understand what's making your essay work as well as what's detracting from it, then you're better able to improve it. Don't get distracted from this important work by grammatical errors, spelling mistakes, or other minutiae; there will be time to correct them later.

Third, learn to take full advantage of all the capabilities of the computer, but also recognize its limitations. Cutting and pasting make experimenting with different organizational strategies a breeze; word-processing programs identify problems with grammar, spelling, and syntax; the search function can locate repetitive or problematic wording; and so on. You should familiarize yourself with, and use, all of the tools your computer provides and be thankful that you barely know the meaning of the word *white-out*. But you should also remember that the computer is just a tool with limits and that you must be its master. Like any tool, it can create new problems in the process of solving old ones. When it comes to grammar, syntax, and spelling, for instance, you should always pay attention to your program's queries and suggestions. But if you let it make all the decisions, you may end up with an essay full of malapropisms at once hilarious and tragic (one student essay consistently referred to human beings as *human beans*!) or of sentences that are all exactly the same size and shape—all perfectly correct, and all perfectly boring. Also, because the computer makes cutting and pasting so easy and only shows an essay one screen at a time, it's much easier to reorganize but much harder to recognize the effects of doing so. During revision, then, you should at times move away from the computer screen. Print out a hard copy periodically so that you can assess your essay as a whole, identifying problems that you can return to the computer to fix.

18.4.1 Assessing the Elements

The first step in revision is to make sure that all the elements or working parts of the essay are indeed working. To help with that process, run through the following checklist in order to identify the strengths and weaknesses of your draft. Try to answer each question honestly.

Thesis
- [ ] Is there *one* claim that effectively controls the essay?
- [ ] Is the claim debatable?
- [ ] Does the claim demonstrate real thought? Does it truly illuminate the text and the topic?

Structure

BEGINNING
- [ ] Does the introduction establish a clear motive for readers, effectively convincing them that there's something worth thinking, reading, and writing about here?
- [ ] Does it give readers all (and only) the basic information they need about the text, author, and/or topic?
- [ ] Does the introduction clearly state the central claim or thesis? Is it obvious which claim is the thesis?

MIDDLE
- [ ] Does each paragraph state one debatable claim? Is the main claim always obvious? Does everything in the paragraph relate to, and help to support and develop, that claim?
- [ ] Is each of those claims clearly related to (but different from) the thesis?
- [ ] Are the claims/paragraphs logically ordered?
- [ ] Is that logic clear? Is each claim clearly linked to those that come before and after? Are there any logical "leaps" that readers might have trouble taking?
- [ ] Does each claim/paragraph clearly build on the last one? Does the argu-

ment move forward, or does it seem more like a list or a tour through a museum of interesting observations?

☐ Do any key claims or steps in the argument seem to be missing?

TIP: You may be better able to discover structural weaknesses if you:

1. re-outline your draft as it is. Copy your thesis statement and each of your topic sentences into a separate document. Then pose the above questions. OR
2. read through the essay with highlighters of various colors in hand. As you read, color-code parts that could be restatements of the same or closely related ideas. Then reorganize to match up the colors.

ENDING

☐ Does the conclusion give readers the sense that they've gotten somewhere and that the journey has been worthwhile?

☐ Does it indicate the implications of the argument, consider relevant evaluative questions, and/or discuss questions that remain unanswered?

Evidence

☐ Is there ample, appropriate evidence for each claim?

☐ Are the appropriateness and significance of each fact—its relevance to the claim—perfectly clear?

☐ Are there any weak examples or inferences that aren't reasonable? Are there moments when readers might ask, "But couldn't that fact instead mean this?"

☐ Is all the evidence considered? What about facts that might complicate or contradict the argument? Are there moments when readers might think, "But what about this other fact?"

☐ Is each piece of evidence clearly presented? Do readers have all the contextual information they need to understand a quotation?

☐ Is each piece of evidence gracefully presented? Are quotations varied by length and presentation? Are they ever too long? Are there any unnecessary block quotations, or block quotations that require additional analysis? (For more specific explanations and advice on effective quotation, see 20.1.)

Though you want to pay attention to all of the elements, first drafts often have similar weaknesses. There are three especially common ones:

- *Mismatch between thesis and argument or between introduction and body*
  Sometimes a first or second draft ends up being a tool for discovering what your thesis really is. As a result, you may find that the thesis of your draft (or your entire introduction) doesn't fit the argument you've ended up making. You thus need to start your revision by reworking the thesis and introduction. Then work your way back through the essay, making sure that each claim or topic sentence fits the new thesis.

- *The list, or "museum tour," structure*
  In a draft, writers sometimes present each claim as if it were just an item on a list (*First, second,* and so on) or as a stop on a tour of ideas (*And this is also important . . .*). But presenting your ideas in this way keeps you and your readers from making logical connections between ideas. It may also

prevent your argument from developing. Sometimes it can even be a symptom of the fact that you've ceased arguing entirely, falling into mere plot summary or description. Check to see if numberlike words or phrases appear prominently at the beginning of your paragraphs or if your paragraphs could be put into a different order without fundamentally changing what you're saying. At times, solving this problem will require wholesale rethinking and reorganizing. But at other times, you will just need to add or rework topic sentences. Make sure that there's a clearly stated, debatable claim up-front and in charge of each paragraph and that each claim relates to, but differs from, the thesis.

- *Missing sub-ideas*
You may find that you've skipped a logical step in your argument—that the claim you make in, say, body paragraph 3 actually depends on, or makes sense only in light of, a more basic claim that you took for granted in your draft. In that case, you'll need to create and insert a new paragraph that articulates, supports, and develops this key claim.

18.4.2 Enriching the Argument

Step 1 of the revision process aims to ensure that your essay does the best possible job of making your argument. But revision is also an opportunity to go beyond that—to think about ways in which your overall argument might be made more thorough and complex. In drafting an essay our attention is often and rightly focused on emphatically staking out a particular position and proving its validity. This is the fundamental task of any essay, and you certainly don't want to do anything at this stage to compromise that. At the same time, you do want to make sure that you haven't purchased clarity at the cost of oversimplification by, for example, ignoring evidence that might undermine or complicate your claims, alternative interpretations of the evidence you do present, or alternative claims or points of view. Remember, you have a better chance of persuading readers to accept your point of view if you show them that it's based on a thorough, open-minded exploration of the text and topic. Don't invent unreasonable or irrelevant complications or counterarguments. Do try to assess your argument objectively and honestly, perhaps testing it against the text one more time. Think like a reader rather than a writer: Are there points where a reasonable reader might object to, or disagree with, the argument? Have you ignored or glossed over any questions or issues that a reasonable reader might expect an essay on this topic to address?

18.4.3 Editing and Proofreading

Once you've gotten the overall argument in good shape, it's time to focus on the small but important stuff—words and sentences. Your prose should not only convey your ideas to your readers but also demonstrate how much you care about your essay. Flawless prose can't disguise a vapid or illogical argument, but faulty, flabby prose can destroy a potentially persuasive and thoughtful one. Don't sabotage all your hard work by failing to correct misspelled words, grammatical problems, misquotations, incorrect citations, or typographical errors. Little oversights make all the difference when it comes to clarity and credibility.

Though you will want to check all of the following aspects of your essay, it will probably be easier to spot mistakes and weaknesses if you read through the essay several times, concentrating each time on one specific aspect.

Every writer has individual weaknesses and strengths, and every writer tends to be overly fond of certain phrases and sentence structures. With practice, you will learn to watch out for the kinds of mistakes to which you are most prone. Eventually, you can and should develop your own *personalized* editing checklist.

Sentences

- ☐ Does each one read clearly and crisply?
- ☐ Are they varied in length, structure, and word order?
- ☐ Is my phrasing direct rather than roundabout?

> **TIPS:**
> 1. Try circling, or using your computer to search for, every preposition and *to be* verb. Since these can lead to confusion or roundabout phrasing, weed out as many as you can.
> 2. Try reading your paper aloud or having your roommate read it to you. Note places where you stumble, and listen for sentences that are hard to get through or understand.

Words

- ☐ Have I used any words whose meaning I'm not sure of?
- ☐ Are the idioms used correctly? Is my terminology correct?
- ☐ Do my key words always mean *exactly* the same thing?
- ☐ Do I ever use a fancy word or phrase where a simpler one might do?
- ☐ Are there any unnecessary words or phrases?
- ☐ Do my metaphors and figures of speech make literal sense?
- ☐ Are my verbs active and precise?
- ☐ Are my pronoun references clear and correct?
- ☐ Do my subjects and verbs always agree?

Mechanics

- ☐ Is every quotation correctly worded and punctuated?
- ☐ Is the source of each quotation clearly indicated through parenthetical citation?
- ☐ Have I checked the spelling of words I'm not sure of? (Remember that spell-checks won't indicate how to spell every word and that they sometimes create mistakes by substituting the wrong word for the misspelled one.)
- ☐ Are my pages numbered?
- ☐ Does the first page of my essay clearly indicate my name (and any other required identifying information), as well as my essay's title?

18.5 CRAFTING A TITLE

Complete your essay by giving it a title. As any researcher trying to locate and assess sources by browsing titles will tell you, titles are extremely important. They're the first thing readers encounter and a writer's first opportunity to create a good impression and to shape readers' expectations. Every good essay deserves a good title. And a good title is one that both *informs* and *interests*. Inform readers by telling them both the work(s) your essay will analyze and something about your topic. Interest them with an especially vivid and telling word or a short phrase from the literary work.

19 THE RESEARCH ESSAY

Writing a research essay may seem like a daunting task that requires specialized skills and considerable time and effort. Research does add a few more steps to the writing process, so that process will take more time. And those steps require you to draw upon, and develop, skills somewhat different from those involved in creating other kinds of essays. But a research essay is, after all, an essay. Its core elements are those of any essay, its basic purpose exactly the same—to articulate and develop a debatable claim about a literary text. As a result, this kind of essay draws upon many of the same skills and strategies you've already begun to develop. Similarly, though you will need to add a few new steps, the writing process still involves getting started, planning, drafting, and revising—exactly the same dance whose rhythms you've already begun to master.

Indeed, the only distinctive thing about a research essay is that it requires the use of secondary sources. Though that adds to your burden in some ways, it can lighten it in others. Think of secondary sources not as another ball you have to juggle but as another tool you get to add to your toolbelt: you're still being asked to build a cabinet, but now you get to use a hammer *and* a screwdriver. This chapter will help you make the best use of this powerful tool.

19.1 TYPES AND FUNCTIONS OF SECONDARY SOURCES

Whenever we write an essay about literature, we engage in a conversation with other readers about the meaning and significance of a particular work (or works). Effective argumentation always depends on imagining how other readers are likely to respond to, and interpret, the literary text. As the "Reading Poetry in Context" chapters in this anthology demonstrate, however, almost all texts and authors are the subject of actual public conversations, often extending over many years and involving numerous scholarly readers. A research essay can be an opportunity to investigate this conversation and to contribute to it. In this case, your secondary sources will be works in which literary scholars analyze a specific text or an author's body of work.

The Context chapters also show that each literary work is significantly shaped by, and speaks to, its author's unique experience and outlook, as well as the events and debates of the era in which the author lived. So a research assignment can be an opportunity to learn more about a particular author, about that author's canon, or about the place and time in which the author lived and worked. The goal of the essay will be to show how context informs text or vice versa. Secondary sources for this sort of research essay will be biographies of the author, essays or letters by the author, and/or historical works of some kind.

Generally speaking, three types of secondary sources are used in essays about literature: *literary criticism, biography,* and *history.* The goal of a particular essay and the kinds of questions it raises will determine which kind of sources you use.

In practice, however, many secondary sources cross these boundaries. Biographies of a particular author often offer literary critical interpretations of that author's work; works of literary criticism sometimes make use of historical or biographical information; and so on. And you, too, may want or need to draw on more than one kind of source in a single essay. Your instructor will probably give you guidance about what kinds of sources and research topics or questions are appropriate. So make sure that you have a clear sense of the assignment before you get started.

Unless your instructor indicates otherwise, *your* argument should be the focus of your essay, and secondary sources should be just that—secondary. They should merely serve as tools that you use to deepen and enrich your argument about the literary text. They shouldn't substitute for it. Your essay should never simply repeat or report on what other people have already said.

Thus even though secondary sources are important to the development of your research essay, they should not be the source of your ideas. Instead, as one popular guide to writing suggests,* they are sources of:

- *opinion* (or *debatable claims*)—other readers' views and interpretations of the text, author, or topic, which "you support, criticize, or develop";
- *information*—facts (which "you interpret") about the author's life; the text's composition, publication, or reception; the era during, or about which, the author wrote; or the literary movement of which the author was a part;
- *concept*—general terms or theoretical frameworks that you borrow and apply to your author or text.

Again, any one source will likely offer more than one of these things. For example, the excerpt from Stephen Gould Axelrod's "Jealous Gods" in chapter 13 provides Axelrod's *opinion* on (or interpretation of) Sylvia Plath's "Daddy"; *information* about the status of the domestic poem in the 1950s; and *concepts* drawn from Freud's theories of psychological development.

Nonetheless, the distinction between opinion (debatable claim) and information (factual statement) is crucial. As you read a source, you must discriminate between the two. And when drawing upon sources in your essay, remember that an opinion about a text, no matter how well informed, isn't the same as evidence. Only facts can serve that function. Suppose, for example, that you are writing an essay on "Daddy." You claim that the speaker adopts two voices, that of her child self and that of her adult self—an opinion also set forth in Axelrod's "Jealous Gods." You cannot prove this claim to be true by merely saying that Axelrod makes the same claim. Like any debatable claim, this one must be backed up with evidence from the primary text.

In this situation, however, you must indicate that a source has made the same claim that you do in order to:

- give the source credit for having this idea or stating this opinion before you did (see 19.4.1);
- encourage readers to see you as a knowledgeable and trustworthy writer,

---

* Gordon Harvey, *Writing with Sources* (Indianapolis: Hackett, 1998) 1.

one who has taken the time to explore, digest, and fairly represent others' opinions;

• demonstrate that your opinion isn't merely idiosyncratic because another informed, even "expert," reader agrees with you.

Were you to disagree with the source's opinion, you would need to acknowledge that disagreement in order to demonstrate the originality of your own interpretation, while also (again) encouraging readers to see you as a knowledgeable, careful, trustworthy writer.

You will need to cite sources throughout your essay whenever you make (1) a claim that complements or contradicts the opinion-claim of a source, or (2) a claim that requires secondary-source information or concepts. In essays that draw upon literary critical sources, those sources may prove especially helpful when articulating motive (see 19.1.1).

> Tip: In addition to being secondary sources of the type you might use in a research essay, many of the pieces excerpted in the "Reading Poetry in Context" chapters draw on other secondary sources. Look over these pieces to see what kinds of sources professional literary critics use and how they use them.

19.1.1 Source-Related Motives

Not all research essays use sources to establish motive. However, this is one technique you can use to ensure that your own ideas are the focus of your essay and to demonstrate that (and how) your essay contributes to a literary critical conversation rather than just reporting on it or repeating what others have already said.

In addition to the general motives described above (17.3.1), writing expert Gordon Harvey has identified three common source-related motives:

1. Sources offer different opinions about a particular issue, thus suggesting that there is still a problem or a puzzle worth investigating.

   > [A]lmost all interpreters of [*Antigone*] have agreed that the play shows Creon to be morally defective, though they might not agree about the particular nature of his defect. [examples] . . . I want to suggest [instead] that. . . .
   > —Martha Nussbaum, "*The Fragility of Goodness . . .*"

2. A source (or sources) makes a faulty claim that needs to be challenged or clarified.

   > Modern critics who do not share Sophocles' conviction about the paramount duty of burying the dead and who attach more importance than he did to the claims of political authority have tended to underestimate the way in which he justifies Antigone against Creon. [examples]   —Maurice Bowra, "*Sophoclean Tragedy*"

3. Sources neglect a significant aspect or element of the text, or they make a claim that needs to be further developed or applied in a new way.

   > At first sight, there appears little need for further study of the lovers in *Far from the Madding Crowd*, and even less of their environment. To cite but a few critics, David Cecil has considered the courtship of Bathsheba, Virginia Hyman her moral

development through her varied experience in love, George Wing her suitors, Douglas Brown her relation to the natural environment, Merryn Williams that of Gabriel Oak in contrast to Sergeant Troy's alienation from nature, and, most recently, Peter Casagrande Bathsheba's reformation through her communion with both Gabriel and the environment. To my knowledge, none has considered the modes or styles in which those and other characters express love and how far these may result from or determine their attitude to the land and its dependents, nor the tragic import in the Wessex novels of incompatibility in this sense between human beings, as distinct from that between the human psyche and the cosmos.

—Lionel Adey, "Styles of Love in *Far from the Madding Crowd*,"
Thomas Hardy Annual 5 (London: Macmillan, 1987)

19.2 RESEARCH AND THE WRITING PROCESS

Keeping in mind the overall goal of making secondary sources secondary, you have two options about when and how to integrate research into the writing process: (1) you may consult sources in the exploratory phase, using them to generate potential topics and theses for your essay, or (2) you may consult sources during (or even after) the planning or drafting phases, using them to refine and test a tentative thesis. Each approach has advantages and disadvantages.

19.2.1 Using Research to Generate Topic and Thesis

You may consult secondary sources very early in the writing process, using them to help generate your essay topic and thesis (or several potential ones from which you will need to choose). This approach has three advantages. First, you approach the research with a thoroughly open mind and formulate your own opinion about the text(s) only after having considered the range of opinions and information that the sources offer. Second, as you investigate others' opinions, you may find yourself disagreeing, thereby discovering that your mind isn't nearly as open as you'd thought—that you do, indeed, have an opinion of which you weren't fully aware. (Since you've discovered this by disagreeing with a published opinion, you're well on your way to having a motive as well as a thesis.) Third, because you begin by informing yourself about what others have already said, you may be in less danger of simply repeating or reporting.

The potential disadvantage is that you may become overwhelmed by the sheer number of sources or by the amount and diversity of information and opinion they offer. You may agree with everyone, being unable to discriminate among others' opinions or to formulate your own. Or you may find that the conversation seems so exhaustive that you despair of finding anything new to add. If you take this approach, you should maximize the advantages and minimize the disadvantages by keeping in mind a set of clearly defined motive-related questions.

If your sources are works of literary criticism, your goal is to answer two general questions: *What's the conversation about? How can I contribute to it?* To answer those questions, it helps to recall the various motives described in section 19.1.1. Turn them into questions that you can pose about each source:

☐ Do the critics tend to disagree about a particular issue? Might I take one side or another in this debate? Might I offer an alternative?

☐ Do any critics make a claim that I think deserves to be challenged or clarified?

☐ Do the critics ignore a particular element or aspect of the text that I think needs to be investigated? Do any of the critics make a claim that they don't really develop? Or do they make a claim about one text that I might apply to another?

If your sources are historical or biographical, you will instead need to ask questions such as:

☐ Is there information here that might help readers understand some aspect of the literary work in a new way?

☐ Does any of this information challenge or complicate my previous interpretation of the text, or an interpretation that I think other readers might adopt if they weren't aware of these facts?

19.2.2 Using Research to Refine and Test a Thesis

Because of the potential problems of consulting secondary sources in the exploratory phase of the writing process (19.2.1), your instructor may urge you to delay research until later—after you've formulated a tentative thesis, gathered evidence, or written a complete rough draft. This approach may be especially appealing when you begin an assignment with a firm sense of what you want to write. The chief advantage of this approach is that you can look at secondary sources more selectively and critically, seeking information and opinions that will deepen, confirm, or challenge your argument. And since you've already formulated your opinion, you may be in less danger of becoming overwhelmed by others'.

There are, however, several things to watch out for if you take this approach. First, you must be especially careful not to ignore, distort, or misrepresent any source's argument in the interest of maintaining your own. Second, you must strive to keep your mind open, remembering that the goal of your research is to *test* and *refine* your opinion, not just to *confirm* it. A compelling argument or new piece of information may well require you to modify or broaden your original argument. Third, you still need to pose the general questions outlined above (19.2.1).

19.3 THE RESEARCH PROCESS

Regardless of when you begin your research, the process will involve four tasks:

- creating and maintaining a working bibliography;
- identifying and locating potentially useful secondary sources;
- evaluating the credibility of sources;
- taking notes.

19.3.1 Creating a Working Bibliography

A working bibliography lists all the sources that you *might* use in your research essay. It is a "working" document in two ways. For one thing, it will change throughout the research process—expanding each time you add a potentially useful source and contracting when you omit sources that turn out to be less relevant than you anticipated. Also, once you have written your essay, your working bibliography will evolve one last time, becoming your list of works cited. For another thing, you can use your bibliography to organize and keep track of your research "work." To this end, some researchers divide the bibliography into three parts: (1) sources that they need to locate, (2) sources that they have located and think they will use, and (3) sources that they have located but think they probably won't use. (Keeping track of "rejects" ensures, first, that you won't have to start from scratch if you later change your mind; second, that you won't forget that you've already located and rejected a source if you come across another reference to it.)

Because you will need to update your bibliography regularly and because it will ultimately become the kernel of your list of works cited, you should consider using a computer. In that case, you'll need to print a copy or take your laptop along each time you head to the library. However, some researchers find it helpful to also or instead use notecards, creating a separate card for each source. You can then physically separate cards dedicated to sources to be located, sources already located, and "rejected" sources. Just in case your cards get mixed up, however, you should also always note the status of the source on the card (by writing at the top "find," "located," or "rejected").

Regardless of the format you use, your record for each source should include all the information you will need in order both to locate the source and to cite it in your essay. Helpful location information might include the library in which it's found (if you're using multiple libraries), the section of the library in which it's held (e.g., "Reference," "Stacks"), and its call number. As for citation or publication information, it's tempting to ignore this until the very end of the writing process, and some writers do. But if you give in to that temptation, you will, at best, create much more work for yourself down the road. At worst, you'll find yourself unable to use a great source in your essay because you can't relocate the necessary information about it. To avoid these fates, note down all facts you will need for a works cited entry (see 20.2.2). Finally, consider noting where you first discovered each source, just in case you later need to double-check citation information or to remind yourself why you considered a source potentially useful or authoritative. (Though you can use abbreviations, make sure they're ones you'll recognize later.)

Here are two sample entries from the working bibliography of a student researching Adrienne Rich's poetry. Each entry includes all the required citation information, as well as notes on where the student discovered the source and where it is located.

Sample Working Bibliography Entries

Boyers, Robert. "On Adrienne Rich: Intelligence and Will." Salmagundi 22–23 (Spring–Summer 1973): 132–48. Source: *DLB* 5. Loc.: UNLV LASR AS30.S33

Martin, Wendy. American Triptych: Anne Bradstreet, Emily Dickinson, Adrienne Rich. U of North Carolina P, 1984. Source: *LRC/CLC*. UNLV Stacks PS310.F45 M3 1984

Once you locate a source, double-check the accuracy and thoroughness of your citation information and update your working bibliography. (Notice, for example, that this student will need to check *American Triptych* to find out the city where it was published and then add this information to her bibliography.)

19.3.2 Identifying and Locating Sources

Regardless of your author, text, or topic, you will almost certainly find a wealth of sources to consult. Your first impulse may be to head straight for the library catalog. But the conversation about literature occurs in periodicals as well as books, and not all contributions to that conversation are equally credible or relevant. For all these reasons, consider starting with one of the reference works or bibliographies described in this section. Then you can head to the catalog armed with a clear sense of what you're looking for.

Once you find one good secondary source, you can use its bibliography to refine your own. Checking the footnotes and bibliographies of several (especially recent) sources will give you a good sense of what other sources are available and which ones experts consider the most significant.

REFERENCE WORKS

Your library will contain many reference works that can be helpful starting points, and some may be accessible via the library's Web page. Here are six especially useful ones.

Literature Resource Center (LRC)

One online source to which your library may subscribe is Gale's *Literature Resource Center*. Designed with undergraduate researchers in mind, it's an excellent place to start. Here you can access and search:

- all the material in two of the reference works described below (*Dictionary of Literary Biography* and *Contemporary Authors*) and in both Merriam-Webster's *Encyclopedia of Literature* and Gale's For Students series (*Literature of Developing Nations for Students*, etc.);
- much (though not all) of the material contained in Gale's Literary Criticism series (another of the reference works described below);
- selected full-text critical essays (or articles) from more than 250 literary journals.

Depending upon your library's subscription arrangement, *LRC* may also give you access to the *MLA Bibliography* (from 1963) and/or to the Twayne's Authors series (both described below).

You can search the database in numerous ways, but you should probably start with an author search. Results will appear as a list of sources divided into four files: Biographies; Literary Criticism, Articles, and Work Overviews; Bibliographies (of works by and about the author); Additional Resources (such as author-focused Web sites). You can access each file or list by simply clicking on the appropriate tab. (There will be a good deal of overlap among the files.) You can then click any item on the list in order to open and read it. Once an item is open, you can also print or e-mail it by clicking on the appropriate icons and following the directions.

If your library doesn't subscribe to *LRC*, consider starting with the printed reference works listed below. Because each is a multivolume work, you will need to consult its cumulative index to find out which volumes contain entries on your author. None of these series can keep up to the minute with the literary critical conversation about a particular author or work, and all offer only selective bibliographies. Such selectivity is both the greatest strength and the greatest limitation of these reference works.

Dictionary of Literary Biography (DLB)

One of the most important and authoritative reference works for students of literature, the *Dictionary of Literary Biography* covers primarily British and American authors, both living and dead. Each volume focuses on writers working in a particular genre and period. Written by a scholar in the field, each entry includes a photo or sketch of the author, a list of his or her publications, a bibliography of selected secondary sources, and an overview of the author's life and work. The overviews are often very thorough, incorporating brief quotations from letters, interviews, reviews, and so on. You will find multiple entries on any major author, each focusing on a particular portion of his or her canon. The volume titles will give you a good sense of which entry will be most relevant to you. Entries on W. B. Yeats, for example, appear in volume 10, *Modern British Dramatists, 1900–1945;* volume 19, *British Poets, 1880–1914;* volume 98, *Modern British Essayists,* First Series; and volume 156, *British Short-Fiction Writers, 1880–1914: The Romantic Tradition.*

Contemporary Authors: A Biobibliographical Guide to Current Authors and Their Works (CA)

Gale's *Contemporary Authors* focuses on twentieth- and twenty-first-century writers from around the world and in a range of fields (including the social and natural sciences). In terms of content, its entries closely resemble those in the *DLB* (see above). But *CA* entries tend to be much shorter.

Literary Criticism (LC)

Also published by Gale, the Literary Criticism series is, in effect, a series of series, each of which covers a particular historical period. (See below for individual series titles, as well as information about the periods covered by each one.) Each entry includes a very brief overview of the author's life and work. (There is often overlap between these overviews and those in *CA.*) But there are two key differences between the *LC* series and both the *DLB* and *CA.* First, the *LC* series includes entries devoted entirely to some individual works, as well as entries on an author's entire canon. Second, the bulk of each entry is devoted to excerpts (often lengthy) from some of the most important reviews and literary criticism on an author and/or work, and coverage extends from the author's day up to the time when the *LC* entry was written. Each entry concludes with a bibliography of additional secondary sources. The *LC* series will thus give a lot of guidance in identifying authoritative sources, as well as access to excerpts from sources that your library doesn't own.

Here are the titles of the five series, along with information about the period each one covers. To identify the appropriate series, you will need to know the year in which your author died.

- Contemporary Literary Criticism (living authors and those who died from 1960 on)
- Twentieth-Century Literary Criticism (authors who died 1900–1959)
- Nineteenth-Century Literature Criticism (authors who died 1800–1899)
- Literature Criticism from 1400 to 1800 (authors [except Shakespeare] who died 1400–1799)
- Shakespearean Criticism

The Critical Heritage

For some major authors, you can find information and excerpts like those offered by *LC* within the individual volumes of the Critical Heritage series. Unlike the reference works described above, this series is a collection of discrete publications such as *The Brontës: The Critical Heritage*. Each will be held not in the reference department, but in the section of the stacks devoted to scholarship on a specific author. You will thus need to search your library's catalog to find it. These volumes are not regularly updated, so each will give a good sense of your author's reception only up to the time it was published.

Twayne's Authors

The Twayne's Authors series incorporates three distinct series: Twayne's United States Authors, Twayne's English Authors, and Twayne's World Authors. Each volume in each series is a distinct book focusing on one author and typically offering both biographical information and interpretation of major works. All aim to be generally accessible and introductory. (As the publishers themselves put it, "The intent of each volume in these series is to present a critical-analytical study of the works of the writer; to include biographical and historical material that may be necessary for understanding, appreciation, and critical appraisal of the writer; and to present all material in clear, concise English.") Yet because each volume is the work of an individual specialist, it represents that scholar's particular point of view (or opinion), and volumes differ a good deal in terms of organization, approach, and level of difficulty.

Each volume will be held not in the reference department, but in the section of the stacks devoted to scholarship on a specific author. To find it, you will need to search the catalog.

MLA INTERNATIONAL BIBLIOGRAPHY

For much more thorough, up-to-date lists of secondary sources—especially periodical articles—you should consult scholarly bibliographies. In terms of literary criticism, the most comprehensive and useful general bibliography is *The MLA International Bibliography of Books and Articles on the Modern Languages and Literatures*. Since 1969, the *MLA Bibliography* has aimed to provide a comprehensive list of all scholarship published anywhere in the world on literature and modern languages, including books, dissertations, book chapters, and articles in over two thousand periodicals. Though it doesn't quite live up to that aim, it comes closer than any other reference work. (The *Bibliography* in fact began in 1922 but initially included only American scholarship; international coverage began in 1956, but the range of publications remained limited until 1969.) Updated annually, the bibliography is available in print, CD-ROM, and online versions, so what the bibliography encompasses, how many years it covers, and how you use it will depend on the version you consult.

In the print version, each volume lists articles and books published in a specific year, so you should start with the most recent volume and then work your way backward through earlier volumes. Each volume is arranged by nationality or language, then by period, then by author and title.

The CD-ROM and online versions allow you to do topic or keyword searches to find all relevant publications, regardless of the year of publication. Ask a librarian for help with accessing and searching the database.

ONLINE AND CARD CATALOGS

Your library's catalog will guide you to books about the author's work. However, the title of a potentially useful book may be too general to indicate whether it covers the text and topic in which you're interested. If your library's catalog is online, use keyword searches to limit the number and range of books that the computer finds.

The books that you find through a catalog search will lead you to a section of the library where other books on your subject are held (because each will have a similar Library of Congress call number). Even if you locate the books you were looking for right away, take a moment to browse. Books shelved nearby probably cover similar topics, and they may prove even more useful than the ones you originally sought. You can also do this kind of browsing online because most online catalogs offer the option of moving from the record of one book to the records of those that appear just before and after it in the catalog.

THE INTERNET

With its innumerable links and pathways, the Internet seems the perfect resource for research of any kind. And in fact some excellent online resources are available to students of literature. *Bartleby.com* is a good, general information site. Here you can access and search several reference works, including the *Columbia Encyclopedia,* the *American Heritage Dictionary of the English Language,* and the eighteen-volume *Cambridge History of English and American Literature,* as well as full-text versions of numerous poems and works of fiction and nonfiction.

There are also many scholarly sites dedicated to specific authors, works, and literary periods. Most sites provide links to others. One site that is especially useful as a gateway to thousands of more specific sites is *The Voice of the Shuttle* <http://vos.ucsb.edu/>.

If you don't find an appropriate link on *The Voice of the Shuttle,* you will probably want to conduct a search using one of the commonly available search engines. Searches using keywords such as "Yeats" or "poetry" will lead you to thousands of possible matches, however, so you should limit your search by creating search strings longer than one word. Read onscreen directions carefully to make sure that the search engine treats the search string as a unit and doesn't find every mention of each individual word.

Despite the obvious benefits of the Internet, you should be cautious in your use of online sources for two reasons. First, although many sites provide solid information and informed opinion, many more offer misinformation or unsubstantiated opinion. Unlike journal articles and books, which are rigorously reviewed by experts before they are accepted for publication, many Internet sources are posted without any sort of review process, and authorship is often difficult to pin down. As a result, you need to be especially careful to identify and evaluate the ultimate source of the information and opinions you find in cyberspace. (For more on evaluating sources, see 19.3.3.)

Second, because the Internet enables you to jump easily from one site to another and to copy whole pages of text merely by cutting and pasting, you may lose your place and be unable to provide readers with precise citations. More serious, you may lose track of where your own words end and those of your source begin, thereby putting yourself at risk of plagiarizing (see 19.4.1). In addition, the Internet is itself constantly mutating; what's there today may not be there tomorrow. All this makes it difficult to achieve the goal of all citation: to enable readers to retrace your steps and check your sources. When you find sites that seem potentially useful, bookmark them if you can. If not, make sure that you accurately write down (or, better, copy directly into a document) the URL of each, as well as the other information you will need for your list of works cited: the author's name, if available; the site or page title; the date the site was last revised or originally published; and the date you accessed it. If the material on the site has been taken from a printed source, note all of the particulars about this source as well.

As a general rule, Internet sources should supplement print sources, not substitute for them.

19.3.3 Evaluating Sources

Not all sources are equally reliable or credible. The credibility and persuasiveness of your essay will depend, in part, on the credibility of the sources you draw on. This is a good reason to start with reference works that will guide you to credible sources.

Nonetheless, it is very important to learn how to gauge for yourself the credibility of sources. As you do so, keep in mind that finding a source to be credible isn't the same as agreeing with everything it says. At this stage, concentrate on whether the opinions expressed in a source are worthy of serious consideration, not on whether you agree with them. Here are some especially important questions to consider:

1. *How credible is the publisher (in the case of books), the periodical (in the case of essays, articles, and reviews), or the sponsoring organization (in the case of Internet sources)?*

   Generally speaking, academics give most credence to books published by academic and university presses and to articles published in scholarly or professional journals because all such publications undergo a rigorous peer-review process. As a result, you can trust that these publications have been judged credible by more than one recognized expert. For periodicals aimed at a more general audience, you should prefer prominent, highly respected publications such as the *Los Angeles Times* or the *New Yorker* to, say, the *National Enquirer* or *People* magazine.

   Internet sources are not subjected to rigorous review processes, but many sites are created and sponsored by organizations. Be sure to identify the sponsoring organization and carefully consider its nature, status, and purpose. The last part of the domain name will indicate the kind of organization it is: the suffix *.com* indicates that the ultimate source is a *company* or commercial, for-profit enterprise; *.org*, a nonprofit or charitable *organization*; *.gov*, a *government* agency; and *.edu*, an *educational* institution. Though you will often find more reliable information via *.gov* or *.edu* sites, this won't always be the case. *Bartleby.com* is, for example, only one of many extremely useful commercial sites, whereas many *.edu* sites feature the work of students who may have much less expertise than you do.

2. *How credible is the author? Is he or she a recognized expert in the relevant field or on the relevant subject?*

Again, publication by a reputable press or in a reputable periodical generally indicates that its author is considered an expert. But you can also investigate further by checking the thumbnail biographies that usually appear within the book or journal (typically near the beginning or end). Has this person been trained or held positions at respected institutions? What else has he or she published?

3. *How credible is the actual argument?*

Assess the source's argument by applying all that you've learned about what makes an argument effective. Does it draw on ample, appropriate, convincing evidence? Does it consider all the relevant evidence? Are its inferences reasonable? Are its claims sound? Does the whole seem fair, balanced, and thorough? Has the author considered possible counterarguments or alternative points of view?

Finally, researchers in many fields would encourage you to consider the source's publication date and the currency of the information it contains. In the sciences, for example, preference is almost always given to the most recently published work on a given topic because new scholarly works tend to render older ones obsolete. In the humanities, too, new scholarly works build on old ones. You should consult recently published sources in order to get a sense of what today's scholars consider the most significant, debatable questions and what answers they offer. Though originality is as important in the humanities as in other scholarly fields, new work in the humanities doesn't necessarily render older work utterly obsolete. For example, a 1922 article on Wordsworth's Immortality Ode may still be as valid and influential as one published in 2002. As a result, you should consider the date of publication in evaluating a source, but don't let age alone determine its credibility or value.

19.3.4 Taking Notes

Once you've acquired the books and articles you determine to be most credible and potentially useful, it's a good idea to skim each one. (In the case of a book, concentrate on the introduction and on the chapter that seems most relevant.) Focus at this point on assessing the relevance of each source to your topic. Or, if you're working your way toward a topic, look for things that spark your interest. Either way, try to get a rough sense of the overall conversation—of the issues and topics that come up again and again across the various sources.

After identifying the sources most pertinent to your argument, begin reading more carefully and taking notes. Again, some researchers find it easier to organize (and reorganize) notes by using notecards, creating one card for each key point. (If you use this method, make sure that each card clearly indicates the source author and short title because cards have a tendency to get jumbled.) Today, however, most researchers take notes on the computer, creating a separate document or file for each source.

Regardless of their form, your notes should be as thorough and accurate as possible. Be thorough because memory is a treacherous thing; it's best not to rely too heavily on it. Be accurate to avoid a range of serious problems, including plagiarism (see 19.4.1).

Your notes for each source should include four things: summary, paraphrase, and quotation, as well as your own comments and thoughts. It's crucial to visually discriminate among these by, for instance, always recording your own comments and thoughts in a separate computer document or file or on a separate set of clearly labeled or differently colored notecards.

Whenever you write down, type out, or paste in more than two consecutive words from a source, you should:

- place these words in quotation marks so that you will later recognize them as quotations;
- make sure to quote with absolute accuracy every word and punctuation mark;
- record the page where the quotation is found (in the case of print sources).

Keep such quotations to a minimum, recording only the most vivid or telling.

In lieu of extensive quotations, try to summarize and paraphrase as much as possible. You can't decide how to use the source or whether you agree with its argument unless you've first understood it, and you can best understand and test your understanding through summary and paraphrase. Start with a two- or three-sentence summary of the author's overall argument. Then summarize each of the relevant major subsections of the argument. Paraphrase especially important points, making sure to note the page on which each appears.

You may want to try putting your notes in the form of an outline. Again, start with a brief general summary. Then paraphrase each of the major relevant sub-claims, incorporating summaries and quotations where appropriate.

Especially if you're dealing with literary criticism, it can be useful to complete the note-taking process by writing a summary that covers all of your sources. Your goal is to show how all the arguments fit together to form one coherent conversation. Doing so will require that you both define the main questions at issue in the conversation and indicate what stance each source takes on each question— where and how their opinions coincide and differ. This kind of summary can be especially helpful when you haven't yet identified a specific essay topic or crafted a thesis because it may help you to see gaps in the conversation, places where you can enter and contribute.

19.4 INTEGRATING SOURCE MATERIAL INTO THE ESSAY

In research essays, you can refer to sources in a number of ways. You can

briefly allude to them:

Many critics, including Maurice Bowra and Bernard Knox, see Creon as morally inferior to Antigone.

summarize or paraphrase their contents:

According to Maurice Bowra, Creon's arrogance is his downfall. However prideful Antigone may occasionally seem, Bowra insists that Creon is genuinely, deeply, and consistently so (2108).

quote them directly:

For Bowra, Creon is the prototypical "proud man" (2107); where Antigone's arrogance is only "apparent," Creon's is all too "real" (2108).

With secondary sources, be very careful about how often you quote and when and how you do so. Keep the number and length of quotations to a minimum. After all, this is *your* essay, and you should use your own words whenever possible, even to describe someone else's ideas. Save quotations for when you really need them: when the source's author has expressed an idea with such precision, clarity, or vividness that you simply can't say it any better; or when a key passage from your source is so rich or difficult that you need to analyze its ideas and language closely. As with primary texts, lengthy quotation will lead the reader to expect sustained analysis. And only rarely will you want to devote a large amount of your limited time and space to thoroughly analyzing the language of a source (as opposed to a primary text). (For more on responsible and effective quotation, see 20.1.)

One advantage of direct quotation is that it's an easy way to indicate that ideas derive from a source rather than from you. But whether you are quoting, summarizing, or paraphrasing a source, use other techniques as well to ensure that there's no doubt about where your ideas and words leave off and those of a source begin (see 19.4.1). A parenthetical citation within a sentence indicates that something in it comes from a specific source, but unless you indicate otherwise, it will also imply that the entire sentence is a paraphrase of the source. For clarity's sake, then, you should also mention the source or its author in your text, using signal phrases (*According to X*; *As X argues*; *X notes that*, etc.) to announce that you are about to introduce someone else's ideas. If your summary of a source goes on for more than a sentence or two, keep on using signal phrases to remind readers that you're still summarizing someone else's ideas rather than stating your own, as in this example from an essay about William Faulkner's story "A Rose for Emily".

> The ways of interpreting Emily's decision to murder Homer are numerous. . . . For simple clarification, they can be summarized along two lines. One group finds the murder growing out of Emily's demented attempt to forestall the inevitable passage of time—toward her abandonment by Homer, toward her own death, and toward the steady encroachment of the North and the New South on something loosely defined as the "tradition" of the Old South. Another view sees the murder in more psychological terms. It grows out of Emily's complex relationship to her father, who, by elevating her above all of the eligible men of Jefferson, insured that to yield what one commentator called the "normal emotions" associated with desire, his daughter had to "retreat into a marginal world, into fantasy" (O'Connor 184).
>
> These lines of interpretation complement more than critique each other. . . . Together, they de-emphasize the element of detection, viewing the murder and its solution not as the central action but as manifestations of the principal element, the decline of the Grierson lineage and all it represents. Recognizing the way in which the story makes use of the detective genre, however, adds another interpretive layer to the story by making the narrator . . . a central player in the pattern of action.
> —Lawrence R. Rodgers, " 'We All Said . . .' "

> NOTE: In the first paragraph, Rodgers summarizes other critics' arguments in his own words, briefly but clearly. To ensure that we know he's about to summarize, he actually announces this intention ("*For simple clarification, they can be summarized* . . . "). As he begins summarizing each view, he reminds us that it is a "view," that he's still not describing his own thoughts. Finally, he uses this unusually long summary to make a very clear and important point: *everyone except me has ignored this element!*

19.4.1 Using Sources Responsibly

Both the clarity and the credibility of any research essay depend upon the responsible use of sources. And using sources responsibly entails accurately representing them and clearly discriminating between your own words and ideas and those that come from sources. Since ideas, words, information, and concepts not directly and clearly attributed to a source will be taken as your own, any lack of clarity on this score amounts to *plagiarism.* Representing anyone else's ideas or data as your own, even if you state them in your own words, is plagiarism—whether you do so intentionally or unintentionally; whether ideas are taken from a published book or article, another student's paper, the Internet, or any other source. Plagiarism is the most serious of offenses within academe because it amounts to stealing ideas, the resource most precious to this community and its members. As a result, the punishments for plagiarism are severe—including failure, suspension, and expulsion.

To avoid both the offense and its consequences, you must always:

- put quotation marks around any quotation from a source (a quotation being any two or more consecutive words or any one especially distinctive word, label, or concept);
- credit a source whenever you take from it any of the following:
  —a quotation (as described above);
  —a nonfactual or debatable claim (an idea, opinion, interpretation, evaluation, or conclusion) stated in your own words;
  —a fact or piece of data that isn't common knowledge; or
  —a distinctive way of organizing factual information.

To clarify, a fact counts as common knowledge—and therefore doesn't need to be credited to a source—whenever you can find it in multiple, readily available sources, none of which seriously question its validity. For example, it is common knowledge that Sherman Alexie is Native American, that he was born in 1966, and that he published a collection of short stories entitled *Ten Little Indians.* No source can "own" or get credit for these facts. However, a source can still "own" a particular way of arranging or presenting such facts. If, for example, you begin your essay by stating—in your own words—a series of facts about Alexie's life in exactly the same order they appear in, say, the *Dictionary of Literary Biography,* then you would need to acknowledge that by citing the *Dictionary.* When in doubt, cite. (For guidance about *how* to do so, see 20.2.)

20 QUOTATION, CITATION, AND DOCUMENTATION

The bulk of any essay you write should consist of your own ideas expressed in your own words. Yet you can develop your ideas and persuade readers to accept them only if you present and analyze evidence. In essays about literature, quotations are an especially privileged kind of evidence. If your essay also makes use of secondary sources, you will need to quote (selectively) from some of these as well. In either case, your clarity and credibility will depend on how responsibly, effectively, and gracefully you move between others' words and your own. Clarity and credibility will also depend on letting your readers know—through precise citation and documentation—exactly where they can find each quotation and each fact or idea that you paraphrase. This chapter addresses the issue of *how* to quote, cite, and document texts and sources. (For a discussion of *when* to do so, see 17.4 and 18.4.)

20.1 EFFECTIVE QUOTATION

When it comes to quoting, there are certain rules that you must follow and certain strategies that, though not required, will help to make your argument more clear and effective.

20.1.1 Rules You Must Follow

1. Generally speaking, you should reproduce a quotation exactly as it appears in the original: include every word and preserve original spelling, capitalization, italics, and so on. However, there are a few exceptions:

   • When absolutely necessary, you may make minor changes to the quotation as long as (a) they do not distort the sense of the quotation, and (b) you clearly acknowledge them. For instance:

   —Additions and substitutions (e.g., of verb endings or pronouns) may be necessary in order to reconcile the quotation's grammar and syntax with your own or to ensure that the quotation makes sense out of its original context. Enclose these additions and changes in brackets.

   —Omit material from quotations to ensure you stay focused only on what's truly essential. Indicate omissions with ellipsis points unless the quotation is obviously a sentence fragment.

Notice how these rules are applied in the following two examples:

Sethe, like Jacobs, experiences the wish to give up the fight for survival and die, but while Jacobs says she was "willing to bear on" "for the children's sakes" (127), the reason that Sethe gives for enduring is the physical presence of the baby in her womb: "[I]t didn't seem such a bad idea [to die], . . . but the thought of herself stretched out dead while the little antelope lived on . . . in her lifeless body grieved her so" that she persevered (31).

When Denver tries to leave the haunted house to get food for her mother and Beloved, she finds herself imprisoned within her mother's time—a time that, cling-ing to places, is always happening again: "Out there . . . were places in which things so bad had happened that when you went near them it would happen again. . . ."
—Jean Wyatt, "Giving Body to the Word: The Maternal Symbolic in
Toni Morrison's *Beloved*," *PMLA* 108 (May 1993): 474–88

NOTE: In the first example, Wyatt uses brackets to indicate two changes, the capi-talization of "it" and the addition of the words "to die." Ellipses indicate that she's omitted a word or words within the sentence that follows the colon. However, she doesn't need to begin or end the phrases *"willing to bear on"* and *"for the children's sake"* with ellipses because both are obviously sentence fragments. In the second example, notice that Wyatt does need to end the quotation with ellipsis points. Even though it reads like a complete sentence, this isn't the case; the sentence continues in the original text.

—Occasionally, you may want to draw your readers' attention to a par-ticular word or phrase within the quotation by using italics. Indicate this change by putting the words "emphasis added" (not underlined or in italics) into your parenthetical citation.

Like his constant references to "Tragedy," the wording of the father's question dem-onstrates that he is almost as hesitant as his daughter to confront death head-on: "When will you look *it* in the face?" he asks her (34; emphasis added).

• Although you should also accurately reproduce original punctuation, there is one exception to this rule: when incorporating a quotation into a sentence, you may *end* it with whatever punctuation mark your sen-tence requires. You do not need to indicate this particular change with brackets.

Whether portrayed as "queen," "saint," or "angel," the same "nameless girl" "looks out from all his canvases" (Rossetti, lines 5–7, 1).

NOTE: In the poem quoted ("In an Artist's Studio"), the words *queen* and *angel* are not followed by commas. Yet the syntax of this sentence requires that commas be added. Similarly, the word *canvases* is followed by a comma in the poem, but the sentence requires that this comma be changed to a period.

2. When incorporating short quotations into a sentence, put them in quo-tation marks and make sure that they fit into the sentence grammatically and syntactically. If necessary, you may make changes to the quotation (e.g., altering verb endings or pronouns) in order to reconcile its grammar and syntax with your own. But you should—again—always indicate changes with brackets.

It isn't until Mr. Kapasi sees the "topless women" carved on the temple that it "occur[s] to him . . . that he had never seen his own wife fully naked" (333).

3. **When quoting fewer than three lines of poetry, indicate any line break with a slash mark, any stanza break with a double slash mark.**

Before Milton's speaker can question his "Maker" for allowing him to go blind, "Patience" intervenes "to prevent / That murmur" (lines 8–9), urging him to see that "God doth not need / Either man's work or his own gifts . . ." (lines 9–10).

"The cane appears // in our dreams," the speaker explains (Dove, lines 15–16).

4. **Long quotations—four or more lines of prose, three of poetry—should be indented and presented without quotation marks to create a *block quotation*. In the case of poetry, reproduce original line and stanza breaks.**

Whereas the second stanza individualizes the dead martyrs, the third considers the characteristics they shared with each other and with all those who dedicate them-selves utterly to any one cause:

> Hearts with one purpose alone
> Through summer and winter seem
> Enchanted to a stone
> To trouble the living stream. (lines 41–44)

Whereas all other "living" people and things are caught up in the "stream" of change represented by the shift of seasons, those who fill their "Hearts with one purpose alone" become as hard, unchanging, and immoveable as stones.

5. **Unless they are indented, quotations belong in double quotation marks; quotations within quotations get single quotation marks. However, if everything in your quotation appears in quotation marks in the original, you do not need to reproduce the single quotation marks.**

The words of Rufus Johnson come ringing back to the reader: " 'Listen here,' he hissed, 'I don't care if he's good or not. He ain't *right!* ' " (468).

As Rufus Johnson says of Sheppard, "I don't care if he's good or not. He ain't *right!*" (468).

6. **Follow a word-group introducing a quotation with whatever punctuation is appropriate to your sentence. For instance:**

—**If you introduce a quotation with a full independent clause (other than something like *She says*), separate the two with a colon.**

Ironically, Mr. Lindner's description of the neighborhood's white residents makes them sound exactly like the Youngers, the very family he's trying to exclude: "They're not rich and fancy people; just hard-working, honest people who don't really have much but . . . a dream of the kind of community they want to raise their children in" (1986).

—**If you introduce or interrupt a quotation with an expression such as *she says* or *he writes*, use a comma (or commas) or add a *that*. Likewise, use a comma if you end a quotation with an expression such as *he says*, unless the quotation ends with a question mark or exclamation point.**

Alvarez claims, "The whole poem works on one single, returning note and rhyme . . ." (1214).

Alvarez suggests that "The whole poem works on one single, returning note and rhyme . . ." (1214).

"The whole poem," Alvarez argues, "works on one single, returning note and rhyme . . ." (1214).

"Here comes one," says Puck. "Where art thou, proud Demetrius?" asks Lysander (Shakespeare 3.2.400–401).

—If quoted words are blended into your sentence, use the same punctuation (or lack thereof) that you would if the words *were not* quoted.

Miriam Allott suggests that the odes, like "all Keats's major poetry," trace the same one "movement of thought and feeling," which "at first carries the poet . . . into an ideal world of beauty and permanence, and finally returns him to what is actual and inescapable."

Keats's poetry just as powerfully evokes the beauty of ordinary, natural things—of "the sun, the moon, / Trees," and "simple sheep"; of "daffodils" and "musk-rose blooms" (*Endymion*, lines 13–14, 15, 19); of nightingales, grasshoppers, and crickets; of "the stubble-plains" and "barred clouds" of a "soft-dying" autumn day ("To Autumn," lines 25–26).

When the narrator's eighty-six-year-old father asks her to tell him a "simple story" with "recognizable people" and a plot that explains "what happened to them next" (31), he gets "an unadorned and miserable tale" whose protagonist ends up "Hopeless and alone" (31).

7. Commas and periods belong inside quotation marks, semicolons outside. Question marks and exclamation points go inside quotation marks if they are part of the quotation, outside if they aren't. (Since parenthetical citations will often alter your punctuation, they have been omitted in the following examples.

Wordsworth calls nature a "homely Nurse"; she has "something of a Mother's Mind."

"You have a nice sense of humor," the narrator's father notes, but "you can't tell a plain story."

What does Johnson mean when he says, "I don't care if he's good or not. He ain't *right!*" ?

Bobby Lee speaks volumes about the grandmother when he says, "She was a talker, wasn't she?"

20.1.2 Useful Strategies

1. Make the connection between quotations and inferences as seamless as possible. Try to put them next to each other (in one sentence, if possible). Avoid drawing attention to your evidence as evidence. Don't waste time with phrases such as *This statement is proof that . . .*; *This phrase is significant because . . .*; *This idea is illustrated by . . .*; *There is good evidence for this . . .*; and

the like. Show why facts are meaningful or interesting rather than simply saying that they are.

INEFFECTIVE QUOTING	EFFECTIVE QUOTING
Wordsworth calls nature a "homely Nurse" and says she has "something of a Mother's mind" (lines 81, 79). This diction supports the idea that he sees nature as a beneficent, maternal force. He is saying that nature is an educator and a healer.	Wordsworth describes nature as a beneficent, maternal force. A "homely Nurse" with "something of a Mother's Mind," nature both heals and educates (lines 81, 79).
Tennyson advocates decisive action, even as he highlights the forces that often prohibited his contemporaries from taking it. This is suggested by the lines "Made weak by time and fate, but strong in will, / To strive, to seek, to find, and not to yield" (lines 69–70).	Tennyson advocates forceful action, encouraging his contemporaries "To strive, to seek, to find, and not to yield" (line 70). Yet he recognizes that his generation is more tempted to "yield" than earlier ones because they have been "Made weak by time and fate" (line 69).

2. Introduce or follow a quotation from a source (as well as a paraphrase or summary) with a *signal phrase* that includes the source author's name; you might also include the author's title and/or a bit of information about his or her status, if that information helps to establish credibility.

   In his study of the Frankenstein myth, Chris Baldick claims that "[m]ost myths, in literate societies at least, prolong their lives not by being retold at great length, but by being alluded to" (3)—a claim that definitely applies to the Hamlet myth.

   Oyin Ogunba, himself a scholar of Yoruban descent, suggests that many of Soyinka's plays attempt to capture the mood and rhythm of traditional Yoruban festivals (8).

   As historian R. K. Webb observes, "Britain is a country in miniature" (1).

   To avoid boring your readers, vary the content and placement of these phrases while always choosing the most accurate verb. (*Says,* for example, implies that words are spoken, not written.) You may find it useful to consult the following list of verbs that describe what sources do.

   Verbs to Use in Signal Phrases

affirms	considers	explains	insists	shows
argues	contends	explores	investigates	sees
asks	demonstrates	finds	maintains	speculates
asserts	describes	focuses on	notes	states
believes	discusses	identifies	observes	stresses
claims	draws atten-	illustrates	points out	suggests
comments	tion to	implies	remarks	surmises
concludes	emphasizes	indicates	reports	writes

3. Lead your readers into fairly long quotations by giving them:
   - a clear sense of what to look for in the quotation;
   - any information they need to understand the quotation and to appreciate its significance. Quite often, contextual information—for instance, about who's speaking to whom and in what situation—is crucial to a

quotation's meaning; this is especially true when quoting dialogue. Also pay attention to pronouns: if the quotation contains a pronoun without an obvious referent, either indicate the specific referent in advance or add the appropriate noun into the quotation. (Again, place added words in brackets.)

INEFFECTIVE QUOTING	EFFECTIVE QUOTING
A Raisin in the Sun seems to endorse traditional gender roles: "I'm telling you to be the head of this family . . . like you supposed to be" (1980); "the colored woman" should be "building their men up and making 'em feel like they somebody" (1949).	*A Raisin in the Sun* seems to endorse traditional gender roles. When Mama tells Walter "to be the head of this family from now on like you supposed to be" (1980), she affirms that Walter, rather than she or Ruth or Beneatha, is the rightful leader of the family. Implicitly she's also doing what Walter elsewhere says "the colored woman" should do— "building their men up and making 'em feel like they somebody" (1949).
Julian expresses disgust for the class distinctions so precious to his mother: "Rolling his eyes upward, he put his tie back on. 'Restored to my class,' he muttered" (490).	Julian professes disgust for the class distinctions so precious to his mother. At her request, he puts back on his tie, but he can't do so without "[r]olling his eyes" and making fun of the idea that he is thereby "[r]estored to [his] class" (490).

NOTE: Here, the more effective examples offer crucial information about who is speaking (*"When Lena tells Walter"*) or what is happening (*"At her request, he puts back on his tie"*). They also include statements about the implications of the quoted words (*"she affirms that Walter . . . is the rightful leader of the family"*). At the same time, background facts are subordinated to the truly important, evidentiary ones.

4. Follow each block quotation with a sentence or more of analysis. It often helps to incorporate into that analysis certain key words and phrases from the quotation.

The second stanza of the poem refers back to the title poem of *The Colossus,* where the speaker's father, representative of the gigantic male other, so dominated her world that her horizon was bounded by his scattered pieces. In "Daddy," she describes him as

> Marble-heavy, a bag full of God,
> Ghastly statue with one grey toe
> Big as a Frisco seal
>
> And a head in the freakish Atlantic
> Where it pours bean green over blue
> In the waters off beautiful Nanset.

. . . Here the image of her father, grown larger than the earlier Colossus of Rhodes, stretches across and subsumes the whole of the United States, from the Pacific to the Atlantic ocean.   —Pamela J. Annas, *"A Disturbance of Mirrors"*

5. Be aware that even though long (especially block) quotations can be effective, they should be used sparingly. Long quotations can create information overload or confusion for readers, making it hard for them to see what is most significant. When you quote only individual words or short

phrases, weaving them into your sentences, readers stay focused on what's significant, and it's easier to show them why it's significant, to get inferences and facts right next to each other.

6. Vary the length of quotations and the way you present them, using a variety of strategies. Choose the strategy that best suits your purpose at a specific moment in your essay, while fairly and fully representing the text. It can be very tempting to fall into a pattern—always, for example, choosing quotations that are at least a sentence long and introducing each with an independent clause and a colon. But overusing any one technique can easily render your essay monotonous. It might even prompt readers to focus more on the (inelegant) way you present evidence than on its appropriateness and significance.

20.2 CITATION AND DOCUMENTATION

In addition to indicating which facts, ideas, or words derive from someone else, always let your readers know where each can be found. You want to enable readers not only to "check up" on you, but also to follow in your footsteps and build on your work. After all, you hope that your analysis of a text will entice readers to reread certain passages from a different point of view.

At the same time, you don't want information about how to find others' work to interfere with readers' engagement with your work. Who, after all, could really make sense of an essay full of sentences such as these: (1) *"I know not 'seems,' " Hamlet claims in line 76 of Act 1, Scene 2*, and (2) *On the fourth page of her 1993* PMLA *article (which was that journal's 108th volume), Jean Wyatt insists that Morrison's "plot . . . cannot move forward because Sethe's space is crammed with the past."*

To ensure that doesn't happen, it is important to have a system for conveying this information in a concise, unobtrusive way. There are, in fact, many such systems currently in use. Different disciplines, publications, and even instructors prefer or require different systems. In literary studies (and the humanities generally), the preferred system is that developed by the Modern Language Association (MLA).

In this system, parenthetical citations embedded in an essay are keyed to an alphabetized list of works cited that appears at its end. Parenthetical citations allow the writer to briefly indicate where an idea, fact, or quotation appears, while the list of works cited gives readers all the information they need to find that source. Here is a typical sentence with parenthetical citation, as well as the works cited entry to which it refers.

Sample Parenthetical Citation

> In one critic's view, "Ode on a Grecian Urn" explores "what great art means" not to the ordinary person, but only "to those who create it" (Bowra 148).

> NOTE: Here, the parenthetical citation indicates that readers can find this quotation on page 148 of some work by an author named Bowra. To find out more, readers must turn to the list of works cited and scan it for an entry, like the following, that begins with the name "Bowra."

Sample Works Cited Entry

> Bowra, C. M. The Romantic Imagination. Oxford: Oxford UP, 1950.

This example gives a basic sense of how parenthetical citations and the list of works cited work together in the MLA system. Note that each parenthetical citation must "match up" with one (and only one) works cited entry.

The exact content of each parenthetical citation and works cited entry will depend upon a host of factors. The next two sections focus on these factors.

20.2.1 Parenthetical Citation

THE GENERIC PARENTHETICAL CITATION: AUTHOR(S) AND PAGE NUMBER(S)

The generic MLA parenthetical citation includes an author's name and a page number (or numbers). If the source has two or three authors, include all last names, as in (Gilbert and Gubar 57). If it has four or more, use the first author's name followed by *et al.* (Latin for "and others") in roman type, as in the second example below. In all cases, nothing but a space separates author's name(s) from page number(s).

> Most domestic poems of the 1950s foreground the parent-child relationship (Axelrod 1230).

> Given their rigid structure, it is perhaps "[n]ot surprisin[g]" that many sonnets explore the topic of "confinement" (Booth et al. 1022).

Notice the placement of the parenthetical citations in these examples. In each one the citation comes at the end of the sentence, yet it appears *inside* the period (because it is part of the sentence) and *outside* the quotation marks (because it isn't part of the quotation). Such placement of parenthetical citations should be your practice in all but two situations (both described in the next section).

VARIATIONS IN PLACEMENT

In terms of placement, the first exception is the block quotation. In this case, the parenthetical citation should immediately *follow* (not precede) the punctuation mark that ends the quotation.

> As historian Michael Crowder insists, Western-style education was the single "most radical influence on Nigeria introduced by the British" because it
>> came to be seen as a means not only of economic betterment but of social elevation. It opened doors to an entirely new world, the world of the white man. Since missionaries had a virtual monopoly on schools, they were able to use them as a means of further proselytization, and continued to warn their pupils of the evils of their former way of life. (195)

The second exception is the sentence that either incorporates material from multiple sources or texts (as in the first example below) or refers both to something from a source or text and to your own idea (as in the second example below). In either situation, you will need to put the appropriate parenthetical citation in mid-sentence right next to the material to which it refers, even at the risk of interrupting the flow of the sentence.

> Critics describe Caliban as a creature with an essentially "unalterable natur[e]" (Garner 458), "incapable of comprehending the good or of learning from the past" (Peterson 442), "impervious to genuine moral improvement" (Wright 451).

> If Caliban is "incapable of . . . learning from the past" (Peterson 442), then how do we explain the changed attitude he seems to demonstrate at the end of the play?

VARIATIONS IN CONTENT

The generic MLA citation may contain the author's name(s) and the relevant page number(s), but variations are the rule when it comes to content. The six most common variations occur when you do the following:

1. *Name the author in a signal phrase*
    Parenthetical citations should include only information that isn't crucial to the sense and credibility of your argument. Yet in nine cases out of ten, information about *whose* ideas, data, or words you are referring to is crucial in precisely this way. As a result, it is usually a good idea to indicate this in your text. When you do so, the parenthetical citation need only include the relevant page number(s).

    According to Steven Gould Axelrod, most domestic poems of the 1950s foreground the parent-child relationship (1230).

    Jefferson's "new generation" are, in Judith Fetterley's words, just "as much bound by the code of gentlemanly behavior as their fathers were" (619).

2. *Cite a poem or play*
    In the case of most poetry, refer to line (not page) numbers.

    Ulysses encourages his men "To strive, to seek, to find, and not to yield" (line 70).

    In the case of classic plays, indicate act, scene, and line numbers, and separate them with periods.

    "I know not 'seems,' " Hamlet claims (1.2.76).

3. *Cite multiple works by the same author or a work whose author is unknown*
    When citing multiple works by the same author or an anonymous work, you will need to indicate the title of the specific work to which you refer. Either indicate the title in your text, putting only the page number(s) in a parenthetical citation (as in the first example below), or create a parenthetical citation in which the first word or two of the title is followed by the page number(s) (as in the third example below). In the latter case, you should format the title words exactly as you would the full title, using quotation marks for essays, short stories, and short poems, and using italics or underlining for books.

    As Judith Fetterley argues in "A Rose for 'A Rose for Emily,' " Jefferson's younger generation is just "as much bound by the code of gentlemanly behavior as their fathers were" (619).

    Jefferson's "new generation" is, in Judith Fetterley's words, just "as much bound by the code of gentlemanly behavior as their fathers were" ("A Rose" 562).

    Arguably, Jefferson's "new generation" is just "as much bound by the code of gentlemanly behavior as their fathers were" (Fetterley, "A Rose" 619).

4. *Cite a source quoted in another source*
    When quoting the words of one person as they appear in another author's work, mention the person's name in a signal phrase. Then create a par-

enthetical citation in which the abbreviation "qtd. in" is followed by the author's name and the relevant page number(s).

Hegel describes Creon as "a moral power," "not a tyrant" (qtd. in Knox 2108).

5. *Cite multiple authors with the same last name*
   In this case, you should either use the author's full name in a signal phrase (as above) or add the author's first initial to the parenthetical citation (as below).

Beloved depicts a "a specifically female quest powered by the desire to get one's milk to one's baby" (J. Wyatt 475).

6. *Cite multiple sources for the same idea or fact*
   In this case, put both citations within a single set of parentheses and separate them with a semicolon.

Though many scholars attribute Caliban's bestiality to a seemingly innate inability to learn or change (Garner 458; Peterson 442; Wright 451), others highlight how inefficient or problematic Prospero's teaching methods are (Willis 443) and how invested Prospero might be in keeping Caliban ignorant (Taylor 384).

7. *Cite a work without numbered pages*
   Omit page numbers from parenthetical citations if you cite:

   · an electronic work that isn't paginated;
   · a print work whose pages aren't numbered;
   · a print work that is only one page long;
   · a print work, such as an encyclopedia, that is organized alphabetically.

   If at all possible, mention the author's name and/or the work's title in your text (so that you don't need any parenthetical citation). Otherwise, create a parenthetical citation that contains, as appropriate, the author's name and/or the first word(s) of the title.

8. *Italicize words that aren't italicized in the original*
   If you draw your readers' attention to a particular word or phrase within a quotation by using italics or underlining, your parenthetical citation must include the words "emphasis added."

Like his constant references to "Tragedy," the wording of the father's question demonstrates that he is almost as hesitant as his daughter to confront death head-on: "When will you look *it* in the face?" he asks her (34; emphasis added).

20.2.2 The List of Works Cited

The alphabetized list of works cited should appear at the end of your completed essay. It must include all, and only, the texts and sources that you cite in your essay; it also must provide full publication information about each one.

If you're writing a research essay and have created and maintained a working bibliography, that bibliography will become the core of your works cited list. To turn the former into the latter, you will need to:

- delete sources that you did not ultimately cite in your essay;
- add an entry for each primary text you did cite;
- delete notes about where you found sources (call numbers, etc.).

FORMATTING THE LIST OF WORKS CITED

The list of works cited should appear on a separate page (or pages) at the end of your essay. (If you conclude your essay on page 5, for example, you would start the list of works cited on page 6.) Center the heading "Works Cited" (without quotation marks) at the top of the first page, and double-space throughout.

The first line of each entry should begin at the left margin; the second and subsequent lines should be indented 5 spaces or ½ inch.

Alphabetize your list by the last names of the authors or editors. In the case of anonymous works, alphabetize by the first word of the title other than *A*, *An*, or *The*.

If your list includes multiple works by the same author, begin the first entry with the author's name and each subsequent entry with three hyphens followed by a period. Alphabetize these listings by the first word of the title, again ignoring the words *A*, *An*, or *The*.

FORMATTING WORKS CITED ENTRIES

The exact content and style of each entry in your list of works cited will depend upon the type of source it is. Following are examples of some of the most frequently used types of entries in lists of works cited. For all other types, consult the sixth edition of the *MLA Handbook*.

Book by a single author or editor

> Webb, R. K. Modern England: From the Eighteenth Century to the Present. New York: Columbia UP, 1969.
> Wu, Duncan, ed. A Companion to Romanticism. Oxford: Blackwell, 1998.

Book with an author and an editor

> Keats, John. Complete Poems. Ed. Jack Stillinger. Cambridge: Belknap-Harvard UP, 1982.

Book by two or three authors or editors

> Gallagher, Catherine, and Thomas Laqueur, eds. The Making of the Modern Body: Sexuality and Society in the Nineteenth Century. Berkeley: U of California P, 1987.

Book by more than three authors or editors

> Zipes, Jack, et al. The Norton Anthology of Children's Literature. New York: Norton, 2005.

Introduction, preface, or foreword

> O'Prey, Paul. Introduction. Heart of Darkness. By Joseph Conrad. New York: Viking, 1983. 7-24.

Essay, poem, or any other work in an edited collection or anthology

> Shaw, Philip. "Britain at War: The Historical Context." A Companion to Romanticism. Ed. Duncan Wu. Oxford: Blackwell, 1998. 48-60.

Yeats, W. B. "The Lake Isle of Innisfree." <u>The Norton Introduction to Poetry</u>. 9th ed. Ed. Alison Booth, J. Paul Hunter, and Kelly J. Mays. New York: Norton, 2006. 1285.

Multiple short works from one collection or anthology

Booth, Alison, J. Paul Hunter, and Kelly J. Mays, eds. <u>The Norton Introduction to Poetry</u>. 9th ed. New York: Norton, 2006.
Frost, Robert. "The Road Not Taken." Booth, Hunter, and Mays. 1247-48.
Keats, John. "Ode to a Nightingale." Booth, Hunter, and Mays. 1098-99.

Article in a reference work

"Magna Carta." <u>Encyclopaedia Britannica</u>. 14th ed. 630–35.

Article in a scholarly journal

Wyatt, Jean. "Giving Body to the Word: The Maternal Symbolic in Toni Morrison's <u>Beloved</u>." *PMLA* 108 (May 1993): 474-88.

Article in a newspaper or magazine

McNulty, Charles. "All the World's a Stage Door." <u>Village Voice</u> 13 Feb. 2001: 69.

Review or editorial

Leys, Simon. "Balzac's Genius and Other Paradoxes." Rev. of <u>Balzac: A Life</u>, by Graham Robb. <u>New Republic</u> 20 Dec. 1994: 26-27.

NOTE: The first name here is that of the reviewer, the second that of the author whose book is being reviewed.

Internet site

<u>U.S. Department of Education (ED) Home Page</u>. US Dept. of Education. 12 Aug. 2004 <http://www.ed.gov/index.jhtml>.
<u>Yeats Society Sligo Home Page</u>. Yeats Society Sligo. 12 Nov. 2004 <http://www.yeats-sligo.com/>.

Article on a Web site

Padgett, John B. "William Faulkner." <u>The Mississippi Writers Page</u>. 29 Mar. 1999. 8 Feb. 2004 <http://www.olemiss.edu/depts/english/ms-writers/dir/faulkner_william/>.

NOTE: The first date indicates when material was published or last updated. The second date indicates when you accessed the site.

21 **SAMPLE RESEARCH PAPER**

The student essay below was written in response to the following assignment:

> Write an essay of 10–15 pages that analyzes at least two poems by any one author in your text and draws upon three or more secondary sources. At least one of these sources must be a work of literary criticism (a book or article in which a scholar interprets your author's work).

Richard Gibson's response to this assignment is an essay that explores the treatment of religion in four poems by Emily Dickinson; Gibson asks how conventional that treatment was in its original historical and social context. Notice that Gibson uses a variety of sources: literary critical studies of Dickinson's poetry; Dickinson biographies; historical studies of nineteenth-century American religious beliefs and practices; letters written by and to Dickinson; and a dictionary. At the same time, notice that Gibson's thesis is an original, debatable interpretive claim about Dickinson's poetry and that he supports and develops that claim by carefully analyzing four poems.

Richard Gibson
Professor William Barksdale
English 301
4 March 2004

Keeping the Sabbath Separately:
Emily Dickinson's Rebellious Faith

Gibson establishes a motive for his essay by first stating a claim about Dickinson's poetry that a casual reader might be tempted to adopt and then pointing out the problems with that claim in order to set up the more subtle and complex claim that is his thesis.

When cataloguing Christian poets, it might be tempting to place Emily Dickinson between Dante and John Donne. She built many poems around biblical quotations, locations, and characters. She meditated often on the afterlife, prayer, and trust in God. Yet Dickinson was also intensely doubtful of the strand of Christianity that she inherited; in fact, she never became a Christian by the standards of her community in nineteenth-century Amherst, Massachusetts. Rather, like many of her contemporaries in Boston, Dickinson recognized the tension between traditional religious teaching and modern ideas. And these tensions, between hope and doubt, between tradition and modernity, animate her poetry. In "Some keep

---

Gibson 2

the Sabbath going to church—," "The Brain—is wider than the Sky—," "Because I could not stop for Death—," and "The Bible is an antique Volume," the poet uses traditional religious terms and biblical allusions. But she does so in order both to criticize traditional doctrines and practices and to articulate her own unorthodox beliefs.

In some ways, Emily Dickinson seemed destined by birth and upbringing to be a creature of tradition. After all, her ancestry stretched back to the origin of the Massachusetts Bay Colony; her ancestor Nathaniel Dickinson "was among the four hundred or so settlers who accompanied John Winthrop in the migration that began in 1630" (Lundin 8). Winthrop and his followers were Puritans, a group of zealous Christians who believed in the literal truth and authority of the Bible; the innate corruption of humanity; the doctrine of salvation by faith, not works; and the idea that only certain people were "predestined" for heaven (Noll 21). A few decades after his immigration, Nathaniel Dickinson moved to western Massachusetts, where he and his descendants would become farmers and stalwarts in local churches (Lundin 9). Although Emily Dickinson's grandfather, Samuel Fowler Dickinson, and her father, Edward Dickinson, would give up farming to become lawyers, they, too, subscribed to the articles of their inherited religion (9). In short, for more than three hundred years prior to her birth, Emily Dickinson's family faithfully adhered to the Puritan tradition.

From early life to her year at college, Dickinson received an education that was "overwhelmingly religious" and traditional (Jones 295). The daily routine of the Dickinson household included prayer and readings from the Bible (296). She also received religious teaching regularly at the First Congregational Church and its "Sabbath [Sunday] school" (296). In her weekday schooling, Dickinson read textbooks such as The New England Primer and Amherst resident Noah Webster's spelling book that included "catechisms," or methodical teachings in religious doctrine and morality (296).

In the early nineteenth century, though, traditional churchgoers in western Massachusetts began to look warily to the east, especially to Boston, where nontraditional religious thinking had developed among both the "liberal Congregationalists" and the "free-thinking rationalists," or "deists" (Noll 138–42, 143–45). Because these theologies were

Gibson does a great job of establishing key terms— "traditional religious teaching," "modern ideas," and "unorthodox beliefs." Notice how he repeats these terms and variations on them throughout the essay in order to link his various subideas.

Gibson simply paraphrases because his focus is the information in the source, not its words. Nonetheless, Gibson uses parenthetical citations to indicate where in the source one can find this information.

Gibson omits the author's name in this parenthetical citation because he is referring to the source indicated in the preceding parenthetical citation.

Gibson refers readers to all the pages in the source that discuss the debate to which he refers—not just to those pages where the quoted phrases appear.

distinctly European and philosophical, they won few converts outside Boston (143, 145). The greater threat was Unitarianism, which had sprung up in Congregational churches. The Unitarians rejected many of the foundational beliefs of the Puritans and instead "promoted a benevolent God, a balanced universe, and a sublime human potential" (284). Former Unitarian minister and transcendentalist philosopher Ralph Waldo Emerson, an author whom Dickinson admired, gained national attention through his writings and speeches on self-reliance and the individual's "direct access" to the "divine spirit" that is behind all "religious systems" (Doriani 18; Norberg xiii–xv). Binding these Bostonian theologies together is an agreement that reason should be applied to religious beliefs. Each then concluded that some—or, in a few minds, most—of the traditional Christian doctrines (to which Amherst adhered) should be abandoned or revised.

Many Bostonian thinkers were influenced by recent developments in science and philosophy that contested the traditional Christian conception of the universe and of the Bible's literal truth. Earlier generations of scientists and philosophers had postulated that the universe obeys fixed laws, which led to ongoing debates about whether the miracles described in the Bible were plausible, even possible (Noll 108). The new astronomy discredited biblical passages describing irregular movements of the sun and the stars. The foremost contemporary dispute, though, concerned the age of the universe. The traditional Christian interpretation of the Bible stated that the universe had existed for about six thousand years (Lundin 32). Early-nineteenth-century geologists, though, had discovered fossils and rock formations that suggested that the Earth was significantly older. Some Christians dug in their heels, while others, like Amherst College professor Edward Hitchcock, attempted to "reconcile orthodoxy and the new geology"—an effort in which the young Dickinson "took comfort" (32). The intellectual scene of Massachusetts at the time of Dickinson's youth thus offered many competing answers to questions about divinity, the historicity of the Bible, and the cosmos. The reign of the old Puritan beliefs over the minds of New England was beginning to wane.

Dickinson herself began to confess doubts about her ability to join the First Congregational Church while still a teenager. In nineteenth-century Amherst, "to 'become a Christian' and

Gibson uses double quotation marks to enclose words he's taken from a source, single quotation marks to enclose words quoted in that source.

Gibson 4

join the church" required "only" that one "subscribe to the articles of faith and offer the briefest of assurance [sic] of belief in Christ" (Lundin 51). At age fifteen, though, Dickinson felt unable to do even this much, writing to her friend Abiah Root that she "had not yet made [her] peace with God." Unable to "feel that [she] could give up all for Christ, were [she] called to die," she asked her friend to pray for her, "that [she] may yet enter into the kingdom [of God], that there may be room left for [her] in the shining courts above" (8 Sept. 1846).

During her stay at Mount Holyoke Women's Seminary, from September 1847 to May 1848, Dickinson was frequently invited, even pressured, to become a Christian. Mary Lyon, headmistress of the college, "laid stress on the salvation of souls" and asked her "students to classify themselves according to their religious condition at the beginning of the year" (Jones 314). Asked to identify herself as a "No-Hoper," "Hoper," or "Christian," Dickinson chose the first of these options (Lundin 40–41). A few months into the school year, she informed Root that "there is a great deal of [religious] interest here and many are flocking to the ark of safety." Dickinson confessed, though, that she "[had] not yet given up to the claims of Christ," but was "not entirely thoughtless on so important & serious a subject" (17 Jan. 1848). In her final letter to Root from Mount Holyoke, Dickinson describes herself as "filled with self-recrimination about the opportunities [for salvation] [she had] missed," fearful that she might never "cast her burden on Christ" (16 May 1848). She thus left Mount Holyoke just as she came to it—a "No-Hoper."

Many critics, including recent biographer Roger Lundin, see the year at Mount Holyoke as a turning point in Emily Dickinson's life, the time when it became clear that she would never "become a Christian" according to Amherst's standards (47–48). Dickinson would never join the First Congregationalist Church and, by the age of thirty, stopped going to services altogether (99). She would likewise never join the Unitarians. Many of her spiritual ideas would resemble those of the transcendentalist Emerson, yet important distinctions remained (171). Throughout her life, she wrote to Christian friends, including ministers, on spiritual topics, despite their doctrinal differences (Lease 50–51). Dickinson thus eschewed New England's religious congregations and asserted her independence in spiritual matters. Yet she always remained

The term *sic* indicates that a spelling or grammar problem within the quotation is present in the original. Gibson encloses the term in brackets to indicate that it is his addition.

In order to make quoted material fit grammatically and syntactically into his sentences, Gibson changes pronouns and adds explanatory words, enclosing all changed or added words in brackets.

The author's name is omitted from this parenthetical citation because it is included in the sentence.

interested in the traditional perspective, and, as a poet, she relied on the traditional terminology in order to relate her new thinking.

Dickinson's well-known poem "Some keep the Sabbath going to church—," which she wrote around 1860, demonstrates this tendency. The opening line places the poem's events on the "Sabbath," the day of worship in Judeo-Christian traditions (Oxford). Thus, while the speaker does not follow her traditional peers "to Church," she nonetheless observes the traditional day (line 1). The speaker finds a "Bobolink," a native bird, to be the service's "Chorister" (line 3), the official term for the leader of a church choir (Oxford). A few lines later, the speaker calls this bird "Our little Sexton," the title of the manager of the church grounds. Normally, the sexton "[tolls] the Bell, for Church" (line 7), yet this sexton "sings" (line 8). The "Orchard" where she sits resembles an important part of church architecture, "a Dome." In this intimate setting, "God preaches, a noted Clergyman— / and the sermon is never long" (lines 9–10). The sermon satisfies two desires that most people have at church: first, to encounter God, and, second, not to be bored. In this natural scene "instead of getting to Heaven, at last— / [She's] going, all along" (lines 11–12).

The poem is so pleasant that it is easy to overlook the fact that its central message, that staying at home can be a spiritual experience, is subversive, for church attendance was important in traditional Congregationalist towns like Amherst (Rabinowitz 64–77). In fact, the word "some" might be an understatement, as, in 1860, most citizens in Amherst probably attended a church on Sunday. The speaker's situation instead resembles Emerson's 1842 description of the transcendentalists, those "lonely" and "sincere and religious" people who "repel influences" and "shun general society" (104–05). Furthermore, the speaker claims access to God without the aid of a religious community, a pastor, or a sacred text, all of which, as seen above, were essential to Puritan religious experience. In this poem, then, the speaker frames her spiritual experience in traditional terms and even keeps a few of the traditional practices, yet she simultaneously describes the benefits of departing from traditional practice.

While "Some keep the Sabbath going to church—" reveals Dickinson's changes in practice, "The Brain—is wider than the

This citation refers to a line in the poem, not to a page number. The page number is indicated in the list of works cited.

A slash mark indicates a line break.

Gibson 6

Sky—," composed perhaps two years later, shows her shift in theology. The speaker asserts a confidence in the power of the human intellect that resembles that of Boston's nontraditional thinkers. In each stanza, she invites the reader to measure the brain by comparing it to some other enormous entity. First, she finds that the brain "is wider than the Sky" and urges the reader to "put them side by side" and see that "the one the other will contain / with ease" and the reader "beside" (lines 1–4). Second, she observes that the brain "is deeper than the sea" and, again, urges the reader to "hold them" and see that "the one the other will absorb / as Sponges—Buckets—do" (lines 5–8). The speaker has a complicated imaginative method: her materials thus far are all physical—brain, sky, sea—but the qualities that she compares are mixed—physical length and depth versus metaphysical length and depth.

In the third stanza, when the speaker observes that the brain "is just the weight of God" (line 9), she introduces theological material into her experiment. She asks the reader to "Heft," or weigh (Oxford), the two "Pound for Pound" and forecasts that "they will differ—if they do— / as Syllable from Sound" (lines 10–12). The poet switches from physical science to linguistics in this closing simile, the meaning of which divides scholars. William Sherwood argues that "each syllable is . . . finite" and "includes only a fraction of the total range of sound," yet "at the same time the syllable is the instrument by which sound is articulated" (127–28). Robert Weisbuch tries to take into account the context of the simile, arguing,

> We must take the qualifying "if they do" ironically.
> The difference of weight between "Syllable" and
> "Sound" is at once minute and absolute, the differ-
> ence of a hair. It is the difference between the thing
> itself and its imperfect, itemized explanation. It is the
> difference, say, between paraphrase and poetry,
> poetry and thought. The brain is not quite and not at
> all the weightless weight of God. (84)

Weisbuch is right to note that the phrase "if they do" is ironic, as "Syllable" and "Sound" undeniably differ. Sherwood helpfully argues that these are differences in quantity and clarity. Thus, though the brain "As Syllable" is, ultimately, less than "the weight of God," it is more intelligible, perhaps more intelligent, than "the total range of sound."

The speaker of this poem is of a scientific bent; her

Gibson carefully leads the reader from one section of his essay to another with a transitional sentence that first summarizes the claim developed in the last section and then articulates the claim that he will develop in the next section.

Gibson's reference to "scholars" tells the reader that he's about to describe and consider other interpretations.

Because this quotation is over four lines, it is indented to create a **block quotation.** Gibson doesn't need to enclose the whole quotation in quotation marks, but he does use quotation marks to set off words quoted within the quotation.

Rather than letting other scholarly interpreters have the last word, Gibson concludes the paragraph by stating his own interpretive claim.

measurements of length, depth, and weight recall the instruction in science that Dickinson received throughout her schooling (Jones 309; Lundin 30). Yet the speaker also believes that there are things beyond or outside the physical world of science and is just as eager to apply her scientific method to them. She perceives both that the human intellect is enormously expansive and that there is a God behind the cosmos. The divinity that she describes, though, is not the one her ancestors worshipped in Amherst: the speaker's God is more like a force than a person, more like the spirit of the universe than its sovereign. In "Some keep the Sabbath going to church—" Dickinson's orchard still seemed planted in Amherst. In "The Brain—is wider than the Sky," it becomes conspicuously a satellite of Boston.

> Again, notice how Gibson touches back on key terms: "Amherst," "Boston," "traditional theology," etc.

This departure from traditional theology caused Dickinson to revise her vision of the afterlife, as suggested by her 1863 "Because I could not stop for Death—." The poem begins by personifying Death as a carriage-driver (lines 1–3). This personification of death echoes several biblical passages; Dickinson's Death "may," for example, "represent one of the Four Horsemen of the Apocalypse" (Bennett 208). The poet's "kindly" personification is, of course, both more benevolent than the destructive biblical figure and, with his carriage, more modern (line 2). The carriage ride takes the speaker past a school, "Fields of Gazing Grain," the "Setting Sun," and then "[pauses]" at a "House," before proceeding "toward Eternity" (lines 9, 11, 12, 17, 24). The "House" "[seems] / a Swelling of the Ground," and is, in fact, a grave (lines 10–11). Thus, the carriage drives the speaker through the stages of life—from youth to maturity, decline, death, and, ultimately, the afterlife.

Although Dickinson may draw her image of Death from the Christian tradition, her Death drives the speaker into a distinctly nontraditional afterlife. The speaker tells the reader early on that Death's carriage "[holds]" "Immortality" and then, in the closing stanza, that she has "surmised" that the carriage's direction is "toward Eternity" (lines 3, 4, 23, 24). In the Puritan theological tradition, death leads to Heaven or Hell, paradise or perdition. Yet Dickinson's carriage does not drive toward either destination; rather, the afterlife is just a continuous movement, a continuation of consciousness. "Some keep the Sabbath going to church—" prepared us, quite subtly, for this conception of the afterlife; there, too, Heaven is not a not place one "[gets] to," "at last," but a state to which one can be "going all along" (lines 11–12). In "Because I could not stop for Death—," the speaker sounds neither blissful nor pessimistic about this state. Her consciousness has adapted to her new existence: "centuries" pass now, "and yet / [it] feels shorter than the Day" when she "first surmised" the carriage's direction (lines 21–23). The word "surmised," though, signals that she is not entirely certain about what, if anything, is to come.

Uncertainty about the afterlife would remain with Dickinson throughout her life and, in 1882, would result in her asking the Reverend Washington Gladden, a somewhat unorthodox Congregationalist, "Is immortality true?" (Lease 50; Gladden). At this time, one of Dickinson's friends, a pastor, had recently died and another friend had become seriously ill (Gladden). Gladden's attempt to reassure her of the truth of immortality draws mostly from his argument that the authoritative figure "Jesus Christ taught" immortality. At the same time, he admits that "absolute demonstration there can be none of this truth."

In perhaps the same year, Dickinson wrote "The Bible is an antique Volume," which shows a mix of skepticism and optimism about the source of Gladden's arguments. The first three lines undermine the Bible's authority; it is an "antique Volume," authored by "faded Men / at the suggestion of Holy Spectres." The poet then provides a list of biblical "Subjects" that "reads like the playbill of a cheap traveling show" (Lundin 203): Eden is "the ancient Homestead"; Satan "the brigadier"; Judas "the Great Defaulter"; David "the Troubadour"; and sin "a distinguished Precipice / others must resist" (lines 4–10). The speaker then uses quotation marks to show her dissatisfaction with religious categories, saying, "Boys that 'believe' are very lonesome / other boys are 'lost' " (lines 11–12). Thus far, the speaker has given us every reason to abandon the Bible—she has discredited its authors, shown the silliness of its subjects, and revealed the tragic culture that surrounds it.

Yet the speaker believes that "had but the Tale [the Bible] a warbling Teller— / all the Boys would come" (lines 13–14). A "warbling Teller" is one whose voice is "thrilling," "ardent," or "friendly" (Bennett 430). For an example, she borrows the poet Orpheus from Greek mythology. His "Sermon," unlike the one the "believing" and "lost" boys now hear, "captivated— / it

No page number is needed in the parenthetical citations for Gladden because the source is only one page long (see Works Cited).

Notice how Gibson leads the reader from one idea/ paragraph to the next with a transition sentence that states the coming paragraph's main idea (This poem "shows a mix of skepticism and optimism about the" Bible) by referring back to the concerns of the last paragraph ("Gladden's arguments").

did not condemn" (lines 15–16). In addition to drawing distinct lines between the saved and the damned, like headmistress Mary Lyon, Puritans often used condemnation, in the now-infamous "fire and brimstone" style, to rouse the immoral to seek salvation (Lundin 11–12; Rabinowitz 5). Instead Dickinson here favors a passionate or intellectual response to a captivating speech over a moral response to a condemning one. She remains a believer in "the emotional force of the Scriptures and [their] expositors," even if she doubts the Bible's historical accuracy and rejects the claims of traditionalist preachers (Doriani 198). The implication of these closing lines, then, is that the Bible is—when read in the right spirit—still a valuable "Volume" for building a community. The Bible has reduced religious authority, but, when performed properly, retains inspirational power. The subtle magic of the poem is that Dickinson herself, in her parodies of biblical "Subjects," enlivens the Bible, "captivates" readers with the old "Tale" through her "warbling" poem.

Though Emily Dickinson might not be a "Christian poet" in the traditional sense of the term, she does beautify and hand down a few beloved pieces of her inheritance, New England Puritanism. She "[keeps] the Sabbath," but at home. She imagines eternity, but without a Heaven or a Hell. She calls the Bible's authors "faded men," but frequently enlivens their "antique" passages in her poems. Over the years, her ideas about God, the universe, and the afterlife changed, but her yearnings to encounter the divine and to experience immortality remained. Emily Dickinson may have physically withdrawn from Amherst society, yet her mind did not withdraw from the intellectual struggles between traditional Amherst and modern Boston. Her spiritual questions and insights are distinctively personal and deeply honest; she is neither a purely skeptical nor a purely religious poet. Her intellect kept her, to her death in 1886, a "No-Hoper" by Mary Lyon's standards, yet, for modern readers, who understand her doubts and share her longings, she is a refreshingly hopeful poet.

Gibson begins his conclusion by returning to the issue he raised in his introduction (Dickinson's status as a "Christian poet"). He then summarizes his argument by briefly reiterating his key points and using a few key words from Dickinson to do so, thus reminding us of how grounded his argument is in textual evidence. Finally, he moves from summarizing his argument to considering its implications for our overall view of Dickinson's poetry.

Gibson 10

Works Cited

Bennett, Fordyce R. A Reference Guide to the Bible in Emily Dickinson's Poetry. Lanham: Scarecrow, 1997.

Dickinson, Emily. "Because I could not stop for Death." Dickinson, Complete Poems 350.

- - -. "The Bible is an antique Volume." Dickinson, Complete Poems 644.

- - -. "The Brain—is wider than the Sky—." Dickinson, Complete Poems 312.

- - -. The Complete Poems of Emily Dickinson. Ed. Thomas H. Johnson. Boston: Little, 1960.

- - -. Letters. Ed. Thomas H. Johnson. Vol. 1. Cambridge: Belknap, 1958.

- - -. "Some keep the Sabbath going to church." Dickinson, Complete Poems 153–54.

- - -. "To Abiah Root." 8 Sept. 1846. Dickinson, Letters 36.

- - -. "To Abiah Root." 17 Jan. 1848. Dickinson, Letters 60.

- - -. "To Abiah Root." 16 May 1848. Dickinson, Letters 67–68.

Doriani, Beth M. Emily Dickinson: Daughter of Prophecy. Amherst: U of Massachusetts P, 1996.

Gladden, Washington. "To Emily Dickinson." 27 May 1882. Letter 752a of Emily Dickinson: Selected Letters. Ed. Thomas H. Johnson. Cambridge: Belknap, 1971. 282.

Jones, Rowena Revis. "The Preparation of a Poet: Puritan Directions in Emily Dickinson's Education." Studies in the American Renaissance, 1982. Boston: Twayne, 1982.

Lease, Benjamin. " 'This World is not Conclusion': Dickinson, Amherst, and 'the local conditions of the soul.' " Emily Dickinson Journal 3.2 (1994): 38–55.

Lundin, Roger. Emily Dickinson and the Art of Belief. 2nd ed. Grand Rapids: Eerdmans, 2004.

Noll, Mark A. America's God: From Jonathan Edwards to Abraham Lincoln. New York: Oxford UP, 2002.

Norberg, Peter. Introduction. Essays and Poems by Ralph Waldo Emerson. New York: Barnes and Noble Classics, 2004. xiii–xxxiii.

The Oxford English Dictionary. 2nd ed. 1989.

Rabinowitz, Richard. The Spiritual Self in Everyday Life: The Transformation of Personal Religious Experience in Nineteenth-Century New England. Boston: Northeastern UP, 1989.

Sherwood, William R. Circumference and Circumstance: Stages in the Mind and Art of Emily Dickinson. New York: Columbia UP, 1968.

Weisbuch, Robert. "The Necessary Veil: A Quest Fiction." Emily Dickinson. Ed. Harold Bloom. New York: Chelsea, 1985.

Critical Approaches

Few human abilities are more remarkable than the ability to read and interpret literature. A computer program or a database can't perform the complex process of reading and interpreting—not to mention writing about—a literary text, although computers can easily exceed human powers of processing codes and information. Readers follow the sequence of printed words and as if by magic re-create a scene between characters in a novel or play, or they respond to the almost inexpressible emotional effect of a poem's figurative language. Experienced readers can pick up on a multitude of literary signals all at once. With rereading and some research, readers can draw on information such as the author's life or the time period when this work and others like it were first published. Varied and complex as the approaches to literary criticism may be, they are not difficult to learn. For the most part schools of criticism and theory have developed to address questions that any reader can begin to answer.

As we noted in the introduction, there are essentially three participants in what could be called the literary exchange or interaction: the *text*, the *source* (the *author* and other factors that produce the text), and the *receiver* (the *reader* and other aspects of *reception*). All the varieties of literary analysis concern themselves with these aspects of the literary exchange in varying degrees and with varying emphases. Although each of these elements has a role in any form of literary analysis, systematic studies of literature and its history have defined approaches or methods that focus on the different elements and circumstances of the literary interaction. The first three sections below—"Emphasis on the Text," "Emphasis on the Source," and "Emphasis on the Receiver"—describe briefly those schools or modes of literary analysis that have concentrated on one of the three elements while de-emphasizing the others. These different emphases, plainly speaking, are habits of asking different kinds of questions. Answers or interpretations will vary according to the questions we ask of a literary work. In practice the range of questions can be— to some extent *should* be—combined whenever we develop a literary interpretation. Such questions can always generate the thesis or argument of a critical essay.

Although some approaches to literary analysis treat the literary exchange (text, source, receiver) in isolation from the world surrounding that exchange (the world of economics, politics, religion, cultural tradition, and sexuality—in other words, the world in which we live), most contemporary modes of analysis acknowledge the importance of that world to the literary exchange. These days, even if a literary scholar wants to focus primarily on the text or its source or receiver, she or he will often incorporate some of the observations and methods developed by theorists and critics who have turned their attention toward the changing world surrounding the formal conventions of literature, the writing process and writer's career, and the reception or response to literature. We describe the work of such theorists and critics in the fourth section below, "Historical and Ideological Criticism."

Before expanding on the kinds of critical approaches within these four categories, let's consider one example in which questions concerning the text, source, and receiver, as well as a consideration of historical and ideological questions, would contribute to a richer interpretation of a text. To begin as usual with preliminary questions about the *text:* What is "First Fight. Then Fiddle." (see p. 270)? Printed correctly on a separate piece of paper, the text would tell us at once that it is a poem because of its form: rhythm, repeating word sounds, lines that leave very wide margins on the page. Because you are reading this poem in this book, you know even more about its form (in this way, the publication *source* gives clues about the *text*). By putting it in a section with other poetry, we have told you it is a poem worth reading, rereading, and thinking about. (What other ways do you encounter poems, and what does the medium of presenting a poem tell you about it?)

You should pursue other questions focused on the text. What *kind* of poem is it? Here we have helped you, especially if you are not already familiar with the sonnet form, by grouping this poem with other sonnets. Classifying "First Fight. Then Fiddle." as a sonnet might then prompt you to interpret the ways that this poem is or is not like other sonnets. Well and good: you can check off its fourteen lines of (basically) iambic pentameter, and note its somewhat unusual rhyme scheme and meter, in relation to the rules of **Italian** and **English sonnets.** *Why* does this experiment with the sonnet form matter?

To answer questions about the purpose of form, you need to answer some basic questions about *source,* such as: *When* was this sonnet written and published? *Who* wrote it? What do you know about Gwendolyn Brooks, about 1949, about African American women and/or poets in the United States at that time? A short historical and biographical essay answering such questions might help put the sonnetness of "First Fight. Then Fiddle." in context. But assembling all the available information about the source and original context of the poem, even some sort of documented testimony from Brooks about her intentions or interpretation of it, would still leave room for other questions leading to new interpretations.

What about the *receiver* of "First Fight. Then Fiddle."? Even within the poem a kind of audience exists. This sonnet seems to be a set of instructions addressed to "you." (Although many sonnets are addressed by a speaker, "I," to an auditor, "you," such address rarely sounds like military commands, as it does here.) This internal audience is not of course to be confused with real people responding to the poem. How did readers respond to it when it was first published? Can you find any published reviews, or any criticism of this sonnet published in studies of Gwendolyn Brooks?

Questions about the receiver, like those about the author and other sources, readily connect with historical questions. Would a reader or someone listening to this poem read aloud respond differently in the years after World War II than in an age of global terrorism? Does it make a difference if the audience addressed by the speaker *inside* the poem is imagined as a group of African American men and women or as a group of European American male commanders? (The latter question could be regarded as involving questions about the text and the source as well as about the receiver.) Does a reader need to identify with any of the particular groups the poem fictitiously addresses, or would any reader, from any background, respond to it the same way? Even the formal qualities of the text could be examined through historical lenses: the sonnet form has been associated with prestigious European literature, and with themes of love and mortality, since the Renaissance. It is significant that a twentieth-century African American poet chose *this* traditional form to twist "threadwise" into an antiwar protest.

The above are only some of the worthwhile questions concerning this short, intricate poem. (We will develop a few more thoughts about it in illustrating different approaches to the text and to the source.) Similarly, the complexity of critical approaches far exceeds our four categories. While a great deal of worthwhile scholarship and criticism borrows from a range of theories and methods, below we give necessarily simplified descriptions of various critical approaches that have continuing influence. We cannot trace a history of the issues involved, or the complexity and controversies within these movements. Instead think of what follows as a road map to the terrain of literary analysis. Many available resources describe the entire landscape of literary analysis in more precise detail. If you are interested in learning more about these or any other analytical approaches, consult the works listed in the bibliography at the end of this chapter.

EMPHASIS ON THE TEXT

This broad category encompasses approaches that minimize the elements associated with the author/source or the reader/reception to focus on the work. In a sense any writing about literature presupposes recognition of form, in that it deems the object of study to *be* a literary work, and to belong to a type or genre of literature, as Brooks's poem belongs with sonnets. Moreover, almost all literary criticism notes some details of style or structure, some *intrinsic* features such as the relation between dialogue or narrated summary, or the pattern of rhyme and meter. But *formalist* approaches go further by foregrounding the design of the text as inherent to the meaning of the whole work.

Some formalists, reasonably denying the division of content from form (since the form is part of the content or meaning), have more controversially excluded any discussion of *extrinsic* matters such as the author's biography or questions of psychology, sociology, or history. This has led to accusations that formalism, in avoiding relevance to actual authors and readers or to the world of economic power or social change, also avoids political issues or commitments. Some historical or ideological critics have therefore argued that formalism supports the powers that be, since it precludes protest. Conversely, some formalists charge that any extrinsic—that is, historical, political, ideological, as well as biographical or psychological—interpretations of literature reduce the text to a set of more or less cleverly encoded messages or propaganda. A formalist might maintain that the inventive wonders of art exceed any practical function it serves. In practice influential formalisms have generated modes of *close reading* that balance attention to form, significance, and social context, with some acknowledgment of the political implications of literature. In the early twenty-first century the formalist methods of close reading remain influential, especially in classrooms. Indeed, *The Norton Introduction to Literature* adheres to these methods in its presentation of elements and interpretation of form.

New Criticism

One strain of formalism, loosely identified as the New Criticism, dominated literary studies from approximately the 1920s to the 1970s. New Critics rejected both of the approaches that prevailed then in the relatively new field of English studies: the dry analysis of the development of the English language, and the misty appreciation and evaluation of great works. Generally, New Criticism minimizes consideration of both the source and the receiver, favoring the intrinsic qualities of a unified literary work. Psychological or historical information about the author, the intentions or feelings of authors or readers, and any philosophical or socially relevant "messages" derived from the work all are out of bounds in a New Critical reading. The text in a fundamental way refers to itself: its medium is its message. Although interested in ambiguity and irony as well as figurative language, a New Critical reader establishes the organic unity of the unique work. Like an organism, the work develops in a synergetic relation of parts to whole.

A New Critic might, for example, publish an article titled "A Reading of 'First Fight. Then Fiddle.'" (The method works best with lyric or other short forms because it requires painstaking attention to details such as metaphors or alliteration.) Little if anything would be said of Gwendolyn Brooks or the poem's relation to modernist poetry. The critic's task is to give credit to the poem, not the poet or the period, and if it is a good poem, implicitly, it can't be merely "about" World War II or civil rights. New Criticism presumes that a good literary work symbolically embodies universal human themes and may be interpreted objectively on many levels. These levels may be related more by tension and contradiction than harmony, yet that relation demonstrates the coherence of the whole poem.

Thus the New Critic's essay might include some of the following observations. The title—which reappears as half of the first line—consists of a pair of two-word imperative sentences, and most statements in the poem paraphrase these two sentences, especially the first of them, "First fight." Thus an alliterative two-word command, "Win war" (line 12), follows a longer version of such a command: "But first to arms, to armor" (line 9). Echoes of this sort of exhortation appear throughout. We, as audience, begin to feel "bewitch[ed], bewilder[ed]" (line 4) by a buildup of undesirable urgings, whether at the beginning of a line ("Be deaf," line 11) or the end of a line ("Be remote," line 7; "Carry hate," line 9) or in the middle of a line ("Rise bloody," line 12). It's hardly what we would want to do. Yet the speaker makes a strong case for the practical view that a society needs to take care of defense before it can "devote" itself to "silks and honey" (lines 6–7), that is, the soft and sweet pleasures of art. But what kind of culture would place "hate / In front of . . . harmony" and try to ignore "music" and "beauty" (lines 9–11)? What kind of people are only "remote / A while from malice and from murdering" (lines 6–7)? A society of warlike heroes would rally to this speech. Yet on rereading, many of the words jar with the tone of heroic battle cry.

The New Critic examines not only the speaker's style and words but the order of ideas and lines in the poem. Ironically, the poem defies the speaker's command; it fiddles first, and then fights, as the **octave** (first eight lines) concern art, and the **sestet** (last six) concern war. The New Critic might be delighted by the irony that the two segments of the poem in fact unite, in that their topics—octave on how to fiddle, sestet on how to fight—mirror each other. The beginning of the poem plays with metaphors for music and art as means of inflicting "hurting love" (line 3) or emotional conquest, that is, ways to "fight." War and art are both, as far as we know, universal in all human societies. The poem, then, is an organic whole that restates ancient themes.

Later critics have pointed out that New Criticism, despite its avoidance of extrinsic questions, had a political context of its own. The affirmation of unity for the artwork and humanities in general should be regarded as a strategy adapted during the Cold War as a counterbalance to the politicization of art in fascist and communist regimes. New Criticism also provided a program for literary reading that is accessible to beginners regardless of their social background, in keeping with the opening of college-level English studies to more women, minorities, and members of the working class. By the 1970s these same groups had helped generate two sources of opposition to New Criticism's ostensible neutrality and transparency: critical studies that emphasized the politics of social differences (e.g., feminist criticism); and theoretical approaches, based on linguistics, philosophy, and political theory, that effectively distanced nonspecialists once more.

Structuralism

Whereas New Criticism was largely a British and American phenomenon, structuralism and its successor, poststructuralism, derive primarily from French theorists. Strains of structuralism also emerged in the Soviet Union and in Prague, influenced by the demand for a science of criticism that would avoid direct political confrontation. Each of these movements was drawn to scientific objectivity—difficult to attain in literature, arts, and other "humanities"—and at the same time wary of political commitment. Politics, after all, had been the rallying cry for censorship of science, art, and inquiry throughout centuries and in recent memory.

Structuralist philosophy, however, was something rather new. Influenced by the French linguist Ferdinand de Saussure (1857–1913), structuralists sought an objective system for studying the principles of language. Saussure distinguished between individual uses of language, such as the sentences you or I just spoke or wrote (*parole*), and the sets of rules of English or any language (*langue*). Just as a structuralist linguist would study the interrelations of signs in the *langue* rather than the variations in specific utterances in *parole*, a structuralist critic of literature or culture would study shared systems of meaning, such as genres or myths that pass from one country or period to another, rather than a certain poem in isolation (the favored subject of New Criticism).

Another structuralist principle derived from Saussure is the emphasis on the arbitrary association between a word and what it is said to signify, the *signifier* and the *signified*. The word "horse," for example, has no divine, natural, or necessary connection to that four-legged, domesticated mammal, which is named by other combinations of sounds and letters in other languages. Any language is a network of relations among such arbitrary signifiers, just as each word in the dictionary must be defined using other words in that dictionary. Structuralists largely attribute the meanings of words to rules of differentiation from other words. Such differences may be phonetic (as among the words "cat" and "bat" and "hat") or they may belong to conceptual associations (as among the words "dinky," "puny," "tiny," "small," "miniature," "petite," "compact"). Structuralist thought has particularly called attention to the way that opposites or dualisms such as "night" and "day" or "feminine" and "masculine" define each other through their differences rather than in direct reference to objective reality. For example, the earth's motion around the sun produces changing exposure to sunlight daily and seasonally, but by linguistic convention we call it "night" between, let's say, 8 p.m. and 5 a.m., no matter how light it is. (We may differ in opinions about "evening" or "dawn." But our "day" at work may begin or end in the dark.) The point is that arbitrary labels divide what in fact is continuous.

Structuralism's linguistic insights have greatly influenced literary studies. Like New Criticism, structuralism shows little interest in the creative process or in authors, their intentions, or their circumstances. Similarly, structuralism discounts the idiosyncrasies of particular readings; it takes texts to represent interactions of words and ideas that stand apart from individual human identities or sociopolitical commitments. Structuralist approaches have applied less to lyric poetry than to myths, narratives, and cultural practices, such as sports or fashion. Although structuralism tends to affirm a universal humanity as the New Critics might do, its work in comparative mythology and anthropology challenged the absolute value that New Criticism tended to grant to time-honored canons of great literature.

The structuralist would regard a text not as a self-sufficient icon but as part of a network of conventions. A structuralist essay on "First Fight. Then Fiddle." might ask why the string is plied with the "feathery sorcery" (line 2) of the "bow" (line 7). These words suggest the art of a Native American trickster or primitive sorcerer, while at the same time the instrument is a disguised weapon: a stringed bow with feathered arrows (the term "muzzle" is a similar pun, suggesting an animal's snout and the discharging end of a gun). Or is the fiddle—a violin played in musical forms such as bluegrass—a metaphor for popular art or folk resistance to official culture? In many folk tales a hero is taught to play the fiddle by the devil or tricks the devil with a fiddle or similar instrument. Further, a structuralist reading might attach great significance to the sonnet form as a paradigm that has shaped poetic expression for centuries. The classic "turn" or reversal of thought in a sonnet may imitate the form of many narratives of departure and return, separation and reconciliation. Brooks's poem repeats in the numerous short reversing imperatives, as well as in the structure of octave versus sestet, the eternal oscillation between love and death, creation and destruction.

Poststructuralism

By emphasizing the paradoxes of dualisms and the ways that language constructs our awareness, structuralism planted the seeds of its own destruction or, rather, deconstruction. Dualisms (e.g., masculine/feminine, mind/body, culture/nature) cannot be separate-but-equal; rather they take effect as differences of power in which one dominates the other. Yet as the German philosopher of history Georg Wilhelm Friedrich Hegel (1770–1831) insisted, the relations of the dominant and subordinate, of master and slave readily invert themselves. The master is dominated by his need for the slave's subordination; the possession of subordinates defines his mastery. As Brooks's poem implies, each society reflects its own identity through an opposing "they," in a dualism of civilized/barbaric. The instability of the speaker's position in this poem (is he or she among the conquerors or the conquered?) is a model of the instability of roles throughout the human world. There is no transcendent ground—except on another planet, perhaps—from which to measure the relative positions of the polar opposites on Earth. Roland Barthes (1915–1980) and others, influenced by the radical movements of the 1960s and the increasing complexity of culture in an era of mass consumerism and global media, extended structuralism into more profoundly relativist perspectives.

Poststructuralism is the broad term used to designate the philosophical position that attacks the objective, universalizing claims of most fields of knowledge since the eighteenth century. Poststructuralists, distrusting the optimism of a positivist philosophy that suggests the world is knowable and explainable, ultimately doubt the possibility of certainties of any kind, since language signifies only through a chain of other words rather than through any fundamental link to reality. This argument derives from structuralism, yet it also criticizes structuralist universalism and avoidance of political issues. *Ideology* is a key conceptual ingredient in the poststructuralist argument against structuralism. Ideology is a slippery term that can broadly be defined as a socially shared set of ideas that shape behavior; often it refers to the values that legitimate the ruling interests in a society, and in many accounts it is the hidden code that is officially denied. (We discuss kinds of "ideological" criticism later.) Poststructuralist theory has played a part in a number of critical schools introduced below, not all of them focused on the text. But in literary criticism, poststructuralism has marshaled most forces under the banner of deconstruction.

Deconstruction

Deconstruction insists on the logical impossibility of knowledge that is not influenced or biased by the words used to express it. Deconstruction also claims that language is incapable of representing any sort of reality directly. As practiced by its most famous proponent, the French philosopher Jacques Derrida (1930–2004), deconstruction endeavors to trace the way texts imply the contradiction of their explicit meanings. The deconstructionist delights in the sense of dizziness as the grounds of conviction crumble away; *aporia*, or irresolvable doubt, is the desired, if fleeting, end of an encounter with a text. Deconstruction threatens *humanism,* or the worldview that is centered on human values and the self-sufficient individual, because it denies that there is an ultimate, solid reality on which to base truth or the identity of the self. All values and identities are constructed by the competing systems of meaning, or *discourses*. This is a remarkably influential set of ideas that you will meet again as we discuss other approaches.

The traditional concept of the author as creative origin of the text comes under fire in deconstructionist criticism, which emphasizes instead the creative power of language or the text, and the ingenious work of the critic in detecting gaps and contradictions in writing. Thus like New Criticism, deconstruction disregards the author and concentrates on textual close reading, but unlike New Criticism, it features the role of the reader as well. Moreover, the text need not be respected as a pure and coherent icon. Deconstructionists might "read" many kinds of writing and representation in other media in much the same way that they might read Milton's *Paradise Lost,* that is, irreverently. Indeed, when deconstruction erupted in university departments of literature, traditional critics and scholars feared the breakdown of the distinctions between literature and criticism and between literature and many other kinds of text. Many attacks on literary theory have particularly lambasted deconstructionists for apparently rejecting all the reasons to care about literature in the first place and for writing in a style so flamboyantly obscure that no one but specialists can understand. Yet in practice Derrida and others have carried harmony before them, to paraphrase Brooks; their readings can delight in the play of figurative language, thereby enhancing rather than debunking the value of literature.

A deconstructionist might read "First Fight. Then Fiddle." in a manner somewhat similar to the New Critic's, but with even more focus on puns and paradoxes and with resistance to organic unity. For instance, the two alliterative commands, "fight" and "fiddle," might be opposites, twins, or inseparable consequences of each other. The word "fiddle" is tricky. Does it suggest that art is trivial? Does it allude to a dictator who "fiddles while Rome burns," as the saying goes? Someone who "fiddles" is not performing a grand, honest, or even competent act: one fiddles with a hobby, with the books, with car keys in the dark. The artist in this poem defies the orthodoxy of the sonnet form, instead making a kind of harlequin patchwork out of different traditions, breaking the rhythm, intermixing endearments and assaults.

To the deconstructionist the recurring broken antitheses of war and art, art and war cancel each other out. The very metaphors undermine the speaker's summons to war. The command "Be deaf to music and to beauty blind," which takes the form of a *chiasmus,* or X-shaped sequence (adjective, noun; noun, adjective), is a kind of miniature version of this chiasmic poem. (We are supposed to follow a sequence, fight then fiddle, but instead reverse that by imagining ways to do violence with art or to create beauty through destruction.) The poem, a lyric written but imagined as spoken or sung, puts the senses and the arts under erasure; we are somehow not to hear music (by definition audible), not to see beauty (here a visual attribute). "Maybe not too late" comes rather too late: at the end of the poem it will be too late to start over, although "having first to civilize a space / Wherein to play your violin with grace" (lines 12–14) comes across as a kind of beginning. These comforting lines form the only heroic couplet in the poem, the only two lines that run smoothly from end to end. (All the other lines have **caesuras, enjambments,** or balanced pairs of concepts, as in "from malice and from murdering" [line 8].) But the violence behind "civilize," the switch to the high-art term "violin," and the use of the Christian term "grace" suggest that the pagan erotic art promised at the outset, the "sorcery" of "hurting love" that can "bewitch," will be suppressed.

Like other formalisms, deconstruction can appear apolitical or conservative because of its skepticism about the referential connection between literature and the world of economics, politics, and other social forms. Yet poststructuralist linguistics provides a theory of *difference* that clearly pertains to the rankings of status and power in society, as in earlier examples of masculine/feminine, master/slave. The *Other,* the negative of the norm, is always less than an equal counterpart. Deconstruction has been a tool for various poststructuralist thinkers—including the historian Michel Foucault (1926–1984), the feminist theorist and psychoanalyst Julia Kristeva (b. 1941), and the psychoanalytic theorist Jacques Lacan (1901–1981).

EMPHASIS ON THE SOURCE

As the above examples suggest, a great deal can be drawn from a text without any reference to its source or author. For millennia many anonymous works were shared in oral or manuscript form, and even after printing spread in Europe it was not necessary to know the author's name or anything about him or her. Yet criticism from its beginnings in ancient Greece has been interested in the designing intention "behind" the text. Even when no evidence remained about the author, a legendary personality has been invented to satisfy readers' curiosity. From the

legend of blind Homer to the latest debates about biographical evidence and por-
traits of William Shakespeare, literary criticism has been accompanied by interest
in the author's life.

Biographical Criticism

This approach reached its height in an era when humanism prevailed in literary
studies (roughly 1750s to 1960s). At this time there was widely shared confidence
in the ideas that art and literature were the direct expressions of the artist's or
writer's genius and that criticism of great works supported veneration of the great
persons who created them. The lives of some famous writers became the models
that aspiring writers emulated. Criticism at times was skewed by social judgments
of personalities, as when Keats was put down as a "Cockney" poet, that is, London-
bred and lower-class. Many writers have struggled to get their work taken seriously
because of mistaken biographical criticism. Women or minorities have at times
used pseudonyms or published anonymously to avoid having their work put down
or having it read only through the expectations, negative or positive, of what a
woman or person of color might write. Biographical criticism can be diminishing
in this respect. Others have objected to reading literature as a reflection of the
author's personality. Such critics have supported the idea that the highest literary
art is pure form, untouched by gossip or personal emotion. In this spirit some
early twentieth-century critics as well as modernist writers such as T. S. Eliot, James
Joyce, and Virginia Woolf tried to dissociate the text from the personality or polit-
ical commitments of the author. (The theories of these writers and their actual
practices did not quite coincide.)

In the early twentieth century, psychoanalytic interpretations placed the text in
light of the author's emotional conflicts, and other interpretations relied heavily
on the author's stated intentions. (Although psychoanalytic criticism entails more
than analysis of the author, we will introduce it as an approach that primarily
concerns the human source[s] of literature; it usually has less to say about the
form and receiver of the text.) Author-based readings can be reductive. All the
accessible information about a writer's life cannot explain the writings. As a young
man D. H. Lawrence might have hated his father and loved his mother, but all
men who hate their fathers and love their mothers do not write fiction as powerful
as Lawrence's. Indeed, Lawrence cautioned that we should "trust the tale, not the
teller."

Any kind of criticism benefits, however, from being informed by the writer's
life and career to some extent. Certain critical approaches, devoted to recognition
of separate literary traditions, make sense only in light of supporting biographical
evidence. Studies that concern traditions such as Irish literature, Asian American
literature, or literature by Southern women require reliable information about the
writers' birth and upbringing and even some judgment of the writers' intentions
to write *as* members of such traditions. (We discuss feminist, African American,
and other studies of distinct literatures in the "Historical and Ideological Criti-
cism" section, although such studies recognize the biographical "source" as a start-
ing point.)

A reading of "First Fight. Then Fiddle." becomes rather different when we know
more about Gwendolyn Brooks. An African American, she was raised in Chicago
in the 1920s. These facts begin to provide a context for her work. Some of the

biographical information has more to do with her time and place than with her race and sex. Brooks began in the 1940s to associate with Harriet Monroe's magazine, *Poetry*, which had been influential in promoting modernist poetry. Brooks early received acclaim for books of poetry that depict the everyday lives of poor, urban African Americans; in 1950 she was the first African American to win a Pulitzer Prize. In 1967 she became an outspoken advocate for the Black Arts movement, which promoted a separate tradition rather than integration into the aesthetic mainstream. But even before this political commitment, her work never sought to "pass" or to distance itself from racial difference, nor did it become any less concerned with poetic tradition and form when she published it through small, independent black presses in her "political" phase.

It is reasonable, then, to read "First Fight. Then Fiddle.," published in 1949, in relation to the role of a racial outsider mastering and adapting the forms of a dominant tradition. Perhaps Brooks's speaker addresses an African American audience in the voice of a revolutionary, calling for violence to gain the right to express African American culture. Perhaps the lines "the music that they wrote / Bewitch, bewilder. Qualify to sing / Threadwise" (lines 3–5) suggest the way that the colonized may transform the empire's music rather than the other way around. Ten years before the poem was published, a famous African American singer, Marian Anderson, had more than "qualif[ied] to sing" opera and classical concert music, but had still encountered the color barrier in the United States. Honored throughout Europe as the greatest living contralto, Anderson was barred in 1939 from performing at Constitution Hall in Washington, D.C., because of her race. Instead she performed at the Lincoln Memorial on Easter Sunday to an audience of seventy-five thousand people. It was not easy to find a "space" in which to practice her art. Such a contextual reference, whether or not intended, relates biographically to Brooks's role as an African American woman wisely reweaving classical traditions "threadwise" rather than straining them into "hempen" (line 5) ropes. Beneath the manifest reference to the recent world war, this poem refers to the segregation of the arts in America. (Questions of source and historical context often interrelate.)

Besides readings that derive from biographical and historical information, there are still other ways to read aspects of the *source* rather than the *text* or the *receiver*. The source of the work extends beyond the life of the person who wrote it to include not only the writer's other works but also the circumstances of contemporary publishing; contemporary literary movements; the history of the composition and publication of this particular text, with all the variations; and other contributing factors. While entire schools of literary scholarship have been devoted to each of these matters, any analyst of a particular work should bear in mind what is known about the circumstances of writers at that time, the material conditions of the work's first publication, and the means of dissemination ever since. It makes a difference in our interpretation to know that a certain sonnet circulated in manuscript in a small courtly audience or that a particular novel was serialized in a weekly journal.

Psychoanalytic Criticism

With the development of psychology and psychoanalysis toward the end of the nineteenth century, many critics were tempted to apply psychological theories to literary analysis. Symbolism, dreamlike imagery, emotional rather than rational logic, a pleasure in language all suggested that literature profoundly evoked a mental and emotional landscape, often one of disorder or abnormality. From mad poets to patients speaking in verse, imaginative literature might be regarded as a representation of shared irrational structures within all *psyches* (i.e., souls) or selves. While psychoanalytic approaches have developed along with structuralism and poststructuralist linguistics and philosophy, they rarely focus on textual form. Rather, they attribute latent or hidden meaning to unacknowledged desires in some person, usually the author or source behind the character in a narrative or drama. A psychoanalytic critic could focus on the response of readers and, in recent decades, usually accepts the influence of changing social history on the structures of sexual desire represented in the work. Nevertheless, psychoanalysis has typically aspired to a universal, unchanging theory of the mind and personality, and criticism that applies it has tended to emphasize the authorial source.

FREUDIAN CRITICISM

For most of the twentieth century, the dominant school of psychoanalytic critics was the Freudian, based on the work of Sigmund Freud (1856–1939). Many of its practitioners assert that the meaning of a literary work exists not on its surface but in the psyche (some would even claim, in the neuroses) of the author. Classic psychoanalytic criticism read works as though they were the recorded dreams of patients; interpreted the life histories of authors as keys to the works; or analyzed characters as though like real people they have a set of repressed childhood memories. (In fact, many novels and most plays leave out information about characters' development from infancy through adolescence, the period that psychoanalysis especially strives to reconstruct.)

A well-known Freudian reading of *Hamlet*, for example, insists that Hamlet suffers from an Oedipus complex, a Freudian term for a group of repressed desires and memories that corresponds with the Greek myth that is the basis of Sophocles' play *Oedipus the King*. In this view Hamlet envies his uncle because the son unconsciously wants to sleep with his mother, who was the first object of his desire as a baby. The ghost of Hamlet Sr. may then be a manifestation of Hamlet's unconscious desire or a figure for his guilt for wanting to kill his father, the person who has a right to the desired mother's body. Hamlet's madness is not just acting but the result of this frustrated desire; his cruel mistreatment of Ophelia is a deflection of his disgust at his mother's being "unfaithful" in her love for him. Some Freudian critics stress the author's psyche and so might read *Hamlet* as the expression of Shakespeare's own Oedipus complex. In another mode psychoanalytic critics, reading imaginative literature as symbolic fulfillment of unconscious wishes much as an analyst would interpret a dream, decipher objects, spaces, or actions that appear to relate to sexual anatomy or activity. Much as if tracing out the extended metaphors of an erotic poem by Donne or a blues or Motown lyric, the Freudian reads containers, empty spaces, or bodies of water as female; tools, weapons, towers or trees, trains or planes as male.

Psychoanalytic criticism, learning from Freud's ventures in literary criticism, has favored narrative fiction with uncanny, supernatural, or detective elements. Plots with excessive, inexplicable fatalities seem to express wishes unconsciously shared by all readers as well as the writer. The method has often been applied to writers of such stories whose biographies are well documented. The life and works of Edgar Allan Poe (1809–1849) therefore have attracted psychoanalytic readings. An orphan who quarreled with the surrogate father who raised him, Poe seems to have been tormented by an unresolved desire for a mother figure. A series of beloved mother figures died prematurely, including his mother and Mrs. Allan, the woman who raised him. He became attached to his aunt and fell in love with her daughter, Virginia Clemm, whom he married in 1836 when she was thirteen, and who died of tuberculosis in 1847. He famously asserted that the most apt subject of poetry is the death of a beautiful woman. In Poe's "The Raven" a macabre talking bird intrudes in the speaker's room and induces an obsession with the dead beloved, a woman named Lenore. In a Freudian reading Poe's "The Cask of Amontillado" appears to transpose a fantasy of return to the womb—an enclosed space holding liquids—into a fulfilled desire to kill a male rival.

JUNGIAN AND MYTH CRITICISM

Just as a Freudian assumes that all human psyches have similar histories and structures, the Jungian critic assumes that we all share a universal or collective unconscious (as well as having a racial and individual unconscious). According to Carl Gustav Jung (1875–1961) and his followers, the unconscious harbors universal patterns and forms of human experiences, or archetypes. We can never know these archetypes directly, but they surface in art in an imperfect, shadowy way, taking the form of archetypal images—the snake with its tail in its mouth, rebirth, mother, the double, the descent into hell. In the classic quest narrative, the hero struggles to free himself (the gender of the pronoun is significant) from the Great Mother, to become a separate, self-sufficient being (combating a demonic antagonist), surviving trials to gain the reward of union with his ideal other, the feminine anima. In a related school of *archetypal criticism,* influenced by Northrop Frye (1912–1991), the prevailing myth follows a seasonal cycle of death and rebirth. Frye proposed a system for literary criticism that classified all literary forms in all ages according to a cycle of genres associated with the phases of human experience from birth to death and the natural cycle of seasons (e.g., Spring/Romance).

These approaches have been useful in the study of folklore and early literatures as well as in comparative studies of various national literatures. While most myth critics focus on the hero's quest, there have been forays into feminist archetypal criticism. These emphasize variations on the myths of Isis and Demeter, goddesses of fertility or seasonal renewal, who take different forms to restore either the sacrificed woman (Persephone's season in the underworld) or the sacrificed man (Isis's search for Osiris and her rescue of their son, Horus). Many twentieth-century poets were drawn to the heritage of archetypes and myths. Adrienne Rich's "Diving into the Wreck," for example, self-consciously rewrites a number of gendered archetypes, with a female protagonist on a quest into a submerged world. Most critics today, influenced by poststructuralism, have become wary of universal patterns. Like structuralists, Jungians and archetypal critics strive to compare and unite the ages and peoples of the world and to reveal fundamental truths. Rich, as a feminist poet, suggests that the "book of myths" is an eclectic anthology that needs to be revised. Claims of universality tend to obscure the detailed differences between cultures and often appeal to some idea of *biological determinism.* Such determinism diminishes the power of individuals to design alternative life patterns and even implies that no literature can really surprise us.

LACANIAN CRITICISM

As it has absorbed the indeterminacies of poststructuralism under the influence of thinkers such as Jacques Lacan and Julia Kristeva, psychological criticism has become increasingly complex. Few critics today are direct Freudian analysts of authors or texts, and few maintain that universal archetypes explain the meaning of a tree or water in a text. Yet psychoanalytic theory continues to inform many varieties of criticism, and most new work in this field is affiliated with Lacanian psychoanalysis. Lacan's theory unites poststructuralist linguistics with Freudian theory. The Lacanian critic, like a deconstructionist, focuses on the text that defies conscious authorial control, foregrounding the powerful interpretation of the critic rather than the author or any other reader. Accepting the Oedipal paradigm and the unconscious as the realm of repressed desire, Lacanian theory aligns the development and structure of the individual human *subject* with the development and structure of language. To simplify a purposefully dense theory: The very young infant inhabits the Imaginary, in a preverbal, undifferentiated phase dominated by a sense of union with Mother. Recognition of identity begins with the Mirror Stage, ironically with a disruption of a sense of oneness. For when one first looks into a mirror, one begins to recognize a split or difference between one's body and the image in the mirror. This splitting prefigures a sense that the *object* of desire is Other and distinct from the subject. With difference or the splitting of subject and object comes language and entry into the Symbolic Order, since we use words to summon the absent object of desire (as a child would cry "Mama" to bring her back). But what language signifies most is the lack of that object. The imaginary, perfectly nurturing Mother would never need to be called.

As in the biblical Genesis, the Lacanian "genesis" of the subject tells of a loss of paradise through knowledge of the difference between subject and object or Man and Woman (eating of the Tree of the Knowledge of Good and Evil leads to the sense of shame that teaches Adam and Eve to hide their nakedness). In Lacanian theory the Father governs language or the Symbolic Order; the Word spells the end of a child's sense of oneness with the Mother. Further, the Father's power claims omnipotence, the possession of male prerogative symbolized by the Phallus, which is not the anatomical difference between men and women but the idea or construction of that difference. Thus it is language or culture rather than nature that generates the difference and inequality between the sexes. Some feminist theorists have adopted aspects of Lacanian psychoanalytic theory, particularly the concept of *the gaze.* This concept notes that the masculine subject is the one who looks, whereas the feminine object is to be looked at.

Another influential concept is *abjection.* Julia Kristeva's theory of abjection most simply reimagines the infant's blissful sense of union with the mother and the darker side of such possible union. To return to the mother's body would be death, as metaphorically we are buried in Mother Earth. Yet according to the theory, people both desire and dread such loss of boundaries. A sense of self or *subjectivity* and hence of independence and power depends on resisting abjection. The association of the maternal body with abjection or with the powerlessness symbolized by the female's Lack of the Phallus can help explain negative cultural images of women. Many narrative genres seem to split the images of women between an angelic and a witchlike type. Lacanian or Kristevan theory has been well adapted to film and to the fantasy and other popular forms favored by structuralism or archetypal criticism.

EMPHASIS ON THE RECEIVER

In some sense critical schools develop in reaction to the excesses of other critical schools. By the 1970s, in a time of political upheaval that placed a value on individual expression, a number of critics felt that the various routes toward objective criticism had proven dead ends. New Critics, structuralists, and psychoanalytic or myth critics had sought objective, scientific systems that disregarded changing times, political issues, or the reader's personal response. New Critics and other formalists tended to value a literary canon made up of works that were regarded as complete, unchanging objects to be comprehended as if spatially in a photograph according to timeless standards.

Reader-Response Criticism

Among critics who challenged New Critical assumptions, the reader-response critics regarded the work not as what is printed on the page but as what is experienced temporally through each act of reading. In effect the reader performs the poem into existence the way a musician performs a score. Reader-response critics ask not what a work means but what a work does or, rather, what it makes a reader do. Literary texts especially leave gaps that experienced readers fill according to expectations or conventions. Individual readers differ, of course, and gaps in a text provide space for different readings or interpretations. Some of these lacunae are temporary—such as the withholding of the murderer's name until the end of a mystery novel—and are closed by the text sooner or later, though each reader will in the meantime fill them differently. But other lacunae are permanent and can never be filled with certainty; they result in a degree of uncertainty or indeterminacy in the text.

The reader-response critic observes the expectations aroused by a text, how they are satisfied or modified, and how the reader projects a comprehension of the work when all of it has been read, and when it is reread in whole or in part. Such criticism attends to the reading habits associated with different genres and to the shared assumptions of a cultural context that seem to furnish what is left unsaid in the text.

Beyond theoretical formulations about reading, there are other approaches to literary study that concern the receiver rather than the text or source. A critic might examine specific documents of a work's reception, from contemporary reviews to critical essays written across the generations since the work was first published. Sometimes we have available diaries or autobiographical evidence about readers' encounters with particular works. Just as there are histories of publishing and of the book, there are histories of literacy and reading practices. Poetry, fiction, and drama often directly represent the theme of reading as well as writing. Many published works over the centuries have debated the benefits and perils of reading works such as sermons or novels. Different genres and particular works construct different classes or kinds of readers in the way they address them or supply what they are supposed to want. Some scholars have found quantitative measures for reading, from sales and library lending rates to questionnaires.

Finally, the role of the reader or receiver in literary exchange has been portrayed from a political perspective. Literature helps shape social identity, and social status shapes access to different kinds of literature. Feminist critics adapted reader-response criticism, for example, to note that girls often do not identify with many American literary classics as boys do, and thus girls do not simply accept the idea of women as angels, temptresses, or scolds who should be abandoned for the sake of all-male adventures. Studies of African American literature and other ethnic literatures have often featured discussion of literacy and of the obstacles for readers who cannot find their counterparts within the texts or who encounter negative stereotypes of their group. Thus, as we will discuss below, most forms of historical and ideological criticism include some consideration of the reader.

HISTORICAL AND IDEOLOGICAL CRITICISM

Approaches to the text, the author, and the reader, outlined above, each may take some note of historical contexts, including changes in formal conventions, the writer's milieu, or audience expectations. In the nineteenth century, historical criticism took the obvious facts that a work is created in a specific historical and cultural context and that the author is a part of that context as reasons to treat literature as a reflection of society. Twentieth-century formalists rejected the *reflectivist* model of art in the old historical criticism, that is, the assumption that literature and other arts straightforwardly express the collective spirit of the society at that time. But as we have remarked, formalist rules for isolating the work of art from social and historical context met resistance in the last decades of the twentieth century. In a revival of historical approaches, critics have replaced the reflectivist model with a *constructivist* model, whereby literature and other cultural discourses help construct social relations and roles rather than merely reflecting them. In other words, art is not just the frosting on the cake but an integral part of the recipe's ingredients and instructions. A society's ideology, its inherent system of representations (ideas, myths, images), is inscribed in and by literature and other cultural forms, which in turn help shape identities and social practices.

Since the 1980s historical approaches have regained great influence in literary studies. Some critical schools have been insistently *materialist,* that is, seeking causes more in concrete conditions such as technology, production, and distribution of wealth, or the exploitation of markets and labor in and beyond Western countries. Such criticism usually owes an acknowledged debt to Marxism. Other historical approaches have been influenced to a degree by Marxist critics and cultural theorists, but work within the realm of ideology, textual production, and interpretation, using some of the methods and concerns of traditional literary history. Still others emerge from the civil rights movement and the struggles for recognition of women and racial, ethnic, and sexual constituencies.

Feminist studies, African American studies, gay and lesbian studies, and studies of the cultures of different immigrant and ethnic populations within the United States have each developed along similar theoretical lines. These schools, like Marxist criticism, adopt a constructivist position; literature is not simply a reflection of prejudices and norms, but helps define as well as reshape social identities, such as what it means to be an African American woman. Each of these schools has moved through stages of first claiming *equality* with the literature dominated by white Anglo American men, then affirming the *difference* of their own separate culture, and then theoretically *questioning the terms and standards* of such comparisons. At a certain point in the thought process, each group rejects *essentialism*, the notion of innate or biological bases for the differences between the sexes, races, or other groups. This rejection of essentialism is usually called the constructivist position, in a somewhat different but related sense to our definition above. Constructivism maintains that identity is socially formed rather than biologically determined. Differences of anatomical sex, skin color, first language, parental ethnicity, and eventual sexual practices have great impact on how one is classified, brought up, and treated socially, and on one's subjectivity or conception of identity. These differences are, however, more constructed by ideology and the resulting behaviors than by any natural programming.

Marxist Criticism

The most insistent and vigorous historical approach through the twentieth century to the present has been Marxism, based on the work of Karl Marx (1818–1883). With roots in nineteenth-century historicism, Marxist criticism was initially reflectivist. Economics, the underlying cause of history, was thus the *base,* and culture, including literature and the other arts, was the *superstructure,* an outcome or reflection of the base. Viewed from the Marxist perspective, the literary works of a period were economically determined; they would *reflect* the state of the struggle between classes in any place and time. History enacted recurrent three-step cycles, a pattern that Hegel had defined as *dialectic* (Hegel was cited above on the interdependence of master and slave). Each socioeconomic phase, or *thesis,* is counteracted by its *antithesis,* and the resulting conflict yields a *synthesis,* which becomes the ensuing *thesis,* and so on. As with early Freudian criticism, early Marxist criticism was often overly concerned with labeling and exposing illusions or deceptions. A novel might be read as thinly disguised defense of the power of bourgeois industrial capital; its appeal on behalf of the suffering poor might be dismissed as an effort to fend off a class rebellion.

As a rationale for state control of the arts, Marxism was abused in the Soviet Union and in other totalitarian states. In the hands of sophisticated critics, however, Marxism has been richly rewarding. Various schools that unite formal close reading and political analysis developed in the early twentieth century under Soviet communism and under fascism in Europe, often in covert resistance. These schools in turn have influenced critical movements in North American universities through translations or through members who came to the United States; New Criticism, structuralist linguistics, deconstruction, and narrative theory have each borrowed from European Marxist critics.

Most recently, a new mode of Marxist theory has developed, largely guided by the thinking of Walter Benjamin (1892–1940) and Theodor Adorno (1903–1969) of the Frankfurt School in Germany, Louis Althusser (1918–1990) in France, and Raymond Williams (1921–1998) in Britain. This work has generally tended to modify the base/superstructure distinction and to interrelate public and private life, economics and culture. Newer Marxist interpretation assumes that the relation of a literary work to its historical context is *overdetermined*—the relation has multiple determining factors rather than a sole cause or aim. This thinking similarly acknowledges that neither the source nor the receiver of the literary interaction is a mere tool or victim of the ruling powers or state. Representation of all kinds, including literature, always has a political dimension, according to this approach; conversely, political and material conditions such as work, money, or institutions depend on representation.

Showing some influence of psychoanalytic and poststructuralist theories, recent Marxist literary studies examine the effects of ideology by focusing on the works' gaps and silences: ideology may be conveyed in what is repressed or contradicted. In many ways Marxist criticism has adapted to the conditions of consumer rather than industrial capitalism and to global rather than national economies. The revolution that was to come when the proletariat or working classes overthrew the capitalists has never taken place; in many countries industrial labor has been swallowed up by the service sector, and workers reject the political Left that would seem their most likely ally. Increasingly, Marxist criticism has acknowledged that the audience of literature may be active rather than passive, just as the text and source may be more than straightforward instructions for toeing the political line. Marxist criticism has been especially successful with the novel, since that genre more than drama or short fiction is capable of representing numerous people from different classes as they develop over a significant amount of time.

Feminist Criticism

Like Marxist criticism and the schools discussed below, feminist criticism derives from a critique of a history of oppression, in this case the history of women's inequality. Feminist criticism has no single founder like Freud or Marx; it has been practiced to some extent since the 1790s, when praise of women's cultural achievements went hand in hand with arguments that women were rational beings deserving equal rights and education. Contemporary feminist criticism emerged from a "second wave" of feminist activism, in the 1960s and 1970s, associated with the civil rights and antiwar movements. One of the first disciplines in which women's activism took root was literary criticism, but feminist theory and women's studies quickly became recognized methods across the disciplines.

Feminist literary studies began by denouncing the misrepresentation of women in literature and affirming women's writings, before quickly adopting the insights of poststructuralist theory; yet the early strategies continue to have their use. At first, feminist criticism in the 1970s, like early Marxist criticism, regarded literature as a reflection of patriarchal society's sexist base; the demeaning images of women in literature were symptoms of a system that had to be overthrown. Feminist literary studies soon began, however, to claim the *equal* worth if distinctive themes of writings by women and men. Critics such as Elaine Showalter (b. 1941), Sandra M. Gilbert (b. 1936), and Susan Gubar (b. 1944) featured the canonical works by women, relying on close reading with some aid from historical and psychoanalytic methods. Yet by the 1980s it was widely recognized that a New Critical method would leave most of the male-dominated canon intact and most women writers still in obscurity, because many women had written in different genres and styles, on different themes, and for different audiences than had male writers.

To affirm the *difference* of female literary traditions, some feminist studies claimed women's innate or universal affinity for fluidity and cycle rather than solidity and linear progress. Others concentrated on the role of the mother in human psychological development. According to this argument, girls, not having to adopt a gender role different from that of their first object of desire, the mother, grow up with less rigid boundaries of self and a relational rather than judgmental ethic. The dangers of these intriguing generalizations soon became apparent. If the reasons for women's differences from men were biologically based or were due to universal archetypes, there was no solution to women's oppression, which many cultures worldwide had justified in terms of biological reproduction or archetypes of nature.

At this point in the debate, feminist literary studies intersected with poststructuralist linguistic theory in *questioning the terms and standards* of comparison. French feminist theory, articulated most prominently by Hélène Cixous (b. 1935) and Luce Irigaray (b. 1932), deconstructed the supposed archetypes of gender written into the founding discourses of Western culture. We have seen that deconstruction helps expose the power imbalance in every dualism. Thus man is to woman as culture is to nature or mind is to body, and in each case the second term is held to be inferior or Other. The language and hence the worldview and social formations of our culture, not nature or eternal archetypes, constructed woman as Other. This insight was helpful in avoiding essentialism or biological determinism.

Having reached a theoretical criticism of the terms on which women might claim equality or difference from men in the field of literature, feminist studies also confronted other issues in the 1980s. Deconstructionist readings of gender difference in texts by men as well as women could lose sight of the real world, in which women are paid less and are more likely to be victims of sexual violence. Some feminist critics with this in mind pursued links with Marxist or African American studies; gender roles, like those of class and race, were interdependent systems for registering the material consequences of people's differences. It no longer seemed so easy to say what the term "women" referred to, when the interests of different kinds of women had been opposed to each other. African American women asked if feminism was really their cause, when white women had so long enjoyed power over both men and women of their race. In a classic Marxist view, women allied with men of their class rather than with women of other classes. It became more difficult to make universal claims about women's literature, as the horizon of the college-educated North American feminists expanded to recognize the range of conditions of women and literature worldwide. Feminist literary studies have continued to consider famous and obscure women writers; the way women and gender are portrayed in writings by men as well as women; feminist issues concerning the text, source, or receiver in any national literature; theoretical and historical questions about the representation of differences such as gender, race, class, and nationality, and the way these differences shape each other.

Gender Studies and Queer Theory

From the 1970s, feminists sought recognition for lesbian writers and lesbian culture, which they felt had been even less visible than male homosexual writers and gay culture. Concurrently, feminist studies abandoned the simple dualism of male/female, part of the very binary logic of patriarchy that seemed to cause the oppression of women. Thus feminists recognized a zone of inquiry, the study of gender, as distinct from historical studies of women, and increasingly they included masculinity as a subject of investigation. As gender studies turned to interpretation of the text in ideological context regardless of the sex or intention of the author, it incorporated the ideas of Michel Foucault's *History of Sexuality* (1976). Foucault helped show that there was nothing natural, universal, or timeless in the constructions of sexual difference or sexual practices. Foucault also introduced a history of the concept of homosexuality, which had once been regarded in terms of taboo acts and in the later nineteenth century became defined as a disease associated with a personality type. Literary scholars began to study the history of sexuality as a key to the shifts in modern culture that had also shaped literature.

In the 1980s, gender had come to be widely regarded as a discourse that imposed binary social norms on human beings' diversity. Theorists such as Donna Haraway (b. 1944) and Judith Butler (b. 1956) insisted further that sex and sexuality have no natural basis; even the anatomical differences are representations from the moment the newborn is put in a pink or blue blanket. Moreover, these theorists claimed that gender and sexuality are *performative* and malleable positions, enacted in many more than two varieties. From cross-dressing to surgical sex changes, the alternatives chosen by real people have collaborated with the critical theories and generated both writings and literary criticism about those writings. Perhaps biographical and feminist studies face new challenges when identity seems subject to radical change and it is less easy to determine the sex of an author.

Gay and lesbian literary studies have included practices that parallel feminist criticism. At times critics identify oppressive or positive representations of homosexuality in works by men or women, gay, lesbian, or straight. At other times critics seek to establish the equivalent stature of a work by a gay or lesbian writer or, because these identities tended to be hidden in the past, to reveal that a writer *was* gay or lesbian. Again stages of *equality* and *difference* have yielded to a *questioning of the terms of difference*, in this case what has been called queer theory (the stages have not superseded each other). The field of queer theory hopes to leave everyone guessing rather than to identify gay or lesbian writers, characters, or themes. One of its founding texts, *Between Men* (1985), by Eve Kosofsky Sedgwick (b. 1950), drew upon structuralist insight into desire as well as anthropological models of kinship to show that, in canonical works of English literature, male characters bond together through their rivalry for and exchange of a woman. Queer theory, because it rejects the idea of a fixed identity or innate or essential gender, likes to discover resistance to heterosexuality in unexpected places. Queer theorists value gay writers such as Oscar Wilde, but they also find queer implications regardless of the author's acknowledged identity. This approach emphasizes not the surface signals of the text but what the audience or receiver might detect. It encompasses elaborate close reading of varieties of work; characteristically, a leading queer theorist, D. A. Miller (b. 1948), has written in loving detail about Jane Austen and about Broadway musicals.

African American and Ethnic Literary Studies

Critics sought to define an African American literary tradition as early as the turn of the twentieth century. A period of literary success in the 1920s, known as the Harlem Renaissance, produced some of the first classic essays on writings by African Americans. Criticism and histories of African American literature tended to ignore and dismiss women writers, while feminist literary histories, guided by the Virginia Woolf's classic *A Room of One's Own* (1929), neglected women writers of color. Only after feminist critics began to succeed in the academy and African American studies programs were established did the whiteness of feminist studies and masculinity of African American studies became glaring; both fields have for some time corrected this problem of vision. The study of African American literature followed the general pattern that we have noted, first striving to claim equality, on established aesthetic grounds, of works such as Ralph Ellison's magnificent *Invisible Man* (1952). Then in the 1960s the Black Arts or Black Aesthetic emerged. Once launched in the academy, however, African American studies has been devoted less to celebrating an essential racial difference than to tracing the historical construction of a racial Other and a subordinated literature. The field sought to recover genres in which African Americans have written, such as slave narratives, and traced common elements in fiction or poetry to the conditions of slavery and segregation. By the 1980s feminist and poststructuralist theory had an impact in the work of some African American critics such as Henry Louis Gates Jr. (b. 1950), Houston A. Baker Jr. (b. 1943), Hazel V. Carby (b. 1948), and Deborah E. McDowell (b. 1951), while others objected that the doubts raised by "theory" stood in the way of political commitment. African Americans' cultural contributions to America have gained much more recognition than before. New histories of American culture have been written with the view that racism is not an aberration but inherent to the guiding narratives of national progress. Many critics now regard race as a discourse with only slight basis in genetics but with weighty investments in ideology. This poststructuralist position coexists with scholarship that takes into account the race of the author or reader or that focuses on African American characters or themes.

In recent years a series of fields has arisen in recognition of the literatures of other American ethnic groups, large and small: Asian Americans, Native Americans, and Chicano/as. Increasingly, such studies avoid romanticizing an original, pure culture or assuming that these literatures by their very nature undermine the values and power of the dominant culture. Instead, critics emphasize the *hybridity* of all cultures in a global economy. The contact and intermixture of cultures across geographical borders and languages (translations, the "creole" speech made up of native and acquired languages, dialects) may be read as enriching themes for literature and art, albeit they are caused by economic exploitation. In method and in aim these fields have much in common with African American studies, though each cultural and historical context is very different. Each field deserves the separate study that we cannot offer here.

New Historicism

Three interrelated schools of historical and ideological criticism have been important innovations in the past two decades. These are part of the swing of the pendulum away from formal analysis of the text and toward historical analysis of context. New historicism has less obvious political commitments than Marxism, feminism, or queer theory, but it shares their interest in the power of discourse to shape ideology. Old historicism, in the 1850s–1950s, confidently told a story of civilization's progress from the point of view of a Western nation; a historicist critic would offer a close reading of the plays of Shakespeare and then locate them within the prevailing Elizabethan "worldview." "New Historicism," labeled in 1982 by Stephen Greenblatt (b. 1943), rejected the technique of plugging samples of a culture into a history of ideas. Influenced by poststructuralist anthropology, New Historicism tried to take a multilayered impression or "thick description" of a culture at one moment in time, including popular as well as elite forms of representation. As a method, New Historicism belongs with those that deny the unity of the text, defy the authority of the source, and license the receiver—much like deconstructionism. Accordingly, New Historicism doubts the accessibility of the past; all we have is discourse. One model for New Historicism was the historiography of Michel Foucault, who as we have said insisted on the power of discourses, that is, not only writing but all structuring myths or ideologies that underlie social relations. The New Historicist, like Foucault, is interested in the transition from the external powers of the state and church in the feudal order to modern forms of power. The rule of the modern state and middle-class ideology is enforced insidiously by systems of surveillance and by each individual's internalization of discipline (not unlike Freud's idea of the superego).

No longer so "new," the New Historicists have had a lasting influence on a more narrative and concrete style of criticism even among those who espouse post-structuralist and Marxist theories. A New Historicist article begins with an anecdote, often a description of a public spectacle, and teases out the many contributing causes that brought disparate social elements together in that way. It usually applies techniques of close reading to forms that would not traditionally have received such attention. Although it often concentrates on events several hundred years ago, in some ways it defies historicity, flouting the idea that a complete objective impression of the entire context could ever be achieved.

Cultural Studies

Popular culture often gets major attention in the work of New Historicists. Yet today most studies of popular culture would acknowledge their debt instead to cultural studies, as filtered through the now-defunct Center for Contemporary Cultural Studies, founded in 1964 by Stuart Hall (b. 1932) and others at the University of Birmingham in England. Method, style, and subject matter may be similar in New Historicism and cultural studies: both attend to historical context, theoretical method, political commitment, and textual analysis. But whereas the American movement shares Foucault's paranoid view of state domination through discourse, the British school, influenced by Raymond Williams and his concept of "structures of feeling," emphasizes the possibility that ordinary people, the receivers of cultural forms, may resist dominant ideology. The documents examined in a cultural-studies essay may be recent, such as artifacts of tourism at Shakespeare's birthplace rather than sixteenth-century maps. Cultural studies today influences history, sociology, communications and media, and literature departments; its studies may focus on television, film, romance novels, advertising, or on museums and the art market, sports and stadiums, New Age religious groups, or other forms and practices.

The questions raised by cultural studies would encourage a critic to place a poem like Marge Piercy's "Barbie Doll" in the context of the history of that toy, a doll whose slender, impossibly long legs, tiptoe feet (not unlike the bound feet of Chinese women of an earlier era), small nose, and torpedo breasts enforced a 1950s ideal for the female body. A critic influenced by cultural studies might align the poem with other works published around 1973 that express feminist protest concerning cosmetics, body image, consumption, and the objectification of women, while she or he would draw on research into the founding and marketing of Mattel toys. The poem reverses the Sleeping Beauty story: this heroine puts herself into the coffin rather than waking up. The poem omits any hero—Ken?—who would rescue her. "Barbie Doll" protests the pressure a girl feels to fit into a heterosexual plot of romance and marriage; no one will buy her if she is not the right toy or accessory.

Indeed, accessories such as "GE stoves and irons" (line 3) taught girls to plan their lives as domestic consumers, and Barbie's lifestyle is decidedly middle-class and suburban (everyone has a house, car, pool, and lots of handbags). The whiteness of the typical "girlchild" (line 1) goes without saying. Although Mattel produced Barbie's African American friend, Christie, in 1968, Piercy's title makes the reader imagine Barbie, not Christie. In 1997 Mattel issued Share a Smile Becky, a friend in a wheelchair, as though in answer to the humiliation of the girl in Piercy's poem, who feels so deformed, in spite of her "strong arms and back, / abundant sexual drive and manual dexterity" (lines 8–9), that she finally cripples herself. The icon, in short, responds to changing ideology. Perhaps responding to generations of objections like Piercy's, Barbies over the years have had feminist career goals, yet women's lives are still plotted according to physical image.

In this manner a popular product might be "read" alongside a literary work. The approach would be influenced by Marxist, feminist, gender, and racial studies, but it would not be driven by a desire to destroy Barbie as sinister, misogynist propaganda. Piercy's kind of protest against indoctrination has gone out of style. Girls have found ways to respond to such messages and divert them into stories of empowerment. Such at least is the outlook of cultural studies, which usually affirms popular culture. A researcher could gather data on Barbie sales and could interview girls or videotape their play, to establish the actual effects of the dolls. Whereas traditional anthropology examined non-European or preindustrial cultures, cultural studies may direct its "field work," or ethnographic research, inward, at home. Nevertheless, many contributions to cultural studies rely on methods of textual close reading or Marxist and Freudian literary criticism developed in the mid-twentieth century.

Postcolonial Criticism and Studies of World Literature

A Web site on the invention of the Barbie doll says that Barbies are sold in over 150 countries around the world and that "more than one billion Barbie dolls (and family members) have been sold since 1959, and placed head-to-toe, the dolls would circle the earth more than seven times" <http://www.ideafinder.com/ history/inventions/story081.htm>. Such a global reach for an American toy begins to seem less like play and more like imperial domination. In the middle of the twentieth century, meanwhile, the remaining colonies of the European nations struggled toward independence. French-speaking Frantz Fanon (1925–1961) of Martinique was one of the most compelling voices for the point of view of the colonized or exploited countries, which like the feminine Other had been objectified and denied the right to look and talk back. Edward Said (1935–2003), in *Orientalism* (1978), brought a poststructuralist analysis to bear on the history of colonization, illustrating the ways that Western culture feminized and objectified the East. Postcolonial literary studies developed into a distinct field in the 1990s in light of globalization and the replacement of direct colonial power with international corporations. In general this field cannot share the optimism of some cultural studies, given the histories of slavery and economic exploitation of colonies and the violence committed in the name of civilization's progress. Studies by Gayatri Chakravorty Spivak (b. 1942) and Homi K. Bhabha (b. 1949) have further mingled Marxist, feminist, and poststructuralist theory to reread both canonical

Western works and the writings of people from beyond centers of dominant culture. Colonial or postcolonial literatures may include works set or published in countries during colonial rule or after independence, or they may feature texts produced in the context of international cultural exchange, such as a novel in English by a woman of Chinese descent writing in Malaysia.

Like feminist studies and studies of African American or other literatures, the field is inspired by recovery of neglected works, redress of a systematic denial of rights and recognition, and increasing realization that the dualisms of opposing groups reveal interdependence. In this field the stage of difference came early, with the celebrations of African heritage known as *Négritude*, but the danger of that essentialist claim was soon apparent: the Dark Continent or wild island might be romanticized and idealized as a source of innate qualities of vitality long repressed in Enlightened Europe. Currently, most critics accept that the context for literature in all countries is hybrid, with immigration and educational intermixing. Close readings of texts are always linked to the author's biography and literary influences and placed within the context of contemporary international politics as well as colonial history. Many fiction writers, from Salman Rushdie to Jhumpa Lahiri, make the theme of cultural mixture or hybridity part of their work, whether in a pastiche of Charles Dickens or a story of an Indian family growing up in New Jersey and returning as tourists to the supposed "native" land. Poststructuralist theories of trauma, and theories of the interrelation of narrative and memory, provide explanatory frames for interpreting writings from Afghanistan to the former Zaire.

Studies of postcolonial culture retain a clear political mission that feminist and Marxist criticism have found difficult to sustain. Perhaps this is because the scale of the power relations is so vast, between nations rather than the sexes or classes within those nations. Imperialism can be called an absolute evil, and the destruction of local cultures a crime against humanity. Today some of the most exciting literature in English emerges from countries once under the British Empire, and all the techniques of criticism will be brought to bear on it. If history is any guide, in later decades some critical school will attempt to read the diverse literatures of the early twenty-first century in pure isolation from authorship and national origin, as self-enclosed form. The themes of hybridity, indeterminacy, trauma, and memory will be praised as universal. It is even possible that readers' continuing desire to revere authors as creative geniuses in control of their meanings will regain respectability among specialists. For the elements of the literary exchange—text, source, and receiver—are always there to provoke questions that generate criticism, which in turn produces articulations of the methods of that criticism. It is an ongoing discussion worth participating in.

BIBLIOGRAPHY

For good introductions to the issues discussed here, see the following books, from which we have drawn in our discussion and definitions. Some of these provide bibliographies of the works of critics and schools mentioned above.

Alter, Robert. *The Pleasure of Reading in an Ideological Age.* New York: Norton, 1996. Rpt. of *The Pleasures of Reading: Thinking about Literature in an Ideological Age.* 1989.

Barnet, Sylvan, and William E. Cain. *A Short Guide to Writing about Literature.* 10th ed. New York: Longman, 2005.

Barry, Peter. *Beginning Theory: An Introduction to Literary and Cultural Theory*. 2nd ed. Manchester: Manchester UP, 2002.

Bressler, Charles E. *Literary Criticism: An Introduction to Theory and Practice*. 3rd ed. Upper Saddle River: Prentice, 2003.

Culler, Jonathan. *Literary Theory: A Very Short Introduction*. Oxford: Oxford UP, 1997.

Davis, Robert Con, and Ronald Schleifer. *Contemporary Literary Criticism: Literary and Cultural Studies*. 4th ed. New York: Addison, 1999.

During, Simon. *Cultural Studies: A Critical Introduction*. New York: Routledge, 2005.

———. *The Cultural Studies Reader*. New York: Routledge, 1999.

Eagleton, Mary, ed. *Feminist Literary Theory: A Reader*. 2nd ed. Malden: Blackwell, 1996.

Eagleton, Terry. *Literary Theory: An Introduction*. 2nd rev. ed. Minneapolis: U of Minnesota P, 1996.

Groden, Michael, and Martin Kreiswirth. *The Johns Hopkins Guide to Literary Theory and Criticism*. Baltimore: Johns Hopkins UP, 1994.

Hawthorn, Jeremy. *A Glossary of Contemporary Literary Theory*. 3rd ed. London: Arnold, 1998.

Leitch, Vincent B. *American Literary Criticism from the Thirties to the Eighties*. New York: Columbia UP, 1989.

———, et al. *The Norton Anthology of Theory and Criticism*. New York: Norton, 2001.

Lentricchia, Frank. *After the New Criticism*. Chicago: U of Chicago P, 1981.

Macksey, Richard, and Eugenio Donato, eds. *The Structuralist Controversy: The Languages of Criticism and the Sciences of Man*. 1972. Ann Arbor: Books on Demand, n.d.

Moi, Toril. *Sexual-Textual Politics*. New York: Routledge, 1985.

Murfin, Ross, and Supryia M. Ray. *The Bedford Glossary of Critical and Literary Terms*. Boston: Bedford, 1997.

Piaget, Jean. *Structuralism*. Trans. and ed. Chaninah Maschler. New York: Basic, 1970.

Selden, Raman, and Peter Widdowson. *A Reader's Guide to Contemporary Literary Theory*. 3rd ed. Lexington: U of Kentucky P, 1993.

Todorov, Tzvetan. *Mikhail Bakhtin: The Dialogic Principle*. Trans. Wlad Godzich. Minneapolis: U of Minnesota P, 1984.

Turco, Lewis. *The Book of Literary Terms*. Hanover: UP of New England, 1999.

Veeser, Harold, ed. *The New Historicism*. New York: Routledge, 1989.

———. *The New Historicism Reader*. New York: Routledge, 1994.

Warhol, Robyn R., and Diane Price Herndl. *Feminisms*. 2nd ed. New Brunswick: Rutgers UP, 1997.

Wolfreys, Julian. *Literary Theories: A Reader and Guide*. Edinburgh: Edinburgh UP, 1999.

Glossary

Boldface words within definitions are themselves defined in the glossary.

allegory as in **metaphor**, one thing (usually nonrational, abstract, religious) is implicitly spoken of in terms of something concrete, but in an allegory the comparison is extended to include an entire work or large portion of a work.

alliteration the repetition of initial consonant sounds through a sequence of words—for example, "While I *n*odded, *n*early *n*apping" in Edgar Allan Poe's "The Raven."

allusion a reference—whether explicit or implicit, to history, the Bible, myth, literature, painting, music, and so on—that suggests the meaning or generalized implication of details in the story, poem, or play.

ambiguity the use of a word or expression to mean more than one thing.

analogy a comparison based on certain resemblances between things that are otherwise unlike.

anapestic a metrical form in which each foot consists of two unstressed syllables followed by a stressed one.

archetype a **plot** or **character** element that recurs in cultural or cross-cultural **myths**, such as "the quest" or "descent into the underworld" or "scapegoat."

assonance the repetition of vowel sounds in a sequence of words with different endings—for example, "The de*a*th of the po*e*t was k*e*pt from his po*e*ms" in W. H. Auden's "In Memory of W. B. Yeats."

aubade a morning song in which the coming of dawn is either celebrated or denounced as a nuisance.

auditor someone other than the reader—a **character** within the fiction—to whom the story or "speech" is addressed.

ballad a narrative poem that is, or originally was, meant to be sung. Characterized by repetition and often by a repeated refrain (recurrent phrase or series of phrases), ballads were originally a folk creation, transmitted orally from person to person and age to age.

ballad stanza a common **stanza** form, consisting of a quatrain that alternates four-beat and three-beat lines; lines 1 and 3 are unrhymed iambic tetrameter (four beats), and lines 2 and 4 are rhymed iambic trimeter (three beats).

blank verse the verse form most like everyday human speech; blank verse consists of unrhymed lines in **iambic pentameter**. Many of Shakespeare's plays are in blank verse.

caesura a short pause within a line of poetry; often but not always signaled by punctuation. Note the two caesuras in this line from Poe's "The Raven": "Once upon a midnight dreary, while I pondered, weak and weary."

canon when applied to an individual author, *canon* (like **oeuvre**) means the sum total of works written by that author. When used generally, it means the range of works that a consensus of scholars, teachers, and readers of a particular time and culture consider "great" or "major." This second sense of the word is a matter of debate since the literary canon in Europe and America has long been dominated by the works of white men. During the last several decades, the canon in the United States has expanded considerably to include more works by women and writers from various ethnic and racial backgrounds.

concrete poetry poetry shaped to look like an object. Robert Herrick's "Pillar of Fame," for example, is arranged to look like a pillar. Also called **shaped verse**.

confessional poem a relatively recent (or recently defined) **kind** in which the speaker describes a state of mind, which becomes a **metaphor** for the larger world.

connotation what is suggested by a word, apart from what it explicitly describes. *See* **denotation**.

controlling metaphors metaphors that dominate or organize an entire poem. In Linda Pastan's "Marks," for example, the controlling metaphor is of marks (grades) as a way of talking about the speaker's performance of roles within her family.

conventions standard or traditional ways of saying things in literary works, employed to achieve certain expected effects.

criticism *See* **literary criticism**.

culture a broad and relatively indistinct term that implies a commonality of history and some cohesiveness of purpose within a group. One can speak of southern culture, for example, or urban culture, or American culture, or rock culture; at any one time, each of us belongs to a number of these cultures.

dactylic the metrical pattern in which each foot consists of a stressed syllable followed by two unstressed ones.

denotation a direct and specific meaning. *See* **connotation**.

descriptive structure a textual organization determined by the requirements of describing someone or something.

discursive structure a textual organization based on the form of a treatise, argument, or essay.

dramatic irony a plot device in which a **character** holds a position or has an expectation that is reversed or fulfilled in a way that the character did not expect but that we, as readers or as audience members, have anticipated because our knowledge of events or individuals is more complete than the character's.

dramatic monologue a monologue set in a specific situation and spoken to an imaginary audience.

dramatic structure a textual organization based on a series of scenes, each of which is presented vividly and in detail.

echo a verbal reference that recalls a word, phrase, or sound in another text.

elegy in classical times, any poem on any subject written in "elegiac" **meter**; since the Renaissance, usually a formal lament on the death of a particular person.

English sonnet *see* **Shakespearean sonnet**.

enjambment running over from one line of poetry to the next without stop, as in the following lines by Wordsworth: "My heart leaps up when I behold / A rainbow in the sky."

epic a poem that celebrates, in a continuous narrative, the achievements of mighty **heroes** and **heroines**, usually in founding a nation or developing a **culture**, and uses elevated language and a grand, high style.

epigram originally any poem carved in stone (on tombstones, buildings, gates, and so forth), but in modern usage a very short, usually witty verse with a quick turn at the end.

extended metaphor a detailed and complex **metaphor** that stretches through a long section of a work.

figurative usually applied to language that uses **figures of speech**. Figurative language heightens meaning by implicitly or explicitly representing something in terms of some other thing, the assumption being that the "other thing" will be more familiar to the reader.

figures of speech comparisons in which something is pictured or figured in other, more familiar terms.

free verse poetry characterized by varying line lengths, lack of traditional **meter**, and nonrhyming lines.

genre the largest category for classifying literature—fiction, poetry, drama. *See* **kind** and **subgenre**.

haiku an unrhymed poetic form, Japanese in origin, that contains seventeen syllables arranged in three lines of five, seven, and five syllables, respectively.

heroic couplet rhymed pairs of lines in **iambic pentameter**.

hexameter a line of poetry with six feet: "She comes, | she comes | again, | like ring | dove frayed | and fled" (Keats, *The Eve of St. Agnes*).

iamb a metrical foot consisting of an unstressed syllable followed by a stressed one.

iambic pentameter a metrical form in which the basic foot is an **iamb** and most lines consist of five iambs; iambic pentameter in English: "One com | mon note | on ei | ther lyre | did strike" (Dryden, "To the Memory of Mr. Oldham")

imagery broadly defined, any sensory detail or evocation in a work; more narrowly, the use of **figurative** language to evoke a feeling, to call to mind an idea, or to describe an object.

imitative structure a textual organization that mirrors as exactly as possible the structure of something that already exists as an object and can be seen.

Italian sonnet *see* **Petrarchan sonnet**.

limerick a light or humorous verse form of mainly **anapestic** verses of which the first, second, and fifth lines are of three feet; the third and fourth lines are of two feet; and the rhyme scheme is *aabba*.

literary criticism the evaluative or interpretive work written by professional interpreters of texts. It is "criticism" not because it is negative or corrective, but rather because those who write criticism ask hard, analytical, crucial, or "critical" questions about the works they read.

lyric originally, a poem meant to be sung to

the accompaniment of a lyre; now, any short poem in which the **speaker** expresses intense personal emotion rather than describing a narrative or dramatic situation.

meditation a contemplation of some physical object as a way of reflecting upon some larger truth, often (but not necessarily) a spiritual one.

memory devices also called *mnemonic devices;* these devices—including rhyme, repetitive phrasing, and **meter**—when part of the structure of a longer work, make that work easier to memorize.

metaphor (1) one thing pictured as if it were something else, suggesting a likeness or **analogy** between them; (2) an implicit comparison or identification of one thing with another unlike itself without the use of a verbal signal. Sometimes used as a general term for **figure of speech.**

meter the more or less regular pattern of stressed and unstressed syllables in a line of poetry. This is determined by the kind of "foot" (**iambic** and **dactylic,** for example) and by the number of feet per line (five feet = pentameter, six feet = hexameter, for example).

monologue a speech of more than a few sentences, usually in a play but also in other genres, spoken by one person and uninterrupted by the speech of anyone else. *See* **soliloquy.**

motif a recurrent device, formula, or situation that deliberately connects a poem with common patterns of existing thought.

myth like **allegory,** myth usually is symbolic and extensive, including an entire work or story. Though it no longer is necessarily specific to or pervasive in a single **culture**—individual authors may now be said to create myths—myth still seems communal or cultural, while the symbolic can often involve private or personal myths. Thus stories more or less universally shared within a culture to explain its history and traditions are frequently called myths.

narrative structure a textual organization based on sequences of connected events usually presented in a straightforward chronological framework.

occasional poem a poem written about or for a specific occasion, public or private.

octameter a line of poetry with eight feet: "Once u | pon a | midnight | dreary | while I | pondered, | weak and | weary" (Poe, "The Raven").

octave the first eight lines of the Italian, or Petrarchan, sonnet. See also **sestet.**

ode a lyric poem characterized by a serious topic and formal tone but no prescribed formal pattern. See Keats's odes and Shelley's "Ode to the West Wind."

oeuvre the sum total of works verifiably written by an author. See **canon.**

onomatopoeia a word capturing or approximating the sound of what it describes; *buzz* is a good example.

oxymoron a **figure of speech** that combines two apparently contradictory elements, as in *wise fool (sophomore).*

paradox a statement that seems contradictory but may actually be true, such as "That I may rise and stand, o'erthrow me" in Donne's "Batter My Heart."

parody a work that imitates another work for comic effect by exaggerating the style and changing the content of the original.

pastoral a poem (also called an eclogue, a bucolic, or an idyll) that describes the simple life of country folk, usually shepherds who live a timeless, painless (and sheepless) life in a world full of beauty, music, and love.

pentameter a line of poetry with five feet: "Nuns fret | not at | their con | vent's nar | row room" (Wordsworth).

personification (or *prosopopeia*) treating an abstraction as if it were a person by endowing it with humanlike qualities.

Petrarchan sonnet also called **Italian** sonnet; a **sonnet** form that divides the poem into one section of eight lines (**octave**) and a second section of six lines (**sestet**), usually following the *abbaabba cdecde* rhyme scheme or, more loosely, an *abbacddc* pattern.

protest poem a poetic attack, usually quite direct, on allegedly unjust institutions or social injustices.

referential when used to describe a poem, play, or story, *referential* means making textual use of a specific historical moment or event or, more broadly, making use of external, "natural," or "actual" detail.

reflective (meditative) structure a textual organization based on the pondering of a **subject, theme,** or event, and letting the mind play with it, skipping from one sound to another or to related thoughts or objects as the mind receives them.

represent to verbally depict an image so that readers can "see" it.

rhyme scheme the pattern of end rhymes in a poem, often noted by small letters, e.g., *abab* or *abba,* etc.

rhythm the modulation of weak and strong (or stressed and unstressed) elements in the flow of speech. In most poetry written before the twentieth century, rhythm was often expressed in regular, metrical forms; in prose and in **free verse**, rhythm is present but in a much less predictable and regular manner.

scanning/scansion *Scansion* is the process of *scanning* a poem, analyzing the verse to show its **meter**, line by line.

sestet the last six lines of the **Italian**, or Petrarchan, **sonnet**. See also **octave**.

sestina an elaborate verse **structure** written in **blank verse** that consists of six **stanzas** of six lines each followed by a three-line stanza. The final words of each line in the first stanza appear in variable order in the next five stanzas, and are repeated in the middle and at the end of the three lines in the final stanza, as in Elizabeth Bishop's "Sestina."

setting the time and place of the **action** in a story, poem, or play.

Shakespearean sonnet also called an English sonnet; a **sonnet** form that divides the poem into three units of four lines each and a final unit of two lines (4+4+4+2 structure). Its classic rhyme scheme is *abab cdcd efef gg*, but there are variations.

shaped verse another name for **concrete poetry**; poetry that is shaped to look like an object.

simile a direct, explicit comparison of one thing to another, usually using the words *like* or *as* to draw the connection. *See* **metaphor**.

situation the context of the literary work's **action**, what is happening when the story, poem, or play begins.

soliloquy a monologue in which the **character** in a play is alone and speaking only to him- or herself.

sonnet a fixed verse form consisting of fourteen lines usually in **iambic pentameter**. *See* **Italian sonnet** and **Shakespearean sonnet**.

spatial setting the place of a poem, story, or play.

speaker the person, not necessarily the author, who is the voice of a poem.

Spenserian stanza a **stanza** that consists of eight lines of **iambic pentameter** (five feet) followed by a ninth line of iambic **hexameter** (six feet). The rhyme scheme is *ababbcbcc*.

spondee a metrical foot consisting of a pair of stressed syllables ("Dead set").

stanza a section of a poem demarcated by extra line spacing. Some distinguish between a stanza, a division marked by a single pattern of **meter** or rhyme, and a verse paragraph, a division governed by thought rather than sound pattern.

structure the organization or arrangement of the various elements in a work.

style a distinctive manner of expression; each author's style is expressed through his/her **diction**, **rhythm**, **imagery**, and so on.

subject (1) the concrete and literal description of what a story is about; (2) the general or specific area of concern of a poem—also called **topic**; (3) also used in fiction commentary to denote a **character** whose inner thoughts and feelings are recounted.

syllabic verse a form in which the poet establishes a precise number of syllables to a line and repeats it in subsequent **stanzas**.

symbol a person, place, thing, event, or pattern in a literary work that designates itself and at the same time figuratively represents or "stands for" something else. Often the thing or idea represented is more abstract, general, non- or superrational; the symbol, more concrete and particular.

symbolic poem a poem in which the use of **symbols** is so pervasive and internally consistent that the larger referential world is distanced, if not forgotten.

syntax the way words are put together to form phrases, clauses, and sentences.

technopaegnia the art of "shaped" poems in which the visual force is supposed to work spiritually or magically.

temporal setting the time of a story, poem, or play.

terza rima a verse form consisting of three-line **stanzas** in which the second line of each stanza rhymes with the first and third of the next.

tetrameter a line of poetry with four feet: "The Grass | divides | as with | a comb" (Dickinson).

tetrameter couplet rhymed pairs of lines that contain (in classical **iambic**, **trochaic**, and **anapestic** verse) four measures of two feet or (in modern English verse) four metrical feet.

theme (1) a generalized, abstract paraphrase of the inferred central or dominant idea or concern of a work; (2) the statement a poem makes about its subject.

tone the attitude a literary work takes toward its **subject** and **theme**.

topic (1) the concrete and literal description of what a story is about; (2) a poem's general or specific area of concern. Also called **subject**.

tradition an inherited, established, or customary practice.

traditional symbols **symbols** that, through years of usage, have acquired an agreed-upon significance, an accepted meaning. *See* **archetype**.

trochaic a metrical form in which the basic foot is a **trochee**.

trochee a metrical foot consisting of a stressed syllable followed by an unstressed one ("Homer").

villanelle a verse form consisting of nineteen lines divided into six **stanzas**—five tercets (three-line stanzas) and one quatrain (four-line stanza). The first and third lines of the first tercet rhyme, and this rhyme is repeated through each of the next four tercets and in the last two lines of the concluding quatrain. The villanelle is also known for its repetition of select lines. A good example of a twentieth-century villanelle is Dylan Thomas's "Do Not Go Gentle into That Good Night."

word order the positioning of words in relation to one another.

Permissions Acknowledgments

Text

DIANE ACKERMAN: "Sweep Me through Your Many-Chambered Heart" from *Jaguar of Sweet Laughter: New and Selected Poems* by Diane Ackerman, copyright © 1991 by Diane Ackerman. Reprinted by permission of Random House, Inc.

VIRGINIA HAMILTON ADAIR: "Cutting the Cake," Copyright © 1996 by Virginia Hamilton Adair, "God to the Serpent," Copyright © 1996 by Virginia Hamilton Adair, "Peeling an Orange," Copyright © 1996 by Virginia Hamilton Adair, from *Ants on the Melon* by Virginia Hamilton Adair. Used by permission of Random House, Inc.

ELIZABETH ALEXANDER: "West Indian Primer" from *The Venus Hottentot* by Elizabeth Alexander. Copyright © 1990. Reprinted by permission of the author.

SHERMAN ALEXIE: "On the Amtrak from Boston to New York City", from *First Indian on the Moon"* by Sherman Alexie. Copyright © 1993 by Sherman Alexie. Reprinted by permission of Hanging Loose Press.

AGHA SHAHID ALI: "Postcard from Kashmir" from *The Half-Inch Himalayas* by Agha Shahid Ali. Copyright © 1987 by Wesleyan University Press. Reprinted by permission of the publisher.

A. ALVAREZ: "Sylvia Plath" from *The Savage God*. Copyright © 1971 by A. Alvarez. Reprinted by permission of the author and Gillon Aitken Associates Ltd.

A. R. AMMONS: "Needs" from *Collected Poems 1951–1971* by A. R. Ammons. Copyright © 1968 by A. R. Ammons. Reprinted by permission of W. W. Norton & Company, Inc.

MAYA ANGELOU: "Africa" from *Oh Pray My Wings Are Gonna Fit Me Well* by Maya Angelou. Copyright © 1975 by Maya Angelou. Reprinted by permission of Random House, Inc.

PAMELA J. ANNAS: excerpt from *A Disturbance in Mirrors: The Poetry of Sylvia Plath* by Pamela J. Annas. Copyright © 1988 by Pamela J. Annas. Reproduced with permission of Greenwood Publishing Group, Inc. (Westport, CT).

JOHN ASHBERY: "City Afternoon," Copyright © 1974 by John Ashbery, from *Self-Portrait in a Convex Mirror* by John Ashbery. Used by permission of Viking Penguin, a division of Penguin Group (USA), Inc. "Paradoxes and Oxymorons" from *Shadow Train* by John Ashbery. Copyright © 1980, 1981 by John Ashbery. Reprinted by permission of Geoges Borchardt, Inc, on behalf of the author. "Of the Light," from *Your Name Here* by John Ashbery. Copyright © 2000. Reprinted by permission of Farrar, Straus & Giroux, Inc.

MARGARET ATWOOD: "Death of a Young Son by Drowning" from *Selected Poems 1966–1984* by Margaret Atwood. Copyright © 1990 Oxford University Press. Reprinted by permission of the publisher. "Death of a Young Son by Drowning" from *The Journals of Susanna Moodie* by Margaret Atwood. Copyright © 1976 by Oxford University Press. Reprinted by permission of Houghton Mifflin Company. All rights reserved. "Siren Song" from *You Are Happy, Selected Poems 1966–1984* by Margaret Atwood. Copyright © 1990 by Margaret Atwood. Reprinted by permission of Oxford University Press. All rights reserved. "Siren Song" from *Selected Poems 1965–1975* by Margaret Atwood. Copyright © 1976. Reprinted by permission of Houghton Mifflin Company. All rights reserved.

W. H. AUDEN: "As I Walked Out One Evening", Copyright 1940 & renewed 1968 by W.H. Auden, "In Memory of W.B. Yeats", copyright 1940 & renewed 1968 by W.H. Auden, "Musee des Beaux Arts", copyright 1940 & renewed 1968 by W.H. Auden, "Stop All the Clocks", copyright 1940 & renewed 1968 by W.H. Auden, from *Collected Poems* by W.H. Auden. Used by permission of Random House Inc.

STEVEN GOULD AXELROD: excerpt from *Sylvia Plath: The Wound and the Cure of Words* by Steven

BUSON: "Coolness" and "Listening to the moon" from *The Essential Haiku: Versions of Basho, Buson & Issa,* edited and with an introduction by Robert Hass. Introduction, selection, and translation copyright © 1994 by Robert Hass. Reprinted by permission of HarperCollins Publishers, Inc.

FRED CHAPPELL: "Recovery of Sexual Desire After a Bad Cold" from *Source* by Fred Chappell. Copyright © 1985. Reprinted by permission of Louisiana State University Press.

KAREN CHASE: "Venison." Originally published in *The New Yorker.* Copyright © 1995 by Karen Chase. Reprinted by permission of Harold Matson Co., Inc.

HELEN CHASIN: "The Word *Plum*" from *Coming Close and Other Poems* by Helen Chasin. Copyright © 1968 by Helen Chasin. Reprinted by permission of Yale University Press.

KELLY CHERRY: "Alzheimer's" from *Death and Transfiguration.* Copyright © 1997. Reprinted by permission of Louisiana State University Press.

MARILYN CHIN: "Summer Love" from *The Phoenix Gone, The Terrace Empty* by Marilyn Chin (Minneapolis: Milkweed Editions, 1994). Copyright © 1994 by Marilyn Chin. Reprinted by permission of Milkweed Editions.

CHIYOJO: "Whether astringent" from *One Hundred Famous Haiku,* selected and translated by Daniel Buchanan. Reprinted by permission of Japan Publications, Inc.

JUDITH ORTIZ COFER: "The Changeling" from *Prairie Schooner,* volume 66, number 3 (fall 1992). Copyright © 1992 by the University of Nebraska Press. Reprinted by permission of the publisher.

HENRI COLE: "White Spine" from *The Visible Man* by Henri Cole. Copyright © 1998 by Henri Cole. Reprinted by permission of Farrar, Straus and Giroux, LLC.

BILLY COLLINS: "Morning" and "Taking Off Emily Dickinson's Clothes" from *Picnic, Lightning* by Billy Collins. Copyright © 1998. Reprinted by permission of the University of Pittsburgh Press. "The Blues" from *The Art of Drowning* by Billy Collins. Copyright © 1995. Reprinted by permission of the University of Pittsburgh Press. "Sonnet", copyright © 2001 by Billy Collins, from *Sailing Around the Room Alone.* Used by permission of Random House, Inc.

MARTHA COLLINS: "Lies" from *Some Things Words Can Do.* Copyright © 1998 by Martha Collins. Reprinted by permission of the author.

WENDY COPE: "Emily Dickinson" and "From Strugnell's Sonnets IV", and "Engineer's Corner" from *Making Cocoa for Kingsley Amis* by Wendy Cope. Reprinted by permission of Faber & Faber Ltd.

HART CRANE: "To Emily Dickinson" from *Complete Poems of Hart Crane* edited by Marc Simon. Copyright © 1933, 1958, 1966 by Liveright Publishing Corporation. Copyright © 1986 by Marc Simon. Reprinted by permission of Liveright Publishing Corporation.

COUNTEE CULLEN: "Yet Do I Marvel" and "Saturday's Child", from *Color* by Countee Cullen. Copyright © 1925 by Harper & Brothers, copyright renewed 1952 by Ida M. Cullen. Reprinted by permission of Thompson and Thompson, New York, NY on behalf of Amistad Research Center. "From The Dark Tower", from *Copper Sun* by Countee Cullen. Copyright © 1927 by Harper & Brothers, copyright renewed 1954 by Ida M. Cullen. Reprinted by permission of Thompson and Thompson, New York, NY on behalf of Amistad Research Center.

E. E. CUMMINGS: "l(a" and "(ponder,darling,these busted statues" from *Complete Poems: 1904–1962* by E. E. Cummings, edited by George J. Firmage. "l(a" copyright © 1958, 1986, 1991 by the Trustees for the E. E. Cummings Trust. "(ponder,darling,these busted statues," copyright © 1926, 1954, 1991 by the Trustees for the E. E. Cummings Trust. Copyright © 1985 by George James Firmage. "Buffalo Bill's" and "in Just-" from *Complete Poems: 1904–1962* by E. E. Cummings, edited by George J. Firmage. Copyright © 1923, 1951, 1991 by the Trustees for the E. E. Cummings Trust. Copyright © 1976 by George James Firmage. Reprinted by permission of Liveright Publishing Corporation.

WALTER DE LA MARE: "Slim Cunning Hands" from *The Complete Poems of Walter de la Mare.* Reprinted by permission of the Literary Trustees of Walter de la Mare and the Society of Authors as their representative.

LORNA DEE CERVANTES: "Refugee Ship," by Lorna Dee Cervantes is reprinted with permissions from the publisher of *The Americas Review* (Houston: Arte Publico Press- University of Houston ©1991)

GREG DELANTY: "The Blind Stitch" from *The Blind Stitch* by Greg Delanty. Copyright © 2001 by Carcanet Press Ltd. Reprinted by permission of the publisher.

BABETTE DEUTSCH: "The falling flower..." from *Poetry Handbook: A Dictionary of Terms* by Babette Deutsch. Copyright © 1974, 1969, 1962, 1957 by Babette Deutsch. Reprinted by permission of HarperCollins Publishers, Inc.

JAMES DICKEY: "Cherrylog Road" and "The Leap" from *Poems, 1957–1967*. Copyright © 1964 and 1967 by Wesleyan University Press. Reprinted by permission of the publisher.

EMILY DICKINSON: #249 [Wild nights! Wild nights!], #341 [After a great pain, a formal feeling comes], #467 [We do not play on Graves—], #479 [She dealt her pretty words like blades—], #569 [I reckon—when I count at all—], #632 [The Brain—is wider than the Sky—], #657 [I dwell in possibility], #712 [Because I could not stop death], #754 [My life had stood a loaded gun], #832 [The wind begun to knead the grass], #875 [I stepped from plank to plank], #986 [A narrow fellow in the grass], and #216 [Safe in their alabaster chambers]. Reprinted by permission of the publishers and the Trustees of Amherst College from *The Poems of Emily Dickinson* edited by Thomas H. Johnson (Cambridge, Mass.: The Belknap Press of Harvard University Press). Copyright © 1951, 1955, 1979, 1983 by the President and Fellows of Harvard College. Reprinted by permission of the publishers and the Trustees of Harvard College.

CHITRA BANERJEE DIVAKARUNI: "Indian Movie, New Jersey" from *Leaving Yuba City* by Chitra Banerjee Divakaruni. Copyright © 1997 by Chitra Banerjee Divakaruni. Used by permission of Doubleday, a division of Bantam Doubleday Dell Publishing Group, Inc.

SUSAN DONNELLY: "Eve Names the Animals" from *Eve Names the Animals* by Susan Donnelly. Copyright © 1985 by Susan Donnelly. Reprinted by permission of Northeastern University Press.

RITA DOVE: "Fifth Grade Autobiography" from *Grace Notes* by Rita Dove. Copyright © 1989 by Rita Dove. Reprinted by permission of W. W. Norton & Company, Inc. "Hattie McDaniel Arrives at the Coconut Grove" from *American Smooth* by Rita Dove. Copyright © 2004 by Rita Dove. Reprinted by permission of W. W. Norton & Company, Inc. "Parsley," copyright © 1983 by Rita Dove, from *Museum* by Rita Dove (Carnegie-Mellon University Press, 1983). Reprinted by permission of the author. "Daystar," copyright © 1986 by Rita Dove, from *Thomas and Beulah* by Rita Dove (Carnegie-Mellon University Press, 1986). Reprinted by permission of the author. "The House Slave," copyright © 1980 by Rita Dove, from *The Yellow House on the Corner* by Rita Dove (Carnegie-Mellon University Press, 1986). Reprinted by permission of the author.

W. E. B. DUBOIS: "Two Novels: Home to Harlem and Quicksand," from *Crisis (June 1928)*. Reprinted with the permission of Crisis Publishing Co., Inc.

CAROL ANN DUFFY: "Mrs. Sisypus" and "Mrs. Midas" from *The World's Wife*. Used by permission of Macmillian Publishers Ltd.

STEPHEN DUNN: "Dancing with God" from *Between Angels* by Stephen Dunn. Copyright © 1989 by Stephen Dunn. Used by permission of W.W. Norton & Company. "After Making Love" and "Poetry" from *Loosestrife* by Stephen Dunn. Copyright © 1996 by Stephen Dunn. Used by permission of W.W. Norton & Company.

T. S. ELIOT: "Journey of the Magi" from *Collected Poems 1909–1962* by T. S. Eliot. Copyright © 1936 by Harcourt, Inc. Copyright © 1963, 1964 by T. S. Eliot. Reprinted by permission of Harcourt, Inc. and Faber & Faber Ltd. "The Love Song of J. Alfred Prufrock" from *Collected Poems 1909–1963*. Reprinted by permission of Faber & Faber Ltd.

JAMES A. EMANUEL: "Emmett Till" from *Whole Grain: Collected Poems, 1958–1989* by James A. Emanuel. Reprinted by permission of the author. "Jazzanatomy" and "Ray Charles" from *Jazz from the Haiku King* by James A. Emanuel. Reprinted by permission of Broadside Press.

LOUISE ERDRICH: "Jacklight" from *Jacklight: Poems* by Louise Erdrich. Copyright © 1984 by Louise Erdrich. Reprinted by permission of the Wylie Agency, Inc.

JAROLD RAMSEY: "The Tally Stick." Reprinted by permission of the author.

DUDLEY RANDALL: "Ballad of Birmingham" from *Cites Burning* by Dudley Randall. Reprinted by permission of Broadside Press.

JOHN CROWE RANSOM: "Bells for John Whiteside's Daughter," copyright © 1924 by Alfred A. Knopf, In, a division of Random House, Inc. and renewed 1952 by John Crowe Ransom, from *Selected Poems* by John Crowe Ransom. Used by permission of Alfred A. Knopf, a division of Random House, Inc.

HENRY REED: "Lessons of the War: Judging Distances" from *Collected Poems* by Henry Reed, edited by Jon Stallworthy. Copyright © 1991 the Executor of Henry Reed's Estate. Reprinted by permission of Oxford University Press.

ISHMAEL REED: "beware: do not read this poem," copyright © 1972 by Ishmael Reed. Reprinted by permission of Ishmael Reed.

ADRIENNE RICH: "Living in Sin," "Planetarium," "Aunt Jennifer's Tigers," "At a Bach Concert," "Storm Warnings," "Snapshots of a Daughter-in-Law," "Diving Into the Wreck," "For the Record," "Four: history" from "Inscriptions," Poem 3 of "Contradictions: Tracking Poems," "Delta," "Dialogue," and "Power," from *The Fact of a Doorframe: Selected Poems 1950–2001* by Adrienne Rich. Copyright © 2002 by Adrienne Rich. Copyright © 2001, 1999, 1995, 1991, 1989, 1986, 1984, 1981, 1967, 1963, 1962, 1961, 1960, 1959, 1958, 1957, 1956, 1955, 1954, 1953, 1952, 1951 by Adrienne Rich. Copyright © 1978, 1975, 1973, 1971, 1969, 1966 by W. W. Norton & Company, Inc. Used by permission of the author and W. W. Norton & Company. "Two Songs," copyright © 1993 by Adrienne Rich. Copyright © 1966 by W. W. Norton & Company, Inc, from *Collected Early Poems: 1950–1970* by Adrienne Rich. Used by permission of the author and W. W. Norton & Company. Excerpts from "A Communal Poetry" and "How Does a Poet Put Bread on the Table?" from *What Is Found There: Notebooks on Poetry and Politics* by Adrienne Rich. Copyright © 1993 by Adrienne Rich. Used by permission of the author and W. W. Norton & Company. "Modotti" from *Midnight Salvage: Poems 1995–1998* by Adrienne Rich. Copyright © 1999 by Adrienne Rich. Used by permission of the author and W. W. Norton & Company. Excerpt from "When We Dead Awaken: Writing as Re-Vision" and "Why I Refused the National Medal for the Arts" from *Arts of the Possible: Essays and Conversations* by Adrienne Rich. Copyright © 2001 by Adrienne Rich. Used by permission of the author and W. W. Norton & Company.

ALBERTO ALVARO RÍOS: "Advice to a First Cousin" and "Mi Abuelo." First published in *Five Indiscresions: A Book of Poems* (Sheep Meadow Press). Copyright © 1985 by Alberto Ríos. Reprinted by permission of the author.

THEODORE ROETHKE "My Papa's Waltz," copyright © 1942 by Hearst Magazines, Inc.; "The Waking," copyright © 1953 by Theodore Roethke; from *The Collected Poems of Theodore Roethke* by Theodore Roethke. Used by permission of Doubleday, a division of Random House.

LIZ ROSENBERG: "Married Love" from *The Fire Music* by Liz Rosenberg. Copyright © 1986. Reprinted by permission of the author. "The Silence of Women" from *Children of Paradise* by Liz Rosenberg. Copyright © 1994. Reprinted by permission of the University of Pittsburgh Press.

CHRISTINA ROSETTI: "Cobwebs" and "In the Artist's Studio" from *The Complete Poems of Christina Rossetti, Volume III,* edited by R. W. Crump. Reprinted by permission of Louisiana State University Press.

MURIEL RUKEYSER: "Reading Time: 1 Minute 26 Seconds" from *A Muriel Rukeyser Reader* (New York: W. W. Norton, 1994). Copyright © 1994 by William L. Rukeyser. Reprinted by permission of International Creative Management, Inc.

MARY JO SALTER: "Welcome to Hiroshima," copyright © 1984 by Mary Jo Salter, from *Henry Purcell in Japan* by Mary Jo Salter. Reprinted by permission of Alfred A. Knopf, Inc. "Home Movies: A Sort of Ode," copyright © 1999 by Mary Jo Salter, from *A Kiss in Space: Poems by Mary Jo Salter*. Used by permission of Alfred A. Knopf, Inc.

YVONNE SAPIA: "Grandmother, A Caribbean Indian, Described by My Father" from *Valentino's*

Simon & Schuster Adult Publishing Group. "Byzantium" and "A Last Confession" from *The Collected Works of W. B. Yeats, Volume 1: The Poems*. Revised and edited by Richard J. Finneran. Copyright © 1933 by Macmillan Publishing Company; copyright renewed © 1961 by Bertha Georgie Yeats. Reprinted with the permission of Scribner, a division of Simon & Schuster Adult Publishing Group.

CYNTHIA ZARIN: "Song," from *Fire Lyric* by Cynthia Zarin, copyright © 1993 by Cynthia Zarin. Used by the permission of Alfred A. Knopf, Inc, a division of Random House, Inc.

Illustrations

Facsimile of Keats's "To Autumn." Autograph Manuscript draft (MS Keats 2.27) courtesy of Houghton Library. Reprinted by permission of the Houghton Library, Harvard University.

John Keats. Portrait by Joseph Severn. Reprinted by courtesy of the National Portrait Gallery, London.

George Keats. Sketch by Joseph Severn. Photographed by Chris Warde Jones. Reprinted with the kind permission of the Keats–Shelley Memorial House, Rome.

Tom Keats. Sketch by Joseph Severn. Reprinted with the kind permission of the Keats–Shelley Memorial House, Rome.

John Hamilton Reynolds. Miniature by Joseph Severn. Reprinted by permission of the Corporation of London from the Collections at Keats House, Hampstead.

Adrienne Rich, 1972. Photograph by Sissy Krook. Reprinted by permission of the photographer.

Adrienne Rich in the classroom, circa 1978. Photograph by Lynda Koolish, Ph.D. Reprinted by permission of the photographer.

Adrienne Rich today. Copyright © by Jason Langer, photographer. Reprinted by permission.

Sylvia Plath. Courtesy of the Sylvia Plath Collection, Mortimer Rare Book Room, Smith College.

Sylvia Plath's father, Otto Plath. Courtesy of the Estate of Aurelia S. Plath and the Lilly Library.

BIOGRAPHICAL SKETCHES

Virginia Hamilton Adair. Mount Holyoke Archives and Special Collections.

John Ashbery. Christopher Felver/Corbis.

Margaret Atwood. K. C. Armstrong/Corbis.

W. H. Auden. Corbis.

Basho. Asian Art & Archaeology, Inc./Corbis.

Earle Birney. Library of Toronto.

Elizabeth Bishop. Bettmann/Corbis.

William Blake. Bettmann/Corbis.

Louise Bogan. Bettmann/Corbis.

Evan Boland. Stanford Daily.

Roo Borson. Cameron Hayne.

Gwendolyn Brooks. AP/Wide World Photos.

Elizabeth Barrett Browning. Bettmann/Corbis.

Robert Browning. Bettmann/Corbis.

Robert Burns. Bettmann/Corbis.

Samuel Taylor Coleridge. Bettmann/Corbis.

Billy Collins. AP/Wide World Photos.

Wendy Cope. Courtesy of Faber & Faber Ltd.

Countee Cullen. Bettmann/Corbis.

E. E. Cummings. Library of Congress.

James Dickey. Oscar White/Corbis.

Emily Dickinson. Bettmann/Corbis.

John Donne. Bettmann/Corbis.

Rita Dove. Fred Viebahn.

Carol Ann Duffy. Colin McPherson/Corbis.

Paul Laurence Dunbar. Corbis.

Stephen Dunn. Matt Valentine.

T. S. Eliot. Hulton-Deutsch Collection/ Corbis.

James A. Emanuel. Godelieve Simons.

David Ferry. Stephen Ferry.

Anne Finch. © National Portrait Gallery, London.

Robert Frost. E. O. Hoppé/Corbis.

Allen Ginsberg. AP/Wide World Photos.

Thomas Gray. John Giles Burckhardt/The Bridgeman Art Library.

Angelina Grimke. Moorland-Spingam Research Center, Howard University.

Thomas Gunn. Christopher Felver/Corbis.

Thomas Hardy. Bettmann/Corbis.

Robert Hass. Barbara Hall.

Seamus Heaney. Christopher Felver/Corbis.

Anthony Hecht. Bettmann/Corbis.

George Herbert. Michael Nicholson/Corbis.

Robert Herrick. Hulton-Deutsch Collection/ Corbis.

Gerald Manley Hopkins. The Granger Collection, New York.

Andrew Hudgins. Photograph by Jo McCulty. Courtesy of Overlook Press.

Langston Hughes.

Ben Jonson. Corbis.

John Keats. Bettmann/Corbis.

Galway Kinnell. Christopher Felver/Corbis.

Etheridge Knight. Photograph by Judy Ray. American Poetry Review Collection, University of Pennsylvania.

Yusef Komunyakaa. Don Getsug Studios.

D. H. Lawrence. Hulton-Deutsch Collection/ Corbis.

Irving Layton. Dominika Dittwald.

Emma Lazarus. Bettmann/Corbis.

Amy Lowell. Bettmann/Corbis.

Andrew Marvell. Mary Evans Picture Library.

Claude McKay. Corbis.

Archibald MacLeish. Bettmann/Corbis.

James Merrill. Oscar White/Corbis.

Edna St. Vincent Millay. Underwood & Underwood/Corbis.

John Milton. Stefano Bianchetti/Corbis.

Marianne Moore. Bettmann/Corbis.

Pat Mora. Cheron Bayna.

Paul Muldoon. Christopher Felver/Corbis.

Ogden Nash. Hulton-Deutsch Collection/ Corbis.

Howard Nemerov. Bettmann/Corbis.

Sharon Olds. Christopher Felver/Corbis.

Mary Oliver. Barbara Savage Cheresh. Courtesy of Beacon Press.

Wilfred Owen. Hulton-Deutsch Collection/ Corbis.

Dorothy Parker. AP/Wide World Photos.

Linda Pastan. Margaretta K. Mitchell.

Katherine Philips. By William Finden. Michael Nicholson/Corbis.

Sylvia Plath. Courtesy of the Sylvia Plath Collection, Mortimer Rare Book Room, Smith College.

Alexander Pope. After Hoare. Michael Nicholson/Corbis.

Ezra Pound. E. O. Hoppé.

Henry Reed. Royal Literary Fund.

Adrienne Rich. Courtesy of the author.

Alberto Alvaro Ríos. Lupika Barron-Ríos.

Theodore Roethke. Bettmann/Corbis.

Liz Rosenberg. Courtesy of the author.

Christina Rossetti. Bettmann/Corbis.

Mary J. Salter. Joanna Eldredge Morrissey.

William Shakespeare. Droeshout engraving. Chris Hellier/Corbis.

Sir Philip Sidney. Hulton-Deutsch Collection/Corbis.

Cathy Song. John Eddy.

Audio Companion

Index of Authors

Index of Titles and First Lines